The **Rough Guide** to

Washington DC

written and researched by

Jules Brown

this edition researched and updated by

JD Dickey

**ROUGH
GUIDES**

NEW YORK • LONDON • DELHI

www.roughguides.com

▲ Cherry blossoms and the Washington Monument

Introduction to

Washington DC

Accurately regarded as the most powerful place on earth, Washington DC more than fulfills its reputation as a monumental – some would say daunting – imperial city with lovely Neoclassical buildings arrayed along grand boulevards, some of the finest museums in North America, an affecting set of war memorials honoring centuries of fallen soldiers, and scads of high-powered politicians, lobbyists, and bureaucrats charting the course of the rest of the country, as well as the world. With the gleaming white images of America's three branches of government – represented by the White House, Capitol, and Supreme Court – dominating the landscape, it's easy to be stunned by the spectacle of so much power in such a small space, but thankfully Washington DC is more than just the memorials, monuments, and museums of the National Mall and Capitol Hill. Beyond these areas, there is, in fact, a flesh-and-blood city, whose vibrant neighborhoods can prove nearly as compelling.

Perhaps surprisingly, Washington DC is actually a pretty progressive town, with a wide range of lively bohemian and upscale-liberal areas, and a population of Latin American immigrants and African Americans who offer their own alternative histories and rich culture in contrast to the sanitized federal versions. And with a population of less than 600,000 residents (it's smaller than just about every foreign capital you could think of), Washington has a certain manageability – from the ease of riding its Metro system to the pleasures of walking and biking around – that separates it from the huge, sprawling American cities from which the capital's political elite are drawn.

Given that it would become the consummate power center, it seems fitting that DC's very founding was the result of political wrangle. In the late eighteenth century, Congress acceded to the demands of the Northern states to assume their Revolutionary War debts, but squeezed a key concession for the South: rather than being sited in New York or Philadelphia, the new federal capital would be built from scratch on the banks of the Potomac River, midway along the eastern seaboard. And while not actually *in* the South, Washington (in the Territory – later District – of Columbia) was very definitely *of* the South. French architect Pierre L'Enfant planned the city on a hundred-square-mile diamond-shaped parcel of land donated by the tobacco-rich states of Virginia and Maryland. John F. Kennedy famously pointed out its contradictions in his wry comment that Washington was "a city of Southern efficiency and Northern charm."

> **It's easy to be stunned by the spectacle of so much power in such a small space**

Even more important than DC's geographical location was its unique experimental nature – a modern, planned capital built for a disparate collection of states seeking security in unity. As a symbol of union, its finest hour came within a century of its founding – the city that was built largely by slaves became the frontline headquarters of the fight against slavery

▼ Fountain, National Gallery of Art Sculpture Garden

DC for free

While European capitals regularly figure as some of the world's most expensive cities, the cost of a visit to Washington DC can come as a refreshing surprise. It's possible, of course, to spend a fortune on five-star hotels and top-of-the-line restaurants, but since so much of your day-to-day itinerary is free, it's easy to get by on the cheap. Virtually every museum and gallery, including the celebrated Smithsonian museums, has complimentary entry, and most have a free program of events, too – from children's activities to evening concerts. Of the engaging tours of the White House, Congress, Supreme Court, Bureau of Engraving and Printing, and Library of Congress, none costs a penny. Most of the famous presidential memorials, historic houses, cemeteries, concerts on the Mall, Fourth of July fireworks, and even the National Zoo are offered gratis as well. You will need to spend five dollars a day on a Metro transport pass if you're not to exhaust yourself completely, but that seems a small price to pay for accessing the biggest range of free attractions in the country.

when, during the Civil War, Abraham Lincoln directed the Union troops from the capital's halls and offices. After the war, thousands of Southern blacks arrived in search of a sanctuary from racist oppression, and since the 1930s DC has been both a predominantly black city and a federal fortress: shunned by the white political aristocracy, the city is run as a virtual colony of Congress, where residents have only nonvoting representation and couldn't even participate in presidential elections until the 1960s. Suffering an endless cycle of boom and bust, the city has one of the country's highest crime rates and appalling levels of unemployment, illiteracy, and drug abuse. And to demagogues everywhere, "Washington" is a dirty word for titanic bureaucracy, a place said to be inhabited by venal politicians isolated from Middle America by the fabled Beltway, the looping freeway that encircles the city and is used as a metaphor for America's political gridlock. Nonetheless, twenty million visitors come to the capital each year for entertainment and edification, making it one of the most visited destinations in the country – and now on the rebound after a two-year slump following the 9/11 attacks. Kept away from the city's peripheral dead zones, visitors find a scrubbed, policed, and largely safe downtown swath, where famous landmarks follow world-class museums with uplifting regularity. Even better, most of what you see in Washington is free, and getting around is easy on foot or by rail. But with repositories of history and culture around almost every corner here, it's well worth a little planning to keep yourself from getting overwhelmed.

What to see

There's no better way to come to grips with the city than by taking a two-mile stroll along the grassy centerpiece of the **National Mall**, the city's major destination. You'll come back here time and again to view the powerful tributes to Washington, Lincoln, Jefferson, FDR, and war veterans, or to browse the collections of the outstanding Smithsonian museums and the National Gallery of Art. At the Mall's eastern end, the US Capitol marks the geographic center of the city, as all neighborhoods and quadrants radiate out from its familiar white, cast-iron dome. **Capitol Hill** is one of DC's oldest neighborhoods, rich in nineteenth-century row houses, and ripe for a stroll from the Capitol itself to other defining buildings like the Supreme Court and Library of Congress. South of the Mall, two of the most popular

> **Twenty million visitors come to the capital each year, making it one of the most visited destinations in the country**

attractions in DC – the Federal Bureau of Engraving and Printing and the US Holocaust Memorial Museum – are the undisputed highlights of the city's **Waterfront** area, though the thriving Fish Wharf, several seafood restaurants, and the Navy Museum are also worth a visit. North of the Mall, the heavily visited section around the **White House** and **Foggy Bottom** contains headquarters for numerous federal bureaucracies and international institutions, as well as heavyweight attractions like the Corcoran Gallery of Art, Renwick Gallery, Kennedy Center, and infamous Watergate Complex.

▼ Korean War Veterans Memorial

Between the White House and Union Station, **Old Downtown** was where nineteenth-century Washington first set out its shops and services, along the spine of Pennsylvania Avenue. After years of neglect, it's now undergoing spirited renovation – especially around the so-called Penn Quarter – with revitalized streets, plazas, galleries, and restaurants. Wedged between Old Downtown and the Mall, the **Federal Triangle** is highlighted by the National Archives and an array of splendid Neoclassical buildings.

In the business district of **New Downtown**, along and around K Street, you'll find a slew of fancy hotels and top-notch restaurants – though little else, since the place shuts down at night. More engagingly, the historic townhouses and mansions of chic **Dupont Circle** hold a gaggle of low-key museums and an expanding enclave of art galleries, not to mention some of DC's best clubs and eateries. To the north, the fun and funky hipster zone of **Adams–Morgan** gets trendier by the day for its diners and live-music venues, while, to the east, the historic black neighborhood of **Shaw** boasts the thriving nightlife corridor of U Street.

West of New Downtown, the long-standing neighborhood of **Georgetown**

World cuisines

In a city where the world's bureaucratic elite gather, it's not surprising that the traditional food of most nations is available at local restaurants, and, for a quick bite, you're never far from a taco, bagel, panino, sub, chili dog, blini, empanada, or pizza. Certain specialties are well worth seeking out: Vietnamese cafés and restaurants (especially across the river in northern Virginia) are typically excellent; Ethiopian dining is big in Adams-Morgan; and gourmet Italian, suit-and-tie continental, and New American dining enclaves satisfy the expense-account crowd. And if you're in the mood for all-American crab cakes and a grilled strip steak, clubby saloon-style restaurants pepper Georgetown and Old Downtown, among other areas. For a rundown of the scene, plus our recommendations, turn to p.262.

is the quintessential hangout of the chattering classes (as well as university students), who make the many good shops, galleries, bars, and restaurants here their own. To the north, the first bona fide city suburbs were in the **Upper Northwest**, where well-to-do areas like Woodley Park and Cleveland Park boast such sights as the enjoyable National Zoo, landmark National Cathedral, and the glades, dales, and riverbanks of Rock Creek Park.

Although there's little to see in the dicey areas of Northeast and Southeast Washington – aside from isolated places like the National Arboretum and National Shrine of the Immaculate Conception – if you venture across

Rally on Capitol Hill

the Potomac into Virginia, to **Arlington**, you'll reach the region's other major memorials: Arlington National Cemetery and the Marine Corps Memorial – as well as the walled-off precinct of the Pentagon. Farther out from the city, excellent day trips include jaunts to historic **Old Town Alexandria**; the family estate of George Washington, **Mount Vernon**; and lesser-known, but still intriguing, sights like **Woodlawn Plantation** and **Gunston Hall**.

When to go

Without question, the best times to visit Washington DC are in the spring and fall, when the weather is at its most appealing – moderate temperatures and mild precipitation – plus, in April, DC's famous cherry trees are in bloom. By contrast, summer in the capital is not very hospitable, with hot and humid days made worse by throngs of visitors packed cheek-to-jowl at the major attractions. Winter, at least for weather, is equally unpleasant, with ice-cold temperatures, plenty of snow and

Row houses in Georgetown

City of Masons

The US capital was designed, constructed, and ruled by Freemasons from its inception through much of the twentieth century. While some have seen sinister implications in this secretive group – indeed, an actual Anti-Mason Party collected votes in early American elections – others have marveled at the way it's fostered a sense of inclusiveness among political leaders who might otherwise have little to do with each other. The hallmarks of Masonry can be found almost everywhere in town, from the planning of the city itself to the placement and physical shape of its major buildings, to the mysterious character of American currency, and the fact that George Washington – himself a Masonic leader – placed the cornerstone of the US Capitol in a ceremony rich with Masonic symbolism. For a glimpse of Masonry in action you won't have to look far: many current institutions (such as the National Museum of Women in the Arts) occupy former Masonic temples, while gleaming icons such as the Scottish Rite Temple and George Washington Masonic Memorial (both open to the public) are eye-popping architectural spectacles built around the symbols and emblems of the secret society.

rain, and howling winds blowing in off the Potomac River. However, the one appeal of winter over summer is the relative lack of visitors – you're likely to have many sights to yourself, or, at the very least, you can expect some relief from the school groups and tour buses that are legion during the rest of the year.

Washington DC climate

	Jan	Feb	Mar	Apr	May	Jun	Jul	Aug	Sep	Oct	Nov	Dec
Average daily temperature												
max (°F)	42	44	53	64	75	83	87	84	78	67	55	45
max (°C)	6	7	12	18	24	28	31	29	26	19	13	7
min (°F)	27	28	35	44	54	63	68	66	59	48	38	29
min (°C)	-3	-2	2	7	12	17	20	19	15	9	3	-2
Average rainfall												
inches	3.4	3	3.6	3.3	3.7	3.9	4.4	4.3	3.7	2.9	2.6	3.1
mm	86.4	76.2	91.4	83.8	94	99.1	111.8	109.2	94	73.7	66	78.7

27

things not to miss

It's not possible to see everything that Washington has to offer in one trip – and we don't suggest you try. What follows is a selective taste of the city's highlights: stirring memorials and savory meals, street-level stimuli and tranquil urban retreats, all arranged in five color-coded categories, which you can browse through to find the very best things to see and experience. All highlights have a page reference to take you straight into the guide, where you can find out more.

01 Ford's Theatre Page **175** • Abraham Lincoln was gunned down by Confederate sympathizer John Wilkes Booth at this theater, where you can see incredible items like the actual murder weapon and a bloodstained piece of Lincoln's overcoat.

02 **The US Capitol** Page 99 •
The citadel of world democracy or an
icon of imperial hegemony, depending on
your view, the Capitol's design was meant to
evoke the Classical ideals that influenced the
country's founders.

03 **Mount Vernon** Page 241 • Take
the best day trip from the city out
to George Washington's Virginia estate, his
home for forty years and his burial place.

04 **Sessions of the Supreme Court** Page 109 •
Oral arguments at the highest court in the
land are heard from October through April,
and are open to the public on a first-come,
first-served basis.

05 **Fourth of July celebrations** Page 309 • DC is the place to be on the
Fourth of July, offering a spirited parade along Constitution Avenue NW, free music and
concerts, and, of course, a grand display of fireworks.

06 **Thomas Jefferson Building, Library of Congress** Page 112 • This magnificent Renaissance Revival building is filled with marble, murals, and mosaics. A prized copy of the Gutenberg Bible is among the many treasures on display.

07 **Chesapeake Bay seafood** Page 125 • Concoct a great picnic of a mess of steamed crabs at the country's oldest continuous fish market, down on the Washington Channel, which still sells the daily catch from boats and trailers.

08 **Arlington National Cemetery** Page 228 • Deservedly the nation's most famous military cemetery, where myriad white crosses sit in perfect rows to mark the graves of nearly a quarter-million US soldiers. An eternal flame, lit by Jackie Kennedy, burns at JFK's grave.

09 **Biking along the C&O Canal** Page 223 • Escape the city for a historic, evocative journey on a lovely fourteen-mile bike ride along the canal towpath from Georgetown to the tumbling waters at Great Falls.

10 **Nighttime tours** Page 34 • Moonlight tours of dramatically lit monuments and memorials are available, and, on chilly winter evenings, some of the area's most famous sights open their doors for candlelight visits.

12 Vietnam Veterans Memorial Page **59** • Arguably the most affecting war memorial to be found anywhere, this dramatic, black-granite chevron carved into the earth is engraved with the names of the 58,000 men who died in the jungles of Southeast Asia.

11 US Botanic Garden Page **106** • The most elaborate and crowded of the city's gardens includes a set of greenhouses, highlighted by the lush vegetation of the Jungle Room, that display foliage from around the world.

13 The White House Page **130** • You'll have to jump through a number of hoops if you want to tour the president's house these days, but the Executive Mansion is still a must for a glimpse inside the most famous address in America.

14 National Air and Space Museum Page **83** • The most popular sight in Washington, and an essential stop for anyone interested in historic airplanes and spacecraft – from the Wright Flyer to *Apollo 11* to transcontinental air balloons.

15 Rock Creek Park Page 213 • Six miles and 1800 acres set along a forest and gorge offer rugged trails for hiking, winding paths for cycling and rollerblading, and nineteenth-century remnants like a functional grist mill and parts of a Civil War fort.

16 National Cherry Blossom Festival Page 308 • When DC's beautiful cherry trees are blooming in late March and early April around the Tidal Basin, the city celebrates with a holiday parade, pageants, concerts, fireworks, and lantern-lighting.

17 Frederick Douglass National Historic Site Page 127 • The preserved Victorian residence where the civil-rights pioneer lived in his 60s and 70s holds key mementos from Douglass's life, plus artifacts like Abraham Lincoln's cane.

18 Adams-Morgan restaurants Page 265 • Savor the most eclectic selection of eateries in DC's funkiest neighborhood, where you can gorge on anything from Ethiopian to Salvadoran to Thai.

xiv

19 National Cathedral Page 209 • The sixth-biggest cathedral in the world is a Gothic Revival icon of American religion and politics, hosting regular services attended by Washington's elite.

20 **Free summer concerts** Page 297 • Whether it's listening to an outdoor music jam in Rock Creek Park, dropping in at the National Zoo for "Sunset Serenades" on Thursday nights, or enjoying the eclectic stylings of the Navy and Marine bands, the warmer months boast plenty of complimentary concerts.

22 **National Museum of American History** Page **60** • Artifacts from nearly four hundred years of American and pre-American history are on display here in a hodgepodge that includes Judy Garland's ruby slippers from *The Wizard of Oz* and the original Star-Spangled Banner.

21 **National Gallery of Art tours** Page **71** • It's impossible to take in the museum's enormous collection in one gulp, so latch onto one of the excellent free guided tours, which concentrate on gallery highlights or particular periods and painters.

23 **Ben's Chili Bowl** Page **279** • Sitting along the historic U Street corridor, this venerable diner doles out the city's best chili dogs and cheese fries.

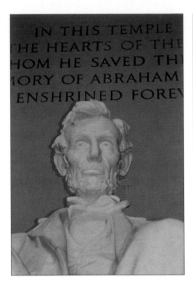

24 **Lincoln Memorial** Page **56** • This Greek temple on a knoll is the best-loved and most dramatic of the city's presidential memorials.

25 **Rare bears** Page **211** • The National Zoological Park is more than a mere animal display, with its wetlands, nature trails, and botanic gardens, but celebrity pandas Mei Xiang and Tian Tian always take center stage.

26 **The Whistler Collection** Page **94** • The works of James McNeill Whistler dominate the Freer Gallery of Art: some 1200 pieces, in addition to his gloriously decorated Peacock Room, are on display.

27 **Eastern Market** Page **114** • Visit DC's longest-serving indoor market, then grab a coffee and crabmeat sandwich in a nearby café; outside, on weekends, you can buy flowers, antiques, and assorted junk.

Contents

Using this Rough Guide

We've tried to make this Rough Guide a good read and easy to use. The book is divided into seven main sections, and you should be able to find whatever you want in them.

Color section

The front color section offers a quick tour of Washington DC. The **introduction** aims to give you a feel for the place, with suggestions on where to go. We also tell you what the weather is like and when the best times to visit are. Next, our author rounds up his favorite aspects of DC in the **things not to miss** section – whether it's great food, amazing sights, or a special activity. Right after this comes the Rough Guide's full **contents** list.

Basics

The basics section covers all the **pre-departure** nitty-gritty to help you plan your trip and the practicalities you'll want to know once there. This is where to find out about money and costs, Internet access, transportation, car rental, local media – in fact just about every piece of **general practical information** you might need.

The City

This is the heart of the Rough Guide, divided into user-friendly chapters, each of which covers a city neighborhood or day-trip destination. Every chapter starts with an **introduction** that helps you to decide where to go, followed by an extensive tour of the **sights**, all plotted on a local **map**.

Listings

Listings contain all the consumer information needed to make the most of your stay, with chapters on **accommodation**, places to **eat** and **drink**, **nightlife** and **cultural** venues, **shopping**, **sports**, and **festivals**.

Contexts

Read contexts to get a deeper understanding of how Washington DC ticks. We include a brief **history**, plus a look at the inner workings of the US government, along with reviews of dozens of **books** and **films** relating to the city.

small print and Index

Apart from a full **index**, which covers maps as well as places, this section includes publishing information, credits, and acknowledgments, and also has our contact details in case you want to send in updates and corrections to the book – or suggestions as to how we might improve it.

Color maps

The back color section contains nine detailed **maps** and plans to help you explore the city up close, navigate the Metro system, and locate the sights recommended in the guide.

Chapter list

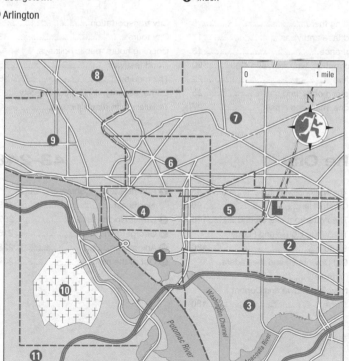

Contents

Listings

Contexts

small print and Index

Color maps

Basics

Basics

Getting there

Unless you live along America's eastern seaboard, the easiest way to get to Washington DC is to fly. Three airports serve the Washington metropolitan area: Reagan National (DCA), the city's domestic airport, located just south of town along the Potomac; Dulles International (IAD), the main international airport, about 45 minutes west, in Virginia; and Baltimore-Washington International (BWI), about an hour north of downtown DC, in Maryland.

Amtrak provides **train service** to DC within the US and Canada, though this is typically a leisurely and expensive option; Greyhound and Peter Pan **buses** are cheaper, albeit less enjoyable, options. DC is easily accessible **by car**, but you might not want to drive once you've reached the city, as it has an outstanding – and safe – public transit system.

Countless travel operators offer **organized tours** and DC-centered holiday packages. Some specialized tours take you to nearby Revolutionary and Civil War battlefields, while others include two or three days in DC as part of a longer East Coast tour, camping holiday, or adventure trip.

Shopping for air tickets and passes

Within the US and Canada, prices for flights to DC are usually relative to the date of departure, length of stay, and seat availability. If you're booking from abroad, tickets will be the most expensive during Europe's high season – June to August, despite this being DC's hottest and most humid period – less pricey in spring and fall, and cheapest during winter, excluding the Christmas and New Year's holiday period. If you're planning to arrive in DC during any major American holidays, be sure to make reservations well in advance.

For the cheapest fares, tickets usually have to be purchased two to three weeks in advance, and you must have at least one Saturday-night stayover. These tickets are nonrefundable and subject to "change fees," meaning that if you alter your return date or

destination, you pay a fee of $50–100 along with the difference in the two prices. It's usually cheaper to fly during the week than on the weekend. Remember to allow for the extra cost of duty fees and airport taxes of 8 to 15 percent.

You can save yourself time and money by comparing ticket prices through an online travel site, or checking out the various discount travel agents. Some operators specialize in youth or student fares, while others offer a range of services that include traveler's insurance and car rentals. Also, many airlines and travel websites allow you to book your tickets online, often at a discount.

If you're traveling from Europe, Australia, or New Zealand and the US is only one stop on a longer journey, you might want to buy a Round-the-World (RTW) ticket. Some agents can sell you an "off-the-shelf" RTW ticket that will have you touching down in about half a dozen cities; others can create one tailored to your needs, though it will likely be more expensive.

Overseas travelers should keep in mind that all major American airlines offer air passes for flights within the US; these passes are good for people who plan to make a lot of stops but only have a limited amount of time. Passes must be bought in advance and require that you arrive in the US via the airline issuing the passes. All the airlines' deals are similar, involving purchase of at least three coupons (around $450–470 for the first three coupons, $75–90 for every additional one), each valid for a flight of any duration within the US.

9

Online booking agents and general travel sites

Ⓦ **www.cheapflights.com, www .cheaptickets.co.uk, www.cheaptickets .ca.** Deals on flights and packages, and links to destination-related sites.

Ⓦ **www.ebookers.com** Low fares on an extensive selection of flights.

Ⓦ **www.etn.nl/discount** A US hub of consolidator and discount-agent links, maintained by the nonprofit European Travel Network.

Ⓦ **www.expedia.com,** and **www.expedia .co.uk** Discount airfares, travel packages, and destination-specific deals.

Ⓦ **www.flynow.com** Online air travel and reservations.

Ⓦ **www.hotwire.com** Last-minute savings of up to forty percent on regular published fares. Travelers must be at least 18 years old. No refunds, transfers, or changes allowed. Bookings from the US only.

Ⓦ **www.lastminute.com** UK site offering last-minute deals.

Ⓦ **www.opodo.co.uk** Popular UK source for low airfares. Owned by nine major European airlines.

Ⓦ **www.orbitz.com** Comprehensive travel resource with great customer service.

Ⓦ **www.priceline.com, www.priceline .co.uk** Name-your-own-price website with discounts around forty percent off standard fares.

Ⓦ**www.seatguru.com** Very useful site giving you the lowdown on airline amenities and the best and worst seats per airline and airplane model.

Ⓦ **www.smilinjackskyauction.com/airlines .htm** Auctions tickets and travel packages to destinations worldwide. Bookings from the US only.

Ⓦ **travel.yahoo.com** Information about where to eat, sleep, etc.

Ⓦ **www.travelocity.com, www.travelocity .co.uk** Destination guides with deals on airfares, car rental, and lodging.

From the US and Canada

Washington DC is well connected to the rest of the US, as well as Canada, by air, and this is undoubtedly the first transportation choice for most North American travelers. Along the East Coast, Amtrak trains provide a viable option from New England to the mid-Atlantic states, as do buses, though neither option provides significant cost savings from anywhere else in the country.

By plane

The most convenient airport for domestic arrivals into DC is **Reagan National Airport**, just south of the Pentagon and linked to downtown DC by the Metro. Delta, United, US Airways, and American offer shuttles from New York's La Guardia Airport four to six times daily during the week, and slightly less frequently on weekends; US Airways also operates weekday shuttles from Boston. Additional airlines offering regular, daily service to Reagan National are Alaska Airlines (via Seattle), America West (Columbus, Phoenix), Continental (Houston, Newark), Midwest Airlines (Milwaukee), and Northwest (Philadelphia, Minneapolis, Detroit).

Most of the major airlines have nationwide service to **Dulles International**, which is probably where you'll land if you're coming from the West Coast. Southwest Airlines and US Airways have good deals for people who are willing to fly into **Baltimore** (BWI) and reserve in advance.

Fares are lowest in the Northeast corridor. From **New York** and **Boston**, you can pay as little as $120 round-trip, though $150–200 is more typical; fares are around $180–240 from **Chicago** and $200–250 from **Miami**. The price of flights from the **West Coast** is more likely to fluctuate – round-trip tickets from LA can cost as little as $200 (Southwest from LAX to BWI), and from **San Francisco** or **Seattle** they can go for $250, but are more likely to be between $300 and $500.

Air Canada has direct flights to DC from **Toronto** (to Reagan National) and **Montréal** (Reagan National and Dulles); from **Vancouver**, you'll have to change at Toronto. American carriers such as Delta, Northwest, and United also operate flights from these cities, often in combination with Canadian airlines. Special deals bring round-trip fares as low as C$300 from Montréal, though you're more likely to pay C$350–500, and the same from Toronto. From Vancouver, winter getaways start at C$550 round-trip (usually with one stop), though the more usual price is around C$600–700.

Airlines

Air Canada US and Canada ☎1-888/247-2262, ⓦwww.aircanada.ca
Air Tran ☎1-800/247-8726, ⓦwww.airtran.com
Alaska Airlines ☎1-800/252-7522, ⓦwww.alaskaair.com
America West ☎1-800/235-9292, ⓦwww.americawest.com
American ☎1-800/433-7300, ⓦwww.aa.com
American Trans Air (ATA) ☎1-800/435-9282, ⓦwww.ata.com
Continental ☎1-800/523-3273, ⓦwww.continental.com
Delta ☎1-800/221-1212, ⓦwww.delta.com
Frontier ☎1-800/432-1359, ⓦwww.flyfrontier.com
JetBlue ☎1-800/JET-BLUE, ⓦwww.jetblue.com
Midwest ☎1-800/452-2022, ⓦwww.midwestairlines.com
Northwest/KLM ☎1-800/225-2525, ⓦwww.nwa.com
Southwest ☎1-800/435-9792, ⓦwww.southwest.com
United ☎1-800/241-6522, ⓦwww.unitedal.com
US Airways US and Canada ☎1-800/428-4322, ⓦwww.usairways.com

Discount travel and flight agents

Air Brokers International ☎1-800/883-3273, ⓦwww.airbrokers.com. Consolidator and specialist in Round-the-World and Circle Pacific tickets.
Airtech ☎ 212/219-7000, ⓦwww.airtech.com. Works directly with airlines to broker standby seats, often at greatly discounted prices.
Educational Travel Center ☎1-800/747-5551, ⓦwww.edtrav.com. Low-cost fares, student and youth discounts, car rental, and tours.
Flight Centre US ☎1-866/WORLD-51, ⓦwww.flightcentre.com; Canada ☎1-888/WORLD-55, ⓦwww.flightcentre.ca. Guarantees lowest airfares.
STA Travel US ☎1-800/329-9537, Canada ☎1-888/427-5639, ⓦwww.statravel.com. Known as "the world's largest student travel organization." Specializes in independent travel.
Student Flights ☎1-800/255-8000, ⓦwww.isecard.com/studentflights. Student and youth fares, plus student IDs and bus passes.
Travel Avenue ☎1-800/333-3335, ⓦwww.travelavenue.com. Full-service travel agent that offers rebates on cruises, tours, and vacation packages.
Travel Cuts US ☎ 1-800/592-CUTS, Canada ☎1-888/246-9762, ⓦwww.travelcuts.com. Specializes in student, youth, and budget travel.

Travelers Advantage ☎1-877/259-2691, ⓦwww.travelersadvantage.com. Discount travel club, with cash-back deals and discounted car rental. Membership required ($1 for three-month trial).
Worldtek Travel ☎1-800/243-1723, ⓦwww.worldtek.com. Discount travel agency for worldwide travel.

Package tours

Booked in the US, a typical three-night jaunt to DC – including round-trip airfare plus three-star, room-only accommodation – starts at about $400 per person when flying from New York, or about $600 when flying from Los Angeles. Another $150–200 gets you upgraded to a room in a superior hotel.

Specialist tour operators

American Express Vacations ☎1-800/346-3607, ⓦwww.americanexpress.com/travel. Flights, hotels, last-minute specials, city-break packages and various specialty tours.
Amtrak Vacations ☎1-800/YES-RAIL, ⓦwww.amtrak.com/services/amtrak-vacations/html. Train or air rail trips throughout the Northeast, plus hotel reservations, car rentals, and sight-seeing tours to DC.
Collette Vacations ☎1-800/340-5158, ⓦwww.collettevacations.com. Choose from traditional tours, independent trips, or a combination of the two. Four- to six-night DC-only trips range from $550 to $1200, and the nine-day "Heritage of America" tour, also covering New York, Pennsylvania, and Virginia, starts at $1700. Prices include meals but exclude airfare/travel to DC.
Contiki Holidays ☎1-888/CONTIKI, ⓦwww.contiki.com. Trips for the 18–35-year-old crowd. The seven-day "Eastern Discovery" tour (from $819, flights extra) includes DC.
Globus and Cosmos ☎1-866/755-8581, ⓦwww.globusandcosmos.com. Deluxe escorted tours. The "Historic East" (eight days, from $1339) and "East Niagara Falls & DC" (seven days, from $1249) tours include significant time in the District. Prices include meals. Request brochures online or via a travel agent.
Insight Vacations ☎1-800/582-8380, ⓦwww.insightvacations.com. Worldwide tours. The "Highlights of New England and Canada" tour, despite its name, includes DC as part of a twelve-day jaunt (from $1384) by motor coach.
Suntrek ☎1-800/SUN-TREK, ⓦwww.suntrek.com. Whistle-stop camping tours, with the East Coast itineraries mixing city stays with adventures in

the great outdoors. The most you get in DC, though, is two nights on the three-week "Swingin' East" tour (from $1084). Meals and personal expenses extra.

Trek America US and Canada ☎1-800/221-0596, ⓦ www.trekamerica.com. Fun, flexible, youth-oriented (18–38-year-olds) camping tours that include DC as part of larger tours of the region. The two-week "Best of the East," departing New York, begins at $824, plus meals and personal expenses.
United Vacations ☎1-888/854-3899, ⓦwww.unitedvacations.com. Custom-make your DC trip with United flights and a good selection of four- and five-star hotels. Car rental and other services can be arranged too.

By train

The sprawling metropolitan area between Boston and Washington has the most dependable **Amtrak** service in the country (☎1-800/USA-RAIL, ⓦwww.amtrak.com). The high-speed, 150mph **Acela** Express has cut the travel time from New York City to Washington DC to two hours and fifty minutes, down from three and a half hours, and six and a half hours from Boston, down from nine hours. If you're traveling from New York City or points south, the Acela is probably the most convenient way to reach Washington, not the least because it drops you right in the middle of town, at Union Station. Amtrak has an arrangement with United Airlines that allows you to fly one leg of your trip to DC and travel the other by rail (**Air Rail** ☎1-800/437-3441).

Round-trip fares for the regular service begin around $150 from **New York** and $180 from Boston. Fares for the reserved-seating express trains can be twice as high. If you're traveling from cities outside the Northeast, ticket prices are comparable to or higher than the equivalent airfare, and if you want any extras, like a sleeping compartment, it will cost you a lot more: the three-day rail journey from **Los Angeles**, for example, costs around $1500 round-trip with an economy sleeper bed, but only $270 without it. In general, Amtrak service isn't a budget option, although some of the journeys are pleasant enough – for example, the Crescent, which travels from New York to New Orleans via DC, makes for a rewarding 24-hour

trip between Washington and the Big Easy, and there is regular Amtrak service to DC from **Toronto** (16hr; C$225 round-trip) and **Montréal** (14hr; C$300), both via New York City. Amtrak often has **seasonal specials**, and students get a fifteen-percent discount on most tickets; check its website or call its toll-free number to inquire about these deals.

Longer-term **rail passes** can be bought in various increments, by both domestic and overseas visitors (the latter must purchase before traveling to North America). These are only worth looking into if DC is part of a longer trip; also worth noting, the passes are not valid for riding the Acela.

By bus

Buses are cheaper and run more frequently than trains, but they take forever and, in a worst-case scenario, you may need to use one of those toilets. **Greyhound** is the chief bus operator to DC (☎1-800/229-9424, ⓦwww.greyhound.com); in addition, **Peter Pan** Bus Lines (☎1-800/343-9999, ⓦwww.peterpanbus.com) offers service to Washington DC from Boston, New York, and **Philadelphia**, sometimes in combination with Greyhound. Standard midweek, round-trip fares for the five-hour trip from **New York City** start just over $100, though they can be as little as $40 with one week's advance purchase. Expect to pay $100–170 from **Boston** (10hr), $120–215 from **Chicago** (18hr), and $230 from **Los Angeles** (60–78hr). Round-trip fares from **Montréal** (13hr) are C$160-300, and around C$250 from **Toronto** (15–18hr); you can book either through the main US portal or on **Greyhound Canada** (☎1-800/661-8747, ⓦwww.greyhound.ca). On all routes, you'll pay a bit more if you travel between Friday and Sunday, though discounted seven-day-advance-purchase tickets and student, senior, and "companion" (two-for-one) fares are often available.

A variety of **bus passes** good for extended periods of time – from a week to sixty days, costing from $220 to $650 – are also available, only worthwhile if DC is part of a longer itinerary. Equivalent passes can be purchased by overseas visitors before leaving home; most travel agents can oblige, as can specialist agents like STA, Trailfinders and Usit Now.

By car

Driving to DC gives you a certain amount of freedom and flexibility, but you'll probably never use your car once you reach the city, since the public transit system is so good. The box below gives an idea of the distances and times involved in driving to DC. Routes into the city are shown on color map 00 and explained in "Arrival," where you'll also find some useful tips on the intricacies of driving in DC itself.

Car rental deals vary wildly, though in general you'll find better prices over the weekend than during the week. You can often realize **significant savings** by booking in advance with a major firm that has representation in DC; most agencies in the city have offices at Reagan National, Dulles International, and BWI airports, and at Union Station. When booking, be sure to get free unlimited mileage and be aware that rates can go up by as much as $200 if you want to pick up the car in one location and leave it at another. If you choose not to pay until you arrive, take a written confirmation of the price with you. Always read the small print carefully for details on Collision Damage Waiver (sometimes called Liability Damage Waiver), a form of insurance that often isn't included in the initial rental charge but can be worth having. This insurance specifically covers the car you are driving (you are, in any case, insured for damage to other vehicles). At around $15 a day, it can add substantially to the total rental cost, but without it you (and, by extension, your own insurance company) are liable for every scratch to the car, even those that aren't your fault. Then again, don't be

suckered into insurance you already have; call your credit card company to see if it offers free insurance if you use your card to pay. **If you are under 25**, be prepared for hefty surcharges on top of the usual rates.

Car rental companies

Alamo US ☎ 1-800/GO-ALAMO, ⓦ www.alamo .com

Avis Canada ☎ 1-800/272-5871, US ☎ 1-800/230-4898, ⓦ www.avis.com

Budget Canada ☎ 1-800/472-3325, US ☎ 1-800/527-0700, ⓦ www.budget.com

Dollar ☎ 1-800/800-3665, ⓦ www.dollar.com

Enterprise ☎ 1-800/726-8222, ⓦ www .enterprise.com

Hertz Canada ☎ 1-800/263-0600, US ☎ 1-800/654-313001, ⓦ www.hertz.com

National ☎ 1-800/962-7070, ⓦ www.nationalcar .com

Thrifty ☎ 1-800/847-4389, ⓦ www.thrifty.com

From the UK and Ireland

There are daily **nonstop flights** to Washington DC from **London Heathrow** with British Airways, United Airlines, and Virgin Atlantic; BMI British Midland flies nonstop from **Manchester** daily except Tuesday. These flights take about eight hours, though return flights are always an hour or so shorter due to tail winds. Outbound flights usually leave Britain mid-morning, and inbound flights from the US usually arrive in the early morning. Other airlines serving DC, including Air Canada, Air France, American, Continental, Delta, Icelandair, KLM/Northwest, Lufthansa, and US Airways, fly from Heathrow or **London Gatwick** via their respective American or European hubs. These flights can add an extra two to five hours to your trip each way, depending on how long you have to wait for your connection.

Return fares to Washington DC can cost more than £500 between June and August

---

Distances and driving times to DC

Boston: 350 miles (8hr)
Chicago: 710 miles (16hr)
Los Angeles: 2690 miles (3 days)
Miami: 1057 miles (24hr)
Montréal: 610 miles (14hr)

New York: 240 miles (5hr 30min)
San Francisco: 2845 miles (3 days)
Seattle: 2868 miles (3 days)
Toronto: 570 miles (12hr)

and at Christmas, though £400–440 is the more typical range. Prices in winter often fall to under £300. The nonstop flights from Heathrow tend to be among the cheapest. With BMI British Midland, you can usually add on a connecting domestic flight to Manchester from one of the other UK regional airports for no extra cost; with other airlines, add-on fares from UK regional airports to London cost around £80–90 return. More flexible tickets to DC, requiring less advance-booking time or allowing changes or refunds, often cost an additional £100–120.

There are no nonstop flights from Ireland to Washington DC. Air France, Aer Lingus, and Delta offer service **from Dublin** via Paris, New York (or Manchester), and Atlanta, respectively. The trip takes between ten and fifteen hours. Other airlines, such as Virgin Atlantic and United, will route you through London, which takes about the same amount of time. Alternatively, you could arrange your own Dublin-to-London flight with low-cost airlines like easyJet or Ryanair and pick up a connecting flight to DC. Return fares from Dublin to DC start at around €650 in the low season, rising to €750–800 in high season. Although Dulles is often the first choice for international travelers to DC, you may be able to save up to €100 by landing in Baltimore's BWI airport, though you'll likely have to connect in London.

Airlines

Aer Lingus UK ☎0845/084 4444, Ireland ☎ 0818/365 000, ⓦwww.aerlingus.ie
Air Canada UK ☎08705/247 226, ⓦwww.aircanada.ca
Air France UK ☎0845/359 1000, Ireland ☎01/605 0383, ⓦwww.airfrance.com
American UK ☎0845/778 9789, ⓦwww.aa.com
British Airways UK ☎0870/850 9850, Ireland ☎1800/626 747, ⓦwww.britishairways.com
British Midland (BMI) UK ☎0870/607 0555, Ireland ☎01/407 3036, ⓦwww.flybmi.com
Continental UK ☎0845/607 6760, Ireland ☎1890/925 252, ⓦwww.flycontinental.com
Delta UK ☎0800/414767, Ireland ☎01/407 3165, ⓦwww.delta.com
easyJet UK ☎0871/750 0100, ⓦwww.easyjet.com

Icelandair UK ☎020/7874 1000, ⓦwww.Icelandair.net
KLM/Northwest UK ☎0870/507 4074, ⓦwww.klm.com
Lufthansa UK ☎0845/773 7747, Ireland ☎01/844 5544, ⓦwww.lufthansa.com
Ryanair UK ☎0871/246 0000, Ireland ☎0818/30 30 30, ⓦwww.ryanair.com
United UK ☎0845/844 4777, Ireland ☎1800/535 300, ⓦwww.unitedairlines.co.uk
US Airways UK ☎0845/600 3300, Ireland ☎1890/925 065, ⓦwww.usairways.com
Virgin Atlantic UK ☎01293/450 150, Ireland ☎ 01/873 3388, ⓦwww.virgin-atlantic.com

Discount travel and flight agents

Apex Travel Ireland ☎01/241 8000, ⓦwww.apextravel.ie. Specialists in flights to Australia, East Asia, and the US. Consolidators for British Airways, American, and SAS Scandinavian.
Aran Travel First Choice Ireland ☎091/562 595, ⓦwww.firstchoicetravel.ie. Low-cost flights worldwide.
Bridge the World UK ☎0870/443 2399, ⓦwww.bridgetheworld.com. Long-haul travel specialists with Round-the-World tickets and tailor-made packages geared toward backpackers.
ebookers UK ☎0870/010 7000, ⓦwww.ebookers.com; Ireland ☎01/241 5689, ⓦwww.ebookers.ie. Allows you to create tailor-made itineraries online.
Flight Centre UK ☎0870/890 8099, ⓦwww.flightcentre.co.uk. Guarantees lowest airfares.
Flights4Less UK ☎0871/222 3423, ⓦwww.flights4less.co.uk. Airline consolidator and tour operator. Offers package deals and independent, tailor-made itineraries. Part of Lastminute.com.
Flynow UK ☎0870/444 0045, ⓦwww.flynow.com. Deals directly with airlines, hotels, car rental companies, and other service providers.
Joe Walsh Tours Ireland ☎01/676 0991, ⓦwww.joewalshtours.ie. Long-established travel agency and tour operator.
Lee Travel Ireland ☎021/427 7111, ⓦwww.leetravel.ie. Comprehensive, independent travel agency.
McCarthy's Travel Ireland ☎021/427 0127, ⓦwww.mccarthystravel.ie. Offers business, wedding, honeymoon, pilgrimage, skiing, and other packages.
North South Travel ☎01245/608 291, ⓦwww.northsouthtravel.co.uk. Profits go to NST Development Trust, a charity that supports grassroots projects in disadvantaged areas of Asia, Africa, and Latin America.

Premier Travel UK ☎ 028/7126 3333, ⓦ www
.premiertravel.uk.com. Group travel, business
travel, car rentals, travel insurance, and daily
specials.

Rosetta Travel UK ☎ 028/9064 4996, ⓦ www
.rosettatravel.com. Travel bargains with flights
leaving from Belfast.

STA Travel UK ☎ 0870/160 0599, ⓦ www
.statravel.co.uk. Known as "the world's largest
student travel organization." Specializes in
independent travel.

Trailfinders UK ☎ 020/7938 3939, ⓦ www
.trailfinders.com; Ireland ☎ 01/677 7888, ⓦ www
.trailfinders.ie. One of the best-informed and most
efficient agents for independent travelers.

Travel Bag UK ☎ 0870/890 1456, ⓦ www
.travelbag.co.uk. Independent travel agency whose
consultants specialize in specific destinations.

Travel Care UK ☎ 0870/112 0085, ⓦ www
.travelcare.co.uk. Flights, holiday deals, and city
breaks around the world.

Usit Now Northern Ireland ☎ 028/9032 7111,
ⓦ www.usitnow.com; Republic of Ireland ☎
0818/200 020, ⓦ www.usit.ie. Specialists in
student, youth, and independent travel.

World Travel Centre Ireland ☎ 01/416 7007,
ⓦ www.worldtravel.ie. Experts in long-haul flights
from Ireland.

Package tours

Numerous companies offer package deals
from the UK to Washington DC, mostly
short city breaks from three to five days. For
a three-day trip, typical rates will run around
£600–650 per person in the high season,
and drop to around £450–500 in the off-
season. Around £100 more gets you a
five-star or superior-grade hotel package.
If you plan to see more of the US than just
DC, fly-drive deals – which include car rental
when buying a transatlantic ticket from an
airline or tour operator – are always cheaper
than renting on the spot. Most specialist
companies offer **fly-drive packages**, but
watch out for hidden extras, such as local
taxes, "drop-off" charges, and redundant
insurance costs.

Specialist tour operators

American Holidays Belfast ☎ 028/9023 8762,
Dublin ☎ 01/673 3840, ⓦ www.american
-holidays.com. Package deals from Ireland to all
parts of the US and Canada.

Bales Worldwide UK ☎ 0870/241 3208, ⓦ www
.balesworldwide.com. Independent tour operator
offering escorted tours and tailor-made trips.

British Airways Holidays ☎ 0870/240 0747,
ⓦ www.baholidays.co.uk. An exhaustive range of
package and tailor-made holidays around the
world.

CIE Tours International Ireland ☎ 01/703 1888,
ⓦ www.cietours.ie. Wide range of escorted bus
tours.

Contiki Tours UK ☎ 020/8290 6777, ⓦ www
.contiki.co.uk. Trips for the 18–35-year-old crowd.
The seven-day "Eastern Discovery" tour (from £565,
flights extra) includes DC.

Kuoni Travel UK ☎ 01306/747 002, ⓦ www
.kuoni.co.uk. Flexible holiday packages to long-haul
destinations.

My Travel UK ☎ 0870/2387777, ⓦ www
.uk.mytravel.com. Large tour company offering
packages, cruises, tailor-made itineraries, and
more.

Thomas Cook Holidays ☎ 0870/0100 437,
ⓦ www.thomascook.co.uk. City breaks in either
three- or four-star accommodations.

TravelScene ☎ 0870/777 4445, ⓦ www
.travelscene.co.uk. Tailor-made trips and budget
city breaks.

TrekAmerica ☎ 01295/256 777, ⓦ www
.trekamerica.co.uk. Camping tours catering to
18–38-year-olds. DC is included in larger tours of
the region. The two-week "Best of the East" tour,
departing New York, costs from £562 (flights and
meals not included).

Twohigs Ireland ☎ 01/677 2666, ⓦ www.twohigs
.com. Specialists in travel to the US, as well as
Australia, Africa, and East Asia.

United Vacations ☎ 0870/606 2222, ⓦ www
.unitedvacations.co.uk. One-stop agent for
tailor-made holidays, city breaks, fly-drive deals, pre-
booked sight-seeing tours, and more.

Virgin Holidays ☎ 0870/220 2788, ⓦ www
.virginholidays.co.uk. City breaks with hotel stays in
Arlington, VA or DC. Flights with Virgin Atlantic.

From Australia and New Zealand

As there are no direct flights to Washington DC from Australia or New Zealand, the
quickest way to get there is to fly via **Los
Angeles** with Qantas, American, or United.
Qantas and American offer nonstop flights
to LAX from Auckland and Sydney, while
Air New Zealand and United connect Auckland via Sydney. It might be cheapest to fly
from Los Angeles to New York City, but,
of course, there will be an extra fare to get

you finally to DC (around $120 round-trip). Specialist agents can help sort out your options and advise about US air passes, which are the cheapest way to fly to DC from whichever American hub you've arrived at.

Return fares to the US East Coast sometimes go for less than A$2200/NZ$2550, though ticketed through to DC they're more likely to cost around A$2400/NZ$2750. Unless you're specifically looking at a short-term city visit, it's going to be a better value for most people to consider buying a **Round-the-World ticket**. The most basic of these, which start at around A$2400/NZ$2750, buys you as many as five stopovers, often including New York. You may have to pick a ticket with more stopovers to get DC specifically included, but it's still unlikely to cost you more than A$2800/NZ$3200.

Airlines

Air France Australia ☎ 1300/361 400, New Zealand ☎ 09/308 3352, ⓦ www.airfrance.com
Air New Zealand Australia ☎ 13 24 76, ⓦ www.airnz.com.au; New Zealand ☎ 0800/737 000, ⓦ www.airnz.co.nz
American Australia ☎ 1300/130 757, New Zealand ☎ 0800/887 997, ⓦ www.aa.com
British Airways Australia ☎ 1300/767 177, New Zealand ☎ 0800/274 847 or 09/356 8690, ⓦ www.britishairways.com
Cathay Pacific Australia ☎ 13 17 47, New Zealand ☎ 0508/800 454 or 09/379 0861, ⓦ www.cathaypacific.com
Continental Australia ☎ 1300/361 400, New Zealand ☎ 09/308 3350, ⓦ www.continental.com
Delta Australia ☎ 02/9251 3211, New Zealand ☎ 09/379 3370, ⓦ www.delta.com
Japan Airlines (JAL) Australia ☎ 02/9272 1111, New Zealand ☎ 09/379 9906, ⓦ www.jal.com
KLM/Northwest Australia ☎ 1300/303 747, New Zealand ☎ 09/309 1782, ⓦ www.klm.com
Korean Air Australia ☎ 02/9262 6000, New Zealand ☎ 09/914 2000, ⓦ www.koreanair.com.au
Lufthansa Australia ☎ 1300/655 727, New Zealand ☎ 0800/945 220, ⓦ www.lufthansa.com
Malaysia Airlines Australia ☎ 13 26 27, New Zealand ☎ 0800/777 747, ⓦ www.malaysia-airlines.com
Qantas Australia ☎ 13 13 13, New Zealand ☎ 0800/808 767 or 09/357 8900, ⓦ www.qantas.com

Thai Airways Australia ☎ 1300/651 960, New Zealand ☎ 09/377 3886, ⓦ www.thaiair.com
United Australia ☎ 13 17 77, New Zealand ☎ 09/379 3800, ⓦ www.united.com
Virgin Atlantic Australia ☎ 02/9244 2747, New Zealand ☎ 09/308 3377, ⓦ www.virgin-atlantic.com

Discount travel and flight agents

Flight Centre Australia ☎ 13 31 33, ⓦ www.flightcentre.com.au; New Zealand ☎ 0800/243 544, ⓦ www.flightcentre.co.nz. Guarantees lowest airfares.
Holiday Shoppe New Zealand ☎ 0800/808 480, ⓦ www.holidayshoppe.co.nz. Great deals on flights, hotels, packages, and tours.
OTC Australia ☎ 1300/855 118, ⓦ www.otctravel.com.au. Cheap hotels, flights, and getaway deals.
STA Travel Australia ☎ 1300/733 035, New Zealand ☎ 0508/782 872, ⓦ www.statravel.com. Known as "the world's largest student travel organization." Specializes in independent travel.
Student Uni Travel Australia ☎ 02/9232 8444, ⓦ www.usitworld.com/services/aus.htm; New Zealand ☎ 09/379 4224, ⓦ www.usitworld.com/countries/nz/. Caters to student, youth, and backpacker markets. Round-the-World tickets, adventure tours, traveler's insurance, and travel passes.
Trailfinders Australia ☎ 02/9247 7666, ⓦ www.trailfinders.com.au. One of the best-informed and most efficient agents for independent travelers.
travel.com Australia ☎ 1300/130 482 or 02/9249 5444, ⓦ www.travel.com.au; New Zealand ☎ 0800/468 332, ⓦ www.travel.co.nz. Books flights, car rentals, and accommodations.

Specialist tour operators

Adventure World Australia ☎ 02/8913 0755, ⓦ www.adventureworld.com.au; New Zealand ☎ 09/524 5118, ⓦ www.adventureworld.co.nz. Specializes in adventure travel throughout the world.
Australian Pacific Touring Australia ☎ 1800/675 222 or 03/9277 8555, New Zealand ☎ 09/279 6077, ⓦ www.aptours.com. Package tours and independent US travel.
Canada and America Travel Specialists Australia ☎ 02/9922 4600, ⓦ www.canada-americatravel.com.au. Accommodation, train travel, adventure sports, car and RV rentals, bus passes, cruises, escorted tours, and independent travel throughout North America.
Contiki Holidays Australia ☎ 02/9511 2200, New Zealand ☎ 09/309 8824, ⓦ www.contiki.com.

Trips for the 18–35-year-old crew. The seven-day "Eastern Discovery" tour (from A$1280, NZ$1670) includes DC.

Sydney Travel ☎ 02/9250 9320, ⓦ www .sydneytravel.com.au. US flights, accommodations, city breaks, and car rental.

United Vacations Australia ☎ 1300/887 870, ⓦ www.unitedvacations.com.au. Tailor-made

itineraries with departures from several Australian airports.

USA Travel Australia ☎ 02/9250 9320, ⓦ www .usatravel.com.au. Good deals on flights, accommodations, city stays, car rental and trip packages.

Viator ⓦ www.viator.com. Books local tours and sight-seeing trips in cities around the world.

Red tape and visas

Keeping up with the constant changes to US **entry requirements** since 9/11 can sometimes seem to be a hopeless task. Several times a year the American government announces new, often harsher, restrictions on foreign entry into the country, adding considerably to the red tape involved in visiting it. Nonetheless, there are several basic rules that apply to these requirements, which are detailed (and should be frequently checked for updates) on the US State Department website ⓦ www.travel.state.gov.

As of 2004, under the **Visa Waiver Program**, if you're a citizen of the UK, Ireland, Australia, New Zealand, most Western European states, or other selected countries like Singapore, Japan, and Brunei (27 in all), and visiting the United States for less than ninety days, you need an onward or return ticket, a Machine Readable Passport (MRP), and a visa waiver form. The MRP requirement is a recent manifestation (November 2004) of America's security clampdown, and requires certain high-tech protections built into the passport against fraud, counterfeiting, and so on. It is up to the various countries covered by the Visa Waiver Program to provide such passports to its citizens; for more information, inquire at American embassies or consulates (see below). The **Visa Waiver Form** (an I-94W) will be provided either by your travel agency, or by the airline during check-in or on the plane, and must be presented to Immigration on arrival. The same form covers entry across the US borders with Canada and Mexico. If you're in the Visa Waiver Program and intend to work, study, or stay in the country for more than ninety days, you must apply for a regular

visa through your local US embassy or consulate. UK citizens must apply in person at the US Embassy in London (see below), under rules adopted in 2003, and have "British Citizen" stated on their passports.

By 2005, Visa Waiver Program countries will include "biometric identifiers" – like digitally scanned fingerprints and headshot photographs– in their citizens' passports, just as non-Visa Waiver Program countries are required to do. To stay up-to-date on this issues visit ⓦ www.dhs.gov/us-visit or ⓦ www.travel.state.gov/vwp.

Canadian citizens, who have not always needed a passport to get into the US, should make sure to have it handy when seeking to enter the country. If you're planning to stay for more than ninety days, you'll need a visa, which you can apply for by mail through the US embassy or nearest US consulate. If you cross the US border by car, be prepared for US Customs officials to possibly search your vehicle.

Citizens of non-waiver countries should contact their local US embassy or consulate for details of current entry requirements, as they often need to have both a valid passport and a non-immigrant visitor's visa. To obtain a visa, complete the application form available at most travel agencies or dozens of sites on the Internet, and send it with the appropriate fee, two photographs, and a passport – valid for at least six months from the end of your planned stay – to the nearest US embassy or consulate. Visas are not issued to convicted criminals or those with ties to radical political groups; complications also arise if you are HIV-positive or have TB, hepatitis, or other major communicable diseases. Furthermore, the US government now fingerprints all visitors to the US from countries not covered by the Visa Waiver Program, and applies spot background checks looking for evidence of past criminal or terrorist connections.

For further information or to get a visa extension before your time is up, contact the nearest **US Citizenship and Immigration Service office**, whose address will be at the front of the phone book, under the Federal Government Offices listings, or call ☎ 1-800/877-3676. You can also contact the National Customer Service Center at ☎ 1-800/375-5283. The local USCIS office for Washington DC is at 4420 N

Fairfax Drive, Arlington, VA 22203 (Mon–Fri 7.30am–2pm; 🖰 uscis.gov). Immigration officials will assume that you're working in the US illegally, and it's up to you to prove otherwise. If you can, bring along an upstanding American citizen to vouch for you, and be prepared for potentially hostile questioning. Under no circumstances are visitors who have been admitted under the Visa Waiver Program allowed to extend their stays beyond ninety days.

US embassies abroad

For a list of foreign embassies and consulates in Washington DC, see "Directory."
Australia Moonah Place, Yarralumla, Canberra, ACT ☎ 02/6214 5600, 🖰 usembassy-australia.state.gov/index.html
Canada 490 Sussex Drive, Ottawa, ON K1P 5T1 ☎ 613/238-5335, 🖰 www.usembassycanada.gov
Ireland 42 Elgin Rd, Ballsbridge, Dublin 4 ☎ 01/668-7122, 🖰 www.usembassy.ie
New Zealand 29 Fitzherbert Terrace, Thorndon, Wellington ☎ 04/462 6000, 🖰 www.usembassy.org.nz
UK 24 Grosvenor Square, London W1A 1AE ☎ 020/7499 9000, visa hotline ☎ 09068/200290, 🖰 www.usembassy.org.uk

Insurance

Although not compulsory, international travelers should have some form of travel insurance. The US has no national healthcare system, and it can cost an arm and a leg (so to speak) having even minor medical treatment. Many insurance policies can be adapted to reflect the coverage you want – for example, sickness and accident benefits can often be excluded or included at will. If you do take medical coverage, verify if benefits will be paid during treatment or only after your return home, and whether there is a 24-hour medical emergency phone number. If you need to make a claim, keep receipts for medicines and medical treatment. Also, if you have anything stolen from you, you must file an official police report.

A typical **travel insurance** policy also provides coverage for the loss of baggage, tickets, and a certain amount of cash or travelers' checks, as well as the cancellation or curtailment of your trip. Most policies exclude so-called dangerous sports unless an extra premium is paid; this should not be a consideration if you're just visiting the city itself.

Before buying travel insurance, **check that you're not already covered.** Credit card companies, home-insurance policies, and private medical plans sometimes cover you and your belongings when you're abroad. Most travel agents, tour operators, banks, and insurance brokers will be able to help you, or you could consider the travel insurance offered by Rough Guides. Remember when securing baggage insurance, to make sure that the per-article limit – typically under $800/£500 – will cover your most valuable possession.

Health

For emergencies or ambulances, dial ☎**911**. If you have medical or dental problems that don't require an ambulance, most hospitals will have a walk-in **emergency room**; for the nearest hospital, check with your hotel or dial ☎**411**. Should you need to see a **doctor**, lists can be found in the *Yellow Book* under "Clinics" or "Physicians and Surgeons." A basic consultation fee is around $60–120, and medications aren't cheap either – keep all your receipts for later insurance claims. Many minor ailments can be remedied by items available in **drugstores**. Foreign visitors should bear in mind that some pills available over-the-counter at home need a prescription in the US, and local brand names can be confusing; ask for advice at any drugstore's pharmacy.

Rough Guides travel insurance

Rough Guides offers its own low-cost travel insurance, customized for our readers. It's available to anyone, of any nationality and any age, traveling anywhere in the world. For a policy quote or to buy online visit at ⊛www.roughguides.com/insurance.

Information, websites, and maps

The main sources of information for the District are the DC Chamber of Commerce and the Washington DC Convention and Tourism Corporation. Both of these offices can send you brochures, visitor guides, events calendars, and maps in advance of your trip, and answer any questions once you've arrived; however, only the Chamber of Commerce visitor center is set up for walk-in visits. There are also numerous DC-related websites, most with fully searchable databases. These let you read up on the hottest new restaurants and clubs and can help you plan your sight-seeing itinerary around the capital.

Information

Before leaving for DC, it's worth contacting one of the organizations listed below under "Tourism offices" to help plan your trip. Call ahead for information or visit their websites; the Convention and Tourism Corporation in particular has reams of helpful information online, from an events calendar to hotel-and-tour packages.

On arrival, you'll find maps and other guides available in the airports, Union Station, and hotels. The most useful item to pick up is the free *Washington DC Visitors Guide*, with listings, reviews, and contact numbers. Once in the city, your first stop should be the **DC Visitor Information Center**, Ronald Reagan Building, 1300 Pennsylvania Ave NW (Mon–Fri 8am–5.30pm, Sat & Sun 9am–4pm; ☎1-866/DC-IS-FUN, ⊛www.dcvisit.com), which can help with maps, tours, and regionwide information.

Out and about in DC, other resources include the **White House Visitor Information Center**, which has details on the Executive Mansion along with National Park sights all over the District, and the **Smithsonian Institution Building** on the Mall, which is the best stop for Smithsonian museum information. You'll also come across National Park Service rangers – in kiosks on the Mall, at the major memorials – who should also be able to answer general queries. One of the most conveniently located ranger sites is the **Ellipse Visitor Pavilion** (daily 8am–3pm; ⊛www.nps.gov/whho/PPSth), on the east side of the Ellipse (in front of the White House) near the bleacher seats. **National Park Service Headquarters** runs an information office (Mon–Fri 9am–5pm; ☎ 202/208-4747), inside the Department of the Interior at 1849 C St NW, that has information about all the city's national monuments and memorials. Additionally, neighborhoods like Georgetown and cities like Alexandria have their own visitor centers covering their respective sights.

As far as **local newspapers and magazines** go, you can't go wrong armed with a free copy of the weekly *City Paper* (available in stores, bars, and restaurants), which has listings of entertainment and cultural events; the free monthly *Where: Washington* magazine (from major hotels and terminals), which provides tourist-oriented information; the glossy *Washingtonian* magazine ($3.95 at newsstands and bookstores), geared toward the wine-loving, jet-setter crowd; and Friday's *Washington Post*. Many neighborhoods and all universities issue free weekly or monthly papers, full of news, reviews, and listings.

Tourism offices

Alexandria in the Ramsay House, 221 King St, Alexandria, VA 22314 ☎703/838-4200 or 1-800/388-9119, ⊛www.funside.com. Daily 9am–5pm.

Arlington 735 S 18th St, Arlington, VA 22202 ☎703/228-5720 or 1-800/677-6267, ⊛www.arlingtonvirginiausa.com. Daily 9am–5pm.

DC Chamber of Commerce 1300 Pennsylvania Ave NW, Washington DC 20005 ☎202/347-7201, ⓕ638-6762, ⊛www.dcchamber.org. Mon–Fri 8am–5.30pm, Sat & Sun 9am–4pm.

Georgetown 3242 M St NW, Washington DC

20007 ☎ 202/303-1600, ⓦ www.georgetowndc
.com. Wed–Fri 9am–4.30pm, Sat & Sun 10am–
4pm.
**National Park Service National Capital
Region** 1849 C St NW, Washington DC 20240
☎ 202/208-4747, ⓦ www.nps.gov. Mon–Fri
9am–5pm.
**Washington DC Convention and Tourism
Corporation (WCTC)** 901 7th St NW, 4th Floor,
Washington DC 20001 ☎ 202/789-7000; in the
UK ☎ 020/8877 4521 or 01235/824482 for
information pack; ⓕ 202/789-7037, ⓦ www
.washington.org.
White House Visitor Center 1450 Pennsylvania
Ave NW, Washington DC 20004 ☎ 202/208-1631,
ⓦ www.nps.gov/whho/WHVC. Daily 7.30am–4pm.
Maps, brochures, and information about major city
sights.

Special events lines

Dial-A-Museum ☎ 202/357-2020 Mon–Sat
9am–4pm; 900 Jefferson Drive SW, Washington DC
20560. Smithsonian Institution exhibits and special
events.
Dial-A-Park ☎ 02/619-7275. Events at National
Park Service facilities.
Post-Haste ☎ 202/334-9000. *Washington
Post* information line for news, weather, sports,
restaurants, events, and festivals.

Useful websites

Throughout the guide, websites are listed for
those museums and other attractions that
have them (most do), along with hotels and
venues. Beyond these, however, a handful
of useful sites are well worth a look when
preparing your trip to DC, and can offer a
particular slant or inside information on the
District that you may not find elsewhere.

Art and culture

Embassy Events ⓦ www.embassyevents
.com. Lists musical events, art shows, lectures,
food and wine dinners, and other activities hosted by
respective countries' embassies. Also allows you to
look inside those marvelous buildings around Dupont
Circle and Kalorama.
National Academies Arts Exhibitions ⓦ www
.nationalacademies.org/arts. Information about art
and photography exhibitions and concerts held in
science-oriented buildings.
Washington Art ⓦ www.washingtonart.com.
Website where DC-area visual artists display

their work online. Includes exhibition information,
discussion forums, and links to other local art sites.
An associated poetry quarterly, *Beltway* (ⓦ www
.washingtonart.com/beltway), publishes the work of
area poets and lists relevant news and events.

Newspapers and magazines

City Paper ⓦ www.washingtoncitypaper.com.
DC's alternative news weekly. Strong on reviews
(both mainstream and off-the-wall), local events, and
classified ads.
The Hill ⓦ hillnews.com. Aimed at those who can't
get enough of inside-the-Beltway news, gossip, and
intrigue. Covers current events, committee hearings,
lobbying, campaign activity, and spirited punditry.
Washington Post ⓦ www.washingtonpost.com.
The online version of the city's best newspaper, with
a full, searchable database, entertainment guide, and
visitor information.
Washingtonian ⓦ www.washingtonian.com. The
online restaurant guide is the best part of the site;
otherwise, plenty of information about living and
working in DC, with a heavy upper-middle-class slant.

Politics

American Politics Journal ⓦ www
.americanpolitics.com. Online, left-leaning political
magazine providing a "moderate and humorous look
at Beltway shenanigans," with daily updates, articles,
and features by politicians, journalists, lobbyists, and
other insiders.
American Presidents ⓦ www
.americanpresidents.org. Everything you ever
wanted to know about every president, from George
Washington to George Dubya, featuring biographies,
portraits, inaugural addresses, links to reference
material, quick facts, and video clips.
Polling Report ⓦ www.pollingreport.com. Covers
trends in American public opinion on everything from
religion to pop culture. Essential reading for political
horse-race bettors.
Thomas ⓦ thomas.loc.gov. Online resource for
legislative information. The only site with biographies
of every member of Congress since 1774, the full
text of the Constitution, committee reports, roll calls
of votes, and much more.

Tourism

Cultural Tourism DC ⓦ www.culturaltourismdc
.orgⓦwww.dcheritage.org. Good information on
smaller museums, historic houses, and neighborhood
highlights. Allows you to build a customized guide to
what you want to see.

Explore DC ⓦ www.exploredc.org. Up-close look at federal buildings, presidential sites, and places showcasing African-American history and culture. Its online tours of Civil War battlefields, historic architecture, and notable parks and gardens are particularly good.

Station Masters ⓦ www.stationmasters.com. Very effective site highlighting major attractions, buildings, and roads around individual Metrorail stations. Gives the location of parking facilities, station escalators and elevators, and train routes.

White House Historical Association ⓦ www .whitehousehistory.org. Online tours of the president's house, plus special features on the various presidents, resources for children and teachers, and a chance to buy a White House Christmas ornament for your tree.

Maps

The **maps** in this guide, along with the free city plans you'll pick up from tourist offices, hotels, and museums, will be sufficient to help you find your way around DC. If you want something a bit more comprehensive, best is the rip-proof, waterproof *Rough Guide Map to Washington DC* ($8.95/£4.99/C$13.50), which details DC's streets (and extends into Virginia) and pinpoints recommended restaurants,

bars, sights, and shops along the way. If you really want to go all out, or are traversing the more unfamiliar outlying parts of the city, you can pick up the comprehensive *Thomas Guide 2004: Washington DC Metro* ($38), a spiral-bound book that provides close-up, exhaustive coverage of even the smallest roads in the area.

If you'll be traveling beyond DC, the **free road maps** issued by each state are usually fine for general driving and route planning. To get hold of one, either write to the state tourist office directly or stop by any state welcome center or visitor center. Rand McNally (ⓦ www.randmcnally.com) produces good commercial state maps, and ranger stations in national parks, state parks, and wilderness areas sell good local hiking maps for $1–3. Camping shops generally have a strong selection as well.

The **American Automobile Association** (☏ 1-800/222-4357, ⓦ www.aaa.com) provides free maps and assistance to its members, and to British members of the AA and RAC. You can visit the local branch at 701 15th St NW, Washington DC 20005 (Mon–Fri 9am–5.30pm; ☏ 202/331-3000, ⓦ www .aaamidatlantic.com).

Arrival

Those traveling to Washington DC by train or bus arrive at the most central locations: Union Station and the downtown Greyhound terminal, respectively. Union Station is easily linked by Metro to the city center, as is Reagan National Airport if you're arriving by plane. From the other airports, you can count on being downtown within sixty to ninety minutes, and the various bus, train, and subway transfers are smooth enough. Taking a taxi from Dulles or Baltimore-Washington International Airport won't save much time, especially if you arrive during rush hour, though filling a cab with three or four people may cost less than if you take one by yourself.

By air

The most convenient destination for domestic arrivals is **National Airport** (DCA; ☏ 703/417-8000, ⓦ www.mwaa.com/national) – officially

Ronald Reagan Washington National Airport – four miles south of downtown and across the Potomac in Virginia. By car or by bus it takes thirty minutes to an hour to reach the center of town from the airport, depending on traffic, though the **National Airport Metro station** is linked directly to Metro Center, L'Enfant Plaza, and Gallery Place-Chinatown on the Blue and Yellow lines, making the subway the clear choice for transit if you don't have too much luggage. A **taxi** downtown costs around $14–17 (including airport surcharge). Another option is the **SuperShuttle** bus (24hr service; one-way $14), which drops you at your hotel.

The area's biggest airport, and one of the five busiest in the country, **Dulles International** (IAD; ⊤703/572-2700, ⊛www.mwaa.com/dulles), 26 miles west in northern Virginia, handles most international and some domestic flights. The drive to or from downtown can take up to an hour in heavy traffic, and rarely less than forty minutes. **Taxis** downtown run $45–55. There's also a **SuperShuttle** bus from Dulles (24hr service; one-way $22), which will bring you to your hotel. It's cheaper, if a little more time-consuming, to take the **Washington**

Flyer Express bus (every 30min, Mon–Fri 5.45am–10.15pm, Sat & Sun 7.45am–10.15pm; one-way $8, round-trip $14; ⊛www.washfly.com) to the **West Falls Church Metro station**, a thirty-minute trip, from where it's a twenty-minute train ride into downtown DC. However, the most inexpensive option is to take public transit all the way into town: catch **Metrobus #5A** from the airport, which connects with the Metro-rail at the Rosslyn and L'Enfant Plaza Metro stations.

Other international and domestic arrivals land at **Baltimore-Washington International Airport** (BWI; ⊤301/261-1000, ⊛www.bwiairport.com), 25 miles northeast of DC and ten miles south of Baltimore. This, too, is up to an hour's drive from downtown DC, with taxis costing around $55 (agree on the price before setting off). **SuperShuttle** buses into Washington (daily 24hr; one-way $30-32) will drop you off at your hotel, but it's cheaper to take the

Leaving DC: getting to the airports

Give yourself plenty of time to get to the airport, especially if you're driving: it can take up to thirty minutes to reach National, and around an hour to get to Dulles or BWI without traffic. Once there, security checks can keep you waiting in line for fifteen to 45 minutes, so try to leave ninety minutes to two hours or more before your flight.

Amtrak ⊤1-800/872-7245, ⊛www.amtrak.com. Northbound line from DC's Union Station to BWI rail terminal (every 30min, 5.25am–10pm); regular service $13, Acela Express $38.

MARC commuter rail ⊤ 410/859-7420, ⊛www.mtamaryland.com. Northbound Penn Line, from Washington Union Station to BWI rail terminal (every 20–60min, Mon–Fri 5.54am–10.35pm), one-way $6.

Metro/bus ⊤202/637-7000 (daily 7am–7pm), ⊛www.wmata.com. To BWI: Metro Green Line to Greenbelt station, where Metrobus #B30 (every 40min, Mon–Fri 6am–10pm, Sat & Sun 8.40am–10pm) continues on to the airport nonstop. To Dulles: Metrobus #5A from L'Enfant Plaza or Rosslyn Metro stations (hourly, Mon–Fri 5.30am–10.30pm, Sat & Sun 5.30–8.30am & noon–10.30pm). To National: Metro Blue or Yellow lines.

SuperShuttle ⊛www.supershuttle.com, 24hr continuous service. To BWI (⊤1-800 /BLUE-VAN or 703/416-6661), $30–32 each way. To Dulles (⊤1-800/BLUE-VAN or 703/416-7884), $22 each way. To National (⊤1-800/BLUE-VAN or 202/296-6662), $14 each way. Pickup on request at your hotel; reservations required.

Washington Flyer Express ⊤1-888/WASH-FLY, ⊛www.washfly.com. To Dulles from West Falls Church Metro: every 30min, Mon–Fri 6.15am–10.45pm, Sat & Sun 8.15am–10.45pm; $8, round-trip $14.

Washington Flyer Taxi ⊤703/661-6655. 24hr metered service to Dulles airport; most cars accept credit cards.

commuter rail from BWI. (A free shuttle service connects the airport with the BWI rail terminal, a 10–15min ride.) The most economical choice is the southbound Penn Line of the Maryland Rail Commuter Service (**MARC**) (every 20–60min, Mon–Fri 4.45am–9.25pm; one-way $6), providing frequent peak-hour departures that take 40–45 minutes to reach Washington's Union Station. The station is also reached from BWI by the quicker daily **Amtrak** trains (every 30 min, 6.20am–midnight; one-way $13) that take a half-hour with regular service, and a mere twenty minutes with the speedier Acela Express trains – which you pay for with a $38 one-way ticket. If you have plenty of time to kill, you can take **public transit** to the city center, riding express bus #B30 from BWI nonstop to Greenbelt Metro station and then catching the Green Line into town, though this route into downtown DC will take you well over an hour.

By train and bus

The grand edifice of **Union Station**, 50 Massachusetts Ave NE, three blocks north of the Capitol, welcomes arrivals from all over the country, including local trains from Baltimore, Richmond, Williamsburg, and Virginia Beach, and major East Coast routes from Philadelphia, New York, and Boston. Train operators include the nationwide **Amtrak** (☎1-800/872-7245, ⓦwww.amtrak.com) and the local **MARC** system (☎1-800/325-7245, ⓦwww.mtamaryland.com), which connects DC to Baltimore, BWI Airport, and suburban Maryland. From the station you can connect to the Metro, rent a car, or catch a taxi outside.

Greyhound (☎1-800/229-9424 or ☎202/289-5154, ⓦwww.greyhound.com) and **Peter Pan** (☎1-800/343-9999, ⓦwww.peterpanbus.com) buses from Baltimore, Philadelphia, New York, Boston, Richmond, and other cities stop at the terminal at 1005 1st St NE at L Street, in an unsavory part of town, five long blocks north of Union Station. The Union Station Metro stop is about a $6 cab ride away, or you can walk a block north to the New York Avenue Metro station, with a southern entrance at M Street.

By car

Driving into DC is a sure way to experience some of the East Coast's worst traffic. The six- to eight-lane freeway known as the **Capital Beltway** (which will expand in certain parts to twelve lanes in a few years) encircles the city at a ten-mile radius from the center and is busy eighteen hours a day (5am–11pm). It's made up of two separate highways: I-495 on the western half and I-95/I-495 in the east. If it's the Beltway you want, follow signs for either.

Approaching the city **from the northeast** (New York/Philadelphia), you need I-95 (south), before turning west on Route 50; that will take you to New York Avenue, which heads directly to the White House, but goes first through a rather bleak industrial wasteland on the northeast edge of town. **From Baltimore** there's the direct Baltimore–Washington Parkway, which also joins Route 50. Indeed, Route 50 is the main route into DC from the east (Annapolis, Maryland, and Chesapeake Bay). **From the south**, take I-95 to I-395, which crosses the river via the George Mason Memorial Bridge – part of the colossal "14th Street Bridge Complex" with multiple spans for mass transit, plus regular highway and express lanes – and deposits you south of the Mall near the waterfront. **From the northwest** (Frederick, MD, and beyond), take I-270 until you hit the Beltway, then follow I-495 (east) for Connecticut Avenue south; this is one of the more attractive entryways into the city, and also one of the slowest. **From the west** (Virginia) use I-66, which runs across the Theodore Roosevelt Bridge to Constitution Avenue, where DC first appears in the image of the Lincoln Memorial. At peak periods in the Beltway, high-occupancy vehicle restrictions apply on I-66 eastbound (6.30–9am) and westbound (4–6.30pm); at these times cars with fewer than three people face a small surcharge at the toll booths. See color map 2 for highways into the city.

Costs, money, and banks

DC may be the nation's capital, but it's a lot more affordable to vacation here than in most big American cities. Nearly all the major museums, monuments, and memorials are free, public transit is cheap and efficient, and the presence of so many students, interns, and public servants means that many bars and restaurants have great deals on drinks and food. That's not to say that you can't spend money; the city has some of the country's finest and most expensive hotels and restaurants, and the odd attraction can be on the pricey side.

Average costs

Accommodation will be your biggest single expense: expect the lowest rate for a double hotel room to be around $100–140/£60–80 a night, though spartan hostels, dingy motels, and a few B&Bs will cost less. This price range can also apply to weekend deals and rooms booked in the less popular winter months (see Chapter 12). Excluding accommodations, count on spending a bare **minimum** of $40/£25 a day, which should cover breakfast, a quick lunch, a budget dinner, and a beer. Taking taxis, having fancier meals, and going out for drinks will mean allowing for more like $70 a day. If you want to go regularly to the theater, rent a car, or take tours, then double that figure.

What's particularly appealing about DC is how much you can do here for **free**: guided tours of the major national museums, the US Capitol, and the White House; outdoor concerts, festivals, parades, and children's events – none of them costs a cent. And although not free, the inexpensive Metro and buses get you to DC's main attractions for $1.20 per ride (or upwards of five bucks a day with a special ticket, like a daily or weekly pass). Where admission is charged, **children** and (usually) **senior citizens** get in for half-price, and full-time **students** (holding an International Student ID Card, or ISIC), anyone under 26 (with International Youth Travel Card) and **teachers** (with International Teacher Card), often receive discounts. Contact youth/student/discount travel agencies for applicable ID cards.

Sales tax in Washington DC is among the lowest in the country at 5.75 percent;

this tax is in addition to the marked price on goods. **Hotel tax** is 14.5 percent, and likewise is added on top of the room rate.

Banks and ATMs

With an **ATM card** and PIN number you'll have access to cash from machines all over DC, though, as anywhere, you'll be charged a total fee of around $3–4 if you use an ATM machine not owned by your bank. Foreign cash-dispensing cards linked to international networks such as Cirrus and Plus are widely accepted; before you travel, ask your bank which branches you can use abroad. To find the nearest ATMs in the capital region, call American Express at ☎1-800/CASH-NOW, Plus at ☎1-800/843-7587, The Exchange at ☎1-800/237-ATMS, or Cirrus at ☎1-800/4-CIRRUS.

The big-name **banks in DC** include East Coast entities like Wachovia and SunTrust. Most banks are open Monday through Friday 9am to 4pm; some stay open until 5pm or 6pm on Friday, and a few are open Saturday 9am–noon. For banking services – particularly currency exchange – outside normal business hours and on weekends, try major hotels or the DC-area branches of Thomas Cook. See "Directory" (pp.330–332) for contact details of downtown banks and Thomas Cook branches.

Travelers' checks

Travelers' checks are universally accepted as cash in stores and restaurants and should therefore be bought in **US dollars only**. The usual fee for travelers' check sales is one or two percent; get them through your bank,

Money: a note for foreign travelers

Given the recent decline in value of the US dollar, one pound sterling will buy $1.70–1.80, a Euro is worth $1.15–1.25, a Canadian dollar 70–80¢, an Australian dollar 65–75¢, and a New Zealand dollar 50–65¢ – all of which makes visiting DC an attractive budget vacation.

US currency comes in bills of $1, $5, $10, $20, $50 and $100 **denominations**. All are the same size, though denominations of $20 or higher have in the last few years been changing shades from their familiar drab green. These days such bills offer more colorful pastels of faint red, yellow, and blue, and other embedded inks and watermarks – all to deter would-be counterfeiters. The dollar comprises one hundred cents, made up of combinations of one-cent pennies, five-cent nickels, ten-cent dimes, and 25-cent quarters. Quarters bearing individual state names and related historical designs are being rolled out one month at a time until 2008. There's also the golden "Sacagawea" dollar coin, named after the Native American woman who assisted Lewis and Clark on their 1804 expedition through the uncharted, western land acquired by the Louisiana Purchase. Very rarely, you may come across the JFK half-dollars (50¢), Susan B. Anthony dollar coins, or Thomas Jefferson two-dollar bills. Change is needed for buses, parking meters, vending machines, and public telephones, so always carry plenty.

When planning your daily DC budget, be sure to allow for **tipping**, which is universally expected. You shouldn't leave a bar or restaurant without tipping at least fifteen percent, unless the service was utterly vile; twenty percent is more like it for good service. The same amount should be added to taxi fares, rounded up to the nearest 50¢ or dollar for convenience. A hotel porter should be tipped $1 a bag, $3–5 for lots of baggage; housekeeping typically gets $1–2 a day; and valet parking attendants receive $1.

or by phone or online with Thomas Cook and American Express. Be sure to have plenty of the $10 and $20 denominations for everyday transactions, and keep the purchase agreement and a record of **check serial numbers** safe and separate from the checks themselves. In the event that checks are lost or stolen, the issuing company will expect you to report the loss immediately; most companies claim you'll have replacements within 24 hours.

Credit cards

For many services, like renting a car or bike or making reservations in a hotel or restaurant, it's expected that you'll be paying or securing your spot with MasterCard, Visa, Diners Club, Discover, or American Express. If you use your credit card in an ATM, remember that all cash advances are treated as loans, with interest accruing daily from the date of withdrawal (with a variable interest rate of as high as twenty percent), and there may be a transaction fee as well.

Wiring money

If you run out of money while abroad, the quickest way to get cash is to contact your bank and have them **wire money** to the one nearest you; it should be considered a last resort. If you must, have someone take cash to the nearest **American Express Moneygram** office (☎1-800/543-4080, also available at participating Thomas Cook branches) and have it instantaneously wired to you, minus a ten-percent commission. For similar, if slightly pricier, services, **Western Union** has offices in major cities (☎1-800/325-6000 in the US, ☎1-800/235-0000 in Canada, ☎0800/833833 in the UK, and ☎1800/649 565 in Australia, ⓦwww .westernunion.com), with credit-card payments subject to an additional $10 fee.

Phone, mail, and email

Given that the military-industrial complex itself had much to do with the creation of the Internet (which it called Arpanet), and the locally based FCC and US Postal Service manage telecommunications and mail delivery, respectively, it's not surprising that Washington DC is one of the most connected cities on the planet. Every major hotel offers rooms equipped with phone and/or Ethernet connections for your computer (though these can be expensive to use), public pay phones are widespread, and there are enough places offering Internet access to keep you up-to-date with your email. You can buy stamps at post offices throughout the downtown area, and mail boxes are easy to find.

Telephones

All telephone numbers in this guide have a **202 area code** (for Washington DC), unless otherwise stated. You do not need to dial the area code within the District. Outside DC, dial 1 before the area code and number. Calls within the greater DC metropolitan area are counted as local even if they require a different code (703 for northern Virginia, or 301 for parts of Maryland, for example). Detailed information about calls, codes, and rates is listed at the front of the **telephone directory** in the *White Pages*.

Telephoning from your hotel room is considerably more expensive than using a pay phone, costing up to $1 for a local call, so you'd be better off using your cell phone for most calls (some budget hotels offer free local calls, however). Long-distance and **international calls** dialed direct are most expensive during daylight hours (7am–6pm), with evening charges slightly reduced (6–11pm), and early morning hours cheapest of all (11pm–7am). If you call overseas from a hotel room phone, expect to be charged a small fortune.

Many major hotels, government agencies, and car rental companies have **toll-free numbers** that are recognizable by their ☎1-800 or ☎1-888 prefixes. Numbers with a ☎1-900 prefix are toll calls, typically sports information lines, psychic hotlines, and phone-sex operators, and will cost you a bundle of money for just a few minutes of use. Worse, perhaps, is swiping a **credit card** at a public pay phone, which can incur astronomical long-distance charges (around $7 per minute), including a mysteriously steep "connection fee."

Telephone charge cards

Most long-distance companies enable customers to make **calling-card** calls that are then billed to their home number. Call your company's customer service line to find out if it provides this service, and if so, what the toll-free access code is.

In the UK and Ireland, it's possible to obtain a free BT **Chargecard** (☎0800/800838), from which all calls made while overseas can be charged to your quarterly domestic account. AT&T (dial ☎0800/890 011, then 1-888/641-6123 when you hear the AT&T prompt to be transferred to the Florida Call Center, free, 24hrs/day) has the **Global Calling Card**, a charge card that can be used in more than two hundred countries, while the **Mercury Calling Card** (☎0500/100 505) can be used in more than sixty countries abroad, including the US, though the fees cannot be charged to a normal phone bill. To call Australia or New Zealand from overseas, telephone charge cards like **Telstra Telecard** or **Optus Calling Card** in Australia and **Telecom NZ's Calling Card** in New Zealand charge calls back to a domestic account or credit card. Apply for cards directly through Telstra (☎1800/038 000), Optus (☎1300/300 937), or Telecom NZ (☎04/801 9000).

An alternative to telephone charge cards is cheap, **prepaid phone cards** allowing calls to virtually anywhere in the world. Various stores, like delis, groceries, and newsstands, sell them; look for signs posted in shop windows advertising rates, which can vary dramatically, and check the fine print to make sure you're getting a good deal. Some cards allow you to add time to them as their minutes elapse through the use of a unique PIN number, while others only have a set number of minutes available. Finally, prepaid calling-card companies may change their rates, policies, or deals on a month-to-month basis, or go out of business altogether, so if you're buying a card, make sure to use it within a reasonable amount of time, lest you end up with a worthless piece of plastic.

Useful telephone numbers

Emergencies ☎911 for fire, police, or ambulance
Directory inquiries for toll-free numbers ☎1-800/555-1212, otherwise 1+area code+555-1212
Local and long-distance directory information ☎411
Operator ☎0
International calls to Washington DC A country's international access code + 1 for the US + 202 for DC
International calls from Washington DC
Australia ☎011 + 61 + number (minus the initial 0 of the area code)
Canada ☎011+ 1 + number (minus the initial 0 the area code)
Ireland ☎011+ 353 + number (minus the initial 0 of the area code)
New Zealand ☎011+ 64 + number (minus the initial 0 of the area code)
UK including Northern Ireland ☎011+ 44 + number (minus the initial 0 of the area code)

Mail

Post offices are usually open Monday through Friday from 9am until 5pm, and Saturday from 9am to noon or 1pm. Stamps can be bought at the full-service windows or automatic vending machines, plus airports, train stations, bus terminals, hotel lobbies, and many shops and newsstands. Ordinary mail weighing up to one ounce and sent within the US costs 37¢, and standard postcards cost 23¢. **Airmail** weighing up to one ounce and sent outside the US costs 80¢; postcards and aerogrammes are 70¢. Allow about a week for delivery of airmail between the US and Europe.

Domestic letters that don't carry a **zip code** are liable to get lost or at least seriously delayed; phone books list zip codes for their service area, and post offices have zip-code directories for major US cities. In this guide zip codes are provided when you may need to write to an establishment in advance of your trip.

Letters sent to you c/o **General Delivery**, known elsewhere as **poste restante**, *must* include the post office zip code and will only be held for thirty days before being returned to sender. A few post offices in DC handle General Delivery, the most convenient of which is the **Benjamin Franklin Post Office**, 1200 Pennsylvania Ave NW, Washington DC 20004 (Mon–Fri 7.30am–5.30pm, Sat 8am–12.30pm; ☎202/842-1444). You can also ask to have mail held at a hotel or, if you're a cardholder, at an American Express office (see "Directory" for details on local offices).

Email

Although the District is otherwise well connected to the Internet, **email** addicts will realize shortly after arrival in the city that DC lacks any real cybercafé culture. If you're not staying somewhere that offers web access (Internet-friendly hotels are noted as such in Chapter 12), you'll be forced to hunt down a FedEx Kinko's or similar spot (look under "Copying" in the *Yellow Book*). You can log on at a major hotel's business center, but that can get pricey fast, so you're better off looking into alternative options like the Martin Luther King Memorial Library, where you can log on for free for up to fifteen minutes at a time. And if you're so inclined before catching a flight at Dulles or National, you can use one of the credit-card-activated Internet kiosks scattered throughout each airport. Finally, keep in mind that by far the easiest way to send and receive email on the road is to sign up with one of the free, web-based email providers like Yahoo! and Hotmail.

City transportation

Most places downtown – including the Mall museums, major monuments, and the White House – are within walking distance of each other, while an excellent public transit system connects downtown to outlying sites and neighborhoods. The Washington Metropolitan Area Transit Authority (WMATA; ⓦwww.wmata .com) operates a subway system (Metrorail) and a bus network (Metrobus), plus you can get around by taxi or bike. Driving a car can involve great frustration, with the District's thick congestion and maddening squares and traffic circles.

The Metro

Washington's subway – the **Metrorail**, or simply the **Metro** – is quick, cheap, and easy to use. It runs on five lines that cover most of the downtown areas and suburbs (with the notable exception of Georgetown), branching out from the center of the District in all directions to just beyond the Capital Beltway, where the outlying stations have lots for commuters' cars. Each line is color-coded and studded with various interchange stations: Metro Center, L'Enfant Plaza, and Gallery Place-Chinatown are the most important downtown, being the most central. Stations are identified outside by the letter "M" on top of a brown pylon; inside, the well-lit, vaulted halls make the Washington Metro one of the safest subway systems in the world – though security

precautions have, as with everything else in town, been tightened since 9/11. Keep in mind that while the system itself may be generally safe, a few of its stations, like Anacostia, are in unsafe neighborhoods.

Although the entire length of the 103 mile system was completed in 2001, thus fulfilling its 1960s design, three new stops are to be added by early 2005: a two-stop Blue Line extension to Largo Town Center in the Maryland suburbs, and, more importantly for visitors, an above-ground Red Line station at New York Avenue, near the Greyhound bus station – a welcome addition since buses arrive in a rather grim neighborhood.

The Metro's **operating hours** are Monday through Thursday 5.30am to midnight, Friday 5.30am to 3am, Saturday 7am to 3am, and Sunday 7am to midnight. Trains

---

Washington Metropolitan Area Transit Authority

For route information and bus and Metro timetables call ☎202/637-7000 (Mon–Thurs 6am–10.30pm, Fri 6am–11.30pm, Sat 7am–11.30pm, Sun 7am–10.30pm) or log on to ⓦwww.wmata.com.

Other helpful numbers
General information ☎202/962-1234
Transit Police ☎202/962-2121 (emergencies only)
Lost and Found ☎202/962-1195 (24hr message; office open Mon–Fri 11am–3pm, also accessible at ⓦwww.wmata.com)
Mobility Link ☎202/962-6464 (help line for people with disabilities)

Passes
For passes and other information, visit:
Metro Center Sales Office 12th and F sts NW at Metro Center Station (Mon–Fri 7.30am–6.30pm)
Metro Headquarters Lobby, 600 5th St NW (Mon–Fri 10am–3pm)
Metro Pentagon Sales Office Upper-level bus bay (Mon–Fri 7am–3.30pm)

run every five to seven minutes on most lines during rush hours, and every ten to twelve minutes at other times. Pick up a copy of the useful **Metro guide** (free, available in most stations), which gives the train and bus routes to the city's various attractions. The entire system is shown on two **Metro System Route Maps** (one for DC/Virginia, one for DC/Maryland; $3 each), available from Metro sales offices (see p.29) and from ADC Map & Travel at 1636 I Street NW (℡202/628-2608). Our color map section at the back of the book also begins with an overview of the Metro system.

Each passenger needs a **farecard**, which must be bought from a machine before you pass through the turnstiles. Fares are based on when and how far you travel and usually cost $1.20 (one-way, peak or off-peak) if you're traveling around downtown, the Mall, and the Capitol (maps and station-to-station ticket prices are posted by the machines, as well as online). **One-way fares** range from $1.20 (base rate) to $3.60; the higher, **peak-rate fares** are charged Monday through Friday 5.30–9.30am and 3–7pm, otherwise the top fare is $2.20. Children under 5 ride free, and seniors are admitted for half of the standard price.

Farecards work like debit cards – you "put in" an amount of money when you purchase the card, and the fare is subtracted after each train ride. If you're going to use the Metro several times, it's worth putting in more money – an additional ten percent credit is added to the value of cards over $20. (Most stations have machines that allow you to buy farecards with debit and credit cards.) Feed the card through any turnstile marked with a green arrow, and then retrieve it. When you do the same thing at the end of your journey, the machine prints out on the card how much money remains. If you've paid the exact amount, the turnstile keeps the card; if you don't have enough money remaining on the card for the journey, insert it into one of the special exit-fare machines, deposit more money, and try the turnstile again. If you plan on catching a bus after your Metro ride, get a **rail-to-bus transfer pass** (good for 85¢ off your bus fare) at the station where you enter the rail system. The self-service transfer machines are on the mezzanine next to the escalator leading to the train platform.

If you plan on making at least five daily trips around central DC, the **Metrorail One Day Pass** ($6) buys unlimited travel after 9.30am on weekdays and all day on the weekend. There's also a **7-Day Fast Pass** ($30), for seven consecutive days' unlimited travel, but a better deal for visitors is the **7-Day Short Trip Pass** ($20), which saves you money and covers almost every sight you'll probably want to see, from the waterfront up to the zoo, and even gets you to National Airport; the only thing outside the covered area is Alexandria, Virginia, for which you'll have to pay a few cents extra. All passes are available at Metro Center station, Metro

Riding the rails in Virginia

The **Virginia Railway Express** (℡703/684-0400 or 1-800/RIDE-VRE, ⊛www.vre.org) can be a good way to see the historic towns spread out over northern Virginia. The mostly bi-level and spacious VRE trains run on two lines that initially link DC's Union Station with L'Enfant Plaza and Alexandria, Virginia. For this segment, the lines run on the same track and can get you from Union Station to King Street, in **Old Town Alexandria**, in less than twenty minutes. The single-use ticket is $4.35, a bit more than the Metro, and takes you to within three-quarters of a mile of the center of Old Town; use Alexandria's DASH bus system or walk east from there.

The real value of VRE, however, is that it can get you out to the appealing "old towns" of **Manassas** and **Fredericksburg**, about an hour south of Union Station, for a very low price ($6–8 one-way). Both places are of great interest to history buffs, being the sites of important Civil War battlefields. See the *Rough Guide to the USA* for accounts of these and other historic areas in the capital region, if you're interested in making day trips beyond the ones outlined in Chapter 11 of this guide.

Headquarters, many area supermarkets, or online through the WMATA website.

Buses

WMATA runs DC's subway and **bus** systems, which operate on largely the same hours (though some buses run until 3am on weekdays). The **base fare** for most bus journeys is $1.20, payable to the driver, though surcharges and zone crossings can raise the price, and express routes will cost $2.50 a ride. The same peak-hour rates on the Metro apply to the buses, and rail transfers cover 85¢ of your bus fare. Two good passes to consider are the **Daily Pass** ($3), which applies to all regular routes and reduces express trips by $1.20, and the **Weekly Pass** ($11), which has the same express-trip reduction and buys seven days' unlimited base-fare trips. Riders of Maryland's **MARC** and Virginia's **VRE** can also use their weekly and monthly rail passes to ride base-rate Metrobus lines for free. Other systems that are covered are in Alexandria (the **DASH**) and en route to Mount Vernon, which you can reach on a **Fairfax Connector** bus. Both systems link with the Metro; for timetable information contact DASH (rides $1; ☎703/370-3274, ⦿www.dashbus.com) or Fairfax Connector (non-express routes 50¢–$1; ☎703/339-7200, ⦿www.fairfaxconnector.com).

Note also that by April 2005, WMATA will have special "Downtown DC Circulators," geared toward tourists and conventioneers, that for 50¢ will take you from Union Station to Georgetown via K Street and the new Washington Convention Center, or alternatively from the Convention Center to the Southwest waterfront by way of 7th Street and the National Mall. Shuttles will run daily from 8am to 9pm, and, if successful, service may be expanded to include a route around the Mall, currently covered by bus lines #13 A/B/F/G.

Useful bus routes

Farragut North to Washington National Cathedral #N2, #N4, #N6 via 18th St, Dupont Circle, Massachusetts Ave, Embassy Row
Foggy Bottom to Cleveland Park #L1 via Virginia Ave, C St, 23rd St, Washington Circle, New Hampshire Ave, Dupont Circle, Connecticut Ave (National Zoological Park), Woodley Park, Cleveland Park
L'Enfant Plaza to McPherson Square #52 via 6th St, Independence Ave, 14th St
Lafayette Square to National Basilica #G8 via H St, 11th St, Rhode Island Ave, 7th St NE
McPherson Square to Woodley Park #L2 via K St, 20th St, Dupont Circle, 18th St (Adams-Morgan), Calvert St, Connecticut Ave (National Zoological Park)
Metro Center to Adams-Morgan #42 via Metro Center (10th and F), H St, Connecticut Ave, Dupont Circle, Columbia Rd (Adams-Morgan)
National Mall to Arlington Memorial Cemetery #13B, #13F via 7th St, Constitution Ave, Lincoln Memorial, Arlington Memorial Bridge
National Mall to Pentagon #13A, #13G via 7th St, Independence Ave, Bureau of Engraving and Printing/Holocaust Museum, 14th St Bridge, Pentagon (then connects to Arlington National Cemetery and loops back to Mall via Constitution Ave)
National Mall to Rock Creek Park #S2, #S4 via Natural History Museum, Old Post Office, 11th St, I St, 16th St (get off at Military Rd, park is short walk west)
Pennsylvania Ave to Georgetown #30, #32, #34, #35, #36 via Eastern Market, US Capitol, Independence Ave, 7th St, Pennsylvania Ave, 15th St, Pennsylvania Ave, Wisconsin Ave (Georgetown)
Union Station to Georgetown #D1, #D3, #D6 via E St, 13th St, K St, Dupont Circle, Q St (Georgetown); return via M St
Union Station to Kennedy Center #80 via Massachusetts Ave, H St, 13th St, K St, 19th St, Virginia Ave, Watergate Complex
Union Station to National Arboretum #X6, #X8 via Massachusetts Ave, Maryland Ave, Bladensburg Rd

Taxis

Taxis complement DC's public transportation system and are especially valuable in outposts like Georgetown and Adams-Morgan, which aren't on the Metro. If you know you're going to be out late in these neighborhoods (or in the dicey district of Shaw), it's a good idea to book a return taxi in advance.

Unlike cabs in most American cities, taxis in DC charge **fares** on a concentric zoned basis. Standard rates are posted in each cab; a ride at the basic rate within one zone costs $5.50. Most crosstown fares, which include the most expensive rides in the city, run from $5 to $17.20; Georgetown to Dupont Circle, for example, costs about $7.60. A $1 surcharge is added during rush hour (Mon–Fri 7–9.30am and 4–6.30pm), and **groups** may be asked to pay up to $2 for each additional passenger (in addition to the first one). Don't be surprised if the driver pulls over to pick up another passenger: this is perfectly legal, provided they don't take you more than five blocks out of the way of your destination, and everybody pays the set amount for their journey. Once you get out of DC, into Maryland or Virginia, you'll pay a metered fare, which can be expensive. Also, taxis from those states are legally allowed to deposit you at your Washington destination, but not to shuttle you from one to the next.

You can either flag cabs down on the street or use the ranks at hotels and transport terminals; there are always cabs available at Union Station. If you call a taxi in advance (see "Directory" for a list of cab companies) there's a $2 surcharge on the fare. For more information, call the **DC Taxicab Commission** at ☎202/645-6005 or visit ⦾www.dctaxi.dc.gov.

Driving

You shouldn't drive in the capital unless you absolutely have to. **Traffic jams** can be nightmarish, the DC street layout is a grid overlaid with unnerving diagonal boulevards, and without a map it's easy to get lost and find yourself in the middle of an unfamiliar urban wasteland. Considering the excellent Metro system, decent buses, and pedestrian-friendly areas, you should think twice about plunking down the money for a rental car. If you must head out of the city by car, either rent one at the end of your stay (at Union Station), or leave your own car at your hotel for the duration – though this will cost $15–30 per night at any decent downtown hotel. For lists of car rental agencies, see p.13.

One-way streets can play havoc with the best-planned driving routes, while the traffic-control system in place during the city's **rush hours** (Mon–Fri 6.30–9.30am & 3–7pm, plus lunchtime) means that many lanes, or even whole streets, **change direction** at particular times of the day and left turns are periodically forbidden. Read the signs carefully. To top it all off, the roads can be treacherous – even on major thoroughfares you'll want to keep an eye out for potholes and ridges.

Parking lots and garages charge from $5/hour to $18/day. Searching for free, **on-street parking** is likely to cost you a lot of time and energy; there are free, limited-wait (two- to three-hour) parking spots around the Mall (Jefferson and Madison Drives, Independence Ave SW) and in West Potomac Park, but they're extremely popular. **Parking meters** tend to operate between 9.30am and 6.30pm, usually allowing a maximum stay of two hours. At other times, just when you think you've found the perfect spot, it will almost certainly be reserved for workers, or on a street that becomes one-way during rush hour, or temporarily illegal to park on because it is rush hour, or rendered useless for countless other reasons. Naturally, the places you might want to drive to for an evening out, like Georgetown, Dupont Circle, or Adams-Morgan, are also short on available parking spaces.

If you're visiting a local resident, however, you can request an on-street **parking permit** from a local police station. You'll need to present your registration and your host will need to provide proof of residence, but this quick and easy process allows you to park in the vicinity of your host's address for up to two weeks (though this doesn't mean that spaces are any less elusive).

Should your car get towed away during your visit, call the local **Department of Motor Vehicles** at ☎202/727-5000 and expect to pay $100 or more to get it back. Vehicles towed away after 7pm on a Friday won't be returned until after 9am the following Monday.

Bikes

True bicycling fans will doubtless want to use their two-wheelers more for sport than transit while in the city, and these opportunities are detailed in chapters concerning "Sports and outdoor activities" and bike-friendly locales such as Rock Creek Park, the C&O Canal, and spots along the Potomac. Given the traffic, few visitors will actually want to brave the DC streets on a bicycle, though several outfits can provide maps and advice on traffic conditions. Bike **rental costs** $25–50 a day, or $100–120 a week (depending on the model and rental company); you'll need to leave a deposit and/or a credit card or passport number. Bikes are permitted on the Metro except on weekdays during rush hour (7–10am and 4–7pm) and on some major holidays, such as the Fourth of July.

Bike rental companies

Better Bikes ☎202/293-2080, ⌨www .betterbikesinc.com. 24hr information line; will deliver anywhere in DC. Has information on bike trails and events.

Big Wheel Bikes 1034 33rd St NW, Georgetown ☎202/337-0254; 2 Prince St, Old Town Alexandria, VA ☎703/739-2300; 3119 Lee Hwy, Arlington, VA ☎703/522-1110; ⌨www.bigwheelbikes. com. Open Wed–Fri 11am–7pm and Sat & Sun 10am–6pm. Georgetown location convenient to C&O Canal and Capital Crescent trails; Alexandria location near Mount Vernon Trail.

Blazing Saddles 445 11th St NW, Old Downtown ☎202/544-0055. Daily 9am–5pm; closed Nov–March.

City tours

There are a number of tour operators eager to show you the many sights of Washington DC, though with just a little research and preparation it's easy to see most things on your own. Some of the more popular tour-bus services, however, are useful, since they allow you to get on and off the bus at will and shuttle you out to the area's far-flung sights. River cruises are also worth considering, especially in summer when the offshore breeze comes as a welcome relief. Specialist tours show you a side of Washington you may not otherwise see, like historic buildings and sites and famous people's homes. For more information, contact Explore DC (☎703/998-2458, ⌨www.exploredc.org) or Cultural Tourism DC (☎202/661-9255, ⌨www.dcheritageculturaltourismdc.org), whose websites list various guided tours and provide a calendar of cultural events.

Building tours

You must make reservations for special, extended, or "VIP" tours of the buildings below. American citizens should contact their congressional representatives well in advance for special tours of government buildings (see box, p.139); these tours will be set for a specific date and time, usually last longer than the regular walk-in tours, and show you areas or rooms not normally open to the public. Make sure to confirm your tour in advance.

Bureau of Engraving and Printing see p.123
Department of State see pp.146–147
Federal Reserve see p.146
Folger Shakespeare Library see pp.111–112

Kennedy Center see p.149
Library of Congress see pp.112–113
National Archives see pp.160–162
Old Executive Office Building see p.138
US Capitol see p.102
Washington National Cathedral see p.210
Washington Post see p.185
White House see p.131

Bicycling

Bike the Sites Inc ☎202/842-BIKE, ⌨www .bikethesites.com. Two- to six-hour guided bike tours of the city's major sights ($40 and up, including bike and helmet), plus tours of Mount Vernon and customized tours of the District. No fixed schedule. Also rents bikes for $25–60 per hour. Tour reservations required.

Buses and trolleys

Gold Line/Gray Line ☎1-800/862-1400 or 301/386-8300, ⊛www.martzgroup.com/GoldLine. Various tours in and around DC, including a two-day tour of downtown sights and Mount Vernon ($80), an evening tour ($56), and trips to Colonial Williamsburg and Monticello (each $70).

Old Town Trolley Tours ☎202/832-9800, ⊛www.historictours.com/washington. Trolleys take you around downtown, the National Mall, Georgetown, and Washington National Cathedral ($26 a day). A "Monuments by Moonlight" tour shows you the Mall's presidential and war memorials after dark ($28). Tickets available at trolley stops and downtown hotels.

Tourmobile ☎202/554-5100 or 1-888/868-7707, ⊛www.tourmobile.com. Narrated bus tours (daily 9.30am–4.30pm) covering downtown and Arlington Cemetery ($20–30), Mount Vernon ($25), and the Mall by night ($20). Tickets available at the office on the Ellipse, kiosks on the Mall (there's one at the Washington Monument) and on the bus itself.

Cruises and river trips

Atlantic Kayak Tours ☎703/838-9072 or 1-800/297-0066, ⊛www.atlantickayak.com. Kayak tours along the Potomac, including 2.5-hour sunset tours highlighting Georgetown's bridges and monuments or the Dyke Marsh Wildlife Area ($44–54 each). Also moonlight tours, full-day trips, and overnight excursions to wildlife areas. No experience is necessary and all equipment is included. Tours run April–Oct only.

Capitol River Cruises ☎1-800/405-5511 or 301/460-7447, ⊛www.capitolrivercruises.com. Forty-five-minute sight-seeing cruises leaving hourly throughout the day (April–Oct noon–9pm) from Georgetown's Washington Harbor, at the end of 31st St NW; $10 per person, reservations not required.

DC Ducks ☎202/966-3825, ⊛www.historictours.com/washington/dcducks.htm. Converted amphibious carriers cruise the Mall and then splash into the Potomac (90min; $28). Hourly departures from Union Station (March–Oct daily 10am–4pm).

Spirit Cruises ☎202/554-8000 or 1-866/211-3811, ⊛www.spiritcruises.com. Swanky two-hour river cruises with bar and bands for $34–50; three-hour dinner cruises for $50–80; or 90min trips to Mount Vernon at night for $25. Tickets and departures from Pier 4, 6th and Water sts SW (Waterfront Metro).

Specialist tours and activities

African American Heritage Tours ☎202/636-9203, ⓔcestours@aol.com. Journeys to local sights important to black history, including the Frederick Douglass National Historic Site and Martin Luther King Jr Memorial. Prices vary; by reservation only.

Capital Helicopters ☎703/417-2150. Twenty-minute helicopter tours ($125 adults; $65 kids) above central DC sights. A minimum of two people required; reservations necessary. Flights are out of National Airport.

Duke Ellington's Neighborhood ☎202/636-9203, ⓔcestours@aol.com. Four-hour bus tour ($20) of the historic U Street/Shaw neighborhood and boyhood home of jazz legend Duke Ellington. Passes by the Mary McLeod Bethune Council House, Lincoln Theatre, Whitelaw Hotel, African American Civil War Memorial, and Howard University. Departures monthly May–Aug; call for schedule.

Goodwill Embassy Tour ☎202/636-4225, ⊛www.dcgoodwill.org. On the second Saturday in May, some of DC's embassy buildings throw open their doors for the day (pre-booked $30; $35 day of). Reserve well in advance. Many embassies also offer free guided tours with reservations; for contact telephone numbers see p.331.

Kalorama House and Embassy Tour ☎202/387-4062, ext18. Various ambassadors' residences and private homes are open to the public for five hours (usually noon–5pm) one day every September; reserve in advance for $18, or pay $20 on the day of the tour.

Scandal Tour ☎202/783-7212. The seamier side of Washington is explored during 90min recounts ($28) of scandals involving the Watergate Hotel, Monica Lewinsky, and more. April–Sept Sat 1pm; by reservation only.

SpyDrive ☎1-866/SPY-TREK, ⊛www.spydrive.com. Two-hour tours ($55–60) of sites in the "spy capital of the world," led by retired FBI, CIA, and KGB officers. The "Robert Hanssen Case" tour covers sites used by the infamous FBI agent for spying and subterfuge.

Walking tours

Anthony S. Pitch ☎301/294-9514, ⊛www.dcsightseeing.com. Highly recommended, two-hour ($15) historical walking tours of Lafayette Square, Georgetown, and Lincoln assassination-related sites led by the amiable Mr Pitch on Sunday mornings at 11am May–Aug (call for schedules).

DC Heritage ☎202/828-9255. Sponsors various tours (90min; around $10) throughout the city, including some on foot that highlight downtown's historic sights and architecture.

Lantern Lights ☎703/548-0100. "Ghost and Graveyard Tour" in Old Town Alexandria of haunted nineteenth-century homes and eerie cemeteries.

Costumed guides tell bone-chilling tales. Tours ($6; April–Sept Wed, Thurs & Sun 7.30pm, Fri & Sat 7.30pm and 9pm) depart from the Ramsay House Visitors Center at 221 King St.

Old Town Walking Tour ☎703/838-4200. Focuses on the history and architecture of Alexandria's historic district ($10; daily Mon–Sat 10.30am, Sun 2.30pm). Departs from the Ramsay House Visitors Center at 221 King St.

Tour DC ☎301/588-8999, ⊛www.tourdc .com. Fascinating hodgepodge of walking tours

that cover various aspects of life among the elite, including Kennedy haunts, important women at Tudor Place, World War II subterfuge on Embassy Row, Georgetown history, and cemetery tours. Saturday tours $15–17 per person; reserve in advance.

Washington Walks ☎202/484-1565, ⊛www .washingtonwalks.com. Two-hour walks through downtown DC, with themes like "Washington Sleeps Here," "Best Addresses," "Most Haunted Houses," and so on (all tours $10 for adults, $5 kids).

Opening hours, public holidays, and festivals

No matter how carefully you've planned your trip to DC, you may find the gates of your favorite park or museum closed if you've forgotten to take holidays and festivals into account. The regular opening hours of specific attractions, monuments, memorials, stores, and offices are given in the relevant listings throughout the guide, and telephone numbers are provided so you can check current information directly before embarking on your trip.

Opening hours

As a general rule, **museums** are open daily 10am to 5.30pm, though some have extended summer hours; a few art galleries, such as the Corcoran, stay open until 8 or 9pm one night a week, often Thursday. Smaller, private museums close for one day a week, usually Monday or Tuesday, and may be open 9am to 4pm or have more limited hours. **Federal office buildings**, some of which incorporate museums, are open Monday through Friday 9am to 5.30pm. Most **national monuments** are open daily 24 hours, though they tend to be staffed only between 8am and midnight, and their gift shops will have more limited hours (typically daily 9am–5.30pm). **Shops** are generally open Monday through Saturday 10am to 7pm; some have extended weekend hours. In neighborhoods like Georgetown, Adams-Morgan, and Dupont Circle, many stores open on Sunday, too, usually noon to 5pm. **Malls** tend to be open Monday through Saturday 10am to 7pm or later, and Sunday noon to 6pm.

While some diners stay open 24 hours, most **restaurants** open daily around 11am for lunch and close at 9 or 10pm. Places that serve breakfast usually open early, between 6 and 8am, serve lunch later, and close in the early or mid afternoon. Dance and live-music **clubs** often won't open until 9 or 10pm; many serve liquor until 2am and then either close for the night or stay open until dawn without serving booze.

In the wake of 9/11, many government buildings **suspended tours** and limited or prohibited public access. Some of these sites have reopened while others remain fortress-like. Also, countless buildings have closed in the last few years for renovation (including the National Portrait Gallery and the American Art Museum, closed until 2006). While these closings are noted in the guide, don't be surprised to find new ones when you arrive.

Public holidays and festivals

On the **national public holidays** listed below, stores, banks, and public and federal offices are likely to be closed all day, as are many clubs and restaurants. Shopping malls, supermarkets, and department and chain stores, however, tend to remain open. The Smithsonian museums and galleries are open every day except Christmas. The traditional **summer tourism season**, when many attractions have extended hours, runs from Memorial Day to Labor Day.

Washington hosts a variety of **annual festivals and events**. America's Christmas Tree is lit each December on the Ellipse in front of the White House; the grandest Fourth of July Parade in the country takes place around the Mall; and every four years in January, the newly inaugurated president proceeds up Pennsylvania Avenue from the US Capitol to the White House.

DC's full **festival calendar** is detailed in Chapter 17. It's important to remember that during certain times, like the National Cherry Blossom Festival in spring, Memorial Day weekend, the Fourth of July, and Labor

Day weekend, it can be very difficult to find accommodations in the city, so it's important to book well in advance.

National holidays

January
1: New Year's Day
3rd Monday: Dr Martin Luther King Jr's Birthday
February
3rd Monday: President's Day
May
Last Monday: Memorial Day
July
4: Independence Day
September
1st Monday: Labor Day
October
2nd Monday: Columbus Day
November
11: Veterans' Day
4th Thursday: Thanksgiving
December
25: Christmas

The media

DC is the most media-savvy city in the United States; much of what makes headlines around the world is born in the capital's press briefings. While you can't get into a White House press conference, you can watch matters unfold on C-SPAN (a no-frills public affairs channel that also broadcasts congressional hearings and House and Senate sessions) and then read about them first-hand in the Washington Post. Nevertheless, overseas visitors will probably find American news coverage too parochial; to keep in touch with day-to-day events back home, you'll have to buy a foreign newspaper, which is easily done in DC.

Newspapers and magazines

DC's major newspaper, the liberal *Washington Post*, is one of America's most respected dailies, landing every morning on the doorsteps of the most powerful people in the world. It routinely wins Pulitzer Prizes, the nation's highest award for journalism, though its most famous one was in the 1970s for its investigation of the

Watergate scandal that brought down the Nixon administration. Top columnists on the paper's opinion pages include political commentator David Broder, conservative George F. Will, neo-conservative Charles Krauthammer, *Slate* editor Michael Kinsley, and liberals like E.J. Dionne. You can read the paper for free on its website Ⓦwww .washingtonpost.com, but registration is required. The only local competitor to the

Post is the conservative, Moonie-published *Washington Times*. There's little reason to read it, unless you're looking to save a dime. The country's one truly national daily, *USA Today* – aka the "McPaper" – is headquartered across the Potomac in Virginia and known for being thick on splashy graphics and thin on investigative journalism. Any upscale hotel will offer you a choice of this paper or the *Post* in the morning.

Free weeklies include the alternative *City-Paper* (ⓦwww.washingtoncitypaper.com), a thick tabloid-sized paper appearing on Thursdays that's known for its progressive slant on current affairs and its arts and entertainment listings, and the gay-oriented *Washington Blade* (ⓦwww.washblade.com) and *Metro Weekly* (ⓦwww.metroweekly.com). Glossy **monthly magazines** include the arts-and-leisure publication *Washingtonian* (ⓦwww.washingtonian.com) and PR-focused *Where: Washington*, plus other local/neighborhood papers and magazines available in bars, restaurants, shops, and hotels.

Newspapers from other US cities, as well as **foreign newspapers and magazines**, can be bought at Union Station, major bookstores, and The Newsroom, 1803 Connecticut Ave NW, Dupont Circle ☎202/332-1489.

TV and radio

The four **television networks** – NBC, ABC, CBS, and Fox – broadcast news and talk shows all morning Monday through Friday until 10am and air their evening local news programs from 5pm to 6.30pm and again at 11pm, also on weekdays. National news is on at 6.30pm. The city's public-TV channel, WETA, is one of the nation's more prominent PBS affiliates, and broadcasts a mix of nature documentaries, political investigations, and history programs (view the programming schedule online at ⓦwww.weta.org/tv). Most hotel rooms have some form of cable TV, though the number of channels available depends on where you stay. Check the daily papers for a list of channels and schedules. Cable news stations include CNN and CNN Headline News, which offers around-the-clock coverage, and Fox News, which provides a right-wing perspective on the day's events. ESPN is your best bet for sports, MTV for youth-oriented music videos and programs, and VH-1 for people outside the MTV demographic. HBO and Showtime present big-budget Hollywood flicks and award-winning shows like *The Sopranos*, while Turner Classic Movies take their programming from the Golden Age of cinema.

The state of commercial **radio** in Washington DC, as elsewhere in America, is pretty dismal: a slew of radio stations are owned by the goliath Clear Channel and Infinity networks, and a few other national heavyweights. For quality news and programming on the radio, tune into WAMU on 88.5 FM (ⓦwww.wamu.org) for National Public Radio broadcasts (Mon–Fri 5–9am & 4–7pm), and independently produced journalism and cultural-affairs shows. NPR also makes its appearance, along with classical-music favorites, on the other public radio station in town, WETA (90.9 FM; ⓦwww.weta.org/fm). Other worthwhile stations are usually broadcast from universities such as George Washington (WRGW 540 AM; ⓦwww.gwradio.com), Georgetown (WGTB 92.3 FM; ⓦwww.wgtb923.com), and Howard (WHUR 96.3 FM; ⓦwww.whur.com), which together play a mix of jazz, folk, blues, hip hop, and alternative rock, along with talk shows and intermittent cultural programs.

TV stations

All of these TV channels' websites offer programming schedules and information, and possibly simulcasts or re-broadcasts of noteworthy shows.

WTTG Fox on 5 ⓦwww.fox5dc.com
WJLA ABC on 7 ⓦwww.wjla.com
WUSA CBS on 9 ⓦwww.wusatv9.com
WDCA UPN on 20 ⓦwww.wdca.com
WETA PBS on 26 ⓦwww.weta.org/tv
WBDC WB on 50 ⓦwww.wbdc.com

Radio stations

All of these radio stations' websites offer programming schedules and information, and possibly simulcasts or re-broadcasts of noteworthy shows.

AM stations

WRGW (540) ⓦwww.gwradio.com. Alternative programming from George Washington University.

WMAL (630) ⓦ www.wmal.com. News, sports, and right-wing talk.

WTEM (980) ⓦ www.wtem.com. Sports talk.

WOL (1450) ⓦ wolam.com. African-American issues are discussed.

WTOP (1500) ⓦ www.wtopnews.com. News, talk, and Baltimore Orioles games.

WPGC (1580) ⓦ www.wpgc955.com. Hip hop, R&B, gospel.

FM stations

WAMU (88.5) ⓦ www.wamu.org. NPR, talk, music, and news.

WPFW (89.3) ⓦ www.wpfw.org. Pacifica Radio: left-leaning news and talk, jazz, and blues.

WCSP (90.1) ⓦ www.c-span.org/watch/cspanradio.asp. C-SPAN Radio: Congress and public affairs coverage.

WETA (90.9) ⓦ www.weta.org/fm. Classical music and NPR news.

WGTB (92.3) ⓦ www.wgtb923.com. Alternative programming from Georgetown University.

WARW (94.7) ⓦ www.947thearrow.com. Classic rock.

WHUR (96.3) ⓦ www.whur.com. Howard University radio: hip hop, jazz, blues, R&B, and cultural programs.

WMZQ (98.7) ⓦ www.wmzqfm.com. Country music.

WHFS (99.1) ⓦ www.whfs.com. Modern rock.

WBIG (100) ⓦ www.oldies100.com. Oldies from the Sixties and Seventies.

WGMS (103.5) ⓦwww.wgms.com. Classical music.

WWZZ (104.1) ⓦ www.moremusic104.com. Pop hits.

WJFK (106.7) ⓦ www.1067wjfk.com. Talk (including Howard Stern).

WRQX (107.3) ⓦ www.mix1073fm.com. Contemporary pop and rock.

WTOP (107.7) ⓦ www.wtopnews.com. News and talk.

Crime, security, and personal safety

For many years Washington has had a poor reputation in terms of crime and personal safety. You'll be assuredly told that it's the "Murder Capital" of the United States, and stories of drug dealers doing business just blocks from the White House are in routine circulation amongst visitors and locals alike. Moreover, the terrorist attack on the Pentagon, anthrax scares on Capitol Hill and at the post office, and repeated Department of Homeland Security advisories have done little to improve the city's image.

It's true, DC ain't Kansas: scan any copy of the *Washington Post* for a rundown of the latest drive-by shootings and drug-war escapades. However, almost all the crime that makes the headlines takes place in neighborhoods (most of NE, SE, and distinct parts of upper NW) that tourists won't be venturing into. When neighborhoods are borderline in terms of personal security, this guide tells you where you should and shouldn't go; if a sight or museum you really want to see is in a risky part of town, take a cab there and back. Otherwise, the places you will be spending most of your time (downtown, along the Mall, in Georgetown), all the major tourist sights, the Metro system, and the main nightlife zones are invariably well guarded, well lit, and well policed. Indeed, the Mall between the US Capitol, White House, and Lincoln Memorial is probably the most heavily policed zone in America.

Security issues

Following the terrorist attacks of September 11, 2001 and the US invasion of Iraq in March 2003, there have been major **security clampdowns** at DC landmarks and institutions. Some buildings, like the US Treasury, are completely closed to the public, while others, like the Pentagon, are open to some degree. While traveling around the capital, you'll soon get used to the city's security regimen. At the biggest-name attractions on the Mall or Capitol Hill, you can expect airport-like security, placing your bags, coats, and personal belongings on conveyor belts and walking through metal detectors. At less-trafficked museums and attractions like the National Building Museum, a guard or two will inspect your bags and other personal items at the door. At minor museums away from the Mall and historic houses, you'll probably only encounter eagle-eyed security guards who will do little to detain you as you enter. Keep in mind that tours of federal and national buildings – including the White House and US Capitol – are subject to cancellation or suspension at any time for security reasons, so call ahead and confirm your plans if you're making a special trip.

Be sure to **carry some form of ID** at all times while in DC. Two pieces should suffice, one of which should have a photo; a passport or driver's license and credit card(s) are best.

Mugging and theft

Most people won't have any security problems in DC, but if something does go wrong, contact the **police** immediately.

DC certainly has its share of **petty crime**. Even in presumably safe neighborhoods like Georgetown and Dupont Circle, you are always vulnerable to theft or muggings. Keep your wits about you in crowds, make sure your wallet or purse is secured, and, of course, avoid parks, parking lots, and dark streets at night. After the Metro has closed down, take taxis home from bars, restaurants, and clubs.

Always be careful when using **ATMs**, especially in untouristed areas. Try to use machines near downtown hotels, shops, or offices, and during the daytime. (ATMs outside tourist areas are prime spots to be mugged.) If the worst does happen, it's advisable to hand over your money and afterwards find a phone and dial ☎**911**, or hail a cab and ask the driver to take you to the nearest police station. Here, report the theft and get a reference number on the report so you

can claim insurance and/or travelers' check refunds. Call the local Travelers Aid (see the "Directory") for practical advice about hospitals and emergency services.

To avoid being the victim of **hotel room theft**, lock your valuables in the room safe when you leave, and always keep doors locked when you're in the room.

Having bags that contain travel documents stolen can be a big headache, so make photocopies of everything important before you travel and keep them separate from the originals. **If your passport is stolen** (or if you lose it), call your country's embassy or consulate (see list on p.331), and pick up an application form for a replacement one, or have one sent to you. Complete the application and return it to your embassy or consulate with a notarized photocopy of your ID and a reissuing fee, often around $30. The process of issuing a new passport can take up to six weeks, so plan accordingly.

Keep a record of the numbers of your **travelers' checks** separate from the actual checks; if you lose them, call the issuing company on the toll-free number below. The missing checks should be reissued within a couple of days, and you can request an emergency advance to tide you over in the meantime.

Finally, remember that you should never flash money around, leave your wallet open or count money in public, and look panicked, even if you are. Also, it goes without saying that you should *never* hitchhike anywhere in DC, or indeed the entire US.

Emergency numbers for lost cards and checks

American Express Cards ☎1-800/528-4800, ⓦ www.americanexpress.com
American Express Checks ☎1-800/221-7282
Citicorp Checks ☎1-800/645-6556, ⓦ www.citicorp.com
Diners Club ☎1-800/234-6377, ⓦ www.dinersclub.com
Discover ☎1-800/DISCOVER, ⓦ www.discovercard.com
MasterCard ☎1-800/826-2181, ⓦ www.mastercard.com
Thomas Cook/MasterCard Checks ☎1-800/223-9920, ⓦ www.travelex.com or www.thomascook.co.uk

Visa Cards ☎1-800/847-2911, ⊛www.visa.com
Visa Checks ☎1-800/227-6811

Car crime and safety

There are certain precautions you can take
to keep yourself safe from crime when driving **rented cars**. Not driving in DC itself is
actually the best precaution: it's not necessary, since public transportation and cheap
taxis can get you most places you'd want
to go. On longer trips, pick up your rental
car on the day you leave the city. Any car
you rent should have nothing on it – like a
special license plate – to distinguish it as a
rental car. When driving, under no circumstances should you immediately stop if you
are "accidentally" rammed by the driver
behind you; instead, drive on to the nearest
well-lit and busy spot and phone the police
at ☎**911**. Keep doors locked and hide valuables out of sight, either in the trunk or the
glove compartment, and leave any valuables you don't need for your journey back in
your hotel safe. Should a relatively uncommon "**carjacking**" occur, in which you're
told to hand over your car at gunpoint, you
should flee the vehicle as quickly as possible, get away from the scene, and then call
the police. If your car breaks down at night
while on a major street, activate the **emergency flashers** to signal a police officer for
assistance; during the day, if possible, find
the nearest phone and/or phonebook and
call for a tow truck. Should you be forced to
stop your car on a freeway, pull over to the
right shoulder of the highway – never the left
– and activate your flashers. Wait for assistance either in your vehicle while strapped
in by a seat belt or on a safe embankment
nearby.

Breaking the law

Aside from speeding or committing parking
violations, one of the most common ways
visitors to DC get into trouble is by **jaywalk-
ing** – crossing the street against red lights
or away from intersections. Fines can be
stiff, and police officers may not be sympathetic if your defense is that you didn't know
it was illegal.

Alcohol laws can also trip up foreigners,
especially if you're unaware that the legal
drinking age here is 21, and that alcohol
consumption in public spaces is illegal. The
same is true for misdemeanor **marijuana**
possession, which may get you thrown
out of the country – or into jail for larger
amounts.

Travelers with disabilities

Given the celebrated passage of the Americans with Disabilities Act (ADA) in
the 1990s, Washington DC is among the most accessible cities in the world for
travelers with disabilities. All public buildings, including hotels and restaurants,
must be wheelchair-accessible and provide accommodating restroom facilities.
Almost all street corners have dropped curbs, subway stations are equipped with
elevators, and buses have lowering platforms for boarding. Even movie theaters – that last holdout for equal access – have been forced by courts in recent
years to allow people in wheelchairs to have a reasonable, unimpeded view of
the screen.

Transportation

It's a good idea for people with special
needs to tell their travel agents this when

booking their trips. A **medical certificate**
of your fitness to travel, provided by your
doctor, is also useful; some airlines or

insurance companies may insist on it. American **air carriers** must by law accommodate those with disabilities, and some even allow attendants of those with serious conditions to accompany them for a reduced fare. **Amtrak** has train cars with special accommodations, wheelchair assistance at train platforms, free travel for guide dogs, and fifteen-percent discounts on fares, with 24 hours' advance notice. Passengers with hearing impairment can get information by calling ☎1-800/523-6590 or checking out ⊚www.amtrak.com. By contrast, traveling by **Greyhound** and Amtrak Thruway bus connections can be problematic. Buses are not equipped with platforms for wheelchairs, though intercity carriers are required by law to provide assistance with boarding, and disabled passengers may be able to get priority seating. Those unable to travel alone, and in possession of a doctor's certificate, may receive two-for-one fares. Call Greyhound's ADA customer assistance line for more information (☎1-800/752-4841, ⊚www.greyhound.com).

Major car rental companies can provide vehicles with hand controls for drivers with leg or spinal disabilities, though these are usually available only on the pricier models. Parking regulations for disabled motorists are now uniform: license plates must carry a three-inch, square international access symbol, and a placard bearing this symbol must be hung from the car's rearview mirror. The *Handicapped Drivers Mobility Guide* is a good resource published by the **American Automobile Association**. The local AAA branch is at 701 15th St NW (Mon–Fri 9am–5.30pm; ☎202/331-3000, ⊚www .aaamidatlantic.com).

Access in the city

The **Washington Convention and Tourism Corporation** (see p.21) produces a free handout on the city's accessibility for people with disabilities; call ☎202/789-7000 or visit ⊚www.washington.org. Each station on the **Metro** system has an elevator (with Braille controls) to the platforms, the trains' wide aisles can accommodate wheelchairs, seventy percent of Metro buses have lowering platforms, and reduced fares and priority seating are available. The Metro

website (⊚www.wmata.com) outlines the system's features in some detail under "Accessibility." There is also a free guide offering complete information on Metro access for the disabled at Metro stations, or you can call ☎202/637-7000 or 638-3780 (TDD). Travelers who are visually impaired or wheelchair-bound can call **Mobility Link** at ☎202/962-6464 for further information.

Most **monuments and memorials** in DC have elevators to viewing platforms and special parking facilities, and at some sites large-print brochures and sign-language interpreters are available. The **White House** has a special entrance reserved for visitors in wheelchairs. (Call ☎202/619-7222 for more information on any site operated by the National Park Service.) The **Golden Access Passport**, issued free to US citizens with permanent disabilities (⊚www.nps.gov/fees_passes), is a lifetime pass to federally operated parks, monuments, historic sites, and recreation areas that charge admission fees. It also provides a fifty-percent discount on fees for camping, boat-launching, and parking. The pass must be picked up in person from the applicable sites.

All **Smithsonian museums** are wheelchair-accessible, and with notice staff can serve as sign-language interpreters or provide large-print, Braille, or recorded material. The free *Smithsonian Access* is available in large print, Braille, or audio cassette; call ☎202/357-2700 or 357-1729 (TTY). It's also available, as is an accessibility map, online at ⊚www.si.edu. To receive a copy of the *Zoo Guide for Visitors with Disabilities* call ☎202/673-4989 or -4823.

In addition, most new downtown **shopping malls** have wheelchair ramps and elevators. **Union Station** is fully accessible, as are the **Kennedy Center** and **National Theatre**, both of which also have good facilities for visitors with hearing or vision impairments.

Information and contacts

Australia and New Zealand

Australian Council for Rehabilitation of the Disabled (ACROD) PO Box 60, Curtin, ACT 2605

⊤02/6282 4333, ⓦwww.acrod.org.au. Provides lists of travel agencies and tour operators.
Barrier-Free Travel 36 Wheatley St, North Bellingen, NSW 2454 ⊤02/6655 1733. Fee-based service providing accessibility information.
Disabled Persons Assembly Level 4, Wellington Trade Centre, 173–175 Victoria St, Wellington ⊤04/801 9100, ⓦwww.dpa.org.nz. Resource center with lists of travel agencies and tour operators.

Canada

Canadian National Institute for the Blind (CNIB) ⊤604/431-2121, ⓦwww.cnib.ca. Assistance and information for the visually impaired.
Western Institute for the Deaf and Hard of Hearing 2125 W 7th Ave, Vancouver V6K 1X9 ⊤604/736-7391 (voice) or 736-2527 (TDD), ⓦwww.widhh.ca. Travel advice for the hearing-impaired.

UK and Ireland

Access Travel 6 The Hillock, Astley, Lancashire M29 7GW ⊤01942/888844, ℻891811, ⓦwww .access-travel.co.uk. Helps travelers secure wheelchair-accessible accommodations, adapted vehicles, nursing services, and more.
Holiday Care 7th Floor, Sunley House, 4 Bedford Park, Croydon, Surrey CR0 2AP ⊤0845/124 9971, ℻124 9972, Minicom ⊤0845/124 9976, ⓦwww .holidaycare.org.uk. Offers free lists of accessible accommodations in the US and other destinations. Provides information on supplemental funding for vacations.
Irish Wheelchair Association Blackheath Drive, Clontarf, Dublin 3 ⊤01/818 6400, ⓦwww.iwa.ie. Information about traveling abroad with a wheelchair.
Mencap Holiday Services Optium House, Clippers Quay, Salford Quays, Manchester M52 2XP ⊤0161/888 1200, ⓦwww.mencap.org.uk. Provides information on holiday travel. Publishes an annual guide.
Royal Association for Disability and Rehabilitation (RADAR) 12 City Forum, 250

City Rd, London EC1V 8AF ⊤020/7250 3222, Minicom ⊤020/7250 4119, ⓦwww.radar.org.uk. Information and advice on travel.
Tripscope The Vassall Centre, Gill Ave, Bristol BS16 2QQ ⊤08457/58 56 41, ℻0117/939 7736, ⓦwww.tripscope.org.uk. Provides a national telephone information service with free advice on UK and international travel.

US

Access-Able PO Box 1796, Wheat Ridge, CO 80034 ⊤303/232-2979, ⓦwww.access -able.com. Puts people with disabilities in contact with each other.
Directions Unlimited 720 N Bedford Rd, Bedford Hills, NY 10507 ⊤1-800/533-5343 or 914/241-1700. Offers customized tours for travelers with disabilities.
DisabilityGuide.org ⊤1-800/949-4232. Free online source of information for the Washington metropolitan area. Lists accessible hotels, restaurants, and shopping venues and provides a referral service. Publishes the *Access Entertainment Guide* ($5), which you can order online.
Mobility International USA PO Box 10767, Eugene, OR 97440 ⊤541/343-1284, ⓦwww .miusa.org. Answers travel questions and operates an exchange program for the disabled. Annual membership ($35) includes quarterly newsletter.
Society for the Advancement of Travelers with Handicaps (SATH) 347 Fifth Ave, #610, New York NY 10016 ⊤212/447-7284, ⓦwww .sath.org. Nonprofit organization comprising travel agents, tour operators, hotels and airlines, and travelers with disabilities.
Washington Ear, Inc ⊤301/681-6636, ⓦwww .washear.org. Free services for people with visual disabilities who cannot read print. Supplies large-print and tactile atlases of the DC area.
Wheels Up! ⊤1-888/38-WHEELS, ⓦwww .wheelsup.com. Online service that provides discounted airfares, tours, and cruises. Publishes a free monthly newsletter.

The City

The City

1

The National Mall

Laid out along two miles between the US Capitol and the Potomac River is nothing less than the cultural and political axis of the United States, the **National Mall** (ⓦwww.nps.gov/nama). Long serving as a choice venue for protest movements of every stripe, it's also the prime target for nearly every visitor to DC. The showpiece expanse is filled with many of the city's biggest-ticket attractions, including nine Smithsonian **museums** – such as the national museums for Air and Space, Natural History, and American History – and the National Gallery of Art. It also contains several of the city's (and the country's) most iconic **monuments and memorials**, dedicated to presidents Washington, Jefferson, Lincoln, and Roosevelt, and to veterans of the Korean War, Vietnam War, World War I, and World War II. The 2000-foot-long, 160-foot-wide Reflecting Pool, supposedly inspired by the Taj Mahal's landscaping and Versailles's pools and canals, runs through the middle of the western half of the Mall, between the Washington Monument and the Lincoln Memorial.

The Mall's central spot in a planned capital city has made it an eyewitness to some of the most historically significant **social and political events**: the 1963 March on Washington brought Dr Martin Luther King Jr to the steps of the Lincoln Memorial to deliver his "I have a dream" speech; in 1967, at the height of the anti-Vietnam War protests, the March on the Pentagon began at those same steps. Three decades later, in 1995, controversial minister Louis Farrakhan, of the Nation of Islam, led hundreds of thousands of black men to the Mall for the Million Man March. On several occasions, the AIDS Memorial Quilt – a patchwork of 40,000 individual squares remembering America's AIDS victims – has covered the full mile from the Capitol to the Washington Monument. For all its grandeur and tumult, however, the Mall is also a place to relax and party, notably at the annual Festival of American Folklife and on the Fourth of July (see "Festivals and parades" chapter).

As a visitor to Washington, you'll find the Mall almost inescapable on any tourist-oriented route. Given a normal appetite for museums, galleries, and monuments (and a fair constitution), you could get around most of the Mall's major sights in three days or so. But it's better to return at various times during your stay, if only to avoid complete cultural overload. Many of the attractions lend themselves to being seen with a combination of other city sights: the western monuments with the White House and Foggy Bottom (Chapter 4); the Jefferson and Roosevelt memorials with the sights along the Waterfront (Chapter 3); and the museums on the Mall's north side interspersed with a stroll around Old Downtown (Chapter 5).

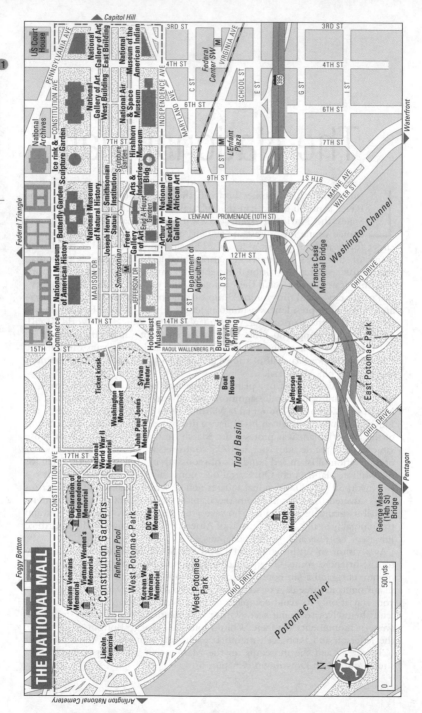

THE NATIONAL MALL

▲ Foggy Bottom
▲ Federal Triangle
▲ Capitol Hill
▲ Arlington National Cemetery

US Court House

National Archives

Ice rink & Sculpture Garden

National Gallery of Art West Building

National Gallery of Art East Building

National Museum of the American Indian

National Air & Space Museum

Hirshhorn Museum

Arts & Industries Bldg

Smithsonian Institution

National Museum of African Art

Arthur M Sackler Gallery

Freer Gallery of Art

Enid A Haupt Garden

Joseph Henry Statue

National Museum of Natural History

National Museum of American History

Butterfly Garden

Dept of Commerce

Department of Agriculture

Holocaust Museum

Bureau of Engraving & Printing

L'Enfant Plaza

Federal Center SW

Washington Channel

Francis Case Memorial Bridge

East Potomac Park

Ticket kiosk

Washington Monument

Sylvan Theater

John Paul Jones Memorial

National World War II Memorial

Declaration of Independence Memorial

Vietnam Veterans Memorial

Vietnam Women's Memorial

Korean War Veterans Memorial

DC War Memorial

Lincoln Memorial

Reflecting Pool

Constitution Gardens

West Potomac Park

Boat House

Tidal Basin

Jefferson Memorial

FDR Memorial

George Mason (14th St) Bridge

Potomac River

Ohio Drive

▲ Waterfront
▲ Pentagon

PENNSYLVANIA AVE
CONSTITUTION AVE
3RD ST
4TH ST
6TH ST
7TH ST
9TH ST
INDEPENDENCE AVE
MADISON DR
JEFFERSON DR
12TH ST
14TH ST
15TH ST
17TH ST
MARYLAND AVE
VIRGINIA AVE
C ST
D ST
E ST
G ST
I ST
SCHOOL ST
3RD ST
4TH ST
6TH ST
L'ENFANT PROMENADE (10TH ST)
RAOUL WALLENBERG PL
MAINE AVE
WATER ST
OHIO DRIVE
395

N

0   500 yds

Some history

Despite the size and prominence the Mall enjoys today, from the early to mid-nineteenth century it was something of an embarrassment – a wild, stagnant piece of land that some saw as a metaphor for the country's then-unrealized potential.

A 400-foot-wide avenue leading west from the Capitol was at the heart of French military engineer **Pierre Charles L'Enfant**'s original 1791 plan for the city; along it, he envisioned gardens and mansions for the political elite. Also, a commemorative monument to George Washington was to stand at the point where a line drawn west from the Capitol met one drawn south from the President's Mansion (what is today the White House). Due to lack of funds, work didn't start on the Washington Monument until 1848, by which time any prospect of the Mall transforming itself from a muddy, bug-infested swamp into a splendid, pleasant avenue was laughable: cows, pigs, and goats grazed on the open land, while the malodorous city canal (linking the C&O Canal in Georgetown with the Anacostia River) ran along the north side, stinking with rotting refuse, spoiled fish, entrails, and dead animals from Washington's Center Market on 7th Street.

Following the construction of the **Smithsonian Institution Building** between 1849 and 1855, eminent landscape gardener Andrew Jackson Downing was hired to design an elegant green space in keeping with L'Enfant's plan. However, the money only stretched to one tree-planted park near the Smithsonian, and people dared not venture there at night, since it quickly became the haunt of ruffians and ne'er-do-wells. What's more, by 1855, work had been halted on the nearby Washington Monument, which stood incomplete for the next twenty years as little more than a chunky granite stump. The Mall continued to deteriorate and, as the city grew, its south side became home to meat markets and warehouses, while the grand avenue L'Enfant imagined was crisscrossed by the ungainly tracks of the Baltimore and Potomac Railroad.

During the **Civil War**, President Lincoln was determined to continue building as "a sign we intend the Union shall go on," and postwar Reconstruction saved the Mall from further decline. The city canal was filled in (it's now Constitution Avenue), Center Market was closed, a Board of Public Works was established to build sewers, sidewalks, and streets, mature trees were planted, and, in 1884, the Washington Monument was finally completed. Several of Downing's other plans were resurrected, extending beyond the Mall to incorporate the grassy Ellipse and the gardens on either side of the White House, finally placing the Mall at the ornamental heart of the city.

With the 1881 addition of the **Arts and Industries Building** (meant to be used as overflow space for the then-named "National Museum"), the Mall came to be seen as a logical site for grand public institutions: the US Botanic Garden opened here in 1902, the Museum of Natural History in 1911, and the Freer Gallery – the Smithsonian's first art museum – in 1923.

Led by Senator James McMillan, members of the 1901 **McMillan Commission**, charged with improving the Mall and the city's park system, returned from Europe fired up with plans to link the Mall with a series of gardens and memorials, and to demolish the unsightly railroad station (later replaced by Union Station). Not everyone concurred, however: powerful House Speaker Joseph Cannon railed that he "would rather see the Mall sown in oats than treated as an artistic composition." But McMillan's proposals prevailed and, following the completion of the Lincoln Memorial in 1922, the Mall was extended west of the Washington Monument for the first time, reaching to the banks of the Potomac River and incorporating the grounds known today as

West Potomac Park (though much of the watery turf of the western Mall still had to be filled in and made to resemble something other than a swamp). More improvements were made in the 1930s, under the auspices of President Roosevelt's New Deal-era Works Progress Administration (WPA), including the planting of the city's now-famous elm trees, and the **National Park Service** was granted stewardship of the Mall and its monuments.

The erection of the Jefferson Memorial in 1943 completed the Mall's initial triumvirate of **presidential monuments**. The monument's architect, John Russell Pope, also designed the contemporaneous National Gallery of Art. The 1960s and 1970s ushered in **museums** of American History and Air and Space, the Hirshhorn Museum, and the National Gallery's East Building. In the 1980s, the Sackler Gallery and the National Museum of African Art were opened. The dedication of the Vietnam Veterans Memorial (1982), the Korean War Veterans Memorial (1995), and the FDR Memorial (1997) demonstrated that there was still space for **further additions**. In 2004, the Mall welcomed the long-awaited National World War II Memorial – which sits on the former site of the Rainbow Pool between the Lincoln Memorial and the Washington Monument – and the National Museum of the American Indian, in a prime spot between the National Air and Space Museum and the US Botanic Garden.

The planning of a capital city

It is sometimes called the City of Magnificent Distances, but it might with greater propriety be termed the City of Magnificent Intentions; for it is only on taking a bird's-eye view of it from the top of the Capitol that one can at all comprehend the vast designs of its projector, an aspiring Frenchman.

Charles Dickens, *American Notes*, 1842

In 1790, the year after George Washington was inaugurated in New York City as the first US president, it fell to Congress to decide upon a **permanent site** for the country's capital. Since independence, Congress had met in a half-dozen cities, and many others in both the North and the South had competing claims and loud promoters. Ultimately the decision came down to **political wrangling**: in return for Congress assuming the states' debts from the Revolutionary War (a key Northern demand), the new federal capital would be in the upper South, somewhere on the sparsely populated banks of the Potomac River.

With the help of Major Andrew Ellicott, a surveyor from Maryland, and the black mathematician and scientist Benjamin Banneker, Washington – a mean surveyor himself – suggested a diamond-shaped, hundred-square-mile site at the confluence of the Potomac and Anacostia rivers. It seemed a canny choice: centering on the confluence, and thus ripe for trade, the site incorporated the ports of Alexandria in Virginia and Georgetown in Maryland; it would have its own port in Anacostia, and – no small matter for Washington – it was only eighteen miles upriver from his home at Mount Vernon. Maryland ceded roughly seventy square miles of land, Virginia thirty; all Washington had to do was find someone to **plan the city**, which Congress decreed would be named Washington City, in the Territory (later District) of Columbia, itself a reference to Christopher Columbus. (Thomas Jefferson thought up both monikers.)

Washington recommended **Major Pierre Charles L'Enfant**, a former member of his Continental Army staff and a fellow Freemason, who was renowned for his successful redesign of New York's Federal Hall prior to Washington's inauguration. Within a year L'Enfant had come up with an ambitious plan to transform a

Monuments and memorials

The Mall is easily laid out for navigation: **monuments and memorials** lie to the west, **museums** sit to the east, and the Washington Monument stands between them. Most visitors make a beeline for this central monument; from there it's easy to visit the World War II Memorial, drop down to the Tidal Basin and the Jefferson and FDR memorials, continue on a clockwise path to the Korean War Veterans Memorial, the Lincoln Memorial, and the Vietnam Veterans Memorial, then wind up on the north side of the Washington Monument. Next you can head to the eastern side of the Mall, if there's any time left in the day.

Other than the Washington Monument, the various memorials and monuments on the western Mall are **not easily accessible by Metro**, and you'll have to walk at least two-thirds of a mile to get to them. The closest stops are Foggy Bottom-GWU and Farragut West to the north, and Smithsonian to the southeast. For a completely different approach, you can arrive from the west via the Arlington Cemetery stop, arriving at the Lincoln Memorial by way of the striking Arlington Memorial Bridge. The best approach, however,

swampy wilderness into a modern imperial city, adding diagonal avenues on top of Jefferson's idea for a conventional street grid, and radiating them from ceremonial squares and elegant circles. A "Grand Avenue" (later known as the Mall) formed the centerpiece; government buildings were assigned their own plots; a central canal linked the city's ports; and sculptures, fountains, and parks punctuated the design. L'Enfant's initial inspiration was the city of Paris and the seventeenth-century palace of Versailles, though Jefferson himself proposed the sites of the **US Capitol** and the **President's Mansion**. The plan named avenues after the fifteen states that existed in 1791, placing avenues named after Northern states north of the Capitol, Southern ones to the south; the most populous states – Virginia, New York, Pennsylvania, and Massachusetts – were represented by the longest avenues.

Washington was delighted with the scheme, though the existing landowners were less than pleased with the injunction to donate any land needed for public thorough-fares. Moreover, L'Enfant found himself in constant dispute with the District commissioners who had been appointed by Washington to oversee the construction. His obstinacy cost him his job in 1792, and the design of the US Capitol and White House were both later thrown open to **public competition**. L'Enfant turned down the $2500 he was offered as payment for his services, sued Congress (unsuccessfully) for $100,000, harried the legislature with his grievances for the rest of his life, and died in penury in 1825.

For decades L'Enfant's plan seemed full of empty pretensions as Washington DC struggled to embody even a faint shadow of its inspired plan. Any number of nine-teenth-century observers commented upon the absurd contrast between such "vast designs" and the less-than-impressive reality. But for all that, this unique attempt to create a capital city that could define a nation was a remarkable enterprise, and itself inspired future state capitals (the first was Indianapolis in the 1820s) to be built from scratch at central geographic and political locations. Perhaps the last word should be with nineteenth-century abolitionist and orator Frederick Douglass, who said: "It is our national center. It belongs to us, and whether it is mean or majestic, whether arranged in glory or covered with shame, we cannot but share its character and its destiny."

may be to take Bus #13, which loops around the Mall to Arlington and back, or the Tourmobile, which runs along Constitution Avenue (see "City tours" and "City transportation" in Basics).

The Washington Monument

15th St NW at Constitution Ave ☎202/426-6841 or 1-800/967-2283, ⊛www.nps.gov/wamo; Smithsonian Metro. Daily 9am–5pm.

If there's one structure that symbolizes DC, other than the US Capitol, it's surely the **Washington Monument** – an unadorned marble obelisk built in memory of the first American president. Simple, elegant, majestic, and, above all, huge, it's immediately recognizable from all over the city (and from planes landing at nearby Reagan National Airport), providing the Mall and the capital with a striking central ornament.

To honor George Washington's achievements, L'Enfant's original city plan proposed an equestrian statue at the intersection of the south axis of the White House and the west axis of the Capitol – an idea which even the modest Washington himself approved of. Yet by the time of Washington's death in 1799, no progress had been made on the statue, though a small stone marker was later placed on the proposed spot by Thomas Jefferson in 1804 (the "Jefferson Pier" is still visible today). Impatient at Congress's apparent lack of enthusiasm for the work, in 1833 Chief Justice John Marshall and a very aged James Madison established the National Monument Society to foster a design competition and subscription drive. From this emerged US Treasury architect **Robert Mills's** hugely ambitious scheme to top a colonnaded base containing the tombs of Revolutionary War-era heroes with a massive obelisk; L'Enfant's original idea received a nod with the addition of a statue of Washington driving a horse-drawn chariot.

The Society took one look at the meager subscriptions and settled for the **obelisk** on its own, which proved to be a wise decision. Early excavations revealed that L'Enfant's chosen spot was too marshy to build on, and when the cornerstone was finally laid on July 4, 1848, it was on a bare knoll 360ft east and 120ft south of the true intersection (which explains why the monument is off-center on the map). By 1853, when funds ran out, the monument was just 152ft high, and stayed that way for almost 25 years – grievously truncated, bordered by the fetid Washington Canal, the site roamed by cattle awaiting slaughter at a nearby abattoir. Mark Twain later likened it to a "factory chimney with the top broken off," while the *New York Tribune*, in an almost universally held opinion, condemned it as a "wretched design, a wretched location."

After the Civil War, Congress finally authorized government funds to complete the monument and appointed **Lieutenant Colonel Thomas Casey** of the Army Corps of Engineers to the work. Casey suffered his own tribulations, not least of which was the discovery that the original marble source in Maryland had dried up; you can still see the transition line at the 150-foot level, where work resumed with marble of a slightly different tone. At long last, by December 1884, the monument was finally complete. The tallest all-masonry structure on the planet, it stands just over 555ft tall, measures 55ft wide at the base, tapers to 34ft at the top, and is capped by a small aluminum pyramid.

A seventy-second **elevator ride** deposits you at the 500-foot level, from where the views – glimpsed through surprisingly narrow windows on all four sides – are, of course, tremendous. Back on ground level, an exterior **bronze statue** of

Washington faces east towards the Capitol. Almost 7ft high, this is a faithful copy of the renowned statue by eighteenth-century French sculptor Jean-Antoine Houdon, which was commissioned for the Virginia State Capitol in Richmond and placed there in 1796. Washington, wearing the uniform of commander-in-chief of the Continental Army, holds a cane in one hand and is flanked by a bundle of rods and a plowshare, signifying authority and peace, respectively.

Due to security concerns, the grounds around the monument are presently being redesigned. When the project is complete, concentric stone rings on the sloping knoll below the pillar will serve to deter terrorism by preventing vehicles from getting too close to the structure. For now there are temporary barriers to keep you from wandering around the grounds, so to visit the monument you must pick up a free ticket from the 15th Street kiosk (on the Mall, south of Constitution Ave; daily 8am–4.30pm); the ticket will allow you to turn up at a fixed time later in the day. You'll need to get to the kiosk early, as **tickets** often run out well before noon. You can avoid any uncertainty by reserving ahead at ☏1-800/967-2283 and paying a $2 service fee per ticket.

National World War II Memorial

17th St SW at Independence Ave, ☏202/426-6841, ✉www.nps.gov/nwwm; Smithsonian or Farragut West Metro. Daily 24hr, staffed 8am–midnight.

The **National World War II Memorial** opened in 2004 to much acclaim, and great relief. Although some feared that it would disrupt the Mall's scenic views or become an overblown statement of victory, neither fear was realized, and the memorial stands as a thoroughly moving statement of duty and sacrifice.

The site roughly occupies the former footprint of the Mall's Rainbow Pool on the western edge of the Washington Monument. Two arcs on each side of a **central fountain** have a combined total of 56 stone pillars (representing the number of US states and territories at the time of the war) that are decorated with bronze wreaths. In the middle of each arc stands a short tower, one called "Atlantic" and the other "Pacific," and within each tower are four interlinked bronze eagles and a sculpted wreath, which, despite its bulk, seems to float above you in mid-air.

Beyond the carefully considered architecture and the FDR and Eisenhower **quotes** that are chiselled on the walls, a concave wall of four thousand golden stars reminds you of the 400,000 fallen US soldiers – a number matched only by the colossal carnage of the Civil War.

Near the memorial, a veteran's history project aims to record and catalogue the war stories of American veterans before these former soldiers are no longer able to tell them. If you have recollections you'd like to share, inquire at the visitor center, on the south side of the memorial, about the best way to record them for posterity.

The DC War Memorial and John Paul Jones statue

A bit south of the World War II Memorial is perhaps the Mall's most overlooked monument: the **DC War Memorial**, hidden in a grove of trees just north of Independence Avenue. This rather humble edifice is basically a small, circular, Neoclassical temple built in 1931 to commemorate local soldiers who fought in World War I. Usually free from tourists or any visitors whatsoever, it

George Washington

The Washington family, originally from the north of **England**, emigrated to America in 1656, a decade after the English Civil War (during which they had been fierce loyalists) and the establishment of Oliver Cromwell's military dictatorship. George Washington was born on February 22, 1732, on his wealthy family's plantation in Westmoreland County, Virginia. Although most of what is known about Washington's early life comes from various fawning and fictitious nineteenth-century biographies, it is clear that he received intermittent schooling and excelled in most outdoor pursuits. Because he wasn't his family's first-born son (primogeniture was a big deal in the Cavalier country of north Virginia), he stood to inherit little property other than a small farm on the Rappahannock River. Washington therefore taught himself how to be a **surveyor**, and in 1748 assisted in the surveying of the new port of Alexandria (see "Out of the city" chapter).

At the age of 21 Washington was appointed by Virginia's governor to travel into the Ohio Valley to ascertain the strength of the French forces, which had been steadily encroaching on British turf. This experience led him to be appointed **lieutenant-colonel** in the Virginia Regiment and, later, aide-de-camp in the French and Indian War, in which he gained his first battle experience (a bad defeat, though Washington gained local respect for his leadership qualities). Finishing the war as regimental commander, he was subsequently elected to the **Virginia House of Burgesses** in Williamsburg. Giving up his commission, in January 1759 he married the wealthy **Martha Dandridge Custis** – who had two children from a previous marriage – and settled at **Mount Vernon** after his eldest brother died. For a time Washington led the bucolic life of a gentleman plantation owner, a lifestyle buttressed by a large number of slaves. George and Martha never had any children of their own, but later became guardians to the youngest two of Martha's grandchildren by her first marriage.

Still serving in the House of Burgesses throughout the 1760s, Washington developed a reputation for honesty and good judgment, and was one of the Virginian delegates at the **Continental Congress** in 1774; the following year, when British soldiers clashed with American volunteers at Lexington and Concord, confrontation turned into revolution. At a second meeting of the Continental Congress in June 1775, the 43-year-old Washington was appointed **commander-in-chief** of the nascent American forces – as much for the fact that he was from Virginia (Congress wanted to combine the existing New England militia with a general who would also attract Southern volunteers) as for his military experience, which was fairly modest.

Washington had his limitations as a battlefield tactician; due to early mistakes, his under-equipped Continental Army lost more battles than it won. But he did have a knack for imposing order and hierarchy onto the fledgling army, and retaining the respect of his forces during trying times. (Throughout the war, Washington shared his soldiers' hardships by spending the winters with them in his northern redoubts, rather than at Mount Vernon.) He was also a fine judge of talent in his subordinates and promoted such key figures as Friedrich von Steuben and Nathaniel Greene, both of whom proved to be excellent tacticians and strategists. Without

offers a quiet and relaxing respite from the hubbub of the Mall – a place to take a break before you wade once more into the throngs of visitors.

Due south of the World War II Memorial and east of the DC War Memorial stands the proud **statue of John Paul Jones** – stranded on a traffic island at 17th Street and Independence Avenue. If the sculpted figure of America's first naval hero looks a bit pensive, it's only appropriate: ironically, the World War II Memorial, which is in his line of sight, honors the alliance of the US with Britain – the European power Jones spent years trying to intimidate with his surprise coastal raids and aggressive nautical tactics.

Washington's strengths, the American army could have easily fallen apart: there was often little money to pay, clothe, or supply the American militiamen, so they regularly deserted; the locals, and often Congress, too, proved unsupportive; and, to top it all off, Washington was ill-served by traitors in his camp. Nonetheless, he never gave in to calls to march against the Congress and grab a Caesar-like stranglehold over the government.

Indeed, after the battle at **Yorktown** in 1781 and the establishment of peace two years later, Washington resisted demands to assume an American "kingship," resigned his commission, and returned to Mount Vernon – a noble act that led many to describe him as a modern "Cincinnatus," after the Roman general who did much the same thing thousands of years earlier (and also led to the establishment of the Society of the Cincinnati; see p.189). However, four years later, at the **Constitutional Convention** in Philadelphia, Washington was back in the political arena. Called to safeguard the Revolution by devising a permanent system of government for the nation, the Convention unanimously elected Washington its presiding officer, as he was the only man able to command universal respect. Once the Constitution had been drawn up and ratified, there was only one realistic choice for the post of first **President of the United States**; in February 1789, George Washington was unanimously elected to the position.

Washington defined the uncharted role of president while developing the relationship between the executive and other **branches of government**. It's doubtful anyone else could have contained the machinations of various members of his cabinet, as the Federalists and Republicans skirmished for influence. Surprisingly, the commander-in-chief often defied expectations by siding with his Federalist, New Yorker Treasury secretary, Alexander Hamilton, over Virginia Republicans Thomas Jefferson and Edmund Randolph.

Despite severe provocation by both sides, Washington kept America out of the war between England and France that was instigated by the French Revolution. During his first term, he even negotiated the political minefield that was choosing the site of the new federal capital. The **capital city** was promptly named after him, and the president laid the cornerstone of the US Capitol in 1793. However, he never lived in Washington or the White House – which wasn't finished until 1800 – shuttling instead between New York, Philadelphia, and other northeastern cities.

Washington was elected to a **second term** in 1793 and would undoubtedly have been granted a third, but in 1797 he was 65 and wanted nothing more than to retire to his farm. Delivering a farewell address to both houses of Congress, he went home to Mount Vernon, where he died two and a half years later on December 14, 1799 from a fever said to have been induced by being caught out in a snowstorm. Congress adjourned for the day, and even the British and French fleets lowered their flags in respect. Martha lived until May 1802, and on her death, Washington's will freed all their slaves. George and Martha are buried together on the grounds of Mount Vernon.

The Jefferson Memorial

West Potomac Park, southeast bank of the Tidal Basin near 15th St SW and Ohio Drive ☏202/426-6841, @www.nps.gov/thje; Smithsonian Metro. Daily 8am–midnight.

Although **Thomas Jefferson** was America's first Secretary of State, its third president, author of the Declaration of Independence, and the closest thing to a Renaissance Man produced in Enlightenment-era America, it took until 1943 for his memorial to be built. It wasn't for the want of inspiration, as Jefferson was a speaker of six languages who practiced law, studied science, mathematics, and archeology, and was an accomplished musician and keen botanist as well as a lucid writer and self-taught architect of considerable prowess. By the twentieth century, though, the memorial site proved contentious: the US Capitol, Washington Monument, White House, and Lincoln Memorial were already in place, and the obvious site lay on the southern axis, south of the Washington Monument. Many bemoaned the destruction of some of the city's famous cherry trees when the ground around the Tidal Basin was cleared (a few protesters even chained themselves to the trunks), while others argued that the memorial would block the view of the river from the White House. More practically, the site proved difficult to reach, since the basin blocked direct access from the north. This, in fact, provides much of its charm today, as the sinuous walk around the tree-lined basin makes for a fine approach.

If the site had its critics, then so did the memorial. When **John Russell Pope** – architect of the National Gallery of Art – revealed his plans for a Neoclassical, circular, colonnaded structure with a shallow dome housing a nineteen-foot-high bronze statue, some said it was too similar to the Lincoln Memorial. The design, however, was in keeping with Jefferson's own tastes: not only was it influenced by the Greek and Renaissance Revival styles that Jefferson had helped popularize in the United States after his stint as ambassador to France in the 1780s, but it also echoed closely the style of Jefferson's own (self-designed) country home at Monticello, in Charlottesville, Virginia.

Today the Jefferson Memorial is one of the most recognizable and harmonious structures in the city: a white marble temple, reminiscent of the Pantheon, with steps down to the water's edge and framed by the cherry trees of the Tidal Basin. The standing bronze statue of Jefferson, by **Rudulph Evans**, gazes determinedly out of the memorial, while the inscription around the frieze sets the high moral tone, trumpeting: "I have sworn upon the altar of God eternal hostility against every form of tyranny over the mind of man." (Though missing is his more pointed comment, "The tree of liberty must be refreshed from time to time with the blood of tyrants and patriots. It is its natural manure.") Inside, on the walls, four more texts flank the statue, including words from the 1776 Declaration of Independence. On the lower level, a small **museum** devoted to Jefferson has historical displays and mementos from his era, and the area in front of the site occasionally hosts musicians and other entertainers who perform during the city's spring and summer celebrations, notably April's National Cherry Blossom Festival (see "Festivals and parades" chapter).

The Tidal Basin

The **Tidal Basin** fills most of the space between the Lincoln and Jefferson memorials. This large inlet, formerly part of the Potomac River, was created in 1882 to prevent flooding, while the famous **cherry trees** – a gift from Japan – were planted around the edge in 1912. The annual Cherry Blossom Festival in early April celebrates their blooming with concerts, parades, and displays of Japanese lanterns. To take it all in from the water, rent a pedal boat from the **Tidal Basin Boat House**, 1501 Maine Ave SW (March–Sept Mon–Fri 10am–6pm, Sat & Sun 10am–7pm; two-seaters $8/hr, four-seaters $16/hr; ☎202/484-0206), a real treat for children, and a great way to experience waterside views of several famous monuments and memorials.

The long spit of East Potomac Park south of the Jefferson Memorial has more cherry trees, while if you walk around the western side of the basin, following

Ohio Drive, you pass the FDR Memorial before reaching the **statue of John Ericsson**, south of the Korean War Veterans and Lincoln memorials. Ericsson, the Swedish-born inventor of the screw-propeller, also designed the ironclad warship *Monitor* – known in its day as a "tin can on a raft" – which, in 1862, held its own against the Confederate vessel *Virginia* in the first naval conflict between ironclad ships.

The Franklin Delano Roosevelt Memorial

West Potomac Park, southwest bank of the Tidal Basin ☎202/376-6704 or 619-7222, ⊛www.nps.gov/fdrm; Smithsonian Metro or #13 bus from Constitution or Independence avenues. Daily 24hr, staffed 8am–midnight.

DC's most recent presidential memorial, honoring **Franklin Delano Roosevelt**, president from 1933 to 1945, would never have been built had it been up to FDR himself. Accepting that he would one day be so commemorated, he favored only a small stone monument on Pennsylvania Avenue (see p.158), but after his death, others insisted on a far more impressive tribute. Designed by Lawrence Halprin and dedicated in 1997, the memorial spreads across a seven-acre site on the banks of the Tidal Basin and is made up of a series of interlinking granite outdoor galleries – called "rooms" – punctuated by waterfalls, statuary, sculpted reliefs, groves of trees, and shaded alcoves and plazas. It's among the most successful – and popular – of DC's memorials, and has an almost Athenian quality to its open spaces, resting-places, benches, and inspiring texts. On a bright spring or fall day, with the glistening basin waters and emerging views of the Washington Monument and Jefferson Memorial, it's one of the finest places in the city for a contemplative stroll.

A wartime leader and architect of the New Deal, Roosevelt's political spirit is captured in a series of carved **quotations**, appearing on the walls, that defined his presidency – perhaps most famously in the words "The only thing we have to fear is fear itself." The four galleries of rustic stone (one for each of his terms in office) turn upon seminal periods: in the second gallery stand George Segal's sculpted figures of a city breadline, a Dustbowl couple in a rural doorway, and an elderly man listening to one of Roosevelt's famous radio fireside chats; in the third gallery, alongside a **seated statue of FDR** and the heartfelt message "I have seen war . . . I hate war," a tangle of broken granite blocks represents the World War II years. The memorial's most beloved element, however, sits at FDR's feet, where a sculpture of his dog Fala attracts countless children and shutterbugs, its pert bronze ears rubbed shiny from all the attention. The memorial ends in the fourth gallery, where a timeline of dates and events is inscribed in the steps, and a statue of perhaps Roosevelt's greatest ally, his wife, Eleanor, stands.

There's great significance, too, in something most visitors don't notice about the memorial, namely that it is fully accessible to people in wheelchairs. At the age of 39, FDR contracted polio, which left him paralyzed from the waist down – a fact largely kept from the American people during his run for the governorship of New York and, later, the presidency of the United States. Believing that public knowledge of his disability would hurt his political career, FDR was almost always pictured standing while making speeches, and he only used his wheelchair in private. (Reporters and photographers aided him in this deception.) In his memorial, FDR is portrayed simply as being seated – his legs largely covered by the flowing cape he wore at the 1945 Yalta conference with Winston Churchill and Joseph Stalin.

The Korean War Veterans Memorial

West Potomac Park, southwest side of Reflecting Pool ☎202/619-7222, ⊕www.nps.gov/kwvm; Smithsonian or Foggy Bottom-GWU Metro. Daily 24hr, staffed 8am–midnight.

Continuing clockwise from the FDR Memorial, the **Korean War Veterans Memorial** lies south of the Reflecting Pool, just a few minutes' walk from the Lincoln Memorial. Dedicated in July 1995 (and largely funded by private contributions), its centerpiece is a Field of Remembrance with nineteen life-size, heavily armed combat troops sculpted from stainless steel. The troops advance across a triangular plot with alternating rows of stones and plant life and head toward the Stars and Stripes positioned at the vertex. A reflecting black granite wall, with the inscription "Freedom is not free" and an etched mural, depicting military support crew and medical staff, flank the ensemble. Although it's generally a moving piece, the soldiers' faces are cruder and less expressive than those of the presidents and other war heroes sculpted along the Mall.

A plaque at the flagstand proclaims, "Our nation honors her sons and daughters who answered the call to defend a country they never knew and a people they never met." Indeed, almost 55,000 Americans were killed in the conflict on the Korean peninsula, with another 8000 missing in action and more than 103,000 wounded. Unlike those who fought in Vietnam, the American soldiers sent into battle by President Truman on behalf of the South Korean government went, tenuously, in the name of the United Nations. The memorial lists the fifteen other countries who volunteered forces, with Britain, France, Greece, and Turkey in particular suffering significant losses. While the memorial honors soldiers from allied countries, it doesn't give the number of Korean casualties: by some estimates, about three million (North and South) Korean civilians died – in addition to half a million North Korean, 50,000 South Korean, and possibly one million Chinese soldiers.

The memorial has a CD-ROM database (inquire at the visitor center), in which you can type the name of a fallen veteran and call up and print out the soldier's rank, serial number, unit, casualty date, and photograph; you can also find some of this information online at ⊕www.koreanwar.org.

The Lincoln Memorial

West Potomac Park at 23rd St NW ☎202/4426-6841, ⊕www.nps.gov/linc; Foggy Bottom-GWU Metro. Daily 24hr; staffed 8am–midnight.

The **Lincoln Memorial** needs no introduction. As one of the country's most recognizable symbols, it represents both the United States' political ideology and its culture of social activism. The memorial is perpetually host to speeches, protests, events, and marches; less tempestuously, it effortlessly provides a backdrop for some of the most stirring photographs in town. The Reflecting Pool, the Washington Monument, and the US Capitol lie to the monument's east, and the Potomac River and Arlington National Cemetery are to its west. This solemn, inspirational memorial is the best-loved of all the city's commemorative icons.

Proposals to erect a monument to the sixteenth president were raised as early as 1865, the year of Lincoln's assassination. While there was no shortage of ideas, there was a struggle to determine an appropriate tribute and site. One early plan suggested building a Lincoln Highway between Washington and Gettysburg, while arch-Neoclassicist John Russell Pope submitted four designs (including a vast pyramid and a stone funeral pyre), all of which were rejected. In 1901 the McMillan Commission finally approved the construction of a Greek temple in the marshlands of the newly created West Potomac Park, though House overlord Joe Cannon inveighed, "I'll never let a memorial to Abraham Lincoln be erected in that goddamned swamp." Nonetheless work began on the memorial in February 1914 under the aegis of New York architect **Henry Bacon**.

The memorial's 36 Doric columns symbolize the number of states in the Union at the time of Lincoln's death, while bas-relief plaques on the attic parapet commemorate the country's 48 states at the time of the memorial's completion in 1922 (Alaska and Hawaii get a mere inscription on the terrace). But for all its restrained beauty, the temple is upstaged by what is inside – the seated statue of Lincoln by **Daniel Chester French** (1850–1931), which faces out through the colonnade. French certainly succeeded in his intention to "convey the mental and physical strength of the great war President": full of resolve, a steely Lincoln clasps the armrests of a thronelike chair with determined hands, his unbuttoned coat falling to either side. The American flag is draped over the back of the chair. It's a phenomenal work, one that took French thirteen years to complete, fashioning the nineteen-foot-tall statue from 28 blocks of white Georgia marble.

Climbing the steps to the memorial and meeting the seated Lincoln's gaze is one of DC's most profound experiences. After your introductions, look out over the Reflecting Pool and down the length of the Mall, then turn back and gaze at the **murals** on the north and south walls. Jules Guerin painted these images, which represent (on the north wall) Fraternity, Unity of North and South, and Charity, and (on the south wall) Emancipation and Immortality. Underneath the murals are carved inscriptions of Lincoln's two most celebrated **speeches** – the Gettysburg Address of November 19, 1863 (the speech that Lincoln himself thought a "flat failure"), and Lincoln's Second Inaugural Address of March 4, 1865, in which he strove "to bind up the nation's wounds" caused by the Civil War.

Although Lincoln is inextricably linked to the nation's abolition of slavery and long struggle with civil rights, ironically, at the memorial's dedication in May 1922, President Warren G. Harding and Lincoln's surviving son, Robert, watched the proceedings from the speakers' platform while Dr Robert Moton – the president of the Tuskegee Institute who was scheduled to make the principal address – was forced to watch from a roped-off, racially segregated area. The memorial thereafter became a centerpiece in demonstrations urging the recognition of civil rights: Spanish Civil War veterans from the Abraham Lincoln Brigade marched here in 1938; a year later, on Easter Sunday, black opera singer Marian Anderson performed from the steps to a crowd of 75,000,

Lincoln and the Gettysburg Address

Abraham Lincoln's **Gettysburg Address** was astonishing for its brevity – the official photographer at the military cemetery's dedication hadn't gotten his equipment ready before the president sat down again. Edward Everett, former senator and one-time Secretary of State, spoke first at the ceremony; later he claimed that he wished he had come close to expressing in two and a half hours what Lincoln had expressed in two and a half minutes. Yet the president's speech was poorly received: Lincoln was convinced that the audience had failed to appreciate its fine nuances, while the *Chicago Times* lambasted its "silly, flat, and dish-watery utterances." Other newspapers had a keener sense of history – *Harper's Weekly*, for example, thought it "as simple and felicitous and earnest a word as was ever spoken."

having been refused permission by the Daughters of the American Revolution to appear at their nearby Constitution Hall. Anderson pointedly dedicated her performance to "the ideals of freedom for which President Lincoln died." Groups from the American Nazi Party to the Black Panthers have exercised their First Amendment rights at the memorial (as anyone can, provided you don't climb on the statue or hang banners from the building). But perhaps the memorial's brightest day was August 28, 1963, when, during the March on Washington for Jobs and Freedom, Dr Martin Luther King Jr delivered his "I have a dream" speech to 200,000 people who had gathered here. Five years later, in May and June 1968, after King's assassination, his successors brought the ill-fated Poor People's March to the memorial (see the "Resurrection City" box, below).

The Reflecting Pool and Constitution Gardens

The view from the Lincoln Memorial would lose a significant part of its appeal were it not for the lengthy **Reflecting Pool** that reaches out from the cenotaph's steps toward the Washington Monument. The reflections in the water of both the memorial and the monument are stunning, particularly at night when everything is lit.

Like the Lincoln Memorial, the pool was built in 1922, inspired supposedly by none less than the Taj Mahal's landscaping and Versailles's pools and canals. Though the surrounding area of West Potomac Park was originally to be landscaped, "temporary" cement-board munitions and office buildings erected around the pool during both world wars proved hard to remove. Reconstruction was only seriously considered when President Nixon suggested the grounds be re-imagined as a Tivoli Gardens-style park in time for the country's bicentennial. However, financial concerns and aesthetic considerations produced, in 1976, the less flamboyant **Constitution Gardens**, a fifty-acre area of trees and dells surrounding a kidney-shaped lake on the north side of the Reflecting Pool. A plaque on the island in the center commemorates the 56 signatories of the Declaration of Independence; every September 17, Constitution Day, the signing of the Constitution is celebrated in the gardens by, among other things, an outdoor naturalization service for foreign-born DC residents.

Resurrection City

At the time of Dr Martin Luther King Jr's 1968 assassination, the civil-rights leader was planning a second march on the capital, which his successors saw to fruition. Under the auspices of the Southern Christian Leadership Conference, the **Poor People's March** (planned for May 14–June 28, 1968) converged on Washington from Mississippi, its organizers determined to force Congress to take a serious stand against poverty and unemployment. The 3000 marchers set up camp around the Reflecting Pool, in view of the US Capitol, and called their shantytown structures Resurrection City. Water and electricity were supplied, and churches and charities brought in food, but rain was heavy and the mud-caked camp quickly lost its momentum. Many residents left early; those who stayed were joined at the Lincoln Memorial by a crowd of 50,000 on June 19, Solidarity Day, to listen to a Peter, Paul, and Mary concert, and to hear various fiery speeches. However, the turnout was much lower than expected, and, with an ebbing of public support, the dispirited camp was dissolved a week later as city police cleared away the tents.

The Vietnam Veterans Memorial

Henry Bacon Drive and Constitution Ave at 21st St NW ℡202/634-1568, @www.nps.gov/vive; Foggy Bottom-GWU Metro. Daily 24hr, staffed 8am–midnight.

If you proceed clockwise around the Reflecting Pool from the Lincoln Memorial, you'll hit the **Vietnam Veterans Memorial** – one of the most poignant tributes to be found anywhere. The Vietnam veterans who conceived of having a memorial in Washington intended to record the sacrifice of every person killed or missing in action without making a political statement. Once the grounds had been earmarked, a national competition was held in 1980 to determine the memorial's design, and a 21-year-old Yale student from Ohio named **Maya Lin** won. (The original design is held and sometimes displayed in the Library of Congress's Jefferson Building.) Lin decided that the names of the fallen would be the memorial and chose to record them on walls of reflective black granite that point to the city's lodestones – the Lincoln Memorial and Washington Monument – and gradually draw you into a rift in the earth. The **names** of the 58,191 American casualties of the Vietnam War are etched into east and west walls that each run for 250ft, slicing deeper into the ground until meeting at a vertex 10ft high; they appear in chronological order (1959–75), and each has appended either a diamond (a confirmed death) or cross (missing in action). It's a sobering experience to walk past the ranks of names and the untold experiences they represent, not least for the friends and relatives who come here to leave tokens at the foot of the walls and make rubbings of the names. Brass-bound directories on each side of the memorial list the names and their locations for anyone trying to find a particular person, and a ranger is on hand until midnight to answer questions. The annual Veterans Day ceremony held at the memorial on November 11 is one of the most emotional in the city, with the memorial walls decked in wreaths and overseen by military color-guards.

Ironically, the memorial's non-political stance came to be seen by some ex-soldiers as a political act itself, and lobbyists successfully argued for a separate martial statue to be added just south of the site. Heralded by a sixty-foot flagpole flying the Stars and Stripes, the **Three Servicemen Statue** depicts young soldiers who, despite bulging weaponry and ammunition, have an air of vulnerability all too easy to understand in the bewildering maelstrom of Vietnam.

More lobbying – in particular by Diane Evans, a former army nurse – led to the creation of the **Vietnam Women's Memorial** in 1993, which stands in a grove of trees at the eastern end of the main site. Few realize that 11,000 American women were stationed in Vietnam (eight were killed), while almost a quarter of a million provided support services throughout the world during the conflict. The bronze sculpture, by Glenna Goodacre, shows one nurse on her knees, exhausted; one tending a wounded soldier (in a pose vaguely reminiscent of a *pietà*); and a third raising her eyes to the sky in trepidation. None of the servicewomen bears insignia, emphasizing the universal intent of the sculpture.

Museums and galleries

There are nine **museums and galleries** along the Mall, most of them national in name and scope, and all but one (the National Gallery of Art) coming under

Smithsonian practicalities

Of the nine excellent **Smithsonian Institution museums** on the Mall, the original building – known as the Smithsonian **Castle** – today serves as the main information center (another early Smithsonian museum, today's Arts and Industries Building, is presently closed for renovation). Other sites and museums sit at some distance from the Mall: the Renwick Gallery, across the street from the White House, focuses on arts and crafts from the nineteenth to the twenty-first century; the National Postal Museum is across from Union Station on Capitol Hill; the American Art Museum and the National Portrait Gallery, in Old Downtown, are closed for refurbishment until 2006; the Anacostia Museum lies south of the eponymous river in a grim part of town; the National Zoological Park is a few miles north of the Mall around Rock Creek Park; and the Steven F. Udvar-Hazy Center, opened in late 2003, is a branch of the National Air and Space Museum, way out in Chantilly, Virginia, and accessible by car or shuttle. The Cooper-Hewitt National Design Museum is also part of the Smithsonian, but, in New York City, is even further away.

All Smithsonian museums and galleries are **open daily all year** (except Christmas Day) from 10am until 5.30pm; some have extended spring and summer hours. Admission is free, though charges are levied for some special exhibitions. For details on **current exhibitions and events**, pick up the free *My Smithsonian* brochure at one of the museums, or a copy of the *Smithsonian Access* brochure for visitors who are disabled by calling ☏202/633-1000 or 357-1729 (TTY) (Mon–Fri 9am–5pm, Sat & Sun 10am–4pm). The Smithsonian's homepage is ⊛www.si.edu or www .smithsonian.org; there's a 24-hour recorded announcement at ☏202/357-2020. (To read about the history of the Institution, see the "Smithsonian story" box, p.90.)

the aegis of the Smithsonian Institution. Since they're all **free**, expect them to be packed with families and school groups, and plan to get jostled around and thwarted from seeing the most popular exhibits. Winter and off-season weekdays are best for viewing the museums, while, during other times of the year, mornings (10am–11am) may be marginally better than afternoons. At the top of many lists are the kid-friendly national museums for Air and Space, Natural History, and American History, and the more serious National Gallery of Art. Less-visited standouts include the Hirshhorn Museum for modern art and sculpture, the National Museum of Asian Art (with its separate Sackler and Freer galleries), and the National Museum of the American Indian. The route below continues the one left off in the "Monuments and memorials" section, heading east from the Washington Monument on a clockwise path from the Reflecting Pool.

National Museum of American History

14th St NW and Constitution Ave ☏202/357-2700, ⊛www.americanhistory.si.edu; Federal Triangle or Smithsonian Metro. Daily 10am–5.30pm, June–Aug closes 6.30pm.

The major museums east of the Washington Monument begin with a procession of big-name Smithsonian institutions. The first of these, on the north side of the Mall, is the **National Museum of American History** – less scholarly center than an entertaining hodgepodge of castoffs and antiques from nearly four hundred years of American and pre-American history. Each floor is a serendipitous delight: George Washington's wooden teeth, Jackie Kennedy's designer dresses, and Judy Garland's ruby slippers in *The Wizard of Oz* are set among didactic displays tracing the country's development from colonial times. You could easily spend a full day poking around the displays, but three to four hours would be a reasonable compromise – and to stick to this time frame, you'll have to be selective.

The museum's roots lie in prodigious bequests made to the original Smithsonian Institution, beginning with pieces left over from Philadelphia's 1876 Centennial Exhibition. Each item collected was destined for the "National Museum" (now the Arts and Industries Building), but since this meant displaying stuffed animals alongside portraits, postage stamps, and patent models, the Smithsonian was soon forced to specialize. An attempt was made to direct part of the collection by founding a National Museum of History and Technology in 1954, for which this dull modernist take on a Beaux Arts building was erected a decade later. The final name change in 1980 was a belated acceptance of the constant underlying theme: that the museum of "American History" firmly relates its exhibits to the experiences of the American people.

Museum practicalities

There's a good **museum shop** and **bookstore**, as well as the main **cafeteria**, on the lower level. The first floor has an ice cream parlor (in the Palm Court), a café serving coffee, fruit, and snacks (next to a 1950s-style automatic vending machine, known as an Automat), and a functioning **post office** counter inside a transplanted nineteenth-century general store (by the Constitution Avenue entrance). Ask at the information desks for details about free **tours**, **lectures**, and **events**, including demonstrations of antique musical instruments, printing presses, and machine tools. The desks, at both Mall (second-floor) and Constitution Avenue (first-floor) entrances, are staffed from 10am to 4pm.

First floor

For the most part, the displays on the first floor come very close to the original idea behind the museum: showcasing the technological advancements and the economic, industrial, and agricultural prowess that brought the US to its position of global power. If you're mainly at the museum for the sections on popular culture and political activity, you'll find little of interest on the first floor – with one notable exception. The museum's installation of the famous **Woolworth Lunch Counter** (the site of one of the South's seminal civil-rights protests) is here, currently part of the Brown v. Board of Education exhibit running until May 2005. There's also a trove of personal narratives, important historic documents, photographs, and mementos concerning the battle against segregation and racism throughout the US.

Because of the museum's ongoing reconstruction of its first floor, many of the familiar science-and-technology rooms have been rearranged and may or may not be on display when you visit. One good place to begin is "**Science in American Life**," which covers every scientific development you can think of from recent decades – including cell phones, birth control, microwave ovens, nylon, nuclear power, and plastics. Within the "Science in American Life" exhibit is the interactive "**Hands On Science Center**," where you can, among other things, identify fossils, take intelligence tests, and use DNA fingerprinting methods to solve a crime. The similarly interactive "**Information Age**" traces communications from Morse's first telegraph to modern information technology. Some of the most remarkable relics are the early models from Alexander Graham Bell's first experiments with the telephone, a device he exhibited to universal amazement at the 1876 Centennial Exhibition in Philadelphia; only thirteen years later, the first public pay phone, a bulky box, was installed in Hartford, Connecticut. Among other diversions, you can listen to

Architecture of the Mall's museums

Although the architecture of the monuments and memorials on the western half of the National Mall is a straightforward take on Neoclassical temples mixed with sleek modern designs, the eastern side is a different story: the various museums there are a hodgepodge of intriguing, sometimes headache-inducing, styles.

The 1964 **National Museum of American History**, despite its splendid collections inside, is quite possibly the ugliest museum on the Mall: it's nothing more than a Brutalist concrete box with giant projecting panels on its facade. Next door, the domed, Neoclassical 1911 **National Museum of Natural History** is much better, with a pleasing set of marble arches and columns (although two blander wings were added in the 1960s).

Continuing east along the north side of the Mall you'll find two buildings of the **National Gallery of Art**, as well as the **Sculpture Garden** and seasonal ice-skating rink. Built in 1941 by John Russell Pope, what is now known as the West Building (at 7th and Constitution) was DC's last great Neoclassical ornament to be set directly on the Mall. With its domed rotunda and sweeping front steps, it's a veritable palace of pink Tennessee marble, though one that was not to everyone's taste: a critic complained it was "hollow and pompous . . . an outdated extravaganza." This is not a charge that could be fairly leveled at I.M. Pei's 1978 East Building, which is across 4th Street and connected to the main building by an underground tunnel. Using the same pink marble of the original building, Pei created a thoroughly modern, interlocking triangular design with a multi-story atrium and expansive interior spaces.

Directly across the Mall from the East Building is Canadian architect Douglas Cardina's **National Museum of the American Indian**. Here Cardina fashioned a modernist reaction to an ancient style; he created a curving, almost undulating stone-and-glass building with earth-toned colors, a terraced facade, and forest and wetland landscapes on an awkward triangular plot. Designed to recall Western landscapes, the structure's visual symbolism is nonetheless archly contemporary, and more rewarding than the monstrosity to its west. The 700-foot-long **National Air and Space Museum** lies between 4th and 7th streets and is a rather dull spread of squat marble boxes split by glass frames. Gordon Bunshaft's cylindrical 1974 **Hirshhorn Museum**, farther along the south side of Independence Avenue, is a

excerpts from early radio programs, deal with a 911 emergency call, or watch archival newsreel and movie footage. The development of computers is shown with the thirty-ton ENIAC (Electronic Numerical Integrator and Computer), built for the US Army during World War II, which could compute a thousand times faster than any existing machine, but took up a thirty-by-fifty-foot room. There are up-to-the-minute computer-based presentations in the Multimedia Theater, and at the end of the section – if you can kick the kids off the consoles – you can explore the world of the "virtual Smithsonian," which allows you to tour the exhibits in a digital format. Around the corner, and beyond the stairway, is a stand-alone mock-up of Julia Child's kitchen – more of an interest to classic TV fans than serious foodies.

The recently installed "**America on the Move**" exhibit is one of the highlights of the museum, an unapologetic celebration of urban, rural, and long-distance transit from the nineteenth century to the present. It covers nineteen rooms and has its own booklet and map, so you can zip right to your favorite section without difficulty. The exhibition starts with the locomotive in the post-Civil War era, and in rough chronological order covers the cultural, economic, and social impact of transportation up to the modern age. To most visitors, the main story here will be familiar: how the US began with covered concrete cylinder balanced on fifteen-foot stilts above a sculpture-laden plaza. The museum has been likened to everything from a monumental donut to a spaceship poised for takeoff.

At this point you're at possibly the most rewarding stretch of the Mall, with five museums and galleries imaginatively situated on the blocks between 9th and 12th streets. The **Smithsonian Institution Building**, known more commonly as the "Castle," is the most prominent of them all. Completed in 1855 by James Renwick, its Gothic towers and battlements jut out into the Mall halfway between the US Capitol and the Washington Monument. Architect and sculptor Horatio Greenhough mocked it at the time as a "medieval confusion," but today it's considered a triumph; its central tower is the only structure other than the Washington Monument to rise above the trees.

Between the Castle and the Hirshhorn Museum is the **Arts and Industries Building**, the Mall's second public construction, built in 1881 to house exhibits from Philadelphia's 1876 Centennial Exhibition. The building is positively jaunty compared to the Castle, with its playful polychromatic brick-and-tile patterns and Victorian verve.

The adjacent **National Museum of African Art** and **Arthur M. Sackler Gallery** were built a century after their neighbor, the Arts and Industries Building. Both were designed by the same Boston architectural firm and opened in 1987. The twin embellished, granite-and-limestone cubes are connected by an underground passage; indeed, all the gallery space at both museums is underground – a reflection of the shortage of room along this part of the Mall. Outside, between the buildings, sits the flower-filled **Enid A. Haupt Garden** (daily: June–Sept 7am–8pm; Oct–May 7am–5.45pm), where you'll find several topiary bison (live animals were once kept here in pens so that nineteenth-century Smithsonian curators could study their expressions).

Charles A. Platt's **Freer Gallery of Art**, a granite-and-marble Italianate palazzo, completes this museum grouping. It was added to the corner plot at 12th and Independence in 1923 and can be reached by underground passage from the Sackler Gallery.

wagons and trains (shown with a huge locomotive from the Southern Railway), was revolutionized by early automobiles (from the first car to make a transcontinental trip, in 1903, to later Model Ts, Studebakers, and Chryslers), and ended up having to deal with urban gridlock and finding alternative means of transit (a walk-in Chicago elevated train is a highlight). Beyond this tale are equally interesting side stories of the new age in transportation – from the old East Coast docks giving way to transpacific container shipping in the 1960s, to the roadside cultures that developed around highways like Route 66, to the emergence of crudely functional "tourist cabins" in the 1930s, shown here with a re-creation of a creepy little Maryland shotgun shack. The story ends in an eye-popping room titled "Los Angeles and the World," with 21 video monitors, light boxes, and electronic news ticker showing how Southern California has emerged as the nation's busiest automotive center and largest US port – all set to the hypnotic rhythms of the Red Hot Chili Peppers' "Californication."

"America on the Move" takes up much of the east side of the first floor, though a few lingering oddments from America's olden days are still present. Among these are the rump version of "**American Maritime Enterprise**" – which has model boats, seafaring paraphernalia, and an entire ship's steam engine on two levels – and truncated rooms devoted to "Power Machinery"

NATIONAL MUSEUM OF AMERICAN HISTORY: FLOOR PLAN

⊠ Elevator
Ⓡ Restroom

FIRST FLOOR

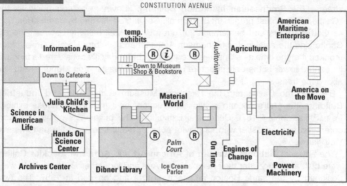

CONSTITUTION AVENUE

Information Age

temp. exhibits

Ⓡ ⓘ Ⓡ

← Down to Museum Shop & Bookstore

↓ Down to Cafeteria

Julia Child's Kitchen

Science in American Life

Hands On Science Center

Archives Center

Dibner Library

Material World

Ice Cream Parlor

Palm Court

Ⓡ   Ⓡ

On Time

Auditorium

Agriculture

American Maritime Enterprise

America on the Move

Engines of Change

Electricity

Power Machinery

SECOND FLOOR

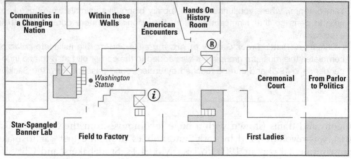

Communities in a Changing Nation

Within these Walls

American Encounters

Hands On History Room

Ⓡ

Washington Statue

ⓘ

Star-Spangled Banner Lab

Field to Factory

First Ladies

Ceremonial Court

From Parlor to Politics

MALL

THIRD FLOOR

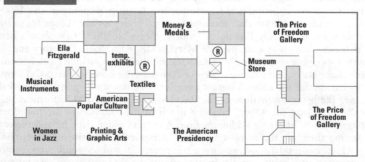

Ella Fitzgerald

temp. exhibits

Ⓡ

Musical Instruments

Textiles

American Popular Culture

Money & Medals

Ⓡ

The Price of Freedom Gallery

Museum Store

Women in Jazz

Printing & Graphic Arts

The American Presidency

The Price of Freedom Gallery

(big drills), "Agriculture" (giant combines), "On Time" (pocket watches to atomic clocks), and "Electricity," which celebrates Thomas Edison's light bulb and Ben Franklin's kite-flying.

Second floor

Many of the museum's social and political exhibits occupy the second floor. Entering from the Mall, it's difficult to miss Horatio Greenhough's much-ridiculed **statue of George Washington**, commissioned in 1832 during the centennial of Washington's birth. Greenhough was paid $5000 by Congress and in 1841 came up with an imperial, seated, toga-clad Washington with swept-back hair, bare torso, and sandals (mothers reputedly covered their children's eyes at its public unveiling).

Continuing clockwise around the floor, the history of African-American migration from 1915 to 1940 is recounted in "**Field to Factory**," telling how the demand for unskilled labor, stimulated by World War I, saw an unprecedented move by hundreds of thousands of African-Americans from the fields of the South to the factories of the North. The "Great Migration" proved a momentous change, establishing strong black communities in diverse Northern cities; most of the documents, photographs, and exhibits recount the experiences of individuals – from the recorded voices of migrants as they traveled north on the (segregated) trains, to the re-creations of the new domestic situations they encountered on a farm in southern Maryland or in a Philadelphia tenement. Beyond here is the "Star-Spangled Banner" exhibit, and then "**Communities in a Changing Nation**," with nineteenth-century America showcased through various social environments – a slave cabin from South Carolina, an indigent peddler's cart, a wealthy Gothic Revival bedroom interior. From here it's a quick move to "**Within These Walls**," where two hundred years of history are brought into focus through the stories of five families and their Massachusetts home, which has literally been transplanted and its skeleton made visible, from the core wooden structure to accrued layers of paint and grime. Continuing on, "**American Encounters**" focuses on New Mexico, looking at how sixteenth- and seventeenth-century Hispanic invasions and, later, tourism have affected the native communities – in particular, the pueblo Indians of Santa Clara and Chimayo. Traditional and contemporary applied art, in the shape of ornate rugs, chests, figurines, and ceramics, sits alongside photographs, videos, and recordings of narrative stories, music, and dance.

For many visitors, the museum's key attraction is the faded and battered red, white, and blue flag that inspired the writing of the US national anthem: the **Star-Spangled Banner** itself, which survived the British bombing of Baltimore harbor during the War of 1812. With dimensions of about 30ft by 34ft, and (backed by heavy linen) weighing 150 pounds, it has fifteen stars and fifteen stripes, representing the fifteen states in the Union at the time of the war.

There was no fixed design for the national flag in the early days of the new republic, and arguments raged over the relative prominence to be given to existing and future states. Congress eventually settled on the more familiar thirteen stripes (for the number of original colonies), while adding a new star to the flag each time a state joined the Union. Following decades of exposure to light and pollution, the flag is currently under long-term restoration, though it's still on view in the conservation lab. Here, workers lying on a giant horizontal gantry laboriously try to fix long-term damage done to the banner, while crowds press their noses against the glass angling for a better look. Alongside this window, a series of documents and artifacts illuminate the flag's history and role in American life.

The Star-Spangled Banner

After burning the Capitol and White House in Washington DC in August 1814, the British turned their attention toward nearby Baltimore, then America's third-largest city, which was defended by the garrison at **Fort McHenry**. To reinforce his defiance of the superior British force, the commander ordered the making of a large American flag, which was hoisted high above the fort in Baltimore harbor. The British attacked on the night of September 13, subjecting fort and harbor defenses to a ferocious bombardment, which the Americans could scarcely counter with their low stocks of weaponry. **Francis Scott Key**, a 35-year-old Georgetown lawyer and part-time poet, witnessed the battle. Attempting to negotiate the release of American prisoner Dr William Beanes, Key was being held on board a British ship that night and, come "dawn's early light," was amazed to see not only that the flag was still "so gallantly streaming," but that the cannons of the outnumbered Americans had forced the British to withdraw.

Taking the bombardment as his inspiration, Key rattled off a poem titled "The Defense of Fort McHenry," which he set to the tune of a contemporary English drinking song called "To Anacreon in Heaven." The first public performance of the song took place in Baltimore a month after the battle, and it soon became an immensely popular rallying cry, despite being notoriously difficult to sing. Union troops adopted it during the Civil War, and it became the armed forces' anthem in 1916 – although it didn't become the official **national anthem** until Herbert Hoover issued a decree in 1931. Despite Key's original title, the song became known as the "Star-Spangled Banner" almost immediately; indeed, the felicitous phrase had already occurred to Key in an earlier poem celebrating the exploits of Stephen Decatur against the Barbary pirates, which contained the words "the star-spangled flag." Less inspiringly, these days the most prominent landmark with Key's name on it is a freeway bridge in Georgetown (see p.225).

The rest of the East Wing is devoted to presidential life in and beyond the White House, centered around the **Ceremonial Court**, designed to resemble the Cross Hall of the White House as it appeared after its 1902 renovation. The Smithsonian managed to purloin some of the original architectural bits and pieces that are incorporated here into the design, as are displays of glass, porcelain, tinware, and silver from the White House collections. More satisfying is the cabinet displaying presidents' personal items: Washington's telescope, Grant's leather cigar case, Nixon's gold pen, Wilson's golf clubs, Jefferson's eyeglasses, and Theodore Roosevelt's toiletry set.

Off the Ceremonial Court, "**First Ladies**" begins with portraits of each presidential wife, from Martha Washington onwards. Though there's an attempt to provide biographical padding, and exhibits exhort viewers to appreciate First Ladies as political partners or preservers of White House culture and history, the real fun here is in the frocks. Helen Herron Taft was the first to present her inaugural ball gown to the Smithsonian for preservation, starting a tradition that allows the museum to display a backlit collection of considerable interest, if not always taste. Other outfits provide revealing historical snapshots: Jackie Kennedy's simple brocaded dress and jacket raised hemlines in America almost overnight. There's access from the Ceremonial Court to "**From Parlor to Politics**," covering the history of women and political reform (1890–1925), with informative, if not necessarily creative or insightful, exhibits on women's clubs, the temperance movement, and voting rights.

Third floor

More or less, the third floor is devoted to American culture, presidents, and armed forces. Many items of the first-named category are simply unclassifiable and have ended up in a grab-bag section called "**American Popular Culture**," on display in cases at the top of the escalators in the West Wing. Most visitors make a beeline for these, gawking in reverence at – among other things – Dorothy's slippers from *The Wizard of Oz* (silver in the original Frank Baum stories, but changed to ruby-red to hype the Technicolor process), Muhammad Ali's boxing gloves, Michael Jordan's NBA jersey, a Babe Ruth-autographed baseball, Dizzy Gillespie's trumpet, and a Star Trek phaser. The rest of the rooms are organized thematically, covering "Women in Jazz" – with recordings of such figures as Ella Fitzgerald and Sarah Vaughn – as well as musical instruments, textiles, money, and medals. Amid the racks of English and American porcelain, eighteenth-century grand pianos, and coins and notes from around the world is a display on the life and work of DC native and jazz legend Duke Ellington. There is also an exhibit of *fai* (circular stone money of the West Pacific Yap Islands), which was up to 12ft in diameter and had to be carried around on poles.

The east side of the third floor is more consistently interesting, starting with "**The American Presidency: A Glorious Burden**," which focuses on various aspects of presidential life, revealing everything from the ways in which the chief executive has communicated with his public to how the office has fared under the gaze of Hollywood's lens. The exhibition displays a fascinating array of objects, including George Washington's general's uniform and Revolutionary War sword, the "fireside chat" microphone through which Franklin Roosevelt soothed an America mired in the Great Depression, and a pair of Mao and Nixon table-tennis paddles, souvenirs from the days of "Ping Pong Diplomacy." In a section devoted to "**Assassinations and Mourning**," you'll find one of the Smithsonian's most prized relics – the top hat Abraham Lincoln wore to Ford's Theatre on the last night of his life. By contrast, a stroke of luck and a fifty-page speech in just the right place spared Theodore Roosevelt's life as the former president was stumping to win another term; a display case contains the speech's first page, complete with bullet hole. With a flair for the theatric even while grievously wounded, Roosevelt would finish the speech before being ushered away to patch up his wound. Elsewhere is the Rough Rider's most cherished legacy: the teddy bear. An avid hunter, Roosevelt apparently inspired the creation of this children's toy when he refused to shoot a captured bear cub on a hunting trip.

As if the surfeit of war memorials around town didn't already remind you, "**The Price of Freedom**" covers America's longstanding support of, and occasional ambivalence to, its armed forces. This brand-new permanent exhibit, which opened November 2004, brings together a number of military-oriented artifacts from previous Smithsonian collections, and arrays them on a chronological course that begins with the Colonial-era French and Indian War and proceeds up to today's welter of global conflicts. One indisputable highlight is the oak gunboat *Philadelphia*, the oldest US man-of-war in existence. In 1776, in a campaign against the British on Lake Champlain, 63 men lived on this tiny ship for three months, suffering extraordinary privation – there was no upper or lower deck and only a canvas cover to protect them from the elements. Also on display is General Washington's linen tent (his campaign headquarters during the Revolutionary War) alongside his camp chest complete with tin plate and coffeepot. Numerous weapons also make appearances, from Colonial muskets to modern machine guns, as do model-ship displays and artillery pieces.

National Museum of Natural History

10th St NW and Constitution Ave ☎202/357-2700, ⊛www.nmnh.si.edu; Federal Triangle or Smithsonian Metro. Daily 10am–5.30pm, June–Aug closes 6.30pm.

Founded in 1911, the **National Museum of Natural History** is one of DC's oldest museums, with its early collection partly based on specimens the Smithsonian commissioned from the game-hunting Theodore Roosevelt on his African safaris. Roosevelt "collected" thousands – from lions and rhinos to gazelles and cheetahs, many of which are still on display. It also happens to be one of the best places in the capital to take visiting children.

Indeed, the museum's imposing three-story entrance rotunda feels like the busiest and most boisterous crossroads in all DC, with troops of screeching school kids chasing each other nonstop around a colossal African elephant. Hundreds of other stuffed animals, tracing evolution from fossilized four-billion-year-old plankton to dinosaurs' eggs and beyond, are all around. Given that the museum owns more than 120 million specimens and artifacts, it can be forgiven for failing to exhibit some of them with sufficient gusto (there are, after all, only so many things you can do with a trayful of pinned butterflies). And after wading through massive crowds that hog the space in the most renowned sections, you might just feel like retreating to the lower level's deserted "Birds of DC" display, with countless ducks, sparrows, and egrets gazing out from behind glass cases.

You'll need to go early to avoid the busiest times, especially in summer and during school holidays; stop by the **information desk** at the elephant's hooves to pick up floor plans, check on any temporary exhibitions, and ask about the **free guided tours** (Sept–June Mon–Fri 10.30am & 1.30pm), which show you the highlights in around an hour. These tours are particularly helpful, since this is one of the Smithsonian's most confusingly laid-out museums. Schedules and information about the films at the museum's **IMAX theater** and programs at the multi-screened, interactive Immersion Cinema are also available at the desk. The soaring, glass-domed **Atrium Café** serves a variety of foods (10am–5pm), along with a buffet dinner, and hosts jazz music concerts and special IMAX screenings ($8; call ☎202/633-7400 for schedule; ⊛www.mnh.si.edu/imax).

First floor

The first floor is typically the busiest and most aggravating part of the museum – if not of DC. Unlike the National Air and Space Museum (another kid-friendly favorite), there's just not enough space to get around easily, and you'll have to squeeze past countless other visitors if you want to have any hope of getting a peek at the big-ticket items. Without a doubt, the **Dinosaurs** section is justifiably the most popular area, with hulking skeletons reassembled in imaginative poses and accompanied by informative text. The massive Diplodocus, the most imposing specimen, was discovered in Utah in 1923, at what is now Dinosaur National Monument. The museum's pride and joy, however, is the 65-million-year-old triceratops (dubbed "Hatcher"), which, these days, is more paleontologically accurate following a high-tech face-lift. Stay in this section long enough to tour the related displays on the **Ice Age**, **Ancient Seas**, **Fossil Mammals**, and **Fossil Plants** – each covering mollusks, lizards, giant turtles, and early fish in exhaustive, engaging detail with the aid of diagrams, text, and fossils. One curious attraction along the way is the hulking pair of menacing – and dopey-looking – giant ground sloths, Ice Age herbivores which didn't stand much of a chance after all the snow melted. Near the end

△ The National Mall at night

of the circuit, you'll unexpectedly get a look at what is claimed to be an early-human form of burial, though the display's centerpiece – a nearly naked cave man tied up with ropes in a dank hole – looks more like something out of *Pulp Fiction* than *Nova*.

Taking up a good chunk of the west side of the first floor is the **Hall of Mammals**, opened in 2003, which, given its layout, is even more congested than the Dinosaurs section. Some 300 replicas focus on mostly fur-wearing, milk-producing creatures in a variety of simulated environments. If you can, check out the African savanna animals, which strive to drink at a watering hole in the same desperate manner in which viewers pry for a look at them, and the various big cats, chimps, shrews, moles, dogs, and other creatures that are biologically related to *Homo sapiens*. To brush up on your Darwin, the Evolution Theater fills you in on all the details you missed while sleeping through biology class.

Although the museum has gotten rid of some of its most outdated displays, it still has a ways to go before it deals successfully with its ethnographical collections, particularly those related to Asian, Pacific, and South American cultures. There are plans to hive the ethnographical items in their own museum, but, for now, entire galleries continue to raise hackles with their 1950s-style attitudes (check out the "Man and the Manlike Apes" window for a taste of this). Some dioramas seem more like something out of a Disney flick than a museum display: the Dem, for example, "until recently lived in a Stone Age culture," while other native folks have all the color and humanity of waxwork dummies. A related section on the second floor involves "**Western Cultures**," though this is as much historical and cultural as it is anthropological – the displays veering between ancient Egypt, Greece, and Rome, and showcasing a number of ancient artifacts (such as death masks, iconic statues, votive offerings, tools, ritual beads, and coffins) and mercifully few dioramas. Unfortunately, since the section is something of a hodgepodge – though better researched and contemporary than those previously mentioned – it's also somewhat flat and unengaging in its presentation.

Much more imaginative is the "**African Voices**" exhibit on the first floor, which does as well as can be expected for a section covering people from an entire continent. Bursting with colorful displays, films, and tunes – plus tools, garments, icons, and trinkets – Africans tell their stories in their own voices, in testimonials and on video monitors, suggesting the wide range of languages and religions practiced on the continent. Best are items like a huge "antelope mask" for tribal rituals, an "airplane coffin" from Ghana in the shape of a KLM jet, and a section on the global reach of African mudcloth, detailing the intersection of native symbolism and Western consumerism.

Second floor

Other galleries are upstairs on the second floor, where a predictable array of reptiles – snakes, gila monsters, and lizards among them – and various animal bones give way to the splendid **Insect Zoo**, sponsored, ironically, by the Orkin pest-control company. Here, many of the exhibits are actually alive, which may or may not be a recommendation. Behind screens – with notices pleading, unsuccessfully, "Please do not tap the glass" – are imprisoned tarantulas, roaches, crickets, bird-eating spiders, worms, termites, and a thriving bee colony. A staff member with the most unenviable job in the world sits in one corner with assorted creepy-crawlies wandering up and down his arms; kids generally can't wait to grab a bug, while cowering adults try hard not to flinch. If you can stomach this sort of entertainment, stick around for one of the daily tarantula feedings (Tues–Sun 11.30am, 12.30pm & 1.30pm). Less creepy insects are on display outside in the **Butterfly Garden**, on the 9th Street side of the museum. Wetland, wooded, meadow, and urban habitats are on view at all times, although, as you might imagine, there's not much to see in the winter.

The **Hall of Geology, Gems, and Minerals** draws regular streams of wide-eyed visitors. Center of attention here are the astounding exhibits from the National Gem Collection, notably the legendary 45-carat **Hope Diamond** once owned by Marie Antoinette, and the subject of a legendary curse. Crowds stare as if hypnotized at the well-guarded rock as it rotates in its display case. Also popular are a pair of the French queen's diamond earrings and a genuine crystal ball that is the world's largest flawless quartz sphere. In addition, the exhibit offers answers to mysteries like why diamonds sparkle, and there are full investigations of related geological phenomena – from plate tectonics and meteors to earthquakes and volcanoes – which are uniformly excellent, well researched, and up-to-date.

Also prominent is the museum's rock and mineral selection. Scientists have identified around 4000 minerals so far and it seems like each one is represented here in its glorious shape, texture, and color. Hunt around and you'll even find an example of Smithsonite – a needle-like crystal mined for zinc – named after Smithsonian Institution benefactor James Smithson, who first recognized it as a distinct mineral. Almost as fascinating is the recent "**Mine Gallery**," which is probably unique to any museum, anywhere. Here, in a small, curving tunnel, the Smithsonian has assembled actual walls from mine tunnels across the country – from a Missouri lead mine's rocky panels to those bearing zinc, copper, and microcline. All of them have terrific displays and background information.

Before leaving the second floor, take a moment to puzzle over the rare **giant squid**. Scientists don't know quite where it lives, but reckon it grows up to 50ft long. Also on hand is a second, smaller specimen, the taningia – another deep-sea squid, which possesses the largest light-producing organs of any known animal.

National Gallery of Art – West Building

Constitution Ave, between 4th and 7th sts NW ☎202/737-4215, ☜www.nga.gov; Archives-Navy Memorial Metro. Mon–Sat 10am–5pm, Sun 11am–6pm.

Despite having a prime spot on the Mall and sitting cheek-to-jowl with other Smithsonian museums, the estimable **National Gallery of Art** is not part of the Smithsonian Institution. You can't hope to see the whole of the museum in one visit, and many concentrate on seeing what they can in the sizable **West Building**, the original gallery structure (see pp.81–82 for the newer **East Building**). The entire first floor (where most of the art can be found) has almost one hundred display rooms, full of works ranging from thirteenth-century Italian to nineteenth-century European and American art. To make best use of limited time, latch on to one of the daily **free tours** and programs; pick up a schedule at the gallery's information desks located on the main floor (Mall entrance) and the ground floor (Constitution Ave at 6th St). The most popular rooms – typically anything related to Rembrandt, Vermeer, and French Impressionism – tend to be busiest mid-afternoon and on weekends.

It's vital to note that in the permanent galleries of the West Building, parts of the collection are rotated or sent out on tour, while many rooms, even entire

NATIONAL GALLERY OF ART: WEST BUILDING MAIN FLOOR

Special Exhibitions

East Garden Court

18th & 19th c. American

18th & 19th c. British

18th & 19th c. Spanish & French

19th c. French

East Sculpture Hall

Elevator

R Restroom

Constitution Avenue (Ground Floor Entrance)

Rotunda

Coat-room

Micro Gallery

Mall Entrance

Downstairs: Sculpture galleries ◄

13th–15th c. Italian

West Sculpture Hall

16th c. Italian

West Garden Court

17th & 18th c. Spanish, Italian & French

17th c. Dutch & Flemish

Downstairs: Temporary exhibits ►

15th–16th c. German, Dutch & Flemish

Building the National Gallery

The **National Gallery of Art** is the legacy of financier **Andrew Mellon**, who began buying the works of European Old Masters in his late 20s. Mellon's ties to the US government in the 1930s – as Secretary of the Treasury and ambassador to Britain – persuaded him that there were means to create a national art gallery in Washington. His own collection certainly begged to be seen by a wider public: among the 121 paintings in Mellon's eventual bequest to the gallery were a score of pieces bought in 1931 from the USSR government, which plundered the works in the Hermitage to prop up its faltering economy. (Stalin made a similar fire sale in the 1930s that led to the build-up of the collection of the Hillwood Museum; see p.215.)

President Franklin D. Roosevelt opened the original National Gallery of Art, designed by **John Russell Pope**, in March 1941. Despite its name, it wasn't (and isn't) a government institution; however, the museum was at once perceived to be of national importance and scope. Now known as the **West Building**, Pope's symmetrical, Neoclassical gallery is overwhelming at first sight, especially when approached from its sweeping steps off the Mall. On the main floor, two wings without external windows stretch for 400ft on either side of a central rotunda, whose massive dome is supported by 24 black Ionic columns. The central, vaulted corridors of each wing serve as sculpture halls, and both wings end at an internal, sky-lit, fountain- and plant-filled garden court.

Remarkably, the West Building was virtually empty at its inauguration in 1941, since Mellon's bequest, substantial though it was, filled only five of the rooms. However, following an influx of gifts and purchases, by the 1970s it was clear that the original building couldn't hold everything. In 1978 **I.M. Pei** completed the modernist, triangular **East Building**, utilizing a block of land between 3rd and 4th streets that Mellon had earmarked as the site of any future expansion. Pei's initial challenge was to deal with the awkwardly shaped land, which he managed by making only the marble walls permanent; the rest of the internal structure can be shaped at will, according to the dictates of the various temporary exhibitions. The East Building has an entrance on 4th Street, although an underground concourse, with a moving walkway, connects it with the West Building. The concourse also has more display space, a very good bookstore, an espresso bar, and a large café – topped by pyramidal skylights and bordered by a glassed-in waterfall. The museum's most recent addition, the **Sculpture Garden**, is outside, between the West Building and the National Museum of Natural History. The garden also has a popular ice-skating rink, where skaters circle well into the winter nights amid sculptures from the post–World War II era.

sections, have in recent years been closed for renovation – so if there's something you specifically want to see, call ahead to make sure it's on view. The West Building's collection starts in Room 1 of the West Wing and proceeds chronologically, beginning with thirteenth- to fifteenth-century Italian art and wrapping up with nineteenth-century French art. To track down the specific location of a particular work, visit the **Micro Gallery** (main floor, Mall entrance), in which an interactive computer system allows you to locate and view some 1700 works in the gallery. The system can also access biographies of more than 650 artists, provide the historical and cultural background of a work or artistic period, and print you a map of a self-selected tour. Alternatively, you can search the collection via the museum's excellent website. Special exhibitions and installations are detailed in a monthly calendar, which also lists the free classical music concerts (Sept–June, usually Sun 7pm) held in the West Building's serene West Garden Court.

Thirteenth- to fifteenth-century Italian art (Rooms 1–15)

The gallery's oldest works are the stylized thirteenth-century Byzantine **icons** (holy images) in which an enthroned Mary holds the small figure of an adult Christ. The Sienese artist **Duccio di Buoninsegna** was one of the first to move beyond strict Byzantine forms; the faces of the subjects in his *Nativity*, a panel taken from the base of his *Maestà* altarpiece in Siena Cathedral, display genuine emotion. The artist **Sassetta**, also from Siena, produced eye-opening works like the St Anthony Triptych (1440), employing colors and designs that, to the modern eye, are somewhat odd, but also had made him popular with some twentieth-century avant-gardists. Much more influential, however, was the Florentine artist **Giotto**, whose humanism and use of perspective would eventually lead to the Renaissance. Giotto's *Madonna and Child* (completed by 1330) marks an extraordinary departure in its attempt to create believable human figures.

The collection then moves to fifteenth-century Florence, the home of the Renaissance. The prominent *tondo* (circular painting) depicting the *Adoration of the Magi* (c.1445) was started by the monk **Fra Angelico** but completed by **Fra Filippo Lippi**, who invested the biblical scene with his full range of emotive powers. **Domenico Veneziano**'s naked *Saint John in the Desert* (c.1445) would have been considered blasphemous before the Renaissance, when nudity was almost exclusively associated with the concept of sin. But for dynamic realism there's nothing to compare with **Andrea del Castagno**'s decorative shield showing *The Youthful David* (c.1450) preparing to fling his sling; Florentines would have understood that Goliath's decapitated head at David's feet was a warning to any of their city's enemies.

In other rooms relating to Florentine artists, all eyes are drawn to **Leonardo da Vinci**'s *Ginevra de' Benci* (1474), an engagement portrait done when Leonardo was only 22, and the only work by the artist in the US. The painting's subject is a 16-year-old Florentine beauty with alabaster skin sitting before a spiky juniper bush – an image meant to symbolize chastity, and to be a pun on her name, Ginevra, and the Italian word for juniper, *ginepro*. Works by **Sandro Botticelli** include his rendering of the *Adoration of the Magi* (early 1480s), set in the ruins of a Classical temple from which the frame of a new structure, representing Christianity, rises.

Other Renaissance-era Italian paintings not to miss include **Andrea Mantegna**'s *Judith with the Head of Holofernes*, where a calm Judith, resembling a Classical statue, clutches the severed head of the Assyrian leader, and **Benvenuto di Giovanni**'s five-panel "pentatych" of Jesus surrounded by various spindly, grotesque onlookers.

Sixteenth-century Italian art (Rooms 16–28)

By the beginning of the sixteenth century, new artistic ideas were emerging in other Italian cities, and the accomplished Bellini family was at the forefront of the scene. Nowhere is this more evident than in **Giovanni Bellini**'s *The Feast of the Gods*, which depicts deities feasting to bawdy excess in a bucolic setting. Bellini created this painting between 1511 and 1514, just a few years before his death in 1516. In 1529, **Titian**, his former pupil, restyled it by removing a grove of trees and adding a striking mountain in the background. Titian would become the finest Venetian painter of all, his revealing portraits and mythological scenes making him one of the most famous European artists, as well as court painter to Spain's Charles V. The gallery's diverse Titian collection includes an image of *Saint John the Evangelist on Patmos* (c.1547) and *Venus with a Mirror* (c.1555).

The High Renaissance artist **Raphael** has only one major piece here. In his renowned *Alba Madonna* (1510), the Virgin and Child are seated on the ground, leaning against a tree stump – intended to emphasize their humility. Although the painting was completed after Raphael moved from Florence to Rome, the *tondo*, the round shape of the painting, was primarily a Florentine style, and the figures of Jesus and John the Baptist suggest that Raphael had studied the cherubic sculptures of the most famous Florentine artist, Michelangelo.

The Late Renaissance yields the Mannerist era, and **Bronzino**'s striking *A Young Woman and Her Little Boy* (c. 1540) is a highlight of this period. Here the favored court portraitist creates almost doll-like figures, with their fair skin and precocious features.

Fifteenth- to eighteenth-century Spanish art (Rooms 29–34, 36–37, and 52)

In the grip of the Counter-Reformation, Spanish art remained deeply spiritual in character, with individual works designed to inspire devotion and piety. The paramount artist of this time was **El Greco**, and the gallery is distinguished for having the most important El Greco collection outside of Spain. Its *Christ Cleansing the Temple* (c.1570) portrays Jesus, leather whip in hand, laying into assorted traders and moneylenders. More typical of the artist's style, though, is the dour *Laocoön* (1610–14), in which the Trojan priest and his two sons are attacked by serpents sent by the Greek gods. From the same period, *Saint Jerome* (c. 1610) – in retreat in the desert and about to beat his chest with a rock – expresses perfectly the emphasis the Spanish Church placed on the concept of blood penance.

Francisco de Zurbarán, well known for his religious portraits, was responsible for *Saint Lucy*, a typical spiritual study, though one with an accompanying shock as your eyes are drawn to those of the saint: hers have been plucked out and laid on a dish that she holds in her hand. Zurbarán's contemporary, **Diego Velázquez**, was the finest Spanish painter of the seventeenth century. He was court painter to Phillip IV by age 24 and spent the rest of his life creating powerful portraits for his patron. Velázquez did, however, occasionally return to domestic scenes, as in the unfinished *Needlewoman* (1640).

Spain's greatest eighteenth-century artist was the flamboyant **Francisco de Goya** who, beginning in 1789, was court painter to Charles IV. The gallery owns several of his works, primarily portraits, including the famous *Señora Sebasa Garcia*, in which the artist abandons background entirely to focus on the elegant *señora*.

Seventeenth- and eighteenth-century French and Italian art (Rooms 29–34 and 36–37)

France's leading seventeenth century painters – like **Georges de la Tour** and popular landscapist **Claude Lorrain** – often set off for Rome, the capital of the Baroque scene. Having spent much of his life in and around Rome, Lorrain's ideas of natural beauty, as represented in *Landscape with Merchants* (c.1630), were firmly Italian, and the careful balance of light and dark in la Tour's *The Repentant Magdalene* (1640) recalls the artist's debt to the preeminent painter of the chiaroscuro style, Caravaggio (whose works, unfortunately, cannot be found in this museum).

Elsewhere in this section, however, the emphasis is strictly Italian. Notable are Bolognese artist **Annibale Carracci**'s *River Landscape* (c.1590), an early Baroque piece in which nature is the subject; **Bernardo Bellotto**'s *The Fortress* *of Königstein*, created for Augustus of Poland; and **Canaletto**'s rendering of the entrance to the Grand Canal and of St Mark's Square in Venice.

Fifteenth- and sixteenth-century German, Dutch, and Flemish works (Rooms 35, 38–41)

Albrecht Dürer is a principal figure among early German Northern Renaissance masters. His visits to Italy had a direct influence on his art; *Madonna and Child* (1496–99), for example, grafts realistic Renaissance figures onto a landscape backdrop typical of Northern European religious paintings of the time.

Also worth checking out are **Matthias Grünewald**'s agonized *The Small Crucifixion* – one of only twenty Grünewald paintings in existence, and the only one in the US – and portraits by **Hans Holbein the Younger**, whose pudgy *Edward VI as a Child* (c.1538) is an image of Henry VIII's heir and son with his third wife, Jane Seymour. The painting's Latin inscription judiciously encourages Edward to emulate the virtues of his father.

The gallery's early Flemish and Dutch works show the new techniques made possible by the revolutionary change from painting with quick-drying egg-based tempera to using slow-drying oil, which allowed artists to build up deep color tones. Acclaimed fifteenth-century artist **Jan van Eyck** was one of the first to adopt the new technique; his *Annunciation* (1434) shows a remarkable depth of color and texture. Even more striking is the tiny panel by **Rogier van der Weyden** of *Saint George and the Dragon*, also executed in the mid-1430s. Van der Weyden used the realism pioneered by van Eyck and applied it to a medieval subject, paying incredible attention to detail (he probably used a magnifying glass to paint individual tree branches and pinprick windows). Also worth checking out are **Hieronymus Bosch**'s *Death and the Miser* (1485–90), a gloriously ghoulish tour de force, and **Quentin Massys**'s grotesque *Ill-Matched Lovers* (c.1520).

Seventeenth-century Dutch and Flemish art (Rooms 42–50)

The mood changes with a swath of **Anthony van Dyck** portraits of assorted Italian, English, and Flemish nobility. Van Dyck was an immensely popular portraitist, perhaps due in part to his flattery of his subjects (elongating their frames, painting them from below to enhance their stature, idealizing their features). His earliest portrait here, *Portrait of a Flemish Lady* (1618), was painted when Van Dyck was just 19. His teacher, **Peter Paul Rubens** offers the striking *Daniel in the Lions' Den* (1613–15), in which virtually life-sized lions bay and snap around an off-center Daniel.

Rembrandt's *The Mill* – a brooding study of a cliff-top mill, backlit under black thunderclouds – is a famous image, with its dark and light connotations of good and evil, and one that influenced nineteenth-century British artists like J.M.W. Turner.

Also worth a look are **Pieter de Hooch**'s depictions of quiet domestic households, such as those in *A Dutch Courtyard* and *The Bedroom*, and **Jan Steen**'s festive *The Dancing Couple* (1663). Portraits of bourgeois gentlemen in ruffled collars and tall hats were bread-and-butter work for **Frans Hals**, and several of these pieces are on display here.

Of all the genre artists from this period, only **Johannes Vermeer** is still widely known – perhaps now more than ever, thanks to best-selling books and a movie based on his life and works. Vermeer created just 45 paintings in his entire career, and but 35 survive. Of these, the gallery owns and displays in turn *Girl with the Red Hat* (c. 1665), *Woman Holding a Balance* (c. 1664), and *A*

Lady Writing (c. 1665), contemplative scenes all set – like most of his works – in his parents' house, which he later inherited. The jury is still out on whether a fourth painting, *Girl with a Flute* (c. 1665), is genuine.

Eighteenth- and early nineteenth-century French art (Rooms 53–56)

Marble busts of Voltaire by **Jean-Antoine Houdon** – who also did sculptures of George Washington (see p.51) – usher in the gallery's eighteenth-century French painting and sculpture collection. The main attraction, however, is arch-Neoclassicist **Jacques-Louis David**'s portrait of *Napoleon in his Study at the Tuileries* (1812). Revolutionary-turned-imperial propagandist, David meant the sword, crisp uniform, military papers, and imperial emblems to bolster Napoleon's heroic image, while his slightly disheveled appearance, the dying candles, and the time on the clock in the background illustrate that he's been up all night working for the good of the country.

By way of contrast, **Jean-Siméon Chardin**'s still lifes and everyday scenes impress with their subtlety and elegance of detail; indeed, Chardin's influence continues to be as great as ever. Elsewhere, works by **Antoine Watteau** include the delightfully absurd *Italian Comedians* (1720) – a group portrait of clowns and players – and the decorative Rococo style of the oval panel depicting *Ceres*, the Roman goddess of the harvest, surrounded by the signs of the summer zodiac, Gemini, Cancer, and Leo.

There's also a major showing of **Jean-Honoré Fragonard**, who knocked out his Rococo "fantasy portraits" in as little as an hour. In *A Young Girl Reading* (c. 1776), the neck ruff and bodice are etched in the paint using the wooden end of the brush, while the lines of the book are mere blurred traces of paint. *The Swing* (1765) is a more artful work; its images of flounced dresses and petticoats had erotic connotations for contemporaneous viewers. For some art lovers, the figure who combines all these influences – David's dramatic compositions, Chardin's subtlety, and Fragonard's elegance – is **Jean-Auguste-Dominique Ingres**, whose wondrous *Madame Moitessier* (1851) is a highlight of pre-Impressionist French art. Indeed, the figure of this darkly clad matron, with her stern expression, pearls, and rosy garland, has been described by one critic as "the most imperial and commanding of Ingres's female portraits."

Eighteenth- and nineteenth-century British art (Rooms 57–59, 61, 63)

The gallery's few **British works** include pieces by William Hogarth, George Stubbs, and George Romney, along with contemporary eighteenth-century court rivals Joshua Reynolds and Thomas Gainsborough. Also usually on display are works by two American artists who enjoyed great popularity during their time in England: Benjamin West, the first American artist to study in Europe, and Gilbert Stuart, pictorial chronicler of the early American presidents. Stuart's *The Skater* (1782) depicts a nonchalant, black-clad ice-skating gent whose sheer cheek was beyond compare in Britain at the time.

Other works are firmly within the British tradition, particularly the harmonious landscapes by **John Constable** and the sea and river scenes of **J.M.W. Turner**, which run the gamut from the gentle *Approach to Venice* (1844) – which John Ruskin described as "the most perfectly beautiful piece of color of all that I have seen produced by human hands" – to *Keelmen Heaving in Coals by Moonlight* (1835), a light-drenched harbor scene set in the industrial north of England. The early *Junction of the Thames and the Medway* (1807) displays the artist's signature hazy color and dramatic nautical themes. Finally, take care also to see **Henry Fuseli**'s striking *Oedipus Cursing His Son, Polynices* (1786), in which the tragic figure points dramatically to his son with the stern visage of an Old Testament patriarch.

Eighteenth- and nineteenth-century American art (Rooms 60, 62, 64–71)

The gallery's enormously eclectic collection of eighteenth- and nineteenth-century American art is one of its most popular. Pick of the collection for many is the line of portraits by **Gilbert Stuart** of the leading American men of his age. Stuart painted the likeness of George Washington more than a hundred times during his career; the two examples here are the early *Vaughan Portrait* (1795) and the more familiar *Athenaeum Portrait* (1810–15) – later the model for Washington's image on the dollar bill. Following his success with Washington, Stuart became, in effect, the American court artist, painting the next four presidents – Adams, Jefferson, Madison, and Monroe – and more than a thousand other portraits (the National Gallery alone has 41).

In contrast to the youthful Stuart, **John Singleton Copley** was already in his mid-30s when he decided to study painting in Europe. Copley made his name internationally with *Watson and the Shark* (1778), whose depiction of a shark attack off the coast of Cuba caused a stir in London at the time, as such dramatic scenes were usually reserved for the martyrdom of saints. The work was likely commissioned by Brook Watson, the subject of the work, who survived his ordeal to eventually become Lord Mayor of London, although Watson apparently neglected to tell Copley that sharks have neither lips nor ears. You'll also find works by **Benjamin West**, whose splendid historical scenes include *The Battle of La Hogue* (1778), which pits seventeenth-century English and French naval forces against each other: the heroic English admiral directs operations from close quarters while the French dandy is more concerned about losing his wig than with the hand-to-hand combat raging around him. Portraiture here includes works by two of West's pupils, **Thomas Sully** and **John Trumbull** (who was later responsible for the murals in the Capitol) and **Rembrandt Peale**'s thoughtful and somewhat precious *Rubens Peale with a Geranium* (1801), wherein the artist's earnest, bespectacled brother looks even more ready to wilt than his potted plant.

By the nineteenth century, American artists were addressing the theme of territorial expansion head-on. *The Notch of the White Mountain* (1839) by **Thomas Cole** is typical in its vibrant use of color, though more monumental are Cole's four *Voyage of Life* (1842) paintings. The series's symbolically haunting images follow a figure from childhood to old age, and are believed to be a warning against the fervent Manifest Destiny that was fueling westward expansion. At around the same time, the German-born **Albert Bierstadt** captured the shimmering, turquoise *Lake Lucerne* (1858) framed by mountains; the painting was a hit, and the progenitor of his extremely successful Rocky Mountains landscapes. Other images of the American wilderness include **George Inness**'s *The Lackawanna Valley* (1855), which shows a steam train puffing through a Pennsylvanian landscape of felled trees, and **Frederic Edwin Church**'s *El Rio de Luz* (1877), depicting a glorious vista of hazy sunshine beaming across a primordial, almost jungle-like riparian terrain.

Taking a break in the National Gallery of Art

For **food** and **drink**, head down a level from the main floor of the West Building or across to the East Building, noting as you go **Salvador Dalí's** *Last Supper*, which overlooks the escalators down to the Concourse.

Cascade Café Concourse level (Mon–Sat 10am–3pm, Sun 11am–4pm). Serves soups, salads, sandwiches, pizza, entrees, and desserts.

Espresso and Gelato Bar Concourse level (Mon–Sat 10am–4.30pm, Sun 11am–5.30pm). Gelato, panini, and an espresso bar.

Garden Café West Building, ground floor (Mon–Sat 11.30am–3pm, Sun noon–6.30pm). Lunch daily; open later on Sunday for those attending the classical concerts in the Garden Court. For reservations call ☎202/216-2480.

Pavilion Café Sculpture Garden (Mon–Thurs & Sat 10am–6pm, Fri 10am–8pm, Sun 11am–6pm). Pleasant lunch spot near outdoor artworks, with Mall views.

Terrace Café East Building, upper level (Sun 11am–3pm). Brunch spot with buffet courses, regular jazz music, and decent views of visitor activity in building atrium.

Philadelphia-based **Thomas Eakins's** work introduces the gallery's late nineteenth-century collection; however, Eakins's light touch is atypical of the post-Civil War period. **Albert Pinkham Ryder's** ultra-dark and often bleak yellow-and-black paintings convey much, despite their small sizes; the most vivid here is *Siegfried and the Rhine Maidens* (1891), a swirling, tortured Wagnerian landscape of bent trees and gnarled bodies, of which the artist said, "I worked for forty-eight hours without sleep or food, and the picture was the result." **James Abbott McNeill Whistler** is dominant too; his standout work here is *The White Girl* (1862), subtitled *Symphony in White, No. 1*. The full-length 1862 study of the artist's mistress is of secondary importance to his use of contrasting shades of white, from dress to drapes to flowers. Other prominent nineteenth-century works include **George Caleb Bingham's** sprightly *Jolly Flatboatmen* (1846) and the crude but strangely intriguing animals of **Edward Hicks's** *Peaceable Kingdom* (1834), surely one of the century's most inexplicably enduring images.

Nineteenth-century French art (Rooms 80–93)

The most popular rooms in the West Building are those containing the exceptional collection of nineteenth-century French paintings, with every Impressionist, post-Impressionist, Realist, and Romantic artist of note represented. There are always crowds before **Claude Monet's** works, among them two facades of Rouen Cathedral. From 1892 onwards, Monet painted more than thirty of these facades, almost all from the same close-up viewpoint, but at different times of the day and in varied conditions. The paintings were reworked in his studio, and a score of them finally exhibited in Paris in 1895. Significant, too, are *The Japanese Footbridge* (1899), whose water-lily theme he was to return to again and again until his death in 1926; his *Woman with a Parasol* (1875), whose emphasis is more the vibrant summer light than its subjects (namely Monet's wife and child); and two of the dozens of studies he made of the town of Argenteuil, where he had a floating studio on the river.

There are also female portraits by the American-in-Paris **Mary Cassatt**, whose work you can usually find with the French Impressionists. Among her pieces here are the flat blocks of color and naturalistic models in *Mother and*

Child (c.1905), and the earlier *Woman with a Red Zinnia* (1891) and *The Boating Party* (1894). Other Impressionists – and their precursors – on display include the likes of Pissarro, Manet, and Degas, all of whose work the thick crowds find delightful, though more seasoned fans may find wanting in spots.

Later developments, such as Symbolism and post-Impressionism, are explored in contiguous rooms. Works by **Vincent van Gogh** include *The Olive Orchard* (1889), a subject he found to be spiritual and complex, and the *Farmhouse in Provence* (1888), filled with strikingly rich colors. **Paul Gauguin**'s powerful *Self-Portrait* (1889) includes a halo, an apple tree, and a serpent.

The gallery's **Cézanne** collection contains still lifes, portraits, and landscapes from most periods of the artist's long life. Cézanne was 27 when he completed *The Artist's Father* (1866). Cézanne *père*, a banker, did not approve of his son's desire to become an artist and opposed his move to Paris in the 1860s. Paul retaliated by perching his father uncomfortably in a high-backed chair in front of an image of one of Paul's paintings.

This section of the gallery finishes with a flourish, highlighting works by **Henri de Toulouse-Lautrec**, whose dancers, madams, and café patrons evoke his peregrinations around the fleshpots of Montmartre. There is also **Edgar Degas**'s dreamlike *Four Dancers* (1899), one of his last large paintings. It's a swirl of motion which could be four young ballerinas in different poses, or one single dancer moving through a routine – rather like a flip-book of sketches laid flat on the canvas.

Sculpture, decorative arts, prints, and drawings

The ground floor hosts changing exhibitions of sculpture, decorative arts, prints, and drawings. The gallery owns more than two thousand pieces of **sculpture**, including many Italian and French pieces from the fourteenth to eighteenth centuries, and nineteenth-century French pieces by Rodin, Degas, and Maillol among others. Also worth seeking out are Honoré Daumier's 36 small portrait busts, intended for use in his printed caricatures; Houdon's contemplative head of George Washington; Gianlorenzo Bernini's marvelous bust of Baroque titan Francesco Barberini; Giovanni della Robbia's elegant *Young Christ*; Paul Manship's streamlined, modern *Diana and a Hound* and similarly sleek *Dancer and Gazelles* (1916); and an anonymous early Baroque sculpture of the fabled she-wolf suckling Romulus and Remus, recounting the legendary birth of Rome.

Among the **decorative arts** are Flemish tapestries; eighteenth-century French furniture; Renaissance majolica, chalices, and religious paraphernalia; Chinese porcelain; engraved medals; and stained-glass windows by Renaissance artist Giovanni di Domenico. Equally impressive is the gallery's collection of **prints and drawings** – 65,000 works, from the eleventh to the twentieth centuries. Selections on display are necessarily limited and tend to be exhibited only for short periods, but if you're sufficiently geared up you can make an appointment to see particular works by calling ☎202/842-6380.

The Sculpture Garden and ice-skating rink

Adjacent to the West Building, the **Sculpture Garden** (Mon–Sat 10am–5pm, Sun 11am–6pm) exhibits a small but impressive selection of contemporary sculpture around the popular ice-skating rink. The garden is more engaging than its Hirshhorn counterpart (see p.89), with floating cubes and eight-ton slabs of elegantly twisted steel scattered across a six-acre enclosure. Entering from the Mall, you'll see one of Alexander Calder's stabiles – a bright, six-legged sheet metal titled *Cheval Rouge*. Nearby, Roy Lichtenstein's *House I* (1996/1998) is a skewed comic-book image made into a pancake-flat sculpture of a house, and Barry Flanagan's pensive rabbit posing as the *Thinker on a Rock* (1997) is an irreverent ode to Rodin's nineteenth-century tour de force. There are also representative works by Joan Miró, David Smith, Louise Bourgeois, Sol LeWitt, and Isamu Noguchi, and the spiky blue threads and titanic red wheel of Claes Oldenburg, and Coosje van Bruggen's gargantuan *Typewriter Eraser* (1999), which guards the western gate along Constitution Avenue. Don't miss the installation of one of Hector Guimard's famed Art Nouveau entrances to the Paris Metro (1902), done with sweeping, sinewy lines and curvaceous letters – so enticing it's a bit of a disappointment the entrance only covers a concrete slab.

At the center of the garden, an **ice-skating rink** (Mon–Thurs 10am–11pm, Fri & Sat 10am–midnight, Sun 11am–9pm) doubles as a **fountain** in the summer. Two-hour skating sessions begin on the hour from November through March (weather permitting). Skates are available for rent and lockers are on hand to stow your valuables.

Overlooking it all is the *Pavilion Café* (see p.79), a pleasant spot to grab a bite, with pastries, salads, sandwiches, beer, wine, and coffee.

National Gallery of Art – East Building

Constitution Ave, between 3rd and 4th sts NW ☎202/737-4215, ✪www.nga.gov; Archives-Navy Memorial Metro. Mon–Sat 10am–5pm, Sun 11am–6pm.

Although the National Gallery's **East Building** was opened in 1978 to accommodate the ever-expanding collection of twentieth-century European and American art, there still isn't enough exhibition space to display the gallery's entire collection. This is partly due to **I.M. Pei**'s audacious modern design, which is dominated by public areas and a huge atrium. Since the exhibition spaces are often taken up with special shows, the gallery's own holdings may not be on display at all when you visit. So if there's something you specifically want to see, call ahead to make sure it's there.

Two or three items are always present, but that's only because they're too big to keep shifting around. Outside the 4th Street entrance is **Henry Moore**'s bronze *Knife Edge Mirror Two Piece*, a male and female representation whose sensuous line and form contrast with the sharp angles of the building (Moore collaborated with Pei before deciding on its exact structure). Inside, dominating the atrium, a huge steel-and-aluminum mobile by **Alexander Calder** hangs from the ceiling, its red and black (and one blue) paddle-like wings moving slowly with the air currents. Also in the atrium, **Joan Miró**'s stunning tapestry *Woman* is usually on display, along with **Max Ernst**'s stern and mildly creepy sculpture *Capricorn*.

Early European Modernism and Impressionism

Twentieth-century exhibitions begin chronologically on the upper level and include pre-1945, mostly European works. Perhaps the most famous name you'll find here is **Pablo Picasso**. His collection includes the Blue Period pieces *The Tragedy* (1903) and *Family of Saltimbanques* (1905), plus 1910's *Nude Woman*, which Picasso completed after fully turning to Cubism. This piece particularly challenged contemporary audiences with a dissection of anatomy suggestive of X-ray photography. Also in this area, and usually displayed near the Picasso pieces, **Henri Matisse**'s restrained early works give way to his exuberant *Pianist and Checker Players* (1924), depicted in his own apartment in Nice.

On the ground floor, French paintings bridge the early-modern and Impressionist eras; highlights include **Edouard Manet**'s evocative images in *Oysters* (1862) and *A King Charles Spaniel* (1866); **Georges Seurat**'s study for his cornerstone of Pointillism, *La Grande Jatte*; **Degas**'s compelling portrait *Rene de Gas* (1855), and pieces by Monet, Renoir, Sisley, Bonnard, Morisot, Vuillard, and Toulouse-Lautrec. Also noteworthy is a self-portrait by **Henri Fantin-Latour**, who chose to depict himself glowering strangely with his head down.

Modern American works

Not far from the French pieces on the ground level are rooms devoted to American art up to World War I. Works include **Childe Hassam**'s *Allies Day, May 1917*, a packed New York streetscape of flags and crowds; **John Marin**'s *Grey Sea* (1938), a moody study of form and color; **Marsden Hartley**'s pointed and stylized *Landscape No. 5*; **Grant Wood**'s bucolic ode to *Haying* (1939); **John Sloan**'s evocative *The City from Greenwich Village* (1922); and **Edward Hopper**'s poignant, if not well-known, *Cape Cod Evening* (1939). **George Bellows**'s assured portrait of *Florence Davey* (1914) in no way prepares you for his other paintings, notably the brutal prizefight pictures *Club Night* (1907) and *Both Members of This Club* (1909), in which you can almost feel the heat as the crowd bays for blood. There's a similar energy in Bellows's brilliantly realized *Blue Morning* (1909), set on a New York construction site.

Post-1945 art (mostly American) is usually shown downstairs in the lower levels. **Andy Warhol**'s works are as familiar as they come, with classic serial examples of *32 Soup Cans*, *Let Us Now Praise Famous Men*, and *Green Marilyn*. Separate rooms are often set aside for the works of artists using huge canvases: the gallery owns large, hovering slabs of blurry color by **Mark Rothko**, as well as the thirteen stations of the cross by **Barnett Newman**, a series of big canvases built around the visual rhythm of black-and-white stripes. There's also **Robert Rauschenberg**'s splattered, stuffed-bird sculpture known as *Canyon*, and **Jasper Johns**'s *Field Painting* and *Target*, which are among his more influential works. Other highlights include **Chuck Close**'s *Fanny/Fingerpainting* (1985), a mighty portrait of an elderly black woman realized from a brilliantly marshaled canvas of finger splotches; **Jackson Pollock**'s *Number 1, 1950 (Lavender Mist)*, a spray of finely drizzled, multicolored drippings; **Clyfford Still**'s big, jagged shards of color, often without titles; compelling sculptures by Louise Bourgeois and David Smith; and delightfully odd works by **Claes Oldenburg**, such as *Clarinet Bridge* (1992) and, best of all, *Soft Drainpipe – Red (Hot) Version* (1967), a huge, soft-red sculpture that looks as much like a drooping phallus as anything under the sink.

National Museum of the American Indian

Jefferson Drive between 3rd and 4th sts SW ☏202/357-2700, ●www.nmai.si.edu; Federal Center SW Metro. Daily 10am–5.30pm.

Continuing clockwise around the mall, skirting the Capitol Reflecting Pool and heading back west along Jefferson Drive, you'll hit the **National Museum of the American Indian**, the newest of the Mall's museums, opened to the public in September 2004. It's instantly recognizable by its curvaceous modern form with undulating walls the color of yellow earth – designed to represent the natural American landscape. This stone-and-glass building with muted hues, terraced facade, and surrounding replicas of forest and wetland landscapes sits on an awkward triangular plot, but is nonetheless in a position of prominence in the shadow of the Capitol dome.

Planned in the mid-1990s, the museum was nine years in development. It's intended to recognize and honor the many **tribes** – like the Iroquois, Sioux, Navajo, Cherokee, and others – who occupied the continent before white settlers arrived in the sixteenth and seventeenth centuries. The collections reach back thousands of years and incorporate nearly a million objects from nations spread out from Canada to Mexico. Some of the items on display include woven garments, musical instruments, totem poles, artwork, kachina dolls, and canoes, as well as ceremonial masks, headdresses, and outfits. The museum also sponsors periodic musical and dance events, along with lectures, films, and other cultural presentations.

National Air and Space Museum

Independence Ave and 6th St SW ☏202/357-2700, ⊛www.nasm.si.edu; L'Enfant Plaza Metro. Daily 10am–5.30pm.

If there's one museum people have heard about in DC, and just one they want to visit, it's the **National Air and Space Museum**. Since opening in 1976, it's become the most popular cultural attraction in the city – and supposedly the entire country – capturing the imagination of almost ten million people every year. The excitement begins in the entrance gallery, which throws together some of the most celebrated flying machines in history, like Lindbergh's *Spirit of St Louis* and looming Cold War-era missiles. More than twenty monstrous galleries on two floors containing objects the size of, well, spaceships mean that even on the busiest days it's not too much of a struggle to get close to the exhibits. You may have to wait a while to get into the **IMAX theater**, but otherwise the worst lines are in the cafeteria.

The **information desk** is at the Independence Avenue entrance; here you can catch a free tour (daily 10.15am & 1pm) and inquire about shuttle pickup to the **Udvar-Hazy Center** satellite museum (see pp.246–247). If you want to visit the **Einstein Planetarium** or see an IMAX movie in the Lockheed Martin Theater (each is $8 per show, $13 for two), buy tickets when you arrive or book in advance (☏202/633-4629). Come early to eat in the self-service **cafeteria**, which has a great view of the Capitol dome. Finally, don't even think of entering the **museum shop** without wads of cash or the stamina to endure relentless demands from kids or companions for model spaceships, Klingon T-shirts, and florid stunt kites.

The first floor

The National Air and Space Museum's entry hall, known as "**Milestones of Flight**," is a huge atrium filled with all kinds of flying machines, rockets, satellites, and assorted aeronautic gizmos that are bolted to the floor, hung from the rafters, and couched in cylindrical holes. For many the highlight is peeking up at the *Spirit of St Louis*, which flew into history on May 20, 1927, when 25-year-old Charles Lindbergh piloted it during the first solo transatlantic crossing. (Lindbergh took off from Long Island and landed near Paris almost 34 hours later.) When he wanted to see where he was headed, Lindbergh either had to use a periscope or bank the plane, since his gas reserve tank was mounted where the windscreen should have been.

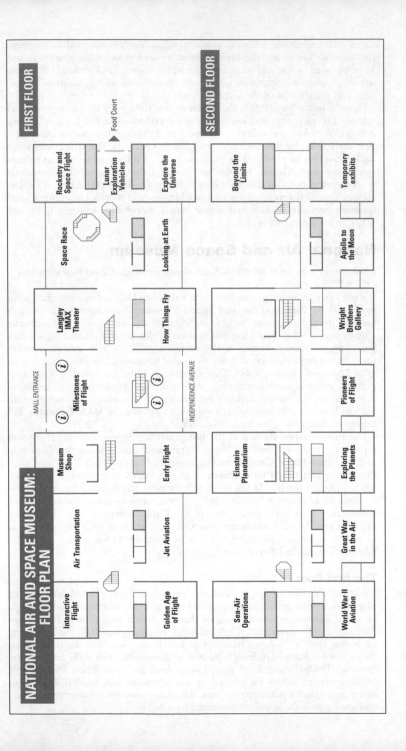

NATIONAL AIR AND SPACE MUSEUM: FLOOR PLAN

FIRST FLOOR

Rocketry and Space Flight

Lunar Exploration Vehicles

Explore the Universe

Space Race

Looking at Earth

▲ Food Court

Langley IMAX Theater

How Things Fly

MALL ENTRANCE

Museum Shop

(i) Milestones of Flight

(i) Early Flight

(i) (i)

INDEPENDENCE AVENUE

Air Transportation

Jet Aviation

Interactive Flight

Golden Age of Flight

SECOND FLOOR

Beyond the Limits

Temporary exhibits

Apollo to the Moon

Wright Brothers Gallery

Pioneers of Flight

Einstein Planetarium

Exploring the Planets

Great War in the Air

Sea-Air Operations

World War II Aviation

Elsewhere you can see spy planes, the Sputnik satellite, sound-barrier-breaking fighters, mail planes, and Cold War-era missiles – ominously, the drab green one is an actual (disarmed) ICBM, the Minuteman III, with enough killing power to wipe out several cities. Less portentously, there's the well-anchored satellite Skylab – looking like a shiny gold tin can – which you can wait in line off the second-floor balcony, and the almost sculptural red form of the gondola for the Breitling Orbiter 3, the first balloon to circumnavigate the earth, in 1999. Traveling at the height of a passenger jet, the balloon averaged 185mph and journeyed some 28,000 miles.

Although the west side of the first floor – with fighters like the Messerschmidt, a Hughes aircraft, and air transporters by Boeing and Douglas Aircraft – certainly has its fans, most of the action is on the east side of the floor. The "Space Race" and "Rocketry and Space Flight" galleries make for a good introduction to outer-space aeronautics, though the huge engines in the latter gallery can get tedious after a while.

"**Space Race**" traces the development of space flight, from machines as diverse as a V2 rocket (Hitler's secret weapon and the world's first ballistic missile system) to an array of space suits from different eras. Highlights here include Wiley Post's early version of a "pressure suit," which resembles something out of a 1950s sci-fi flick with its tin-can helmet, leather gloves, metal collar, and rubber tubes poking out, and a Mark V deep-sea diver's suit from 1900, a distant cousin of the outfits worn by 1960s astronauts on their moonwalks.

A display of lunar exploration vehicles starts with unmanned probes – the *Ranger*, *Lunar Orbiter*, and *Surveyor* – and gives way to the ludicrously flimsy lunar module *Eagle*, in which Neil Armstrong and Edwin "Buzz" Aldrin made their historic descent to the moon ("Houston . . . the *Eagle* has landed"). The *Eagle* itself isn't on display, but the *LM-2* – a backup model built for the moon-landing program that was never used – is. If told the module was made out of tin foil, cans, and coat hangers, you could believe it.

Nearby, "**Rocketry and Space Flight**" traces the history of rocketry from the black-powder rockets used in thirteenth-century China to Robert Goddard's experiments with liquid fuel in 1926, which pointed the way to eventual space flight. On a lighter note, coverage of sci-fi stalwarts Jules Verne and Buck Rogers includes a delightful re-creation of the former's notion of a spaceship: basically a riveted-iron capsule with cushy, red-velvet interior and rich wooden cabinets for storage below the plush seats.

Given the demise of manned space travel in recent years, it's not surprising that the museum's newer galleries reflect a shift in focus. The most vivid example of this shift is "**Explore the Universe**," which is not about floating around the moon, but instead peering out at distant galaxies from the earth and earth-orbiting satellites. The collection here is impressive, and you'll no doubt get more out of the display if you have even a faint understanding of astronomy, astrophysics, or cosmology. The arsenal of high-tech, high-ticket items includes spectroscopes and spectrographs, X-ray telescopes for hunting down the dark matter that may compose four-fifths of the universe's mass, early observation tools like reflecting telescopes, chunky lenses, and curious "Armillary Spheres," a giant backup mirror for the Hubble space telescope, and, best of all, a replica of the huge, forbidding metal cage used for telescopes at California's Mount Wilson Observatory.

The other galleries on the first floor are much less eventful. If your time is limited, the most engaging is "**Early Flight**," where you can see Otto Lilienthal's glider (1894), which first inspired the Wright brothers, whose success in turn provided the impetus for the resourceful Herman Ecker. A year after teaching himself to fly in 1911, Ecker built his *Flying Boat* using bits and pieces bought at hardware stores. The early technology explored by people like Ecker and the Wrights is also covered in "**How Things Fly**," an interactive room aimed at those who need a refresher course to understand the museum's exhibits. It's worth glancing, too, at "**Looking at Earth**," where aerial photographs include pictures of San Francisco after the 1906 earthquake (snapped from a kite), 1860 photos of Boston taken from a balloon, and German castles recorded by camera-carrying pigeons.

The second floor

Those who want to recount early twentieth-century world-war heroism will be drawn to the west side of the second-floor galleries: the "**Great War in the Air**" bursts with dog-fighting biplanes, and "**World War II Aviation**" has a classic set of American and foreign fighters. On the east side, "**Beyond the Limits**" details how computers have affected flight and features touch-screen workstations, a cockpit simulator, a model of a Cray-1 supercomputer, and cruder push-button models. Aside from these galleries, however, the focus of the second floor is in three key rooms; the first two cover the seminal figures who brought air travel into being.

In 2003 the museum finally gave Orville and Wilbur Wright the full recognition they deserve, dedicating an entire room – whimsically labeled "**Wright Cycle Co.**" – to the siblings who pioneered aeronautics, despite being bicycle manufacturers at the outset. Indeed, one of their five remaining two-wheelers is on display here, along with their tool cases, Orville's mandolin case, various medals, a 1905 model for an automobile, and a Korona camera similar to the one they used to record history. Naturally, though, the focus is the handmade Wright Flyer, sitting prominently in the middle of the gallery, in which the Wright brothers made the first powered flight in December 1903 at Kitty Hawk, North Carolina. Just 20ft above the ground, that flight lasted twelve seconds and covered 120ft; within two years the Wrights were flying over twenty miles at a time, but there was little interest in their progress. Indeed, in the rush for the skies, the Smithsonian Institution was supporting the efforts of a noted engineer (and its third Secretary), Samuel Pierpoint Langley, who conspicuously failed to fly any of his experimental planes. It was forty years before the Institution formally recognized the brothers' singular achievement, while the original Wright Flyer was only accepted into the Smithsonian fold in 1985.

Next door, the "**Pioneers of Flight**" gallery recounts similarly courageous endeavors, including the balloon basket of Captain Hawthorne Grey, who in May 1927, in a dashing but pointless gesture, reached a height of 42,470ft – only to run out of oxygen. More successfully, in 1923 the *Fokker T-2* was the first airplane to make a nonstop flight across North America – a journey that took 26 hours and 50 minutes. Just twelve years earlier, and after only twenty hours of flying lessons, Cal Rogers had attempted to pick up the $50,000 prize offered by William Randolph Hearst to the first pilot to fly coast-to-coast in less than thirty days. Rogers eventually managed the journey in a patched-up biplane, but it took him two months, seventy landings, and several crashes. The museum's most poignant airplane is the bright-red *Lockheed Vega*, flown solo across the Atlantic in May 1932 by Amelia Earhart, who disappeared five years later over the Pacific attempting an around-the-world flight.

Needless to say, most visitors make a beeline for **"Apollo to the Moon,"** the most popular and crowded room in the museum. The main gallery centers on the *Apollo 11* (1969) and *17* (1972) missions, the first and last flights to the moon. There are Neil Armstrong's and Buzz Aldrin's spacesuits, a Lunar Roving Vehicle (basically a golf cart with a garden seat), *Apollo 17*'s flight-control deck, tools, navigation aids, space food, clothes, and charts, and an astronaut's survival kit (complete with shark repellent). In a side room, each space mission is detailed, beginning in May 1961 when, on a fifteen-minute flight aboard *Freedom 7*, Alan B. Shepard Jr became the first American in space. Also on view are items from John Glenn's brave mission to become the first American to orbit the earth, with the launch of *Friendship 7* in 1962. Glenn went around the earth three times in five hours and saw four sunsets in a craft barely big enough to hold an astronaut; his spacesuit is preserved here, as are the toothpaste tubes used to squeeze food into his mouth. A separate memorial commemorates the three men who died on the *Apollo* launchpad in 1967 – Virgil Grissom, Edward H. White II, and Roger Chaffee. A memorial plaque in Arlington Cemetery (see p.231) commemorates another major US space disaster – the explosion of the space shuttle *Challenger* in 1986.

Finally, the most hardcore of aeronautics buffs will certainly enjoy a trip out to the **Steven F. Udvar-Hazy Center** in suburban Virginia (see "Out of the city" chapter), where you can get a look at flying craft too big even to fit into the main museum's capacious digs.

Hirshhorn Museum and Sculpture Garden

Independence Ave at 7th St SW ☎202/357-2700, ⊛www.hirshhorn.si.edu; L'Enfant Plaza or Smithsonian Metro. Museum daily 10am–5.30pm; Sculpture Garden daily 7.30am–dusk.

The **Hirshhorn Museum** is an unmissable, cylindrical drum of a building that, with its concrete facade and monumental scale, is a perfect example of late modernist architecture at its most inhuman. Luckily, the art inside is much better, an extensive collection of late nineteenth- and twentieth-century works based on the mighty bequest of Latvian immigrant, stockbroker, and uranium magnate Joseph H. Hirshhorn, whose vast fortune enabled him to collect art on a grand scale. Hirshhorn's original bequest in 1966 included 4000 paintings and 2600 sculptures, and by the time of his death in 1981, the overall number of pieces had risen to more than 12,000. Not surprisingly, it's impossible for the museum to display more than a fraction of its collection at any one time – and for you to get a full impression of what's on display in just one visit. In addition to the permanent collection, there are changing exhibitions of contemporary art, thematic shows, and a **sculpture garden** with the *Full Circle* outdoor **café** (summer lunch only). There are **free guided tours** of the permanent collection (Mon–Fri 10.30am & noon, Sat & Sun noon & 2pm), and good art **films** are shown a couple of evenings a week (☎202/357-1300 for details).

Museum orientation

The Hirshhorn's two upper floors are split into inner and outer loops, with its main galleries circling along the nearly windowless exterior wall, and sculpture from two centuries residing in the glass-enclosed inner exhibition halls overlooking the fountain. American and European sculpture and modern art from the turn of the twentieth century to the 1960s occupy the third-floor galleries, while contemporary works and special exhibitions are on the second floor along with European sculpture spanning the period 1850 to 1935. The most contemporary works are in the lower-level galleries, where the exhibits are frequently rotated. Keep in mind that the museum's spaces are often rearranged and entire arcs of each floor periodically off-limits, so if there's something you specifically want to see, call ahead to make sure it's there.

European and American sculpture

If the museum has one recognized strength, it's the nineteenth-century **French sculpture** collection, considered one of the best of its kind outside France. **Jean-Baptiste Carpeaux**, principal French sculptor of the mid-nineteenth century, is represented, along with **Auguste Rodin**, whom he directly influenced. Of various bronzes by **Henri Matisse**, most notable is *The Serf*, a stumpy portrait of a downtrodden spirit, while alongside **Edgar Degas**'s usual muscular ballerinas are energetic studies of women washing, stretching, and emerging from a bath. Masks and busts by **Pablo Picasso** trace his (and sculpture's) growing alliance with Cubism: contrast the almost jaunty bronze *Head of a Jester* (1905) with the severe *Head of a Woman*, produced just four years later. A similar exercise is possible with a series of five exemplary bronze heads by Matisse of his wife Jeanette (1910–13), which clearly show the journey from Realism to Cubism. Abstraction gets further along with **Brancusi**, whose *Torso of a Young Man* is rather too similar to a brass, cylindrical phallus.

There's an abundance of 1950s **Henry Moore** here, from the rather gentle *Seated Figure Against a Curved Wall* to the more imposing *King and Queen*, a regal pair of seated five-foot-high bronze figures whose curved laps and straight backs look as inviting as chairs. Look, too, for *Kiln Man*, **Robert Arneson**'s self-portrait as a brick chimney, with little cigar-smoking heads of the artist ready for firing inside. It's also hard to miss **Nam June Paik**'s *Video Flag* (1985–96), composed of seventy thirteen-inch monitors, with a flurry of images spanning the presidents from Truman to Clinton, all the while managing to resemble a fluttering American flag. Several big-name artists get entire rooms to themselves; if you're a fan, you'll delight in **Sol LeWitt**'s optical-illusion-like "Wall Drawings," which bracket his *13/11* (1985), a white-painted wooden lattice of cubes on the floor. Also enticing is the work of **Joseph Cornell**, who receives an entire room devoted to his art boxes; in these, little found objects and curiosities are arrayed behind glass, the most enchanting of them being the *Medici Princess* (c.1952), in which a replica of a fetching Mannerist-era portrait by Bronzino stares out from behind blue glass, while an open drawer below is filled with intriguing castoffs such as bracelets, pearls, a Tuscan map, and a powder-blue feather. Less familiar artists also get their due, among them **Lucas Samaras**, whose forbidding *Book No. 6* (1962) is made of straight pins, and the arch-Futurist **Giacomo Balla**, whose vigorously jagged painted-metal pieces look ready to rip your hand off if you get too close.

European and American painting

As with its sculpture collection, the Hirshhorn's cache of **modern paintings** has several strengths (de Kooning, Bacon) and some weaknesses (few women, no Kandinsky, and, despite his sculpture on display, no Matisse). The set starts with figurative paintings from the late nineteenth and early twentieth century and winds its way toward Abstract Expressionism and Pop Art. Along the way, separate rooms showcase the various major currents of the past century, from the surrealism of Salvador Dalí, Max Ernst, and Joan Miró to the organic abstractions of Alexander Calder.

American art makes a particularly good showing: there are portraits by John Singer Sargent, Mary Cassatt, and Thomas Eakins (including a strong study of Eakins's wife), and representative works by Winslow Homer, Albert Bierstadt, Marsden Hartley, and Edward Hopper. In addition, Hirshhorn's collection of work by Abstract Expressionist **Willem de Kooning** is one of the most impressive anywhere, although changing displays, loans, and special exhibitions wreak havoc with formal viewing plans. There's a rotating selection of paintings by the likes of Georgia O'Keeffe, Robert Rauschenberg, Louise Bourgeois, Clyfford Still, Piet Mondrian, Jasper Johns, Roy Lichtenstein, and Andy Warhol – in short, just about every noteworthy twentieth-century artist. Other third-floor highlights include the Directions Gallery, where newer, often international, work is exhibited, and the Abram Lerner Room, which affords panoramic views of the Mall and a place to rest your feet.

Downstairs, the second level is given over to special exhibitions, with the remaining galleries featuring a thematically linked showing of selected works from the contemporary collection. More **contemporary art** is on display on the lower level, where you're likely to find works by widely known artists like Warhol and Johns, as well as those of artists currently setting the art periodicals abuzz.

The Sculpture Garden

Much of the Hirshhorn's monumental sculpture is contained in the **Sculpture Garden**, a sunken concrete arbor across Jefferson Drive on the Mall side of the museum. In May and October, there are special free tours (call for times). **Roy Lichtenstein**'s towering *Brushstroke* (1996), a formalized sculpture of one of his signature painted images, oversees the garden. Other works include **Rodin**'s *Monument to the Burghers of Calais* and **Matisse**'s four human *Backs* in relief (1919–30). Many of the artists represented inside the museum appear in the garden too – Henry Moore, naturally, but also **Aristide Maillol** (in particular, a graceful *Nymph* of 1930) and Henri Laurens, Joan Miró, and David Smith. Of the lesser-known works, several stand out, like **Gaston Lachaise**'s proud, bronze *Standing Woman (Heroic Woman)* from 1932. The pond is fronted by **Alexander Calder**'s *Six Dots over a Mountain* (1956); for a more impressive Calder, make for the museum entrance on Independence Avenue, where his *Two Disks* (1965) sit on five spidery legs tall enough for you to walk under.

Minor Smithsonian attractions

Sitting between the Smithsonian Castle and the Hirshhorn Museum, the Arts and Industries Building is another fitting holdover from the Victorian era, with its playful polychromatic brick-and-tile patterns. However, despite its enticing design and historic value as one of the Smithsonian's founding structures, the building is undergoing renovation and won't be open to the public any time soon. Still on view, though, are the regular children's programs at its **Discovery Theater** (@www .discoverytheater.si.edu), while right outside is the popular **carousel**. Even more appealing are the lovely **Enid A. Haupt Gardens** (daily: June–Sept 7am–8pm; Oct–May 7am–5.45pm) nearby, where you'll find several topiary bison and well-tended plots of decorative flowers.

The Smithsonian story

It's strange to consider that an Englishman endowed the fundamentally American institution of the Smithsonian, but that's exactly what happened. **James Smithson**, a gentleman scientist and the illegitimate son of the first Duke of Northumberland, was raised as James Lewis Macie but took his natural father's name after his mother's death in 1800. Despite never visiting the US, he bequeathed half a million dollars "to found at Washington, under the name of the Smithsonian Institution, an establishment for the increase and diffusion of Knowledge" – provided that his surviving nephew should die without an heir. His nephew did just that in 1835, six years after Smithson's death, though it took Congress until 1846 to decide first whether to accept the money, and then what sort of institution would fit the bill. In the end, the vote was for a multi-use building that would hold a museum, art gallery, and laboratory: the original Smithsonian Institution Building, known as "the Castle," was completed in 1855.

For all its wealth, however, the Smithsonian had a shaky start; it wasn't at all clear how it should diffuse the knowledge proposed by its benefactor. Matters slowly improved under the stewardship of the Smithsonian's first Secretary, **Joseph Henry**, who tried to direct the institution primarily toward scientific research, but a new wrinkle occurred when America observed its centennial in 1876. The government invited its constituent states and forty foreign nations to display a panoply of inventions and exhibits that would celebrate contemporary human genius. The subsequent Centennial Exhibition in Philadelphia was a roaring success, though at its close most of the exhibits were abandoned by their owners, who couldn't afford to take or ship them home. Congress made the Smithsonian responsible for the items and approved funds for a new "National Museum" (now the Arts and Industries Building) to house them. Opened in 1881 in time to host President Garfield's inaugural ball, the building soon became rooted in people's consciousness as the "nation's attic," since quite apart from the Centennial exhibits – which included an entire American steam locomotive and Samuel Morse's original telegraph – the Smithsonian also made acquisitions that weren't of a strictly educational nature. Over the years, as the National Museum filled to bursting, most of the Smithsonian holdings were farmed out to new, specialized museums.

Only the central rotunda and four of the original exhibit halls remain from the Arts and Industries Building's first design, and the nearby Castle houses the main visitor center, whose fine marble-pillared Great Hall suggests the grandeur of the Smithsonian's holdings.

Smithsonian Institution Building

1000 Jefferson Drive SW ☏202/357-2700, ✉www.si.edu; Smithsonian Metro. Castle open daily 9.30am–5.30pm.

Easily the most striking edifice on the Mall, the **Smithsonian Institution Building** is widely known as "the **Castle**" for its ruddy brown sandstone, nave windows, and slender steeples. It serves as headquarters for the Smithsonian Institution, an independent trust holding 140 million artifacts in sixteen museums (and one zoo). Inside you can see a twenty-minute video highlighting the role of the institution, interact with touch-screen Smithsonian information displays and electronic wall maps, and check out scale models of all the major city plans for DC, from L'Enfant's designs onwards. You can also stop by the information desk for the latest details on events at all the galleries. The high-ceiling **Commons Restaurant**, a nineteenth-century beauty with Victorian-era touches and courtly charm, may well be one of the nicest settings on the Mall to pause for a meal, but it's also likely the priciest (call ☏202/357-2957 for reservations).

Smithsonian founder **James Smithson**, who never visited America in life, found a place here in death: his ornate, Neoclassical tomb stands in an alcove just off the Mall entrance. It was placed here in 1904, 75 years after his death in Italy. Sadly, his tomb records his age incorrectly, since he was 64 and not 75 when he died. Also, out on the Mall, in front of the building's entrance, the resplendent robed statue is not of Smithson, as you might suppose, but of first Smithsonian Secretary, Joseph Henry.

National Museum of African Art

950 Independence Ave SW ☏202/357-4600, ⊛www.nmafa.si.edu; Smithsonian Metro. Daily 10am–5.30pm.

In the same area of the Mall as the Smithsonian Building, the **National Museum of African Art** has the nation's foremost collection of traditional sub-Saharan Africa art, including some six thousand diverse sculptures and artifacts culled from a wide variety of tribal cultures, displayed in a series of permanent galleries and bolstered by special exhibitions. In many ways, the museum is one of applied art, though the application of a particular piece is not always clear. In part this is due to the techniques of early collectors, who tended not to concern themselves with recording information about their goods. In most cases, even the artist's name is unknown, and attempting to date a piece is fraught with difficulty. On the whole, most of the works are nineteenth- or twentieth-century – some are older, but because most African art is made from wood or clay, it tends not to survive for long. For an overview of the collection, the free guided **tours** (daily except Fri) are an excellent introduction (pick up a schedule at the ground-floor information desk). It's also worth noting that the **gift shop** on the first level is one of DC's most intriguing, selling woven and dyed fabrics and clothes as well as the usual books and postcards.

The Kerma and Benin collections

The Nubian trading city of **Kerma**, 180 miles south of the present Egypt–Sudan border, flourished between 2500 and 1500 BC. Most of what is known about the city is derived from the excavations of royal tombs, discovered at huge cemeteries lost in the desert for centuries. On display are ceramic bowls (perfectly round, despite being hand-formed), including one with a hippo head for a spout, and carved legs and delicate ivory animal figures from the ceremonial beds used to carry the dead to the cemetery for burial. As in Egypt, Nubian royalty were buried with hundreds of "volunteers," who "allowed themselves to be buried alive" to serve their masters in the afterlife. Ivory inlays from these burial beds come in the form of an ibex, hyenas, vultures, and the hippo god Taweret – standing up and wearing a skirt.

More coherent is the adjacent gallery's display of royal art from the Kingdom of **Benin**, home of Edo-speaking people in what is now Nigeria. It's a small collection of highly accomplished works relating to the rule of the *Oba*, or king, some dating back as far as the fifteenth century. Best pieces here are the copper-alloy heads (made using the sophisticated lost-wax casting technique), some of which depict an erstwhile *Oba*, although one is of a defeated enemy – that he's not Edo is indicated by the four raised scars over each eye (the other heads have only three). There's a picture of the current *Oba* on the gallery wall, in resplendent orange, whose ceremonial headdress and neck-ruff echo those depicted on the copper heads, evidence that the same royal style has prevailed for more than five hundred years. Look also for *Oba* figures flanked by attendants, carrying swords or musical instruments, and bearing weapons like muskets – most likely to fend off Europeans, depicted here as pointy, wide-eyed goofballs riding horses. Finally, among these items are splendid pendants and plaques, some with the red earth of Benin still on them, and a figure of an *Oba* holding a smaller *Oba* figure, holding a smaller *Oba* figure holding a smaller *Oba* …

The rest of the collection

The other galleries make efforts to contextualize the objects on display. In "**Images of Power and Identity**," the emphasis is on political, religious, and ceremonial art – mostly from West and Central Africa – which includes some of the museum's most elaborate holdings. The exhibition contains the museum's two oldest pieces – rounded, stylized, terra-cotta equestrian and archer figures from Mali (thirteenth to fifteenth century) – and also includes the only work in the museum for which the artist is known. Olowe of Ise, an artist to royalty among the Yoruba people of Nigeria, was responsible for the carved wooden palace door that stands 6ft high and depicts in relief a king seated on a horse, his wives ranked above him, and soldiers and daughters below. Remarkably, the door was carved from a single piece of wood. Several works (fertility fetishes) represent a woman and child; note especially the worn wooden carving from Nigeria that would have sat at one end of a ceremonial drum. From Cameroon, a wooden sculpture of a regal male figure holds his chin in his hand (a sign of respect), his decorative bead clothing covered with symbolic representations of spiders (a wily opponent) and frogs (fecundity).

There's much to learn, too, about the African concepts of divinity and beauty: a carved figure from the Ghanaian Asante people shows a seated male and female with disk-shaped heads, a form considered to be the aesthetic ideal. One of the most engaging works, a headrest from the Luba people of the Congo, is supported by two caryatid figures who, if you look around the back, have their arms entwined.

The "**Art of the Personal Object**" displays chairs, stools, and more headrests, mostly carved from wood using an adze, as well as assorted ivory snuff containers (two from Angola with stoppers shaped like human heads), beer straws (from Uganda), carved drinking horns, combs, pipes, spoons, baskets, and cups. Especially interesting are the Mozambique headrest that looks like a cross between a dachshund and an elephant, the "hair knives" meant for cutting through tangles, and a drinking horn with geometric sunburst designs.

Arthur M. Sackler Gallery

1050 Independence Ave SW ☎202/357-4880 or 357-2700, ✉www.asia.si.edu; Smithsonian Metro. Daily 10am–5.30pm.

As you finish up the National Mall museum circuit, you come to the two institutions that make up the National Museum of Asian Art. The first, the angular, pyramidal **Arthur M. Sackler Gallery**, displays its artworks and devotional objects from Asia in comfortable, well-lit, underground galleries (the other, connected by an underground passage and described on pp.94–97, is the Freer Gallery). Research physician, publisher, and art collector Arthur M. Sackler originally donated about a thousand pieces to the Smithsonian, and coughed up $4 million toward the museum's construction. The permanent collections are featured below; temporary exhibitions might cover themes such as South Asian textiles and village arts, contemporary Japanese ceramics, splendid fifteenth- to seventeenth-century illuminated Indian manuscripts, or early Islamic texts from Iran, gorgeously colored in gilt, silver, lapis lazuli, and crushed-stone pigments. The gallery's standout Vever Collection is an unrivaled group of works related to the art of the Islamic book, such as manuscripts and calligraphy, from the eleventh to the nineteenth centuries.

The **information desk** (daily 10am–4pm) at ground level should be your first stop. Ask about the highly informative free guided **tours** (Thurs–Tues 12.15pm). The gallery also has a **shop**, with a fine range of prints, fabrics, ceramics, and artistic gewgaws, and an Asian art research **library**, shared with the Freer Gallery and open to the public (Mon–Fri 10am–5pm).

The Arts of China

The permanent exhibitions are located on the first level; the most prominent one is "**The Arts of China**," which highlights the Sackler's collection of 3000-year-old Chinese bronzes. As early as the fifteenth century BC, ritual wine containers were being fashioned from bronze and showing decoration, such as the faces and tails of dragons, that would become ever more refined. By the time of the late Shang Dynasty (twelfth and eleventh centuries BC), the decorative motifs were outstanding; artisans were now producing elegant bronze vessels with bold designs. All the decorated detail was produced using intricate clay molds – there was no carving of the surface after casting. The subsequent Western and Eastern Zhou dynasties (1050–221 BC) refined the vessels further, with the bird now appearing as the major motif (many of the pieces on display feature bird-shaped handles, or show wispy reliefs of plumage and feathers). Jade pendants also depicted birds and, more commonly, intricate dragon shapes. The technique used to create these items was just as impressive – since jade is too hard to be carved, the lapidaries would rub an abrasive paste across the surface with wood or bamboo to shape and polish the stone. The Sackler's collection of later Chinese art reveals other skills, notably those of the ceramicists of the Tang Dynasty (618–907) who produced multicolored temple guard figures, designed to ward off evil spirits with their fearsome expressions. The last Chinese dynasty, the Qing (1644–1911), witnessed the flourishing of the imperial scholars, who would place so-called "scholar's rocks" (natural pieces of stone resembling mountains) on their desks to encourage lofty thoughts. From this period, too, date the Sackler's remarkably well-preserved carved wooden cabinets and book stands, showing a simple, understated decoration that English and Scandinavian craftsmen would later adopt as their own. By way of contrast, Qing imperial porcelain was richly embellished with symbolic figures and motifs, like a plate depicting a young boy holding a pomegranate full of seeds, or a cockerel and ladies holding fans with painted butterflies, symbolizing fertility.

Luxury Arts of the Silk Route Empires

The "**Luxury Arts of the Silk Route Empires**" exhibit, in the underground link to the Freer, intends to show the historic free flow of artistic ideas between Central, West, and East Asia and the Mediterranean world. The decorative forms seen in medieval Western metalwork and ceramics are echoed in silver Syrian bowls, Persian plates, and Central Asian swords and buckles; note also the beautifully worked, fourth-century Iranian silver drinking vessel (called a *rhyton*) shaped in the form of a gazelle. Here, too, you'll find more Tang Dynasty ceramics, utilizing either simple white porcelain or vibrant tricolored glazes, as well as contemporaneous silverware – from everyday items like a ladle and stem cup to a fine mirror, inlaid with a winged horse and dragon motif. The "Buddhist Heavenly Beings" – floating angelic figurines of gold that once formed part of an altar set – are from the same period.

Other displays

"**Sculpture of South and Southeast Asia**" traces the spread of devotional sculpture across the continent. The earliest piece here is from ancient Gandhara (now part of Pakistan and Afghanistan), a third-century carved head of the Buddha whose features were directly influenced by images from Greece and Rome, with which Gandhara traded. Later Hindu temple sculpture from India includes bronze, brass, and granite representations of Brahma, Vishnu, and Shiva; there's also a superb thirteenth-century stone carving of the elephant-headed Ganesha, the remover of obstacles – his trunk burnished by years of illicit touching by museum visitors. From India, Hinduism and Buddhism spread to the Khmer kingdom (Cambodia), which in addition to adopting classical Indian styles also developed its own naturalistic artistic style. On a thirteenth-century temple lintel, male figures are shown entwined with vines alongside an unidentified female goddess with conical crown and sarong.

"**Metalwork and Ceramics from Ancient Iran**" displays a collection of vessels, weapons, and ornaments made between 2300 and 100 BC. Many of the ceramic vessels here are animal-shaped or painted with animal motifs, while a ceramic trio from northern Persia resemble metal, such was the craftsman's skill in firing. There's great dexterity, too, displayed in the metalwork, particularly the bronze and copper finials (ornamental pole tops) depicting demons (denoting magical powers) or vegetation (fertility).

Freer Gallery of Art

Jefferson Drive at 12th St SW ☎202/357-4880 or 357-2700, ✉www.asia.si.edu; Smithsonian Metro. Daily 10am–5.30pm.

Opened in 1923, the **Freer Gallery of Art** was the first Smithsonian museum devoted exclusively to art. The airy Italian Renaissance palazzo of granite and marble has long been considered one of the city's most aesthetically pleasing museums, with small, elegant galleries encircling a herringbone-brick courtyard furnished with splashing fountain. Design appeal aside, the gallery's abiding interest lies in its unusual juxtaposition of Asian and American art, including more than 1200 prints, drawings, and paintings by James McNeill Whistler – the largest collection of his works anywhere. The galleries on the third level hold selections from the permanent collection, only a fraction of which is on display. Pick up a current floor plan at the **information desk** by the Mall entrance, where you can also inquire about the free, daily (except Wed) highlights **tour**. From the Freer, it's possible to reach the Sackler Gallery via a shared underground passageway.

The original owner of the gallery's collection was **Charles Lang Freer**, an industrialist who made a fortune building railroad cars in Detroit and then spent it on what was at the time considered to be obscure Asian art. Freer bought his first piece, a Japanese fan, in 1887, and thirteen years later retired at the age of 44 to concentrate on his collection, adding Chinese jades and bronzes, Byzantine illuminated manuscripts, Buddhist wall sculptures, and Persian metalwork during five trips to various Asian countries. Freer also began to put together a series of paintings by contemporary American artists whose work he thought complemented his Asian collection. Dwight William Tryon, Thomas Wilmer Dewing, and Abbott Henderson Thayer benefited from Freer's patronage, though the most profitable relationship was with the London-based Whistler, practically all of whose works ended up in Freer's hands. In 1912 Freer embarked upon a plan to endow and build a gallery to hold his collection. He was delighted with the plans drawn up by Charles Platt, but sadly never saw their fruition. Work began in 1916, but was interrupted by the outbreak of World War I; Freer died in 1919, and the gallery didn't open for another four years.

James McNeill Whistler

Not surprisingly, **James Abbott McNeill Whistler** (1834–1903) dominates the scene at the Freer. Born in Lowell, Massachusetts, Whistler moved first to Paris as an art student, from which time dates a *Self-Portrait* (1857) found here. In it, Whistler is wearing a flat-brimmed hat, looking very much the man at ease with Left Bank life. After moving to London in the early 1860s, Whistler not only began to collect modish Japanese prints and *objets*, but embraced their influences in a series of vibrant works, starting with *The Golden Screen* (1865), which depicts a seated woman in Japanese dress in front of a fine painted screen. Freer, attracted by the Oriental flavor of Whistler's art, made a special journey to London to introduce himself, returning on several occasions over the years to buy more of the painter's work.

An unfinished portrait of Freer (1902), started during his last visit just before Whistler's death, hangs in the gallery. Other works include studies incorporating a red Oriental fan (a prop dear to Whistler's heart), and various examples of the tonal experiments that fascinated the artist, who constantly repeated and developed shades of color to harmonious effect. Don't miss a grouping of three highly evocative *Nocturnes*, which use combinations of blue, silver, gray, and gold to illuminate the hazy colors and soft forms of landscapes at Chelsea, Bognor, and Valparaiso Bay. Also striking, *Arrangement in White and Black* (1873) contrasts the ghostly white dress and parasol of Whistler's mother, Maud Franklin, with the dark shades of the background; and *The Little Red Glove* (1896–1902) harmonizes glove and bonnet with the subject's auburn hair. Many of Whistler's works are signed with a butterfly monogram, a Japanese device.

Besides these works, Whistler is also represented by the magnificent **Peacock Room**, whose origins can be traced to the commissioned painting, *The Princess From the Land of Porcelain*. This painting hung above the fireplace in the London dining room of Frederick Leyland, a Liverpudlian shipowner and Whistler patron, who had commissioned interior designer Thomas Jeckyll to add a framework of latticework shelves and gilded leather panels to the room's walls so that he might display his fine collection of Chinese porcelain. Whistler happened to be working on another project in the house at the time and, taking advantage of Leyland's absence on business, decided to restyle Jeckyll's work. Using a technique similar to Japanese lacquerware, he covered the leather-clad walls, ceiling, shelving, and furnishings with rich blue paint, gold-painted peacock feathers, gilt relief decor, and green glaze; above the sideboard he placed two golden painted peacocks trailing a stream of feathers – the aggressive-looking birds supposedly emblematic of the relationship between painter and patron. Nonetheless, Whistler's idea was to present his art as a harmonious whole (the room's full title incorporates the phrase *Harmony in Blue and Gold*), much as the Japanese did; the room was at once a framed picture and an object of applied art, like an Oriental lacquer box. This artistic hijack outraged Leyland, who refused to pay Whistler for the work. Completed in 1877, the room met a mixed critical reception, though Whistler's friend Oscar Wilde, for one, thought it "the finest thing in color and art decoration the world has known." After Leyland's death, the room and its contents passed into the hands of a London art gallery, which later sold it to Freer. Restoration has returned the iridescent colors to their nineteenth-century best, the framed shelves filled with blue-and-white porcelain to show what Leyland's original dining room might have looked like.

Other American artists

The museum's other American art is less gripping, though it is interesting to trace what attracted Freer to many of the works. Note the Oriental-style calligraphic brush strokes of the trees in the foreground of *Winter Dawn on Monadnock*, just one of the Impressionist landscapes by **Abbott Handerson Thayer** (1849–1921), who was heavily influenced by Freer's Asian art collection, which he knew well. **Thomas Wilmer Dewing** comes closer to Whistler's mood with *The Four Sylvan Sounds* (1896), a folding painted screen clearly of Asian influence. Contemporaries considered Dewing to be elitist, and Freer didn't have much competition for his works, though he doubtless had to bid higher for paintings by the more popular **John Singer Sargent**, whose *Breakfast in the Loggia* (1910), a scene in the arcaded courtyard of a Florentine villa, was bought to remind him of the gallery he planned to build in DC.

Asian art

Things pick up again with the Freer's collection of **Japanese art**, in particular the painted folding screens that so delighted Whistler. Called *byobu* (protection from the wind), these depict the seasons or themes from Japanese literature and range from two to ten panels long. Other choice items include the nineteenth-century porcelain dish shaped like Mount Fuji and – one of the oldest pieces here – a twelfth-century standing Buddha of wood and gold leaf. **Korean ceramics**, like wine bottles, tea bowls, and ewers, date from the tenth to the fourteenth centuries and show a uniform jade-like glaze. They're remarkably well preserved, many having been retrieved from aristocratic tombs or surviving as venerated objects handed down through the generations.

Other rooms are devoted to **Chinese art**, ranging from ancient jade burial goods to a series of ornate bronzes (1200–1000 BC), including ritual wine servers in the shape of tigers and elephants. There's also a stunning series of ink-on-paper hand scrolls, though the calligraphy (literally "beautiful writing") isn't just confined to paper – jars and tea bowls, even ceramic pillows, are painstakingly adorned. Freer also made three trips to Egypt, and many of the exhibits date from his last trip in 1909, when he bought a remarkable collection of richly colored glass vessels, bronze figurines, and carved plaques, most around 4000 years old. Later Freer spread his net to incorporate pieces of **Buddhist, South Asian, and Islamic art**. A remarkably well-preserved Pakistani stone frieze from the second century AD details the life of Buddha, while the South Asian art collection sports some of the most delicate pieces yet: temple sculpture, colorful devotional texts, and gold jewelry set with rubies and diamonds. Elsewhere, Turkish ceramics (many repeating garden motifs) are displayed alongside a fine inlaid Persian pen box (thirteenth century) emblazoned with animal heads and engraved with the name of the artist and the owner.

2

Capitol Hill

Famously the focus of American lawmaking, **Capitol Hill** is a political showpiece without compare. Its most potent symbol, the towering silhouette of the white-domed **US Capitol**, home to the US Congress, tops the shallow knoll at the eastern end of the Mall. The building – whose Neoclassical design is meant to evoke the ideals of ancient Greece and Rome that inspired the founding fathers – is the political and geographical center of the city, and many of DC's diagonal boulevards lead directly to it.

Around the Capitol sit more essential components of American government, including the **Supreme Court** and **Library of Congress**; a few attractions like the historic **Sewall–Belmont House**, the lush **US Botanic Garden**; and various federal office buildings, which reach as far as the two C streets, north and south of the Capitol, and east to 2nd Street. For many, that is the extent of the neighborhood, but the Hill is actually home to diverse residential areas, where politicians, aides, lobbyists, and even common folk live. The southeast stretches of **Pennsylvania Avenue**, and the bustling **Eastern Market**, just off the avenue, provide a few worthy distractions, while **Lincoln Park**, with its memorial to the Great Emancipator, marks the neighborhood's eastern limit. The spruced-up area around grand old **Union Station** lies to the north.

As a neighborhood, Capitol Hill has faced a lengthy climb to respectability. When Pierre L'Enfant and his surveyors began laying out the city, the cross drawn on what was then Jenkins Hill was the focus of a grand, Baroque-styled city plan. The US Capitol was erected on the site of that cross, and in 1800 Congress moved in. But this marshy outpost was slow to develop: it froze in the bitter winters and sweltered in the harsh summers; from their boarding houses around the Capitol, legislators had to trudge the muddy length of Pennsylvania Avenue for an audience with the president in the White House. After the **War of 1812** broke out, the British diverted a force away from Quebec and upstate New York and made a play for Washington and Baltimore – a plan designed more to shame the American government than to achieve any immediate tactical goal. The Capitol was the first to burn, prompting many to suggest abandoning the city altogether and setting up political shop somewhere more hospitable.

However, with the conclusion of the war, the damaged structures were rebuilt, and as the capital and the federal government grew in stature in later years, so too did the Hill. During the nineteenth century, rows of elegant **townhouses**, which today form the keystone of Capitol Hill's status as a protected historic district, began to appear. Eventually, major federal institutions that had been housed since 1800 in the ever-expanding Capitol complex moved into new homes of their own: first the Library of Congress in 1897 (whose oldest building has been refurbished), then the Supreme Court in 1935.

Old Downtown — Bus Terminal

N

CAPITOL HILL

I ST

NORTH CAPITOL ST

H ST

G ST

MASSACHUSETTS

National Postal Museum

Union Station

M

Union Station

Columbus Meml Fountain

5TH ST

6TH ST

MORRIS PL

7TH ST

8TH ST

PICKFORD PL

9TH ST

H ST

G ST

F ST

ACKER ST

E ST

LEXINGTON PL

NEW JERSEY AVE

2ND ST

1ST ST

F ST

NW

NE

4TH ST

3RD ST

E ST

UNION STATION PLAZA

LOUISIANA

DELAWARE AVE

Taft Memorial

Russell

Senate Office Buildings

Dirksen

Hart

C ST

Sewall-Belmont House

CONSTITUTION AVE

Stanton Park

MASSACHUSETTS AVE

MARYLAND AVE

MARYLAND

PENNSYLVANIA AVE

Peace Monument

US Capitol

Future visitor center

Supreme Court

2ND ST

3RD ST

4TH ST

5TH ST

A ST

Lincoln Park

Capitol Reflecting Pool

Grant Meml

Garfield Meml

Capital Guide Kiosk

Visitor Facility

US Botanic Garden

Jefferson Bldg

Library of Congress

Folger Shakespeare Library

John Adams Bldg

EAST CAPITOL ST

A ST

F

National Mall

Bartholdi Fountain

Rayburn

INDEPENDENCE AVE

Longworth Cannon

Madison Bldg

SEWARD

NORTH CAROLINA AVE

Eastern Market

C ST

Federal Center SW

M

VIRGINIA AVE

CANAL ST

SOUTH CAPITOL ST

C ST

House Office Bldgs

D ST

NEW JERSEY AVE

Capitol South

M

Folger Park

Ebenezer Church

PENNSYLVANIA AVE

SQUARE

6TH ST

7TH ST

8TH ST

9TH ST

Eastern Market

AVE

D ST

M

SE   Marion Park

0   200 yds

Waterfront SE

CAFÉS & RESTAURANTS					
America	2	Mr Henry's	18	Capitol City Brewing Co.	1
B. Smith's	3	The Monocle	7	Capitol Lounge	11
Banana Café & Piano Bar	23	Murky Coffee	17	The Dubliner	5
Bistro Bis	6	Remington's	21	Hawk 'n' Dove	15
Bread and Chocolate	19	Taverna		Kelly's Irish Times	4
Café Berlin	9	the Greek Islands	13	Phase One	24
Las Placitas	22			Politiki	14
Le Bon Café	10	**BARS & CLUBS**		Tune Inn	16
Market Lunch	12	Bullfeathers	20	Two Quail	8

ACCOMMODATION	
Bull Moose B&B	E
Capitol Hill Suites	G
Hereford House	H
Holiday Inn on the Hill	D
Hotel George	B
Hyatt Regency Washington	C
Phoenix Park	A
William Penn House	F

Later in the twentieth century, massive office buildings were erected to accommodate legislators and their staff, reflecting the government's growth in stature, size, and bureaucratic red tape.

The US Capitol

East end of the Mall, Capitol Hill ☎202/225-6827 for tour information, ☎202/224-3121 general information, ⊕www.house.gov, www.senate.gov, www.aoc.gov; Capitol South or Union Station Metro. Daily tours 9am–4.30pm.

The towering, rib-vaulted dome of the **US Capitol** (visible from all over the city) soars between north and south wings, respectively occupied by the

Senate and **House of Representatives**, the two legislative bodies that make up Congress. The building, with its grand halls and statues, committee rooms, and ornate chambers, is one of the few places in the District where you get a tangible sense of the immense power wielded by the nation's elected officials. Unlike the White House – where you're kept away from any real action – when Congress is in session, you can watch from third-floor galleries as elected leaders get down to business (though with evolving security requirements, you may need approval from your local representative to do so; check the above websites for current information).

The Capitol is the only building in DC without an address, as it stands foursquare at the center of the street plan: the city quadrants extend from the building, and the numbered and lettered streets count away from its central axis. For the same reason, the building doesn't have a front or a back, simply an "East Front" and a "West Front." The **public entrance** is at the East Front, where, from 1829 to 1977, all the presidents were inaugurated. In 1981 Ronald Reagan was sworn in on the west side, and the five inaugurations since then

Capitol conflicts

In 1812, Thomas Jefferson declared the US Capitol "the first temple dedicated to the sovereignty of the people, embellishing with Athenian taste the course of a nation looking far beyond the range of Athenian destinies." Indeed the building has been an iconic symbol of democracy for more than two centuries, and the foot of the US Capitol has been an obvious hub for **political demonstrations**. In 1894, Jacob S. Coxey led an "army" of unemployed people from Ohio and points west to demand a public works program to create jobs; he was arrested for trespassing, and the few hundred men with him slunk off home. After World War I, unemployed soldiers – the so-called "Forgotten Men" of the era – camped outside the Capitol; fifty years later the weary citizens of the Poor People's March of May 1968 set up makeshift tents and shelters they called "Resurrection City" (see p.58). More recently, in 1995, Nation of Islam leader Louis Farrakhan harangued white America from the terrace steps while addressing attendees of the Million Man March.

On occasion, the building itself has come **under attack**. Shots were fired in the Capitol in 1835, and in 1915, 1971, and 1983 various aggrieved protestors detonated bombs in the building (no one was injured). The worst attack was in the summer of 1998, when a lone gunman stormed the building, killing two Capitol police officers and injuring several members of the public. This event led to calls for the building to be made secure, and an underground visitor's center – where tourists are to be screened and inspected before entering the building – was planned in response and will open in 2006.

It was, of course, the 2001 terrorist attacks in DC and New York City that really led to clarion calls for restricting public access to the building. To add to the fears on high, in October 2001 an already jittery Capitol Hill was made even more so following a shipment of anthrax to the office of Senate Majority Leader Tom Daschle. Congress suspended its session for a week, tours of the Capitol were canceled for several months, and many offices were closed for decontamination.

While it will likely be some time before a new balance between security and liberty is reached (as far as the public's access to government buildings goes), one can be fairly sure that the Capitol's open-door policy will be less freewheeling than in the past. With the anthrax crime yet to be solved and the threat of terrorism always present, the Hill has an atmosphere of heightened security and occasional paranoia, so visitors are well advised to avoid making off-color jokes about terrorism or violence while here – the focus of the nation's democracy is also the focus of its fears.

have followed this precedent. When Congress is in session (from January 3 until close of business, usually in the fall) the lantern above the dome is lit, and flags fly above Senate or House wings.

Some history

A chaste plan, sufficiently capacious and convenient for a period not too remote, but one to which we may reasonably look forward, would meet my idea in the Capitol.

George Washington, 1792

In 1792, just a few years after the Constitution was ratified and a new federal government empowered, the design of the seat of that government, the US Capitol, was thrown open to public competition. **Dr William Thornton**, an amateur whose grand Neoclassical offering brought a splendor deemed appropriate for Congress's meeting place, won the competition. On September 18, 1793, in a ceremony rich with Masonic symbolism, the cornerstone of the Capitol was laid by second-term president George Washington. By the time the government moved to DC from Philadelphia seven years later, however, the Capitol was nowhere near completion.

When Congress assembled for the first time in the brick-and-sandstone building on November 22, 1800, only a small north wing housing the Senate Chamber, the House of Representatives, the Supreme Court, and the Library of Congress was ready. (Elsewhere, President John Adams moved into an unfinished White House; see p.133.) The building's ceilings leaked, and the furnaces installed to heat the structure produced intolerable temperatures. Adams's successor, **Thomas Jefferson** (the first president inaugurated inside the Capitol), appointed the respected **Benjamin Latrobe** as surveyor of public buildings in an attempt to speed up work, and by 1807 a south wing had been built for the House of Representatives. In addition, Latrobe added a second floor to the north wing, allowing separate chambers for the Supreme Court and the Senate.

British troops burned down the Capitol and the White House in 1814. With President Madison having fled the city, Washington DC's future was uncertain. Nonetheless, Congress met for four years in a quickly built "Brick Capitol" (see box, p.102) on the site of today's Supreme Court, and restoration work continued on what was left of the original Capitol – which wasn't much.

Latrobe found the building's interior gutted and the surviving exterior walls blackened by smoke (the British soldiers had stacked up all the furniture they could find and lit a bonfire). His grandiose ideas for rebuilding and expanding the Capitol found few admirers, and in 1817 he was replaced by **Charles Bulfinch**. The reconstructed wings were reopened in 1819, and in 1826 the Capitol finally appeared in a form that Thornton might have recognized, complete with a central rotunda topped by a low wooden dome clad in copper.

By the 1850s Congress had again run out of space. Plans were laid to build magnificent, complementary wings on either side of the building and to replace the dome with something more substantial. In 1857 the new south wing accommodated the **House Chamber**, and two years later the **Senate Chamber** moved to the new north wing. The **Civil War** threatened to halt work on the **dome**, but Abraham Lincoln, recognizing the Capitol as a potent symbol of the Union, was determined that the building should be completed. A cast-iron dome was painstakingly assembled, though the work was hampered by the presence of Union troops stationed in the building (some

The Brick Capitol

When the British marched into Washington in August 1814, they promptly burned down the Capitol and, in the words of Alistair Cooke, "the rest of the new public buildings that in those days were all that distinguished Washington from a fishing town on a marsh." It was a supreme humiliation, and one that revived the bitter debate about Washington's suitability as the nation's capital. President Madison, a native Virginian, gave the Northern dissenters no chance to agitate: he returned to the city at the earliest opportunity and directed the building of a temporary Brick Capitol. Hastily designed by Benjamin Latrobe, it was erected on the site of today's Supreme Court – land then occupied by a tavern and vegetable garden. Here, in 1817, James Monroe became the first president to take the oath of office in an outdoor public ceremony in Washington.

When the US Capitol was finally restored in 1819 and the government moved back in, the Brick Capitol became home to the Circuit Court of DC until the new City Hall was finished. From 1824 to 1861 the building was a lodging house, and from 1861 to 1867 it was a prison. It was later replaced by three row houses, which were in turn demolished to make way for the Supreme Court in 1935.

soldiers insisted on shinning up and down hundred-foot ropes draped from the Rotunda walls for amusement). But in December 1863 the glorious project came to fruition. Hoisted on top of the white-painted dome was the nineteen-foot-high **Statue of Freedom** by sculptor Thomas Crawford. Resplendent in a feathered helmet and clutching a sword and shield, the statue is also known as "Armed Liberty."

Give or take a few minor additions, the US Capitol hasn't changed much since this last burst of construction. The surrounding terraces were added after the Civil War, and when extra office space was required in the last century, separate **House and Senate office buildings** were built in the streets on either side of the Capitol. The Capitol's columns were replaced in the 1950s, and the original ones moved out to the National Arboretum (see p.205). The East Front was extended in 1962 and faced in marble to prevent the original sandstone from deteriorating further, and, so far, the West Front – now the oldest part of the building – has avoided modern accretions, though it was restored in the 1980s.

Visiting the Capitol

With all the terrorism and war-making of recent years, access to the nation's highest legislative body has become more restricted. The West Front is guarded and gated, and anyone not here on official business is barred entrance, while the East Front is being completely reconstructed to make way for an underground visitor's center scheduled to open in 2006. To enter the building, you'll need to drop by the **Capitol Guide Service kiosk** near the southwest side of the complex (near the James Garfield statue, 1st St SW at Maryland Ave) and pick up free tickets. It's important to get there as early as possible: tickets are handed out beginning at 9am, but lines often form well in advance. Once you have your tickets, you can wait at the **South Visitor Receiving Facility**, on the south side of the House of Representatives building, until your reserved tour begins; if you visit between April and September, expect to wait in line for one or two hours. Lines are shorter in winter, and the place is generally less busy on Sundays and during lunchtime most other days. Finally, although the sites listed below have typically been open for tours in the past, continuing security clampdowns may make some of them off-limits during your visit.

The Rotunda

Standing in the **Rotunda**, you're not only at the center of the US Capitol, but at point zero of the entire District. William Thornton, the Capitol's first architect, took Rome's Pantheon as his model, so it's no wonder that this is a magnificent space: 180ft high and 96ft across, with the dome canopy decorated by Constantino Brumidi's mighty **fresco** depicting the *Apotheosis of Washington*. The fresco took the 60-year-old Brumidi almost a year to complete and shows George Washington surrounded by symbols of democracy, arts, science, and industry, as well as female figures representing the thirteen original states. Brumidi had a hand, too, in the **frieze** celebrating American history that runs around the Rotunda wall, beginning with Columbus's arrival in the New World and ending with the Civil War.

From the floor, it's hard to see much detail of either frieze or fresco, and eyes are drawn instead to the eight large **oil paintings** that hang below the frieze. Four of the paintings depict events associated with the "discovery" and settlement of the country (like, again, Columbus's arrival and the Pilgrims' embarkation), though most notable are the four Revolutionary War pieces by **John Trumbull**, who trained under Benjamin West, the first American artist to study in Europe. These paintings (1818-24) are still in the eighteenth-century British vein, with rigid figures and martial pomp and ceremony. Three of them portray military leaders giving up their commands – two because of wartime surrenders (Burgoyne and Cornwallis) and one because of the end of war (Washington before Congress) – and one shows the signing of the Declaration of Independence. All in all, they made for a prominent start for the burgeoning American art scene.

Busts and statues of prominent American leaders fill in the gaps in the rest of the Rotunda. Washington, Jefferson, Lincoln, and Jackson are all here, along with a modern bust of Dr Martin Luther King Jr and a gold facsimile of the Magna Carta. In such august surroundings thirty people – including ten presidents, members of Congress, military leaders, and eminent citizens – have been **laid in state** before burial. The most recently honored was fortieth president Ronald Reagan, who died in June 2004. Reagan was the first commander-in-chief honored in this manner since President Lyndon Johnson died in 1973.

National Statuary Hall

From the Rotunda you move south into one of the earliest extensions of the building – the section that once housed the chamber of the **House of Representatives**. The acoustics here are such that, from his desk, John Quincy Adams could supposedly eavesdrop on opposition members on the other side of the room.

After the House moved into its new wing in 1857, the chamber was used for various temporary purposes (novelist Anthony Trollope bought gingerbread from a market stall in here) until Congress decided to turn it into the **National Statuary Hall** and invited each state to contribute two statues of its most famous citizens. Around forty statues are still on display in the hall, with the others scattered around the corridors in the rest of the building; few are of any great distinction. Adelaide Johnson's 1921 *Suffrage Monument*, which was moved here after languishing in the Crypt for much of its existence, certainly grabs your attention. The statue shows women's rights pioneers Susan B. Anthony, Lucretia Mott, and Elizabeth Cady Stanton poking their heads out of a large, mostly uncut block of granite, as if entombed there. Although the work is hardly an aesthetic triumph and has been criticized as unbefitting the importance of these key figures, it is one of only six statues of women in the entire building.

Old Senate Chamber

North of the Rotunda is the **Old Senate Chamber**. This splendid semicircular gallery, with its embossed rose ceiling, was built in 1810 and reconstructed from 1815 to 1819, after the British had done their worst damage to the city. The Senate met here until 1859, when it moved into its current quarters. The Supreme Court moved in and stayed until 1935, when it, too, was given a new home. After that the Old Senate Chamber sat largely unused until it was restored to its mid-nineteenth-century glory for the Bicentennial. Its furnishings are redolent of that period; the members' desks are reproductions, but the gilt eagle topping the vice president's chair is original, as is the portrait of George Washington by Rembrandt Peale.

Contemporary engravings helped restorers reproduce other features of the original Senate chamber, like the rich red carpet emblazoned with gold stars. As Charles Dickens noted when he visited, the original carpet received severe punishment from "tobacco-tinctured saliva" despite the provision of a cuspidor by every desk – the universal disregard of which led to "extraordinary improvements on the pattern which are squirted and dabbled upon it in every direction." If visitors dropped anything on the floor, they were enjoined "not to pick it up with an ungloved hand on any account." Despite such expectoration, members of this Senate chamber participated in some of the most **celebrated debates** of the era: in 1830 the great orator Daniel Webster of Massachusetts fiercely defended "Liberty and the Union" in a famous speech lasting several hours; over two days in 1850 Henry Clay pleaded his succession of compromises to preserve the Union (brandishing a fragment of Washington's coffin for emphasis); and in 1856, Senator Charles Sumner of Massachusetts – having argued forthrightly against the Kansas-Nebraska Bill (which allowed for extending slavery into the new territories) and branding slavery a "harlot" – was caned senseless at his desk by Preston Brooks, an incensed congressman from South Carolina. Both men became heroes to their respective sides of the Mason-Dixon line.

Old Supreme Court and the Crypt

Before 1810, the Senate met on the floor below the **Old Senate Chamber**, in a room that architect Benjamin Latrobe later revamped to house the Supreme Court, which sorely needed a permanent home. While the work was being carried out, Supreme Court sessions were often held in an inn opposite the Capitol, and once the British had delayed matters by burning the rest of the building, the nation's highest tribunal was forced to meet in rented townhouses on the Hill. By 1819, however, the Court had settled in this chamber, where it remained until 1860, when it moved again – this time upstairs, to the chamber just vacated by the Senate.

The **Old Supreme Court Chamber** served as a law library until 1950, after which it too was restored to its mid-nineteenth-century appearance. Its dark, comfortable recesses resemble a gentleman's club (which, in many ways, it was). Some of the furnishings are original, including the desks, tables, and chairs, as are the busts of the first five chief justices.

The **Crypt** lies underneath the Rotunda, on the same level as the Old Supreme Court Chamber. Lined with Doric columns, it was designed to house George Washington's tomb, a plan that was never realized (Washington's buried with his wife, Martha, at Mount Vernon). The Crypt instead is an **exhibition center**, displaying details of the plans submitted for the 1792 architectural competition and details about the Capitol's construction.

House and Senate chambers

With beefed-up security measures, public access to the **House and Senate chambers** has been sharply cut back; it's even hard to get into the visitors' galleries since currently they're not part of the official Capitol tour. If you're an American citizen, you can try applying to your representative's or senator's office in advance for a pass valid for the entire (two-year) session of Congress. For more information call ☎202/225-6827 or visit ⓦwww.house.gov or www .senate.gov.

The chambers may well be empty, or deep in torpor, when you show up, which is fine if all you want is a flavor of either place. If you're lucky, you may watch members introduce legislation or even vote on various bills or issues. The House chamber is the more striking of the two, with its decorative frieze and oil paintings; from here the president addresses joint sessions of Congress and delivers his annual **State of the Union** speech. The Senate chamber is perhaps more widely recognized these days, as it was the setting for the final chapter of President Clinton's impeachment trial.

Legislative offices

You can get a lot closer to senators and representatives in their offices than in the Capitol; access is usually quite open, with obstacles consisting mainly of a few security guards and scanners.

The six legislative office buildings contain the **committee rooms** where most of the day-to-day political activity takes place (hearings have been open to the public since the 1970s). The first of these office buildings – named for past politicians – was built in 1908–09, and the last in 1982; they follow the pattern of the Capitol in that the Senate office buildings (Russell, Dirksen, and Hart) are to the north and the House office buildings (Cannon, Longworth, and Rayburn) are to the south. A senator's office is easy to identify by an American flag and his or her state flag outside in the corridor. Committee hearings, usually held in the morning, are listed in the *Washington Post*'s "Today in Congress" section. Unless you turn up early, you may not get in, especially to anything currently featured on the TV news.

Only in the Senate Hart Building, on Constitution Avenue NE at 2nd Street, is there any artwork of note: dominating the atrium is Alexander Calder's monumental black *Mountains and Clouds*. This was the artist's last work, and the only one to combine a separate mobile and stabile. The **Hart Building**, with its towering atrium and sizable glass windows, is also the only architecturally appealing structure out of the six offices, the others featuring the same grim passageways and dim fluorescent lighting that critics claim characterize all of Washington.

West of the Capitol

Facing the National Mall, the West Front of the Capitol provides a striking image of imperial power that is heightened by the mirror image shown in the **Capitol Reflecting Pool** at its base. The pool itself, with its surrounding benches and sloping wall, is an excellent spot to rest before tackling the museums on the Mall, plus it provides an important function with its aesthetic form: the shallow watery expanse was laid out as part of a lightweight roof to shelter the subterranean channel of the 395 freeway below, as anything heavier would have been unsuitable for covering such a wide area.

West Front memorials

A low-key memorial to peace and a monument to the assassinated twentieth president, James Garfield (shot only four months after his inauguration), sit at the junction of the Capitol grounds with Pennsylvania Avenue NW and Maryland Avenue SW, respectively. The **Garfield Memorial** is in the vicinity of the Capitol Guide Service kiosk, where you can pick up tickets for tours of the Capitol (see p.102). However, the most significant structure sits between the memorial and monument, the 250-foot-long **Ulysses S. Grant Memorial**, honoring the general-in-chief of the Union forces under President Lincoln during the Civil War. Dedicated in 1922, the monument depicts a somber Grant on horseback, guarded by lions, flanked by a charging cavalry unit on one side and an artillery unit moving through thick mud on the other. Sculptor Henry Merwin Shrady spent twenty years on the work, using uniformed soldiers-in-training as his models. In waging total war on the Confederate forces from 1864 to 1865, Grant secured final victory for Lincoln, thus preserving the Union. Contemporaries talked of his personal shortcomings and of his fearsome drinking habits, but Lincoln knocked back all complaints, saying, "I wish some of you would tell me the brand of whiskey that Grant drinks. I would like to send a barrel of it to my other generals."

North of the Reflecting Pool toward Union Station, a small park bordered by Constitution and Louisiana avenues contains the **Robert A. Taft Memorial**, a statue and sixty-foot-high, concrete bell tower erected in 1958. The memorial honors the veteran senator (and son of President William Howard Taft), who during the mid-twentieth century was known simply as "Mr. Republican."

US Botanic Garden

245 1st St SW ☎202/225-8333, ⊛www.usbg.gov. Daily 10am–5pm.

The centerpiece of the popular **US Botanic Garden**, which sits near a corner of the National Mall, is a **conservatory** crowned by the eighty-foot-tall **Palm House**, the result of a recent renovation that transformed a 1933 Victorian-style building into a state-of-the-art greenhouse. More than four thousand plants are on display, including colorful ranks of tropical, subtropical, and desert species in climate-controlled rooms. Of particular note are the orchid section, where two hundred of the garden's twelve thousand varieties are visible at any one time, and the **Jungle Room**, stuffed with equatorial trees and humid almost to the point of discomfort.

While the garden's roots can be traced to early proponents like George Washington and Thomas Jefferson, it was Lt Charles Wilkes's 1838–42 expedition to the South Seas that really got things going. The irascible Wilkes, said to be

△ National Postal Museum

the model for the Captain Ahab character in Herman Melville's seafaring epic, *Moby Dick*, returned to America after four years and nearly 90,000 miles with a collection of ten thousand plants from around the world. These specimens formed the core of a revitalized garden; a cycad dating back to Wilkes's journey is still on view.

Bartholdi Fountain

South of the Botanic Garden, across Independence Avenue at 1st Street SW, is a small demonstration garden next to the thirty-foot-high **Bartholdi Fountain**, submitted by French sculptor Frédéric-Auguste Bartholdi to the 1876 Centennial Exhibition in Philadelphia. (A decade later Bartholdi would create the Statue of Liberty, one of America's most enduring icons.) Congress bought the fountain in 1877 for display on the Mall (it moved to this site in 1932), where its original gas lamps – illuminated at night – made it a popular evening hangout. Today the fountain is often deserted, but is as good a spot as any to catch your breath before taking the long walk down the Mall.

East of the Capitol

All the other notable buildings and institutions of Capitol Hill – like the **Supreme Court** and **Library of Congress** – lie on the east side of the Capitol, within half a dozen blocks of each other. Here, in the charming and historic East Capitol neighborhood, amid the grand old Georgian and Federal townhouses, a few historic old homes, such as the Sewall-Belmont House, add to the picturesque setting, making it a good spot for a daytime walk. It's worth being wary after dark though: for all its upscale trappings, Supreme Court justice David Souter was mugged here in 2004, not far from his home.

The Supreme Court

1st St and Maryland Ave NE ☎202/479-3211, ⊛www.supremecourtus.gov or ⊛www.scus.gov; Union Station or Capitol South Metro. Mon–Fri 9am–4.30pm.

The third – and easily the most respected – branch of American government, the judiciary, has its apex at the **Supreme Court of the United States**. Not only is the court the familiar judge of what is and isn't constitutional, it's also the nation's final arbiter for disputes between states, between the federal government and states, between federal and state judges, and between individuals appealing all kinds of legal decisions – from boundary disputes to death-penalty sentences. Since it was established at the Constitutional Convention of 1787, the Court has functioned as both the guardian and interpreter of the **Constitution**, but only really began flexing its muscles in the 1800s under the sway of Chief Justice John Marshall (see box, pp.110–111). Its familiar motto is "Equal Justice For All" – the legend inscribed upon the architrave above the double row of eight columns facing 1st Street.

Oddly, for such a linchpin of the American political system, the Supreme Court was forced to share quarters in the US Capitol until 1935, when, on the prompting of Chief Justice (and former president) William Howard Taft, it was finally granted its own building. Seventy-year-old **Cass Gilbert**, known primarily for his neo-Gothic Woolworth Building in New York, was perhaps an unusual choice for architect, but his marble temple did indeed reflect the dignity and importance of the Supreme Court, as he hoped it would. In response to its warm reception, Gilbert said, "It is receiving so much favorable praise that I am wondering what is wrong with it."

The facade of the building glistens as natural light bounces off the bright white marble, and "Contemplation of Justice" and "Guardian of Law" **sculptures** flank the wide steps down to 1st Street. Solemn, if not pompous, the sculptures' effect is lightened somewhat by the relaxed representations on the **pediment** over the main entrance: here, among allegorical Greek figures, are Chief Justice Taft as a Yale student, Chief Justice Marshall reclining, and architect Gilbert and sculptor Robert Aitken clad in togas.

Inside, the main corridor – known as the **Great Hall** – has a superb carved and painted ceiling, white walls lined with marble columns, and busts of all the former chief justices. At the end of the corridor is the surprisingly compact **Court Chamber**, with damask drapes and a molded plaster ceiling done up in gold leaf, flanked by more marble columns. A frieze runs around all four sides, its relief panels depicting various legal themes, allegorical figures, and ancient and modern lawgivers. When in session, the Chief Justice sits in the center of the **bench** (below the clock), with the most senior justice on his right and the next in precedence on his left; the rest sit in similar alternating fashion so that the most junior justice sits on the far right (left as you face the bench). Curiously, the chairs for each justice are made in the Court's own carpentry shop.

Although you could once reach the ground floor via the building's wondrous spiral staircases, today, in a more security-obsessed era, you'll have to content yourself with an elevator ride. The lower floor has its own Great Hall (overseen by a mighty statue of Chief Justice Marshall lounging in his chair) and a permanent exhibition about the Court. A free, short movie fills you in on the Court's legal and political background, while architectural notes, sketches, and photos trace the history of the building itself. You'll also find restrooms, a gift shop, a snack bar, and a cafeteria on this level.

Visiting the Court

The Court is **in session** from October through June. Between the beginning of October and the end of April, oral arguments are heard every Monday, Tuesday, and Wednesday from 10am to noon and 1pm to 3pm for two weeks each month. (In May and June, the Court works out its rulings and presents them to the public.) The sessions, which almost always last one hour per case, are **open to the public** on a first-come, first-served basis. Arrive by 8.30am if you really want one of the 150 seats, and keep in mind that for some high-profile cases, such as those involving abortion rights or freedom of speech, people sometimes wait in line overnight. More casual visitors simply join a separate line, happy to settle for a three-minute stroll through the standing gallery. When Court is not in session, guides give **lectures** in the Court Chamber (Mon–Fri 9.30am–3.30pm; hourly on the half-hour).

Sewall-Belmont House

144 Constitution Ave NE ☎202/546-1210, ⊕www.sewallbelmont.org; Union Station Metro. Tues–Fri 11am–3pm, Sat noon–4pm. $3.

North of the Supreme Court, across Constitution Avenue at 2nd Street, is the red-brick townhouse known as the **Sewall–Belmont House**, one of the oldest private residences in the city. The dainty building, overwhelmed by the surrounding Senate office monoliths to its west, was built in 1800 by Robert

The supremacy of the Supreme Court

The Supreme Court was established by the Constitution to oversee the balance between the federal government and the states, and between the legislative and executive branches of government. It comprises nine justices who are appointed by the president and approved by the Senate. Once approved, the justices are in for life ("during good behavior," per the Constitution) and can only be removed by impeachment.

The Court (and the associated system of district courts) convened for the first time in February 1790. At the end of the following year, the ratification of the Bill of Rights in effect gave the Supreme Court an additional role: to defend the liberties enshrined in the Bill, directing the country as to what was and wasn't constitutional. However, it wasn't until 1803 and the case of *Marbury v Madison* that the Court's power of judicial review – the ability to declare a law or action of Congress or the president unconstitutional – was established. Since then, the Supreme Court has repeatedly shaped the country's social and political legacies by ruling on the constitutionality of subjects as diverse as slavery (in the 1857 Dred Scott case), segregation (1896's *Plessy v Ferguson*), civil rights (1954's *Brown v Board of Education*), abortion (1973's *Roe v Wade*), and freedom of the press (Pentagon papers in the early 1970s).

Because the country relies on an eighteenth-century document as the basis of its twenty-first-century political structure, the Supreme Court has its work cut out providing interpretive rulings. In practice, this leads to a great deal of arguing in front of the Supreme Court justices. That said, even though it's the country's final court of appeal, each year the Supreme Court takes only about five percent of the seven thousand cases lower courts ask it to hear. (The cases chosen are determined by the so-called "Rule of Four," meaning at least four justices have agreed to hear a case.) The Court grants these cases *certiorari* – the prospect of making a case "more certain" by agreeing to review it – and then hears written and oral arguments. After the deliberations, one justice is made responsible for writing the opinion, which serves as the latest interpretation of that particular constitutional issue. The justices don't

Sewall and rented in 1801 to Albert Gallatin, Treasury secretary to presidents Jefferson and Madison. Gallatin participated in negotiations for the Louisiana Purchase (1803), which was signed in one of the front rooms. In 1814, while the Capitol was burning, a group of soldiers under Commander Joshua Barney retreated to the house and fired upon the British. This resistance, however, only stirred the British to set the house ablaze. Unlike the Capitol, it wasn't too badly damaged; enough of it survived, in fact, for Gallatin to negotiate the war-ending Treaty of Ghent here. The treaty was actually signed in the Octagon, in nearby Foggy Bottom.

In 1929, the house was sold to the **National Woman's Party** and was home for many years to Alice Paul, the party's founder and author of the 1923 Equal Rights Amendment. The house still serves as party headquarters and maintains a museum and gallery dedicated to the country's women's and suffrage movements. A short film fills in some of the background of the house, a short tour makes much of the period furnishings, and the carriage house contains the country's earliest feminist library. Portraits, busts, and photographs of all the best-known activists adorn the halls and wall, starting in the lobby with sculptor Adelaide Johnson's busts of Susan B. Anthony, Elizabeth Cady Stanton, and Lucretia Mott, the trio that Johnson would memorialize with her sculpture *Suffrage Monument* in the Capitol (see pp.103–104). Other mementos include the desks of both Alice Paul and Susan B. Anthony, and the banner used to picket the White House during World War I when the call for universal suffrage reached its loudest pitch.

all have to agree: they can concur in the majority decision even if they don't accept all the arguments, or they can produce a dissenting opinion, which might be cited in future challenges to particular laws.

The makeup of the Supreme Court is of the utmost relevance to the opinions it will produce. Not surprisingly, presidents over the years have thought it useful to have politically sympathetic justices on the bench and have made appointments accordingly. But things don't always go as planned: the most famous example of this is President Eisenhower's selection of California governor Earl Warren to the bench in the 1950s. Instead of ruling like a rock-ribbed Republican, as Ike thought he would, Warren ended up being perhaps the most liberal-minded chief justice in the court's history. Also, the process is tinged with an element of chance, dependent upon the longevity of the incumbent justices: both Eisenhower and Richard Nixon appointed four justices, while Jimmy Carter appointed none. Controversial Supreme Court nominees can be rejected by the Senate, as were two of Nixon's plus Reagan's ultra-conservative hopeful, Robert Bork. George H. W. Bush's second appointee, Clarence Thomas, only scraped through after the highly publicized hearings following lawyer Anita Hill's allegations of sexual harassment.

Whichever way the Court leans, and despite its firm roots in the Constitution, it depends ultimately on the mood of the people for its authority. If it produces opinions that are overwhelmingly opposed by inferior courts, or by the president or Congress, there's not much it can do to enforce them. Indeed, Congress has the constitutional right (Article 3, Section 2) to restrict the Court's jurisdiction – a notion proposed by FDR when he tired of the Court's constant interference with his New Deal legislation. Perhaps unique among federal institutions, the Supreme Court has generally retained the respect of the American people for its perceived impartiality in defending the Constitution against partisan politics, even if that was temporarily threatened by its decision in *Bush v Gore*, which determined the 2000 presidential election.

Before visiting, it may be worth a phone call to verify the site's accessibility. The building is in line for an overdue renovation to preserve its internal structure and may be periodically closed in coming years.

Folger Shakespeare Library

201 E Capitol St ☎202/544-7077, ⊛www.folger.edu; Union Station or Capitol South Metro. Mon–Sat 10am–4pm.

The renowned **Folger Shakespeare Library**, on the south side of the Supreme Court, is an unexpected burst of Art Deco architecture, with a sparkling white marble facade split by geometric window grilles, and panel reliefs depicting scenes from the Bard's plays. The look inside, however, is quite different: a dark oak-paneled Elizabethan Great Hall features carved lintels, stained glass, Tudor roses, and a sculpted ceiling.

Founded in 1932, the Folger holds more than 300,000 books, manuscripts, paintings, and engravings and honors Shakespeare's work and culture. The **Great Hall** displays changing exhibitions about the playwright and various Elizabethan themes; the reproduction Elizabethan Theater hosts lectures and readings as well as medieval and Renaissance music concerts by the Folger Consort (see p.296); and an Elizabethan garden on the east lawn grows herbs and flowers common in the sixteenth century.

It's a good idea to visit when a free ninety-minute **guided tour** is being offered (Mon–Fri 11am, Sat 11am & 1pm); every third Saturday (April–Oct

10am & 11am), a guide also lectures on the intricacies of the garden. The library itself – another sixteenth-century reproduction – is open to the public only during the Folger's annual celebration of Shakespeare's birthday (usually the Saturday nearest April 23). In the **Shakespeare Gallery**, next to the Great Hall, there's a permanent multimedia exhibit entitled "The Seven Ages of Man," which offers a computer-assisted glimpse of the Folger's holdings and the intricacies of Shakespeare's life and work.

Finally, as you'd expect, the **gift shop** sells everything from the Stratford lad's plays to jokey T-shirts based on Shakespearean quotations.

The Library of Congress

Jefferson Bldg, 1st St SE at Independence Ave ☎202/707-8000, ⊛www.loc.gov; Capitol South Metro. Mon–Sat 10am–5.30pm.

The **Library of Congress** is the nation's official copyright office and the world's largest library (it's said that, on average, ten items per minute are added to its holdings). Books are just part of its unimaginably large collection: 128 million items, from books, maps, and manuscripts to movies, musical instruments, and photographs, are kept on 530 miles of shelving spread out over three buildings – where they stay, as the Library of Congress does not circulate its materials beyond the complex.

When Congress convened in 1800 in the new, if incomplete, Capitol, it was considered imperative to fund a library for the use of its members. Five thousand dollars was made available to buy books for a Library of Congress, which was housed in a small room in the original north wing. Calamitously, the carefully chosen reference works were all lost when the British burned the Capitol in 1814, an act that prompted **Thomas Jefferson** to offer his considerable **personal library** as a replacement; this collection comprised more than six thousand volumes, which Jefferson had accumulated during fifty years of service at home and abroad, picking up, he said, "everything which related to America." A year later, Congress voted to buy this stupendous private collection for almost $24,000 – a massive sum at the time.

Jefferson's sale laid the foundation for a well-rounded collection, but another fire in 1851, this time accidental, caused severe damage. From that point, the library was forced to rely on donations and select purchases until it received two major boosts. In 1866 it acquired the thousands of books hitherto held by the **Smithsonian Institution**, and in 1870 it was declared the national copyright library – in theory, adding to its shelves a copy of every book published and registered in the United States (though the odd title sometimes escapes its grasp). Not surprisingly, the library soon outgrew its original home, and in 1897 the exuberantly eclectic **Thomas Jefferson Building** opened across from the Capitol, complete with domed octagonal Reading Room and adorned with hundreds of mosaics, murals, and sculptures. The building was projected to have enough space to house the library until 1975, but by the 1930s it was already too full. In the surrounding blocks, the **John Adams Building** was erected in 1939, followed by the **James Madison Memorial Building** in 1980.

Visiting the Library

The magnificent **Jefferson Building** is the library's unquestioned centerpiece. At its visitor center (ground-level entrance on 1st St SE) you can learn about the building's highlights and get a calendar of events for upcoming concerts and lectures. You're allowed to wander around inside, but you'd do well to catch one of the free library **tours** (Mon–Sat 10.30am, 11.30am, 1.30pm, 2.30pm & 3.30pm; last tour Sat at 2.30pm) or watch the continuously running twelve-minute **film** on the history of the library.

The Renaissance Revival building is anchored by its **Great Hall**, rich with marble walls and numerous medallions, inscriptions, murals, and inlaid mosaics. A treasured copy of the **Gutenberg Bible** is on display, while upstairs the visitor's gallery overlooks the octagonal marble-and-stained-glass **Main Reading Room**, a beautiful space whose columns support a 125-foot-high dome. The mural in the dome canopy, the **Progress of Civilization**, represents the twelve nations said to have contributed most to world knowledge.

The library's huge collection is showcased on the second floor in the "**American Treasures**" gallery, where themed cabinets – "Civil Society," "Mapping," "Technology," and so on – display some of the nation's most significant documents. The exhibits are periodically rotated, but you may see such diverse pieces as Walt Whitman's Civil War notebooks, the original typescript of Martin Luther King Jr's "I have a dream" speech, Martha Jefferson's household inventory (with a record of ducks and geese butchered), and numerous music scores, historic photographs, early recordings, magazines, and baseball cards. Changing exhibitions of especially significant documents, such as those associated with Washington, Lincoln, and Jefferson, receive central billing, while other exhibits are downstairs on the ground floor. There, the **Gershwin Room** preserves George's Steinway and Ira's typewriter, and the **Swann Gallery** puts on temporary shows extracted from the library's unrivaled collection of American caricature and cartoon art.

Using the Library

Anyone over 18 carrying photo ID can use the library, and some one million readers and visitors do so each year. To find what you're looking for, head for the information desks or touch-screen computers in the Jefferson or Madison buildings. The **Main Reading Room** in the Jefferson Building is just one of 22 reading rooms, and the rules are the same in each. This is a research library, which means you can't take books out; in some reading rooms you have to order what you want from the stacks. You can also access papers, maps, and musical scores, and the advent of the **National Digital Library** means that many now come in machine-readable format (the desks in the Main Reading Room are wired for laptops and there are CD-ROM indexes). Major exhibitions, as well as prints, photographs, films and speeches, are also available online. For research advice, call ☎202/707-6500; for reading room hours and locations, call ☎202/707-6400.

Pennsylvania Avenue SE

To most visitors, the section of **Pennsylvania Avenue** running southeast from the Capitol will be much less familiar than the stretch running northwest from it, where the presidential inaugural parade is held. Still, over the course of six blocks or so, you can find some of DC's more appealing ethnic restaurants and noteworthy bars, and a gentrifying scene that attracts increasing numbers of yuppies looking for affordable digs. There are also restored townhouses and splashes of green at places like Folger Square, Seward Square, and Marion Park. Although you shouldn't wander around the district south of E Street on your own, two churches there stand out and can be safely visited in daylight The utilitarian red-brick **Ebenezer United Methodist Church**, 420 D St SE (Mon–Fri 8.30am–3pm, Sun service 11am; ☎202/544-1415), is the neighborhood's oldest black congregation. Founded in 1805, the church was the site of DC's first public school for black people; it was a short-lived affair (1864–65), but a pioneering one, since the teachers were paid out of federal funds. The current building dates from 1897, and if you call in advance someone will be on hand to show you around (otherwise you can check it out on your own). On the 4th Street side stands a wooden model of "Little Ebenezer," the original frame church that stood on this site. Farther south, but unlikely to be open, **Christ Church** at 620 G St SE is an early work (1806) by Capitol architect Benjamin Latrobe, notable mainly to architecture buffs for its charming Gothic Revival facade.

Eastern Market

7th and C sts SE ⊕www.easternmarket.net. Tues–Fri 10am–6pm, Sat 8am–6pm, Sun 8am–4pm.

If you're taking a stroll in the East Capitol neighborhood, you may wonder what all the hubbub is surrounding what looks like an ancient brick train station. Upon entering, you'll find that this forbidding, windowless 1873 structure has nothing to do with trains, but is instead home to **Eastern Market**, in continuous operation since the nineteenth century. Designed by Adolph Cluss with less flamboyance than his Arts and Industries Building on the Mall, the building hosts a welter of vendors doing roaring business selling seafood, deli meats, sides of beef, and other foodstuffs. The stalls spill onto the sidewalk on the weekend, when you can buy produce and flowers (Sat 10am–5pm), or antiques and junk (Sun 10am–5pm). On either side, along 7th Street, delis, coffee shops, antique stores, and clothes shops make it one of the Hill's more appealing hangouts.

East Capitol Street and Stanton Park

East Capitol Street, one of the city's four axes and one of the first streets on the Hill to be settled, starts between the Supreme Court and the Library of Congress's Jefferson Building. For its first ten or so blocks, its wide, tree-lined reach is peppered with wooden and brick townhouses, some dating from before the Civil War, others sporting the trademark late Victorian turrets and "rusticated" (roughened) stonework. The typical row house at 316 A St NE was home to black orator and writer **Frederick Douglass** when he first moved to the capital in 1870 to take up the editorship of the *New National Era*, a newspaper championing the rights of African-Americans. His family owned no. 318, too, and Douglass lived here with his first wife, Anna, until 1877, when they moved to the grander Cedar Hill in Anacostia (see Chapter 3). From here, it's just a few blocks north to **Stanton Park**, where there's an equestrian statue of Revolutionary War general **Nathaniel Greene**, who had a significant role in the 1781 battle of Yorktown, which basically guaranteed America's independence from Britain.

Lincoln Park

In 1876, on the eleventh anniversary of Abraham Lincoln's assassination, the slain sixteenth president was honoured in **Lincoln Park**, farther along East Capitol Street between 11th and 13th streets. In the presence of President Grant, **Frederick Douglass** read aloud the Emancipation Proclamation to the assembled thousands as the "Freedom Memorial" was unveiled in the center of the park. To contemporary eyes the memorial may seem a bit paternalistic

– the bronze statue portrays Lincoln, proclamation in one hand, standing over a kneeling slave, exhorting him to rise – but it was actually daring for its day. Working from a photograph, sculptor Thomas Ball re-created in the slave the features of **Archer Alexander**, the last man to be seized under the Fugitive Slave Act, which empowered slaveowners to capture escaped slaves even if they fled to free states. Under Lincoln's gaze, Alexander is breaking his own shackles.

It wasn't until a century later, in 1974, that a monument was erected in DC specifically to honor the achievements of a black American, or, indeed, a woman. Facing Lincoln, across the park, is a memorial remembering **Mary McLeod Bethune**, educator, women's rights leader, and special advisor to Franklin Delano Roosevelt. Robert Berks, also responsible for the 8-foot head of JFK in the Kennedy Center, depicts Bethune leaning on her cane, reaching out to two children and passing on, as the inscription says, her legacy to youth. (Across town near Logan Circle stands another memorial to Bethune, the Bethune Council House; see p.186.)

The neighborhood degenerates east of the park. In the daylight, peer up East Capitol Street to **RFK Stadium** in the distance (see p.315), but don't head there on foot.

Union Station and around

At Capitol Hill's northern limit, **Union Station** stands at the center of a re-development plan that was designed to revitalize a formerly neglected part of the city. In addition to the station, try to make time for the Smithsonian's **National Postal Museum**, located just opposite, which should appeal to casual visitors as well as those obsessed by philately.

Union Station

On the border of the north side of Capitol Hill and the eastern fringe of Old Downtown is DC's magnificent **Union Station**, 50 Massachusetts Ave NE. Some 20,000 square feet larger than New York City's Grand Central Terminal, the huge Beaux Arts building is alive with skylights, marble detail, and statuary, culminating in a 96-foot-high coffered ceiling whose model was no less than ancient Rome's Baths of Diocletian. Outside, the facade is studded with allegorical statuary and etched with prolix texts extolling the virtues of trade, travel, and technology. On the east side of the building are stations for the Metro, Amtrak, Virginia Rail Express, and MARC; on the lower gallery there's a food court and a movie theater; and on the upper floor are stores, restaurants, car rental agencies, and ticket counters. Back on the east side, near Gate D, is a statue honoring A. Phillip Randolph, founder of the Brotherhood of Sleeping Car Porters union and one of the prime movers in the 1963 March on Washington for Jobs and Freedom.

The station was built in 1908 after the McMillan Commission decreed an end to the chaos caused by the separate lines and stations that crisscrossed the city. Its architect, **Daniel H. Burnham**, a member of the commission, produced a classic building of monumental proportions to house the train sheds and waiting rooms. For five decades, Union Station sat at the head of an expansive railroad network that linked the country to its capital: hundreds of thousands of people arrived in the city by train, catching their first glimpse of the Capitol dome through the station's great arched doors – just as the wide-eyed James Stewart does at the beginning of Frank Capra's 1939 film *Mr Smith Goes to Washington*. Incoming presidents arrived at Union Station by train for their inaugurations (Truman was the last) and were met in the specially installed Presidential Waiting Room; some, like FDR and Eisenhower, left in a casket after lying in state at the Capitol. Come the 1960s, though, and with the gradual depletion of train services, Union Station was left unkempt and underfunded. An ill-conceived scheme turned it into a visitor's center during the 1976 Bicentennial, and it wasn't fully restored until 1988.

It's also worth taking a turn outside in Union Station Plaza, the landscaped approach to the station that stretches all the way down to the Capitol grounds. The **Columbus Memorial Fountain** in front of the station was dedicated in 1912 and features a statue of the Genovese explorer standing on the prow of a ship, between two lions and male and female figures representing the old and new worlds. A replica of Philadelphia's **Liberty Bell** stands nearby.

National Postal Museum

Massachusetts Ave NE at N Capitol Ave ☎202/357-2700, ◉www.si.edu/postal; Union Station Metro. Daily 10am–5.30pm.

Having finished the design for Union Station, Burnham turned his attention to a new **City Post Office** opposite the station to replace the Romanesque colossus in the Federal Triangle. Built between 1911 and 1914, it was a working post office until 1986, when it was renovated at a cost of $200 million, in part to house the **National Postal Museum**. (A research library and a brew-pub are also in the renovated structure.) Before you descend to the lower-level galleries, take time for a quick look at the building itself, whose white Italian marble reaches are some of the most impressive in the city. Also, look up and read how the postal service is "Messenger of Sympathy and Love. . .Consoler of the Lonely. . . Enlarger of the Common Life" and "Carrier of News and Knowledge," among other claims.

The collection

The museum is one of the Smithsonian's quiet triumphs. The collection, from the National Museum of American History, includes sixteen million artifacts, but since many of these are stamps, only a few of which are on display, it's not that daunting a show. Indeed, the museum's strength is in its selectivity, judiciously placing the history of the mail service within the context of the history of the United States itself.

Escalators down to the galleries dump you in "**Moving the Mail**," which features soaring models of early mail planes – from a 1911 Wiseman-Cooke craft that vaguely resembles the Wright Flyer to a 1939 Stinson Reliant monoplane – as well as an 1851 mail coach with bourgeois riders inside, and a walkthrough Southern Pacific rail car with artifacts and a video on display. Beyond here is "**Binding the Nation**," which begins with the **first postal route**, the seventeenth-century King's Best Highway between New York and Boston – a dark and spooky tour through a primeval wood. The story continues with small models of steamships and clipper ships, and a crude "mud wagon" that did the literal dirty work of nineteenth-century mail delivery. Saddles and spittoons, among other artifacts, represent the relay-rider system of the famed **Pony Express**, which lasted for only two years (1860–61); although it cut mail delivery times in half (from San Francisco to New York in thirteen days), the founding partners lost $30 on every letter carried. In the end, without government backing, the private enterprise collapsed. This exhibit concludes with a sobering reminder of the modern dangers of sorting the mail in the wake of terrorism and anthrax-related fears. Elsewhere in the museum are other oddments related to postal-service history. The most interesting of these include a recreation of a 1916 Pennsylvania postal cage, weird and wonderful rural mailboxes (including one made from car mufflers in the shape of a tin man), a paddle punch used to fumigate letters during Philadelphia's 1890 yellow fever outbreak, and a winter-weather mail car with track wheels and skis attached. Only in "**Stamps and Stories**" do you get a look at the museum's philatelic collection (up until this point, there's barely a stamp in sight). Here you'll find some splendid curiosities as well as frequently rotated exhibitions; you might see anything from ultra-rare vintage stamps to detailed coverage of famous series, like Ducks of America.

Before leaving, you can print out your own free, **personalized postcard** from the machines in the lobby, then buy a stamp in the stamp store and mail it home.

The Waterfront and around

M ost visitors to Washington DC spend much, if not all, of their time on the National Mall and Capitol Hill, so it's not surprising that other areas in the vicinity are often ignored. The **Waterfront** region south of the Mall, along the Potomac and Anacostia rivers, is one such spot and it's easy to understand why: this vast terrain's assorted sights are unified by little other than their proximity to the water, and few decent food and drink options exist in the spaces between. But if you have a day or so to spare, several places are easily toured and well worth a look, most prominently the United States Holocaust Memorial Museum and the Bureau of Printing and Engraving, just a few blocks from the Mall; the Potomac waterfront's marinas and fish market; the Navy Museum with its cache of nautical artifacts; and the Anacostia Museum and Frederick Douglass National Historic Site, in the historic Anacostia community. Much of the **Southwest** area around the Potomac's Washington Channel is accessible by public transit, but a bigger effort will be required to reach the limited attractions in the dicier **Southeast** neighborhoods along the Anacostia River. Visitors are advised to head directly to the individual sights listed there – and then come straight back again.

Some history

For a century after the city was founded, DC's nearest accessible riverbanks (in today's West Potomac Park) were too marshy and malarial to develop. The only practicable wharves and piers were those built along the Channel, but they, too, stagnated and only began to flourish after the Tidal Basin was created in 1882.

Despite the undeveloped character of the nearby river, Southwest thrived as a fashionable neighborhood in the early nineteenth century because it was close to the Capitol. But in the 1870s, the railroad arrived and sliced its way through the area, diminishing its social cachet and causing the wealthy to flee north. The people left behind were mostly poor blacks who worked at the goods yards, storage depots, and wharves. The work eventually dried up, the swamp–ridden housing became increasingly dilapidated, and by the 1920s the area had degenerated into a notorious slum.

The US government eventually recognized the potential to create a central-ized business district in Southwest. Low-rent housing was demolished and families were displaced to make room for federal agencies like the Department of Agriculture. More buildings were added in the 1930s and 1960s, and the rather haphazardly developed commercial buildings and piers that lined the north bank of the Channel were redeveloped to lure visitors.

Along the Potomac River

The main course of the Potomac River is separated from the Southwest and Waterfront developments by the Washington Channel and East Potomac Park, which begins south of the Tidal Basin and continues down to the junction of the Anacostia River south of Fort McNair. The park itself is pleasant enough – walkable, with nice views across to Virginia, plus there are tennis courts, fishing grounds, and a public pool, though it offers little of interest beyond these things. Rather, the area's limited attractions lie along the Washington Channel, starting just east of the Tidal Basin and south of the Mall, where the **Holocaust Museum** and **Bureau of Engraving and Printing** are always major destinations for visitors. Continuing southeast, the **Fish Wharf** is a favorite spot to buy a soft-shelled crab or two, and there are a few pockets of interesting architecture here and there. However, on the streets just inland, the massive plazas and superstructures housing the federal bureaucracy are drab and inhumanly scaled, and of interest only to rabid fans of mid-twentieth-century modernist architecture. On weekdays, there's little life here after 6pm, and on weekends there's even less.

South of the Mall: the federal buildings

The federal government's grunt work is done in concrete fortresses just south of the National Mall. Almost all the agencies here are bounded by Independence Avenue, 3rd Street, E Street, and 14th Street, and are served by two Metro stations: Federal Center SW and L'Enfant Plaza. The block between 3rd and 4th streets is taken up by the hulking **Department of Health and Human Services** – the only federal building in the area open to the public, and home to the government's **Voice of America** offices (free 40min tours Mon–Fri 10.30am, 1.30pm & 2.30pm, reservations required; ☎202/619-3919, ⓦwww .voa.gov). The entrance is around the back, on C Street between 3rd and 4th.

The VOA is one of the world's biggest international broadcasters. It was established in 1942 as part of the war effort and given its own charter in 1960, as part of the US Information Agency, to transmit programs overseas that promote US values and culture. It's still a powerful propaganda machine, which is why its broadcasts have often been jammed by various disaffected foreign powers. Guided tours walk you through the studios from where broadcasts are made in 53 languages and transmitted to 91 million listeners in 120 countries. One place you won't hear the VOA, however, is in Washington DC – or anywhere else in the nation for that matter: a 1948 act prohibits the government from proselytizing to its citizens by radio.

The Southwest's other federal buildings occupy a no-man's-land between 4th and 14th streets. Apparently it wasn't for want of trying that the area appears so dreary: the Department of Transportation (between D and E at 7th) was designed by **Edward Durrell Stone**, who managed to make the Kennedy Center (see pp.149–152) stand out in similarly unpromising surroundings, and

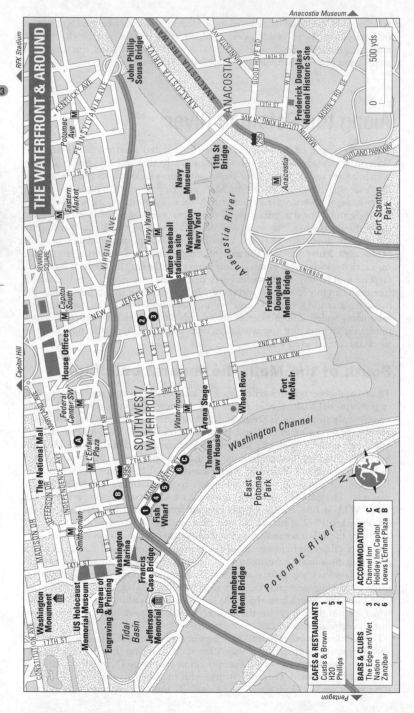

THE WATERFRONT & AROUND

Anacostia Museum ▲

▲ RFK Stadium

John Phillip Sousa Bridge

ANACOSTIA FREEWAY

Frederick Douglass National Historic Site

ANACOSTIA

295

SUITLAND PARKWAY

Fort Stanton Park

Anacostia M

GOOD HOPE RD

MORRIS RD SE

MINNESOTA AVE

16TH ST

13TH ST

W ST

MARTIN LUTHER KING JR AVE

11th St Bridge

Navy Museum

Washington Navy Yard

Anacostia River

Frederick Douglass Meml Bridge

ROBBINS ROAD

Fort McNair

2ND ST NW

4TH AVE SW

Wheat Row

Washington Channel

East Potomac Park

Potomac River

Rochambeau Meml Bridge

N

Z

Future baseball stadium site

Navy Yard M

M

3RD ST

2ND ST SE

1ST ST

SOUTH CAPITOL ST

NEW JERSEY AVE

M Capitol South

House Offices

SEWARD SQUARE

KENTUCKY AVE

PENNSYLVANIA AVE

Potomac Ave M

Eastern Market M

11TH ST

VIRGINIA AVE

M Federal Center SW

Capitol Hill ▲

MARYLAND AVE

The National Mall

JEFFERSON DR

INDEPENDENCE AVE

E ST SW

D ST

Smithsonian M

12TH ST

9TH ST

7TH ST

L'Enfant Plaza M

A

B

395

MAINE AVE

WATER ST

SOUTHWEST/ WATERFRONT

Waterfront M

3RD ST

4TH ST

6TH ST

Arena Stage

Thomas Law House

Fish Wharf

1 4 5

6 C

2 3

Washington Marina

Francis Case Bridge

MADISON DR

CONSTITUTION AVE

14TH ST

17TH ST

Washington Monument

US Holocaust Memorial Museum

Bureau of Engraving & Printing

Tidal Basin

Jefferson Memorial

▲ Pentagon

0   500 yds

CAFÉS & RESTAURANTS
Custis & Brown   1
H2O   5
Phillips   4

BARS & CLUBS
The Edge and Wet   3
Nation   2
Zanzibar   6

ACCOMMODATION
Channel Inn   C
Holiday Inn Capitol   A
Loews L'Enfant Plaza   B

even **I.M. Pei** has had a hand in some of the various plazas and streetscapes. The closest thing here to modern swagger, though, is the curving double-Y-shaped concrete structure from the late 1960s that holds the Department of Housing and Urban Development (D St between 7th and 9th), whose architect, **Marcel Breuer**, gave more than a nod to his Bauhaus origins. The only semblance of old-fashioned style emerges in the oldest (and westernmost) agency, the Department of Agriculture (Independence Ave between 12th and 14th): sited here since 1905, the original building on the north side of Independence Avenue is connected by slender arches to the much larger 1930s Neoclassical structure across the avenue.

Beyond the buildings themselves, the main focus of Southwest development in the 1960s and 1970s was **L'Enfant Plaza**, at D Street between 9th and 10th streets, where there's now a central Metro station. It's easy to feel a twinge of sympathy for Pierre L'Enfant – alone among the city's spiritual founders, he gets not a monument but a barren 1960s concrete square and subway station as his memorial.

United States Holocaust Memorial Museum

14th St between C St and Independence Ave SW ☏202/488-0400, ⊛www.ushmm.org; Smithsonian Metro. Daily 10am–5.30pm.

One of the city's most disturbing and unforgettable experiences is visiting the **United States Holocaust Memorial Museum**, which presents an intimate look at the persecution and murder of six million Jews by the Nazis. Upon entry, you are given a card containing biographical information about a real Holocaust victim whose fate you then follow throughout the museum. This approach personalizes the genocide, but the exhibits also emphasize the wider historical machinations that allowed Hitler to assume power in the first place. The solemn mood throughout is reflected by the museum's stark architecture and evocative design: half-lit chambers, a floor of ghetto cobblestones, an obscenely cramped barracks building, and an external roofline that resembles the guard towers of a concentration camp. Despite its bleak subject matter, the museum is one of the more popular (and crowded) attractions in DC. You don't need tickets to see the special exhibitions or to enter the museum and the interactive Wexner Learning Center, but you do need tickets with fixed entry times to get into the permanent exhibit, "The Holocaust." **Tickets** are free but limited to four per person. You can pick them up beginning at 10am daily at the 14th Street entrance, but be sure to arrive before mid-morning or they'll likely be sold out. Advance tickets can be purchased through Tickets .com (☏1-800/400-9373).

The **permanent exhibition** spans the museum's second, third, and fourth floors; you start at the top and work your way down. The main galleries are not considered suitable for children under the age of 11, but the feature "Remember the Children: Daniel's Story" is designed for those over the age of 8. The 14th Street entrance is at first-floor level, where you'll find the **information desk**, children's exhibit, and museum shop. From there stairs lead down to the auditoriums and special exhibition area at the concourse level. The amount of items on display requires most visitors to spend at least three hours in the museum. There are rest areas throughout, and a contemplative **Hall of Remembrance** is on the second floor. The **Wexner Learning Center**, on the same floor, has computer stations that allow you to access text, photographs, films, and other resources. There's also a **café** (8.30am–4.30pm) in the Ross Administrative Center, at 100 Raoul Wallenberg Place, outside the museum's 15th Street entrance.

The fourth floor

The first rooms on the fourth floor use storyboards, newspaper articles, and film clips to chronicle the "**Nazi Assault**" and rise to power from 1933 to 1939. What begins as a boycott of Jewish businesses and book-burning quickly leads to the organized looting of Jewish shops and the parading of German women who had "defiled" their race by associating with Jews. From there, anyone who didn't fit the Nazi ideal, like gays (who were forced to wear an identifying pink triangle), blacks, gypsies, and Freemasons were persecuted and imprisoned. Beyond a glass wall etched with the names of the hundreds of Eastern European Jewish communities wiped off the map forever, a towering stack of photographs from 1890 to 1941 records the breadth of life in just one of them – the *shtetl* (community) of Eishishok, in what's now Lithuania. The pictures vividly show street scenes, ceremonies, and parties, as well as families and individuals.

The third floor

The third floor covers the era of Hitler's "**Final Solution**," beginning with the first gassing of Jews at a death camp in Poland in December 1941. Jews were transported to the camps from the ghettos in which they'd been incarcerated, and although there was resistance to the Nazis in the ghettos, this was ultimately futile. Some 33,000 Jews were slaughtered at Babi Yar in Kiev following the German invasion of the Ukraine capital in 1941. Although many Jews had fled the city before occupation, the ones who remained were murdered in retaliation for explosions, presumably set off by Soviet engineers, that blew up German headquarters and other buildings. In the Warsaw uprising of 1943, the resistance held out for a month despite having no real weapons or supplies. Eventually all the surviving Jews were brought to the camps in packed freight cars; you can walk through one here that stands on railroad tracks taken from the camp at Treblinka.

The most harrowing part of the exhibition deals with life and death within the concentration camps. A pile of blankets, umbrellas, scissors, cutlery, and other personal effects taken from the hundreds of thousands of prisoners underscores that they expected to be put to work but were instead mostly gassed within hours. A re-created barracks building from Auschwitz provides the backdrop for the oral memories of some survivors, as well as a shocking film of gruesome medical experiments carried out on selected prisoners.

As the museum clearly – and uncomfortably – shows, America knew of Auschwitz as early as May 1944 but, despite demands to bomb it, Assistant Secretary of War John J. McCloy argued that its destruction "might provoke even more vindictive action by the Germans." Survivors later testified that they would have welcomed such terminal liberation: "Every bomb that exploded... gave us new confidence in life," records one witness. The third floor ends with photographic coverage of the Eishishok *shtetl* and its experience with the Final Solution. In contrast to the photos on the fourth floor, these pictures show the destruction, in just two days, of a town and community that had existed for more than nine hundred years, and the slaughter of its residents.

The second floor

As the Nazi front collapsed across Europe during 1945, many groups became involved in efforts to aid the Jews. The "**Last Chapter**" on the second floor recounts the heroism of individuals and the response of certain governments (the Danish in particular). Much of the floor details the Allied forces' liberation of the camps: film reels show German guards being forced to bury mountains of bodies in mass graves, while locals were made to tour the camps to witness the extent of the horror. Although Nazis were later prosecuted during the Nuremberg trials, most of those responsible for the planning, maintenance, and administration of the camps were never tried; thousands of others were treated leniently or acquitted altogether. In a few cases, former Nazis like Werner von Braun – the creator of the Nazi's V-2 missile that was manufactured at forced-labor camps – were hired by the US and USSR governments during the Cold War. Von Braun went on to develop missiles and rockets for the US after World War II and become director of NASA's Marshall Flight Center.

The Bureau of Engraving and Printing

14th and C sts SW ℡202/622-2000, ⊛www.moneyfactory.com; Smithsonian Metro. Mon–Fri 10am–2pm.

The bland bureaucratic buildings found east of 14th Street and south of Independence Avenue are virtually indistinguishable from each other, with one exception – the **Bureau of Engraving and Printing**, where US currency, government securities, and postage stamps are created. Although its name is a bit dry, the Bureau offers one of DC's most popular tours; each year nearly half a million people take the twenty-minute tour of what is, effectively, a large printing plant. That may not sound like an attraction of interest, but keep in mind that the presses here crank out millions of dollars in currency every day, and $120 billion a year.

The Bureau was established in 1862, when President Lincoln empowered six employees to initiate business in the attic of the Treasury Building, sealing up blocks of $1 and $2 bills that had been printed by private banks. By 1877, all **US currency** was produced by the Bureau, which moved into its current home in 1914. Today, almost three thousand employees work either here or at a second plant in Fort Worth, Texas. US currency has undergone significant changes in the last 140 years; huge denominations like the $50,000 bill, for example, have long since disappeared from general circulation. In recent years, the $20, $50, and $100 bills have seen their standard, drab-green color improved with soft pastels, and hidden security stamps and watermarks have been embedded in an attempt to thwart would-be counterfeiters.

Between March and August you must pick up tickets for **tours** in advance from 10am to 2pm, but you can, and should, start waiting in line at 8am, as tickets are often gone by 11.30am. The rest of the year you can show up later, just before 10am, without tickets, though you'll still have to wait in line. A forty-minute Congressional/VIP tour that provides an in-depth, behind-the-scenes look at the plant is available for those who make arrangements through their representative's office (Mon–Fri 8.15am & 8.45am, also May–Aug 4pm). Contact the tour office at ℡202/874-2330 or 1-866/874-2330 for any tour information. If you care only to drop by the **visitors center** – perhaps to purchase an overpriced bag of shredded currency that you can send to the folks back home – it's open daily from 8.30am to 3pm.

The tour

The Department's history unfolds in a video that plays in the main corridor as you wait in line for the tour to begin. What everyone really wants to see, though, is the dough, which you glimpse during the march through claustrophobic viewing galleries looking down on the printing presses. The making of US currency is a surprisingly low-tech operation: hand-engraved dyes are used to create intaglio steel plates, from which the bills are printed in

△ Catch of the day at the fish market

sheets of 32, checked for defects, and loaded into large barrows. On a separate press, they're then overprinted with serial numbers and seals, sliced up into single bills by ordinary paper-cutters, and stacked into "bricks" of four thousand notes before being sent out to the twelve Federal Reserve Districts, which issue the notes to local banks. Key facts, fired out amid lame jokes by the guides, include the tidbit that the bills aren't made from paper at all, but from a more durable fabric that's three-quarters cotton. Even so, the most used note, the dollar, lasts only eighteen months on average. Those whose job it is to spot flaws in the currency appear to visitors as a line of people with their heads in their hands gazing at bundles of notes. These workers undergo a rigorous two-year apprenticeship, scrutinize one sheet of bills per second, and log eight-hour days with two twenty-minute breaks and a thirty-minute lunch. All but one in a thousand misprinted bills are caught.

Benjamin Banneker Memorial Circle

From the printing plant, following D Street east to 10th Street and south over the freeway, you'll reach **Benjamin Banneker Memorial Circle**, where there's a viewpoint over the Washington Channel and the rest of the Waterfront. A memorial and fountain here honors Banneker, an African-American born in Maryland in 1731 to a former slave. Almost entirely self-taught, Banneker distinguished himself as a mathematician, astronomer, and inventor before being invited, at the age of 60, to assist in the surveying of the land for the new capital. He also published several editions of a successful almanac and spent the last years before his death in 1806 corresponding with Thomas Jefferson, who he hoped would abandon his prejudices against the intelligence of African-Americans.

The Washington Channel and around

The developed waterfront of the Potomac's **Washington Channel** is accessible by Metro at 4th and M streets SW. Most people come here to eat seafood at one of the **restaurants** along Maine Avenue or Water Street SW, west of 7th; all have terraces and patios with views across to **East Potomac Park**. Otherwise, the two main attractions here are near the towering Francis Case Bridge. The **Washington Marina**, filled with pricey nautical craft, provides a good backdrop for various summer fairs and events, though is typically of little interest to landlubbers. Adjacent is the **Fish Wharf** (daily 7.30am–8pm), with the oldest continuously operating fish market in the country. The fishmongers will do their best to sell you their wares, even if you're only browsing. Impressive displays include huge trays of Chesapeake Bay fish, shrimp, clams, oysters and, especially, Maryland blue crabs, which are available live or steamed. There's nowhere to sit and eat, but you can head to the waterside promenade for a picnic.

Further down Maine Avenue, east of 7th Street, the **Arena Stage** (see p.299) is one of the most accomplished playhouses in the city and provides a good target for theater lovers, while the **Thomas Law House**, N and 6th streets SW (c.1794–96), one of DC's oldest surviving townhouses, is worth a look for its stately Federal architecture. If you cut past here to 4th Street, you can see **Wheat Row** (1315–1321 4th St SW), a strip of Federal houses built around the same time and part of the Harbor Square residential development at 4th between N and O streets. The houses are striking for their elegant, early-American design, unique for surviving DC's 1960s urban renewal (compare them to their bland, modern surroundings), and unusual for being some of the first edifices built on speculation, with the promise of rising property values in the future.

Channel and river collide south of here with the spit of land occupied by the off–limits **Fort McNair**. Fortified in 1791, the base became home to the **Washington Arsenal** in 1804, though its buildings were blown up by the British in 1814 and later destroyed by an explosion that killed 21 people in 1864. At the **US Penitentiary**, built in the 1820s on the arsenal grounds, the conspirators in the Lincoln assassination were imprisoned, tried, and executed.

Along the Anacostia River

Unlike the Potomac, the **Anacostia River**'s waterfront has not been the subject of a redevelopment project. The river courses through run-down, impoverished **Southeast** Washington, just south of the US Capitol. The few attractions here are the **Navy Museum**, the **Frederick Douglass National Historic Site**, and the **Anacostia Museum** – a lesser-known member of the Smithsonian Institution family.

Washington Navy Yard

The **Washington Navy Yard** was one of the first naval yards in the country. Established in 1799, it has been in continuous operation ever since, excluding an interruption that began in 1812, when the commander burned the base to prevent the invading British Army from capturing it. Shipbuilding ceased here in 1874, but ordnance production continued until 1962. Since then the base has served as a naval supply and administrative center, and today would be of little or no interest were it not for its terrific Navy Museum. Before entering the Yard, you'll need to show photo ID to the guard at the gate (designed by Benjamin Latrobe in 1804) at 9th and M, just a few blocks east of the Navy Yard Metro station. As with all federal sites, call ahead to make sure it hasn't been closed for security reasons.

Navy Museum

805 Kidder Breese St SE ☏202/433-4882, ⊛www.history.navy.mil; Navy Yard Metro. Mon–Fri 9am–4pm, Sat & Sun 10am–5pm.

Unless you're an active member of the military, you must make reservations to visit the **Navy Museum**, housed in the Navy Yard's former gun factory in Building 76. The museum traces the history of the US Navy since it was created in 1794 in response to attacks on American ships by Barbary pirates. Displays include uniforms, ship figureheads, vicious cat-o'-nine-tail whips, and a walk-through frigate gun-deck. Separate galleries detail every US Naval conflict from the War of 1812 to the present day, while permanent exhibits highlight everything from US Polar explorations begun in the 1840s to the necessity of submarines in combat and intelligence operations. Also on display are the exploits of early naval hero Stephen Decatur, who captured three boats during hand-to-hand fighting at Tripoli in 1804, and whose house (see p.137) is one of DC's more estimable structures. The World War II displays are par-ticularly affecting; you can sit in anti-aircraft guns, watch crackly archive film footage, and view an account of the sinking of a PT 109 patrol boat by a Japanese destroyer on August 2, 1943. The boat's commander, John Fitzgerald Kennedy, towed the boat's badly burned engineer ashore, despite an injured back. Finally, the mildly diverting USS *Barry*, a destroyer docked outside the museum, has its mess room, bridge, and quarters open to the public.

Anacostia

On the south side of the Anacostia River, across from the Navy Yard, is Washington's most notorious neighborhood. **Anacostia**'s name derives from the area's original Native American inhabitants, the tobacco-growing Nacotchtanks, who were later called the Nacostines. The Nacotchtanks were supplanted by nineteenth-century merchants seeking homes close to the Capitol, who were in turn displaced in the 1850s by the white working and middle class encouraged to settle in what developers called Uniontown. The neighborhood thrived during post-Civil War Reconstruction, primarily due to the building of the 11th Street Bridge, which connected Anacostia with the rest of DC. But the "white flight" to the suburbs gathered speed in the 1950s, and by 1970 more than 95 percent of Anacostia's residents were black – and largely abandoned by the city authorities. The 1968 riots damaged much of the area's infrastructure and confidence, and the neighborhood still suffers grievously from underfunding, dilapidated housing, unemployment, and crime.

There are, of course, pockets with handsome old houses and revitalized commercial centers, but much of Anacostia is a dangerous scene for outsiders who don't know where they're going. The two attractions reviewed here are best reached by cab from Anacostia Metro station.

Frederick Douglass National Historic Site

1411 W St SE ☎202/426-5961, ⊛www.nps.gov/frdo. Daily: May–Sept 9am–5pm, Oct–April 9am–4pm.

Frederick Douglass – former slave, abolitionist leader, and blistering orator – was 60 years old when, in 1877, he moved to the white brick house known as **Cedar Hill**. Its mixed Gothic Revival–Italianate architecture, 21 rooms, and fifteen acres were typical of the homes built twenty years earlier in what was then called Uniontown, though at that time they were sold only to whites. Douglass, DC's newly appointed US marshal, was the first to break the racial barrier, paying $6700 for the property and living out the last eighteen years of his life here.

You can reserve a place on one of the home's free hourly **tours** by calling ☎1-800/967-2283 (a handling fee of $2 is charged; it's also possible to take a tour without reservations). The tours begin in the **visitors center** below the house, where a short docudrama and a few exhibits provide details about Douglass's life. Next you're led up the steep green hill for a rather dry tour around the house. Cedar Hill was a substantial piece of property for its time, and Douglass entertained leading abolitionists and suffragists here while talking in the parlors or eating in the dining room. Mementos on display include President Lincoln's cane, given to Douglass by Mary Lincoln, and a desk and chair from Harriet Beecher Stowe. Family portraits capture his first wife, Anna, who died in 1882; his second wife, Helen, who was much younger and – shockingly for hidebound DC – white; and his five children, two of whom served with distinction in Massachusetts's black 54th regiment during the Civil War.

Most of the fixtures and fittings are original and illustrate middle-class life in late nineteenth-century Washington. Douglass kept chickens and goats outside in the gardens and the only water source was a rainwater pump, but inside the

Frederick Douglass (1818–95) was born into slavery as Frederick Bailey on a Maryland estate in 1818. His exact birth date and father's identity (Bailey was his mother's name) are unknown, though it was rumored he was the son of a white man, perhaps his owner. At the age of 8 he was sent to work as a house servant in Baltimore, where, although it was illegal to educate slaves, the owner's wife taught him to read and he taught himself to write. By 1834 Frederick had been hired out to a nearby plantation, where he was cruelly treated; his first attempt to escape, in 1836, failed. Later, apprenticed as a ship caulker in Baltimore's docks, Frederick attended an educational association run by free blacks and met his first wife, Anna Murray. With money borrowed from her and equipped with a friend's passbook, Frederick fled to New York in 1838 disguised as a free seaman. Anna followed him and they were married later that year, moving to Massachusetts where Bailey – now working as a laborer – became Douglass (after a character from Sir Walter Scott's *Lady of the Lake*) to confound the slave-catchers.

Douglass became active in the **abolitionist movement**, lecturing about his life for the Massachusetts Anti-Slavery Society during the 1840s and risking capture when, in 1845, at just 27 years old, he published his autobiography, *Narrative of the Life of Frederick Douglass, an American Slave*. It was a resounding success, forcing the increasingly famous Douglass to leave for England for fear he'd be recaptured. After he spent two years on the lecture circuit, friends raised the money to buy his freedom and Douglass returned home. His views were slowly changing, and in a break with pacifist white abolitionists, he founded his own newspaper, the *North Star* (later renamed *Frederick Douglass' Paper*), in Rochester, New York, in 1847. In it, Douglass began increasingly to explore the idea of political rather than moral reform as a means of ending slavery. His reputation as a compelling orator and writer grew, and another autobiography, *My Bondage and My Freedom*, appeared in 1855. Meanwhile, Douglass extended his interests to **women's suffrage** (a bold move at the time), discussing issues with such luminaries as Susan B. Anthony, Lucretia Mott, and Elizabeth Cady Stanton.

When President Lincoln issued the Emancipation Proclamation in 1863, the country's most respected black leader urged "men of color" to join the war effort, which backfired somewhat when it became clear that his fiery recruitment speeches promised black soldiers an equality in service and conditions that the Union Army didn't offer. With slavery abolished and Reconstruction set in place, in the mid-1860s Douglass turned to pressing for **black suffrage**. He campaigned for Ulysses S. Grant and the Republicans in 1868 and played a major role in pushing through the **Fifteenth Amendment**, granting all male citizens the right to vote – though this caused a temporary rift with his suffragist colleagues since "citizens" still didn't include women.

Douglass and Anna moved to DC in 1870, buying a house on Capitol Hill, where he continued to earn his living lecturing, writing, and, for a while, editing the progressive *New National Era* newspaper. In 1877 he was appointed to the largely ceremonial position of marshal of Washington DC and moved to **Cedar Hill** in Anacostia.

Douglass was made recorder of deeds for the city in 1880, and in 1881 published his third autobiographical work, *Narrative of the Life and Times of Frederick Douglass*. Anna died a year later, and Douglass caused a scandal when he quickly married Helen Pitts, a sharp-witted white secretary almost twenty years his junior. More controversy followed as Douglass was accused of cozying up to successive political administrations that were deemed to have betrayed the aspirations of black Americans ever since Emancipation. Quitting his post as recorder, Douglass eventually regained his reputation. In 1889, at a time when others might have considered retirement, he accepted the post of consul-general in Haiti, where he served for two years.

Back at Cedar Hill, but by now in ill health, Douglass continued to write and speak publicly until his death from a heart attack on February 20, 1895, at the age of 77. His funeral, effectively a state occasion, was held at the Metropolitan AME Church (see p.185) in downtown DC. His writings continued to inspire a new generation of black leaders who took his fight into the twentieth century.

kitchen the domestic staff had access to all the latest technology, like the Universal clothes wringer. Douglass chose to work either in his study, surrounded by hundreds of books, or in the outdoor "Growlery" – a rudimentary stone cabin he used for solitary contemplation.

Anacostia Museum

3

1901 Fort Place SE ☎202/287-2061, ⊛www.si.edu/anacostia. Daily 10am–5pm.

Though well off the beaten path, the Smithsonian's **Anacostia Museum** – like the nearby Frederick Douglass National Historic Site – warrants a visit. However, don't even think about walking here from the Anacostia Metro stop; buses #W2 or #W3 from Howard Road (outside the Metro) stop at the museum, though it's less unnerving to come by taxi. The museum's official mission, as the **Center for African American History and Culture**, is to devote itself to recording and displaying the life of blacks in America, particularly in the upper South (DC, Maryland, Virginia, and the Carolinas). Its permanent collection is mostly historical in nature, holding documents, photographs, books, and personal effects; a favorite item is the fur coat opera singer Marian Anderson wore to her famed 1939 concert on the steps of the Lincoln Memorial, after the racially blinkered Daughters of the American Revolution denied her permission to sing at Constitution Hall. There's also a display of contemporary quilts and a small art collection with works by folk artist Leslie Payne and a sampling of paintings and prints by local artists like Samella Lewis, John Robinson, and Elena Bland. The museum is perhaps best known for its temporary exhibitions, some of which have highlighted black artists and writers, the Great Migration that brought blacks north after the Civil War, and numerous artifacts related to slavery throughout America from the seventeenth to nineteenth centuries. Call or check the website to see what's being shown, or ask for details at the Smithsonian Castle (see p.90) on the Mall. Keep in mind that the museum may be closed for weeks at a time, or longer, while new exhibits are being installed.

The White House and Foggy Bottom

ew residences in the world are as familiar as the **White House**, the elegant Georgian mansion at 1600 Pennsylvania Avenue. Since 1800, when John Adams moved into the unfinished building, it's been home to every US president and has survived the ravages of fire, war, and potential acts of terror to stand as an enduring symbol of American power and democracy.

Along with the US Capitol, the White House was one of two original cornerstones of L'Enfant's master plan for the city. It is now very much in the center of things: to the south lies the National Mall; to the east, the Federal Triangle and the elegant colossus of the Treasury Building; to the north, historic Lafayette Square and the rising towers of New Downtown; and to the west, Foggy Bottom – the bureaucratic district north of Constitution Avenue that runs to the Potomac River. In the early nineteenth century, the upper class entertained the political elite here in stunning homes like the **Octagon**, while today the area is best known for federal buildings such as the **State Department**, and cultural and educational institutions like the **Kennedy Center** and **George Washington University**, the students of the latter bringing a certain zest to the streets' otherwise nine-to-five flavor. The city's first art museum, in what is now the **Renwick Gallery** of arts and crafts, was built here in 1859, though its collection was eventually moved to the nearby **Corcoran Gallery of Art**, one of the country's most respected museums. Less reputable, however, is one of Foggy Bottom's biggest draws: the **Watergate Complex** that was the site of the 1972 break-in that led to President Nixon's unprecedented resignation.

The White House

1600 Pennsylvania Ave NW ☎202/456-7041, special events ☎202/456-2200, tours ☎202/456-7041, ⍟www.whitehouse.gov; McPherson Square or Farragut West Metro. Tours Tues–Sat 7.30–11.30am.

The **White House**, residence and office of the President of the United States, is the most famous house at the most famous address in America. For millions, the idea of touring the president's home and possibly being in the same building as the most powerful man in the world has an almost totemic quality. In the end, however, many visitors are surprised by how small the quarters are and that their tour consists of a lot of waiting around and quick shuffles past railed-off rooms filled with presidential portraits.

Public access can be affected by security concerns. In 1995 the stretch of Pennsylvania Avenue north of the White House was permanently closed to vehicles following two incidents in which shots were fired at the building and a light aircraft crashed into one of the outer walls; for months following September 11, 2001, when a hijacked plane presumably headed for the White House crashed in a Pennsylvania field, the building was entirely closed to the public. Security, therefore, is as tight as you'd imagine.

In the nineteenth century, though there were armed sentries at every door and plainclothes policemen mingled with visitors, virtually anyone could turn up at the president's house without an introduction. In his diary, novelist Captain Frederick Marryat deplored the way a visitor might "walk into the saloon in all his dirt, and force his way to the President, that he might shake him by the one hand while he flourished the whip in the other." As late as the 1920s, the general public was allowed to saunter across the lawns and picnic on the grounds, and President Warren G. Harding would answer the front door himself.

These days, **tours** of the White House are offered to groups of ten or more. You must reserve your tour a month in advance through your US representative or senator (@www.house.gov or @www.senate.gov), whose office will be able to provide further details and possibly link smaller groups together to equal the requisite size. Foreign visitors must contact their embassy in DC to make arrangements. Before your scheduled tour date, be sure to call ahead and confirm everything. The **White House Visitor Center**, 1450 Pennsylvania Ave NW (daily 7.30am–4pm; ☎202/208 1631, @www.nps.gov /whho/WHVC/index.htm), in the Department of Commerce, several blocks southeast of the White House, is worth a visit in its own right. Six permanent exhibits highlight topics like the First Families and White House architecture, plus there are concerts, lectures, free maps and brochures, and a gift shop. It can also provide information on other federally operated sites, museums, and parks, and give you the low-down on current entry requirements and security restrictions for each.

Other parts of the White House are accessible on occasion throughout the year. In April and October the gardens are opened for afternoon tours, and at Christmas there are special evening tours of the festively decorated interior. Contact the visitor center for details.

Some history

Pierre L'Enfant was fired before he could make a start on the White House, then known as the **President's Mansion**, and in 1792 its design was thrown open to competition. **James Hoban**, an Irish immigrant and professional builder won the $500 prize for his Neoclassical design, influenced by the Georgian manor houses of Dublin, which followed President Washington's request for a mansion that would command respect without being extravagant and monarchical. Hoban believed a stone house would give the crucial impression of permanence and stability, though DC had few skilled masons and no quarries. Advertisements were placed in European newspapers before local slaves and Scottish masons from the Potomac region were used for the work. Progress was slow: the masons put down their tools in 1794 in the city's first

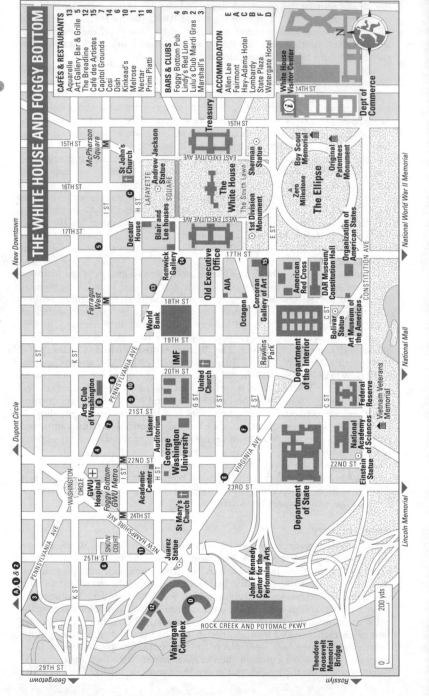

THE WHITE HOUSE AND FOGGY BOTTOM

CAFÉS & RESTAURANTS

Aquarelle	13
Art Gallery Bar & Grille	5
The Breadline	12
Café des Artistes	15
Capitol Grounds	7
Cosi	14
Dish	6
Kinkead's	10
Melrose	1
Nectar	11
Primi Piatti	8

BARS & CLUBS

Foggy Bottom Pub	4
Lindy's Red Lion	9
Lulu's Club Mardi Gras	2
Marshall's	3

ACCOMMODATION

Allen Lee	E
Fairmont	A
Hay-Adams Hotel	C
Lombardy	B
State Plaza	F
Watergate Hotel	D

Federal Triangle

Pennsylvania Avenue

New Downtown

Dupont Circle

A, 1 & 2

Georgetown

Rosslyn

Lincoln Memorial

National Mall

National World War II Memorial

N

White House Visitor Center

Dept of Commerce

14TH ST

15TH ST

Treasury

EAST EXECUTIVE AVE

McPherson Square

St John's Church

Andrew Jackson Statue

16TH ST

LAFAYETTE SQUARE

I ST

H ST

17TH ST

The White House

The South Lawn

WEST EXECUTIVE AVE

Decatur House

Blair and Lee houses

1st Division Monument

Sherman Statue

Zero Milestone

E ST

The Ellipse

Boy Scout Memorial

Original Patentees Monument

Renwick Gallery

Old Executive Office

17TH ST

Farragut West

18TH ST

World Bank

19TH ST

AIA

Octagon

Corcoran Gallery of Art

American Red Cross

DAR Museum/ Constitution Hall

Organization of American States

Art Museum of the Americas

CONSTITUTION AVE

C ST

Bolivar Statue

Rawlins Park

Department of the Interior

L ST

K ST

IMF

20TH ST

G ST

United Church

F ST

E ST

C ST

Federal Reserve

Vietnam Veterans Memorial

PENNSYLVANIA AVE

Arts Club of Washington

21ST ST

Lisner Auditorium

George Washington University

National Academy of Sciences

Einstein Statue

WASHINGTON CIRCLE

GWU Hospital

GWU Metro

Foggy Bottom-

Academic Center

I ST

H ST

22ND ST

22ND ST

Department of State

St Mary's Church

23RD ST

24TH ST

VIRGINIA AVE

E

NEW HAMPSHIRE AVE

SNOW COURT

25TH ST

Juarez Statue

John F Kennedy Center for the Performing Arts

Watergate Complex

ROCK CREEK AND POTOMAC PKWY

29TH ST

Theodore Roosevelt Memorial Bridge

200 yds

0

pay strike, and the house of gray Virginia sandstone wasn't completed in time to house Washington, whose second term ended in 1797.

America's second president, **John Adams**, moved into the unfinished building on November 1, 1800, a few days before he lost his bid for re-election; the First Family was forced to hang its laundry in the grand East Room while final touches were put on the mansion. East and west terraces were built during the administration of **Thomas Jefferson**, who had entered the building's design competition under a pseudonym; Jefferson also installed the home's first water closets and hired a French chef. Under **James Madison**, the interior was redecorated by Capitol architect Benjamin Latrobe, who defended copying parts of Jefferson's proposed design by arguing that Jefferson's ideas were lifted in turn from "old French books, out of which he fishes everything." During the **War of 1812**, British soldiers burned down the mansion in August 1814, forcing Madison and his wife to flee; when the troops entered, they found the dining table set for forty, the wine poured in the decanters, and the food cooked in the kitchen. Hoban was charged with reconstructing the building after the war, and it was ready to reopen in 1817 – but with one significant change: to conceal fire damage to the exterior, the house was painted white.

Throughout the nineteenth century, the White House was decorated, added to, and improved upon by each new occupant, though occasionally there were setbacks. To celebrate his inauguration in 1829, **Andrew Jackson** invited some of his rowdy followers back to the White House, who then proceeded to wreck the place, forcing Jackson to spend the first night of his presidency in a hotel. Jackson did, however, redeem himself by installing the building's first indoor bathroom in 1833. Gaslights were added in 1848, central heating and a steam laundry in 1853, the telephone in 1877, and electric lighting in 1891. When President James Garfield lay dying from an assassin's bullet in 1881, enterprising naval engineers cooled his White House bedroom by concocting a prototype air conditioner from a fan and a box of ice (full air-conditioning didn't follow until 1909).

During the Civil War, troops were briefly stationed in the White House's East Room, cooking their dinner in the ornate fireplace, while the South Lawn was used as a field hospital. The East Room is also where seven US presidents have lain in state – the first being **Abraham Lincoln** just after the close of the Civil War in 1865.

It wasn't until **Theodore Roosevelt**'s administration (1901–09) that fundamental structural changes (as opposed to the previous piecemeal ones) were made to the building, as well as expansions to accommodate the president's family and staff. Elevators were added and an executive West Wing – incorporating the president's personal **Oval Office** – was built. The famous Rose Garden was planted outside the Oval Office in 1913 on the orders of President Wilson's wife, Ellen, and was used for ceremonial purposes. An entire residential third floor was added in 1927, an East Wing followed in the 1940s, while, during World War II, a diverse set of improvements included an air-raid shelter, swimming pool (which FDR used for exercise), and movie theater.

Because presidential families lived in the White House during these renovations, the projects were often done too quickly, so that by 1948 the entire building was on the verge of collapse. **Harry Truman** – who had already added a poorly received balcony ("Truman's folly") to the familiar south-side portico – had to move into nearby Blair House for four years while the structure was stabilized. New foundations were laid, all the rooms were dismantled, and a modern steel frame was inserted. The Trumans moved back in 1952,

The role of the presidency

When delegates at Philadelphia's 1787 Constitutional Convention created the role of President of the United States, they had no intention of replacing a British monarchy with an American one. Instead, they devised a federal system of government with separate executive, legislative, and judicial branches and prescribed precise limits on the authority of each. The president was made chief executive, though one whose role was within, rather than above, the government. Indeed, presidential powers were detailed in Article 2 of the **Constitution**, after full discussion of the more fundamental role of Congress in Article 1. Still, this was a step up in prestige from the old **Articles of Confederation** (1783–88), which had no real executive branch whatsoever, and thus no means of enforcing the laws passed by Congress. At first, the president wasn't even directly elected, but instead chosen by an **electoral college** appointed by the states, the idea being to free the presidency from factional influence. The **12th Amendment** (1804) opened up the ballot for president (and vice president) to popular election, though the electoral college remained intact, with electors now being chosen via the party that won a given state. Since the Civil War, three American presidents, including George W. Bush in 2000, lost the popular vote but won the electoral vote.

The Constitution actually has very little to say about the presidency itself. Specific, enumerated powers are few – to make treaties, appoint federal officers, act as commander-in-chief, etc – and this may have been because the Constitution's authors never really agreed on what the president's role should be. The elevation of the presidency is due in part to certain extraordinary leaders who've occupied and enhanced the post over the past centuries, like George Washington, America's trusted first president; Andrew Jackson, who expanded voting rights; Abraham Lincoln, who preserved the Union during the Civil War; Theodore Roosevelt, who dismantled illegal monopolies and trusts; and Franklin Roosevelt, whose unprecedented federal programs sought to lift the country out of the Great Depression.

Constitutionally, the president has sole executive responsibility, although he has come to be assisted by special advisors and a large White House staff. The president oversees fifteen executive departments, whose appointed secretaries form his **Cabinet**, which is more of an advisory forum than a policy-making body. When a new party occupies the White House after an election, the upper-echelon staff at various federal agencies – from the Post Office to the National Security Council – usually changes dramatically to ensure consistency with the new administration's policies (and also to reward the president's loyal followers). Today, roughly two thousand people work directly or indirectly for the Executive Office of the President, while another 100,000 non-strategic federal posts are technically within the presidential fold.

Additional information on the presidency and individual presidents of the United States can be found in Contexts.

and since then there have been no significant alterations – unless you count Nixon's bowling alley, Ford's outdoor pool, and Clinton's jogging track.

The interior

The self-guided **tours** concentrate on rooms on the ground and State (principal) floors. The Oval Office, family apartments, and private offices on the second and third floors are off-limits, and guards make sure you don't stray from the designated route. Once inside, your group is allowed to wander one-way through or past a half-dozen furnished rooms. Though guards will answer questions if they can, the tour is not exactly conducive to taking your time, and in many rooms you can't get close enough to appreciate the paintings or the furniture. Caught up in the flow of the crowd, most people are outside again well within thirty minutes. As if this weren't bad enough, there's a paucity of quality fixtures and fittings on display, and not just because much of the best stuff is kept in private quarters. Until Jackie Kennedy and her Fine Arts Committee put a stop to the practice, each incoming presidential family changed, sold, or scrapped the furniture according to individual taste, while outgoing presidents took favorite pieces with them – you're just as likely to come across White House furniture and valuables in places like Dumbarton House or the Woodrow Wilson House.

The East Wing and East Room

Visitors enter the **East Wing** from the ground floor and traipse first past the Federal-style Library, paneled in timbers rescued from a mid-nineteenth-century refit and housing 2700 books by American authors. Opposite is the Vermeil Room, once a billiard room but now named for its extensive collection of silver gilt; the portraits are of recent First Ladies. Next you move upstairs to the State Floor, where the **East Room** – the largest room in the White House – is the first stop. The East Room has been open to the public since the days of Andrew Jackson. It has been used in the past for weddings, various lyings-in-state, and other major ceremonies, and has a grand appearance with long, yellow drapes, a brown marble fireplace, and glass chandeliers from c.1900. Between the fireplaces hangs the one major artwork on general display: Gilbert Stuart's celebrated 1797 portrait of a steely George Washington, rescued from the flames by Dolley Madison when the British torched the White House.

Green, Blue, and Red rooms, and the State Dining Room

The last rooms on the tour are more intimate in scale. The **Green Room**, its walls lined in silk, was Jefferson's dining room and JFK's favorite in the entire house. Portraits line the walls, Dolley Madison's French candlesticks are on the mantelpiece, and a fine, matching green dinner service occupies the cabinet. The room is now often called upon to host receptions, as is the adjacent, oval **Blue Room**, whose ornate French furniture was bought by President Monroe after the 1814 fire. In 1886, Grover Cleveland was married in here, the only time a president has been married in the White House. The **Red Room** is the smallest of the lot, decorated in early nineteenth-century Empire style and sporting attractive inlaid oak doors. Finally, the oak-paneled **State Dining Room** harks back to the East Room in scale and style and hosts banquets for important guests. (Theodore Roosevelt used to stick his big-game trophies in here.) From here you loop back through the cross halls and exit on the north side of the White House, opposite Lafayette Square.

The South Lawn

The White House is surrounded by greenery, but its most famous patch is the **South Lawn**, the grassy stretch that hosts its most famous outdoor event: the Easter Egg Roll. The Roll is a longstanding tradition that began in 1878 and has been interrupted only by war and particularly foul weather. Although the event changes slightly every year, it usually involves children painting eggs and rolling them across the grass, a White House staffer dressed as the Easter Bunny, and various department heads reading stories and trying to act goofy. To get free tickets for this event, which occurs the Monday after Easter, drop by the Ellipse Visitor Center at 15th and E streets at 7.30am on either the day of the Roll or the Saturday before it. Tickets are first-come, first-served and run out quickly.

The Ellipse

The **Ellipse** is the large green expanse south of the White House. Since 1978 it's been home to the rather stumpy **National Christmas Tree**, a Colorado blue spruce that the president lights every year to mark the start of the holiday season. On the Ellipse's northern edge, at E Street opposite the South Lawn, is the **Zero Milestone**, which marks the point from where all distances on US highways are measured; on its eastern side (along 15th St) is the bronze **Boy Scout Memorial**. Nearby, the simple granite **Monument to the Original Patentees** commemorates the eighteenth-century landowners who ceded land so that the city could be built. At the Ellipse's southeastern corner, the stone **Bulfinch Gatehouse** at Constitution and 15th was one of a pair that stood at the Capitol grounds' western entrance. Today its partner stands across the Ellipse at Constitution and 17th.

Around the White House

If the White House demands attention from the south side – appearing as a gleaming monolith at the edge of a lush green lawn – it's obscured on the east and west by two giant office buildings (the Treasury and Old Executive Office buildings, respectively), and sneaks up on you from the north. The security gates are not so imposing as you approach from **Lafayette Square**, so the northern side is your best bet for an unobscured snapshot of the president's house, and perhaps a chance to see a shadowy figure or two darting around inside.

Lafayette Square and around

The land due north of 1600 Pennsylvania Avenue was originally intended as part of the White House grounds, but in 1804 President Thomas Jefferson divided it in half and created a public park. Until 1824 the park, lined with the houses of cabinet members and other prominent citizens, was known as **President's Square**. Over the years redevelopment threatened the surrounding houses on several occasions, but in the 1960s Jacqueline Kennedy intervened and modern monoliths were erected behind them, rather than in place of them – resulting in one of the stranger visual juxtapositions in the District.

In the park's center is its only statue of an American, the figure of **Andrew Jackson** astride a horse, surrounded by cannons and doffing his hat. Statues of foreign-born Revolutionary leaders are set at the corners of the square. In the southeast corner stands a likeness of the park's namesake, the **Marquis de Lafayette**, who was a Revolutionary War general by the age of 19. Following the war Lafayette was imprisoned in France as a "traitor," but, during a return to the US in 1824, he was feted on the Mall and awarded various honors, including this eponymous park. His statue shows him flanked by French admirals and being handed a sword by a female nude, symbolizing America.

In the northeast corner of the park, a memorial for **Tadeusz Kosciusko**, the Polish freedom fighter and a prominent engineer in Washington's army, features an angry imperial eagle killing a snake atop a globe while the general towers overhead. The inscription at the base is surely one of the District's more memorable lines, taken from Scottish poet Thomas Campbell: "And freedom shrieked as Kosciusko fell!"

Blair and Lee houses

Built by the first US surgeon-general in 1824, **Blair House**, at the south-western corner of Lafayette Square, was named after a prominent Washington real-estate speculator, Francis Preston Blair, and has served as the presidential guest house since the 1940s. Along with hosting foreign dignitaries, both the Truman and Clinton families stayed here while White House renovations were in progress. Next door, the 1860 **Lee House** was where Robert E. Lee was offered – and refused – command of the Union Army. Unfortunately, you can't look inside these residences, but their Federal-style exteriors are worth a glance.

Decatur House

Benjamin Latrobe's red-brick 1819 **Decatur House**, 1610 H St NW (Tues–Sat 10am–5pm, Sun noon–4pm; donation; ☎202/842-0920, ⊛www .decaturhouse.org), is the oldest home on the square. Latrobe built this house for Stephen Decatur, a precocious American hero who performed with distinction in the War of 1812 and as a navy captain fighting Barbary pirates. Decatur lived here only about a year, as he was killed in a duel by Commodore Barron. The Federal-style first floor, studded with naval memorabilia, is decorated in the fashion of the day. Most of the other rooms have Victorian-style inlaid floors, furnishings, mirrors, molding, and the like. If the building's museum is open (it's closed several weeks during the year for preservation work), you can take a free guided tour (30–45min) that begins fifteen minutes after each hour.

Hay-Adams Hotel

Across the street from the Decatur House is the **Hay-Adams Hotel**, H and 16th sts (☎202/638-6600, ⊛www.hayadams.com), an impressive Renaissance Revival building with elegant arches and columns. The hotel sits on the former site of the townhouses of statesman **John Hay** (President Lincoln's private secretary) and his friend, historian and author **Henry Adams**. Their adjacent homes were the site of glittering soirées attended by Theodore Roosevelt and his circle – an association that appealed to hotshot hotel developer Harry Wardman, who jumped at the chance to buy the properties in 1927. Since then, the hotel, which boasted the city's first air-conditioned dining room, has been at the heart of Washington politicking: Henry Kissinger lunched here regularly, Oliver North did much of his clandestine Iran-Contra fundraising here, and the Clintons slept here before Bill's first inauguration.

St John's Church

1525 H St NW ☎202/347-8766, ⊛www.stjohns-dc.org. Mon–Sat 10.30am–2.30pm; free tours after 11am Sun service.

The tiny yellow church across H Street from Lafayette Park was built by **Benjamin Latrobe** in 1815. The handsome, domed Episcopal church was intended to serve the president and his family and is therefore known as the "**Church of the Presidents**"; all since Madison have attended – sitting in the special pew (No. 54) reserved for them – and when an incumbent dies in office, **St John**'s bells ring out across the city. The handsome 1836 building just east of the church, with a grand French Second Empire facade, is today a parish building but, in the nineteenth century, was home to the British Embassy.

Treasury Building

The **Treasury Building**, with its imposing Neoclassical bulk and grand colonnade, flanks the White House to the east and faces 15th Street. Built – or at least begun – in 1836 by Robert Mills, who created the Old Patent Office and Old Post Office, this is commonly judged to be the finest Greek Revival building in DC. During the Civil War, the basement was strengthened and food and arms were stored in the building, as Lincoln and his aides planned to hole up here if the city was attacked. The statue at the southern entrance, facing Hamilton Place, is of **Alexander Hamilton**, first Secretary of the Treasury (and the man on the $10 bill; the Treasury Building itself is on the back). Washington's closest advisor during the president's first administration, he died young in an 1804 duel with Aaron Burr, Jefferson's vice president and scheming Tammany Hall founder. Due to an ongoing renovation and the usual security fears, the building is not currently open to the public, though visitors with political connections may find other means of access (see box, opposite).

Eisenhower Old Executive Office Building

The ornate, gray-granite **Eisenhower Old Executive Office Building**, 17th St and Pennsylvania Ave NW, was built in 1888 to house the State, War, and Navy departments (and recently renamed for the 34th president). Its architect, Alfred B. Mullet, claiming to be inspired by the Louvre, produced an ill-conceived monster of a French Empire-style building with hundreds of freestanding columns, extraordinarily tall and thin chimneys, a copper mansard roof, pediments, porticos, and various pedantic stone flourishes. The design was never terribly popular, but schemes to renovate or rebuild came to nothing, mainly because of the expense involved in tackling such a behemoth. These days its roomy interior provides office space for government and White House staff – indeed, this was where in 2001 incoming Bush administration bureaucrats alleged that outgoing Clinton staffers had vandalized some of the offices, leaving trash in the rooms and removing the "W" keys from computer keyboards. More notoriously, the building was the base of the White House "Plumbers," Nixon's dirty-tricks team, and hosted several of the infamous tape-recorded Watergate-related meetings; it was also where Colonel Oliver North and his secretary, Fawn Hall, shredded documents relating to the Iran-Contra scandal. The building has long housed the offices of the vice president, so security here is almost as tight as at the White House and US Capitol. To view the ornate public rooms, filled with marble and gilt, stained glass, tiled floors, and wrought-iron balconies, you'll need to contact your elected representative and arrange for a tour (see box, opposite).

Renwick Gallery

Pennsylvania Ave at 17th St NW ☎202/633-2850, ⊛www.americanart.si.edu; Farragut West Metro. Daily 10am–5.30pm.

The Second Empire flourishes of the Old Executive Office Building were directly influenced by the earlier, smaller, and much more harmonious

Special access for special visitors

In this era of high security and paranoia, it can seem like every interesting site in DC is being locked down or having its public access dramatically scaled back. In the years since 9/11, places like the White House and Pentagon have reopened to the public, but with many stipulations. However, as with everything in the nation's capital, political connections can get you far; in this case, they can provide access to buildings that are officially off-limits to the public. The Treasury and Eisenhower Old Executive Office buildings offer two good examples: before the terrorist attacks, both were open for tours; afterwards, their entrances were indefinitely sealed to public view. However, if you **contact your elected representative**, it may be possible to set up a Saturday-morning tour of the Eisenhower building (check Ⓦwww .house.gov or Ⓦwww.senate.gov for contacts, or call Ⓣ202/456-2326); alas, gaining access to the Treasury Building is a bit trickier. It helps to have worked on the campaign of, or given money to, your home-district representative, who in turn should occupy a seat on, or better yet be the chair of, a subcommittee overseeing financial or banking matters. In short, the closer you are to your local politician, and the greater prominence he or she has in relation to the department at hand, the better your chances are of getting a **tour**. If you lack these connections, a way around the ungainly requirements of touring the Pentagon, for example (officially only open to veterans and school groups), is to get in touch with an important (home-state) member of the Armed Services or Intelligence Committees; if you're interested in the State Department, see if any members of the Foreign Affairs Committee are from your area. Unfortunately, getting access to the confines of the FBI, Department of Justice, Homeland Security, or the CIA (out in Langley, Virginia) may prove difficult even with a good connection.

Renwick Gallery of American arts and crafts, which lies directly opposite across Pennsylvania Avenue. Started by **James Renwick** (architect of the Smithsonian Castle) in 1859, the handsome red-brick building was originally meant to house the private art collection of financier **William Wilson Corcoran**. Work was interrupted by the **Civil War**, during which the building was requisitioned for use by the Union Army's quartermaster-general. The Southern-sympathizing Corcoran left for Europe in 1862, where he stayed throughout the war. On his return, Corcoran finally got his gallery back (and, having sued, $125,000 from the government in back rent) and opened it to the public. Within twenty years his burgeoning collection had outgrown the site, and the new **Corcoran Gallery** was built just a couple blocks south. At one point, the US Court of Claims took over the Renwick building and, after it vacated, the by-then decrepit building was saved and restored in the 1960s by the Smithsonian, which uses it to display selections from its **American Art Museum**. Until 2006, the Renwick will act as a small version of that very museum, featuring some of its more familiar paintings until it's fully renovated.

The building itself is stunning: an inscription above the entrance announces it to be "Dedicated to Art," and the ornate design reaches its apogee in the upper floor's deep-red **Grand Salon**, a soaring parlor with windows draped in striped damask, paintings stacked four and five high in a vertical column, velvet-covered benches, marble-topped cabinets, and splendid wood-and-glass display cases taken from the Smithsonian Castle. This was the main picture gallery in Corcoran's time; its lofty dimensions meant that there was no difficulty in converting it into a courtroom and judge's chambers during the Court of Claims' tenure. Opposite, the smaller Octagon Room was specifically designed to hold **Hiram Powers**'s nude statue *The Greek Slave* (now in the Corcoran

Gallery), while between the two rooms on the same floor are galleries devoted to American crafts – mostly modern jewelry and furniture, but also sculpture, ceramics, abstracts, and applied art. The first floor hosts temporary exhibitions of contemporary crafts.

The collection

Filled with pieces from the Smithsonian American Art Museum, the Grand Salon is the Renwick's unquestioned highlight. At first glance this one room's collection is staggering, but several key items stand out. Most conspicuous are the huge frames of **Frederic Church**'s *Aurora Borealis* and **Thomas Moran**'s *The Grand Canyon of the Yellowstone*, colossal nature paintings that embody the gung-ho, Manifest Destiny spirit of nineteenth-century America, dramatically depicting the country's grand vistas, however inaccurate or unrealistic at times. Notable portraits here include eighteenth- and nineteenth-century renderings of John Adams (**Gilbert Stuart**), upstanding socialites Betty Wertheimer and Elizabeth Winthrop Chanler (**John Singer Sargent**), merchant's wife Mrs George Watson (**John Singleton Copley**), and an impish St Nicholas (**Robert Walter Weir**).

Other items include the sculpted sitting cherub of the *Will o' the Wisp* (**Harriet Hosmer**) and the aging patriarch of the *Man with the Cat – Henry Sturgis Drinker* (**Cecilia Beaux**). The American collection's best cache of all, however, may be the works of **Albert Pinkham Ryder**, which are typically dark, moody images of twisted landscapes and classical-fiction or mythical allegories rendered in small frames with thick paint. His best pieces here include *Jonah*, a swirling, abstract seascape; *Lord Ullin's Daughter*, poised amid tumultuous waves and perilous rocks; *King Cophetua and the Beggar Maid*, a dark, surreal encounter in a dreamlike terrain; *Moonlight*, and *With Sloping Mast and Dipping Prow*, both oceanic rides into a sea of gloom.

South along 17th Street

From the Eisenhower Old Executive Office Building and the Renwick Gallery, you can stroll south down 17th Street toward Constitution Avenue and take in a number of attractions along the way, including the **Daughters of the American Revolution Museum** and the **Corcoran Gallery of Art** – home to the city's earliest art collection (originally in the Renwick Gallery), though smaller, more offbeat collections nearby are also worth a visit. Keep an eye out for the five-story, iron-framed **Winder Building**, 604 17th St NW, which, in 1848, was the tallest building in Washington and the first to incorporate central heating. Between D and E streets is the white marble headquarters of the **American Red Cross**; look for the Tiffany stained glass in its second-floor assembly-room windows.

Corcoran Gallery of Art

500 17th St NW ☎202/639-1700, ⊛www.corcoran.org; Farragut West Metro. Wed–Mon 10am-5pm, Thurs closes at 9pm. $5.

The **Corcoran Gallery of Art** changed locations at the end of the nineteenth century, moving from what is now the Renwick Gallery to a beautiful Beaux Arts building of curving white marble with a green copper roof, the light and airy interior enhanced by a double atrium. The gallery's mighty American collection includes more than three thousand paintings, from colonial to contemporary, Neoclassical sculpture, and modern photographs, prints, and drawings. Over the years, the permanent collection has expanded to include European works, Greek antiquities, and medieval tapestries. Benefactors continue to bestow impressive gifts, like the large collection of Daumier lithographs donated by Dr Armand Hammer and the seven hundred works by two hundred nineteenth- and twentieth-century artists and sculptors, from Picasso to Calder, left by Olga Hirshhorn (wife of Joseph of the eponymous gallery). A new 140,000-square-foot wing, opening in a few years, will go a long way toward accommodating the museum's burgeoning collection, and the eye-popping sculptural curves of Frank Gehry's design will be sure to stand out amid the current genteel surroundings. Works from the permanent collection are rotated throughout the year, and other pieces are sent out on tour; not everything mentioned below will be on display at any one time. Details of changing exhibitions are available at the **information desk**, inside the main entrance, which is also where you can sign up for the guided tours of the permanent collection. The *Café des Artistes* (☎202/639-1786) has standard salads and sandwiches, but is unique for its signature Sunday-morning **Gospel Brunch** ($24), during which you nosh to the sound of fervent musical evangelizing.

European art

The gallery's collection of European art is a very mixed bag, mainly comprising the 1925 bequest of **Senator William A. Clark**, an industrialist with more money than discretion. William Corcoran's own collection here includes 120 commissioned animal bronzes by French sculptor **Antoine-Louis Barye** (1796–1875), a selection of which is usually on display. These bronzes are graphic representations of animals in combat: a lion attacking a horse, a python crushing a gazelle, etc.

Some of the gallery's most familiar names are in the **Clark Landing**, a two-tiered, wood-paneled gallery accessed on the second floor from the Rotunda. Here you're likely to find mid-level paintings by **Degas**, **Renoir**, **Monet**, **Sisley**, and **Pissarro**, as well as works by **Rousseau** and **Corot**; the latter's *Repose* is a notably sour-faced nude with Pan and his nymphs cavorting in the background. The only other European exhibits of real interest are the ones devoted to six-teenth-century French and Italian works, including some outstanding Italian majolica plates depicting mythological scenes, a thirteenth-century stained-glass window lifted from Soissons Cathedral, and two large, allegorical wool-and-silk French **tapestries** (1506) representing contemporaneous political and historical events. However, the most striking piece of the gallery's European collection is not a painting, but the corner room on the first floor known as the **Salon Doré** (Gilded Room), which originally formed part of an eighteenth-century Parisian home, the Hôtel de Clermont. Senator Clark bought the entire room, intending to install it in his New York mansion; after arriving in Washington, though, the senator housed it here, then bequeathed it to the Corcoran after his death. Framed mirrors (flanked by medallion-holding cherubs) make it seem larger than it actually is, and the rest of the room is filled with floor-to-ceiling hand-carved wood paneling, gold-leaf decor, and ceiling murals.

American art

Most of the Corcoran's American art collection is displayed on the second floor. Approaching through the Rotunda and Clark Landing you'll find

△ Renwick Gallery

paintings by early American artists such as Gilbert Stuart, Thomas Cole, George Inness, and Benjamin West. **Rembrandt Peale**'s equestrian *Washington Before Yorktown* (1824) is striking for its illuminated image of a strong, deliberate general hours before the decisive battle for independence.

The gallery possesses a fine collection of landscapes, starting with the expansive *Niagara* (1857) by **Frederic Edwin Church** and **Albert Bierstadt**'s splendid *The Last of the Buffalo* (1889). While Church concerned himself with the power of nature, Bierstadt here celebrates human endeavor within the natural world, portraying the Native American braves pursuing buffalo so numerous they darken the plain. In marked contrast, **Thomas Cole**'s *The Return* (1837), a mythical medieval scene of an injured knight returning to a priory glowing in the evening light, has little to do with America, though it does display the Hudson River School's penchant for portraying ethereal romance and natural beauty. Artist-cum-inventor **Samuel F.B. Morse**'s *The Old House of Representatives* (1822) was finished in a studio the artist set up in the US Capitol so that he could observe his subjects at work. One room is usually devoted to nineteenth-century portraiture, with formal studies by renowned artists like **John Trumbull** (who painted the Capitol murals) and **Charles Bird King**, who depicts statesman Henry Clay supporting an 1821 resolution for South American independence. Most prominent, though, are **George Peter Alexander Healy**'s presidential portraits of Van Buren, Tyler, Polk, Taylor, Arthur, and Lincoln, commissioned by Congress for display in the White House. Striking also is **Thomas Sully**'s 1845 rendering of Andrew Jackson on horseback, fresh from triumph at the Battle of New Orleans in 1814, though the general looks well beyond the 47 years of age he would have been at the time. For some reason, the gallery's most notorious piece of sculpture is in this room as well. Originally on display in the Renwick Gallery, **Hiram Powers**'s *The Greek Slave* (1846), with her manacled hands and full-length nudity, so outraged contemporary critics that women visitors were prevented from viewing it while men were in the room.

Moving into late nineteenth-century art, the gallery holds works by **John Singer Sargent**, **Thomas Eakins**, and **Mary Cassatt** among others. Sargent is responsible for one of the gallery's most loved pieces – the startling *Simplon Pass* (1911), with its landscape of crags and boulders – as well as more familiar society portraits. Few works, however, are as robust as **Winslow Homer**'s *A Light on the Sea* (1897), depicting a fiercely strong woman swathed in fishing nets and intensely contrasting areas of light and dark. Working women were rare subjects indeed during Homer's time, as were African Americans. **Richard Norris Brooke**'s *A Pastoral Visit* (1881) is a warm, beautifully lit scene out of black life in the rural South. Worth a look also is one of **Cecilia Beaux**'s feline-inspired works, *Sita and Sarita*, in which a pale woman in a luminous white dress sits with a curious black cat perched on her shoulder.

The gallery's pre-World War II collection includes works by **Childe Hassam**, **Rockwell Kent**, **Thomas Hart Benton**, and **Edward Hopper**, whose sailing picture, *Ground Swell* (1939), features a long, smooth sea and horizon, and just a hint of menace. Even better is **George Bellows**'s *Forty-Two Kids*, in which the urchins in question are playing half-naked on the rotting docks of New York's East River. The rest of the second-floor rooms are devoted to special exhibitions and changing selections of prints, drawings, and photographs from the permanent collection. Depending on space, post-war and contemporary American artists, including big names like **Lichtenstein**, **Warhol**, and **de Kooning** may be on display.

DAR Museum

1776 D St NW ℡202/879-3241, ⊛www.dar.org/museum; Farragut West Metro. Mon–Fri 9am–4pm, Sat 9am–5pm; tours Mon–Fri 10am–2.30pm, Sat 9am–4.30pm.

The National Society of the **Daughters of the American Revolution** (DAR) has had its headquarters in Washington for more than a century. Founded in 1890, this thoroughly patriotic (if unswervingly conservative) organization is open to women who can prove descent from an ancestor (male or female) who served the American cause during the Revolution. Fueled by the motto "God, Home, and Country," it busies itself with good-citizen and educational programs, including one designed to promote "correct flag usage" throughout America: the Stars and Stripes adorning the rostrums in the Senate and the House in the US Capitol are gifts from the DAR, and just two of the more than 100,000 given away since 1909.

The organization's original meeting place was the 1905 Beaux Arts Memorial Continental Hall, facing 17th Street, whose main chamber hosted the world's first disarmament conference in 1921. Delegates now meet for their annual congress (the week of April 19, anniversary of the Battle of Lexington) in the massive adjoining **Constitution Hall** on 18th Street, designed with typical exuberance by John Russell Pope in 1929. A blight on the organization's history, however, occurred in 1939, when DAR refused to let peerless black contralto Marian Anderson perform in the hall. Eleanor Roosevelt resigned from the organization in outrage, and Anderson gave her concert instead on Easter Sunday at the Lincoln Memorial to a rapt crowd of 75,000.

The collection

Visitors to the **DAR Museum** (entrance on D St) are shown first into the **gallery**, where a hodgepodge of embroidered samplers and quilts, silverware, toys, kitchenware, glass, crockery, earthenware, and just about anything else the Daughters have managed to lay their hands on over the years are on display. Although exhibits change, there's usually a great selection of ceramics, popular in the Revolutionary and Federal periods (from which most of the collection dates). On request, one of the docents will lead you through the rest of the building, beginning in the spacious, 125,000-volume **genealogical library** that was once the main meeting hall. The library is open to DAR members and non-members ($5 a day) keen to bone up on such topics as *The History of Milwaukee* (in eight alarmingly large volumes) or *The Genealogy of the Witherspoon Family*.

What the Daughters are most proud of, however, are the **State Rooms**, comprising no fewer than 31 period salons, mainly decorated with pre-1850 furnishings, each representing a different state. Few are of any historical or architectural merit, with a handful of exceptions: the New England room has an original lacquered wooden tea chest retrieved from Boston Harbor after the Tea Party in 1773; the California room replicates the interior of an early adobe house; and the New Jersey room displays furniture and paneling fashioned from the wreck of a British frigate sunk off the coast during the Revolutionary War – the overly elaborate chandelier was made from the melted-down anchor.

Organization of American States

17th St at Constitution Ave NW ☎202/458-3000, ⊛www.oas.org; Farragut West Metro. Mon–Fri 9am–5.30pm.

Founded in 1890 "to strengthen the peace and security of the continent," the **Organization of American States** (OAS) is the world's oldest regional organization, with 35 member states from Antigua to Venezuela. Its headquarters occupy one of the more charming buildings in the city, a squat, white Spanish Colonial mansion built in 1910 that faces onto the Ellipse. From the main entrance on 17th Street – fronted by a gaunt statue of Columbus's patron, Queen Isabella of Spain – you pass through fanciful iron gates to a cloistered lobby. The decor here turns almost to whimsy, with a fountain and tropical trees reaching to the wooden eaves and stone frieze above. You can then climb upstairs and walk through the gallery of national flags and busts of OAS founders, and take a peek in the grand Hall of the Americas.

A path leads from the Constitution Avenue side of the building through the so-called Aztec Garden to the smaller building behind. The **Art Museum of the Americas** – officially at 201 18th St NW (Tues–Sun 10am–5pm;

☎202/458-6016, ⊛www.museum.oas.org) – shows exhibits of Central and South American art, highlighted by the goofy surrealism of **Roberto Matta**, the assemblage sculptures of **Marisol Escobar**, and the plump, satirical portraits of **Fernando Botero**, as well as temporary shows focusing on painting, photography, architecture, and more. In the main brick-floored gallery, the walls are lined with lively Latin American ceramics reaching to a wood-beamed roof.

Foggy Bottom

Together with Georgetown, **Foggy Bottom** forms one of the oldest parts of DC, lying between Pennsylvania and Constitution avenues from 17th to 25th streets. It's not exactly the most exciting place – the cultural activities at the **Kennedy Center** and the various government offices set a blandly white-collar, institutional tone – but enough of the buildings, including the historic **Octagon** house, are open to the public, making a walk through the neighborhood rewarding. The nearest Metro stop is Foggy Bottom-GWU, which is convenient for **George Washington University**, Washington Circle, and the Kennedy Center, but is half a dozen blocks and a fifteen-minute walk from Constitution Avenue.

Constitution Avenue

From the Organization of American States building at the corner of 17th Street, **Constitution Avenue** – known as B Street until the 1930s – parades

The murky story of Foggy Bottom

Settled in the mid-eighteenth century, **Foggy Bottom** began as a thriving town on the shores of the Potomac (which reached further north in those days), and was known variously as Hamburg or Funkstown, after its German landlord **Jacob Funk**. Fashionable houses were built on the higher ground above today's E Street, though down by the river, in what's now **West Potomac Park**, it was a different story: filthy industries emptied effluents into the Potomac and the city canal, while workers' housing was erected on the low-lying malarial marshlands, blighted by plagues of rats, rampant poison ivy, and winter mud and fog.

The poor, predominantly black, neighborhood changed radically once the marsh-lands were drained in the late 1800s. Families and industries were displaced by the new West Potomac Park, and the southern limit was now defined by the grand **Constitution Avenue**, which replaced the filled-in city canal. The smarter streets to the north formed the backdrop for a series of federal and international organizations that moved in before and after World War II, as the federal workforce rapidly expanded. In 1802, there were only 291 federal employees; by the 1970s there were over two million; consequently, entire districts like Foggy Bottom were appropriated to warehouse DC's burgeoning share. Nowadays, given the predominance of governmental institutions here and the absence of any real street life outside of **George Washington University**, Foggy Bottom has seamlessly blended with the fabric of official Washington, becoming a wide swath of bureaucracy beginning at Capitol Hill and continuing on to the east bank of the Potomac River.

an attractive line of buildings framed by the greenery of Constitution Gardens across the way. The street isn't necessarily a destination in itself, but it's dotted with interesting sites along the way, from a few architectural highlights on the north side to the Vietnam Veterans Memorial on the south side of the avenue.

Federal Reserve

20th St NW between C St and Constitution Ave ☎202/452-3149 for tours, ☎202/452-3778 for gallery, ☻www.federalreserve.gov; Foggy Bottom-GWU Metro. By advance reservation only, Mon–Fri 11am–2pm.

The first building of any distinction along Constitution Avenue is the enormous, eagle-fronted **Federal Reserve**, designed by Paul Cret, who was also responsible for the OAS and the Folger Shakespeare Library (see pp.111–112). The department headquartered here controls the country's money supply and gold reserves, and issues government securities. Group tours of the 1937 building are available for visitors 18 and over, and include a film giving an overview of the organization's function, as well as a look at the Board Room, where key decisions – like whether to raise US interest rates and, if so, by how much – are made. With a day's notice, you can make a separate reservation to visit the Reserve's decent **art gallery**, which hosts temporary exhibits on Romantic-era French sculpture and American Abstract Expressionism, among other things. Its small permanent collection comprises a hodgepodge of donated pieces, from the bucolic works of Antebellum landscape artist **Thomas Hotchkiss** to the modern color-field paintings of **Ellsworth Kelly**.

National Academy of Sciences

2101 Constitution Ave NW ☎202/334-2000, ☻www.nas.edu; Foggy Bottom-GWU Metro. Mon–Fri 9am–5pm.

Congress created the **National Academy of Sciences** in 1863 to provide the country with independent, objective scientific advice. The building's facade is adorned with Greek inscriptions, and its cold Neoclassical lines are softened by a grove of elm and holly trees at the southwest (22nd St) corner, where Robert Berks's large bronze statue of **Albert Einstein** sits. Einstein is depicted lounging on a granite bench with the universe (in the shape of a galaxy map) at his feet; a piece of paper inscribed with the famous formula from his Theory of Relativity is in his hand.

The Academy also has an **art gallery** that showcases pieces relating to its mission. Paintings, sculptures, and multimedia projects by mostly unknown artists provide fascinating takes on astronomy, anatomy, cosmology, cartography, and other scientific fields. (Every third Thursday, many of the same works pop up at NAS's Old Downtown branch, at 500 5th St NW, which is otherwise closed to the general public, except for a book- and gift shop.) There are also free Sunday-afternoon **music concerts** (Oct–April; see p.296) in its auditorium, featuring the occasional big-name artist, in styles from Baroque to modern.

Department of State

C St between 21st and 23rd sts ☎202/647-3241, ☻www.state.gov; Foggy Bottom-GWU Metro. Tours by appointment only Mon–Fri 9.30am, 10.30am & 2.45pm.

In 1960 the **Department of State** moved out of the Old Executive Office Building and into its own headquarters – a long, white building occupying two entire blocks in the southwest corner of Foggy Bottom. Established in 1789 and helmed by Thomas Jefferson, the nation's oldest and most senior Cabinet agency is effectively the federal foreign office. It's also notoriously circumspect, and it's a wonder that visitors were ever allowed in at all. Although tours were suspended here after 9/11, they have since resumed (though you must reserve at least a month in advance) and allow you to peek at the elegant **Diplomatic Reception Rooms**. During the 1960s, many of these rooms were redecorated and re-furnished to provide more suitable chambers for receiving diplomats and heads of state. Among the wealth of eighteenth- and nineteenth-century paintings and furniture is the desk on which the American Revolution's conclusive Treaty of Paris was signed.

Department of the Interior

1849 C St NW ☎202/208-4743, ⓦwww.doi.gov; Farragut West Metro. Mon–Fri 8.30am–4.30pm; reserve in advance for tours.

The nation's principal landowner and conservation agency, the **Department of the Interior**, is east of the State Department along C Street. One of the earliest federal departments to take up residence in Foggy Bottom, the Department moved into Waddy Butler Wood's granite, square-columned building in 1937. Inside, grand WPA-era murals – like one commemorating Marian Anderson's 1939 concert at the Lincoln Memorial – decorate the walls.

After presenting ID at the reception desk, you'll be directed to the Department's little-visited **museum**, which sheds light on agencies like the Bureau of Land Management, the National Park Service, and the Bureau of Indian Affairs. The wood-paneled museum opened in 1938 and is filled with stuffed bison heads, old saddles, fossils and minerals, paintings by nineteenth-century surveyors of the West, and five elaborate dioramas featuring an Oklahoma land office, coal mine explosion, and frontier fort. There are also regularly changing exhibitions of photography, paintings, or sculpture, much of it drawn from the museum's stock of 145 million items. Around the corner from the museum, a gift shop sells Native American crafts. Elsewhere in the building, the **National Park Service**'s information office (Mon–Fri 9am–5pm) has leaflets on almost every NPS park, museum, and monument in the country; in DC, that includes all the sites on the Mall.

The Octagon

1799 New York Ave NW ☎202/638-3105, ⓦwww.theoctagon.org; Farragut West Metro. Tues–Sun 10am–4.30pm. $3.

Built in 1800, the **Octagon** is one of the city's oldest homes. Today it sits one block north of the Interior Department, and west of the Corcoran Gallery. Although it doesn't have eight sides (debate continues as to what the name actually means), it's nonetheless a classic structure loosely adapted from the Georgian style, whose rather simple brick exterior gives way to curving interior walls, arcing closet doors, and several period rooms open for touring. The circular entry hall sports its original marble floor, while beyond, a swirling, oval staircase climbs up three stories. The house had two master bedrooms and five regular ones to accommodate the owner, his wife, and their fifteen children; most of the rooms are now used as gallery space. In the dining and drawing rooms, period furnishings reveal how the house would have looked in its day – light, with high ceilings, delicate plaster cornicing, and Chippendale accessories. The two portraits in the dining room are of the architect and the owner, and the beautifully carved stone

The many sides of the Octagon

Wealthy Virginian plantation owner **John Tayloe** built his Washington townhouse on a prime corner plot just two blocks from the new President's Mansion. Although no longer set amid fields and flanked by a line of fir trees, the Octagon, now dwarfed by the office buildings behind it, gives a good example of the private homes that once characterized the neighborhood. Tayloe, a friend of George Washington, was so rich and well connected that he could afford to spend the colossal total sum of $35,000 on his house and hire **William Thornton**, who designed the US Capitol, to build it. The **War of 1812** guaranteed the house its place in history. Spared the bonfire that destroyed the President's Mansion – possibly because the French ambassador was in residence at the time – President and Dolley Madison stayed here after they returned from fleeing the city. For six months in 1814–15, the president ran the government from its rooms, and on February 17, 1815, the **Treaty of Ghent**, making peace with Britain, was signed in the study (on a table still kept in the house). For much of the latter part of the nineteenth century, the Octagon was left to deteriorate, but at the turn of the twentieth century, the American Institute of Architects (AIA) bought it and used it as its headquarters until 1973. The AIA – now ensconced in modern premises nearby – still maintains the Octagon, which is open as both a historic house and a museum, with changing exhibitions devoted to architecture, decorative arts, and city history.

mantel in the drawing room is an original, signed and dated 1799. Take a look downstairs at the accessible basement, which gives you an idea of the kind of drudgery servants and slaves underwent while the house owners lived in splendor above.

Northern Foggy Bottom

The **northern side** of Foggy Bottom is rather drab terrain, split between sites for institutional behemoths like the IMF and World Bank (adjacent on G St between 18th and 20th) and the uneventful campus for **George Washington University**. The main campus spreads over several city blocks between F, 20th, and 24th streets and Pennsylvania Avenue; the nicest part is **University Yard**, between G and H, and 20th and 21st streets – a green, rose-filled park surrounded by Colonial Revival buildings. The park's statue of Washington is yet another copy of the famous Houdon image. For more information on the university, visit the Academic Center at 801 22nd St NW (Jan–April & Aug–Oct Mon–Fri 9am–5pm, Sat 10am–3pm; ☎202/994-6602, ⑩www.gwu .edu), where you can pick up a campus map and ask about the occasional student-led historic walking tours of the area (1hr long; Mon–Fri 11am & 3pm, Sept–May also Sat 11am & 2pm).

There are a few scattered points of architectural interest in northern Foggy Bottom. To the east, at 20th and G, the red-brick, Gothic **Lutheran United Church**, built in 1889 for the descendants of the neighborhood's Germanic immigrants, provides a reminder of one aspect of Foggy Bottom's religious history, while on the western side of the GWU campus, the Gothic **St Mary's Church**, 730 23rd St, was the first black Episcopal church in DC. Established in 1886, its construction was paid for by a wealthy band of local citizens who coughed up $15,000 to hire architect **James Renwick**, of Smithsonian Castle and Renwick Gallery fame. Two blocks west on 25th Street (north of H), there's a run of carefully preserved nineteenth-century brick houses with vivid pastel colors; the most interesting ones are in **Snow Court** (off 25th, between I and K), DC's only surviving interior alley, where the homes are only 12ft wide – in the 1880s each one probably housed ten people; nowadays they change hands for a fortune.

The Watergate

If there's a single word synonymous with American political scandal, it's certainly "Watergate (see box overleaf)," which takes its name from the **Watergate Complex** on 25th Street NW at Virginia Avenue. This huge, curving, mid-1960s residential and commercial monster – named for the flight of steps behind the Lincoln Memorial that leads down to the Potomac – has always been a sought-after address, both for foreign ambassadors and the city's top brass. People like Bob and Elizabeth Dole and Caspar Weinberger have maintained apartments here for years, and White House intern Monica Lewinsky lived here before scandal forced her from DC. In 1972, the Democratic National Committee was headquartered in the hotel's sixth floor. On June 17, five men connected to President Nixon's re-election campaign were arrested for breaking into the offices, and two years later, Nixon resigned from the presidency in disgrace. Visitors can come here to shop, sleep (see p.255), and eat (see *Aquarelle*, p.273), but the complex is really more something you'd pass by, rather than tour.

Kennedy Center

2700 F St NW ☎202/467-4600, 🌐www.kennedy-center.org; Foggy Bottom-GWU Metro. Tours Mon–Fri 10am–5pm, Sat & Sun 10am–1pm; reserve at ☎202/416-8340.

Washington didn't have a national cultural center until 1971, when the $78-million white marble monster designed by Edward Durrell Stone was opened. The **John F. Kennedy Center for the Performing Arts** continues to be the city's foremost cultural outlet; it has four main auditoriums, various exhibition halls, a clutch of restaurants and bars, and is home to the **National Symphony Orchestra**, **Washington Opera**, and **American Film Institute**. There's an information desk on your way in, and you're free to wander around. Provided there's no performance or rehearsal taking place, you can look inside the theaters and concert halls (most are open to visitors 10am–1pm). Free 45-minute guided tours depart daily from Level A (beneath the Opera House).

The Grand Foyer itself is a real sight: 630ft long and 60ft high, it's lit by gargantuan crystal chandeliers and contains an eight-foot-high **bronze bust**

> I would walk over my grandmother if necessary to assure the President's re-election.
>
> Charles Colson, special counselor to Richard M. Nixon

The burglars who broke into the headquarters of the Democratic National Committee at the Watergate were in effect breaking into the home of every citizen of the United States. And . . . what they were seeking to steal was . . . their most precious heritage, the right to vote in a free election.

> Sam Ervin, chairman of Senate Investigating Committee

The 1972 presidential election campaign was well under way when five men were arrested at the **Watergate Complex** on June 17. Richard Nixon, running for re-election against Democratic challenger George McGovern, was determined to win a second term, elevating the election race into a moral struggle against encroaching liberal forces, who, crucially, were pushing the anti-Vietnam War message to the top of the political agenda.

After being spotted by a security guard on his rounds, the five men were apprehended in the offices of the Democratic National Committee in the act of tapping the phone of Lawrence O'Brien, the national party chairman. Once arraigned in court, it became clear that these were no ordinary burglars: one, James McCord, worked directly for the **Committee to Re-Elect the President** (known, appropriately, as CREEP), all had CIA connections, and some were later linked to documents which suggested that their escapade had been sanctioned by White House staffer Howard Hunt and election campaign attorney G. Gordon Liddy. To anyone who cared to look, the connections went further still: at the White House, Hunt worked for Charles Colson, Nixon's special counsel, while McCord's direct superior was the head of CREEP, John Mitchell, who also happened to be Attorney General of the United States.

Amazingly, at least in retrospect, hardly anyone looked further. The burglars, together with Hunt and Liddy, were indicted in September 1972 but refused to provide details about any possible collaborators. The Democrats, none more so than McGovern, complained loudly about dirty tricks, but the White House officially denied any knowledge. In the election in November, Nixon won a landslide, carrying 49 out of the 50 states, save only Massachusetts and the District of Columbia.

From such commanding heights, it was remarkable how quickly things unraveled. Initially the only people asking questions were *Washington Post* reporters **Bob Woodward** and **Carl Bernstein**. As the months went by, and aided by a source known to Woodward only as "Deep Throat," the pair uncovered irregularities in the Republican campaign – "dirty tricks" to discredit their opponents – many of which had close, but unprovable, links with the Watergate burglary. To the FBI's annoyance, the stories often relied on verbatim accounts of the FBI's own investigations – someone, somewhere, was leaking information. However, it still proved difficult to generate much interest outside Washington in the matter, and the story would probably have been forgotten but for the impetus provided by the defendants' trial. All pleaded guilty to burglary, but before sentencing in January 1973 the judge made it clear that he didn't believe that the men acted alone; long sentences were threatened. Rather than face jail, some defendants began to talk, including James McCord, who not only implicated senior officials like John Mitchell for the first time but also claimed that secret CREEP funds had been used to finance an anti-Democrat smear campaign, which employed so-called "plumbers" – to stop leaks and patch holes in Nixon's defenses – to work against domestic adversaries (the "enemies" on Nixon's infamous list). This was precisely what Woodward and Bernstein had been trying to prove for months.

As pressure on the administration for answers grew, the Senate established a special investigating committee under Sam Ervin and appointed a special prosecutor, Archibald Cox. The trail now led ever closer to the White House. In a desperate damage-control exercise, Nixon's own counsel, John Dean, was sacked, and the resignations of White House Chief of Staff H.R. Haldeman and domestic affairs advisor John Erlichman were accepted; all, it seemed, were involved in planning the burglary.

In June 1973, the **Watergate hearings**, broadcast on national television, began to undermine Nixon's steadfast denial of any involvement. It transpired that the White House had promised clemency and cash if the burglars remained silent; the CIA had leaned on the FBI to prevent any further investigations; and illegal wiretaps, dirty tricks campaigns, and unlawful campaign contributions were commonplace.

The president continued to stand aloof from the charges, but was finally dragged down by the revelation that he himself had routinely bugged offices in the White House and elsewhere, taping conversations that pertained to Watergate. Famously, it quickly became a matter of "what did the president know and when did he know it." Cox and the Senate committee subpoenaed the **tapes**, but Nixon refused to release them, citing his presidential duty to protect executive privilege. Soon after, he engineered the sacking of Cox in the so-called "Saturday Night Massacre," a move that led to the convening of the House Judiciary Committee, the body charged with preparing bills of **impeachment** – in this case, against the president for refusing to comply with a subpoena. To deflect mounting suspicion, Nixon finally handed over edited transcripts of the tapes in April 1974; despite the erasure of eighteen minutes of conversation, the "smoking gun" transcripts, rather than clearing Nixon of any involvement, simply dragged him further in – many citizens were appalled, for one, to see the great number of "expletive deleted" notations from the tapes, suggesting Nixon was impossibly vulgar and obscene in his common speech. The president, furthermore, at least knew about the cover-up, and there was clear evidence of wrongdoing by key government and White House personnel. A grand jury indicted Mitchell, Haldeman, Erlichman, Dean and others for specific offenses, while the House Judiciary Committee drew up a bill of impeachment against Nixon for committing "high crimes and misdemeanors."

On August 5, 1974, the **Supreme Court** ordered Nixon to hand over his tapes. These proved conclusively that he and his advisors had devised a strategy of bribes and destruction of evidence to cover up White House and CREEP involvement in the Watergate burglary. The president, despite his protestations, had lied to the people, and it was inevitable that he should face impeachment. Urged on by senior Republican senators, on August 8, 1974, Richard Milhous Nixon became the first president to **resign**. Combative to the end, he made no acknowledgment of guilt, suggesting instead that he had simply made errors of judgment.

Vice President **Gerald Ford** succeeded Nixon as president, but not much changed within the new administration: Secretary of State Henry Kissinger, who had a hand in the bombing of Laos and Cambodia and the coup in Chile that installed Augusto Pinochet – campaigns hidden from the American public – kept his job, while Alexander Haig, a key figure in the withholding of the Watergate tapes, was promoted to become head of NATO. To top it all off, Ford formally pardoned Nixon with unseemly haste, allowing him to live out his retirement without controversy in California, but probably costing Ford his 1976 re-election to Jimmy Carter. In a bizarre twist, Richard Nixon slowly rehabilitated himself in the eyes of the political establishment and even the press; when he died in 1995 there was a full turn-out at his funeral by leaders of all political hues – however, the ceremony took place not in official Washington, but in Yorba Linda, California; unlike Ronald Reagan in 2004, Nixon did not lie in state under the Capitol dome or receive official honors at Washington National Cathedral.

of JFK in the moon-rock style favored by sculptor Robert Berks. You can also drop by the Hall of States, where states' flags are hung in the order they entered the Union, and the Hall of Nations, which honors the nations recognized by the US. In addition, each of the theaters and concert halls has its own catalog of artwork, from the **Matisse** tapestries outside the Opera House and the **Barbara Hepworth** sculpture in the Concert Hall, to the **Felix de Welden** bronze bust of Eisenhower above the lobby of the Eisenhower Theatre. The **Roof Terrace** level has the Performing Arts Library – filled with scripts, information on historical performances, and recordings (Tues–Fri 11am–8.30pm, Sat 10am–6pm) – and places to eat. While you're up here, step out onto the terrace for great views across the Potomac to Theodore Roosevelt Island, and north to Georgetown and Washington National Cathedral.

Old Downtown and the Federal Triangle

A few decades ago the older section of DC's Downtown, above the eastern half of the Mall, was a pretty bleak place, blighted by crime and deserted at night, with little of interest other than the architecture of its nineteenth-century Neoclassical buildings and grand New Deal-era structures. In recent years, however, **Old Downtown** has experienced an upsurge of interest, thanks to a steady flow of urban-renewal dollars and the economic boom of the late 1990s; today you'll find a wide range of chic restaurants, niche museums, fancy hotels, and more. Tours of the neighborhood begin with the landmarks along Pennsylvania Avenue NW and include the **Navy Memorial** and grand old **Willard Hotel** North of the avenue, city boosters have re-designated a broad swath of Old Downtown and taken to calling it the **Penn Quarter**, in and around which many of the grander municipal buildings have been converted into fine museums – for example, the Pension Building is now the stunning **National Building Museum**, and the old Library is the **City Museum of DC**. Other key sights include **Ford's Theatre** and the **Museum of Women in the Arts**, from which it's only a short stroll to **Chinatown**, where you can lunch cheaply on noodles and dim sum. Less appealing is the ten-square-block area below Pennsylvania Avenue NW known as the **Federal Triangle**, where eight colossal government buildings hog all the space. It's true that the Triangle has its highlights, but for most visitors it's little more than a buffer separating the sights of Old Downtown from the National Mall.

Some history

The land between the Capitol and the White House, north of the Mall, was the only part of nineteenth-century Washington that remotely resembled a city. A downtown developed in the diamond formed by Pennsylvania, New York, Massachusetts, and Indiana avenues, and fashionable stores and restaurants existed alongside printing presses, shoeshine stalls, oyster sellers, and market traders. Entertainment was provided by a series of popular theaters, including Ford's Theatre, where President Lincoln was shot.

By the late nineteenth century, Pennsylvania Avenue marked the southern limits of Washington society; the shops on its north side were as far as the genteel would venture. The downtown area was given a new lease of life in the 1930s, when the majestic buildings of the Federal Triangle were built, but by the 1960s it was a shambling, low-rent neighborhood that would be badly damaged by the 1968 riots. As established businesses fled to the developing area north of the White House, the faded neighborhood eventually became known as Old Downtown.

In the 1980s, however, Old Downtown began to be rescued from years of neglect. Since then, an enormous amount of money has been pumped into renovations, especially in the easternmost area (south of G St, between 3rd and 12th), now being trumpeted as the Penn Quarter – grafting an agreeable swatch of delis, restaurants, galleries, and landscaping onto the existing historic buildings and cleaned-up streets. Just to the north of here, the opening of the MCI Center (at 7th and F) has sparked another revitalization, and with the new Convention Center north of Mt Vernon Square, this part of downtown DC is sure to remain one of the city's most rapidly evolving areas for years to come.

Along Pennsylvania Avenue NW

Defining the border between Old Downtown and the Federal Triangle (forming its hypotenuse), **Pennsylvania Avenue NW** is one of the District's most famous roads, connecting the Capitol with the White House. In L'Enfant's original design, the avenue was supposed to allow for unimpeded views of both structures, but this changed when Andrew Jackson had the Treasury Building plunked down on the western end. Still, the avenue continues as the site of the president's triumphal January **Inaugural Parade**, which takes him from the Capitol (where he's sworn in) to the White House (where he'll live for the next four years). Thomas Jefferson led the first impromptu parade in 1805; James Madison made the ceremony official; and every president since then has trundled up in some form of conveyance or another – except Jimmy Carter, who famously walked the sixteen long blocks to the White House.

Although Pennsylvania Avenue was to be the center of the new capital's commercial life, its success was hampered by the piecemeal development taking place all around. While fashionable shops operated along its north side, the swamp-ridden reaches to its south (today's Federal Triangle), close to the filthy canal that isolated the city from the Mall, housed a notorious stew of slum housing, bordellos, and cheap liquor joints. Turn-of-the-twentieth-century additions to the avenue – notably the Post Office and the *Willard Hotel* – were part of an early attempt to transform the district's fortunes, but for much of the twentieth century Pennsylvania Avenue was in severe decline. In the 1970s the Pennsylvania Avenue Development Corporation (PADC) formed and enlivened the area with small plazas, memorials framed by newly planted trees, and attractive Victorian flourishes on lampposts and benches.

Pershing Park and around

Beginning at Old Downtown's northwestern end of Pennsylvania Avenue, closest to the White House, the pleasant Pershing Park was named for the commander of the American forces during World War I, popularly known as "Black Jack" for his role as a commander of African-American cavalry soldiers

OLD DOWNTOWN AND THE FEDERAL TRIANGLE

CAFÉS & RESTAURANTS

Andale	28
Burma	12
Café Mozart	3
Corner Bakery	21
Dean & Deluca	22
District Chophouse & Brewery	24
Eat First	10
Ebbitt Express	15
Haad Thai	2
Harry's	27
Hunan Chinatown	11
Jaleo	26
Lei Garden	8
Matchbox	6
Old Ebbitt Grill	14
Red Sage	16
Reeve's Restaurant and Bakery	13
Sky Terrace	18
Ten Penh	29
Tony Cheng	9
Tosca	19

BARS & CLUBS

Capitol City Brewing Co.	4
D.A's RFD Washington	5
Diva	23
ESPN Zone	1
Fadó	7
Gordon Biersch Brewery	20
John Harvard's	25
Platinum	17

ACCOMMODATION

Courtyard by Marriott	F
Harrington	H
Henley Park	C
Hi-Washington DC	A
JW Marriott	G
Marriott at Metro Center	E
Morrison-Clark Inn	B
Red Roof Inn	D

in the 1890s. Pershing's statue stands alongside a sunken terrace that becomes a skating rink in winter. Just to the west, **Hamilton Place** marks the spot where an earlier general, William Tecumseh Sherman (also honored by a statue), presided over the Grand Review of the Union Armies in May 1865; six weeks after Lee's surrender, the victorious troops proudly marched up Pennsylvania Avenue in one of the most stirring military parades ever seen in the capital. It was a show of Union strength tinged with sadness, as President Lincoln had been assassinated only a few weeks earlier.

Willard Hotel

1401 Pennsylvania Ave NW ☎202/628-9100, 🌐www.washington.intercontinental.com; Metro Center Metro.

Looming over the north side of Pershing Park at 14th Street is one of the grand old ladies among Washington hotels, the **Willard** – a Washington landmark for over 150 years. Although a hotel has existed on the site since the city's earliest days, it was after 1850, when Henry Willard gave his name to the place, that it became a haunt of statesmen, politicians, and top brass – including Abraham Lincoln, who was smuggled in here before his first inauguration (during which snipers were placed on the roof). The *Willard*'s opulent public rooms attracted profit-seekers anxious to press their demands on political leaders; it's even believed that the hotel gave rise to the word "lobbyist." A story also tells that Julia Ward Howe wrote *The Battle Hymn of the Republic* while closeted here during the Civil War – supposedly inspired by Union soldiers marching under her window belting out their favorite song, *John Brown's Body*.

In 1901, the *Willard* was renovated and became the splendid Beaux Arts building that you'll find today. It went out of business after the riots of 1968, but a thorough restoration in 1986 recaptured its early style. Drop by the galleried lobby and tread the main corridor's plush carpets to get a feel for where DC's swells and well-heeled still hang out. After spending some time here, you might want to check out the 1917 *Washington Hotel* (see "Accommodation" chapter), on the corner of 15th and F streets, whose rooftop bar provides excellent views across to the White House grounds.

Freedom Plaza

The large, open space known as **Freedom Plaza** lies where Pennsylvania Avenue kinks into E Street (at 13th) and is the site of numerous festivals and open-air concerts. Lined in marble, the square is inlaid with a large-scale representation of Pierre L'Enfant's city plan, crafted in bronze and colored stone, and etched with various laudatory inscriptions. From here the view down Pennsylvania Avenue to the Capitol is splendid, but this is a sweltering place to hang around in summer; the only shade is provided by the statue of **General Casimir Pulaski**, a Polish hero of the Revolutionary War, at the eastern end.

On the plaza's south side, the Corinthian columns and pediments of the Beaux Arts **District Building** offer a glimmer of historic charm, while the restored facade of the **National Theatre** – on this site since 1835, though the current building dates from 1922 – forms part of the **National Place** complex, whose drab exterior hides a three-level shopping mall, **The Shops at National Place** – looking worse for wear these days, with a number of the boutiques now shuttered. At the northeastern corner of the plaza, the elegant **Warner Theatre** (at 13th and E) is a classic 1920s movie house that has been reborn as a performing-arts center.

Old Post Office

1100 Pennsylvania Ave NW ☎202/289-4224, ⊛www.oldpostofficedc.com; Federal Triangle Metro.
Mon–Sat 10am–7pm, Sun noon–8pm, summer Mon–Sat until 9pm.

Two blocks east of Freedom Plaza is the stunning, Romanesque Revival **Old Post Office**, which owes its survival more to the depressed real-estate market of the early twentieth century than it does to civic planners' sense for historic preservation. A longtime candidate for demolition, the former post office (1899–1914) has managed to survive through the decades intact, with its towering granite walls, seven-story atrium, restored iron support beams, and burnished wood paneling. Now known as the **Pavilion**, the site is home to ethnic restaurants and various shops, and features a post office counter from the turn of the twentieth century (Mon–Fri 9am–5pm), still in use at the Pennsylvania Avenue entrance.

The building's **clock tower** is also worth a look (daily Mon–Fri 9am–5.45pm, Sat & Sun 10am–5.45pm, summer Mon–Fri until 7.45pm; ☎202/606-8691, ⊛www.nps.gov/opot); from here park rangers oversee short, free tours up to the **observation deck**, 270ft above Pennsylvania Avenue. The glass-elevator ride allows you to see the building in all its glory, and the view-ing platform (three flights of stairs beyond the elevator) offers a stunning city panorama. On the way back down to the elevator, you can see the **Congress Bells**, replicas of those in Westminster Abbey. A Bicentennial gift from London, they were installed here in 1983.

Back outside on the avenue, **Benjamin Franklin** – "Philosopher, Printer, Philanthropist, Patriot," as his statue has it – gives a cheery little wave. You can park yourself on a bench and look across to the Beaux Arts facade of the 1898 Evening Star Building, with its attractive balconies, pediments, and carvings.

Federal Bureau of Investigation

9th St and Pennsylvania Ave NW ☎202/324-3447, ⊛www.fbi.gov; Archives-Navy Memorial Metro.

Even if you had somehow never heard of the **FBI**, the presence of countless DC tourists wearing T-shirts emblazoned with that acronym would doubtless get your attention. The Bureau's giant, Brutalist home at Pennsylvania Avenue and 9th Street is a clunky modern office that pales by comparison to the Neo-classical-styled Department of Justice across the street. This used to be a favorite spot for visitors who were fans of the *X-Files* and other such TV programs, but since 9/11 tours have been canceled, and the building's ongoing renovation has kept it off-limits to nosy interlopers, T-shirts or not.

From the outside there's not much to look at: the building itself is a 1970s monstrosity named for the organization's notorious Red-baiting, cross-dressing chief, **J. Edgar Hoover**. Established in 1908 with the motto "Fidelity, Bravery, Integrity," the FBI owed its early investigative techniques to those of Scottish immigrant Allan Pinkerton's successful nineteenth-century Pinkerton Detec-tive Agency, and made its reputation in the 1920s and 1930s by battling gang-sters and attempting to enforce Prohibition. Today, ten thousand special agents are employed to fight organized and white-collar crime, pursue drug traffickers and terrorists, and lurk in the shadowy world of counter-intelligence.

Market Square and around

In 1801 the city's biggest outdoor market opened for business at the foot of 7th Street. Known as Center Market, it backed onto the canal along the Mall, where goods barges could be unloaded; out front, top-heavy carts and drays spilled across Pennsylvania Avenue and up 7th Street on the way out of the city. It was a notoriously noxious spot, and there was little clamor when it was demolished in 1870; the **National Archives** (see pp.160–162) was erected on the site in 1935. The concave, colonnaded buildings of the development opposite, known as **Market Square**, are given over to café-restaurants and outdoor seating, while upper-floor apartments have sweeping views over the revitalized Penn Quarter.

US Navy Memorial

701 Pennsylvania Ave NW ☎202/737-2300, ✆www.lonesailor.org; Archives-Navy Memorial Metro. Heritage Center open Tues–Sat 9.30am–5pm, also Mon in summer.

Market Square's circular plaza is covered by an etched representation of the world, circled by low, tiered, granite walls lapped by running water. These elements are part of the **US Navy Memorial**, which also includes a statue of a lone sailor, kit bag by his side, and inscribed quotations from the likes of Themistocles, architect of the Greek naval victory during the Persian Wars, and naval aviator Neil Armstrong. Especially worth a look are the bronze relief panels on the walls, which illustrate different aspects of the Navy's mission in various wars. The imagery and captions can be off-kilter – "LSTs: Fondly Known as Large, Slow Targets" – but you do get a sense of the Navy's focus and spirit. In summer, the **Navy Band** holds regular concerts at the memorial.

Directly behind the memorial, in the easternmost Market Square building at 701 Pennsylvania Ave NW, the **Naval Heritage Center** can tell you more about the service with its changing exhibits. Portraits honor the various presidents who have served in the US Navy: JFK famously commanded a motor torpedo boat and was awarded the Navy and Marine Corps Medal for heroism, and Johnson, Nixon, Ford, and Carter all served with distinction too. George H.W. Bush, then the Navy's youngest bomber pilot, received the Distinguished Flying Cross and three air medals for his endeavors.

FDR Memorial

Across Pennsylvania Avenue from here, in the green plot in front of the National Archives at 9th Street, a small marble memorial commemorates war-time president **Franklin Delano Roosevelt**. It was FDR's wish that any memorial to him erected after his death be "plain, without any ornamentation," and that's what he got – at least at first. Placed here in 1965 on the twentieth anniversary of his death, the monument is inscribed simply "In Memory of Franklin Delano Roosevelt 1882–1945." But despite his request, the much more elaborate FDR Memorial opened on the National Mall in 1997 (see p.55).

East of the memorials

A little farther up on the north side of Pennsylvania Avenue, the turreted, pink-stone **Sears House**, at no. 633, once contained the studio of nineteenth-century photographer Matthew Brady, whose graphic photographs of the slaughter at Antietam in 1862 first brought home the full horror of the Civil War to the American people. A block northeast of the Navy Memorial on Indiana Avenue, small **Indiana Plaza** is taken up by the monument to the victorious Grand Army of the Republic, a triangular obelisk adorned with figures representing Fraternity, Loyalty, and Charity. Back on the south side of Pennsylvania Avenue, the bronze, triple-decker fountain in the corner plot between 6th Street and Constitution Avenue commemorates former Secretary of the Treasury and art maven **Andrew Mellon**, fittingly sited across from the National Gallery of Art, which he funded and filled with paintings. Finally, just before 4th Street NW, the ultramodern stone-and-glass Canadian Embassy sits next to the site for the **Newseum**, a journalism-oriented museum that plans to open in early 2007 after relocating from its former home in Arlington.

The Federal Triangle

The wedge of land formed by 15th Street and Pennsylvania and Constitution avenues, the **Federal Triangle** is the massively scaled area linking the White House and US Capitol, with grand Neoclassical piles presenting imposing facades to the National Mall. Most of these structures were erected in the 1930s in an attempt to graft instant majesty upon the capital of the Free World. The Triangle's nineteenth-century origins, however, were distinctly humble, as a canal-side slum known as Murder Bay. Hoodlums frequented its brothels and taverns, and on hot days the stench from Center Market drifted through the ill-fitting windows of the district's cheap boardinghouses. Few improvements came until the 1920s, when a shortage of office space forced the federal government's hand. The Triangle was bought and redeveloped in its entirety between 6th and 15th streets, following a classical plan that featured buildings opening onto quiet interior courtyards. Although never fully realized, the plan made for a remarkably uniform area. Different architects worked on various projects, but all the buildings have the same characteristics: granite façades, stone reliefs, huge columns and ponderous inscriptions.

The National Aquarium

14th St south of Pennsylvania Ave NW ☎202/482-2825, ⊛www.nationalaquarium.com; Federal Triangle Metro. Daily 9am–5pm. $3.50.

Built in 1931, the thousand-foot-long Department of Commerce was one of the first Federal Triangle buildings to be completed, and today it forms the western side of the Triangle, at 14th Street between E and Constitution. Its main points of interest are that it houses the White House Visitor Center, on the north side of the building, and the **National Aquarium**, on the east side, at 14th Street. Founded in 1873, this is the oldest aquarium in the country, and even though it's been here since 1932, the Department of Commerce's drab gray corridors still seem like a strange environment for fish. There are some 1700 creatures of 260 species here, but despite its impressive-sounding name and central location, the aquarium is one of the city's more disappointing sights: the fish-tank displays don't seem to have been updated in at least twenty years, and the atmosphere is stagnant and depressing. Save your time and effort for the National Museum of Natural History, one long block south and east.

Ronald Reagan Building and around

Across 14th Street, the Beaux Arts-style **District Building**, with its mighty caryatids and bold corner shield emblems, predates all other Federal Triangle edifices. Erected in 1908 to house city council offices, it escaped demolition in the 1920s and 1930s and hung on until 1992, when the mayor's office was moved to Judiciary Square. Since then, the building has been restored as part of the massive adjacent development, the **Ronald Reagan Building**, 1300 Pennsylvania Ave at 14th St NW, the country's second-largest federal building after the Pentagon. Inside, along with the International Trade Center and other offices, you'll find an immense, barrel-vaulted atrium, a food court, restaurant, and exhibition space on the west side, where a colorful, graffiti-covered chunk of the Berlin Wall provides visual contrast to the antiseptic architecture. The main reason you'll possibly want to visit this building, however, is to check out the **DC Chamber of Commerce Visitor Center** (Mon–Fri 8am–5.30pm, Sat & Sun 9am–4pm; ☏202/347-7201, ⊛www.dcchamber.org), which provides maps, tours, and information.

Across the courtyard to the east, and impossible to miss if you're heading toward the Federal Triangle Metro, is the gargantuan **Ariel Rios Building**, a Neoclassical, New Deal-era behemoth that houses both the Environmental Protection Agency and the US Customs Service. Its long colonnade and entablature of lazing nudes provide stark contrast to the bleak modernism of the National Museum of American History across Constitution Avenue.

IRS, Justice Department, and FTC

East across 12th Street, the 1930 **Internal Revenue Service** (IRS) building was the earliest federal structure to grace the Federal Triangle area. Its Neoclassical design is textbook material, though libertarians may take issue with the inscription on the facade: "Taxes are what we pay for a civilized society." Across 10th Street is the Art Deco-influenced **Department of Justice**, in whose enclosed courtyard stands a bust of former Attorney General **Robert F. Kennedy** by Robert Berks, who sculpted the eight-foot-tall bronze bust of JFK in the Kennedy Center. Across 9th Street, you'll see the National Archives (see below), and the area is completed by the suitably triangular-shaped **Federal Trade Commission** (FTC) building, between 7th and 6th streets. Friezes over the building's doors on Constitution Avenue depict images of agriculture, trade, and the control of trade, symbolized by twin exterior statues (at the rounded 6th Street side) of a muscular man wrestling a wild horse.

National Archives

700 Pennsylvania Ave NW ☏202/501-5000, tours ☏202/501-5205, ⊛www.archives.gov; Archives-Navy Memorial Metro. Daily 10am–5.30pm, summer until 9pm.

John Russell Pope's **National Archives** is high Neoclassicism with bells on, showing off 72 ornate Corinthian columns (each 50ft high), a dome that rises 75ft above floor level, and a sculpted pediment, facing Constitution Avenue, topped by eagles. The Archives is responsible for the country's federal records dating back to the 1700s. When the department opened in 1935, its holdings were already formidable; today they are almost unfathomable. What everyone comes to see is the Holy Trinity of American historical records – the **Declaration of Independence**, the US **Constitution**, and the **Bill of Rights** – but the National Archives also comprises hundreds of millions of pages of documents, from war treaties to slave-ship manifests; seven million pictures; 120,000 reels of film; almost 200,000 sound recordings; eleven million maps and charts; and a quarter of a million other artifacts. If you're a researcher, you can apply for an official ID to give you access to the collection; if not, you'll have to wait in line like all the other visitors.

The Declaration of Independence

> We hold these truths to be self-evident: that all men are created equal, that they are endowed by their Creator with certain unalienable rights, that among these are life, liberty, and the pursuit of happiness . . .

Declaration of Independence, Second Continental Congress, 1776

Revolutionary fervor was gaining pace in the American colonies in the early months of 1776, whipped up in part by the demagoguery of **Samuel Adams**'s Sons of Liberty and the publication of **Thomas Paine**'s widely read pamphlet, *Common Sense*, which castigated monarchical government in general and **George III** of England in particular. In May, the sitting Second Continental Congress in Philadelphia advised the colonies to establish their own governments, whose delegates in turn increasingly harried the Congress to declare independence. The die was cast on June 7 when Richard Henry Lee of Virginia moved that "these United Colonies are, and of right ought to be, Free and Independent States." Four days later, while debate raged among the delegates, Congress authorized a committee to draft a formal declaration.

Five men assembled to begin the task: **Thomas Jefferson**, Benjamin Franklin, John Adams, Roger Sherman, and Robert Livingston. Jefferson, an accomplished writer, was charged by the others to produce a draft, which was ready to be presented to Congress by June 28. Despite the evidence of most history books, though, Jefferson didn't simply rattle off the ringing declaration that empowered a nation. For a start, he lifted phrases and ideas from other writers – the "pursuit of happiness" was a common contemporary rhetorical flourish, while the concept of "unalienable rights" had appeared in George Mason's recent **Declaration of Rights for Virginia** (see p.245). Moreover, his own words were tweaked by the rest of the committee and other changes were ordered after debate in Congress, notably the dropping of a passage condemning the slave trade, in an attempt to keep some of the Southern colonies on board. However, by the end of June, Congress had a document that spelled out exactly why Americans wanted independence, who they blamed for the state of affairs (George III, in 27 separate charges), and what they proposed to do about it. Read today, it's still a model of perfect clarity of political thought.

At this point, myths start to obfuscate the real chain of events. After a month of argument – not every delegate agreed with the proposed declaration – Congress finally approved Lee's motion on July 2, 1776. Technically, this was the day that America declared independence from Great Britain, though two days later, on **July 4, 1776**, Congress, representing the "thirteen United States of America," also approved Jefferson's document; within a couple of years, celebrations were being held on the anniversary of the fourth. The only man to actually sign the Declaration on July 4 was **John Hancock**, president of the Continental Congress, who appended his name largely and with such flourish so that the poor-sighted king wouldn't miss it – hence the colloquialism "John Hancock" for someone's signature; other signatures weren't added until August 2 and beyond, since many of the delegates had gone home as soon as the Declaration was drawn up. In any case, if the **War of Independence** didn't go well, those signatures were as good as death warrants and would allow the British to prosecute the signatories for treason and other crimes. And Hancock, as one of the richest and most powerful of delegates, had perhaps the most to lose of all. However, the mood of the occasion was best summed up by Ben Franklin, the oldest of the signatories. With his mordant wit, he reminded his compatriots, "Gentlemen, we must now all hang together, or we shall most assuredly all hang separately."

The Charters of Freedom

The Archives' three key documents, called America's **"Charters of Freedom,"** sit in the magnificent marble Rotunda within state-of-the-art, airtight containers filled with argon gas. The pages of these post-Colonial artifacts are written in elegant calligraphy in closely spaced lines – which, given their faded ink, makes them very hard to read under the low light of the display cases.

Perhaps the most popular of these documents is the **Declaration of Independence.** That it's survived at all since 1776 is rather amazing: not only was the document used as a political, social, and educational tool for the first half-century of its existence – visiting one part of the country after another – an engraving to make copies wasn't even struck until 1823. The following years didn't save the document from further wear and tear, though, as it was still moved around constantly, even within the city itself, until it was finally preserved with limited technology in the 1920s and more modern methods in the early 1950s. The two other documents here are also very important, if not quite as remarkable in their survival. The copy of the **Constitution** is the one signed at the 1787 Constitutional Convention in Philadelphia by twelve of the original thirteen states (Rhode Island signed three years later), while the first ten amendments to the Constitution became the articles of the **Bill of Rights**, and the one on display here is the federal government's official copy. (For more on the Constitution, see "The American system of government," pp.346–350.) Less familiar but still historically significant documents relating to Western US expansion, law, and politics are on view alongside the Charters of Freedom. However, seeing any of these documents can involve a long wait during summer hours, so try to come during non-peak times.

Murals along the Rotunda's walls underscore the documents' significance, with pictures of Thomas Jefferson handing the Declaration of Independence to John Hancock, and James Madison presenting the Constitution to Convention chair George Washington.

The rest of the collection

Although the Charters are the only documents guaranteed to be on display, another historic document that you may find on view is one of the seventeen extant copies of the **Magna Carta**, the famous declaration of rights (for the nobility at least) issued by England's King John in 1215. John's successors all confirmed and reissued the Magna Carter, but later versions lacked some of the original provisions. The document, hand-written in Latin, stopped evolving in 1225, and all future issues, including the one here from 1297, were based on the 1225 version. Its guarantee of certain rights, like trial by jury and equality before the law, directly influenced America's own **Bill of Rights**.

Given that the Archives holds items as diverse as the Louisiana Purchase, with Napoleon's signature, the World War II Japanese surrender document, the Strategic Arms Limitation Treaty of 1972, and President Nixon's resignation letter, it's always worth checking the temporary exhibitions in the surrounding chambers. Also, a shuttle bus can take you to the Archives' Maryland depository, where you can hear selections from the Watergate tapes, which led to Nixon's downfall.

Finally, it's a good idea to take one of the excellent **guided tours**, which show you more of the Archives' holdings, as well as its **genealogy center**; indeed, the Archives' resources were of great help to Alex Haley, author of *Roots*, who spent many hours here tracing his ancestry.

Judiciary Square

Since the city's earliest days, when storehouses served as rank jails for runaway slaves, **Judiciary Square** – east of 5th Street, between E and F streets – has been the central location for its local government and judiciary. The mayor's offices are at One Judiciary Square, and the 1820 Greek Revival-style **Old City Hall** is on D Street between 4th and 5th. In 1881 it saw the murder trial of Charles Guiteau, who shot President James Garfield in the back just four months after his inauguration. The trial site was appropriate, since the outdoor statue of Abraham Lincoln is said to be the first such honor made after his assassination, quickly erected in 1865. The building has since been rechristened as the Superior Court of DC, but is unfortunately fenced off and not open to the public.

Within a few blocks of here stand the US Tax Court, Department of Labor, Municipal Center, and the US Federal Courthouse – all uniformly gloomy and monolithic. The courthouse galleries are open to anyone interested in watching the legal proceedings: the US Federal Courthouse (main entrance on Constitution Ave) sees the most high-profile action, from the trial of various Watergate and Iran-Contra defendants to that of former mayor Marion Barry. This was also where the 1998 grand jury hearings on the Clinton–Lewinsky affair were held, with all the main players appearing to give evidence in person save for the president, who testified via closed-circuit TV from the White House.

National Law Enforcement Officers Memorial

Visitor center at 605 E St NW ☎202/737-3213, ⊛www.nleomf.com; Judiciary Square Metro. Mon Fri 9am–5pm, Sat 10am–5pm, Sun noon–5pm.

The impressive **National Law Enforcement Officers Memorial**, dedicated in 1991, is in the center of Judiciary Square. Walls lining the circular pathways around a reflecting pool are inscribed with the names of more than 17,000 police officers killed in the line of duty, beginning with US Marshall Robert Forsyth, shot dead in 1794. Every year in May, new names are added to the memorial, which has space for 26,000; at the current rate (a police officer is killed every other day on average), it will be full by the year 2100. Directories at the site help you locate a particular name, or you can get assistance at the nearby visitor center, two blocks west.

National Building Museum

401 F Street NW ☎202/272-2448, ⊛www.nbm.org; Judiciary Square Metro. Mon–Sat 10am–5pm, Sun 11am–5pm. $5.

Formerly the Pension Building, the **National Building Museum** was once home to a courthouse and various federal agencies; now it's a stirring museum focusing on architecture and covering topics like urban renewal, high-rise technology, and environmental matters. The permanent exhibition on the second floor, "Washington: Symbol and City," explores the creation of the capital city itself and shows which of the District's planned buildings have come to fruition. Also worth a look are the Pension Commissioner's three-room office suite – with its fireplaces, decorative friezes, and vaulted ceilings – and the winning scale model from the 1910 competition to design the Lincoln Memorial. Free tours (Mon–Wed 12.30pm, Thurs–Sat also 11.30am

Washington DC has always had an anomalous place in the Union. It's a **federal district** rather than a state, with no official constitution of its own, and its citizens are denied full representation under the American political system: they have no senator to defend their interests and only a nonvoting representative in the House (a position the capital city shares with American Samoa, Guam, and the Virgin Islands). And until 1961, when the 23rd Amendment was passed, DC residents weren't permitted to vote in a presidential election.

Although the city has had a mayor and some sort of elected council since 1802, in the early days so many inhabitants were transients – politicians, lobbyists, lawyers, and appointed civil servants – that the local government was denied tax-raising powers; instead, Congress simply appropriated money piecemeal for necessary improvements. In 1871, the District was given **territorial status**. President Grant appointed a governor and city council, and an elected house of delegates and boards of public works and health followed; all adult males (black and white) were eligible to vote. Many of the most significant improvements to the city infrastructure date from this period of limited self-government, with the head of the Board of Public Works, Alexander "Boss" Shepherd, instrumental in dredging sewers, paving and lighting streets, and planting thousands of trees. However, Shepherd's improvements and a string of corruption scandals put the city $16 million in debt. Direct control of DC's affairs passed back to Congress in 1874, which later appointed three commissioners to replace the locally elected officials.

And that was how matters stood for a century, until Congress passed the **Home Rule Act** in 1973. Small improvements had already been effected – the first black commissioner (for a city now predominantly black) was appointed in 1961; later, an elected school board was established. But only in 1974, when the District's first elected mayor in more than a century, **Walter E. Washington**, took office, supported by a fully elected thirteen-member council, did the city wrest back some measure of autonomy. However, Congress still retained a legislative veto over any proposed local laws, as well as keeping a close watch on spending limits.

Washington was succeeded as mayor in 1978 by Democrat **Marion S. Barry**, former civil-rights activist and, some would argue, demagogue without compare. At first, he was markedly successful in attracting much-needed investment; he also significantly increased the number of local government workers, which gave him a firm support base among the majority black population. But longstanding whispers about Barry's turbulent private life – charges of drug addiction in particular – exploded in early 1990, when he was surreptitiously filmed in an FBI sting operation buying and using crack cocaine. Barry spent six months in prison and was replaced as mayor by Democrat **Sharon Pratt Kelly**, a former attorney who, despite her undoubted expertise, signally failed to improve the city's worsening finances. Nor did she endear herself to the city's employees, and in the mayoral election of 1994, Barry made an astounding comeback after admitting to voters the error of his

& 1.30pm; Sun 12.30pm & 1.30pm) give you access to the otherwise restricted third floor – the best spot to view the towering columns' intricate capitals.

As much as any exhibit, the building is of most interest for its architectural details and storied history. In the late 1860s the number of Civil War casualties put a huge strain on the government's pension system. Additional offices were required in which to process claims and payments to veterans and dependents; subsequently, in the 1880s, what became known as the **Pension Building** was erected between 4th and 5th streets, framing the entire north side of Judiciary Square. Emerging from the Metro up the escalators brings you face-to-face with its imposing red–brick facade.

ways. But a year later, a Republican Congress finally tired of the embarrassment of DC's massive budget deficit and revoked the city's home rule charter. A congressionally appointed financial control board was subsequently given jurisdiction over the city's finances, personnel, and various work departments, stripping away what little responsibility the mayor had left.

Barry didn't stand in the 1998 mayoral election and was succeeded by Democrat **Anthony A. Williams**, a former chief financial officer of the control board, who won a resounding two-thirds share of the vote in his first political foray. Perhaps even more significantly, the election results produced for the first time a white majority on the District council. This result, together with the election of an avowed technocrat as mayor, signaled a shift away from the confrontation of the later Barry years.

Washington rebounded under the control board, as deficits became surpluses and city residents could once again afford to be optimistic about their trash being collected. By virtue of its success, the control board put itself out of business in October 2001, and full executive power returned to the mayor and the council ahead of schedule, with Congress (which subsidizes the District) less fearful than before that the federal capital will simply collapse. The city once again seems a worthy place to live: the population appears to have stabilized at last after decades of decline thanks to lower crime rates, tax credits, and the optimism generated by Mayor Williams's leadership and reformist agenda.

But although the District's financial management has improved, a daunting fiscal challenge remains. DC's tax base is too narrow to support the level of services the city requires: two-thirds of the city's workers live (and pay local taxes) in Virginia and Maryland; roughly forty percent of the land is owned by the government (which excuses itself from taxes); and years of middle-class flight to the suburbs has left the population at its lowest level since the 1930s. The obvious solution to this problem – a commuter tax – is a nonstarter for political reasons, while past attempts to raise the income tax have only led to more fleeing to the suburbs. Many residents also reacted with horror to Mayor Williams's dogged, and successful, pursuit of major-league baseball in 2003–04, returning a team to the national capital at a cost of hundreds of millions of dollars – spending money on a sporting luxury when the District's basic schools and services are already woefully underfunded. In reaction to this, the DC Council elected three insurgent members in 2004 to challenge the mayor's policies; sure enough, one of them was Marion Barry himself.

Whoever DC's leaders may be, many believe that achieving **statehood** would solve the District's financial conundrum (its license plates already decry "Taxation Without Representation"). But the crux of granting statehood to DC lies in the realm of national politics: statehood would likely mean that the District's voters, who are overwhelmingly liberal, would send one Democrat to the House and two to the Senate, so the chances of garnering enough Republican support for the option are extremely slim.

General Montgomery C. Meigs sought to honor veterans of both sides of the war with a stunningly designed building. The exterior of the Renaissance-style palazzo is enhanced by a three-foot-high, terra-cotta frieze that runs around the building (between the first and second floors) and depicts various military images, including charging cavalry, wounded soldiers, and marines rowing in a storm-tossed sea. Inside, Meigs maximized the use of natural light in his majestic **Great Hall**, inspired by the generous proportions of Rome's Palazzo Farnese, and created one of the most striking interior spaces anywhere in the US. The hall's centerpiece fountain is surrounded by eight Corinthian columns measuring 8ft across at the base and more than 75ft high; each is made up of 70,000 bricks, plastered and painted to resemble Siena marble. Above the ground-floor Doric arcade, the three open-plan galleried levels, 160ft high, were aired by vents and clerestory windows – opened each day by a young boy employed to walk around on the roof. In the upper-floor niches Meigs planned to put busts of prominent Americans, though this never happened; today, the 244 busts are a repeated series of eight figures (architect, construction worker, landscape gardener, etc) representing the building arts. Not surprisingly, this vast, striking space has been in regular demand since its inception. Grover Cleveland held the first of many presidential **inaugural balls** here in 1885 (when there was still no roof on the building); a century later, it hosted President Reagan's second inaugural ball and President Clinton's first; and every year the televised *Christmas in Washington* special is filmed here.

Marian Koshland Science Museum

500 5th St NW ☏202/334-1201, ⊚www.koshland-science-museum.org. Wed–Mon 10am–5pm. $5.

One of the newest museums in the District, the **Marian Koshland Science Museum** is unique in that it doesn't soft-pedal or dumb down its displays to accommodate the least common denominator; instead it offers an engaging, vigorous presentation of fact, theory, and speculation relating to some of the core scientific and technological issues of the day. Although it's relatively small, this National Academy of Sciences museum aims to provide comprehensive coverage of its limited subjects, delving into the political and cultural debates relating to them. The Koshland has one **permanent exhibition** on the latest, and typically controversial, ideas relating to the expansion of the universe, dark matter, and string theory, and two **temporary exhibits** running until 2006. The first deals with the nature of DNA, from its nucleic-acid construction to its use in tracking down criminals and providing antidotes for pandemic diseases; the second is a complex and multifaceted look at global warming, showing the chemical components of greenhouse gases (notably carbon dioxide and methane) and the potential dangers they pose. Both of these exhibits balance their scientific data with hands-on, user-friendly multimedia elements.

The Penn Quarter

Not to be confused with Pennsylvania Avenue itself, which loosely acts as a southern boundary, the **Penn Quarter**, in the heart of Old Downtown, is the city's official designation for a cache of renovated buildings, new museums, stylish cafés and bars, and other sights that have gone up in the last few years between 3rd and 12th streets, roughly south of G Street. The relatively new **MCI Center**, just to the north, has played an especially big role in the area's revitalization, luring folks to spend money in an area that was once a blighted symbol of urban decay.

DC's downtown area was marred following the **1968 riots**, spurred by the assassination of Dr Martin Luther King Jr. White residents and institutions fled, and urban disinvestment, federal neglect, and suburbanization contributed to the area's steep decline. It took the full development of the Metro system – connecting downtown with the rest of the city – and a new national

Three blocks west of the National Building Museum and in the center of the Penn Quarter, the Greek Revival structure of the **Old Patent Office**, begun in 1836 by Treasury Building and General Post Office architect **Robert Mills**, is among the oldest in the city, though it wasn't completed for thirty years. The building was designed to hold offices of the Interior Department and the Commissioners of Patents, and models of America's patented nineteenth-century inventions were on display – including Eli Whitney's cotton gin, Samuel Colt's pistol, and Robert Fulton's steam engine, as well as items by Thomas Edison, Benjamin Franklin, and Alexander Graham Bell. During the Civil War the building's halls were filled with over two thousand beds and used for emergency hospital services. One of the clerks in the Patent Office, **Clara Barton**, abandoned her duties to work in the hospital and went on to found the American Red Cross in 1881. The poet **Walt Whitman** worked here, too, as an untrained volunteer, dressing wounds and comforting injured soldiers – an experience that led directly to the long series of poems known as *Drum-Taps*, included in the fourth edition (1867) of *Leaves of Grass*. In March 1865, just before the end of the war, Whitman's "noblest of Washington buildings" hosted Lincoln's second inaugural ball, with four thousand people in attendance for a night of dancing and feasting. "Tonight," wrote Whitman later, "beautiful women, perfumes, the violins' sweetness . . . then, the amputation, the blue face, the groan, the glassy eye of the dying."

Despite its heritage, the building was scheduled for demolition in the 1950s, before the Smithsonian stepped into the breach. Today the Old Patent Office building houses two of the city's major art institutions: the **National Portrait Gallery** and the **American Art Museum** (though both are, unfortunately, closed for renovation until July 4, 2006). The galleries occupy separate wings: the American Art Museum on the G Street side; the Portrait Gallery on F Street. For more information call ☎202/357-2700 or check ⊛www.nmaa.si.edu or www.npg.si.edu. Note also that many of the American Art Gallery's holdings, including ones detailed below, are currently on display in the Renwick Gallery's impressive Grand Salon (see p.139).

attitude toward redeveloping urban cores to bring in the masses; now the Penn Quarter is a must-see for all but the most benighted tourists who only come for the Mall and Capitol Hill. Be sure to check out the area's better restaurants and notable attractions, including excellent **Smithsonian museums**, the **International Spy Museum**, and **Ford's Theater**, among other, lesser-known sights.

National Portrait Gallery

8th and F streets NW ☎202/357-2700, ⊛www.nmaa.si.edu; Gallery Place-Chinatown Metro. Closed for renovation until July 4, 2006.

Portraits of prominent citizens were the foundation of many early American art collections (Congress itself commissioned a series of presidential portraits for the White House in 1857), but the **National Portrait Gallery** didn't open until the 1960s. The permanent collection contains more than four thousand images of notables from every walk of life, but perhaps its best-known piece is **Gilbert Stuart**'s celebrated "Lansdowne" portrait of George Washington. In addition to paintings, the gallery contains numerous sculptures and photographs, including more than five thousand plate-glass negatives of the Civil War era by Matthew Brady.

Popular culture images

The most popular area of the gallery's collection comprises portraits of figures from the performing arts. These include **Paul Robeson** as Othello by Betsy Graves Reyneau; a regal portrait of singer **Marian Anderson**; photographs of **Gloria Swanson** and **Boris Karloff**; a bronze bust of **Grace Kelly**; and an almost three-dimensional metallic study of **Ethel Merman** as Annie Oakley by Rosemary Sloat. Perhaps most striking, though, is Harry Jackson's terrific polychrome bronze sculpture of a *True Grit*-era **John Wayne**. American sports icons immortalized here include a pugnacious **Joe Louis** (again by Betsy Graves Reyneau) and a poignant **Arthur Ashe** (Louis Briel), painted in the last few months of his life. Action shots include a painting of **Mickey Mantle** watching as **Roger Maris** hits another homer in the 1961 season, and, best of all, James Montgomery Flagg's depiction of the **Jack Dempsey–Jess Willard** heavyweight championship fight of 1919. Seated to the right of the struggling Willard (in black shorts) is the eager Damon Runyon, who was a sports reporter before he wrote humorous, streetwise stories.

Presidential portraits

As you might expect, the gallery has an impressive collection of presidential portraits. Gilbert Stuart's portrait of **George Washington** (1796), an imperial study of a stalwart man, is one of the star attractions. Some of the other presidential studies are notable for the artists behind them: **Norman Rockwell** created an intentionally flattering portrait of Richard Nixon, while a bust of a relatively carefree, first-term **Bill Clinton** was the work of Jan Wood, a sculptor otherwise best known for her depictions of horses. Alexander Healy, who was commissioned for presidential portraits beginning in the 1850s, produced a moving portrayal of a pensive (and surprisingly handsome) **Abraham Lincoln**, while Civil War painter Ole Peter Hansen Balling was responsible for portraits of presidents Chester A. Arthur and, in what must have been a rush job, **James Garfield**, who was inaugurated in March 1881, shot in July, and died in September. Edmund Tarbell faced a unique challenge when painting **Woodrow Wilson**'s portrait; because the president was always too ill to pose, Tarbell was forced to work entirely from photographs. English portraitist Douglas Chandor's rather raffish **Franklin Delano Roosevelt** painting has FDR in a chic, fur-lined cape and sporting his trademark cigarette holder. This painting was to be part of an (unfinished) study of FDR with Churchill and Stalin at Yalta, which explains the alternative sketches of Roosevelt's hands holding cigarettes, glasses, and pens. Finally, a notorious portrait of Lincoln, taken in February 1865 by war photographer Alexander Gardner, has a crack in the plate running across Lincoln's forehead. After his assassination, many observers saw this, in retrospect, as a terrible omen.

Notable Americans

The gallery's "Notable Americans" collection features portraits of both colonial and Native Americans, with several studies of braves and chiefs by George Catlin, a lithograph of **Sitting Bull**, and a painting of **Pocahontas** in English dress. A bust of **Geronimo** was sculpted by his distant relative, the Apache artist Allan Houser. Industrialists, inventors, and businessmen are pictured alongside churchmen and feminists, so together with Bell, Edison, and Carnegie there's **Belva Ann Lockwood**, the first woman to run for president (in 1884; she got 4149 votes), a bust of **Susan B. Anthony** by Adelaide Johnson (better known for her *Suffrage Monument* statue in the Capitol), and a stuffy portrait of feminist **Elizabeth Cady Stanton**. Marshall D. Rumbaugh's sculpture of **Rosa Parks** shows her manacled between two cops after she refused to give up her seat on the bus in Montgomery, Alabama – their small heads and shaded eyes contrasting with the seamstress's defiant gaze as her handbag dangles beneath her handcuffs.

Literature and the arts

Studies of personalities from literature and the arts include a touching early photograph by Man Ray of **Ernest Hemingway** and his young son, and the extraordinary, bulky, terra-cotta figure of **Gertrude Stein** depicted by Jo Davidson as a tranquil, seated Buddha. Fascinating, too, are Edward Biberman's creepy study of **Dashiell Hammett** in a horrible wool coat, and John White Alexander's 1902 depiction of a transfixed Samuel Clemens (better known as **Mark Twain**). In 1889 Alexander painted **Walt Whitman** as a seated sage, with light streaming through his bushy beard. The collection's most prized piece, however, is Edgar Degas's severe portrait (1880–84) of his friend, Impressionist **Mary Cassatt**, hunched over a chair with a sneer on her face. Cassatt hated the image so much that she had it sold with the understanding that it wouldn't be allowed to go to an American collection where her family and friends might see it.

American Art Museum

8th and G streets NW ☎202/357-2700, ⍰www.nmaa.si.edu; Gallery Place-Chinatown Metro. Closed for renovation until July 4, 2006.

The **American Art Museum** holds one of the city's more enduring art collections. Before the Smithsonian was founded, the federal government had its own art collection, which, together with pieces loaned by prominent Washington citizens, was displayed in the 1840s in the Patent Office. These works were later given over to the Smithsonian, which had yet to find premises for a planned "National Gallery" to house its expanding art collection. Eventually the Smithsonian resorted to displaying its paintings in the Natural History Museum, while Andrew Mellon's bequest to the nation resulted in the founding of a separate National Gallery of Art. Not until the Patent Office building became available did the Smithsonian finally find a home for its 38,000 paintings, prints, drawings, sculpture, photographs, folk art, and crafts – the largest collection of American art, colonial to contemporary, in the world. Stop by in July 2006 for the unveiling of the museum's holdings in its newly renovated space.

Western imagery

The museum scores with its nineteenth-century art of the American West. The collection includes almost four hundred paintings by **George Catlin**, who spent six years touring the Great Plains, painting portraits and scenes of Native American life that he later displayed as part of his "Indian Gallery." His paintings were the first contact many white settlers had with the aboriginal peoples of America, and viewers were fascinated by his lush landscapes showing buffalo herds crossing the Missouri, or those featuring tribes at work and play. The contrast between cultures is best seen in Catlin's 1832 painting of a warrior named Pigeon's Egg Head arriving in Washington DC in full traditional dress, only to return to his tepee encampment in frock coat and top hat, sporting an umbrella and smoking a cigarette. Perhaps Catlin is most interesting for recording civilizations and habitats that survived only briefly after the onslaught of the pioneers – soon after he visited and painted the Plains Mandan tribes, they were wiped out by an epidemic of smallpox, brought by white settlers.

Not all of the collection's scenes are of warriors or hunts, however: Catlin also produced many keenly observed domestic studies, like the painting of a woman with a child in an elaborately decorated cradle, while a 1920 **Joseph Henry Sharp** painting shows Blackfoot Indians making medicine by burning feathers over an open fire. One of Catlin's contemporaries, **John Mix Stanley**, primarily depicted Apache warriors, though one of his works here captures a graphic *Buffalo Hunt* (1845). There's a remarkable bronze statue, too, called *The Indian Ghost Dancer*, by **Paul Wayland Bartlett** (1888), where the dancer is near total exhaustion after hours of trancelike dancing.

Folk art

The museum's **folk art** collection includes some traditional pieces, notably Native American ceramics, but it's the contemporary art that stands out. **Malcah Zeldis**'s exuberant *Miss Liberty Celebration* depicts the Statue of Liberty surrounded by a family group comprising Elvis, Einstein, Lincoln, Marilyn, and Chaplin, and was completed to celebrate the artist's recovery from cancer. The most extraordinary piece here is perhaps **James Hampton**'s so-called *Hampton Throne*, a mystic, cryptic cluster of foil- and gilt-covered lightbulbs, boxes, plaques, wings, altars, and furniture capped by the text "Fear Not." Hampton, a solitary figure who referred to himself as "Saint James," worked in a garage on N Street NW between 1950 and his death in 1964. It's believed that *Hampton Throne* is full of obscure religious references and was unfinished at the time of the artist's death. Incidentally, the work's full title is *The Throne of the Third Heaven of the Nations' Millennium General Assembly*.

Early American art

Many of the museum's heavyweight paintings of **nineteenth- and early twentieth-century** American art are on view at the Renwick Gallery, especially those by Albert Pinkham Ryder, Winslow Homer, Mary Cassatt, John Singer Sargent, and John Singleton Copley. Among the sculpture from this period that's on display is **Daniel Chester French**'s *The Spirit of Life* (1914), a winged sprite with laurel wreath, fashioned by the man who created the powerful seated statue in the Lincoln Memorial. **Hiram Powers** also has sculptures and models on display here. The surface of *America* (1848), a plaster model of crowned Liberty, is punctured by the tips of a series of metal rods, inserted to act as a guide for carving the eventual marble version. *Thomas Jefferson* (1860) shows the same technique, unfortunately making it look as if the frock-coated president has a severe case of acne.

Landscapes and portraits

The excellent collection of American **landscapes** includes *Among the Sierra Nevada Mountains* (1868), a superb example of the dramatic power of **Albert Bierstadt**, whose three long trips to the American West between 1858 and 1873 provided him with enough material for the rest of his career. The painting's striking ethereal light illuminates distant waterfalls, ducks in flight, and snow-capped peaks. There are similar, though smaller, expressions of grandeur in scenes from Lake Placid, the Colorado River, and Niagara Falls, painted

△ National Building Museum

by **Hudson River School** artists like Jasper Francis Cropsey and John Frederick Kensett. Charles Bird King powerfully portrays the original inhabitants of these landscapes in the images of five Pawnee braves wearing red face-paint and ceremonial bead earrings. King studied in London under Benjamin West before moving to Washington DC, where he earned a comfortable living painting society portraits. The steady flow of Native Americans through the capital in the 1820s – there to sign away their land in a series of worthless treaties – prompted him to divert his attentions to recording their likenesses instead. Also rather extraordinary, though in quite a different fashion, is his contemporaneous portrait of *Mrs John Quincy Adams*, obviously uncomfortable with the artist's suggestion that she sit at a harp in an ill-advised crown of feathers.

Twentieth-century art

The museum's **twentieth–century art** collection was formerly displayed in the spectacular 260-foot-long Lincoln Gallery, which runs down the east side of the building. It was here, amid the white marble pillars, that Abraham Lincoln and his entourage enjoyed his second inaugural ball. High-profile names among the modern and contemporary collection include Robert Motherwell, Willem de Kooning, Robert Rauschenberg, Clyfford Still, Ellsworth Kelly, and Jasper Johns. But there are noteworthy pieces from less well-known artists, too, like Leon Golub's red, raw *Napalm Head*, which is painted onto a torn canvas sack, and Marisol's comical *Charles de Gaulle* (1967), depicting the great French president as a rectangular wooden box and head atop a small cart. The museum also owns a decent selection of abstract works by the artists of the **Washington Color School** – primarily Gene Davis, Morris Louis, Kenneth Noland, Thomas Downing, Paul Reed, and Howard Mehring – also known as color-field painting. All tended to stain their canvases with acrylic paint to give greater impact to color and form, methods that first came to public attention in 1965 at a groundbreaking Washington exhibition of modern art.

MCI Center

601 F St NW ☎202/628-3200, 🌐www.mcicenter.com; Gallery Place-Chinatown Metro.

With the 1997 opening of the $200-million, 20,000-seat **MCI Center**, professional sports came back to downtown DC from the suburbs – and with it, on game nights, the crowds and the buzz. The center is the home of the NBA's woeful **Wizards**, the WNBA **Mystics**, and the NHL's **Capitals**; see "Sports and outdoor activities" chapter if you're interested in catching a basketball or hockey game while in town. To serve the crowds, and to encourage more visitors, the center has a sporting goods store and restaurants, including *Nick and Stef's Steakhouse* (see "Eating" chapter), where a private room overlooks the Wizards' practice court.

Along 7th and F streets

The downtown transformation is taking place rapidly along 7th Street, between F and D, where spruced-up buildings form the hub of a nascent arts district studded with galleries. New cafés, bars, and restaurants contribute to the area's growing appeal, perhaps best exemplified by one of 7th Street's finest buildings, **The Lansburgh**, at no. 420 (between D and E). Once a department store, the building's soaring facade now provides a grand frame for the

Shakespeare and Woolly Mammoth theaters. Major improvements are also under way along F Street, between 7th and 10th, though it still has a way to go before it resembles its thriving turn-of-the-twentieth-century commercial self. At 9th and F streets, the elegant Romanesque Revival **Riggs National Bank** Building has been rescued as a Courtyard Marriott hotel (see p.258) and still features its grand 1891 facade, with rough-hewn arches and brick-and-granite cladding.

General Post Office

7th and F sts NW ☎202/628-7177, ⊛www.monaco-dc.com; Gallery Place-Chinatown Metro.

Modeled on a Renaissance palazzo inspired by the ancient Roman Temple of Jupiter, the former **General Post Office**, the city's first marble building, is a Greek Revival masterwork dating back to 1842. Since the post office pulled up stakes later in the nineteenth century, the building has served as site of the US Tariff Commission and, in its present form, the trendy *Hotel Monaco*. With its high-ceilinged offices now remodeled into guest rooms, the luxurious hotel's interiors and public spaces are well worth a look, with wonderfully preserved details and complementary modern touches including vaulted ceilings, marble columns, checkerboard marble floors, spiral stairways, and minimalist contemporary decor.

The International Spy Museum

800 F St NW ☎202/207-0219, ⊛www.spymuseum.org; Gallery Place-Chinatown Metro. Daily 10am–6pm, April–Oct closes 8pm. $13.

The Penn Quarter's newest major attraction, the **International Spy Museum**, is a big part of F Street's revival: it resides in five nineteenth-century buildings, including the Atlas Building, which, fittingly, was home to the US Communist Party from 1941 to 1948. Experts in the field, ranging from former FBI, CIA, and KGB chiefs to specialists in cryptology, disguise, and clandestine photography, helped create the $30-million museum, whose exhibits aim to illuminate the impact of espionage on various historic events and to showcase dozens of nifty gizmos that would earn Q's grudging respect. Despite the steep entrance fee, the museum is one of DC's most popular sites; call ahead for entry information, as tickets can sell out days in advance during the high season.

Crammed full of the kind of Cold War-era gizmos, weapons, and relics that will make readers of Robert Ludlum and Tom Clancy giddy with delight, the museum offers items and displays covering thousands of years of spycraft, beginning with a small model of the infamous Trojan Horse and moving on to cover ancient Rome, imperial China, Elizabethan England, and Civil War-era America. Most of the museum's attention is devoted to America during the years 1939 to 1991, from the beginning of World War II to the end of the Cold War, with a sizable assortment of multimedia exhibits, walk-through re-creations, dioramas, and video clips.

The presentation begins inauspiciously, in hackneyed, Disneyesque fashion, with a **filmstrip** providing a Hollywood-style view of the spy trade and the dubious claim that "the Cold War was clearly the intelligence community's finest hour." After the film, you're led into a series of interesting galleries that cover topics like celebrities fighting the Nazis through subterfuge (notably Marlene Dietrich) and allow you to view **re-creations** of a cramped East Berlin escape tunnel and a darkened "interrogation room" for captured spies. There's even a **video game** based on the spy-coding Enigma machine.

Among these galleries, the standouts are undoubtedly the **artifacts** from the height of the Cold War in the 1950s and 1960s, presented in glass cases and broken down by theme – "Training," "Surveillance," and so on. Some of the many highlights include tiny pistols disguised as lipstick holders, cigarette cases, pipes, and flashlights; oddments like invisible-ink writing kits and a *Get Smart!*-style shoe phone; a colorful and active model of James Bond's Aston Martin spy car; bugs and radio transmitters hidden in ambassadorial gifts (such as a Great Seal of the US given by Russians); ricin-tipped poison umbrellas used to kill Warsaw Pact dissidents; and a rounded capsule containing a screwdriver, razor, and serrated knife – ominously marked, "rectal tool kit." Also highlighted are the many personalities, real and imagined, that make up the colorful world of espionage: Whittaker Chambers and his microfilm-containing pumpkin are here, as are Mata Hari and **celebrity spies** like singer Josephine Baker and Julia Child, the late television

The assassination of Abraham Lincoln

In the days after Robert E. Lee surrendered to Ulysses S. Grant on April 9, 1865, officially ending the Civil War, there was a celebratory mood in Washington DC. On the evening of Good Friday, April 14, 1865, President and Mrs Lincoln went to Ford's Theatre to see top actress Laura Keene perform in the comedy *Our American Cousin*, a play about a yokel who travels to England to claim his inheritance. The president's advisors were never very keen on him appearing in public, but Lincoln, as on previous occasions, overrode their objections. The Lincolns were accompanied by their friends Major Henry Rathbone and his fiancée, Clara Harris; the four took their seats upstairs in the presidential box, just after the play had started.

Conspirators had been plotting to kill the president for weeks. **John Wilkes Booth**, a 26-year-old actor with Confederate sympathies and delusions of grandeur, had first conceived of a plan to kidnap Lincoln during the war and use him as a bargaining chip for the release of Southern prisoners. Booth drew others into the conspiracy, notably **John Surratt**, whose mother owned a rooming house on H Street, where the conspiracy was hatched; John Surratt was already acting as a low-level courier for the secessionist cause. **George Atzerodt** from Maryland was recruited because he knew the surrounding countryside and its hiding places, as was **David Herold**, a pharmacist's clerk in DC; **Lewis Powell** (or Paine, as he was sometimes known) was hired as muscle. With Lee's surrender in April, Booth decided to assassinate the president instead; Herold, Atzerodt, and Powell were to kill Secretary of State **William Seward** and Vice President **Andrew Johnson**. Surratt had already left the group when the talk turned to murder, and the other attacks came to naught: Johnson was left alone by a fearful Atzerodt while Seward, although injured by Powell, later recovered.

At about 10.15pm, during the third act of the play, when only one actor was onstage and the audience was laughing at a joke, the assassin struck. Lincoln's bodyguard had left the box unattended, and Booth took the opportunity to step inside and shoot Lincoln in the back of the head. Major Rathbone grappled with Booth but was stabbed in the arm with a hunting knife and severely wounded. Booth then jumped the 12ft down onto the stage, catching one of his spurs and fracturing a bone in his left leg as he fell. But he was on his feet immediately – most of the audience thought it was part of the play – and shouted "Sic semper tyrannis!" ("Thus ever to tyrants," the motto of the state of Virginia) before running off backstage and into the alley, where he had a horse waiting.

First into the presidential box was **Charles Augustus Leale**, a young army doctor. Lincoln was unconscious and laboring badly, and it was decided to carry chef whose kitchen is on display just a few blocks south at the Museum of American History.

Finally, the museum makes a game effort to show the limitations of catching up with spies in the 1990s – the exploits of respective CIA and FBI moles Aldrich Ames and Robert Hanssen are described – but leaves us hanging without going into depth about the most important question of the last few years: how US intelligence failed to prevent the al Qaeda terrorist network from attacking America on September 11, 2001.

Ford's Theatre and Lincoln Museum

511 10th St NW ☎ 202/347-4833, ⓦ www.fordstheatre.org; Metro Center Metro.

On the west end of the Penn Quarter, the district north of Pennsylvania Avenue has been home to several theaters since the founding of the city, being little more than a stroll from the White House and mansions of Lafayette Square. In 1861, entrepreneur John T. Ford converted a church into an epony-

him to the nearest house to care for him better. Once inside the **Petersen House**, Lincoln was placed in the small back bedroom, where Leale and the other doctors strived to save him. Soon the house was bulging at the seams, as Mrs Lincoln, her son Robert, Secretary of War Edwin Stanton, various politicians and army officers, and, eventually, Lincoln's pastor, arrived to do what they could. Lincoln never regained consciousness and died at 7.22am the next morning, April 15; Stanton spoke for all, declaiming "Now he belongs to the ages" (or, as some historians assert, to the "angels"). Lincoln's body was taken back to the White House, where it lay in state for three days before the funeral.

Booth, meanwhile, had fled on horseback through Maryland with David Herold, stopping at a certain **Doctor Mudd**'s to have his injured leg treated. The pair hid out for several days, but after crossing into Virginia were eventually surrounded by Union troops at a farm. Herold surrendered, and on the same day, April 26, Booth was shot dead while holed up inside. All the other alleged conspirators were soon captured and sent for trial on May 10 in a military court at **Fort McNair**. They were kept chained and hooded and, after six weeks of evidence, Herold, Powell, Atzerodt, and Mary Surratt were sentenced to hang, the punishment being carried out on July 7, 1865. A last-minute reprieve for Mary Surratt – who, although she housed the conspirators, probably knew nothing of the conspiracy – was refused, and she became the first woman to be executed by the US government. Dr Mudd received a life sentence, while the stagehand who held Booth's horse at the theater got six years, though both were pardoned in 1869 by Andrew Johnson, Lincoln's successor. John Surratt, who had fled America, was recaptured in 1867 and also stood trial, but was freed when the jury couldn't agree on a verdict.

Much has been written about the effect of the assassination of Lincoln on the country and its future. He was at the start of his second term as president when he died, and many have held that the slavery question and Reconstruction would have been handled with more skill and grace under his leadership. It's impossible to say, though it is interesting to note the personal effect that the close-quarters assassination may have had on the three other occupants of the presidential box that night: ten years later Mary Lincoln – never the most stable of people – was judged insane and committed; in 1883 Clara Harris (by now Clara Harris Rathbone) was herself shot, by her husband, Henry Rathbone, who died in an asylum in 1911.

mous theater that proved to be popular until April 14, 1865, when, during a performance of *Our American Cousin*, actor and Southern sympathizer John Wilkes Booth shot President Abraham Lincoln. Following Lincoln's assassination, **Ford's Theatre** was draped in black in a show of respect, and it remained closed while the conspirators were pursued, caught, and tried. Ford abandoned attempts to reopen the theater after he received death threats, and the theater was eventually converted into office space. It wasn't until the 1960s that it was restored to its former condition – not only using period furnishings, but operating again as a working theater.

Its greater significance, though, is as a museum documenting Abraham Lincoln's murder. Provided rehearsals or matinees aren't in progress (usually Thurs, Sat & Sun), the theater hosts an entertaining narrative (hourly 9.15am–4.15pm) recounting the events of the fateful night. You can then file up to the circle for a view through glass of the damask-furnished presidential box in which Lincoln sat in his rocking chair; most of the items inside are reproductions. In the basement, the **Lincoln Museum** (daily 9am–5pm; ☎202/426-6924, ⊛www.nps.gov/foth) displays impressive items like the actual murder weapon (a .44 Derringer), a bloodstained piece of Lincoln's overcoat, and Booth's knife, keys, and diary, in which he wrote "I hoped for no gain. I knew no private wrong. I struck for my country and that alone."

Petersen House

516 10th St NW ☎202/426-6924, ⊛www.nps.gov/foth; Metro Center Metro. Daily 9am–5pm.

Having been shot in Ford's Theatre, an unconscious President Lincoln was carried across the street and placed in the back bedroom of a home owned by local tailor William Petersen. Lincoln never regained consciousness and died the next morning. You can walk through the restored **Petersen House**'s gloomy parlor rooms to the small bedroom, where there's a replica of the bed on which Lincoln died (he lay diagonally, since he was too tall to lie straight). Period furniture aside, there's little to see here – the original bloodstained pillow that used to be on the bed has been moved to the theater museum. However, it's interesting to note just how small the room is: Lincoln's immediate family and colleagues were present in the house during his last night, but not all could cram into the room at the same time – something ignored by contemporaneous artists who, in a series of mawkish deathbed scenes popular at the time, often portrayed up to thirty people crowded around the ailing president's bed.

Chinatown and around

DC's version of **Chinatown**, north of the Penn Quarter, stretches no more than a handful of undistinguished city blocks along G and H streets NW, between 6th and 8th. The vibrant triumphal arch over H Street (at 7th), paid for by Beijing in the 1980s, is hopelessly at odds with the neighborhood itself, since it heralds little more than a dozen restaurants and a few grocery stores. In fact, the city's first Chinese immigrants, in the early nineteenth century, didn't live in today's Chinatown (which only began in the early twentieth century) but in the piquant slums of Swampoodle, north of the Capitol. At that time, H Street and its environs were home to small businesses and modest rooming houses. In one of these, during the 1860s, Mary Surratt presided over the comings and goings of her son John and his colleagues, including John Wilkes Booth – all subsequently implicated in the assassination of Abraham Lincoln. A plaque marks the site of the house (then No. 541 H St), now the *Wok and Roll* restaurant at 604 H St NW.

City Museum of Washington DC and around

The grand, Neoclassical old Library building, with its stylish friezes, floor mosaics, and Ionic columns and pilasters, holds the **City Museum of Washington DC**, 801 K St NW (Tues–Sun 10am–5pm; $3; ☎202/383-1800, ⓦwww.citymuseumdc.org; Mt Vernon Square Metro), which is run by the District's Historical Society. The Society, formerly housed in Dupont Circle's glorious Heurich House, set up headquarters here in 2003 and displays photos, artifacts, and other effects, including an old volunteer fireman's helmet, deeds of slave sales and manumission, and various political posters. *Washington Stories*, a daily multimedia show (extra $4), recounts the city's past in the museum's theater, while its **Gibson Reading Room** (Tues–Sun 10am–5pm) provides access to a trove of photos, documents, books, and memorabilia relating to the development of the nation's capital.

Close by is the current main public library, **Martin Luther King Jr Memorial Library**, 901 G St NW (Mon–Thurs 9.30am–9pm, Fri & Sat 9.30am–5.30pm, Sun 1–5pm; ☎202/727-1186, ⓦwww.dclibrary.org), whose sleek lines of black steel and glass announce it as the work of Mies van der Rohe. Inside a large mural by Don Miller depicts the life and death of the esteemed civil rights leader. A block north, the modernist eyesore of the **Washington Convention Center** (H St, between 9th and 11th) still hosts the occasional event, but for conventions has been superseded with a sleeker new version a few blocks north, while the multistory *Grand Hyatt*, 1000 H St NW (see "Accommodation" chapter), is worth popping into for its soaring and impressive atrium. Finally, **1100 New York Avenue** is a former bus terminal with a sprightly Art Deco facade, which is now preserved within an office complex.

Around Metro Center

Metro Center, the downtown hub of the Metro system, has separate exits along G and 12th streets. From either exit you will emerge near **Hecht's** department store, a looming, modern edifice on G Street (between 12th and 13th). Other, more aged department stores in the area haven't done quite so well: Garfinkel's lost its fight for survival more than a decade ago, though its location at 14th and F forms part of the Metropolitan Square and Hamilton Square development. This site retains various historic Beaux Arts facades along 15th Street (facing the Treasury Building), notably the turn-of-the-twentieth-century **B.F. Keith's Theatre** and the **National Metropolitan Bank**; there's also access to the historic *Old Ebbitt Grill* (see "Eating" chapter).

National Museum of Women in the Arts

1250 New York Ave NW ☎202/783-5000, 🖰www.nmwa.org; Metro Center Metro. Mon–Sat 10am–5pm, Sun noon–5pm. $8.

Opened in 1987, the **National Museum of Women in the Arts** houses the most important collection of its kind – more than 2500 works by some 600 female artists, from the sixteenth century to the present day, as well as silverware, ceramics, photographs, and decorative items. Even the building itself, a former Masonic lodge, is striking for its trapezoidal shape, brick-and-limestone facade, and elegant colonnade. The permanent collection is on the third floor, and rotating selections of contemporary works are displayed in the mezzanine level. Temporary exhibitions are on the ground, second, and fourth floors.

Renaissance to Neoclassical art

The permanent collection runs chronologically, starting with works from the Renaissance, like those of **Sofonisba Anguissola** (1532–1625), who was considered the most important female artist of her day. From a noble family, Anguissola achieved fame as an accomplished portraitist before becoming court painter to Phillip II of Spain; her evocative *Double Portrait of a Lady and Her Daughter* is on display, along with the engaging *Holy Family with St John* by her contemporary, **Lavinia Fontana**. A century or so later, Dutch and Flemish women like **Clara Peeters**, **Judith Leyster** and **Rachel Ruysch** were producing still lives and genre scenes that were equal to those of their more famous male colleagues – notice the vivacity of Peeters's *Still Life of Fish and Cat*. On occasion, female artists broke out of their limited environment to paint non-traditional subjects: for example, German-born **Maria Sybilla Merian** superbly crafted engravings of flora and fauna, inspired by her intrepid explorations in Surinam in 1699. Meanwhile, in France, women like **Elisabeth–Louise Vigée–Lebrun** (1755–1842) held sway as court painters, depicting the royalty fluttering around Marie Antoinette. But as a woman artist, Vigée-Lebrun was marginalized, her paintings denied the respect accorded those of her male contemporaries, and she was kept out of the Académie des Beaux-Arts until the 1780s.

Nineteenth-century art

In the nineteenth century, American women artists began to enter the fray. **Lilly Martin Spencer** was inordinately popular as a producer of genre scenes: *The Artist and Her Family at a Fourth of July Picnic* (1864) is typically vibrant, despite the grim wartime period in which it was painted. As Impressionism widened the parameters of art, painters like **Berthe Morisot** (1841–95) and, particularly, **Mary Cassatt** (1844–1926) produced daring (for the time) scenes of nursing mothers, young girls, and mewling babies. Cassatt, like many of her contemporaries, was intrigued by the forms and colors of Asian art; *The Bath* (1898), an etching of mother and baby created with crisp swatches of pale color, was influenced by an exhibition of Japanese woodblocks she had seen in Paris, where she lived from an early age. **Cecilia Beaux** (1863–1942), also inspired by her stay in Paris, was sought after for her rich, expressive portraits such as that of Ethel Page – so much so that she was honored with a commission to paint Theodore and Mrs Roosevelt in 1903. One of Beaux's most striking works, *Sita and Sarita*, is on view at the Corcoran Gallery.

Twentieth-century art

The museum's twentieth-century collection includes classical sculptures by Camille Claudel (1864–1943), paintings by Georgia O'Keeffe and Tamara de Lempicka, linocuts by Hannah Höch, and a cycle of prints depicting the hardships of working-class life by the socialist **Käthe Kollwitz** (1867–1945), part of her powerful *A Weaver's Rebellion* (1893–98). Insightful self-portraits reveal Kollwitz appearing drained by her work in an etching of 1921, and **Frida Kahlo** (1907–54), dressed in a peasant's outfit and clutching a note to Trotsky, dedicating herself to the Revolution. Another, more curious work is Kahlo's *Itzcuintli Dog with Me*, in which she poses next to a truly tiny, strangely adorable mutt. The last gallery reaches into modern times, with striking photographs of figures from the entertainment and literary worlds by Louise Dahl-Wolfe, and contemporary work by sculptors Dorothy Dehner and Louise Nevelson, minimalist Dorothea Rockburne, and Abstract Expressionists Helen Frankenthaler, Lee Krasner, and Elaine de Kooning, among others. One of the highlights is a series of studies for the *Dinner Party*, by **Judy Chicago**, a groundbreaking feminist work from the 1970s.

New York Avenue Presbyterian Church

1313 New York Ave NW ☎202/393-3700, ⊛www.nyapc.org; Metro Center Metro. Daily 9am–1pm, guided tours Sun after 8.45am & 11am services.

Half a block west of the museum, the red-brick **New York Avenue Presbyterian Church** offers a 1950s facsimile of the mid-nineteenth-century church in which the Lincoln family worshipped. The pastor at that time, Dr Gurley, was at Lincoln's bedside at the Petersen House when he died and conducted the funeral service four days later at the White House. Someone in the church's office (on the New York Avenue side) should be able to point out the president's second-row pew, while downstairs in the "Lincoln Parlor" you can see an early draft of his Emancipation Proclamation and portraits of Lincoln and Dr Gurley.

New Downtown and Dupont Circle

Many visitors will bear at least passing acquaintance to the part of the city known as **New Downtown**, if only because that's where many of the better hotels are. Known by several different names – including West Downtown and Midtown – this is where, in the late Victorian era, businessmen and hoteliers first saw the advantage in being just a few blocks from the White House. More than anything else, New Downtown is DC's corporate district, defined as the off-center diamond north of Lafayette Square formed by Pennsylvania, New Hampshire, Massachusetts, and New York avenues. Some of its thoroughfares, like 16th Street and Connecticut Avenue, long had their appeal for historic architecture and the odd museum, but these streets really took off after the panicked flight from Old Downtown following the 1968 riots. These days, the place is primarily ground zero for lobbyists – especially on K Street – and offers a smattering of interesting institutions, museums, and some good restaurants to go along with its upscale accommodation.

Nearby **Dupont Circle** took longer to come into its own, but in recent decades has been an essential destination for its hip restaurants and clubs, gay-friendly merchants, charming old buildings, and contemporary-art galleries. As a symbol of gentrification, the neighborhood is often invoked whenever a formerly down-at-the-heel area becomes chic and trendy, with the threat or promise of it becoming "the next Dupont Circle." Northwest from the Circle itself, turn-of-the-twentieth-century mansions house the denizens of Embassy Row, private galleries cluster near the Phillips Collection, America's first modern art museum, and townhouse museums are peppered around the elite neighborhood of **Kalorama**.

New Downtown

Some of the main thoroughfares (such as 16th Street and Connecticut Avenue) of DC's business zone, **New Downtown**, were developed early on by businessmen and hoteliers with a firm stake in the government's policies toward the private sector, and – with lobbying as feverish now as it's ever been – as many political and economic decisions are still being made here, in these

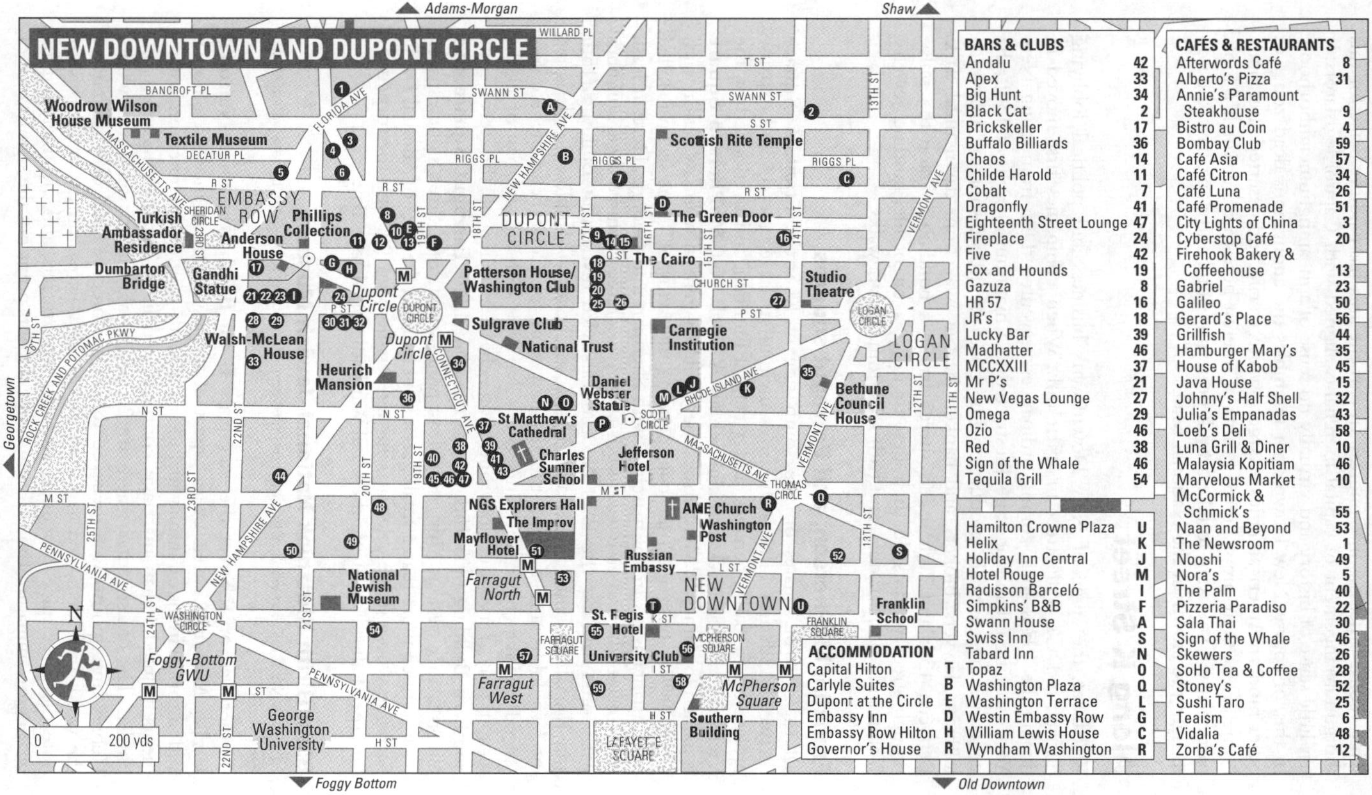

NEW DOWNTOWN AND DUPONT CIRCLE
Adams-Morgan
Shaw
Georgetown
Foggy Bottom
Old Downtown
Woodrow Wilson House Museum
Textile Museum
Turkish Ambassador Residence
Dumbarton Bridge
Anderson House
Phillips Collection
Gandhi Statue
Walsh-McLean House
Heurich Mansion
EMBASSY ROW
DUPONT CIRCLE
Dupont Circle
Patterson House/ Washington Club
Sulgrave Club
National Trust
Scottish Rite Temple
The Green Door
The Cairo
Carnegie Institution
Studio Theatre
LOGAN CIRCLE
Bethune Council House
Daniel Webster Statue
St Matthew's Cathedral
Charles Sumner School
Jefferson Hotel
NGS Explorers Hall
The Improv
Mayflower Hotel
AME Church
Washington Post
Russian Embassy
NEW DOWNTOWN
Franklin School
National Jewish Museum
Farragut North
Farragut West
St. Regis Hotel
University Club
McPherson Square
Southern Building
George Washington University
Foggy-Bottom GWU
LAFAYETTE SQUARE
FRANKLIN SQUARE
0 200 yds
BARS & CLUBS
Andalu 42
Apex 33
Big Hunt 34
Black Cat 2
Brickskeller 17
Buffalo Billiards 36
Chaos 14
Childe Harold 11
Cobalt 7
Dragonfly 41
Eighteenth Street Lounge 47
Fireplace 24
Five 42
Fox and Hounds 19
Gazuza 8
HR 57 16
JR's 18
Lucky Bar 39
Madhatter 46
MCCXXIII 37
Mr P's 21
New Vegas Lounge 27
Omega 29
Ozio 46
Red 38
Sign of the Whale 46
Tequila Grill 54
CAFÉS & RESTAURANTS
Afterwords Café 8
Alberto's Pizza 31
Annie's Paramount Steakhouse 9
Bistro au Coin 4
Bombay Club 59
Café Asia 57
Café Citron 34
Café Luna 26
Café Promenade 51
City Lights of China 3
Cyberstop Café 20
Firehook Bakery & Coffeehouse 13
Gabriel 23
Galileo 50
Gerard's Place 56
Grillfish 44
Hamburger Mary's 35
House of Kabob 45
Java House 15
Johnny's Half Shell 32
Julia's Empanadas 43
Loeb's Deli 58
Luna Grill & Diner 10
Malaysia Kopitiam 46
Marvelous Market 10
McCormick & Schmick's 55
Naan and Beyond 53
The Newsroom 1
Nooshi 49
Nora's 5
The Palm 40
Pizzeria Paradiso 22
Sala Thai 30
Sign of the Whale 46
Skewers 26
SoHo Tea & Coffee 28
Stoney's 52
Sushi Taro 25
Teaism 6
Vidalia 48
Zorba's Café 12
ACCOMMODATION
Capital Hilton T
Carlyle Suites B
Dupont at the Circle E
Embassy Inn D
Embassy Row Hilton H
Governor's House R
Hamilton Crowne Plaza U
Helix K
Holiday Inn Central J
Hotel Rouge M
Radisson Barceló I
Simpkins' B&B F
Swann House A
Swiss Inn S
Tabard Inn N
Topaz O
Washington Plaza Q
Washington Terrace L
Westin Embassy Row G
William Lewis House C
Wyndham Washington R

white-collar offices, as in Congress. In part the area has paid the price for this shotgun arrangement of capital merchants aligned with Capitol legislators: it has little sense of history and virtually no sense of a meaningful neighborhood. In this, of course, New Downtown resembles the anonymous dead zones of other modern American cities – largely white, sterile, and deserted after 6pm. Nonetheless, there are scattered points of interest here that are worth a look, particularly if you want to take a walk near your hotel and don't have the will to fight the crowds at the National Mall.

Along K Street

K Street, the spine of New Downtown's business and political lobbying district, is DC's Wall Street in spirit only. When companies first moved in during the 1970s, local zoning ordinances prevented them from aping New York's soaring urban landscape. Restricted to a maximum height of 130ft, the structures are generally production-line boxes of little distinction in which lobbyists, lawyers, brokers, and bankers beaver away from dawn until dark. Between 13th and 20th streets there's barely a building to raise the pulse, though street vendors do their best to inject a bit of life, hustling jewelry, T-shirts, silk ties, hot dogs, and bath salts from the sidewalks.

Franklin, McPherson, and Farragut squares

Of the trio of squares on the south side of K Street, **Franklin Square** (between 13th and 14th) is the most inviting, its large, tree-covered expanse broken up by paths, benches, and a central fountain, and overlooked by the Victorian-era, red-brick Franklin School. A block west, **McPherson Square** is named for James B. McPherson, the Civil War general who saw action with Grant at Vicksburg and later, commanding the Army of Tennessee, was killed near Atlanta as his troops marched with Sherman into Georgia. Here, at least, late nineteenth- and early twentieth-century architects infused their buildings with some flair, like the 1924 Neoclassical-styled Investment Building (15th and K), whose limestone, Beaux Arts facade belies a completely redesigned modern lobby and interior, the inspired work of Cesar Pelli; the Renaissance Revival arches of the University Club (900 15th St); and, best of all, the scrupulously carved capitals and lion's head plaques of the terra-cotta Southern Building (805 15th St), dating from 1910. **Farragut Square**, two blocks farther west (at 17th), is the least prepossessing of K Street's open spaces; it's not much more than a small green stain beneath the gaze of Admiral David Farragut, whose statue celebrates his reckless heroism ("Damn the torpedoes. Full speed ahead!") during the Civil War battle of Mobile Bay.

B'nai B'rith Klutznick National Jewish Museum

2020 K St NW ☎202/857-6583, ⊛bnaibrith.org/museum. Mon–Thurs 10am–3pm, by reservation only. $5.

Further west on K Street, the exemplary **B'nai B'rith Klutznick National Jewish Museum** covers every aspect of the Jewish experience. Ceremonial and historical items on display include eighteenth-century circumcision instruments, painted Italian marriage contracts, and linen Torah (liturgical scroll) binders. The oldest artifacts here are 2000-year-old incantation bowls, whose Hebrew inscriptions were believed to cast a protective spell over whomever the words were dedicated to. Other pieces show extraordinary workmanship: note the silver spice containers adorned with turrets, and the micrographic writing on miniature Bibles. Enthusiastic docents point out the significance of silver amulets, Torah crowns, and various parchment scrolls; slender metal Torah pointers in the shape of a hand, for example, are designed to avoid having a human hand touch the sacred scroll itself. The museum also covers diaspora groups around the world, including multicultural communities in India and Ethiopia, and has a hall of fame celebrating Jewish-American contributions to sports.

Connecticut Avenue and around

Beyond the National Mall, you could conceivably cover most of Washington DC's other major sights on just two roads: Pennsylvania Avenue NW, starting at the US Capitol and proceeding through Old Downtown to the White House, and from there (after a short detour on 15th and H streets) on to **Connecticut Avenue** NW, leading from New Downtown to Dupont Circle and on to Upper Northwest. Indeed, Connecticut Avenue is arguably the most appealing of all the District's thoroughfares, if only because it links so many interesting neighborhoods – from chic and swank to funky and bohemian – and takes you past all sorts of excellent eateries, boutiques, booksellers, bars, clubs, museums, and galleries along the way. While most of these lie beyond the precinct of New Downtown, it's here where the vital road gets its start.

Mayflower Hotel

The double-bay-fronted **Mayflower Hotel**, 1127 Connecticut Ave NW (☎202/347-3000; Farragut North Metro), has graced its location since 1925, when its first official function was to host President Calvin Coolidge's inaugural ball. Countless other official and unofficial events have taken place here – everything from high-profile diplomatic luncheons to off-the-record journalistic meetings. Designed by the New York architects responsible for Grand Central Terminal, the *Mayflower's* centerpiece is its remarkable 500-foot long **Promenade** – effectively a lobby connecting Connecticut Avenue to 17th Street – which could comfortably accommodate an army division or two. It's rich in rugs, oils, sofas, gilt, and mirrors, as is the hotel's **Grand Ballroom**, in which a dozen incoming presidents have swirled around the dance floor over the years. FDR lived in the *Mayflower* for a while after his inauguration; J. Edgar Hoover lunched here every day when he ran the FBI; and during President Clinton's impeachment proceedings, Monica Lewinsky was interviewed in her suite by Kenneth Starr's prosecutors. Now part of the Renaissance chain, the renovated hotel is an expensive night's rest, but you could also stay somewhere else and still troop through the marvelous public spaces and watch the swells having lunch in the über-chic *Café Promenade* (see "Eating" chapter).

National Geographic Society Explorers Hall

1145 17th St NW ☎202/857-7588, ☻www.nationalgeographic.com/explorer; Farragut North Metro.
Mon–Sat 9am–5pm, Sun 10am–5pm.

The National Geographic Society maintains its headquarters near 17th and M streets. Founded in 1888, it began by funding important expeditions to various uncharted territories; its greatest asset, however, was Gilbert Hovey Grosvenor, founding editor of *National Geographic* magazine, who first conceived that geography could be presented in an exciting way, primarily through spectacular illustrations. At the headquarters building, **Explorers Hall** displays excellent rotating exhibits in the tradition of the magazine's globe-trotting coverage, as well as child-friendly geographic exhibits. Together these cover a range of topics, including global health campaigns, rain-forest protection, indigenous cultures, and the latest trends in science and technology. The hall also hosts frequent events spotlighting explorers, photographers, scientists, and filmmakers, as well as occasional concerts. At the National Geographic **store**, you can choose from a wide selection of maps, globes, videos, photography books, and souvenirs.

Charles Sumner School

1201 17th St NW ☎202/442-6060; Farragut North Metro. Mon–Sat 10am–5pm.

Across M Street from the National Geographic Society, the **Charles Sumner School** honors the nineteenth-century senator nearly clubbed to death in the Old Senate Chamber by pro-slavery Congressman Preston Brooks of South Carolina, who violently objected to Sumner's more enlightened views. To improve the education offered to black children, a separate public high school – the first in the country – was established in the city in 1870. A harmonious red-brick building with a handsome central clock tower, the school is today largely used for conferences, but a free onsite **museum** has a number of mildly interesting exhibits, which range from temporary shows by African-American artists to displays relating to the city's school system.

St Matthew's Cathedral

1725 Rhode Island Ave NW ☎202/347-3215, ⊕www.stmatthewscathedral.org. Mon–Fri & Sun 6.30am–6.30pm, Sat 7.30am–6.30pm.

While not quite on the same level as the National Shrine of the Immaculate Conception, **St Matthew's Cathedral** is still monumental with its flavorful neo-Gothic character, and is an essential stop for anyone interested in spiritual or architectural sites. The centerpiece above the altar is a towering, 35-foot **mosaic** of the church's patron saint; other features include a grand organ with seventy tin pipes, a white-marble altar and pulpit, and four more mosaics depicting the four evangelists (Matthew, Mark, Luke, and John). Beyond its striking appearance, the cathedral is perhaps best known as the place where **JFK**'s funeral mass was held in 1963, and an inlaid plaque honoring the slain president lies in front of the altar; he was buried at Arlington National Cemetery. Kennedy made frequent appearances here, and later (Protestant) presidents as well as just about every notable Catholic politician in Congress have also dropped by. If you want to peer at the bigwig worshippers, church services are open to all; for a better look at the building itself, free tours occur Sunday at 2.30pm, or you can make reservations for a different time.

16th Street and around

Most of the area above K Street was scantily populated until well into the nineteenth century, but post-Civil War expansion changed **16th Street** completely, replacing ramshackle buildings in a predominantly black neighborhood with large mansions, gentlemen's clubs, and patrician hotels, all benefiting from their proximity to the White House. Heading north from the Executive Mansion, the old *Carlton Hotel*, 16th and K streets, has maintained its rich 1920s decor after transforming into the stylish *St Regis* (see "Accommodation" chapter), while a block north, the imposing **Russian Embassy**, at 1125 16th St NW, is a pleasing 1910 Beaux Arts mansion spruced up for diplomatic use. Farther along on 16th Street, the stately *Jefferson Hotel*, at no. 1220 (see "Accommodation" chapter), was built in 1922 and retains its classical arches and iron balconies; the **Metropolitan AME Church** and *Washington Post* building are about a block east (see below); and **Scott Circle**, at Massachusetts and Rhode Island avenues, was once a fashionable nineteenth-century park but is today a traffic roundabout graced with a statue of Union commander General Winfield Scott astride his horse.

Continuing the walk north of Scott Circle, architectural highlights on 16th include the **Carnegie Institution**, at P Street, a pleasing Neoclassical monument with grand columns; the **Cairo**, at Q Street, an 1894 hodgepodge of Moorish, Romanesque, and early-modern Sullivanesque designs whose enormous, 170-foot height caused the District to impose size restrictions for residential buildings; the so-called **Green Door**, 1623 16th St, an 1886 Richardsonian Romanesque mansion with stone cladding, red-brick arches, and turrets; and the astounding Scottish Rite Temple, at no. 1733 (see below).

Metropolitan AME Church

1518 M St NW ☎202/331-1426. Mon–Sat 10am–6pm.

Down on M Street, around lower 16th Street, the large, Gothic, red-brick **Metropolitan African Methodist Episcopal (AME) Church** – built and paid for in 1886 by former slaves – hosted Frederick Douglass's funeral in February 1895. The statesman and orator was brought to lie in state in the church where he had often preached. On the day of the funeral, crowds swamped the street outside, black schools closed for the day, and flags in the city flew at half-mast. This formidable edifice is one of the District's ecclesiastical high points, with its striking, narrow arches and spires, and handsome decorative granite trim. You should be able to look around when the church isn't holding a service.

Washington Post

1150 15th St NW. Hourly tours Mon 10am–3pm; by advance reservation only at ☎202/334-7969.

Walk around the block onto 15th Street to see the offices of the **Washington Post**, the second most famous daily in America after the *New York Times*. The newspaper's reputation is based squarely on the investigative coup of its reporters Bob Woodward and Carl Bernstein, who exposed the Watergate scandal that led to the resignation of President Nixon in 1974. Free **tours** of the modernist offices were suspended in 2001, due to a spate of anthrax attacks on various media organizations around the country, but have since resumed for groups of ten or more, by written request (call for more information). The tours offer a behind-the-scenes look at how the paper is put together – worthwhile if you're interested in journalism, or if you're just a news junkie.

Scottish Rite Temple

1733 16th St NW ☎202/232-3579, ✆www.srmason-sj.org; Dupont Circle Metro. Library Mon–Fri 8am–3pm, tours 8am–2pm.

John Russell Pope's **Scottish Rite Temple**, halfway between New Downtown and the edgy Shaw district, is one of DC's most eye-catching buildings; indeed, in the 1930s, the American Institute of Architects voted it one of the five finest structures in the world. If you're anywhere in the vicinity, you can't possibly miss it, with its towering Ionic columns, ziggurat-like roof, huge base, and ancient-temple design inspired by the Mausoleum at Halicarnassus, one of the Seven Wonders of the Ancient World. Built in 1915 of limestone and granite, this Masonic temple is predictably loaded with arcane symbolism, striking imagery (notably the two sphinxes guarding the place out front), and various inscriptions hailing knowledge, truth, and other values. Unlike many such temples, though, this one has long been accessible to the uninitiated: it's been a **public library** for many decades – housing a voluminous collection of works by fellow Scottish Mason and poet, Robert Burns – and is open for daily **tours**, though you're not likely to receive any answers if you start asking questions about secret rituals and handshakes.

Logan Circle and 14th Street

In the early twentieth century, an influx of black middle-class residents began to fill the roomy Victorian houses around **Logan Circle**, between New Downtown and Shaw. Fashionable Iowa Circle, as it was then known, became Logan Circle in 1930, named for the Civil War general whose impressive equestrian statue lords over the spot. The surrounding Victorians have miraculously survived the neighborhood's slow decline since the 1950s; turrets, terraces, balconies, and pediments in various states of repair signal the fact that this is a protected historic district.

Fourteenth Street, half a block west, was the community's upscale shopping thoroughfare, but was almost completely lost to the 1968 riots. Its rough edges have been largely tamed by the various fringe theater companies, trendy restaurants and bars, and quirky boutiques that have set up shop since; nevertheless it's not the most inviting place to be at night – don't wander the streets alone in the dark.

Bethune Council House

1318 Vermont Ave NW ☎202/673-2402, ⊛www.nps.gov/mamc. Mon–Sat 10am–4.30pm.

In one of the restored townhouses just off Logan Circle, the **Bethune Council House** serves as a memorial to one of DC's most prominent

The rise of Mary McLeod Bethune

Mary McLeod Bethune was born on a cotton farm in South Carolina in 1875, one of seventeen children of poor parents, both ex-slaves. A bright, inquiring child, she was sent to a local school and later entertained thoughts of becoming a missionary in Africa (she was turned down because of her race) before moving to Florida in 1904 to found the Daytona Educational and Industrial School for Negro Girls (later **Bethune-Cookman College**). Starting in a rented room and using homemade materials, Bethune persevered with her intention to train teachers who would serve the African-American community. In 1935, she was recognized with an award from the NAACP, and soon after President **Franklin Roosevelt** asked her to serve as special advisor on minority affairs. Later, as the director of the Division of Negro Affairs in the National Youth Administration, Bethune became the first African-American woman to head a federal office, and was the only woman to work in the ad hoc **"Black Cabinet"** that advised FDR about the implications of his New Deal policies on blacks. In 1945, through the NAACP, Bethune was invited to San Francisco to attend the conference that established the United Nations.

Bethune bought her home on Vermont Avenue in 1942 and lived there for seven years. She also used it as headquarters for the National Council for Negro Women, founded in 1935, which sought to bring various organizations together to fight discrimination more effectively. Her work here formed the basis of her collection of writings called *Legacy*, finished just before her death in 1955, in which she outlined the meaning of her work in a stirring series of messages for those who would follow: "I leave you a thirst for education. I leave you a respect for the use of power. I leave you faith. I leave you racial dignity."

African-American residents. Administered by the National Park Service, the house serves as a research center and archive, though you're welcome to tour the restored rooms, which contain a few of Mary McLeod Bethune's mementos alongside period photographs and changing exhibitions. The memorial to Bethune in Lincoln Park (see p.115) records more of her legacy. The best way to get here is the fifteen-minute walk up Vermont Avenue from McPherson Square Metro, past Thomas Circle.

Dupont Circle

Strictly speaking, **Dupont Circle** is the great traffic roundabout formed at the intersection of such major boulevards as Massachusetts, Connecticut, and New Hampshire avenues with 19th and P streets, making for a ten-spoked wheel that can take forever to drive if you hit it during rush hour. Beyond the Circle itself, this section of Northwest DC is a fun, relaxed neighborhood with a good blend of hipsters, yuppies, and old-timers, plus dining, drinking, and clubbing options for a variety of tastes. Easily accessible on the Metro's Red Line, it's also one of the city's best areas for a walk, loaded with gorgeous townhouses and mansions from the nineteenth and early twentieth centuries, as well as a number of museums, bookstores, and galleries. Along with Connecticut Avenue NW, the other major stretches for nighttime entertainment are the gay-oriented P Street west of the Circle and 17th Street east of it, which have an abundance of frenetic dance clubs and friendly neighborhood bars. **Embassy Row**, just to the northwest along Massachusetts Avenue, is lined with historic Beaux Arts mansions now stuffed with diplomats and staffers, and flying flags of their respective nations out front. One of the best times to visit Dupont Circle is the first weekend in June, when a consortium of ten area museums sponsors the Dupont–Kalorama **Museums Walk Weekend** (@www.dkmuseums.com), featuring free concerts, historic-house tours, and craft fairs.

Some history

Until the Civil War, Pacific Circle – as Dupont Circle was first known – marked the western edge of the city, beyond which the nation's capital petered out into a series of farms, barns, and slaughterhouses. With the postwar boom, however, streets were paved and a bridge was built across Rock Creek to nearby Georgetown. The **British Embassy** was built here in the mid-1870s, and subsequently lawyers and businessmen installed their families in grand Victorian houses. By the turn of the century, Dupont Circle was where all self-respecting industrial barons and high-flying diplomats built their city mansions, often in the favored Beaux Arts style of the time. Massachusetts Avenue, northwest of the Circle, became so popular with foreign legations that it acquired the tag Embassy Row, while the even more secluded residences north of S Street developed into the exclusive neighborhood of **Kalorama** (see p.191) – named in Greek for the "beautiful view" it afforded of the Rock Creek Valley.

Dupont Circle's golden age of soirées and socialites ended at roughly the same time World War II began. Many of its wealthy residents were hit by the 1929 stock market crash and sold out; other mansions were torn down or, the ultimate ignominy, turned into boardinghouses for the postwar influx of federal workers. The Circle became solidly middle-class and, during the 1970s, even vaguely radical, as a younger crowd moved in, attracted by a dilapidated

Dupont Circle

housing stock in which they could strip pine, throw down weave rugs, and demonstrate against the Vietnam War.

Since then, rampant gentrification has long seen off the Dupont Circle hippies, and it's once more an upmarket address, full of designer coffeehouses and swank restaurants, if leavened somewhat by a load of alternative bookstores and unpretentious drinking establishments.

The traffic circle and around

The large traffic island of Dupont Circle is as much a hub as any roundabout in DC, and centers around a **fountain** whose frolicking nude allegorical figures – representing sea, stars, and wind – were meant to honor the naval exploits of Civil War Admiral Samuel Dupont. In modern times the Circle itself has always looked a little ragged at the edges – hip thriller writer George P. Pelecanos, writing about the 1970s, described it as full of "girl-watching businessmen, stoners, cruising homosexuals, short-skirted secretaries, doe-faced chicken hawks eyeing little boys, the whole Dupont stew," but on the whole it's an easygoing hangout with chess-players hogging the permanent tables in the center of the Circle, and a bunch of cafés, bookstores, and restaurants within a few minutes' walk. There are Metro entrances to the northwest and south.

There are almost too many notable examples of historic architecture here to mention, but a few buildings are definite standouts. The Neoclassical **Washington Club**, at 15 Dupont Circle NW and Massachusetts Ave, was formerly the Patterson House, where the Coolidge family, camping out during White House renovations, entertained Charles Lindbergh soon after his solo transatlantic crossing. The swanky **Sulgrave Club**, at 1801 Massachusetts Ave, is another upscale building, with an elegant Beaux Arts design and terra-cotta details, while at 1785 Massachusetts Ave, the **National Trust for Historic Preservation** (☎202/588-6000, ⊛www.nthp.org) occupies the towering edifice once known as the McCormick Apartments. The striking 1922 building has lovely period details, again of a late Beaux Arts flavor; for a closer look, take one of the Trust's tours, offered by reservation only.

Just outside the northwest-side Metro exit, the grand **Blaine Mansion**, at 2000 Massachusetts Ave, is a marvelous red-brick Victorian from 1881 that was once home to three-time presidential candidate James "Slippery Jim" Blaine, whose worst defeat was in 1884, when he became the first Republican nominee to lose the general election since before the Civil War – to Grover Cleveland, who has a DC neighborhood named after him (Cleveland Park).

Heurich House

1307 New Hampshire Ave NW ☎202/429-1894, ⊛www.heurichhouse.org; Dupont Circle Metro. Tours Wed 12.15pm & 1.15pm. $5.

One historic residence that is regularly open to the public is the wondrous **Heurich House**, built in 1894 for German-born brewing magnate Christian Heurich, and a stunning example of the Richardsonian Romanesque popular at the time. With its rough-hewn stone turret and castellations and richly carved wood-and-plaster interior, the mansion – known as "The Brewmaster's Castle" – resembles a miniature medieval fortress. The Historical Society of Washington DC had its headquarters here from 1956 to 2003 (when it moved to the old City Library; see p.177), but the house is once again in the possession of the Heurich family, who still allow weekly tours of the place. These tours take you through many of the restored rooms and focus on the mansion's lavish decor and the lifestyle of its original occupants. On display are the formal parlor, drawing room, and dining room, a music room with a mahogany musicians' balcony, and the basement *Bierstube* (beer room), carved with such Teutonic drinking mottos as "He who has never been drunk is not a good man."

Embassy Row

Embassy Row starts in earnest a few paces northwest up Massachusetts Avenue, where the Indonesian Embassy at no. 2020 occupies the magnificent Art Nouveau **Walsh-McLean House**, built in 1903 for gold baron Thomas Walsh. It's a superb building – with colonnaded loggia and intricate, carved windows – that was once one of high society's most fashionable venues. Soirées here were presided over by Walsh's daughter Evalyn, the last private owner of the Hope Diamond (now in the National Museum of Natural History). Nearby, the Anderson House (see below) merits a visit; the **Cosmos Club**, 2121 Massachusetts Ave, is a swank private entity with an agreeable Beaux Arts style; and the memorial to Tomas Masaryk, at 22nd and Q streets, is a 2002 work that honors the founder of Czechoslovakia with a large brooding statue. There are a number of other statues in this area as well, the most prominent – and incongruous – of which is of **Mahatma Gandhi**, who, with his skinny frame and walking stick, presides over a traffic island at Massachusetts, Q, and 21st.

Although the diplomatic residences in the area are typically closed to the public, occasionally you can take a closer look inside some of them. If you want to know more about a given country's culture (with a heavy PR spin of course), check out ⊛www.embassyevents.org for a listing of art shows, lectures, food fairs, films, and displays taking place at selected embassies here and elsewhere in town. Alternatively, you can drop in on the **Goodwill Embassy Tour** (pre-booked $30, $35 day of; ☎202/636-4225, ⊛www.dcgoodwill.org) on the second Saturday in May, during which some of DC's finest embassy buildings throw open their doors.

Anderson House

2110 Massachusetts Ave NW ☎202/785-2040, ⊛www.thesocietyofthecincinnati.addr.com; Dupont Circle Metro. Tues–Sat 1–4pm.

The **Anderson House** is a veritable palace, built between 1902 and 1905 as the winter residence of Larz Anderson, who served as ambassador to Belgium and Japan. As a Beaux Arts residence it has no equal in the city, its gray-stone exterior sporting twin arched entrances with heavy wooden doors and a colonnaded portico. Inside, original details – cavernous fireplaces, inlaid marble floors, Flemish tapestries, evocative murals, and a grand ballroom – provide a lavish backdrop for diplomatic receptions. Anderson bequeathed this wonderful house to the **Society of the Cincinnati**, as his great-grandfather was a founding member. Established in 1783, the Society – named after Cincinnatus, the legendary Roman general who famously relinquished his command after saving the city from invading hordes – is the oldest patriotic organization in the country and maintains a small museum of Revolutionary War memorabilia here; if you can prove your lineage to an American officer in that conflict, you can apply to become a member. Appropriately enough, **George Washington** was its first President-General, and there's a white marble bust of him in the entrance hall by Thomas Crawford, who sculpted the Freedom figure on top of the Capitol. The best time to visit the Anderson House is when it's offering one of its regular **free concerts** (see p.297), typically classical chamber-music recitals.

Sheridan Circle and around

Farther northwest, at **Sheridan Circle**, an equestrian statue of Union General Phillip H. Sheridan was erected in 1909. Compared to the 60-foot heads of Washington, Jefferson, Lincoln, and Roosevelt that its sculptor, Gutzon Borglum, went on to create at Mount Rushmore, this statue seems positively dainty. On the south side of the Circle, the **Residence of the Turkish Ambassador**, 1606 23rd St, is brimming with Near Eastern motifs; oddly, it wasn't commissioned by the Turks at all but by one Edward Everett, the man who patented the fluted bottle-top. From the Circle, you can duck down 23rd Street to see **Dumbarton Bridge**, guarded on either side by enormous bronze bison. The bridge provides the quickest route into northern Georgetown, emerging on Q Street by Dumbarton House, about twenty minutes from Dupont Circle.

The Phillips Collection

1600 21st St NW ☎202/387-2151, ⒲www.phillipscollection.org; Dupont Circle Metro. Tues–Sat 10am–5pm, Sun noon–7pm, Thurs closes at 8.30pm. $8.

The **Phillips Collection**'s claim to be "America's first museum of modern art" is based on its having opened eight years before New York's Museum of Modern Art. The oldest part of the Georgian Revival brownstone building was the family home of founder **Duncan Phillips**, who lost his father and brother in little over a year and established a gallery in 1921 in their honor. Financed by the family's steel fortune, Phillips bought nearly 2400 works over the years; during the 1920s, he and his wife, Marjorie, became patrons of young artists like Georgia O'Keeffe and Marsden Hartley. The diverse collection includes everyone from Renoir to Rothko, as well as pre-modern artists like Giorgione and El Greco. Because the museum is strong on temporary exhibits, and because it's experiencing an ongoing renovation, it's likely that, when you arrive, some of the pieces below either won't be on view or will have been moved to different rooms. If there's something here that you specifically want to see, be sure to call in advance.

The museum's **main entrance** is in the Goh Annex, on 21st Street. The **permanent collection** is on the first two floors of the annex, and on the first and second floor of the original building; the annex and original building are connected by a "skywalk." **Special exhibitions** are on the annex's third floor, and a **gift shop** is on the original building's ground level. A full program of **cultural events** includes classical music recitals (Sept–May Sun 5pm; free with admission); "Artful Evenings" (Thurs 5–8.30pm), with live music, lectures, and a bar; and weekly tours (Sat 2pm).

The Goh Annex

The permanent collection on the first floor of the **Goh Annex** makes for a rather low-key introduction, usually featuring a handful of **Abstract Expressionist** works from the 1950s, including a characteristically gloomy set of paintings by Rothko, such as his *Orange and Red on Red*; Philip Guston's phantasmagoric *The Native's Return*; and signature pieces by Willem de Kooning and Richard Diebenkorn. The powerhouses are usually kept **one floor up**, and comprise a wistful Blue Period Picasso, Matisse's *Studio, Quai St-Michel*, a Cézanne still life, and no fewer than four van Goghs, including the powerful *Road Menders* (1889). Pierre Bonnard gets a good showing – you have to stand well back to take in the expansive, post-Impressionist scale of *The Terrace* (1918) and *The Palm* (1926). Top billing generally goes to Renoir's *The Luncheon of the Boating Party* (1891), where straw-boater-wearing dandies linger over a long and bibulous feast. Phillips bought the painting in 1923 for $125,000 as part of a two-year burst of acquisition that also yielded Cézanne's *Mont Saint-Victoire* and Honoré Daumier's *The Uprising*. There's an impressive collection of **Degas** works, too – from early scenes like *Women Combing Their Hair* (1875) to the late ballet picture *Dancers at the Bar* (c. 1900), in which the background and hair of the subjects collide in an orange frenzy.

Other **nineteenth-century works** include pieces by Gustave Courbet and Eugène Delacroix (note his wonderful painting of the violinist Paganini in full fiddle). Phillips's catholic taste comes to the fore with the juxtaposition of two paintings of a repentant St Peter: one, fat and bluff, by Goya, the other a more familiar, biblical study by El Greco. An odd choice on the face of it, Phillips bought this latter piece for his modern art museum because he considered El Greco "the first impassioned expressionist."

Main building

If you cross the skywalk and head down the stairs to the main building's **first floor**, you'll hit the oak-paneled "**Music Room**," where Cubist paintings by Georges Braque (a particular favorite of Phillips, who owned thirteen of his works) vie for attention. Beyond here the collection concentrates more on **late nineteenth-** and **early twentieth-century American artists**, featuring pieces like Winslow Homer's bleak *To The Rescue*; James McNeill Whistler's enigmatic *Miss Lilian Woakes,* and Albert Pinkham Ryder's moody and atmospheric *Moonlit Cove* among the highlights. Also worth a look are Charles Sheeler's sleek ode to the modern age, *Skyscrapers*; a few colorful still lifes by Stuart Davis; Jean Arp's striking *Helmeted Head II* and Mondrian's *Painting no. 9.*

The **second floor** features artists championed by Phillips in the 1920s and 1930s, like Milton Avery (who influenced the young Rothko) and Jacob Lawrence – the latter represented by extracts from a powerful series called *The Migration of the Negro*. Better known names abound, too, notably **Edward Hopper**, whose works here include *Sunday* (1926), featuring a man sitting alone on a bleak, empty street, and the much later *Approaching a City*, viewed from the vantage point of sunken train tracks. **Paul Klee's** works range from the stick figures embellishing *Arrival of the Jugglers* (1926) to the kaleidoscopic maze of rectangles, triangles, and trapezoidal shapes in *The Way to the Citadel* (1937).

Kalorama

North of Sheridan Circle, in the exclusive district of **Kalorama**, quiet streets with manicured lawns stretch out to meet Rock Creek Park. Here the city's diplomatic community thrives behind lace curtains and bulletproof glass in row after row of multimillion-dollar townhouse embassies, private homes, and hibiscus-rich gardens. One of the best such examples, the **Hauge House**, lies on the neighborhood's south end, at 24th and S streets. This French Renaissance mansion housed the first Norwegian embassy in 1907, and today it's home to the Cameroon embassy.

If you head up 24th Street toward Kalorama Circle, you'll find spectacular views across Rock Creek Park to Georgetown and beyond. Just to the east, the **Residence of the French Ambassador** at 2221 Kalorama Rd NW is the area's most ambitious building; the Tudor Revival country manor was

He was the perfect prototype of the seventeenth-century Puritan reincarnated.

Alistair Cooke, *America*, 1973

Born **Thomas Woodrow Wilson** in Stanton, Virginia, to a plain-living Presbyterian family, the future president dropped the "Thomas" at a very early age, convinced that the new version would sound better when he was famous. He attended law school and, though he didn't take his final exams, practiced law in Georgia for a year, only to discover that it wasn't his métier. Wilson returned to graduate school to earn his doctorate (making him the only American president to have a PhD) and taught law and political economics for twelve years, eventually rising to become a reforming president of **Princeton University**. Known and respected as an academic writer on political science and a stern critic of government corruption, he might have dedicated his life to these pursuits but for the Democratic Party's need for progressive candidates to run against the splintering Republicans. In 1910 Wilson won election as the **governor of New Jersey** and two years later received the Democratic nomination for president. The split in the Republican Party – with Theodore Roosevelt running on the Bull Moose Party ticket against the incumbent William Howard Taft, a former Republican protégé – gave the Democrats both houses in Congress and let Wilson slip into power.

In his two terms of office, Wilson – a stirring orator (and the last president to write his own speeches) – saw through a batch of reformist legislation that continued Roosevelt's crusade against corporate vice and corruption. The **Federal Reserve** was established to better regulate the banking system, anti-trust laws were strengthened, the **19th Amendment** (for women's suffrage) passed, and labor laws were enacted that at least gave a nod to workers' rights. But Wilson also presided over rather darker events – not least the violent breaking of the Colorado coal strike, leaving 66 people dead, and the entrenchment of segregation in the federal system. Indeed, it's misleading to see Wilson as any kind of liberal; his reforms made capitalism safe in a period of considerable turmoil and were very much part of the turn-of-the-century strengthening of federal power at the expense of individual freedom. It's no coincidence that the **18th Amendment** sanctioning Prohibition was passed during his presidency, and it was Wilson who, upon viewing D.W. Griffith's notoriously racist epic *The Birth of a*

originally built for a mining magnate and sold to the French in 1936 for the then absurdly expensive sum of almost half a million dollars. And unlike the Norwegians, who parted company with their stunning mansion, the French have clung tightly to theirs ever since.

Woodrow Wilson House

2340 S St NW ☎202/387-4062, ◉www.woodrowwilsonhouse.org; Dupont Circle Metro. Tues–Sun 10am–4pm. $5.

Many commanders-in-chief lived in Washington DC before moving into the White House; all but one of them left the moment they retired from public service. **Woodrow Wilson**, the 28th president, spent the last years of his life in a fine Waddy Butler Wood-designed Georgian Revival house that is now open to the public. It's a comfortable home – light and airy, with high ceilings, wood floors, a wide staircase, and a solarium – which, despite his incapacitating stroke in 1919, Wilson aimed to use as a workplace where he could write political science books and practice law. That his second wife,

Nation, famously remarked that the film was "writing history with lightning."

If Wilson was blind to the concerns of workers and minorities, he had a keen political eye for a broader picture, mixed with a high moral tone that brooked no argument. Inspired by his sound analysis of the mood of the American people, and perhaps also by a gut pacifism, he managed to keep America out of **World War I** until 1917. Within four months of his second inauguration, however, the country was at war, prompted ostensibly by unprovoked German attacks on American shipping, though later critics would claim that the government wanted war orders to stimulate the economy. Abandoning his pacifist stance, Wilson instead declared a war "for democracy" and devoted his considerable energies to ending it quickly and imposing a new moral order on the world. This manifested in his championing a **League of Nations**, an idea he took to the peace conference in Paris, seeing it as a "matter of life or death for civilization." However, the president was soon outflanked by the wilier leaders of Britain and France, who took the conference as an opportunity to punish Germany for its misdeeds and produced the **Treaty of Versailles**, which led to crushing unemployment and financial collapse, and, eventually, the rise of the Nazi party. Of course, there was no way Wilson could have foreseen such an outcome – indeed, some historians even claim that while in Paris, Wilson had a bout of Spanish influenza, then widespread around the world, when he signed off on some of the European leaders' more draconian measures.

Returning in June 1919 to sell the League to the American people (and more importantly to the Senate, which has to ratify any treaty by a two-thirds majority), Wilson undertook a draining speaking tour. After a series of blinding headaches he had to cut it short, returning to DC where, on October 2, 1919, he suffered a huge stroke that half-paralyzed him.

His cherished League was finally rejected by the Senate in March 1920, but by then Wilson was almost completely incapacitated. Few people outside government were informed of this, and in what today looks suspiciously like a cover-up, his wife Edith – sixteen years his junior – took on many of the day-to-day decisions in the White House, prompting critics to complain of a "petticoat presidency." As inflation rose and the economy slumped, Warren Harding was swept into power in the 1920 presidential elections, partly undoing Wilson's legacy through misrule and scandal. Wilson, old and infirm, and his wife left the White House for S Street, where crowds greeted him

Edith, a rich jeweler's widow, wanted to stay in DC near her family and friends probably had something to do with the decision to remain; she lived in the house for more than 35 years after Wilson's death. Indeed, Wilson only lived here for three years, and after he passed away was interred in Washington National Cathedral.

Visitors are first ushered into the front parlor, where Wilson liked to receive guests, and then there's plenty to see from there – not least of which is the elevator, installed to help the enfeebled ex-president move between floors, and the bedroom, furnished by Edith as it had been in the White House. The canvas-walled library of the scholarly president (he ran Princeton University before he ran the country) once held eight thousand books, but they were donated to the Library of Congress after his death; the only remaining ones are the 69 volumes of Wilson's own writings. In a separate room is a silent-movie projector and screen that were given to him after his stroke by Douglas Fairbanks Sr. The fully equipped kitchen, straight out of the 1920s, has a blacklead range and provisions stacked in the walk-in pantry.

Textile Museum

2320 S St NW ☎202/667-0441, ⊛www.textilemuseum.org; Dupont Circle Metro. Mon–Sat 10am–5pm, Sun 1–5pm. $5.

Next door to the Woodrow Wilson House, in two equally grand converted residences, the **Textile Museum** presents temporary exhibitions drawn from its 15,000-strong collection of textiles and carpets. The museum had its roots in the collection of **George Hewitt Myers**, who bought his first Asian rug as a student and opened the museum with three hundred other rugs and textile pieces in 1925. Based in his family home and designed by no less an architect than John Russell Pope, the museum soon expanded into the house next door; today both buildings, and the beautiful gardens, are open to the public. Displays might include pre-Columbian Peruvian textiles, Near and Far Eastern exhibits (some dating back to 3000 BC), and rugs and carpets from Spain, South America, and the American Southwest. Other intriguing temporary exhibits cover topics such as contemporary textile design – using computers, photographic imagery, metallic threads, and other oddments – and the intersection of art, craft, and fashion, with objects designed as much to hang on a wall as on a body.

Adams-Morgan, Shaw, and Outer Northeast

Few districts represent the gap between tourist-friendly DC and the "real" DC more than **Adams-Morgan** and **Shaw** do. Unlike the neighborhoods to the south, these offer little in the way of museums or official attractions, and are rarely visited by folks arriving into town on tour buses. However, for residents of the city, they offer some of the liveliest street culture, best independent shops, and richest blend of races and cultures you're likely to find along the Eastern Seaboard outside of New York. Even better, these are the essential spots for freewheeling dance clubs, rock- and punk-music venues, and cheap bars – notably without the stuffy attitudes found around Dupont Circle. With this authentic edge, however, comes a bit of diciness, and if you're coming at night it's best to take a cab between major destinations. Where there are plenty of people around, mainly the lively commercial stretches of 18th Street and U Street, crime isn't as much of a problem, though you're well advised to always stay alert.

Adams-Morgan is one of the few areas in the city with an inexpensive **nightlife scene**, and you should dine out at least once here, since its range of ethnic restaurants is unparalleled in the District. Only in Shaw, to the east, do you have to pick your spots carefully. Once *the* thriving black neighborhood, and home of a vibrant music scene in the 1920s and 1930s, the area is still feeling the effects of its rapid postwar decline, though pockets are slowly being dragged back toward respectability.

Beyond Adams-Morgan and Shaw, the **Outer Northeast** section of DC offers a handful of scattered attractions, like the marvelous **National Arboretum** and the **National Shrine of the Immaculate Conception**, at some remove from its more crime-ridden areas, and accessibile in the daytime with few hassles. Several of the area's sights are also within easy reach of the Metro system.

ADAMS-MORGAN, SHAW & OUTER NORTHEAST

CAFÉS & RESTAURANTS

18th and U Duplex Diner	29
Ben's Chili Bowl	33
Bukom Café	15
Cakelove	39
Cashion's Eat Place	13
Coppi's	40
The Diner	9
Fasika's	6
Florida Avenue Grill	24
Grill from Ipanema	8
Harambe Café	30
I Matti	19
Jolt 'n' Bolt	44
L'Enfant	32
La Fourchette	22
Lauriol Plaza	45
Mama Ayesha's	2
Meskerem	21
Meze	18
Mixtec	14
Pasta Mia	16
Perry's	17
Pizza Mart	12
Tryst	3

ACCOMMODATION

Adams Inn	A
Courtyard by Marriott	H
Kalorama Guest House	C
Normandy Inn	E
Washington Hilton	F
Washington International Student Center	B
Windsor Inn	G
Windsor Park	D

BARS & CLUBS

2:K9		Chi-Cha Lounge	43
9:30 Club		Chief Ike's Mambo Room	1
Bedrock Billiards		Columbia Station	27
Black Cat		Common Share	46
Blue Room		Habana Village	11
Bohemian Caverns		Heaven & Hell	23

Madame's Organ	38	Spy Lounge	25
Millie and Al's	1	Toledo Lounge	20
Polly's Café	27	Twins Jazz	41
Republic Gardens	35	U-topia	37
Rumba Café	23	Velvet Lounge	36

ADAMS-MORGAN

SHAW

DUPONT CIRCLE

KALORAMA

National Shrine and Takoma Park

Georgetown

McMillan Reservoir

Howard University

Howard Hall

Founder's Library

Howard University Hospital

Howard Theatre (site)

African-American Civil War Memorial

African-American Civil War Museum

Lincoln Theatre

Source Theatre

Kalorama Park

Warder House

Meridian Hill Park

Meridian International Center

Pink Palace

Columbia Heights

DC Arts Center

Wyoming Building

Altamont Building

Visions Cinema Bistro Lounge

Phillips Collection

Anderson House

Textile Museum

Woodrow Wilson House Museum

Rock Creek Park

Woodley Park Zoo

Ontario Building

see inset

Adams-Morgan

Nowhere is gentrification faster changing the original, ethnic character of a Washington neighborhood than in **Adams-Morgan**, DC's trendiest district. With every passing month new designer restaurants, stylish bars, and hip stores march farther into the area, if not displacing, then at least beginning to out-number the traditional Hispanic businesses that have thrived here since the 1950s. Spanish signs and notices are still much in evidence, especially along Columbia Road, and the neighborhood certainly celebrates its heritage well at the annual **Latin American Festival** (July) and **Adams-Morgan Day** (Sept) shindigs. For a night out largely free from the braying collegiate antics of Georgetown, you'll find Adams-Morgan's **18th Street** strip a refreshing change: laid-back, open-to-the-sidewalk bars, restaurants, cafés, and clubs with a diverse clientele. Ethiopian arrivals are responsible for some of the neigh-borhood's most highly rated eateries, but you can devour anything here from Argentinian to Vietnamese.

Adams-Morgan is generally thought of as being bounded by Connecticut and Florida avenues and 16th and Harvard streets, though in practice most visitors see little more than the few blocks on either side of the central **Colum-bia Road/18th Street intersection**, where most of the bars and restaurants are situated. The eastern boundary of the neighborhood is marked by 16th Street and Meridian Hill Park – don't stray further east than 16th Street into Shaw. To the west, the boundary is formed by the **National Zoo** and Connecticut Avenue NW, which is where you'll find the nearest **Metro**: from Woodley Park-Zoo Metro on Connecticut Avenue, it's a fifteen-minute walk across the Duke Ellington Bridge to the Columbia Road/18th Street junction. From Dupont Circle Metro it's a steep twenty-minute hike up 19th Street to Columbia Road. By **bus**, take the #L2 from McPherson Square, which travels up 18th Street to Calvert Street; alternately, #42 goes via Metro Center (10th and F), H Street, Connecticut Avenue, Dupont Circle, and up to Columbia Road.

Some history

The neighborhood's **gentrification** is simply turning Adams-Morgan full circle. In the late nineteenth century, its hilly, rural reaches were colonized by wealthy Washingtonians looking for a select address near the power-housing of Dupont Circle. Impressive apartment buildings were erected in the streets off Columbia Road, boasting expansive views and connected to downtown by streetcar. Until World War II some of the city's most prominent politicians and business people lived here, and many of their mansions survive intact. After the war, the city's housing shortage meant that many buildings were converted into rooming houses and small apartments; well-to-do families moved farther out into the suburbs and were replaced by a growing blue-collar population, black and white, and, crucially, by increasing numbers of Latin American and Car-ibbean immigrants, whose population grew rapidly in the 1960s. Concerned that the area was becoming too segregated, a local group fashioned a symbolic name from two local schools: one all-white (Adams), one all-black (Morgan).

Today, Adams-Morgan is regarded as the most racially mixed neighborhood in the city, and for the most part there's a good-natured atmosphere in the streets, where grocery stores and corner cafés sit alongside arty boutiques and sharp bars. Images of Adams-Morgan frequently pop up in movies: *In the Line of Fire*, *Dave*, *A Few Good Men*, and *Enemy of the State* all feature scenes shot in the neighborhood.

Along Columbia Road

Adams-Morgan's Hispanic legacy is at its strongest in the stretch of Columbia Road northeast of 18th Street, a good place to check out the street stalls, jewelry sellers, and thrift stores; a Saturday **market** occupies the southwestern plaza where the two meet. For most visitors that's more than enough activity, though the streets east and west of the two main drags contain a fair amount of interest – Anthony Pitch's **walking tours** of the district (see p.34) can show you more.

Starting from the south, just beyond Dupont Circle along Columbia Road NW, the **Wyoming Building**, no. 2022, is a classic example of the marvelous apartment houses built in the early twentieth century, its mosaic floor, molded ceilings, and marble reception room forming one of DC's loveliest interiors (the Eisenhowers lived here between 1927 and 1935). Adjacent on the south side, at 1919 Connecticut Ave NW, is the **Washington Hilton**, a charmless modern block, but also a historically significant one: this is where, in the driveway roundabout, John Hinckley Jr shot Ronald Reagan in a 1981 assassination attempt, leaving the president and three others gravely wounded, and his press secretary, James Brady, permanently paralyzed. Just to the north, the Italian-Renaissance-style **Altamont Building**, 1901 Wyoming Ave NW, at 20th St, is much more visually striking, with its rooftop terrace and squat towers, barrel-vaulted and gilded lobby, and an adjoining parlor featuring original, Old English-styled furniture..

Most glamorous of all the Adams-Morgan buildings is the cupola-topped **Ontario Building**, way up north at 2853 Ontario Rd (at 18th), built between 1903 and 1906. Its roll call of famous residents has included five-star generals Douglas MacArthur and Chester Nimitz; journalist Janet Cooke, whose Pulitzer Prize-winning story about youth and drugs was later discredited; and *Washington Post* scribe Bob Woodward. Carl Bernstein, Woodward's partner in the Watergate investigation, also lived in Adams-Morgan, in the much less grandiose **Biltmore** apartment building, 1940 Biltmore St, off 19th St, just a couple of blocks south.

Along 18th Street

South of Columbia Road, **18th Street** is the center of DC's melting pot, where yuppies from Kalorama drop in to sample the funky vibe and snap up street wear for a song; venturesome gays and hipsters from Dupont Circle come to imbibe at bars and browse in secondhand bookstores; and African Americans from Shaw visit to support independent boutiques and other minority businesses. The broad mix of visitors is equalled by the wide range of restaurants

The U Link Shuttle

The DC **Metro** system recently made it much easier to access the highlights of Adams-Morgan and its surrounding areas. Starting at the Woodley Park-Zoo Metro station, the **U Link Shuttle** (line #98; 30min trip) travels along Calvert, 18th, and U streets from Adams-Morgan until it reaches the U Street-Cardozo Metro Station. The fare is only 25¢, though you'll pay the full $1.25 for a transfer to another bus line; hours are Mon–Fri 6pm–3am, Sat 10am–3am, Sun 6pm–midnight. If you don't have a car, this is definitely the best way to travel through a dicey area at night – cheaper than a cab, safer than on foot – and it manages to cross a rather wide expanse of the city that lacks subway service.

and stores – including pizza joints, ethnic diners, Latin botanicas, junk emporia, bistros, astrologers and palm-readers, antique sellers, vintage-clothing dealers, book and music shops, coffeehouses, and fringe theaters. The scene is presided over by lines of **Victorian row houses** in various states of disrepair or renovation, with increasing numbers of artists' and yuppies' lofts adding more change and ferment to the neighborhood. The architecture here is more eye-catching than historically unique, but fans of historic buildings can venture a few blocks east toward Meridian Hill.

Meridian Hill

In some ways, the hilltop precinct of **Meridian Hill**, roughly between Florida Avenue and Columbia Road along 16th Street NW, represents the eastern edge of the gentrification shaping Adams-Morgan; the upturn in neighborhood fortunes hasn't quite reached this far – and the area is still edgy enough to dissuade you from walking here after dark. Although the Columbia Heights Metro stop is in the heart of the neighborhood, you might want to tour the area by car before you do too much wandering around. Still, for anyone interested in the high points of Washington **architecture**, this area is a must, no matter how you get here.

Given that almost everything worth seeing lies on, or at most a block off, **16th Street**, it may be tempting to simply combine a stroll up here with one through the northern reaches of New Downtown along the same street. But, again, caution is advised – what looks convenient on a map can involve treks through unexpectedly down-at-the-heel or dangerous pockets. If you're not familiar with the turf under foot, tooling around in a rental car is probably the safest alternative.

Meridian Hill Park

Although it might be hard to believe these days, the area around **Meridian Hill Park**, between Florida Avenue and Euclid Street, was, in the midtwentieth century, one of the swankiest areas of DC – its townhouses and condos sought out by the swells of high society. As with so much in the city, though, the riots of 1968 changed everything, and the panicked rush of white flight, brought on by the proximity to burned-out Shaw, emptied the neighborhood of its upper- and upper-middle-class residents and most of its investment capital. There's been a small rebound since then, though the general area – known as **Columbia Heights** to DC residents – is still a place many avoid. The park itself gives a hint of what things were like in the old days: here you'll find nothing less than a twelve-acre French-style **garden**, finished in 1930, with smartly designed greenery and pathways, well-balanced terraces, and a central series of stepped waterfalls. The park boasts a few other oddments – such as a strange set of **statues**, depicting Joan of Arc, Dante, and one of America's worst presidents, James Buchanan – but the houses surrounding the park are the more eye-popping ornaments.

Around the park

That the streets around the park hold such stunning mansions is largely due to **Mary Henderson**, wife of former senator John Henderson, who felt that either the White House should be relocated to the area or the Lincoln Memorial erected here. Her own marvelous fortress, known as the Henderson Castle, is no longer standing, but its legacy can be seen in some of the homes nearby. One such standout is the so-called **Pink Palace**, on the north side of the park at 2600 16th St, which has been painted many colors but still sports its original Venetian Renaissance windows and overall design. The **Benjamin Warder House**, across the street, is also hard to miss. This stocky version of a Romanesque castle was designed by H.H. Richardson and has been taken apart, rebuilt, and renovated several times since it first went up in 1888; it's now a luxury apartment building (for a look, call ☏202/332-1717 or visit ⊛www.wardermansion.com). The former **Embassy of France**, a block south at 2460 16th St, is a stunning, 1908 version of a High Baroque palace, while, further north, a trio of delightful historic-revival churches, from the 1920s and 1930s, cluster around the intersection of 16th and Columbia Road, of which the **National Baptist Memorial Church** is the most striking, with its colonnaded combination of Baroque and Neoclassical elements.

Meridian International Center

1624–1630 Crescent Place NW ☏202/667-6800, ⊛www.meridian.org; Columbia Heights Metro. Wed–Sun 2–5pm.

The **Meridian International Center** occasionally exhibits the work of global artists and crafts workers, but the interest really lies in the pair of historic-revival mansions that play host to the center and its displays. The first, the John Russell Pope-designed **Meridian House**, was the residence of Irwin Laughlin, a high-powered Spanish ambassador and steel heir who was especially fond of the eighteenth-century French style. The neo-Baroque home features limestone walls, formal European-styled gardens, priceless antiques, sculpted Neoclassical busts, and assorted curiosities and treasures gathered from a lifetime's globe-hopping. Next door, the **White-Meyer House** is where you'll find the Center's displays of worthy international art, but the focus here is again the architecture. This is another revivalist work of Pope's for an ambassador (to France), in the English Georgian style, with an elegant symmetry and balance, Ionic columns, and a vaguely Classical feel. It's a bit less inspired and altogether more restrained than the Meridian House.

Shaw

East of Adams-Morgan and Meridian Hill, the historic district of **Shaw** – roughly north of M Street between North Capitol and 15th streets – is one of the oldest residential areas in DC; it has a rich past and the stirrings of a future, but remains sorely affected by three decades of neglect. You can have a festive time in a night out on **U Street** or a stroll around some of the peripheral historic sights and landmarks covered below, but keep in mind that when you're here, you're away from the safer parts of Northwest DC. Drugs (and the crime that goes with them) are still prevalent, many buildings are run-down, and the atmosphere can be oppressive in places. Don't wander aimlessly and alone in the neighborhood, which can change from borderline to downright threatening in a block or two; head straight for your destination, take cabs when necessary, and keep your wits about you. A good way to see the neighborhood is to take a **walking tour** or sign up for "**Duke Ellington's DC**," a summer bus tour that includes taking in a play and visiting several local sites (see p.34).

Some history

First settled by immigrant whites who built shanty housing along 7th Street after the Civil War, the area was one of the booming city's main commercial arteries and remained busy during the Depression, when the low-rent housing in the alleys on either side began to attract countless black immigrants from the rural Southern states in search of work. Pool halls, churches, cafés, theaters, and social clubs sprang up; a shopping strip developed across on 14th Street; and **U Street** evolved into the "Black Broadway." For years the neighborhood was known simply as "14th and U," eventually taking the name "Shaw" after **Colonel Robert Gould Shaw**, the (white) commander of the Union Army's first black regiment (the Massachusetts 54th) – the unit featured in the film *Glory*. With the all-black **Howard University** at 6th Street, and Griffith Stadium (now Howard University Hospital) at 2401 Georgia Ave attracting massive crowds to its black baseball games, there was a real vibrancy to this corner of DC.

Duke Ellington (1899–1974)

Edward Kennedy Ellington was born in Washington DC (on 22nd St NW), and grew up in Shaw at 1212 T St. A precocious child, nicknamed **"Duke,"** at 15 he was playing ragtime in scratch bands at local cafés; he wrote his first composition, *Soda Fountain Rag*, in 1914. Also an accomplished young artist, Ellington turned down a scholarship to New York's Pratt Institute to instead form "The Washingtonians," a trio with which he played extensively in DC before making the big move to New York in 1923. By 1927, the trio had expanded to become **The Duke Ellington Orchestra**; a year later, it was a permanent fixture at Harlem's **Cotton Club**, where Ellington made his reputation in five tumultuous years, writing early, atmospheric classics like *Mood Indigo* and *Creole Love Call*. Ellington and his orchestra appeared in their first feature film, *Check and Double Check*, in 1930, and by 1932, they had made more than 200 recordings. Established as one of America's finest jazz composers and bandleaders, Ellington set off on his first European tour in 1933, when he took the continent by storm. The following decade saw the penning of his most celebrated works – from *Sophisticated Lady* and *Take the A Train* to *Don't Get Around Much Anymore*.

The Ellington style was unmistakable: melodious ballads and stomping swing pieces alike employed inventive rhythmic devices and novel key changes to inimitable creative effect. In 1943, Ellington was the first popular musician to perform at Carnegie Hall (where he premiered the ambitious *Black, Brown and Beige*) and, despite a decline in **Big Band** popularity after World War II, he managed to keep both his band and personal following largely intact. Ellington spent much of the 1950s and 1960s touring and diversifying his output – recording with younger artists like **Max Roach** and **Charles Mingus**, writing soundtracks for (and appearing in) movies, and composing extended pieces that mixed jazz with classical music. In 1969 he received the **Presidential Medal of Freedom** for his services to music and the arts. By the time of his death in 1974, Duke Ellington had arranged or composed more than six thousand works. Duke married Edna Thompson in 1918 and they had one son, Mercer, though the couple later separated. Mercer went on to play trumpet in his father's band and, after Duke's death, led the Duke Ellington Orchestra.

In DC, the city remembers one of its favorite sons with the **Duke Ellington Birthday Celebration**, a weeklong festival held each year around April 20. The Calvert Street Bridge between Woodley Park and Adams-Morgan was renamed **Duke Ellington Bridge** in his honor, and the city established the **Duke Ellington School of the Arts** in Georgetown (35th and R sts NW; ☎202/337-4022). This public high school offers a four-year course of study for artistically talented youths; free tours are available once a month (except June–Sept) – call for details.

Segregation – entrenched in Washington since the late nineteenth century – ironically secured Shaw's prosperity, since black residents stayed within the neighborhood to shop and socialize. Conversely, desegregation opened up the varied attractions of downtown Washington to Shaw's black inhabitants, and the ensuing decline of the neighborhood was swift. Black middle-class flight to the periphery had been taking place since the turn of the century, with larger Victorian properties bought from suburban-bound whites in fringe neighborhoods such as LeDroit Park, Logan Circle, and the so-called "Striver's Section" of U Street (between 15th and 18th). By the 1960s, the older black streets in Shaw were feeling the pinch, while the riots of 1968 finished them off. News of the assassination of Dr Martin Luther King Jr sparked three days of arson, rioting, and looting that destroyed businesses and lives along 7th, 14th, and H streets. A dozen people were killed, millions of dollars of property lost, and the confidence of nearby businesses in Old Downtown jolted so severely that within a decade that area, too, was virtually abandoned. (The 1968 riots weren't the first to tear Shaw apart. In the summer of 1919, prompted by the violent antics of vigilante white ex-soldiers, five days of rioting – including fierce fighting on U, 7th, and T streets as well as in southwest Washington – left thirty people dead.) Signs of revival are now evident, however – revitalized U Street has a Metro station and once again features on the city's nightlife scene, while **14th Street**, continuing south to Logan Circle (see p.186), has blossomed as an alternative theater district. The process is slow going, though, and for every corporate chain store you spot popping up on U, there's a building freshly abandoned just a few blocks away. The pace of change can be erratic in these parts.

U Street and around

The only part of Shaw most visitors see – and the safest to visit – is the thriving section of **U Street** in the blocks near U Street-Cardozo Metro, where more trendy bars and clubs move in with every passing year. Between the world wars, U Street – known locally as "You" Street – ranked second only to New York's Harlem as America's center of black entertainment. At the splendid **Lincoln Theatre**, built at 1215 U St in 1921, vaudeville shows and movies were bolstered by appearances from the most celebrated jazz performers of the day: Count Basie, Billie Holiday, Cab Calloway, Ella Fitzgerald, and DC's own Duke Ellington among them. The theater now serves as a performing arts center (see p.298). Next door, *Ben's Chili Bowl* (see "Eating" chapter) is a 40-year-old institution frequented by the likes of Bill Cosby and Denzel Washington.

The once-elegant **Howard Theatre**, several blocks east of the U Street scene at 624 T St, opened in 1910 as the first theater in DC built strictly for black patrons, though that didn't stop hip whites from flocking here to see the shows. An unknown **Ella Fitzgerald** won an open-mike contest here; 1940s Big Bands filled the auditorium; and later artists such as James Brown, Smokey Robinson, Gladys Knight, and Martha and the Vandellas lined up to appear; in 1962 the **Supremes** played their first headlining gig here. The theater survived the riots in one piece but closed soon after; today it's being slowly renovated, after standing abandoned for years.

African-American Civil War Memorial and Museum

1200 U St NW ☎202/667-2667, ⊛www.afroamcivilwar.org; U Street-Cardozo Metro. Mon–Fri 10am–5pm, Sat 10am–2pm.

Leave the Metro by the 10th Street exit and you'll emerge near the **African-American Civil War Memorial**, one of the country's few monuments honoring African-American soldiers who fought for the Union. *The Spirit of Freedom* sculpture stands in the center of a granite-paved plaza, partially encircled by a Wall of Honor, along which you'll find the names of the 209,145 United States Colored Troops (and their 7000 white officers) who served. President Lincoln sanctioned the creation of African-American regiments in 1862, and slaves, former slaves, and freedmen joined the fight. The rush to enlist was best summed up by Frederick Douglass, whose words "Who would be free themselves must strike the blow. Better even die free than to live slaves" are inscribed at the site. Sadly, these brave troops were not included in the celebratory Grand Review of the Union Armies along Pennsylvania Avenue after the war's end, an early sign that the battle for equality had only begun.

Three blocks west of the memorial, in the 1903 Italianate **True Reformer Building** – which was designed, built, and financed by African Americans – the associated museum tells the soldiers' largely unknown story as part of its permanent exhibition, "Slavery to Freedom: Civil War to Civil Rights." Composed largely of photographs and documents, the collection begins its African-American history with the original bill of sale for an 11-year-old girl. Other features include a "Descendents Registry," where visitors can look up relatives who may have served with the US Colored Troops, and a "Computer Search For Your Soldier," which employs the Civil War Soldiers and Sailors Names Index to identify troops along with the history of their regiments.

Howard University

2400 6th St NW ☎202/806-2755 or ✉campustour@howard.edu for campus tours; Shaw-Howard University Metro.

The prestigious **Howard University** – named for General Otis Howard, commissioner of the Freedmen's Bureau – was established in 1867 by a church missionary society to provide a school for freed blacks after the Civil War. Its first faculties were in law, music, medicine, and theology, though today hundreds of subjects are taken by almost 13,000 students from over a hundred countries. Famous Howard alumni include Toni Morrison, Jessye Norman, Thurgood Marshall, David Dinkins, Andrew Young, and Shaka Hislop.

Sadly, only one of the original campus buildings remains – **Howard Hall**, 607 Howard Place, a handsome French Second Empire structure built in the 1860s. Many of the other buildings are historic-revivals from the 1930s, and few are better than the **Founder's Library**, a gigantic edifice modeled after Philadelphia's Independence Hall. The library houses the **Moorland-Spingarn Research Center** (Mon–Thurs 9am–4.45pm, Fri 9am–4.30pm; ☎202/806-7240), which contains the country's largest selection of literature relating to black history and culture. The library is open to the public, though as a casual visitor, you're more likely to come for a campus tour.

LeDroit Park

Short of money just a decade after its inauguration, the university sold a plot of land (in the shallow angle formed by Florida and Rhode Island avenues) to developers who then built an exclusive suburb of sixty detached houses. White university staff were the first to take up residence in **LeDroit Park**, as it was known, and well-to-do black families moved into the brick row houses built in the 1880s and 1890s. By 1920 LeDroit Park was a fashionable black neighborhood, and though much of it has decayed over the years, it's been declared a historic district; the best-preserved group of original houses are along the 400 block of U Street. Prominent black citizens continue to be associated with the area – the family of DC's first black mayor, Walter Washington, has owned a house here for years, while Jesse Jackson maintains a property here too. Neo-Gothic, French Second Empire, and Victorian styles predominate, and the neighborhood is accessible from a convenient **Metro station**, Shaw–Howard University, three blocks west.

Outer Northeast

Conventional wisdom dictates visitors stick to the central neighborhoods when visiting DC, but a number of unique, fascinating sites make it worth the effort to venture to some farther-flung parts of the city. Spread across the Outer Northeast section of town are the expansive **National Arboretum**, the monumental **National Shrine of the Immaculate Conception**, the quaint and historic **Takoma Park**, and more. For some sights a car will be necessary, for others there's a Metro station within blocks. Keep in mind, though, that none of these spots is very near the others, and in between you may in fact run across some of those down-at-the-heel neighborhoods that you've been warned to stay away from – so take heed.

National Shrine of the Immaculate Conception

400 Michigan Ave NE ☎202/526-8300, ⊛www.nationalshrine.com. Daily Nov–March 7am–6pm, April–Oct 7am–7pm.

Two of DC's most interesting, and least visited, spots are easily accessible by Metro heading north from Shaw (with a transfer at the Fort Totten station). By way of the Brookland Metro station, the first sight is the largest Catholic church in the US, the **National Shrine of the Immaculate Conception**, which was built in the 1950s. Its grand Byzantine design, looming dome with multicolored mosaics, and towering Roman arch above the entrance would alone make the site an eye-grabber, but added to these features are a sleek bell tower, lovely bas-relief panels, several large buttresses, and a huge circular Celtic *triqnetra*, symbolizing the Trinity – and that's just the exterior. Inside, the church is astoundingly big, with some 75 chapels or alcoves for statues, intricate mosaics showing a fight against a seven-headed serpent (among other scenes), a big pipe organ and even larger baldachino with four great marble columns, and, looming above it all – its eyes seeming to follow you around the church – a jaw-dropping mosaic of Jesus clad in a striking red robe, with jets of flame shooting out from his golden halo. Adjacent to the Shrine is the **Catholic University** campus, along with the **Pope John Paul II Cultural Center**, 3900 Harewood Rd (Tues–Sat 10am–5pm, Sun noon–5pm; ☎202/635-5400, ⊛www.jp2cc.org), which presents exhibits on art, architecture, culture, and faith, and provides information on the life and works of the current head of the Roman Catholic Church.

Takoma Park

After transferring from the Fort Totten Metro station north on the Red Line, you soon come to **Takoma Park**, America's first planned suburb for urban commuters. Today it is one of the country's most avowedly progressive communities and is still largely intact with its original 1880s buildings and design. Some of the stylish historic homes worth checking out include the **Bliss House**, 7116 Maple Ave, an Italianate charmer made of wood but with a painted brick-and-stone facade; the Victorian bungalows along Willow Avenue north of Tulip Street; the **Zigzag Art Deco structure** at 7000 Carroll Ave; and the grand **Cady Lee Mansion**, Chestnut Ave at Eastern, the best of several Queen Anne buildings, rich with gables, gingerbread detailing, a wraparound porch, and slate roof. The Takoma Metro station is right in the middle of this area (on the District border with Maryland), which is an excellent spot for an hour or two of wandering. For neighborhood maps, tours, and information, visit @www .historictakoma.org.

National Arboretum

3501 New York Ave NE ☎202/245-2726, @www.usna.usda.gov. Daily 8am–4.30pm, summer Sat & Sun closes 5pm.

Nestled along the Anacostia River roughly two miles northeast of the Capitol building, the sprawling **National Arboretum** is an oasis of green amid an otherwise grim part of the District. The best time to visit is from mid-April to October, when plenty of plants are in bloom and park access is made easier by **direct bus service** (#X6; Sat & Sun every 40min; $1.10) from Union Station and by **tram tours** (April–Oct Sat & Sun, 10.30am–4pm; $4), forty-minute journeys that meander along the park's 9.5 miles of roadways past ponds, gardens, and plant collections, taking in everything from colorful bursts of azaleas to the woodlands of Japan. At the entrance at 24th and R streets you'll find the **visitor's center**, where you can pick up a visitor's guide, which includes a map, seasonal plant information, and descriptions of the gardens. It's also possible to drive, hike, or bike through the park – although biking *to* the park might be more adventure than you're after.

It's well worth a visit to the surreal gathering of "**Capitol Columns**," which stand in a meadow at the heart of the grounds, supporting open sky. Once part of the US Capitol, the sandstone pillars, crafted in the Neoclassical Corinthian style, presided over every presidential inauguration from Jackson to Eisenhower. They were effectively put out to pasture in the 1950s in order to correct a flaw in the Capitol's design, which caused the columns to appear mismatched relative to the size of the dome. Other Arboretum highlights include the **Dogwood Collection**, best seen in bloom on a late spring afternoon; the **National Grove of State Trees**, a thirty-acre site where trees native to each state (plus the District of Columbia) grow on individual plots; and the clumsily named **Dwarf and Slow-Growing Conifer Collection**, basically a set of little pines, spruces, and firs that make for an off-kilter hillside landscape. Those preferring a short, self-guided walking tour can take in the sights closest to the administration building. Here, in addition to the **National Herb Garden**, you'll find the arboretum's most popular destination, the renowned **National Bonsai and Penjing Museum** (daily 10am–3.30pm), which celebrates the ancient Chinese and Japanese art form of growing tiny trees, with selections from Asia as well as North America. Even if you have no interest in this sort of thing, the odd, sprightly array of miniature plants is really worth a look, with some of the branches and blooms gnarled and twisted almost to a grotesque degree.

Kenilworth Aquatic Gardens

1550 Anacostia Ave NE ☎202/426-6905, ⊛www.nps.gov/kepa; Deanwood Metro. Daily 7am–4pm.

Well off the beaten path, even for the National Park that it is, **Kenilworth Aquatic Gardens** is on the eastern fringe of the District, and definitely worth a look if you're interested in horticulture or natural preserves. Set on seven hundred acres of protected marshlands, the twelve-acre gardens are rich with water lilies and lotuses, and you can take an up-close view of them on an elevated **boardwalk** that hovers over the waterline. Alternately, there are several good paths for exploring this wet terrain, with its many ponds and pools, as you're able to see a pristine part of the Anacostia River – hard to imagine in other parts of the District. The lilies are in bloom from May through September, but at their height in late July, when the park's **Waterlily Festival** provides a very good reason to visit. While the gardens are accessible by the I-295 freeway, you can also reach them by taking the Metro to Deanwood station a few blocks south.

Upper Northwest

n the heights above Georgetown, running up to the District's border, the smart neighborhoods of **Upper Northwest** comprise some of the most exclusive territory in Washington. The upper- and middle-class flight up Connecticut, Wisconsin, and Massachusetts avenues began when a number of nineteenth-century presidents made the cool reaches of rural **Woodley Park** – across Duke Ellington Bridge from Adams-Morgan – their summer home; Grover Cleveland later bought a stone cottage farther north in an area that today is called **Cleveland Park**. Few others could afford the time and expense involved in living a four-mile carriage-ride from the city center until the arrival in the 1890s of the streetcar; within three decades both Woodley Park and Cleveland Park had become bywords for fashionable, out-of-town living, replete with apartment buildings designed by the era's top architects. The tone is no less swish today, with a series of ritzy suburbs stretching into Maryland – on the DC side of the border, **Tenleytown** and **Friendship Heights** have no proper attractions, but offer some decent shopping and dining options.

If you *are* looking for attractions, however, the Upper Northwest's three big ones are the **National Zoo**, part of the Smithsonian Institution; **Washington National Cathedral**, the sixth-largest cathedral in the world; and the wooded expanses of **Rock Creek Park**, largest and most enjoyable of the city's green spaces. Given the elevation of this area, and the rather strenuous effort you'll need to get around it, you're advised to take the **Metro Red Line**, which runs underneath the area in some of the country's deepest subway channels. Alternative routes are to take **Bus** #L2, which runs up Connecticut Avenue from McPherson Square via Adams-Morgan (18th St) to Chevy Chase, and buses #30, #32, #34, #35 and #36, which travel up Wisconsin Avenue from Georgetown to Friendship Heights.

Woodley Park

The first Upper Northwest neighborhood you'll encounter – either north from Georgetown on Wisconsin Avenue or west from Adams-Morgan on Calvert Street – is **Woodley Park**, marked at the intersection of Calvert and Connecticut Avenue with a pair of wondrous hotels that give a hint of the serious money that lurks in the surrounding hills. In 1918, architect Harry L. Wardman, who designed many of the apartment buildings and townhouses here, created the massive **Wardman Park Hotel**, Connecticut Ave NW and Woodley Rd (see "Accommodation" chapter), a red-brick, vaguely Colonial

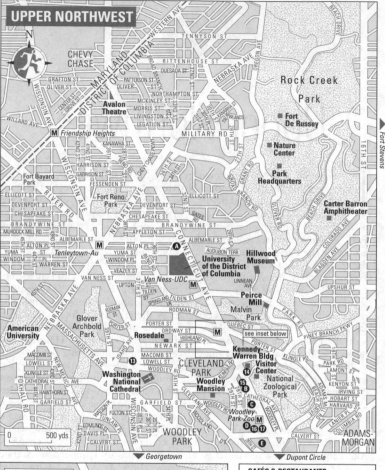

UPPER NORTHWEST

CHEVY CHASE

Avalon Theatre

M Friendship Heights

Fort Bayard Park

Fort Reno Park

M Tenleytown-Au

Glover Archbold Park

American University

Rosedale

Washington National Cathedral

University of the District of Columbia

Van Ness-UDC M

Peirce Mill

Malvin Park

Kennedy-Warren Bldg Visitor Center

Woodley Mansion

CLEVELAND PARK

National Zoological Park

Woodley Park-Zoo M

WOODLEY PARK

Rock Creek Park

Fort De Russey

Nature Center

Park Headquarters

Hillwood Museum

Carter Barron Amphitheater

see inset below

ADAMS-MORGAN

Fort Stevens

0   500 yds

▼ Georgetown   ▼ Dupont Circle

0   100 yds

The Broadmoor

PORTER STREET   QUEBEC STREET

M

Cleveland Park

PORTER   STREET

ORDWAY STREET   ORDWAY STREET

Uptown Theatre

NEWARK   STREET

CLEVELAND PARK

MACOMB   STREET   MACOMB   STREET

Tregaron

208

CAFÉS & RESTAURANTS	
Ardeo	12
Cactus Cantina	13
Firehook Bakery & Coffeehouse	7
Krupin	1
Lebanese Taverna	14
Nam Viet	5
New Heights	16
Sala Thai	2
Spices	9
Vace	11
Woodley Café	15
Yanni's Greek Taverna	3
Yanyu	4
BARS & CLUBS	
Aroma	6
Ireland's Four Provinces	8
Nanny O'Brien's	10
Zoo Bar – Oxford Tavern	17
ACCOMMODATION	
Days Inn	A
Kalorama Guest House	B
Marriott Wardman Park	D
Omni Shoreham	E
Woodley Park Guset House	C

Revival giant whose tower still dominates the local skyline. The hotel has been a phenomenal success, attracting high-profile politicians and social butterflies who entertained guests in the grand public rooms and rented apartments for themselves. Across on Calvert Street, a second landmark followed within a decade, the hybrid Art Deco-style **Shoreham** (now an Omni; see "Accommodation" chapter), which was built in 1930 for $4 million. Since then it's hosted an inaugural ball or gala for every president from FDR to George W. Bush; here President Truman played poker, JFK courted Jackie, Nixon announced his first Cabinet, and, in the celebrated **Blue Room**, Judy Garland, Marlene Dietrich, Bob Hope, and Frank Sinatra entertained the swells.

To check out where relatively staid nineteenth-century presidents passed their summers, head up Connecticut Avenue to Cathedral Avenue and walk west past 29th Street to the **Woodley Mansion**, now the Maret School. This white stucco Georgian was built in 1800 for Philip Barton Key, whose nephew Francis later penned the "Star-Spangled Banner." Its elevation meant that it was a full ten degrees cooler in the summer than downtown, and presidents Van Buren, Tyler, and Buchanan needed no second invitation to spend their summers here.

Cleveland Park

Back on Connecticut Avenue and heading north past the zoo you're soon in **Cleveland Park**, a stylish suburb marked by a few eye-grabbing buildings, including the **Kennedy-Warren Apartments** (no. 3133), a soaring Art Deco evocation of 1930s wealth; the Art Deco **Uptown Theatre** (no. 3426), which has been showing movies since 1936; and the **Broadmoor** (no. 3601), a residential development from 1928 with grand-scale and angular Art Deco versions of Classical motifs. However, it's further west into the hills, around Newark Street and Highland Place, where you'll see the really historic buildings that make this neighborhood unique. These hills hold the area's highest concentration of upper-class residences, dating from its great turn-of-the-twentieth-century expansion: Robert Head, Waddy Butler Wood, and Paul Pelz all built houses here, and it was on Newark Street that Grover Cleveland's (long-demolished) summer house – the one that prompted the whole influx – once stood. Also worth a look are estates like the **Rosedale**, 3501 Newark St NW, featuring the area's oldest structure – a weathered stone building – which dates from 1740, amid later Colonial and early American additions; and the **Tregaron**, 3100 Macomb Ave NW (tours by appointment only at ☎202/243-1827), a stately Colonial Revival that's now used as the campus for the Washington International School. For more on local highlights, contact the **Cleveland Park Historical Society** (☎202/363-6358, ⑩www .clevelandparkdc.org), which also provides information on occasional tours of area homes.

Washington National Cathedral

Massachusetts and Wisconsin aves NW ☎202/537-6200 or 364-6616, ⑩www.cathedral.org/cathedral; Woodley Park-Zoo Metro. Mon–Fri 10am–5.30pm, Sat 10am–4.30pm, Sun 8am–6.30pm. $3 donation.

Washington National Cathedral is the sixth-largest cathedral in the world, a monumental building so medieval in spirit it should surely rise from a dusty old European town plaza rather than a DC suburb. But the cathedral was intentionally set in this location: on the heights of **Mount St Alban**, unaffected by the city's zoning restrictions, the architects would have free rein to produce their masterpiece. Built from Indiana limestone and modeled on the medieval English Gothic style, it's supported by flying buttresses, bosses, and vaults, and shows off striking stained-glass windows, quirky gargoyles, massive columns, and, as an all-American touch, two rows of state flags hanging below the clerestory level. Continual restoration allows the cathedral to always look stunning to visitors, or at least those here to worship in the church. Down below, in the crypt and elsewhere, the ravages of time have made for a rather dank and uninspiring environment.

The idea of a "national church" in the city was first proposed by George Washington, but it was not until a century later that Congress finally granted a charter for what is officially known as the **Cathedral Church of St Peter and St Paul**. In 1907, the foundation ceremony was held, with President Theodore Roosevelt in attendance, and construction on the building began. Architects **George Bodley** (a noted English church architect) and **Henry Vaughan** designed the cathedral, but they were succeeded after their deaths around World War I by **Philip Hubert Frohman**, who spent the next fifty years on the project. Frohman died in 1972, and the cathedral wasn't finished until 1990 (though parts have been in use since the 1920s).

Although a Protestant church, and the seat of the Episcopal Diocese of Washington, it is intended as a national church and hosts services for other denominations as well. Most prominently, it's held services for a number of presidents: **Woodrow Wilson** was commemorated and interred here upon his death in 1924, which was appropriate since much of the work on the building took place during his presidency; the work fascinated him so much that he used to visit the construction site in his chauffeur-driven limousine. Eighty years later **Ronald Reagan**, after first lying in state in the Capitol Rotunda, was honored with a memorial service here before his body was flown back to California for burial. Other presidents, such as **Dwight Eisenhower**, have also received similar honors, though as yet Wilson is the only one to be buried here.

Visiting the cathedral

The center portal in the west facade isn't always open; you may have to enter from the northwest cloister. For a floor plan and information, descend to the **Crypt**, where there's an **information desk** and a huge **gift shop** (daily 9.30am–5pm) that runs nearly the length of the building. **Guided tours** are available on request at the west entrance (Mon–Sat 10–11.30am & 12.45–3.15pm, Sun 12.30–2.30pm; $3); ask one of the docents about them. Phone ahead or check the website for schedules of the many **specialty tours**, which feature everything from the cathedral's gardens to its gargoyles. The 57-acre grounds, or **Cathedral Close** (virtually a small fiefdom), hold cathedral offices, three schools, a college, sports fields, and swimming pool. There is also a **Herb Cottage** (daily 10am–5pm) that sells dried herbs and teas; a **Greenhouse** (Mon–Sat 9.30am–5pm, Sun 10am–5pm) with various plants for sale; and the **Bishop's Garden**, a walled, rose-and-herb garden laid out in medieval style.

It's easiest to reach the cathedral by **bus**, on the #30, #32, #34, #35, or #36 from Pennsylvania Avenue downtown (including Wisconsin Ave via Georgetown), or Bus #N2, #N4, or #N6 from Farragut Square via Dupont Circle and Embassy Row. If you don't mind a twenty-minute walk, you can take the **Metro**. From the Woodley Park-Zoo station, turn left from Connecticut Avenue into Cathedral Avenue and right into Woodley Road to reach the lower-level information center; the west door is around the corner on Wisconsin Avenue. The cathedral's daily worship schedule is: Mon–Sat 7.30am, noon, 2.30pm & 5.30pm (Sat 4pm instead of 5.30pm); Sun 8am, 9am (10am Sept–June), 11am, 4pm & 6.30pm.

The interior

Place yourself first at the west end of the **nave** (completed in 1976) to appreciate the immense scale of the building; it's more than a tenth of a mile to the high altar at the other end. Along the south side of the nave, the first bay commemorates **George Washington**, whose marble statue proclaims him to be "First Citizen, Patriot, President, Churchman and Freemason," while five bays down is **Woodrow Wilson**'s sarcophagus. In the adjacent bay, look up to the **Space Window**, whose stained glass incorporating a sliver of moon rock commemorates the flight of *Apollo II*. On the north side, across from Washington, the **Abraham Lincoln Bay** is marked by a bronze statue of Abe, with Lincoln-head pennies set into the floor. The next berth down is for cathedral architect **Philip Hubert Frohman**, a Catholic whose family received special dispensation to have him buried in this Protestant church. The last bay before the North Transept features a small likeness of **Dr Martin Luther King Jr** above the arch, inscribed "I Have A Dream." On Sunday March 31, 1968, the reverend preached his last sermon here before heading for Memphis, where he was due to lead a march of striking black workers; four days later he was assassinated, with violent repercussions for the poorer sections of the District, as well as other parts of America.

From the **High Altar** – adorned with a six-foot-tall gold cross – there's a splendid view back down along the carved vault to the west rose window. The beautifully intricate **reredos** features 110 figures surrounding Christ in Benediction. An elevator from the south porch at the west end of the nave (near the Washington statue) ascends to the **Pilgrim Observation Gallery**, which affords stupendous city views.

National Zoological Park

3001 Connecticut Ave NW ☎202/673-4800, 🖳www.natzoo.si.edu; Cleveland Park or Woodley Park-Zoo Metro. Grounds daily: April–Oct 6am–8pm, Nov–March 6am–6pm; buildings daily: April–Oct 10am–6pm, Nov–March 10am–4.30pm.

The sloping **National Zoological Park** is part of the Smithsonian Institution, and, with its free admission, is always a popular draw for visitors who make it up this far. Sited between Woodley Park and Adams-Morgan, the zoo sprawls down the steep sides of Rock Creek, with trails through lush vegetation leading past simulations of more than three thousand creatures' home environments. Although founded in 1889 as a traditional zoo, today it thinks of itself as a "BioPark," combining the usual menagerie of giraffes, elephants, lions, and tigers with botanic gardens, a prairie, natural history displays, aquariums, and a wetlands zone called "Amazonia." Note that with a shake-up in the zoo's management (see box overleaf) and the 2004 introduction of an Asia Trail,

---

Music in the cathedral

Carillon recitals Sat 12.30pm, ten-bell peal Sun 11am.
Cathedral choristers Tues–Thurs 5.30pm (school year only).
Choral and classical concerts, indoors and out; call for schedule.
Organ recitals/demonstrations Wed 12.45pm & Sun 4pm.

some of the animals may be moved around or housed in different locations from the ones listed here.

The main entrance on Connecticut Avenue is a ten-minute walk from either **Metro** station, but it's easiest to arrive at the Cleveland Park one; from there the zoo is a level stroll south along Connecticut Avenue; from Woodley Park you'll have to hike uphill. Just inside the gate you'll find the **visitor center,** where you can pick up a map and list of the day's events, including feeding times. From here, two trails loop downhill through the park to Rock Creek: the **Olmsted Walk**, passing most of the indoor exhibits, and the steeper **Valley Trail**, with aquatic exhibits, birds, and "Amazonia." Head down one and back up the other, visiting the side exhibits on the way, and you'll walk more than two miles. Allow a minimum of three hours to do the park justice. A café, restaurant, police post, concession stands, paid parking, and restrooms are scattered throughout the park. In summer the zoo hosts "**Sunset Serenades**," popular events that take place on Thursday evenings and involve musical and cultural entertainment.

Olmsted Walk

Strolling along the **Olmsted Walk**, you'll first notice the usually inactive and sleepy-looking big cats in the **Cheetah Conservation Station**, but a little farther on you'll have your first zoo-celebrity sighting: the **pandas** Mei Xiang and Tian Tian, who arrived from China in 2000 to fill the absence created by the recent deaths of Ling Ling and Hsing Hsing, the famous pair presented by Beijing during Richard Nixon's 1972 visit. The pandas are on view daily from 9am to 4.30pm, and are the constant focus of media interest for their mating activity – or lack thereof.

The path winds down past elephants, giraffes, hippos, and rhinos to the **American Prairie** exhibit, which explains the history of the nation's grasslands and shows off a selection of bison – reminding us of the mere 140,000 that survive nationally out of a population that in the mid-nineteenth century numbered in the tens of millions. The first of the zoo's garden areas, the **American Indian Heritage Garden**, celebrates Native Americans' understanding and use of nature; here you can learn about the healing

Trouble in the cages

It should be no surprise that **political controversy** has, in the case of the National Zoological Park, wended its way up from Capitol Hill into Upper Northwest. As part of the Smithsonian Institution, the zoo has long had a fiscal mandate that ties it to cultural decisions made in the nation's capital, and doesn't allow it to get away with abuses that might be permitted at lesser, more isolated facilities. A case in point occurred in February 2004, when a study found managerial and husbandry problems at the zoo "at all levels," and specifically cited the **deaths** of 23 animals – about one percent of the zoo's creatures – as proof of serious and ongoing neglect, incompetence, and failure. Tragedies included two red pandas dying after munching on open containers of rat poison, and a zebra actually starving to death. This report and the subsequent public outcry led to zoo director Lucy Spelman's resignation and calls from politicians for more oversight and control, and even from some conservatives to ditch the zoo entirely. The *Washington Post* as usual led the way in investigating the problems and for a while the story made headlines across the country. Since then, modest improvements have been made – like tighter checks on animal welfare and more regular park renovations – though what the future holds is anyone's guess.

properties of herbs and plants like the coneflower (used to treat insect bites, venereal disease, and rabies) and the emetic Indian tobacco plant – also known as vomitweed, pokeweed, and gagroot.

Further along, the orangutans are encouraged to leave the confines of the **Great Ape House** and commute to the "**Think Tank**," where scientists and four-legged primates come together to hone their communications skills and discuss world events as part of the fascinating **Orangutan Language Project**. Between Ape House and Think Tank is the **Reptile Discovery Center**, with a full complement of snakes, turtles, crocodiles, alligators, lizards, and frogs. Be sure not to miss the remarkable **komodo dragons**, one of which, Kraken, was the first to be born in captivity outside Indonesia. Since her celebrated birth in 1992, Kraken has grown to a length of 7ft, thanks to a steady diet of rats. The adjacent **Invertebrate Exhibit** covers the lives and loves of everything from ants to coral to octopus. Admission to these two popular centers can be restricted at busy times; be sure to first check their status at the visitor center. Beyond here, the moat-surrounded **island** filled with lions and tigers marks the end of the big animals display, but you might want to duck in and out of the thoroughly unpleasant **bat cave** before heading up the Valley Trail.

Valley Trail

The best thing on the **Valley Trail** is undoubtedly the indoor "**Amazonia**" exhibit, which simulates the habitat along the Amazon River Basin. A cleverly constructed undulating aquarium gets you close to the fish – piranhas included – while bombarding you with informative notes. Next you climb up a level into the humid, creeper-clad rain forest, above the water you've just walked along, familiarizing yourself with roots, leaf mold, forest parasites, and birdcalls.

Further along on the trail, seals and sea lions splash in an outdoor pool, and then it's a slow walk uphill past beaver dams, the bird house, an artificial wetland with cranes and herons, and assorted eagles, antelope, and tapirs. If there's noise coming from the bushes as you go along, it'll be the golden lion tamarins, or South American marmosets – the successful breeding of which is one of the zoo's quiet triumphs; more than one thousand now roam the wild in Brazil, the majority of which were reintroduced by the zoo or descend from this group of Washingtonians.

Rock Creek Park and around

Most visitors overlook the city's major natural preserve, **Rock Creek Park** (ⓦwww.nps.gov/rocr), which divides Upper Northwest from Adams-Morgan and the north-central part of the District. Established in 1890, its 1800 acres spread out above the National Zoo to form a mile-wide tract of woodland west of 16th Street. The Rock Creek Parkway shadows the creek for much of its length, until it hits the zoo (north of which it's known as Beach Drive). A **car** is the easiest way to get around the park; by public transit, you can take the **Metro** to Cleveland Park, which provides access just north of the zoo, or to Friendship Heights, from which **buses** #E2, #E3, and #E4 run up Western Avenue and McKinley Street before cruising along Military Road into the middle of the park. To reach the east side of the park, take Bus #S2 or #S4; both run straight up 16th Street from anywhere north of K Street NW.

Alternatively, you can hop on a **bike** in Georgetown and ride north along the creek. The park is open during daylight hours. It's not a wise idea to come on foot, on your own, or at night, though cross-street traffic is permitted 24 hours a day.

Park highlights

The park has fifteen miles of **trails and paths** that run along both sides of the creek and include tracks, workout stations, bridleways (in the wooded northern section), and a cycle route that runs from the Lincoln Memorial, north through the park, and into Maryland. To the south, Arlington Memorial Bridge links the route to the Mount Vernon Trail in Virginia (see p.234). On weekends (Sat 7am to Sun 7pm), Beach Drive between Military and Broad Branch roads is closed to cars, and rollerbladers happily make the space their own. The park also has ballparks, thirty picnic areas, and the Carter Barron Amphitheater (16th St and Colorado Ave NW; see p.294), which hosts various **summer concerts**.

The sights start at the southern end of the park, a mile above the zoo, where the serene, granite **Peirce Mill** (Wed–Sun noon–4pm; ☎202/282-0927) stands in a beautiful riverside hollow on Tilden Street, near Beach Drive. One of eight nineteenth-century gristmills in the valley, and the last to shut down (in 1897), it produces cornmeal and wheat flour for sale to visitors. You can observe the process, and even have a go yourself with small hand grinders and sifters, though keep in mind that throughout 2004 the mill was closed for renovation and may require more work before it's up and running again.

The **Nature Center** on Glover Road, just south of Military Road (daily 9am–5pm; ☎202/426-6828), acts as the park **visitor center**, with natural history exhibits and details of weekend **guided walks** and self-guided **nature trails**.

Fort Circle Parks

Just on the other side of Military Road from the Rock Creek Nature Center, the remains of Fort De Russey stand as a reminder of the network of defenses that ringed the city during the Civil War, now known as the **Fort Circle Parks** (ⓦwww.nps.gov/rocr/ftcircle). Guarding against Confederate attack from the north, **Fort De Russey** was one of 68 forts erected around the city. The sites of others have been appropriated as small parks on either side of Rock Creek Park itself. East on Military Road from the park to 13th Street NW and north of Missouri Avenue, **Fort Stevens** marks the spot at which the city came closest to falling to Confederate troops during the Civil War. An army of 15,000 soldiers crossed the Potomac in July 1864 and got within 150 yards of the fort before the hastily reinforced Union defense drove them back under a barrage of artillery fire. President Lincoln was in the fort during the attack and mounted the parapet for a better look at the Confederate line, drawing a stinging rebuke from a nearby soldier, who shouted "Get down you damned fool!" at his commander-in-chief. Today, you can somewhat imagine the scene, with the earthen mounds, wooden works, and vintage cannons testifying to the site's importance.

Seven blocks farther north on Georgia Avenue is **Battleground National Cemetery** (daily dawn–dusk), which holds the remains of the Union soldiers killed in the battle to defend Fort Stevens. Buses #70 and #71 run here, up 7th Street (which becomes Georgia Ave NW) from the National Mall, but given Georgia Avenue's rather fearsome reputation you're advised to come and go by taxi.

Hillwood Museum and Gardens

4155 Linnean Ave NW ☎1-877/HILLWOOD, ⊕www.hillwoodmuseum.org; Van Ness-UDC Metro. Tues–Sat 9.30am–5pm; by reservation only. $12.

Just west of Rock Creek and a short distance north of Peirce Mill, the 1923 neo-Georgian manor once known as Arbremont was acquired in the 1950s by **Marjorie Merriwether Post**, heir to the cereal-company fortune, and transformed into a showpiece she renamed Hillwood. These days, the redbrick mansion and its lovely grounds – thick with roses and French- and Japanese-styled gardens – are part of the **Hillwood Museum**, and while the site is handsome enough, what brings people out here is the cache inside. Through her Russian-ambassador husband, in the 1930s Post managed to collect a treasure trove of Fabergé eggs and boxes, Byzantine and Orthodox icons, eighteenth-century glassworks, and other priceless items that today form the core of the museum's collection. There's also an array of French and English decorative-arts items, including tapestries, gilded commodes, porcelain cameos, parquet-inlaid furniture, and so on, but it's the loot from Stalin's USSR that really grabs your attention. In 2001 the museum was reopened after an extensive renovation, which returned some of the estate's original Georgian-styled design and undid some of the more maladroit "improvements" Post made in the 1950s.

The easiest way to get here is by **bus** (following the same routes as for the west side of Rock Creek Park) or **Metro** to the Van Ness-UDC station, from which it's only a short walk south on Connecticut Avenue and then east along Upton Street. Check the museum's website for details.

9

Georgetown

I f there's one place that can lure the masses away from the National Mall and Capitol Hill, it's **Georgetown**. This is true even though, geographically, it's out on a limb – well to the west of downtown, far off the Metro line, and beyond Rock Creek. Despite the area's popularity with well-heeled visitors, Georgetown's relative isolation has engendered an elitism that doesn't need to advertise itself: Jan Morris called it "the most obsessively political residential enclave in the world." The Kennedys moved here before JFK made it to the White House and were followed by establishment figures who have adopted Georgetown as their home (or, more usually, one of their homes): crusading scribbler Bob Woodward, *Washington Post* publisher Katherine Graham and her editor Ben Bradlee, art collector and philanthropist Paul (son of industrial titan Andrew) Mellon, scandal-writer-to-the-stars Kitty Kelley, ponderous novelist Herman Wouk, Elizabeth Taylor (during her marriage to Senator John Warner) – the list goes on and on.

There is, of course, more to Georgetown than its upper-crust inhabitants. The area is at its vibrant best along the spine of **Wisconsin Avenue** and **M Street**, with bars, coffee shops, fashionable restaurants, and antique bookstores in which Georgetown University students rub shoulders with staid old power brokers. Its history is diverting too, and many of the area's buildings date to the early eighteenth century, making it older than the capital itself. Federal-era and shuttered Victorian townhouses hung with flower baskets stud the streets, while a series of stately mansions and handsome parks, gardens, and cemeteries lies north of Q Street. Down on the **C&O Canal**, below M Street, the odd horse-drawn boat fills the waterway, while the tree-shaded towpaths have been turned over to cyclists and walkers; to the north, upper Georgetown is home to the elite of the elite, and while you won't get to poke around any of the private mansions, there are a handful of historic homes that are open to the public.

Unfortunately, Georgetown's most annoying anomaly is that it's not on the **Metro** (Rock Creek and its valley are in the way). And don't even think about driving here: there's nowhere to park. The nearest Metro station is Foggy Bottom-GWU, from which it's a fifteen- to twenty-minute walk up Pennsylvania Avenue and along M Street to the junction with Wisconsin Avenue. Alternatively, approach from Dupont Circle, a similar-length walk west along P Street (or over the Dumbarton Bridge and along Q St; see p.190), which puts you first in the ritzier, upper part of Georgetown – in which case you might want to start your tour with the mansions, parks, and gardens of northern Georgetown. **Buses** #30, #32, #34, #35, and #36 run all the way from Eastern Market, up Capitol Hill, to the Mall, and on to Pennsylvania Avenue until they reach M Street and Wisconsin Avenue; #D1, #D3, and #D6 go via E St, 13th St, K St, and Dupont Circle to Q St in Georgetown and return via M St; and

#G2 runs from Dupont Circle to P and Dumbarton streets. At night you'll find **taxis** relatively easy to come by on the main drags; it's an $8–10 ride to and from most downtown DC locations.

Alternatively, you can take the **Georgetown Shuttle** (Route #2) from the Rosslyn Metro station in Arlington, Virginia – a walk is definitely not recommended on the busy Francis Scott Key Bridge from there – which connects to the Dupont Circle Metro along M and L streets and New Hampshire Avenue; fares are cheap ($1, or 35¢ with subway transfer) and there's a shuttle every ten minutes (Mon–Thurs 7am–midnight, Fri 7am–2am, Sat 8am–2am, Sun 8am–midnight; @www.georgetowndc.com/shuttle.php). Also, Route #1 covers the stretch from the Foggy Bottom-GWU Metro, heading along K Street and going north at Wisconsin Avenue, and then turning around at R Street back in the same direction.

Some history

In the early eighteenth century, when this area was part of Maryland, Scottish merchants began to form a permanent settlement around shoreside warehouses

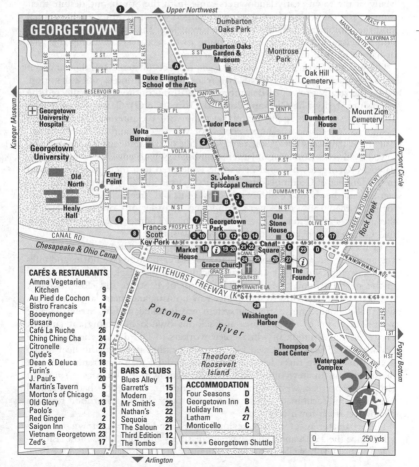

on the higher reaches of the Potomac River (or "Patowmack," as it was then known). Here they oversaw a thriving trade, exporting the plentiful **tobacco** from nearby farms and importing foreign materials and luxuries for colonial settlers. In 1751 the Maryland Assembly granted a town charter to the merchants, who named their flourishing port after their royal protector, George II. Within a decade, "George Towne" was a runaway success, attracting other merchants who built large mansions on estates to the north of the river, and by the 1780s it was America's largest tobacco port.

Once George Washington had selected the Potomac region as the site of the new federal capital, it seemed logical that such a **port** be included in the plans. In 1791, together with Alexandria in Virginia, the town was incorporated within the **federal district**. And while for many years the new Washington City remained little more than an idea, Georgetown continued to prosper; by 1830 it had a population of nine thousand and was thriving with Federal-style brick houses, fashionable stores, well-tended gardens, and even an eponymous university (founded in 1789). By the time of the Civil War, Georgetown was still separate enough from Washington to be considered suspect in Union eyes. Many of the town's early landowners came from the South, but, despite their support for the **Confederate** cause, Georgetown's proximity to the capital (and the Union troops stationed in the town) kept the lid on any overt secessionist feeling, as did Lincoln's suspension of due process (including the writ of habeas corpus) in parts of nearby Maryland.

The war and Georgetown's commercial prospects flickered and died at about the same time. The tobacco trade had recently faltered due to soil exhaustion, while the steady growth of Baltimore and Washington itself badly affected the town's prosperity. The **Chesapeake and Ohio (C&O) Canal**, completed in 1850, represented an attempt to revive trade with the interior, and for a time Georgetown became a regional center for wheat, coal, and timber shipment. But the canal was soon obsolete: the coming of the railroads was swiftly followed by the development of larger steamboats, which couldn't be accommodated by Georgetown's canal or harbor. Relegated to a mere **neighborhood** in the District of Columbia after losing its charter in 1871, Georgetown experienced another blow in 1895 when most of its old street names – some in use for more than 150 years – were abandoned by order of Congress in favor of the numbers and letters of the federal city plan. There was even a suggestion that Georgetown become known as "West Washington."

For much of the late nineteenth and early twentieth centuries, Georgetown was anything but a fashionable place to live. Water-powered foundries and mills provided employment for a growing, predominantly black population, based in the neighborhood of Herring Hill, south of P Street and close to Rock Creek. Gardens were lost to speculative row housing and many larger mansions were subdivided; a noisy streetcar system was installed; and **M Street** became a workaday run of cheap stores and saloons owned by immigrant families. However, a mass influx of white-collar workers to DC during the New Deal era and World War II reversed Georgetown's rather down-at-the-heel image – apartments were turned into houses and Federal mansions renovated. Part of the charm for newcomers was that Georgetown's boundaries – southern river, eastern creek, western university and northern estates – had prevented wholesale, indiscriminate development, and today the neighborhood retains a distinctive, small-town character.

This character is, of course, zealously preserved by Georgetown residents who, since the 1950s and 1960s, have increasingly included DC's most fashionable and politically well-connected residents. Certain historic houses have been lost to developers and some of the streets are overwhelmed by traffic, but since 1967 Georgetown has been registered as a **National Historic Landmark**, which means that new buildings and renovations have to be sympathetic to their surroundings, house facades are color-coordinated, and the canal has been landscaped and preserved as a historic park.

M Street and around

For two centuries, **M Street** has been Georgetown's central artery; it cuts through the lower town before crossing Rock Creek into Foggy Bottom, and is as good an introduction to the area as any, providing you with a vibrant glimpse of Washington society amid old-fashioned row buildings packed cheek-to-jowl with scarcely an alley in between. As elsewhere in Georgetown, the street retains many of its original Federal and later Victorian buildings, though the ground floors of the structures have all long since been converted for retail use. Most new buildings have tended to follow the prevailing red-brick style, none more noticeably so than the elegant *Four Seasons Hotel* between 28th and 29th streets (see "Accommodation" chapter), which acts as an eastern gateway to the heart of the corridor. A short distance down the street, the **Old Stone House** (see below) is one of the District's most venerable structures, and the area's **visitor center**, 3242 M St (☎202/298-9222, ⊛www .georgetowndc.com), is stuffed with all kinds of brochures and information on different aspects of the building.

Shops, restaurants, and bars proliferate around the main M Street/Wisconsin Avenue junction, whose useful landmark is the gold dome of the **Riggs National Bank**. Just beyond is **Georgetown Park**, a high-profile shopping mall at 3222 M St that used to be a site for storing public transit "omnibuses" drawn by horses. A block west, at Potomac Street, the triple-arched, red-brick **Market House** has hosted a public market since the 1860s, even if today the butchered carcasses and patent medicines have made way for a celebrated Dean & Deluca deli. At the junction with 34th Street, the **Francis Scott Key Bridge** (better known as just "Key Bridge") shoots off across the river to Rosslyn. Key, author of the "Star-Spangled Banner," moved to Washington in 1805 and lived in a house here at M Street. His home was later demolished to make way for the **Whitehurst Freeway** – an act of sacrilege only belatedly atoned for by the establishment of **Francis Scott Key Park**, just off the street. The park contains a bronze bust of Key, a sixty-foot flagpole flying the Stars and Stripes, a wisteria-covered arbor, and a few benches from which to peer through the break in the buildings to the river. Walk down the steps here and you're standing on the point at which, in September 1781, General Washington and his ally Jean-Baptiste de Rochambeau, Commander-in-Chief of the French Army in America, prepared to cross the Potomac en route to Mount Vernon and, ultimately, Yorktown, where a decisive victory against the British the following month effectively secured America's independence during the Revolutionary War.

The Old Stone House

3051 M St NW ☎202/895-6070, ⊛www.nps.gov/olst. Wed–Sun noon–5pm; tours by reservation only.

The **Old Stone House** – the only surviving pre-Revolutionary house in DC – sits, incongruously, in the center of the M Street action. It was constructed

△ Canal boat on the C&O canal

in 1765 by a Pennsylvania carpenter and retains its rugged, rough-hewn stone appearance. Built like a small fortress, the three-feet-thick walls are made of craggy rocks quarried from blue fieldstone; its wooden beams are massive oak timbers; and its floor is hard with packed earth. Nonetheless, the fanciful suggestion that Pierre L'Enfant used it as a base while designing the federal city was the only thing that saved it from demolition in the 1950s. Today it's been restored to what it probably looked like in the late eighteenth century, and short **guided tours** lead you through the kitchen and carpenter's workshop downstairs, and paneled parlors and bedrooms upstairs.

N Street to Georgetown University

Potomac Street, a few blocks west of the Old Stone House, is a good route to take you north to **N Street**, which contains some of Georgetown's finest Federal-era buildings. None is open to the public, but several particularly attractive facades appear between 29th and 34th streets. Robert Todd Lincoln (President Lincoln's son) lived out the last decade of his life at **no. 3014**; the house was later purchased by *Washington Post* stalwart Ben Bradlee. Four blocks west is **no. 3307**, which JFK and Jackie owned from 1957 to 1961; Jackie also moved briefly into **no. 3017** after JFK's assassination. There's a cluster of other historic houses on **Prospect Street**, one block south, where late eighteenth-century merchants built mansions like those at **nos. 3425** and **3508**; as the street name suggests, they once possessed splendid views down to the river from which they derived their wealth.

Before you leave lower Georgetown it's worth swinging by **Georgetown University** (☎202/687-3600, ⊛www.georgetown.edu), located on the heights above the river; the **main gate** is at 37th and O streets. Founded in 1789 as the Jesuit Georgetown College, it's the oldest Catholic university in the country. Today, the university and its six thousand students give the neighborhood much of its buzz. The architecture is a bit of a hybrid, ranging from the plain facade of the **Old North** building, which dates from 1795, to the Romanesque details of **Healy Hall**, finished ninety years later. Contact the university for information about tours.

The Kreeger Museum

2401 Foxhall Rd NW ☎202/338-3552, ⊛www.kreegermuseum.org. Tours by reservation only Tues–Fri 10.30am & 1.30pm, Sat without reservation 10am–4pm. $8.

As one of Washington's most obscure cultural attractions, the **Kreeger Museum** is little known mainly because of its location in the hills northwest of Georgetown University (in the sub-district of Foxhall), though it well rewards a visit for its splendid array of twentieth-century modernist art. Housed in an ultra-modern white-walled home designed by Philip Johnson, the museum has open hours on Saturday but shows its collection on 90-minute, reservation-only tours on other days of the week. However you see it, you'll be taking in the works of various major artists – from Impressionists like Monet and Renoir, to early moderns such as Picasso, to Abstract Expressionists like Mark Rothko and Clyfford Still. Also worth a look are the jagged steel monoliths of David Smith; the lean metallic sculptures of Brancusi; James Rosenquist's huge Pop Art diptychs and triptychs; and Edvard Munch's disturbing Scandinavian brand of Expressionism. It's sometimes hard to predict exactly what will be on view at any one time, but the collection is large enough to ensure most modern art fans won't go away disappointed. Additionally, the museum has a number of works by Indian and African artists, and items from the pre-Columbian world.

Georgetown in the movies

Georgetown crops up in many movies that are only incidentally set in Washington DC. Although the house in **The Exorcist** was a stage set, the steep flight of steps down which Father Damien is thrown actually exists (at 36th between M and Prospect); author-screenwriter William Peter Blatty knew it well since he lived nearby. Other movies were filmed on campus at Georgetown University, including the 1980s brat-pack movie **St Elmo's Fire**, in which Rob Lowe, Demi Moore, Emilio Estevez, Judd Nelson, Ally Sheedy, and Andrew McCarthy primp, preen, and throw tantrums all over town as they come to terms with life and love after college. Lawyer-turned-fugitive Will Smith gets a swanky Upper Georgetown pad in **Enemy of the State** (though not much time to enjoy it, as he's arbitrarily pursued from Adams-Morgan to Baltimore). The pseudo-Victorian elegance of the Georgetown Park Mall on M Street has turned up in key scenes in Jean-Claude van Damme's **Timecop** and Arnold Schwarzenegger's **True Lies**, though top Georgetown thriller honors go to Kevin Costner's underrated **No Way Out**. Largely set in the Pentagon, the film does have Costner jogging along the C&O Canal and later chased along the Whitehurst Freeway before escaping into the "Georgetown Metro" station – there is, of course, no such thing – leading to a finale with one of the more unexpected twists in mainstream Hollywood cinema.

Wisconsin Avenue

Georgetown's most bustling area is where M Street meets **Wisconsin Avenue**, the neighborhood's cultural and commercial epicenter. Whereas M Street's offerings tend to be more mainstream chain stores and tourist-friendly boutiques, Wisconsin Avenue caters more to locals and those with a flair for independent shopping. It's not that the shops along Wisconsin (which is at its most enticing from M to Q streets) are necessarily cheap or obscure, but they do have a more creative aspect and irreverent spirit – anything from upstart DC designers and hometown coffeehouses, to modernist galleries and frenetic clubs. The architecture in the vicinity has some highlights too, like **St John's Episcopal Church**, just off Wisconsin at O and Potomac, a quaint Federal structure built in 1806 by US Capitol architect William Thornton to house DC's oldest Episcopal congregation (dating to 1776); the blocky, Neoclassical **Volta Bureau**, three blocks west of Wisconsin at 1537 35th St, built in 1893 as an institute for the deaf (the building was funded by Alexander Graham Bell with money he was awarded by the French government's Volta Prize after inventing the telephone); and the **Duke Ellington School of the Arts** (see p.201), 35th and R streets, a grand Greek Revival high school founded by the jazz great to serve as a magnet for artistically inspired DC youth.

Along the C&O Canal

On a clear summer's day there's no better spot to be in Georgetown than along the **Chesapeake and Ohio (C&O) Canal**, whose eastern extremity feeds into Rock Creek at 28th Street NW. The canal is overlooked on both sides by restored red-brick warehouses, spanned by small bridges, lined with trees, and punctuated by occasional pastel-colored towpath houses. The prettiest central stretch starts at **30th Street**, where the adjacent locks once opened to allow boatloads of coal, iron, timber, and corn from the upriver Maryland estates to pass through. Just to the east, it's hard to visualize what it must have been like in its mid-nineteenth-century glory days – indeed, at some of the now-closed locks, water cascades through and over the wooden beams, and the entire works looks ready to give way at the slightest push.

The Potomac River had been used by traders since the earliest days of settlement in the region, but a series of rapids and waterfalls – like those at Great Falls, just fourteen miles from Georgetown – made large-scale commercial navigation all but impossible. A canal was proposed (George Washington was one of the shareholders) that would follow the line of the river and open up trade as far as the Ohio Valley, but when construction finally finished in 1850,

Activities on the C&O Canal

It's 184 miles from Georgetown to the canal terminus at Cumberland, MD. Along the way, the canal wends its way through highly varied scenery: past waterfalls, through forests, and skirting the ridges and valleys of the Appalachian Mountains.

Canal boats

To sign up for trips on the ninety-foot, mule-drawn **canal boats** – accompanied by park rangers in nineteenth-century costume who work the locks – stop in at the **C&O Canal Visitor Center**, 1057 Thomas Jefferson Street NW (daily April–Oct 10am–4pm; ☎202/653-5190, ⊛www.nps.gov/choh). Tickets cost $8, and there are usually three or four daily departures Wednesday through Sunday from mid-June to early September, with reduced service from April to mid-June and mid-September to late October.

Along the canal

A number of outlets **along the canal** rent boats, canoes, and bikes, including several in the first twenty-mile stretch from Georgetown (see p.314). For a day trip by **bicycle**, Great Falls (see below) – an easy, flat fourteen miles away – is a reasonable destination. You'll need to observe a 15mph speed limit on the towpath, wear a helmet, and give way to all pedestrians and horses. It takes most people a couple of hours to bike to Great Falls from Georgetown, and the only slightly tricky part is just before Lock 15, where you'll have to carry the bike for a couple hundred yards. **Canoes** and **boats** are limited to specific areas (visitor centers and rental outlets can advise) and you shouldn't venture onto the Potomac River, which can be very dangerous, or swim in the canal itself. You can **picnic** anywhere you like, but only light fires in authorized fireplaces. First-come, first-served basic **campsites** are dotted along the entire length of the canal; the one closest to the city is at Swain's Lock, twenty miles from Georgetown.

Great Falls Park

At **Great Falls Park**, fourteen miles from Georgetown, the **Great Falls Tavern Visitor Center**, 11710 MacArthur Blvd, Potomac, MD (daily 10am–4pm; summer closes 5pm; ☎301/299-3613, ⊛www.nps.gov/grfa), has a museum covering the history of the canal. This is the starting point for guided local tours, walks, and canal boat trips (same prices and schedules as in Georgetown). Nearby, a boardwalk offers terrific views of the falls themselves. There's a **snack bar** but no other eating or rental facilities. By car, take MacArthur Boulevard, signposted from Georgetown, or Exit 41W off the Beltway; outside rush hour, it's a 20min drive. There's also a **visitor center** on the Virginia side of the falls (☎703/285-2965) – though no access between the two sides of the canal and the Potomac River – with information on more tours and trails, but no boat trips. Get there by following Route 193 West, also known as Georgetown Pike (Exit 44 off the Beltway); turn right on Old Dominion Drive, from where it's a mile to the entrance station. Parking is $5 for three days of use.

the **C&O** reached only as far as Cumberland in Maryland, 184 miles and 74 locks away. Confederate raiding parties found the barges and locks easy targets during the Civil War and much of the traffic dried up for the duration – doubtless to the satisfaction of the Union troops stationed in Georgetown, who used to swim naked in the canal, offending local sensibilities. Even after the war the canal never attracted sufficient trade, mainly because of competition from the railroads; the last mule-drawn cargo boat was pulled through in the 1920s, after which severe flooding from the Potomac destroyed much of the canal infrastructure. The C&O's historical importance was recognized in 1971 when its entire length was declared a **National Historic Park**, and today scores of visitors hike, cycle, and horse-ride along the restored towpaths; canoeing and boating are allowed in certain sections, too, and the National Park Service offers passenger canal boat services (see p.223).

Along the canal

One of the most appealing stretches of the canal is the short section between **Thomas Jefferson Street** and **31st Street**, where artisan houses dating from the building boom of the mid-nineteenth century have been handsomely restored as shops, offices, and, occasionally, private homes. Thomas Jefferson Street itself is lined with attractive brick houses, some in the Federal style, featuring rustic stone lintels, arched doorways with fanlights, and narrow top-floor dormers. On the south side of the canal, **The Foundry**, 1050 30th St, is just one of the many brick warehouses that line the canal. It was originally built as a machine shop and later served as a veterinary hospital to care for the mules that worked the boats; today it serves as office space. Other warehouses have received similar treatment – like the shops and offices at **Canal Square**, 1054 31st St – and frame either side of the waterway as far up as Francis Scott Key Bridge, five blocks west.

At **Wisconsin Avenue**, south of the canal, you're at the oldest part of Georgetown. This was the first road built from the river into Maryland during colonial times, and was a major route for farmers and traders who used the slope of the hill to roll their barrels down to riverside warehouses. Later, canal boatmen would be lured into the Gothic Revival **Grace Church** on South Street, just off Wisconsin Avenue, by promises of salvation from the earth-bound drudgery of hauling heavy goods from barge to warehouse. Others sought solace in nearby **Suter's Tavern**, where, it's claimed, George Washington met Maryland landowners to discuss the purchase of property so that work could start on the federal city. The tavern was knocked down long ago, but there's a plaque marking its approximate site at 31st and K streets.

The waterfront

South of the C&O Canal, **K Street** was once known as Water Street for the very good reason that it fronted the Potomac River, though land reclamation has now pushed the water a hundred yards or so farther south. K Street's most noticeable feature is what's above it, namely the looming **Whitehurst Freeway** – the elevated road built in the 1950s to relieve traffic congestion on M Street. Cross the road under the freeway and you reach the riverside development of **Washington Harbor** (east of 31st), its interlocking towers and capsules set around a circular, terraced plaza with spurting fountains. The waterfront on either side is due to be landscaped as part of a new **Georgetown Waterfront Park**, and there are views upriver to the Francis

Scott Key Bridge and downriver to Theodore Roosevelt Island and Bridge, as well as of the backs of the Watergate Complex and Kennedy Center. The restaurants and bars in the Harbor complex are all fairly expensive, but there's nothing more relaxing than a summer evening on the terrace, sipping drinks, and watching the boats sculling by. If you'd like to go for a cruise yourself, several boat-rental shops offer the means to explore the calmer waters around the Key Bridge and Roosevelt Island. Good choices include Fletcher's Boat House, 4940 Canal Rd NW (☎202/244-0461, ⓦwww.fletchersboathouse .com), which rents rowboats and canoes, and Thompson Boat Center, 2900 Virginia Ave NW (☎202/333-9543, ⓦwww.thompsonboatcenter.com), with its single and double kayaks, canoes, and rowing shells.

Northern Georgetown

Set on "The Heights" above Q Street, the grand mansions and estates of **northern Georgetown** sat out the upheavals that took place below during the nineteenth and twentieth centuries. Owned by the area's richest merchants, the land here was never exploited for new construction when Georgetown was in the throes of expansion. Today several of the fine homes and beautiful grounds are open to the public.

From the middle of Georgetown, the easiest way to get here is straight up Wisconsin Avenue (Bus #30, #32, #34, #35, or #36 from M St). Alternatively, if you approach from New Downtown, crossing Dumbarton Bridge from Massachusetts Avenue NW (Dupont Circle Metro) puts you directly on Q Street. You can also take the **Georgetown Shuttle** (Route #1; see p.217) as far as Wisconsin Avenue at R Street, from where it's only a short walk east to the major sights.

Tudor Place

1644 31st St NW ☎202/965-0400, ⓦwww.tudorplace.org. Tours Tues–Fri 10am–2.30pm, Sat 10am–3pm, Sun noon–3pm. $6.

Two blocks east of Wisconsin Avenue between Q and R streets, stately **Tudor Place** was designed by William Thornton, who was also responsible for the US Capitol and Georgetown's St John's Episcopal Church. Commissioned in 1805 by Thomas Peter (descendant of one of the area's original Scottish tobacco merchants and son of Georgetown's first mayor) and his wife Martha Custis Peter (granddaughter of Martha Washington), the house displays an incongruity that was rare for the period – Thornton embellished the fundamentally Federal-style structure with a Classical domed portico on the south side. The exterior has remained virtually untouched since and, as the house stayed in the same family for over 150 years, the interior has been spared the constant

---

Garden Day

Each May, the Georgetown Garden Club sponsors its annual **Garden Day**, when private patches of greenery are open to the public. Tickets cost $25 ($30 in May) for the self-guided tour and raise funds for charity and conservation efforts. Watch the local listings magazines for details, call ☎202/333-4953, or visit ⓦwww .georgetowngardentour.com.

"improvements" wrought in Georgetown's other period homes by successive owners. **Guided tours** show you furnishings lifted from the Washington's family seat at Mount Vernon and fill you in on how Martha Peter watched from her bedroom window as British troops burned down the US Capitol in 1814. You're supposed to reserve in advance for the tours, but ringing the bell at the front gate gives you access to the gardens during the day (Mon–Sat 10am–4pm, Sun noon–4pm; free). Walk up the path and bear to the right where a white box holds detailed maps ($2 donation) of the paths, greens, box hedges, arbors, and fountains.

Dumbarton Oaks

1703 32nd St ☏202/339-6401, ⊛www.doaks.org. Tues–Sun 2–5pm. Donation.

One long block east of Wisconsin Avenue, and just north of Tudor Place, the grand estate of **Dumbarton Oaks** encompasses a marvelous red-brick Georgian mansion surrounded by gardens and woods. In 1703, Scottish pioneer Ninian Beall was granted almost 800 acres of land, stretching from the river to Rock Creek, and proceeded to make himself a fortune from the tobacco trade. Although much of the land was later sold by his descendants, more than enough of the coveted northern reaches remained for newcomer William H. Dorsey to create the house and landscaping in 1800. The estate was added to and renovated over the years before being acquired by diplomat **Robert Woods Bliss** in 1920 to house his significant collection of world art. In 1940 the house was handed on to Harvard University (the current owners), and in 1944 its commodious Music Room hosted a meeting of American, Russian, British, and Chinese delegates, whose deliberations led to the founding of the United Nations the following year.

Unfortunately, much of the mansion is not open to the public, though its ten acres of **formal gardens** (entrance at 3101 R St; March–Oct 2–6pm; $6), with their beech terrace, evergreens, rose garden, brick paths, pools, and fountains, provide one of DC's quietest and most relaxing retreats. The estate's highlight, however, and the one part of the mansion open to the public, is its terrific **museum**, featuring the Bliss collection. **Pre-Columbian** art was one of the statesman's obsessions, evident through countless gold, jade, and polychromatic carvings, sculpture, and pendants of Olmec, Inca, Aztec, and Mayan provenance – among them ceremonial axes, jewelry made from spondylus shells, stone masks of unknown significance, and sharp jade "celts" possibly used for human sacrifice. Bliss was equally fascinated by the **Byzantine Empire**, and his silver Eucharist vessels, ivory boxes, and painted icons are all standouts. Ancient items like a second-century porphyry urn and Syrian mosaic of Narcissus are equally impressive. Perhaps most extraordinary is the miniature fourteenth-century mosaic icon of the Forty Martyrs, which depicts – in cubes of enamel paste and semiprecious stone – forty Roman soldiers left to freeze to death because they refused to recant their Christian beliefs. Finally, you can also take a peek in the **Music Room** and see its wondrous paintings and tapestries, walnut chests and credenzas, decorative wooden ceiling, and vintage pianos and harpsichords.

Dumbarton House

2715 Q St NW ☏202/337-2288, ⊛www.dumbartonhouse.org. Hourly tours Tues–Sat 10am–2pm. $5.

Past 27th Street, **Dumbarton House** is one of the oldest homes in Georgetown, built between 1799 and 1804. The construction of the bridge over Rock Creek in 1915 necessitated the house's removal, brick by brick, from farther down Q Street to its present position. Known for a century as "Bellevue," the elegant Georgian mansion housed Georgetown's first salon, as political leaders of the day came to call on Joseph Nourse, registrar of the US Treasury, who lived here until 1813. The following year, as the British overran Washington, Dolley Madison watched the White House burning from Bellevue's windows (the house was the first refuge for the fleeing president and first lady). The **National Society of Colonial Dames of America**, now headquartered here, will provide the historical skinny and escort you slowly through period rooms filled with Federal furniture, early prints of Washington DC, and middling portraits. If you don't have an hour to spare, or an insatiable interest in decorative porcelain that once, possibly, adorned the White House, content yourself instead with a seat in the quiet, restful garden.

Mount Zion and Oak Hill cemeteries

Mount Zion Cemetery, the oldest burial ground in the city, is hidden away down an offshoot of 27th Street (northern side of Q St) and just five minutes from Dumbarton Bridge. Formerly the Old Methodist Burying Ground, the land was bought in 1842 for the burial of members of the Mount Zion Methodist Church, whose membership was unusual for the time – halved between whites and blacks, who themselves were split between freedmen and slaves. (The fine red-brick church still stands at 1334 29th St, at Dumbarton St.) The cemetery has been neglected over the years, with headstones scattered through the tangled undergrowth, but a start has been made in tidying the place up and restoring some of the monumental gravestones. There's still a long way to go, however, before it matches the pristine grounds of the adjacent **Oak Hill Cemetery**, 3001 R St (Mon–Fri 10am–4pm; ☎202/337-2835), whose tiered gravestones you can glimpse through the trees beyond.

Endowed by banker and art collector William Wilson Corcoran, exclusive Oak Hill began receiving Georgetown's wealthy dead in 1849. Dating from that time is the brick **gatehouse** at 30th and R streets, where you enter the lovingly kept grounds that spill down the hillside to Rock Creek. Within the grounds, the diminutive brick-and-sandstone **Gothic chapel** is the sprightly work of James Renwick (architect of the Smithsonian Castle), while to the west stands a marble plinth with a bust of John Howard Payne – author of the treacly "Home Sweet Home." Ask at the gatehouse for directions to the resting homes of the cemetery's other notable names, including Corcoran himself; Edwin Stanton, Secretary of War under President Lincoln; and former Secretary of State Dean Acheson.

10

Arlington

For many visitors, **Arlington** is synonymous with its eponymous cemetery, and rarely do they spend a minute of time around town before heading back to DC proper. But a recent influx of urban refugees has given this relatively tony suburb a more progressive edge and supported a flowering of good restaurants, bars, clubs, and theaters – so sticking around for the evening isn't a bad idea at all.

In the first half of the nineteenth century Arlington was actually part of the District of Columbia. At the time, however, many people felt that Arlington was the northern gateway to where the South began, and in 1846 Virginia demanded back the thirty square miles it had contributed to the capital city 55 years earlier. For many years Confederate commander Robert E. Lee lived on the sloping hills at his **Arlington House**, overlooking the Potomac and beyond, but during the Civil War the federal government confiscated his land to bury the Union dead in what would become **Arlington National Cemetery**. As an act of reconciliation, in the 1930s Arlington Memorial Bridge was dedicated, symbolically connecting the Lincoln Memorial with the dead of both sides of the war now buried in the cemetery.

The Arlington Memorial is one of three bridges (the Francis Scott Key and 14th Street the others) that directly link the suburb to the city; in addition, the **Metrorail** provides easy access on its Orange, Blue, and Yellow lines – the latter two routed through DC's domestic airport, Reagan National, which is also in Arlington. The fact that the **Pentagon**, the country's military headquarters, is sited here only bolsters this close relationship to the capital. Across the Potomac to the immediate east is the pleasant and walkable refuge of **Theodore Roosevelt Island**, while the **Mount Vernon Trail** – which runs to Alexandria and down to George Washington's estate – is to the south.

While its southern neighbor, Alexandria, is still a bit better for **dining** and **shopping**, Arlington does boast a few major malls in the sub-districts of Pentagon City and Crystal City (not themselves destinations), and conveniently, much of the **nightlife** scene is found on Clarendon and Wilson boulevards around the Clarendon and Court House Metro stations, respectively.

Arlington National Cemetery

Across Arlington Memorial Bridge ℡ 703/695-3250, ⊛ www.arlingtoncemetery.org; Arlington Cemetery Metro. Daily: April–Sept 8am–7pm; Oct–March 8am–5pm.

Washington's grand monuments sit across the Potomac from a sea of identical white headstones spreading through the hillsides of **Arlington National Cemetery**. The 600-acre site commemorates the deaths of some quarter-million US soldiers and their dependents, as well as John and Robert Kennedy,

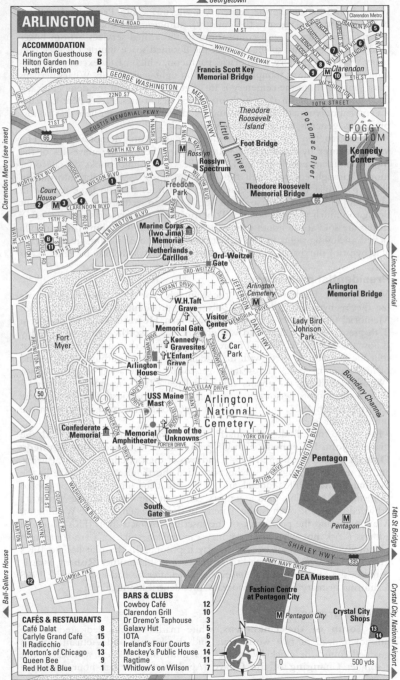

ARLINGTON

▲ Georgetown

ACCOMMODATION

Arlington Guesthouse	C
Hilton Garden Inn	B
Hyatt Arlington	A

CANAL ROAD

M ST

WHITEHURST FREEWAY

Francis Scott Key
Memorial Bridge

GEORGE WASHINGTON

Clarendon Metro

Clarendon

22ND ST

21ST ST

66

NORTH KEY BLVD

18TH ST

WILSON BLVD

N NASH ST

N KENT ST

Rosslyn

Rosslyn
Spectrum

Freedom
Park

Theodore
Roosevelt
Island

Foot Bridge

Little River

Potomac River

FOGGY
BOTTOM

Kennedy
Center

10

ARLINGTON

Theodore Roosevelt
Memorial Bridge

66

Court
House

CLARENDON BLVD

ARLINGTON BLVD

Marine Corps
(Iwo Jima)
Memorial

Netherlands
Carillon

Ord-Weitzel
Gate

ORD-WEITZEL DRIVE

L'ENFANT DRIVE

W.H.Taft
Grave

Visitor
Center

Memorial Gate

Kennedy
Gravesites

L'Enfant
Grave

Arlington
House

USS Maine
Mast

Arlington
Cemetery

JEFFERSON DAVIS HWY

MEMORIAL DRIVE

Arlington
Memorial Bridge

Lady Bird
Johnson
Park

Car
Park

MCCLELLAN DRIVE

Arlington
National
Cemetery

Fort
Myer

50

Confederate
Memorial

Memorial
Amphitheater

Tomb of the
Unknowns

PORTER DRIVE

YORK DRIVE

Boundary Channel

Pentagon

PATTON DRIVE

WASHINGTON BLVD

South
Gate

Pentagon

SHIRLEY HWY

ARMY NAVY DRIVE

395

DEA Museum

Fashion Centre
at Pentagon City

Pentagon City

Crystal City
Shops

COLUMBIA PIKE

Lincoln Memorial

14th St Bridge

Crystal City, National Airport

Clarendon Metro (see inset)

CURTIS MEMORIAL PKWY

FORT MYER DRIVE

OAK ST

A

WILSON BLVD

NORTH KEY BLVD

RHODES ST

PIERCE ST

1

M

A

3

4

M

Court
House

SCOTT

ROLFE ST

15TH ST

COURTHOUSE RD

TROY ST

14TH ST

B

11

13TH ST

WAYNE ST

2ND ST

VEITCH ST

WAYNE ST

ADAMS ST

BARTON ST

WASHINGTON BLVD

COURTHOUSE RD

ARLINGTON BLVD

JEFFERSON DRIVE

GRANT DRIVE

SHERMAN DRIVE

EISENHOWER DRIVE

12

Ball-Sellers House

Clarendon (inset)

Clarendon Metro

5

FRANKLIN ROAD

DANVILLE ST

WILSON BLVD

CLARENDON BLVD

7

6

8

9

M

10

11TH ST

WASHINGTON

10TH STREET

N

0   500 yds

CAFÉS & RESTAURANTS

Café Dalat	8
Carlyle Grand Café	15
Il Radicchio	4
Morton's of Chicago	13
Queen Bee	9
Red Hot & Blue	1

BARS & CLUBS

Cowboy Café	12
Clarendon Grill	10
Dr Dremo's Taphouse	3
Galaxy Hut	5
IOTA	6
Ireland's Four Courts	2
Mackey's Public House	14
Ragtime	11
Whitlow's on Wilson	7

229

▼ 15

▼ C

whose graves here make the cemetery a pilgrimage site. Primarily a military burial ground (the largest in the country), Arlington also holds the remains of other national heroes with connections to the armed services – from boxer (and ex-GI) Joe Louis to the crew of the doomed space shuttle *Challenger*. In many ways the cemetery is America's pantheon, which partly excuses the constant stream of visitors trampling through on sight-seeing tours. What's perhaps most striking about the cemetery is the dignity inherent in the democratically even lines of simple markers and unadorned headstones. Paris's Père Lachaise it's emphatically not: there's a restrained, understated character here that honors presidents, generals, and enlisted personnel alike.

The **Metro** takes you right to the main gates on Memorial Drive. The **visitor center** by the entrance issues **maps** indicating the gravesites of the most prominent people buried here, while various guidebooks on sale offer more thorough coverage; call the office (☎703/607-8052) for information about particular graves. The cemetery is enormous (far too large to take in every plot on a single visit), so if you simply want to see the major sites without doing too much walking, board a **Tourmobile** for a narrated **tour** (see p.34); tickets are sold at the booth inside the visitor center. (Combined Tourmobile tickets, including sights in DC and transportation to Arlington, are also available by prior purchase.) In good weather the cemetery is busy by 9am.

Presidential memorials

Many people head straight for the Kennedy gravesites, though few realize they're bypassing Arlington's only other presidential occupant. Through Memorial Gate, just to the right, lies **William Howard Taft**, the one-term 27th president (1909–13) who was groomed as a worthy successor to Teddy Roosevelt (and in fact did bust more corporate trusts than his predecessor), but split the Republican party with his intransigence. In an outburst near the end of his tenure, he said: "The nearer I get to the inauguration of my successor [Woodrow Wilson], the greater the relief I feel." Taft – uniquely – enjoyed a second, much more personally rewarding career as chief justice of the Supreme Court between 1921 and 1930, and is even commemorated in relief on the building itself (see p.109).

Farther up the hillside is the marble terrace where simple plaques mark the graves of **John F. Kennedy**, 35th US president, his wife **Jacqueline Kennedy Onassis** (laid to rest here in 1994), and two of their children – a son, Patrick, and an unnamed daughter – who both died shortly after birth. Jackie lit the **eternal flame** at JFK's funeral, and ordered that the funeral decor be copied from that of Lincoln's, held a century earlier in the White House. When it's crowded here, as it often is, the majesty of the view across to the Washington Monument and the poignancy of the inscribed extracts from JFK's inaugural address ("Ask not what your country can do for you . . .") are sometimes obscured; come early or late in the day if possible. In the plot behind JFK's grave, a plain white cross marks the gravesite of his brother **Robert**, assassinated in the kitchen of LA's *Ambassador Hotel* after he had just won the 1968 California primary for the Democratic presidential nomination.

Military graves

The **Tomb of the Unknowns**, white marble blocks dedicated to the unknown dead of two world wars and the Korean and Vietnam wars, is guarded round-the-clock by impeccably uniformed soldiers who carry out a somber **Changing of the Guard** (April–Sept every half-hour, otherwise on the hour). The circular, colonnaded **Memorial Amphitheater** behind is the site of special remembrance services. DNA testing in June 1998 provided positive identification of the remains of the previously unknown soldier in the Vietnam War tomb, which – for now – stands empty.

Arlington National Cemetery began as a burial ground for **Union soldiers**, on land taken from Robert E. Lee after he joined the Confederate army at the outset of the Civil War. As a national cemetery, though, it was subsequently deemed politic to honor the dead on both sides of the war; the **Confederate section**, with its own memorial, lies to the west of the Tomb of the Unknowns. Other sections and memorials commemorate conflicts from the Revolutionary War to the Gulf War. Presumably, a section memorializing those who served in Afghanistan and Iraq will be created, as casualties from those wars are already buried here.

The highest concentration of notable military graves is found in the myriad plots surrounding the Tomb of the Unknowns: with a map, and an eye for knots of camera-toting tourists, you'll find the graves of **Audie Murphy**, most decorated soldier in World War II, and boxer **Joe Louis** (born, and buried here, as Joe Louis Barrow), world heavyweight champion from 1937 to 1949. Elsewhere are the graves of **Robert Todd Lincoln,** President Lincoln's son; **John J. Pershing,** commander of American forces in World War I (who has a separate park in his honor in the Federal Triangle); Arctic explorer **Robert Peary**; civil rights leader **Medgar Evers**, shot in 1963 by rampaging racists in the Deep South; astronauts **Virgil Grissom** and **Roger Chaffee** of the ill-fated 1967 *Apollo* flight; tough-guy actor **Lee Marvin**; and thriller-writer **Dashiell Hammett,** a World War II sergeant. The latter honoree is perhaps the most unexpected, as the writer was threatened by official Washington throughout much of his later life – denounced as a subversive by self-appointed moral crusaders, investigated and jailed for "un-American" activities during the McCarthyite witch hunts of the 1950s, and finally hounded by the IRS for tax delinquency.

Group memorials

The most photographed of the many group memorials is the one dedicated to those who died aboard the space shuttle **Challenger**, located immediately behind the amphitheater; adjacent is the memorial to the **Iran Rescue Mission**, whose failure in snatching American embassy workers from their captors doomed Jimmy Carter at the polls in 1980. Both stand close to the mast of the **USS Maine**, whose mysterious destruction in Havana harbor in 1898 – still debated more than a century later – prompted the rise of "yellow journalism" and the short-lived Spanish–American War; both a memorial and a monument to the **Rough Riders**, a devil-may-care cavalry outfit in which a young Theodore Roosevelt made his reputation, commemorate the war itself. More controversial is the memorial inscribed with the names of those killed over Lockerbie, Scotland on **Pan Am flight 103** in the 1988 terrorist explosion; some felt its location in a military cemetery was inappropriate. Dedicated in 1997, the **Women in Military Service** memorial, situated at the main gateway, is the country's first national monument to honor American servicewomen, though there's an honorary group statue at the Vietnam Veterans Memorial.

Arlington House

Sherman Drive, in Arlington National Cemetery ☎703/557-0613, ⊛www.nps.gov/arho; Arlington Cemetery Metro. Daily 9.30am–4.30pm.

Immediately above the Kennedy gravesites, the imposing **Arlington House** has served as a memorial to Confederate commander Robert E. Lee since 1933.

Built in the early nineteenth century by George Washington Parke Custis, the grandson of Martha Washington by her first marriage (the cemetery stands on land that formerly belonged to Custis), the house passed to his daughter, Mary, after his death. Her marriage in 1830 to Lee, a lieutenant in the US Army, was later of enormous consequence: in 1861, Lee was at Arlington House when he heard the news that Virginia had seceded from the Union. Coming from a proud Virginian family, whose number included two signatories of the Declaration of Independence, the West Point-trained Lee was torn between loyalty to his native state and the preservation of the Union that he served. His decision was made more difficult when, at Blair House, just a block from the White House itself, President Lincoln offered Lee command of the US Army. But loyalty to his home won out – Lee resigned his commission and left Arlington for Richmond, where he took command of Virginia's military forces. Mary fled Arlington a month later as Union soldiers consolidated their hold on DC, and the federal government eventually confiscated the estate. The two never returned to Arlington, and as early as 1864 a **cemetery** for the Union dead was established on the grounds of the house, and the mansion itself was used as an ad hoc **camp** for Union soldiers. A year later, Lee – now general-in-chief of the Confederate armies – surrendered to General Grant at Appomattox Court House. After Lee's death, his family took their case to the US Supreme Court; they argued for the return of the family land and succeeded in getting it back in 1874. However, they ultimately had to sell it back to the government Lee had fought against because, despite their earlier wealth and prominence, the clan had fallen on hard times and needed the money – $150,000 in all.

You can explore the house during cemetery opening hours on a free **self-guided tour**. Highlights include the principal bedroom, where Lee wrote his resignation letter from the US Army before the Civil War, and the family parlor, in which he was married; a fair number of the furnishings are original. The architecture is also impressive – the Greek Revival mansion features six thick Tuscan columns and a stately Neoclassical style, adding grandeur to its position on the high ground above the Potomac.

From the grounds the views across the river to the Mall are stunning. No less a man than the **Marquis de Lafayette**, a guest at Arlington House in 1824, thought the aspect "the finest view in the world." Fittingly, the grave of city designer **Pierre Charles L'Enfant** was belatedly sited here in 1909 after the city forgave his feuding over pay for his services.

Marine Corps Memorial and Netherlands Carillon

Arlington Blvd at Meade St ☎703/289-2500, ⊛ www.nps.gov/gwmp/usmc.htm; Arlington Cemetery Metro. Daily 24hr.

Lying to the north, just outside the cemetery walls, is the hugely impressive 78-foot-high bronze **Marine Corps Memorial**. After passing through the **Ord-Weitzel Gate**, it's a twenty-minute walk north of the cemetery's main section, though the easiest approach is to take the **Metro** to the **Rosslyn** station, from which it's a ten-minute, signposted walk. The memorial commemorates the Marine dead of all wars – from the first casualties of the Revolutionary War to the fallen in Iraq – but it's more popularly known as the **Iwo Jima Statue**, after the "uncommon valor" shown by US troops in the bloody World War II battle for the small but strategically essential Pacific island where 6800 lives were lost. In a famous image – inspired by a contemporary photograph – half a dozen marines raise the Stars and Stripes on Mount Suribachi in

February 1945; three of the survivors of the actual flag-raising posed for sculptor Felix W. de Weldon. In summer (June–Aug), the US Marine Corps presents a **parade** and **concert** at the memorial every Tuesday at 7pm, and the annual **Marine Corps Marathon** starts here each October.

Nearby, to the south, rises the **Netherlands Carillon**, a 130-foot-high steel monument dedicated to the Netherlands' liberation from the Nazis in 1945. Given by the Dutch in thanks for American aid, the tower is set in landscaped grounds featuring thousands of **tulips**, which bloom each spring. The fifty bells of the carillon are rung on Saturdays and holidays (May–Sept), at which times you can climb the tower for superlative city views.

The Pentagon

I-395 at Jefferson Davis Hwy ☎703/695-3325, ⊛www.defenselink.mil; Pentagon Metro. Mon–Fri 9am–3pm; by reservation only.

The locus of modern American war-making, the **Pentagon** is the seat of the **US Department of Defense**, and one of the largest chunks of architecture in the world, with a floor area of 6.5 million square feet and five 900-foot-long sides enclosing 17.5 miles of corridors. Terrorists left their mark on this massive structure on 9/11 when they crashed **American Airlines flight 77** into its western flank, killing nearly two hundred people and tearing open a hole almost two hundred feet wide. In the wake of the attack, the military suspended all Pentagon **tours**, though they've since resumed for veterans and school groups of ten or more people; reserve well in advance. If the military does ever loosen the reins a bit and let more people in, the resumed tours, like those in the past, will most likely focus on such statistics as the Pentagon's 284 restrooms and 1700 pints of milk drunk daily by the 25,000 employees. You're better off seeing the giant American flag that covered the 9/11 gash while the building was being repaired; it's on prominent display in the National Museum of American History.

The most interesting thing about the Pentagon is the structure itself, which was thrown together in just sixteen months during World War II to consolidate seventeen different buildings of what in those days was properly called the **War Department**. Efficiency dictated the five-story, five-sided design: with so many employees, it was imperative to maintain quick contact between separate offices and departments – it takes just seven minutes to walk between any two points in the building. Built on swamp- and wasteland, the building was constructed entirely of **concrete** (fashioned from Potomac sand and gravel) rather than the marble that brightens the rest of Washington; President Roosevelt thus neatly avoided boosting the Axis war effort since Mussolini's Italy was then the world's foremost supplier of marble.

Crossing the Potomac by bridge, the **Metro Yellow Line** affords great views of the Pentagon. The Pentagon Metro station, however, no longer allows you to exit directly into the building lobby. Instead, you'll be let out near the bus stop and have to pass through a new, tightly controlled entry complex. If you're interested in shopping, the next two southbound Metro stations let you off near, or directly in, a pair of massive malls at Crystal City and Pentagon City.

DEA Museum

700 Army Navy Drive ☎202/307-3463, ⊛www.deamuseum.org; Pentagon City Metro. Tues–Fri 10am–4pm.

Those interested in military-style power – disappointed perhaps at not being able to tour the Pentagon itself – may enjoy a visit to the **Drug Enforcement**

Agency Museum, across from the Pentagon City Mall. Here you can ignite your enthusiasm for America's ongoing, and seemingly endless, **War on Drugs** with a cache of exhibits designed to persuade you of the fundamental rectitude of hunting down drug kingpins and sending narcotics users and traffickers to prison for long periods of time. In "**Target America**," the museum goes for broke trying to prove the links between stateless terrorist groups and drug barons, undergirding its presentation with a chunk of actual rubble from the World Trade Center. The most elaborate display, though, is the historical timeline of drugs in America, which, through photos, documents, and artifacts, traces the fascination with mind-altering substances, from the mid-nineteenth-century opium wars to beatnik 1950s hopheads to the rise of cocaine in the 1980s and beyond; conveniently left out is corporate America's role in the development of some of the most dangerous drugs. But the museum can be strangely captivating, with a score of vintage pipes, rolling papers, posters, and other oddments on view – surely the one and only place in official Washington where this much drug paraphernalia is on public display.

The Mount Vernon Trail and Theodore Roosevelt Island

If you've had enough of official government sites and are interested in doing a little hiking or biking, the 18.5-mile **Mount Vernon Trail** runs parallel to the George Washington Memorial Parkway, from Arlington Memorial Bridge south seven miles to Alexandria and on to Mount Vernon in Virginia. The trail sticks close to the Potomac for its entire length and runs past a number of sites of historic or natural interest. For more information, and a free **trail guide**, contact the National Park Service in Washington (☎202/619-7222, ⊛www .nps.gov). Those looking for a quieter place for a constitutional should head to **Theodore Roosevelt Island**, a nature park with 2.5 miles of trails that meander through marsh, swamp, and forest. Access to the island, which lies at the start of the Mount Vernon Trail, is via a footbridge on the Arlington side of the Potomac, not far from the Rosslyn Metro station.

Ball-Sellers House

5620 S 3rd St ☎703/379-2123, ⊛www.arlingtonhistoricalsociety.org. April–Oct Sat 1–4pm.

Well to the west of the main riverside section of Arlington, the **Ball-Sellers House** is one of the oldest homes in the area, and is surprisingly well preserved after hundreds of years, offering a nice counterpart to Georgetown's Old Stone House. Both were crafted from rough-hewn oak logs and built largely by their owners in the mid-1700s, with the Ball-Sellers' beams joined together with notches, its roof made of clapboard panels, and the cracks in its walls sealed with mud. What remains, then, is an eye-opening and heartening image of what it took to survive in the north Virginia country before the nascent city of Washington swallowed up the surrounding land (which it would later relinquish). Although it isn't open very often and is only convenient for those going on a driving tour of the area, the house, listed on the National Register of Historic Places, is worth a visit.

Out of the city

B
eyond Washington DC and Arlington, the attractions are farther-flung
but still worthwhile if you have a car or are up for navigating between
Metro and bus lines. Especially in Virginia, you can literally go in any
direction and find some fascinating slice of history, culture, or entertainment. All the places below are within an hour's reach of Washington – perfect if you're limiting your ventures strictly to day trips. Most prominently,
these sights include George Washington's home of **Mount Vernon** and the
wonderfully preserved eighteenth-century town of **Alexandria**, good for its
dining, shopping, and nightlife. There's also the lesser-known, but still intriguing, **Woodlawn Plantation**, where you'll find Frank Lloyd Wright's "Usonian" Pope-Leighey House; **Gunston Hall**, whose owner, George Mason,
prefigured the federal Bill of Rights with his own earlier Virginian version;
the pleasant expanses of **Green Springs Gardens Park**, and the new **Steven
F. Udvar-Hazy Center**, an offshoot of the Smithsonian's National Air and
Space Museum.

The area is so rich and alive with history in part because Virginia was the
first and biggest British colony on the continent; it generated the bulk of its
wealth through a tobacco industry that relied on thousands of imported slaves.
Also, the state had a habit of producing national leaders, including the likes
of George Washington, Thomas Jefferson, and Robert E. Lee. When the Civil
War came, Alexandria – solidly Confederate – was occupied by federal forces
and began a long decline that kept it out of the limelight for many decades; a
good thing, too, for this benign neglect also helped it retain many of its historic
structures, which otherwise would have been lost to gung-ho 1960s urban
renewal, as happened in many other places in Washington DC.

Old Town Alexandria

Six miles south of Washington DC, Alexandria predates the capital considerably,
and its preserved Old Town gives a good idea of what eighteenth-century life
was like for the rich **tobacco farmers** who lived here. First settled by Scots-
man John Alexander in 1699, Alexandria was granted town status fifty years
later – according to tradition, a 17-year-old George Washington assisted in the
preliminary survey (a claim bolstered by the existence of a contemporaneous
parchment map with his name on it in the Library of Congress). By the time of
the Revolution, Alexandria was a booming port and trading center, exporting
wheat and flour to the West Indies, with a thriving social and political scene.

With the establishment of the new capital in 1791, the town was incorporated into the District of Columbia very much against the wishes of its estate- and slave-owning Southern planters, and few were sorry when, in 1846, Virginia demanded its land back from the federal government. Alexandria's Confederate sympathies led to it being occupied by Union troops during the Civil War, which, in turn, led to the town's decline: the new railroad tracks used to move troops and supplies throughout northern Virginia were later employed to carry freight, destroying Alexandria's shipping business in one blow.

What's now known as **Old Town Alexandria** – the compact downtown grid by the Potomac – was left to rot in the later nineteenth century. Many of the warehouses and wharves were abandoned, while other buildings became munitions factories during both world wars. Today, after twenty years of spirited renovation, the Colonial-era streets and converted warehouses are hugely popular attractions, making the town a charming relic just across the water from the nation's capital. Although the town's gift shops, costumed guides, and endless insistence on "authenticity" can become wearing, there are still plenty of fascinating buildings, museums, and tours to merit your interest. Nor is it all preserved in theme-park isolation, since Old Town forms part of the booming commuter town of greater Alexandria. Consequently, you can get here easily on the Metro, and there's more than a few good **cafés** and **restaurants** (see p.268), not to mention some decent **accommodation** (see p.253). It's also prime **shopping** territory, with antiques, crafts, ethnic, folk-art, vintage-clothing, and gift stores on every corner. Good hunting

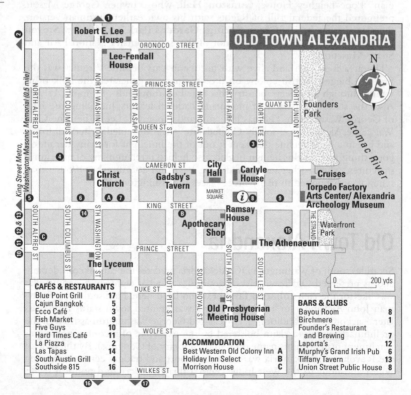

OLD TOWN ALEXANDRIA

CAFÉS & RESTAURANTS

Blue Point Grill	17
Cajun Bangkok	5
Ecco Café	3
Fish Market	9
Five Guys	10
Hard Times Café	11
La Piazza	2
Las Tapas	14
South Austin Grill	4
Southside 815	16

ACCOMMODATION

Best Western Old Colony Inn	A
Holiday Inn Select	B
Morrison House	C

BARS & CLUBS

Bayou Room	8
Birchmere	1
Founder's Restaurant and Brewing	7
Laporta's	12
Murphy's Grand Irish Pub	6
Tiffany Tavern	13
Union Street Public House	8

grounds are at the upper end of King Street (toward the Metro station), along Cameron Street (behind City Hall), and at the Torpedo Factory Arts Center (on the waterfront).

Although the main drags – particularly King Street – are top-heavy with traffic, it's not hard to find areas for peace and quiet here. Cobbled, tree-lined streets with herringbone brick sidewalks are lined with pastel-washed houses featuring boot-scrapers and horse-mounting blocks outside the front door, and cast-iron drainpipes stamped "Alexandria, DC."

Old Town practicalities

The **Metro** station for Old Town Alexandria is King Street (Yellow and Blue lines; 25min from downtown DC), a mile or so from most of the sights; alternatively, you can take **Virginia Railway Express**'s old-fashioned trains (see p.30) to get here from Union Station. Outside King Street station, pick up the local **DASH** bus ($1; for timetable information call ☎703/370-3274, ⓦwww .dashbus.com), which runs down King Street, and get off at Fairfax Street; if you prefer, you can make the twenty-minute walk from the station instead. **Drivers** should follow the George Washington Memorial Parkway south from Arlington and take the East King Street exit. Metered parking in the Old Town is hard to come by and limited to two hours, though a free 24-hour parking pass is available by taking ID and car registration to the visitor center (see below). Cyclists or walkers can get here using the **Mount Vernon Trail**; in Old Town Alexandria, Big Wheel Bikes, 2 Prince St (☎703/739-2300, ⓦwww .bigwheelbikes.com), can rent you a bike to ride to and from Mount Vernon, ten miles away.

Old Town is laid out on a grid and most of the sights lie within the same ten blocks. Guided walks, ghost tours, and river cruises (April–Oct; $8; see p.314) operate during the high season. Note that many sights are closed on Monday, and that opening hours are limited on Sunday.

Alexandria's festivals

Alexandria has a full calendar of **festivals**, many of them linked either to the Scottish connections of the town's original settlers or to the Washington and Lee families. Call the visitor center (☎703/838-4200) or log onto ⓦwww.funside.com for additional information.

January (3rd Sun): music, Lee-Fendall House tours, and other entertainment to celebrate the birthday of Robert E. Lee.

February (3rd weekend): a ball at *Gadsby's Tavern*, a parade, and a mock battle at nearby Fort Ward to celebrate George Washington's birthday; ⓦwww.washington birthday.net.

March: St Patrick's Day parade; ⓦwww.ballyshaners.org.

April (mid): special homes and gardens tours in Old Town; ⓦwww.VAgardenweek .org.

June (mid): waterfront festival with music, fireworks, tours, cruises, and entertainment; ⓦwww.waterfrontfestival.org.

July (last weekend): Virginia Scottish Games, featuring highland dancing and Celtic games, sports, and pastimes; ⓦwww.vascottishgames.org.

December (1st Sat): Scottish Christmas Walk with more dancing and parades; (2nd Sat): candlelight tours of museums and historic houses, accompanied by traditional music; ⓦwww.campagnacenter.org.

Ramsay House

The town's **visitor center**, in the **Ramsay House**, 221 King St (daily 9am–5pm; ☎703/838-4200, ⊚www.funside.com), provides pamphlets and information on countless historic sites and curiosities. The house itself is the oldest in town, built (though not originally on this site) in 1724 for **William Ramsay**, one of Alexandria's founding merchants and later its first mayor. Ramsay had the house transported upriver from Dumfries, Virginia, and placed facing the river, where his ships loaded up with tobacco. The water is now three blocks away: the bluff that the town was built on was excavated after the Revolutionary War, and the earth was used to extend the harbor into the shallow bay, which is why Ramsay House stands so high above the street, its foundations exposed.

Carlyle House and City Hall

When the town was established, Ramsay's fellow merchant, **John Carlyle**, bought two of the most expensive land plots and built Alexandria's finest Colonial-era home. In the 1750s, when all the town's other buildings were constructed of wood, the Georgian, white-sandstone **Carlyle House**, 121 N Fairfax St (Tues–Sat 10am–4.30pm, Sun noon–4.30pm; $4; ☎703/549-2997, ⊚www.carlylehouse.org), made a powerful statement about its owner's wealth. Accounts of Carlyle's business dealings – he ran three plantations and traded numerous slaves – inform the half-hour **guided tour** of the restored house. Contrast the family's draped beds, expensively painted rooms, and fine furnishings with the bare servants' hall, which has actually been over-restored – in the eighteenth century it would have had an earthen floor and no glass in the windows. To their credit, the displays in the mansion don't shy away from presenting the bare, disturbing details of the lives of slaves during the era. Aside from slavery and domestic matters, the tour discusses how the Carlyle House played a role in intercontinental affairs: in August 1755, it was used as **General Braddock**'s headquarters during the planning of the French and Indian War. George Washington was on Braddock's staff, and after the war he frequently visited the house. Less auspiciously, the estate was also the site, a decade later, for Braddock and a handful of British colonial governors to propose the infamous Stamp Act – one of the many actions that propelled the colonists and Britain toward war in the coming years.

Braddock's troops earlier paraded across the way in **Market Square**, off King Street, the heart of Alexandria since its founding. The modern brick terrace around the square sounds one of the few discordant notes in the Old Town, and the Georgian Revival **City Hall** – notable for its quaint steeple – that faces the square looks rather sprightly for such an old building; not surprisingly, it's a post-Civil War reconstruction of an early nineteenth-century Benjamin Latrobe creation. A weekly **farmers' market** still sets up in the City Hall arcades (Sat 5–10am), as it has for more than two hundred years.

Gadsby's Museum Tavern and Christ Church

Gadsby's Museum Tavern, 134 N Royal St (April–Sept Tues–Sat 10am–5pm, Sun 1–5pm; Oct–March Tues–Sat 11am–4pm, Sun 1–4pm; $4; ☎703/838-4242, ⊚www.gadsbystavern.org), occupies two Georgian buildings: the City Hotel from 1792 and the tavern itself from 1785. Downstairs, *Gadsby's Tavern* is still a working restaurant, complete with "authentic" Colonial food and costumed staff. In early American society, anyone who was anyone dropped by here for a visit – from the Marquis de Lafayette to Thomas Jefferson. Short **tours** of the complex by a knowledgeable guide lead you through the old tavern and hotel rooms; candlelight tours in mid-December offer the same scenery, along with other historic buildings, bathed in a romantic glow ($20; ☎703/838-4242).

Three blocks west up Cameron Street, the English-style **Christ Church** (Mon–Sat 9am–4pm, Sun 2–4pm; ⓦwww.historicchristchurch.org), a working branch of the Episcopal diocese, contains the Washington family pew. Identified by a striking red-and-white bell tower, the Georgian edifice, set in a legendary churchyard, was built of brick and finished just before the Revolution. During the Civil War, Union soldiers worshipped here, as did FDR and Churchill on one occasion eighty years later; periodically, the sitting president may drop in for a visit, often to coincide with President's Day or Washington's birthday.

Lee-Fendall House

The Washingtons weren't the only notable family with ties to Alexandria. A descendant of the Lees of Virginia, Phillip Fendall, built his splendid clapboard mansion, the **Lee-Fendall House**, 614 Oronoco St (Tues–Sat 10am–4pm, Sun 1–4pm; $4; ☎703/548-1789, ⓦwww.leefendallhouse.org), in 1785. Much of the furnishing dates from the antebellum era, and the house has been remodeled into the Greek Revival style you see today. Distinguished Revolutionary War general Henry "Light Horse Harry" Lee composed Washington's funeral oration here (in which, memorably, he declared him "first in war, first in peace, and first in the hearts of his countrymen"), and the home has had other famous residents in later years. The most notable of these was powerful labor leader John L. Lewis, who moved in during 1937 as the head of the United Mine Workers, soon created the Congress of Industrial Organizations as a rival to the American Federation of Labor, and helped merge both groups in the 1940s. Lewis lived here until his death in 1969.

Just before the War of 1812 Henry Lee bought his own house on the same block and installed his wife and five children there. This, the boyhood home of Robert E. Lee, 607 Oronoco St, is a red-brick, Federal-era building first owned by a Virginia tobacco planter who occasionally entertained George Washington at dinner. Today it's a private home.

Lyceum and Athenaeum

South of King Street, the **Lyceum**, 201 S Washington St (Mon–Sat 10am–5pm, Sun 1–5pm; ☎703/838-4994, ⓦwww.alexandriahistory.org), houses the town's history museum in a magisterial, 1839 Greek Revival building that was designed to be a centerpiece for the town's cultural pretensions – the evocative name harkening back to Classical hubs for learning, discussion, and public oration. Although the place doesn't quite have the same role today, its changing displays, film shows, and associated art gallery can put some flesh on the town's history; varied exhibits range from old photographs and Civil War documents to locally produced furniture and silverware (the latter an Alexandrian specialty in the nineteenth century).

Five blocks east along Prince Street, the **Athenaeum** (Wed–Fri 11am–3pm, Sat 1–3pm, Sun 1–4pm; ☎703/548-0035, ⓦwww.nvfaa.org), another ancient-styled edifice, with its mighty columns and high pediment, was built as a bank. It's now an art center, where you can check out the latest modern art in a series of galleries, take in music, dance, and theater performances, or listen in on one of the periodic lectures devoted to the arts.

Old Presbyterian Meeting House and Apothecary Shop

The tomb of prominent Alexandria merchant John Carlyle lies in the quiet graveyard of the **Old Presbyterian Meeting House**, 321 S Fairfax St (Mon–Fri 9am–4pm; ☎703/549-6670, ⊛www.opmh.org). The Scottish town founders met here regularly – most prominently in December 1799 for George Washington's memorial service. Despite its historic pedigree and religious importance, the site closed for sixty years beginning in 1889, and was allowed to deteriorate until finally being restored in the 1950s. Nearby a similarly venerable property can be found at 105 S Fairfax St, where patent medicines for Washington were concocted behind the tiny yellow windows of the **Stabler-Leadbeater Apothecary Shop** (Mon–Sat 10am–4pm, Sun 1–5pm; $3; ☎703/836-3713, ⊛www.apothecarymuseum.org), which was founded in 1792 and remained in business until the 1930s; it still displays its original furnishings, herbs, potions, and medical paraphernalia – some eight thousand items in all and well worth a look.

The waterfront

Eighteenth-century Alexandria wouldn't recognize its twentieth-century **waterfront** beyond North Union Street, not the least because the riverbank is several blocks farther east, following centuries of landfill. Where there were once wooden warehouses and wharves heaving with barrels of tobacco, there's now a smart marina and boardwalk, framed by the green stretches of Founders Park to the north and Waterfront Park to the south. Forty-minute **sightseeing cruises** depart (May–Aug Tues–Sun, April & Sept–Oct Sat & Sun only; $8) in front of the Food Pavilion; longer trips run to DC or Mount Vernon and back. For information, contact the Potomac Riverboat Company (☎703/548-9000, ⊛www.potomacriverboatco.com).

Before this whole area was cleaned up in recent decades, the US government built a torpedo factory on the river, which operated until the end of World War II. Restyled as the diverting **Torpedo Factory Arts Center** (daily 10am–5pm; ☎703/838-4565, ⊛www.torpedofactory.org), its three floors contain the studios of more than two hundred artists. All the studios are open to the public, displaying sculpture, ceramics, jewelry, glassware, and textiles in regularly changing exhibitions. Look, too, inside the center's **Alexandria Archaeology Museum** (Tues–Fri 10am–3pm, Sat 10am–5pm, Sun 1–5pm; ☎703/838-4399, ⊛www.alexandriaarchaeology.org), where much of the town's restoration work was carried out, and where you can see ongoing preservation efforts in a laboratory open to the public.

George Washington Masonic Memorial

In a town bursting with Washington mementos, none is more striking than the **George Washington Masonic Memorial**, 101 Callahan Drive (daily 9am–5pm; ☎703/683-2007, ⊛www.gwmemorial.org), whose 333-foot tower – built on top of a Greek temple – looms behind the King Street Metro station, often disappearing into the low-hanging fog during the winter months. The Virginia Freemasons built the memorial in 1932 to honor a "deserving brother," and the tower was designed to resemble nothing less than the long-destroyed Lighthouse at Alexandria, one of the seven wonders of the ancient world. Inside, the glorious visual ode continues with a seventeen-foot bronze **statue** of the general and president, sundry memorabilia, and dioramas depicting events from his life. To see this, and the superb views from the observation platform, you'll have to wait for a forty-minute **tour**, which leaves from the building's main hall (on the half-hour in the morning, on the hour in the afternoon, last tour 4pm). But even from the steps outside, the views across the Potomac to the Washington Monument and Capitol dome in the distance are terrific.

Mount Vernon

3200 George Washington Memorial Pkwy ☎703/780-2000, ✉www.mountvernon.org; Huntington Metro, then Fairfax Connector Bus #101. Daily: April–Aug 8am–5pm; March & Sept–Oct 9am–5pm; Nov–Feb 9am–4pm. $11.

Set on a shallow bluff overlooking the broad Potomac River, sixteen miles south of Washington DC, **Mount Vernon** is among the most attractive historic plantations in the country. George Washington lived on his beloved estate for forty years, during which he ran it as a thriving and progressive farm, anticipating the decline in Virginia's tobacco cultivation and planting instead grains and food crops with great success. When he died, it seemed only fitting that he be buried on its grounds, as his will directed; America's first president lies next to his wife, Martha, in the simple family tomb.

The estate is an extremely popular site for a day trip, and summer weekends, especially, can be very busy. Come early or midweek, if you can, and allow at least two hours to see the house and grounds. You can't eat or drink here, but you're allowed to leave the estate to eat and then return without paying a second admission fee.

To reach Mount Vernon, go first to Huntington Metro (Yellow Line) and then take Fairfax Connector Bus #101 (hourly; ☎703/339 7200, ✉www .fairfaxcounty.gov/connector). It's an easy enough route, though it takes over an hour. A cab from the Metro station costs around $20 (call White Top Cab at ☎703/644-4500). Drivers can follow the George Washington Parkway from DC; there's free parking at the site. The Mount Vernon Trail (see p.234) ends here, too, after starting in Arlington.

Ninety-minute Spirit **cruises** to Mount Vernon depart from Pier 4, 6th and Water streets SW in DC (mid-March to Aug daily, Sept & Oct Fri–Sun only; $34 round-trip; reserve at ☎202/554-8000, ✉www.spiritcitycruises .com/mtvernon), and it's only fifty minutes to Mount Vernon from Old Town Alexandria on cruises offered by the Potomac Riverboat Company (May–Aug daily, April, Sept & Oct Sat & Sun only; $27; ☎703/548-9000, ✉www .potomacriverboatco.com). The **Tourmobile** bus also runs out here – a four-hour trip. The prices of both cruise and Tourmobile trips include admission to the house and grounds.

Some history

George Washington's father, **Augustine**, built a house on the Washington estate in 1735. When he died, the house and lands passed to George's elder brother, Lawrence; after his death in 1752 and his widow's in 1761, the estate went to George. Not that he had an opportunity to spend any real time here early on, since for much of the 1750s he was away on service with the Virginia militia, and then fighting in the French and Indian War. He married in 1759, and it was during the years before 1775 – when he was next called away on

Events at Mount Vernon

Throughout the year, Mount Vernon hosts a range of **festivals** and **special events**. Around the third weekend in February, Washington's **birthday** is celebrated with a wreath-laying ceremony and fife and drum parades; admission to Mount Vernon is free at that time. Each May a three-day festival toasts local **winemakers** in a series of evening events, featuring live jazz and visits to the cellar vaults. In December, special **Christmas tours** re-create the Washingtons' yuletide celebrations and allow access to the third floor of the mansion, which is usually closed. On weekend winter evenings (late Nov to mid-Dec), there are also special **"Mount Vernon by Candlelight"** tours, casting a romantic glow on this historic site. Book ahead for a candlelight visit or for the wine festival; a special admission price applies. For further information, call Mount Vernon or visit its website.

service, as a general in the Continental Army – that Washington came to know his estate. He tripled its size to eight thousand acres, divided it into five separate working farms, and landscaped the grounds; rolling meadows, copses, riverside walks, parks, and even vineyards were all laid out for the family's contemplation and amusement.

Just five hundred acres of the estate remain today, the rest having been split and sold off by the terms of successive wills (including a parcel that became Woodlawn Plantation; see p.245), but there's still more than enough to provide an idea of the former whole. The lifestyle of an eighteenth-century **gentleman farmer** was an agreeable one, in Washington's case supported by the labor of more than two hundred slaves who lived and worked on the outlying farms. The modest house he inherited was enlarged and redecorated with imported materials; formal gardens and a bowling green were added; and the general bred stallions, hunted in his woods, and fished in the river. But Washington did his homework as well. Daily at dawn he made a personal tour of inspection on horseback, sometimes riding twenty miles around the grounds. He studied the latest scientific works on farming, corresponded with experts, and, introducing new techniques, expanded the farms' output to include the production of flour, textiles and even whiskey; often his experimental methods cost him financially. While he was away fighting the Revolutionary War, Washington was forced to turn over the day-to-day operation of his estate to others – who were doubtless thrilled to receive his sixteen-page letters from the front directing the latest farm improvements.

Washington spent eight years away from Mount Vernon during the war, and was prevented from retiring there for good at the end of the fighting: in 1787 he was heading the Constitutional Convention in Philadelphia, and two years later was elected to his first term as US president – news he heard first at Mount Vernon from a messenger who had ridden all the way from Philadelphia. He only visited his house another dozen or so times during his presidency, often for just a few days. When he finally moved back in 1797, at the end of his second term in office, he and Martha had just two and a half years together before his death on December 14, 1799. Out on one of his long estate inspections, he got caught in the snow and succumbed to a fever that killed him (for more on Washington's life, see pp.52–53).

Slave quarters and museum

The path up to the mansion passes various outbuildings, including a renovated set of former **slave quarters**. Ninety slaves lived and worked on the grounds alone, and though there's evidence that Washington was a kinder master than most – for instance, refusing to sell children away from their parents, allowing slaves to raise their own crops, and providing the services of a doctor when needed – they still lived lives of deprivation and overwork. His overseers were continually enjoined to watch the slaves like hawks and guard against theft and slacking. Washington was quick to realize that the move away from tobacco cultivation to more skilled farming made slavery increasingly unprofitable. He stopped buying slaves in the late 1770s, allowing those he owned to learn occupations such as carpentry, bricklaying, and spinning, and to be maintained once they had reached the end of their working lives. After his death, his will freed all of Mount Vernon's slaves, much to the chagrin of his wife, who wanted to retain as much of the family's "property" as possible.

Nearby, a small **museum** traces Washington's ancestry and displays porcelain from the house, medals, weapons, silver, and a series of striking miniatures, by Charles Willson Peale and his brother James, of Martha and her two children by her first marriage. The clay bust of Washington was produced by French sculptor Jean-Antoine Houdon, who worked on it at Mount Vernon in 1785 before completing his famous statue for the Richmond capitol.

The house and grounds

Around the corner, fronting the circular courtyard, stands the **mansion** itself, with the bowling green stretching before it. It's a handsome, harmonious wooden structure, reasonably modest, but sporting stunning views from its East Lawn. The wooden exterior was painted white, beveled and sandblasted to resemble stone; inside, the Palladian windows and bright rooms follow the fashions of the day, while the contents are based on an inventory prepared after Washington's death. Fourteen rooms are open to the public, including portrait-filled parlors, cramped bedrooms, and the chamber where Washington breathed his last on a four-poster bed still in situ. Curiosities in his study include a wooden reading chair with built-in fan and a globe he ordered from London, while in the central hall hangs a key to the destroyed Bastille, presented to Washington by Thomas Paine in 1790 on behalf of Lafayette.

After touring the mansion there's plenty more to see on the **grounds**, including the separate kitchen (set apart from the house because of the risk of fire), storehouse, stables, smokehouse, wash house, overseer's quarters, kitchen garden, and shrubbery. There's also a forest trail nature walk, and you can take a stroll down to the tomb, where two marble **sarcophagi** for George and Martha are set behind iron gates. Washington's will also directed that a new brick vault be erected after his death, since the original family vault on the grounds was in poor shape; the current structure was built in 1831. Nearby lies a slave burial ground, while beyond there's a site where demonstrations of Washington's crop-growing and farming techniques are occasionally held.

The grist mill

Located three miles west of the estate along Highway 235, George Washington's **grist mill** (April–Oct daily 10am–5pm; $4, or $2 with Mount Vernon admission) provides a glimpse into the tedious labor involved with mashing grain to make it usable for other purposes, not unlike at the Peirce Mill in

Rock Creek Park. Guides in period costume go through the rigors of showing how water-power drove the mill, which in turn produced flour from
corn, wheat, and other cereals. The entire experience is much less romantic
than anything else on the estate grounds, though the site also lets you see an
archeological work in progress, as the remains of Washington's own whiskey
distillery are dug up and reconstructed.

Further afield

With so many things to see in the capital region from Maryland to Virginia,
trying to follow a comprehensive inventory of such sights – spread across
four centuries – may prove fruitless as well as exhausting (pick up the *Rough
Guide to USA* if you'd like to give it a go). Rather, the best way to tackle a
larger slice of the DC metropolitan area may well be to limit yourself to **day
trips**: places you can see, with the aid of a car, within an hour or so's drive
of the capital and not get trapped in the seemingly motionless gridlock on
the fearsome Beltway highway loop. The one alternative to cruising around
the area in a rental is to go by train; the Metrorail system is only of limited
use in this regard, but Virginia Railway Express can get you out to more far-
flung locations, notably the old townsites of Manassas and Fredericksburg
and their respective Civil War battlefields, without too much difficulty.

Ultimately, the following selected sights provide nice adjuncts to what
you've already experienced around the District and northern Virginia –
historic architecture and gardens at **Green Springs**, old-fashioned
musical stylings at **Wolf Trap**, stately mansions at **Woodlawn Plantation** and
Gunston Hall, and, the one oddball in the group, the **Pope-Leighey
House** – an unexpected "Usonian" curiosity designed by master architect
Frank Lloyd Wright.

Green Springs Gardens Park

Braddock Rd at Little River Turnpike 236 ☏703/941-7987, ⊛www.co.fairfax.va.us/parks/gsgp.
Grounds daily dawn–dusk, house Wed–Sun noon–4pm.

Several miles west of the city of Alexandria, and east of Pinecrest Golf
Course, the natural expanses of **Green Springs Gardens Park** are a terrific spot for a respite from sight-seeing. Set on 27 acres, the park is based
around the estate of eighteenth-century farmer John Moss. The 1760 red-
brick Georgian manor house is the estate's centrepiece, while the grounds
surrounding the mansion host farmers' markets, bonsai displays, and seasonal
events in the spring, summer, and around Christmas. The official purpose
of the gardens – which hold native Virginia plants – is to educate people
about the best ways to plant and maintain their trees and flowers (an onsite
horticultural library helps too). If you have an interest in this sort of thing,
the display gardens can be impressive, and in separate plots hold the likes
of roses, herbs, shade plants, fruits and vegetables, mixed borders, and more.
One-hour garden **tours** offered four times per month (Aug–Oct periodic
Mon 10am & Wed 7am; $5) provide a good introduction, but more enjoy-
able are the tours that include a **tea service** in the manor house (Aug–Oct
Thurs 1pm; $22).

Woodlawn Plantation and Pope-Leighey House

9000 Richmond Hwy, Alexandria, VA ☎ 703/780-4000, ⊛ www.woodlawnplantation.org, www .popeleighey1940.org. March–Dec daily 10am–5pm. $7.50 each attraction, $13 combined ticket.

Not far from George Washington's grist mill, near the intersection of highways 1 and 235, lie the sprawling grounds of **Woodlawn Plantation**, which were part of the Mount Vernon estate until, after Washington's death in 1799, two thousand acres were ceded to his nephew, **Major Lawrence Lewis**, and Martha Washington's granddaughter, **Eleanor Custis Lewis**. An impressive red-brick Georgian manor house (finished in 1805) was built on the grounds by no less than US Capitol architect William Thornton, who used Palladian design elements and fashioned its decorative trim from local sandstone. However, the substantial labor involved in building the house (all the bricks were fired in a kiln at the site) meant that slave labor was used in abundance. Looking around the estate, you can get a sense of the backbreaking work that was required; this lends an uncomfortable subtext to the graceful design – with its noble marble busts and elegant arched windows and doors – and vividly demonstrates the social extremes that existed in nineteenth-century Virginia.

Perhaps incongruously, Woodlawn Plantation is also the site of a house designed by twentieth-century architect **Frank Lloyd Wright**, whose broad notions of the democratic spirit enabled him to develop "Usonian" homes meant to be affordable for common people. The **Pope-Leighey House** is one such creation, and while the Usonian trend never really caught on – the homes are now collectors' items for the wealthy – it did allow him to experiment with radical concepts within strict limitations of budget, size, and labor. The Pope-Leighey House was not originally built here, but instead moved from another Virginia location when threatened with demolition. Luckily it survived, as this 1200-square-foot residence reveals much about Wright's philosophies: the materials are limited to wood, brick, concrete, and glass; the layout is strongly horizontal, with trellises to control direct sunlight; the clerestory windows employ unique cut-out patterns; and the floor plan is open and the ceilings low – except for that of the living room, which rises to 13ft and occupies about half the overall space of the house.

Gunston Hall

10709 Gunston Rd, off I-95 ☎ 703/550-9220, ⊛ www.gunstonhall.org. Daily 9.30am–5pm. $8.

A short drive south from Mount Vernon, and designed in a similar spirit to the area's other red-brick Georgian manors, **Gunston Hall** is a Colonial-era plantation once owned by **George Mason**, author of the Virginia Declaration of Rights, which the later US Bill of Rights was largely based upon. In both its architecture and decor, Gunston Hall evokes primarily the Federal style, with its striking Neoclassical arches, original boxwood-lined walkway, lovely formal gardens (set on 550 acres that are mostly wooded), and all-around balance and symmetry. This was but one of Mason's many land speculations – the others encompassed some 24,000 acres of property – and like many other planter estates, Mason's had its slaves; a veritable army of them managed the homestead, carefully trimmed the gardens, grew the crops, and made various onsite improvements.

What distinguished Gunston Hall from other plantations, though, was less its attractive landscape and elegant manor, but rather its owner: unlike George Washington and his elite Virginia associates (who would go on to positions of power under the country's new government), George Mason was a fierce **anti–Federalist** who opposed any establishment of a strong central government, especially an executive branch with broad taxing and military power. As a delegate to the 1787 Constitutional Convention, Mason famously said he "would sooner chop off my right hand than put it to the Constitution as it now stands." After voting against the adoption of the document, and thus pitting himself against Washington and his comrades, Mason then made the dire prediction, in print, that the nation would either "produce a monarchy, or a corrupt, tyrannical aristocracy; it will most probably vibrate some years between the two, and then terminate in the one or the other."

The Barns at Wolf Trap

1645 Trap Rd, Vienna, VA ☎703/938-2404, ⊛www.wolftrap.org. Concerts Oct–May; opera June–Sept.

Well to the northwest of Alexandria, via Highway 7, is what some call the Kennedy Center of folk music. In 1966, Congress declared **Wolf Trap** a "National Park for the Performing Arts," meaning that it would be devoted to American music in all its native forms, like bluegrass, jazz, ragtime, Cajun, zydeco, Native American, and countless others. The space for this music could hardly be better – a pair of remodeled **barns** from the eighteenth century (moved here from upstate New York), which provide just the right weathered charm and echoey acoustics that well serve instruments such as banjos, guitars, mandolins, gourds, and washboards. The German barn is the larger of the two, giving you a chance to listen to the music on the "threshing floor" or in a hayloft above. Wolf Trap's other venues include the modern Filene Center and a theatrical stage, but the hoary barns are the definite highlight, and if you come at the right time you're likely to see anyone from established names to up-and-comers with more talent than name recognition; in the summer the barns host local performances of classic operas. Prices can vary widely, so check the website for detailed information.

Wolf Trap is outside the Beltway, between Route 7 and Route 267 (Dulles Toll Road). For directions on how to get there by public transportation, call ☎703/255-1860 – Metro shuttle-bus service is available for most performances. The park has concession stands and a restaurant, but in summer it's nicer to bring a picnic and eat on the grass. Parking is free.

The Steven F. Udvar-Hazy Center

14390 Air and Space Museum Parkway, Chantilly, VA ☎202/357-2700, ⊛www.nasm.si.edu/museum/udvarhazy. Daily 10.30am–5.30pm.

Truly fervent devotees of airplanes and spacecraft can take a shuttle ($7, otherwise parking $12) from the National Air and Space Museum to the **Steven F. Udvar-Hazy Center**, or just make their way out to the Virginia suburb of Chantilly, not far from Dulles Airport, on their own. Everything that's too big to fit into the main building on the Mall is here, spread across 400 million cubic feet. Among the eighty planes and sixty spacecraft are fighters from America's twentieth-century wars, transport craft, and planes used by the postal service, sports enthusiasts, and commercial airlines. As you'll quickly see, though, the entire experience boils down to checking out four huge items: the first, the SR-71 **Blackbird**, is a legendary spycraft that looks like a sleek black missile. It once tooled around 80,000ft in the atmosphere and, well out of Viet Cong artillery range, provided intelligence to American forces in Vietnam. Elsewhere is the B-29 **Enola Gay**, the plane that dropped the first atomic bomb on Hiroshima – though the exhibit features no discussion one way or the other about the morality of nuking civilians. The other two aircraft on display are even more colossal, and more contemporary, and include the Air France **Concorde**, which in 1976 became the only supersonic jet to fly commercially, although now it's no longer in service. Even more eye-opening, the space shuttle **Enterprise**, parked out back, was a prototype for the first space shuttle. This version has no engines, which is just as well since NASA's grounded the entire fleet due to recent tragedies and mechanical foul-ups.

Listings

Listings

Accommodation

Without a doubt, one of the highlights of staying in Washington DC is cozying up in a swank **hotel** in the historic center and having the entire District at your feet, either literally or through the Metro system. Of course, for many this is far from reality, and unless you're willing to drop upwards of $200 a night, you'll probably be out of luck. That said, great options abound beyond the big-name hotels: **bed-and-breakfasts** are certainly viable options, particularly in spots like Dupont Circle; **chain hotels** and motels exist everywhere (and in better neighborhoods than you might expect), with the usual affordable rates; and **hostels** can be found here and there – not in any real abundance, mind you, but frequently enough to allow you to drop anchor in town for less than $40 a night.

Hotels and B&Bs

Standard DC **room rates** begin around $100–120 a night, but, for savvy travelers, there's plenty of room for negotiation. Many hotels discount their rates on weekends (some by up to fifty percent), while prices are low from late fall to winter, and when Congress isn't in session. Always ask if the rate you've been quoted is the best available; often, discount information has to be ferreted out of desk clerks, or cross-checked online. Where places offer particularly good deals, we've said so in the review. Also, since hotels charge by the room, three people can often stay in a double for the same (or at a slightly higher) price as two.

There are hotels in all the main downtown areas, though accommodations near the White House, on Capitol Hill, and in Georgetown tend to be

---

Hotel reservation services

Bed & Breakfast Accommodations Ltd ☎413/582-9888, ℻582-9669, 🌐www.bedandbreakfastdc.com

Bed & Breakfast League ☎202/363-7767, ℻368-8396

Capitol Reservations ☎202/452-1270 or 1-800/847-4832, ℻202/452-0537, 🌐www.capitolreservations.com

Washington DC Accommodations ☎202/289-2220 or 1-800/554-2220, ℻202/338-4517, 🌐www.washingtondcaccommodations.com

business-oriented and pricey. The occasional **budget option** exists in Foggy Bottom and Old Downtown, while most of the chain hotels and mid-range places are in New Downtown – particularly on the streets around Scott and Thomas circles. Outer neighborhoods tend to have a wider selection of smaller, cheaper hotels and B&B-style guest houses, and it's no hardship at all to stay in Dupont Circle, Adams–Morgan, or Upper Northwest; you'll probably be eating and drinking in these places anyway. We've also listed a few options in Arlington and Alexandria, VA, though these towns are easy to see during a day trip from the capital. A number of B&B agencies (see box, p.251) offer rooms in small inns, private homes, or apartments, starting from around $60 per night; a luxury B&B, though, can be every bit as pricey as a hotel, with rates reaching as high as $200–300 a night.

If you're bringing along a car, you're more likely to find free **parking** in the outer neighborhoods; garage parking is available at most downtown hotels, but you'll be charged $20–30 a night for the privilege. Very occasionally, an inn or hotel we list is on the edge of a dicey neighborhood; where safety is an issue, we've said so, and you're advised to take taxis back to your hotel at night in these areas.

In the off-season you'll often be paying less than what's indicated in our reviews. Groups and families should consider the city's suite hotels, where you'll get a kitchen and possibly a separate living room too. One other thing to keep in mind: in summer, DC is hot and humid, and air-conditioning is essential for getting a good night's rest.

Adams-Morgan

Adams Inn 1744 Lanier Place NW ☎202/745-3600 or 1-800/578-6807, ⓦwww.adamsinn.com; Woodley Park-Zoo Metro. Simple B&B rooms in three adjoining Victorian townhouses on a quiet residential street (just north of Calvert St). No TVs, but free breakfast, coffee all day, garden patio, and laundry facilities. Sharing a bath saves you $10. ❸

Courtyard by Marriott 1900 Connecticut Ave NW ☎202/332-9300 or 1-800/321-3211, ⓦwww.courtyard.com/wasnw; Dupont Circle or Woodley Park-Zoo Metro. The top-floor rooms of this hillside hotel have splendid views. Free Internet access, gym, outdoor pool, and good prices for the area, which is a short

walk from the heart of both Dupont Circle and Adams-Morgan. ❹

Kalorama Guest House at Kalorama Park 1854 Mintwood Place NW ☎202/667-6369, ⓕ319-1262; Woodley Park-Zoo Metro. Victorian guest house near Adams-Morgan restaurants. Spacious rooms (and some suites, for $30 more) in four spotless houses filled with period objets and handsome furniture (no TVs). Free breakfast, papers, coffee, and evening sherry. Booking is essential – single rooms are as cheap as $50, or doubles with bath for $80–100, depending on the season. ❸

Normandy Inn 2118 Wyoming Ave NW ☎202/483-1350 or 1-800/424-3729, ⓦwww.jurys.com; Dupont Circle or Woodley Park-Zoo

Accommodation price codes

❶ Under $50	❺ $140–200
❷ $50–70	❻ $200–250
❸ $70–100	❼ $250–300
❹ $100–140	❽ Over $300

The price codes given in the reviews below reflect the average price for a standard double room in peak season (late March to early July), excluding room tax of 14.5 percent. Unless otherwise stated all rooms come with bathroom; breakfast is normally not included.

Metro. Quiet hotel in upscale neighborhood, with comfortable rooms (each with fridge and coffeemaker) and free high-speed Internet access. Coffee and cookies are served daily, and there's a weekly wine and cheese reception. ❹

Washington Hilton 1919 Connecticut Ave NW ☎202/483-3000 or 1-800/445-8667, ⓦwww .hilton.com; Dupont Circle Metro. Massive 1960s convention hotel midway between Dupont Circle and Adams-Morgan. More than 1100 smallish rooms, but most have very good views. Facilities include pool, health club, tennis courts, and bike rental. ❻

Windsor Inn 1842 16th St NW ☎202/667-0300 or 1-800/423-9111, ⓦwww.windsor embassyinns.com. Not too far from the Dupont Circle Metro, with units in twin brick 1920s houses and spacious suites. Some rooms have fridges; ground-floor rooms look onto a terrace. Free continental breakfast, served in the attractive lobby. No onsite parking. ❸

Windsor Park 2116 Kalorama Rd NW ☎202/483-7700 or 1-800/247-3064, ⓦwww .windsorparkhotel.com; Dupont Circle or Woodley Park-Zoo Metro. Pleasant, vaguely Victorian rooms with cable TV, just off Connecticut Avenue. Eight suites available. Continental breakfast included. ❹

Alexandria, VA

Best Western Old Colony Inn 1101 N Washington St ☎703/739-2222, ⓦwww.bestwestern .com; Braddock Road Metro. Less than a mile from the Metro station on the north side of Old Town, this moderately priced choice with standard amenities (plus free breakfast and internet access) is one of the better chain options for the historic center. ❹

Holiday Inn 480 King St, Old Town ☎703/549-6080 or 1-800/368-5047, ⓦwww.holiday innwashingtondc.com; King Street Metro. Alexandria's best-situated hotel, just off Market Square, makes a great base for exploring. There's an indoor pool, and many rooms have balconies overlooking a quiet internal courtyard. The hotel is pet-friendly too. ❺

Morrison House 116 S Alfred St, Old Town ☎703/838-8000 or 1-800/367-0800, ⓦwww .morrisonhouse.com; King Street Metro. Faux Federal-era townhouse (built in 1985) complete with ersatz "authentic" decor, like parquet floors and crystal chandeliers, yet with modern comforts like high-speed Internet connections and designer linens. There's also an acclaimed restaurant. ❻

Arlington, VA

Arlington Guesthouse 739 S 22nd St ☎703/768-0335, ⓦwww.americanguesthouse .com/Arlington.htm; Pentagon City Metro. Bare-bones lodging, but some of the cheapest in the area (down to $55 off-season), and near the Metro. Four rooms have single and double beds, with some dorm units – add $10–20 per extra adult. ❸

Hilton Garden Inn 1333 N Court House Rd ☎1-800/528-4444, ⓦwww.hiltongardeninn .com; Court House Metro. Chain hotel two blocks from the Metro with a business center and gym. Suites have fridges, microwaves, and Internet access. Save $30 by coming on a weekend. ❻

Hyatt Arlington 1325 Wilson Blvd ☎703/525-1234, ⓦwww.arlington.hyatt.com; Rosslyn Metro. Recently renovated corporate property in a prime spot near a Metro station, as well as Georgetown and Arlington National Cemetery, with standard chain features plus gym and Internet access. ❻

Capitol Hill

Bull Moose B&B 101 Fifth St NE ☎202/547-1050 or 1-800/261-2768, ⓦwww .bullmoose-b-and-b.com; Union Station or Capitol South Metro. Turreted brick Victorian evokes themes relating to legendary US president and Bull Moose Party founder Teddy Roosevelt — from the Panama Canal to the charge up San Juan Hill. The ten guest rooms (some en-suite) lack phones, but phone, fax, and Internet access are all available on site. Extras include free continental breakfast, evening sherry, and use of a kitchen. ❹

Capitol Hill Suites 200 C St SE ☎202/543-6000 or 1-800/424-9165; Capitol South Metro. Popular converted apartments whose renovated suites are all equipped with kitchenettes or proper kitchens. Free morning coffee, muffins, and juice, plus Internet access and daily paper. Busy when Congress is in session; on weekends and in August the price drops $50–70. ❻

Hereford House 604 S Carolina Ave SE ☎202/543-0102; Eastern Market Metro. Century-old white, brick townhouse with hardwood floors, small garden, and bright, reasonably sized rooms (no TVs) in residential eastside Capitol Hill, one block from the Metro. Four, somewhat cramped rooms (sharing two bathrooms), plus three more (no breakfast) in a separate house. ❸

Holiday Inn on the Hill 415 New Jersey Ave NW ☎202/638-1616 or 1-800/638-1116, ⍟www .holiday-inn.com; Union Station Metro. Rooms are nothing special, but there's a pool, exercise room, and sports bar and grill dedicated to the Washington Senators, DC's one-time pro baseball team, which departed decades ago. Weekend rates here can be a bargain, from $50–90 less. ❺

Hotel George 15 E St NW ☎202/347-4200 or 1-800/576-8331, ⍟www.hotelgeorge.com; Union Station Metro. Postmodern design meets 1928 Art Deco architecture, resulting in sleek lines, contemporary room furnishings (dark wood and glass, with copious Washington imagery), great marble bathrooms, in-room CD players, and a trendy bar-bistro. Weekend rates are $40–50 cheaper. ❽

Hyatt Regency Washington on Capitol Hill 400 New Jersey Ave NW ☎202/737-1234 or 1-800/233-1234, ⍟www.washingtonregency .hyatt.com; Union Station Metro. Two blocks from the train station, this 800-room luxury hotel features a multistory atrium, pool, and gym – and a few rooms with views of the Capitol. Newly remodeled rooms with sleek black-and-cream furnishings give a modern spritz to formerly staid units. Rate can drop by up to $100 on weekends. ❻

Phoenix Park 520 N Capitol St NW ☎202/638-6900 or 1-800/824-5419, ⍟www.pparkhotel .com; Union Station Metro. Elegant rooms in an Irish-themed hotel loaded with dark wood, paintings, and old-country style, located across from Union Station. Popular with politicos, who frequent its *Dubliner* pub (see "Bars and clubs" chapter). There's a good restaurant, too, serving hearty breakfasts. $300 for basic room, suites start at $100 more. ❽

Dupont Circle

Brickskeller Inn 1523 22nd St NW ☎202/293-1885, ⍟www.thebrickskeller.org; Dupont Circle Metro. A converted apartment house with a stately facade and simple rooms, most of which have sinks; some have a bath and TV. Located above one of the Circle's

oldest and best bars (see p.284). The top-floor rooms have a view of Rock Creek Park. Good weekly rates. ❸

Carlyle Suites 1731 New Hampshire Ave NW ☎202/234-3200 or 1-866/468-3532, ⍟www .carlylesuites.com; Dupont Circle Metro. An Art Deco-styled structure with rooms that are more functional than fancy. Still, with high-speed Internet hookups, kitchenettes with fridges and microwaves, and an on-site café and laundry, it's a good choice for the area. ❹

Dupont at the Circle 1604 19th St NW ☎202/332-5251 or 1-888/412-0100, ⍟www .dupontatthecircle.com; Dupont Circle Metro. Eight handsome rooms – high ceilings, kitchenettes, marble bathrooms – in a Victorian townhouse near the Circle (at Q St). Continental breakfast included. Offers higher-priced packages (for $100–400 over room rate) with quirky names like the "Metrosexual Special" that include wine, chocolates, and facials. ❺

Embassy Inn 1627 16th St NW ☎202/234-7800 or 1-800/423-9111, ⍟www.windsor embassyinns.com; Dupont Circle Metro. Welcoming bed-and-breakfast on a residential street in northeastern Dupont Circle, well placed for bars and restaurants. Free continental breakfast, coffee, and papers, plus an early-evening sherry to speed you on your way. ❹

Embassy Row Hilton 2015 Massachusetts Ave NW ☎202/265-1600 or 1-800/774-1500, ⍟www.hilton.com; Dupont Circle Metro. Smart Embassy Row standard, with marble bathrooms, cable TV, lobby bar, health center, and seasonal rooftop pool. Rates can plummet up to $150 on weekends in low and shoulder seasons. ❼

Radisson Barceló 2121 P St NW ☎202/293-3100 or 1-800/333-3333, ⍟www.radisson .com; Dupont Circle Metro. European-style hotel with good restaurant in the heart of the Dupont Circle nightlife scene. Rooms are spacious, and there's a gym, pool, and sundeck. ❺

Rouge 1315 16th St NW ☎202/232-8000, ⍟www.rougehotel.com; Dupont Circle Metro. Dupont Circle's hippest hotel (though it's actually on nearby Thomas Circle), where the 137 sleek rooms are outfitted with crimson velvet drapes, red leatherette headboards, and postmodern art; minibars are stuffed with the likes of Redi-Whip and condoms. The ground-floor bar-lounge is a definite highlight (and a real weekend scene) where you can indulge in a complimentary cold pizza and Bloody Mary – for breakfast. In case you do want to leave your room, you'll find yourself a quick walk from the Circle's prime haunts. **❼**

Simpkins' B&B 1601 19th St NW T 202/387-1328; Dupont Circle Metro. Victorian townhouse just a minute from the Metro, with six rooms at unbeatable rates for this location. Decor is plain and facilities simple. Guests share two bathrooms, a small kitchen (with free tea and toast), and the cable TV in the lounge; there's also free high-speed Internet access. Call at least two weeks in advance. **❷**

Swann House 1808 New Hampshire Ave NW T 202/265-4414, W www.swannhouse.com; Dupont Circle Metro. Elegant B&B in an 1883 Romanesque Revival mansion with striking red-brick arches, gables, and turrets, a ten-minute walk from both Dupont Circle and Adams-Morgan. There are nine individually decorated rooms – some with working fireplaces – as well as porches and decks for reclining, and a private garden with fountain. Free continental breakfast, afternoon refreshments, and an early-evening sherry to round out the day. **❻**

Westin Embassy Row 2100 Massachusetts Ave NW T 202/293-2100 or 1-800/WESTIN-1, W www.starwood.com/westin; Dupont Circle Metro. This former *Ritz-Carlton* still caters to clubby politicos, media types, and business people who frequent its *Jockey Club* restaurant. Anglo-French country-house chic, with on-site gym and nice rooms with high-speed Internet access. Weekend rates drop to $250, otherwise around $300. **❽**

Foggy Bottom

Allen Lee 2224 F St NW T 202/331-1224 or 1-800/462-0186, W www.allenleehotel .com; Foggy Bottom-GWU Metro. Misleadingly attractive exterior hides musty rooms (with and without private bath) with clunky air-conditioning – inspect a couple before checking in. The place has seen much better days, but is in a convenient location and is certainly cheap for DC, with shared-bath doubles for as low as $62. **❷**

Fairmont 2401 M St NW T 202/429-2400, W www.fairmont.com; Foggy Bottom-GWU Metro. High-class West End oasis with extremely comfortable rooms, pool,

excellent health club, and internal garden courtyard. Upscale new chain owner has topped up the furnishings that much more. Just north of Washington Circle, midway between Foggy Bottom and Georgetown. **❼**

Hay-Adams 800 16th St NW T 202/638-6600 or 1-800/424-5054, W www.hayadams.com; Farragut West or McPherson Square Metro. One of DC's finest hotels, from the gold-leaf and walnut lobby to the sleekly modern rooms, to the suites (which can cost thousands per night) with fireplaces and original cornices, marble bathrooms, balconies, and high ceilings. Upper floors have great views of the White House across the square. Breakfast is served in the Lafayette Room, one of the District's better spots for early-morning power dining. **❽**

Lombardy 2019 Pennsylvania Ave NW T 202/828-2600 or 1-800/424-5486, W www .hotellombardy.com; Foggy Bottom-GWU or Farragut West Metro. Red-brick apartment-style hotel, renovated with modern furnishings, in good Pennsylvania Avenue location, close to two Metro stations. Spacious rooms, most with kitchenettes and coffeemakers; the café has outdoor seating and is solid for breakfast. **❺**

State Plaza 2117 E St NW T 202/861-8200 or 1-800/424-2859, W www.stateplaza.com; Foggy Bottom-GWU Metro. Commodious, stylish suites with fully equipped kitchens and dining area, plus a rooftop sundeck, health club, and good café. There's often room here when other places are full. **❺**

Watergate 2650 Virginia Ave NW T 202/965-2300 or 1-800/424-2736, W www.watergate hotel.com; Foggy Bottom-GWU Metro. Iconic Washington hotel synonymous with bad political behavior, but otherwise a nice spot with comfortable rooms and suites – some with kitchens – and balconies with river views. New owner has increased the style factor and jazzed up the rooms, and the complex offers a gym, shops, and the primo *Aquarelle* restaurant (see "Eating" chapter). Expect to save $80 on weekends. **❼**

Georgetown

Four Seasons 2800 Pennsylvania Ave NW T 202/342-0444 or 1-800/332-3442, W www .fourseasons.com. This modern red-brick pile at the eastern end of Georgetown is one of

DC's most luxurious hotels. Stars, royalty, and business high-rollers hanker after the lavish rooms and suites with views of Rock Creek Park or the C&O Canal. Service is superb, and there's a pool, fitness center, and the *Garden Terrace* bar-lounge. Save $100 on weekends, otherwise $400 or more. ❽

Georgetown Inn 1310 Wisconsin Ave NW ☎202/333-8900 or 1-800/424-2979, ⓦwww .georgetowninn.com. Stylish, red-brick hotel in the heart of Georgetown offering taste-fully appointed rooms (those off the avenue tend to be quieter) with marble bathrooms, plush decor, and high-speed Internet hook-ups. ❻

Holiday Inn Georgetown 2101 Wisconsin Ave NW ☎202/338-4600 or 1-800/465-4329, ⓦwww.holiday-inn.com. The only relative cheapie in Georgetown; it's a bit far up Wis-consin Avenue (on the way toward Upper Northwest), though buses and cabs get you down to M Street pretty quickly. Parking, outdoor pool, and fitness room too. ❹

Latham 3000 M St NW ☎202/726-5000 or 1-800/368-5922, ⓦwww.thelatham.com. Well-sited hotel with rooftop pool, sundeck, and one of the city's finest dining experiences, *Citronelle* (see "Eating" chapter). Some rooms have canal and river views, and there are some superb split-level executive suites with business facilities like high-speed Inter-net access and fax/copy machines. A suite may run $100 more. ❻

Monticello 1075 Thomas Jefferson St NW ☎202/337-0900 or 1-800/388-2410, ⓦwww .hotelmonticello.com. All-suite hotel located off M Street, in an evocative spot near the historic C&O Canal, with spacious standard suites and some two-level penthouses that sleep up to six; all units have a wet bar, microwave, and fridge. Free Internet access in the business center. Summers see a small discount in price, as do some weekends. ❺

New Downtown

Capital Hilton 1001 16th St NW ☎202/393-1000 or 1-800/445-8667, ⓦwww.hilton.com; Farragut North or McPherson Square Metro. Spacious rooms, buzzing lobby-bar, Art Deco trappings, and great location three blocks from the White House. Facilities include an expansive health club and spa complex, and a good sports bar-restaurant.

Weekend rates are among the lowest for quality downtown rooms, some $50–100 below weekday prices. ❼

Governor's House 1615 Rhode Island Ave NW ☎202/296-2100 or 1-800/821-4367, ⓦwww .capitalhotelswdc.com; Dupont Circle or Far-ragut North Metro. Although the exterior is unpromising, it offers a relaxed atmosphere inside with decent-size rooms, some with sofa beds and kitchenettes. There's a popular bar and grill and a pool, plus you can use the nearby YMCA fitness center. Weekend rates are a good deal, as low as $88. ❺

Hamilton Crowne Plaza 14th and K St NW ☎202/682-0111 or 1-800/227-6963, ⓦwww .crowneplaza.com; McPherson Square Metro. Resurrected 1920s Beaux Arts-style hotel with swanky decor, high-speed Internet access, fine city views, and a central, sought-after Franklin Square location. Elegant rooms, lobby espresso bar, health club, and sauna add to the plush atmos-phere. ❽

Helix 1430 Rhode Island Ave NW, near Logan Circle ☎202/462-9001, ⓦwww.hotelhelix.com; Dupont Circle or Farragut North Metro. A prime choice if you're into a young, convivial atmosphere and bright, festive decor that includes multicolored furniture, boomerang shapes, and other eye-popping detail. Rooms come in three flavors – the chill-out "Zone," chic "East," and kid-friendly "Bunk." Save $70 or so on weekends. ❺

Holiday Inn Central 1501 Rhode Island Ave NW ☎202/483-2000 or 1-800/248-0016, ⓦwww .inn-dc.com or www.holidayinn.com; Dupont Circle or Farragut North Metro. One of down-town's better mid-range options, located at Scott Circle, with modern rooms, a rooftop pool, a bar, and free breakfast. Don't let the grim, corporate-modern exterior keep you away. ❺

Jefferson 1200 16th St NW ☎202/347-2200 or 1-800/365-5966, ⓦwww.thejeffersonhotel .com; Farragut North Metro. Patrician land-mark on 16th Street. A bit away from the main action, but still a favorite since the 1920s for its antique-strewn interior with busts, oils, and porcelain at every turn, plus fine restaurant and stylish guest rooms. Weekend rates can fall to less than $200 a night. ❽

Mayflower 1127 Connecticut Ave NW ☎202/347-3000 or 1-800/228-7697, ⓦwww .renaissancehotels.com/WASSH; Farragut North

△ Willard InterContinental

Metro. Beautiful and sumptuous Washington classic, with a promenade – a vast, imperial hall – that, from the lobby, appears to be endless. Smart rooms have subtle, tasteful furnishings, and the terrific *Café Promenade* restaurant (see "Eating" chapter) is much in demand with power diners. If there's one spot in DC where the national and international political elite come to roost, this is it. ❻

St Regis Washington 923 16th St NW ☎202/638-2626 or 1-800/562-5661, ⓦwww .starwood.com/stregis; **McPherson Square Metro.** Just a few blocks north of the White House, President Calvin Coolidge cut the ribbon opening this 1920s Italian Renaissance classic, rich with antiques, chandeliers, and carved wooden ceiling in the lobby that looks right out of a European palace. One of DC's cozier luxury hotels, it features elegant rooms with stylish appointments, plus an on-site gym and business center. ❻

Swiss Inn 1204 Massachusetts Ave NW ☎202/371-1816 or 1-800/955-7947, ⓦwww .theswissinn.com; **McPherson Square Metro.** Cozy townhouse accommodation with air-conditioned rooms featuring kitchenettes, TV, and bath; parking (free on weekends) available. Hosts are multilingual. Book well in advance since prices don't get much better downtown. ❸

Tabard Inn 1739 N St NW ☎202/785-1277, ⓦwww.tabardinn.com; **Dupont Circle Metro.** Three converted Victorian townhouses, two blocks from Dupont Circle, with forty unique, antique-stocked rooms with an odd mix of modern and old-fashioned decor. Laid-back staff, comfortable lounges with romantic fireplaces, a courtyard, and an excellent restaurant. Rates include breakfast and a pass to the nearby YMCA. Save at least $40 if you share a bath. ❺

Topaz 1733 N St NW ☎202/393-3000, ⓦwww .topazhotel.com; **Dupont Circle Metro.** Boutique hotel whose vibrant rooms have padded headboards with polka dots, lime-green striped wallpaper, and funky furniture; several also have space for yoga – complete with workout gear and videos – or treadmills, stationary bikes, and elliptical machines. Weekend rates save $20–30. ❼

Washington Plaza 10 Thomas Circle NW ☎202/842-1300 or 1-800/424-1140, ⓦwww .washingtonplazahotel.com; **McPherson Square Metro.** Convenient location three blocks from the Metro. Seasonal outdoor pool and deck, and great views across the Circle from the large rooms. Tourists mingle with business travelers in the lobby bar. Good weekend discounts. ❺

Washington Terrace 1515 Rhode Island Ave NW ☎202/232-7000, ⓦwww.washingtonterrace hotel.com; **Dupont Circle or Farragut North Metro.** Comfortable rooms, sleek modern decor, marble bathrooms, and outdoor terrace for summer dining. Not too far from the Dupont Circle nightlife scene. Weekend rates start at $159 and include breakfast. ❼

William Lewis House 1309 R St NW ☎202/462-7574 or 1-800/465-7574, ⓦwww.wlewishous .com; **McPherson Square Metro.** Elegantly decorated, gay-friendly B&B set in two century-old townhouses north of Logan Circle, within blocks of the Shaw neighborhood. All ten antique-filled rooms have shared bath. Out back there's a roomy porch and a hot tub set in a garden. Rates include continental breakfast on weekdays and a full American breakfast on weekends. It's ultra-cheap for what you get, so reservations are essential. ❸

Wyndham Washington 1400 M St NW ☎202/429-1700 or 1-800/996-3426, ⓦwww .wyndham.com; **McPherson Square Metro.** Contemporary comfort near Thomas Circle, with soaring atrium, a coffee shop, fitness club, and bars. Lower weekend rates often include breakfast and parking. Formerly the notorious *Washington Vista*, where ex-mayor Marion Barry was arrested in a drug sting. ❼

Old Downtown

Courtyard by Marriott 900 F St NW ☎202/638-4600, ⓦwww.marriott.com; **Gallery Place -Chinatown Metro.** Stunning 1891 Romanesque Revival bank that, following a $25-million renovation, has been converted into a truly original hotel. The lobby overflows with marble columns, elegant bronzework, and grand archways, while the spacious rooms (formerly offices) have varying layouts, and some sport big windows and sweeping views. Also worth a look are the old-fashioned conference rooms – one is housed in the bank's former vault. Save $100 by staying on a weekend. ❼

Grand Hyatt 1000 H St NW ☎202/582-1234 or 1-800/233-1234, ⓦwww.grandwashington .hyatt.com; **Metro Center Metro.** Its location opposite the Convention Center keeps this nearly 900-room hotel busy during the week. The twelve-story atrium and its lagoon, waterfalls, and glass elevators are a definite highlight, and renovated rooms are now properly stylish and modern. Includes an on-site deli-café, a restaurant, and a sports bar. Rates can drop by half on weekends. ❼

Harrington 1100 E St NW ☎202/628-8140 or 1-800/424-8532, ⓦwww.hotel-harrington.com; **Metro Center Metro.** One of the old, classic, and basic downtown hotels, of which few remain these days. Has a prime location near Pennsylvania Avenue. Air-conditioned rooms (singles to quads) have TV, though they're a bit worn around the edges. Still, the prices are tough to beat for the area. Cheap parking. ❸

Henley Park 926 Massachusetts Ave NW ☎202/638-5200 or 1-800/222-8474, ⓦwww .henleypark.com; **Mount Vernon Square-UDC Metro.** Former apartment building north of the Convention Center turned into a smart and stylish, Old World-elegant hotel; it's rather at odds with the borderline neighborhood. Though you should be wary at night, it's just a few blocks north of the happening Penn Quarter. ❻

JW Marriott 1331 Pennsylvania Ave NW ☎202/393-2000 or 1-800/228-9290, ⓦwww .marriott.com; **Metro Center or Federal Triangle Metro.** Flagship Marriott property in one of the best locations in the city; part of the National Place development and overlooking Freedom Plaza (ask for a room facing the avenue). Rooms are up to the elite corporate standard, plus there are several restaurants, a sports bar, and a health club with indoor pool. ❽

Marriott at Metro Center 775 12th St NW ☎202/737-2200 or 1-800/228-9290, ⓦwww .marriott.com; **Metro Center Metro.** Downtown business hotel close to the Convention Center with sizable rooms and a popular bar and grill. Weekends can be a real bargain, often including free breakfast and parking, and knocking up to $120 off the weekday rate. ❽

Monaco 700 F St NW ☎202/628-7177, ⓦwww .monaco-dc.com; **Gallery Place-Chinatown Metro.** Perhaps the most architecturally significant hotel in the area. Opened in 2002 in what was once a grand Neoclassical post office designed by Robert Mills. Nowadays, the offices have been remodeled into ultra-chic accommodation, complete with sophisticated modern rooms (with busts of Jefferson above the armoires), minimalist contemporary decor, and public spaces with marble floors and columns, plus grand spiral stairways. Weekend rates can drop to $170. ❼

Morrison-Clark Inn 1015 L St NW ☎202/898-1200 or 1-800/332-7898, ⓦwww .morrisonclark.com; **Mount Vernon Square-UDC Metro.** Antique-and-lace accommodation in a historic Victorian mansion complete with veranda. Located one block from the new Convention Center and two blocks from the Metro. Fifty-odd rooms in Victorian and other old-fashioned styles, balconies overlooking a courtyard, a comfortable lounge, and a solid restaurant. Although the area can get dicey at night, this is still one of Old Downtown's better deals. ❻

Red Roof Inn 500 H St NW ☎202/289-5959 or 1-800/733-7663, ⓦwww.redroof.com; **Gallery Place-Chinatown Metro.** Reasonable rates for this central location in the Penn Quarter, with Chinatown and the MCI Center on the doorstep. Rooms are merely standard, but there are good weekend and off-season discounts, and kids under 18 stay free. The café serves a buffet breakfast (not included in the room rate), and there's an exercise room with sauna. ❹

Washington 515 15th St NW ☎202/638-5900 or 1-800/424-9540, ⓦwww.hotelwashington .com; **Metro Center Metro.** Historic hotel next to the *Willard*, across from the Treasury Building. Its popular rooftop restaurant-bar, the *Sky Terrace* (see "Bars and clubs" chapter), boasts one of the city's best views. It rarely needs to offer discount rates, but during off-season weekends when Congress isn't in session rates can be reduced by $20 or more. ❺

Willard InterContinental 1401 Pennsylvania Ave NW ☎202/628-9100 or 1-800/327-0200, ⓦwww.washington.interconti.com; **Metro Center Metro.** A signature, truly iconic Washington hotel that dominates Pershing Park near the Treasury Building. In business on and off since the 1850s (most recently since the 1980s), it's a Beaux Arts marvel with acres of marble, mosaics, and glass; a stunning lobby and promenade; finely furnished rooms; and top-drawer clientele thick with politicos, lobbyists, and other honchos. Weekends around $250, weekdays $450. ❽

Upper Northwest

Days Inn 4400 Connecticut Ave NW ⓣ202/244-5600 or 1-800/329-7466, ⓦwww.daysinn.com; Van Ness UDC-Metro. Near the university and a Metro stop, and within reach of Rock Creek Park. Has a colorless, bunker-like exterior, but offers clean, if smallish, rooms with all the usual chain-hotel conveniences. ❸

Kalorama Guest House at Woodley Park 2700 Cathedral Ave NW ⓣ202/328-0860; Woodley Park-Zoo Metro. Victorian charm not far from the Metro in Woodley Park. Two houses (19 rooms, 12 en-suite) offering comfortable brass beds plus free continental breakfast, aperitifs, papers, and coffee. Book well in advance. Rooms with shared bathrooms go for $60, private bathrooms tack on another $20, and suites add another $30 on top of that. ❸

Marriott Wardman Park 2660 Woodley Rd NW ⓣ202/328-2000 or 1-800/228-9290, ⓦwww.marriott.com; Woodley Park–Zoo Metro. Woodley Park's monumentally historic, celebrity-filled hotel-palace that manages to be the largest hotel in DC (and frequent site of political fundraisers), with two pools, a health club, and restaurants bristling with attentive staff. Very good weekend and off-season discounts (down to $160) make this more affordable than you might think, though convention business keeps rooms full most of the year. ❽

Omni Shoreham 2500 Calvert St NW ⓣ202/234-0700 or 1-800/843-6664, ⓦwww.omnihotels.com; Woodley Park–Zoo Metro. Plush, grand, Washington institution bursting with history and overlooking the south chasm of Rock Creek Park. Features swank, comfortable rooms – which have been recently renovated – many with a view of the park, plus an outdoor pool, tennis courts, and the foliage-filled *Garden Court* for drinks. ❼

Woodley Park Guest House 2647 Woodley Rd NW ⓣ202/667-0218 or 1-866/667-0218, ⓦwww.woodleyparkguesthouse.com; Woodley Park-Zoo Metro. Pleasant guest house on residential Woodley Park side street (opposite the *Marriott*). Offers a quiet refuge with 16 rooms (most en-suite), ample parking, and free continental breakfast. It's well located near the Metro, the zoo, and a swath of good restaurants along Connecticut Avenue. Reservations essential. ❸

Waterfront and around

Channel Inn 650 Water St SW ⓣ202/554-2400 or 1-800/368-5668, ⓦwww.channelinn.com; Waterfront Metro. The city's first hotel right on the Waterfront, with some rooms looking across to East Potomac Park. There's free parking, an outdoor pool, a lounge, sundeck and choice of seafood restaurants nearby. ❺

Holiday Inn Capitol 550 C St SW ⓣ202/479-4000 or 1-800/465-4329, ⓦwww.holidayinncapitol.com; L'Enfant Plaza or Federal Center SW Metro. Variously sized rooms within walking distance of the Capitol and Smithsonian museums; includes a bar, restaurant, deli, and seasonal rooftop pool. As with all of this chain's hotels in DC, weekend rates are attractive – around $120. ❺

Loews L'Enfant Plaza 480 L'Enfant Plaza SW ⓣ202/484-1000 or 1-800/235-6397, ⓦwww.loewshotels.com; L'Enfant Plaza Metro. Very chic modern hotel a couple blocks south of the Mall (and north of the Waterfront itself), with direct access to the Metro. Spacious rooms in nineteenth-century French style (but not retro-tacky), most with river or city views, plus health club and rooftop pool. Special winter and weekend rates apply – inquire ahead. ❺

Hostels

Washington DC is hardly prime **hostel** territory, though there are a few cheapies – either actual or de facto hostels – scattered around if you know where to look. Except for the HI-Downtown, these are all pretty far afield, though not necessarily in the middle of nowhere. For rock-bottom alternatives, students can try contacting a **university** such as Georgetown (ⓣ202/687-4560); George Washington, in Foggy Bottom (ⓣ202/994-6688), Catholic, near the National Shrine (ⓣ202/319-5277); and American, in Upper Northwest (ⓣ202/885-3370). All offer a variety of dorms, doubles, and apartments at budget rates in summer (June–Aug). Arrangements must be made well in advance, and you may find there's a minimum stay requirement (as much as thirty days).

HI-Washington DC 1009 11th St NW, Old Downtown ☎202/737-2333, ⓦwww.hiwashingtondc.org; Metro Center Metro. Large (270 beds), clean, and very central hostel near the new Convention Center. Offers free continental breakfast, high-speed Internet access, renovated dorm rooms (male and female), and shared bathrooms, plus kitchen, lounge, laundry, luggage storage, enthusiastic staff, and organized activities. Also offers internships and volunteer opportunities. Open 24hr, but take care at night around here. Members save $3 on daily room rate. $29
Norwich Hostel 4607 Norwich Rd ☎240/472-2572, ⓦwww.hometown.aol.com/dclodging/index.htm; College Park-University of Maryland Metro. Five-bedroom complex way out in College Park, Maryland, but useful because it's near the Green Line Metro (20min to downtown DC), as well as the university. Private doubles and an outdoor deck are available. $1 lifetime membership required. $40 per day, $225 per week.
Washington International Student Center 2451 18th St NW, Adams-Morgan ☎202/667-7681 or 1-800/567-4150, ⓦwww.washingtondchostel.com; Dupont Circle or Woodley Park-Zoo Metro. Backpackers' accommodation in plain, multi-bedded dorm rooms. Offers Internet access, lockers for personal belongings, cable TV, and free pickup from bus and train stations. This is downtown DC's cheapest bed, but you may find the cramped surroundings, shared bathrooms, and "traveling" crowd tiresome after a while. Book at least two weeks in advance. $22
William Penn House 515 E Capitol St SE ☎202/543-5560, ⓦwww.quaker.org/penn-house; Capitol South or Eastern Market Metro. One of the least expensive spots in town, in a prime location just blocks from the Capitol. This Quaker-run hostel doesn't require religious observance, but does prefer (though not demand) that guests be active in progressive causes. Rooms hold 4–10 people, and breakfast is included. There's no curfew, but also no drugs or booze allowed. Morning services available if you're interested. $35

Eating

I n many ways, the Washington **dining** scene is an outlet of its power politics: fancy eateries are constantly in demand by politicians, lobbyists, and
corporate heavyweights, and there's almost as much business conducted
there – quietly, with a wink and a nod over prime rib – as there is in the
dull office corridors of K Street or the Federal Triangle. That said, the tight
competition between DC restaurants ensures that many new contenders on
the culinary scene fall by the wayside, regardless of the quality of their food or
service. Of course, the old-line stalwarts endure decade after decade, and some
of them – most prominently the *Old Ebbitt Grill* – actually serve tempting
entrees; others, though, get by for a while on their deal-making atmosphere
and leave the food as an afterthought. Our listings below naturally focus on
the best places to have an enjoyable meal, and leave the trendy, fly-by-night
joints to the pages of tourist brochures and corporate publicity campaigns.

Although it's generally a few steps behind New York, LA, and San Francisco,
the District keeps up with the times fairly well, and you're apt to find all manner of stylish Asian-fusion and New American restaurants as you would in
any other major city. Moreover, talented chefs and restaurateurs are not above
cloning their successes, so you can expect new offshoots of DC's most popular
eating houses, both in the city and in the suburbs.

As for specific **cuisines**, good Southern and Southwestern American food
isn't hard to find, while Georgetown, in particular, has a rash of renowned
New York-style saloon-restaurants serving everything from oysters to strip
steaks. Continental restaurants tend to be pricey, but there are some good bistros (Georgetown, again), while tapas, tortilla wraps, and, at the city's **diners**,
comfort foods like meat loaf and mac and cheese are abundant on the menus.
Altogether, the Chinese restaurants in Chinatown pale in comparison to Thai
or Vietnamese eateries (the best of which are across the river in Arlington).

Local and independent chains

Major chains – Starbucks, Au Bon Pain, Baja Fresh – can be found throughout the
city ad infinitum, but quirkier independent coffee shops are spreading fast, and there
are a few smaller local chains that are worth keeping an eye out for: Chesapeake
Bagel Bakery and Whatsa Bagel for great stuffed bagels, Julia's Empanadas for the
eponymous Mexican treat, and La Prima/Via Cucina for Italian deli sandwiches and
provisions. And whenever you're in the mood for coffee or tea, drop by Firehook
Bakery & Coffeehouse or Teaism, two very good local chains that have outposts
around the city.

13

EATING

There's also a comparatively large number of Ethiopian restaurants, especially in Adams-Morgan, and fans will be able to track down places serving food from countries as diverse as Argentina, Burma, Greece, and El Salvador.

Finally, for a break from the high-pressure dining scene, DC's **cafés** are good spots to knock back a latte while reading the *Post* or surfing the Internet. For a light meal or snack, they're also hard to beat, and of course can be found almost everywhere.

Neighborhoods

Certain **neighborhoods** tend to attract particular kinds of restaurants: homey trattorias are as scarce downtown as power-dining spots are in Adams-Morgan. Unfortunately, the areas in which visitors spend much of their time – the Mall and around the White House – have few good-value cafés and restaurants, though plenty of street vendors selling bland hot dogs and ice cream.

Happily, the excellent Metro system and sheer number of taxis mean that nowhere is really off-limits when it comes to choosing a restaurant. In Old Downtown, Chinatown is the only central ethnic enclave with its own swath of restaurants, though Penn Quarter, near the MCI Center, has recently emerged as a serviceable dining center. But it's only really in the outer neighborhoods that you can saunter up and down, checking out the options. There are also lots of opportunities to sit outside when the weather's agreeable – patios, sidewalk tables, and open-front windows are all standard in DC.

Georgetown has the most varied selection of dining places – rowdy saloons, diners, ethnic restaurants and some rather sniffy establishments – most of them in the few blocks on either side of the M Street/Wisconsin Avenue intersection. Dupont Circle (chiefly P St and Connecticut Ave) rivals Georgetown for its selection, with a recent influx of flashy new eateries reinvigorating a neighborhood already known for its designer Italian restaurants and coffee shops. DC's most down-to-earth area for dining out is Adams-Morgan, which also has the city's best bargains. Though prices are moving up slowly, 18th Street at Columbia Road is lined with scores of ethnic restaurants, all of which are still pretty good value. There are also pockets of worthwhile eateries east of Capitol Hill, along Connecticut Avenue in Upper Northwest, in Old Town Alexandria, and in scattered patches in northern Virginia – with some especially good Asian diners west of Arlington in far-flung spots like Fairfax and Falls Church.

The **listings** in this chapter are arranged geographically and alphabetically, and correspond to the neighborhoods in the guide. Neighborhood sections are in turn split into two divisions: "Cafés, snacks, and light meals," detailing spots good for a quick bite or a coffee, and "Restaurants." These two categories are not mutually exclusive; you can, of course, eat lunch or dinner at many of the diners, cafés, and coffee shops we've listed, and also perhaps get a light meal at many of the restaurants. At some spots it's essential to reserve a table, and you'll need to book well in advance to eat at the most renowned restaurants.

For listings by cuisine, turn to the box overleaf. For restaurants popular with a gay and lesbian clientele, see Chapter 16, "Gay DC." We've given each restaurant a price category (see box, p.266), which reflects the cost of a three-course meal, per person, excluding drinks, tax, and service. These are only a guideline, however: most people will be hard-pressed to get through three courses in many restaurants, and often you'll be able to eat for less than we suggest; on the other hand, don't forget you have to add the price of drinks to your bill and, in most places, at least fifteen percent for service. To keep the price of

African (also see Ethiopian)
Bukom Café p.266
Harambe Café p.266

American
Afterwords Café p.271
America p.269
Ardeo p.279
Art Gallery Bar & Grille p.273
Capitol City Brewing Company p.278
Carlyle Grand Café p.269
Cashion's Eat Place p.266
Clyde's p.275
Dish p.273
District Chophouse & Brewery p.278
Fran O'Brien's p.276
Hard Times Café p.268
J. Paul's p.275
Martin's Tavern p.275
Melrose p.274
The Monocle p.270
Morton's of Chicago p.269 and p.275
Mr Henry's p.270
New Heights p.280
Nora's p.272
Old Ebbitt Grill p.278
Perry's p.268
Sign of the Whale p.277
Stoney's p.277
Tabard Inn p.277
Two Quail p.270
U-topia p.279
Woodley Café p.280

Asian (also see specific cuisines)
Burma p.270
Café Asia p.276
House of Kabob p.277
Malaysia Kopitiam p.277
Nooshi p.276
Perry's p.268
Spices p.280
Ten Penh p.279
Yanyu p.280

Cajun
Cajun Bangkok p.268

Caribbean
Red Ginger p.275

Chinese
City Lights of China p.272
Hunan Chinatown p.270
Mark's Duck House p.269
Tony Cheng's p.271

Delis and diners
18th and U Duplex Diner p.266
Ben's Chili Bowl p.279
The Diner p.266
Five Guys p.268
Furin's p.274
Harry's p.278
Krupin's p.279
Loeb's Deli p.276
Luna Grill & Diner p.272
Reeve's Restaurant and Bakery p.278

Ethiopian
Fasika's p.266
Meskerem p.267
Zed's p.275

French
Au Pied de Cochon p.274
Bistro Bis p.270
Bistro du Coin p.271
Bistro Français p.274
Café la Ruche p.275
Citronelle p.276
Gerard's Place p.276
La Fourchette p.266

German
Café Berlin p.270
Café Mozart p.277

Greek
Taverna The Greek Islands p.270
Yanni's Greek Taverna p.280
Zorba's Café p.273

Indian
Amma Vegetarian Kitchen p.274
Bombay Bistro p.268
Bombay Club p.276
House of Kabob p.277

meals at a minimum, look for set lunches (from as little as $5) and early-bird dinners (usually served before 7pm); these are not just a feature of inexpensive restaurants, as many fancier establishments maintain sensible prices in the face of a volatile market.

Italian
Aquarelle p.273
Ecco Café p.268
Galileo p.276
I Matti p.266
Il Radicchio p.269
La Piazza p.268
Paolo's p.275
Pasta Mia p.267
Primi Piatti p.274
Tosca p.279

Japanese
Café Asia p.276
Spices p.280
Sushi Taro p.273

Jewish
Krupin's p.279
Loeb's Deli p.276

Mexican/Latin American
Andale p.278
Cactus Cantina p.279
Café Citron p.272
The Grill from Ipanema p.266
Lauriol Plaza p.267
Mixtec p.267

Middle Eastern
Lebanese Taverna p.280
Mama Ayesha's p.267
Meze p.267
Skewers p.273

Pizza
Alberto's Pizza p.271
Coppi's p.279
Pizza Mart p.266
Pizzeria Paradiso p.272
Vace p.279

Seafood
Blue Point Grill p.268
Custis & Brown p.280
Fish Market p.268
Grillfish p.276
H2O p.280
Johnny's Half Shell p.272
Kinkead's p.274
McCormick & Schmicks p.277

Nectar p.274
Phillips p.280

Southern
B. Smith's p.270
Florida Avenue Grill p.279
Old Glory p.275
Red Hot & Blue p.269
Southside 815 p.268
Vidalia p.277

Southwestern
Red Sage p.278
South Austin Grill p.268

Spanish
Gabriel p.272
Jaleo p.278
Las Tapas p.268

Steak
Annie's Paramount Steakhouse p.303
Morton's of Chicago p.000 and p.269, and 275
The Palm p.277

Thai
Bangkok Bistro p.274
Busara p.274
Cajun Bangkok p.268
Haad Thai p.278
Sala Thai p.273, and p.280

Vegetarian-friendly
Amma Vegetarian Kitchen p.274
Café Dalat p.269
Café Luna p.272
Luna Grill & Diner p.272
New Heights p.280
Nora's p.272
Yanyu p.280

Vietnamese
Café Dalat p.269
Four Sisters p.269
Nam Viet p.280
Queen Bee p.269
Saigon Inn p.275
Vietnam Georgetown p.275

Adams-Morgan

All the places listed in Adams-Morgan are within a few blocks of the junction of 18th Street and Columbia Road; the nearest Metro stops (noted below) are a good fifteen-minute walk away.

Cafés, snacks, and light meals

18th and U Duplex Diner 2004 18th St NW ☏202/234-7890; Dupont Circle Metro. Classic comfort foods such as mac and cheese and meat loaf go toe-to-toe with spruced -up favorites like salmon quesadillas. Sun & Mon 6am–11pm, Tues–Sat 6am–12.30am.

The Diner 2453 18th St NW ☏202/232-8800; Dupont Circle or Woodley Park-Zoo Metro. A high ceiling and weathered tile floor make this Adams-Morgan oasis, with chrome-and-red-leather stools, more stylish café than down-at-the-heel diner. Still, you can't go wrong with old favorites like omelets, pancakes, and bacon. Daily 24hr.

Pizza Mart 2445 18th St NW ☏202/234-9700. Clubgoers mop up an evening's worth of drinks with the hefty slices at this hole-in-the-wall pizzeria, one of several decent choices on this major Adams-Morgan strip. Daily 11am–4am.

Tryst 2459 18th St NW ☏202/232-5500; Dupont Circle or Woodley Park-Zoo Metro. Very popular, signature Adams-Morgan hangout where you can enjoy decent pastries and gourmet drinks, but also slurp down wine, beer, and even morning cocktails. Arty and relaxed, with the added bonus of Internet access. Mon–Thurs 6.30am–2am, Fri & Sat 6.30am–3am, Sun 8am–12.30am.

Restaurants

Bukom Café 2442 18th St NW ☏202/265-4600; Dupont Circle or Woodley Park-Zoo Metro. Laid-back restaurant-bar serving delicious African dishes like egusi, a broth of goat meat with ground melon seeds and spinach, and chicken yassa, baked with onions and spices, for around $10. All washed down with African beers and music (live Tues–Sat). Sun–Thurs 4pm–2am, Fri & Sat 4pm–3am. Moderate.

Cashion's Eat Place 1819 Columbia Rd NW ☏202/797-1819; Dupont Circle or Woodley Park-Zoo Metro. Renowned for its clever takes on New Southern cuisine; old-time dishes like casseroles, tarts, corncakes, grits, sweet potatoes, and fruit-and-nut pies are transformed into taste-bud-altering delights – for a rather high price. Tues 5.30–10pm, Wed–Sat 5.30–11pm, Sun 11.30am–2.30pm & 5.30–10pm. Expensive.

Fasika's 2477 18th St NW ☏202/797-7673; Dupont Circle or Woodley Park-Zoo Metro. This twenty-year institution is the most upmarket of the local Ethiopian places, with sidewalk seating and live music three nights a week. Spicy stews are $12 or so; also try the *doro wat* – chicken in pepper sauce – and Ethiopian steak tartare. Mon–Thurs 5–11pm, Fri–Sun noon–midnight. Moderate.

Grill from Ipanema 1858 Columbia Rd NW ☏202/986-0757; Woodley Park-Zoo Metro. Brazilian staples made with flair, highlighted by the *feijoada* (Brazilian meat stew), shrimp dishes, and scrumptious Sunday brunch. Try the baked clams to start, and watch your *caipirinha* (rum cocktail) intake. Mon–Thurs 5–10.30pm, Fri 5–11pm, Sat noon–11pm, Sun noon–10pm. Moderate.

Harambe Café 1771 U St NW, at Florida Ave and 18th ☏202/332-6435; Dupont Circle Metro. Simple, family-run African dining room with some of the cheapest food in town – filling chicken, beef, and lamb wot (spicy stew) served on *injera* bread, plus vegetarian platters and even a few pasta dishes – all accompanied by some great music. Mon–Thurs & Sun noon–1am, Fri & Sat noon–2am. Inexpensive.

I Matti 2436 18th St NW ☏202/462-8844; Dupont Circle or Woodley Park-Zoo Metro. Trendy trattoria-pizzeria with classic pastas, gnocchi, and pizzas, a great selection of antipasti, and grilled meat and fish specials. Dishes like braised rabbit, seared lamb, and grilled sea bass push the price up a notch. Mon–Thurs 5.30–10.30pm, Fri & Sat 5.30–11pm, Sun 5.30–10pm, also Mon–Sat noon–2.30pm. Moderate.

La Fourchette 2429 18th St NW ☏202/332-3077; Dupont Circle or Woodley Park-Zoo

Restaurant prices

These per-person prices include a three-course meal or equivalent, but exclude drinks, tax, and service:

Inexpensive: under $15
Moderate: $15–25

Expensive: $25–40
Very expensive: over $40

Metro. The brasserie's been here forever and the food – French classics served at closely packed tables – is reliable, if not particularly adventurous or surprising. Main bonus is the sidewalk patio. Mon–Fri 11.30am–10.30pm, Sat 10am–11pm, Sun 10am–10pm. Moderate.

Lauriol Plaza 1835 18th St NW ☏202/387-0035; **Dupont Circle Metro.** Serves scrumptious Latin American-styled *ceviche* and grilled meats. The place frequently gets packed with tourists and revelers, and the service can be spotty in such a cramped and busy atmosphere. Sun–Thurs 11am–11pm, Fri & Sat 11am–midnight. Moderate.

Mama Ayesha's 1967 Calvert St NW ☏202/232-5431; **Woodley Park-Zoo Metro.** Middle Eastern favorites like kibbeh, grape leaves, and the rest, with a lamb shank you can really sink your teeth into, plus spicy garlic lamb and chicken staples. Come for dinner, and be prepared to bust a gut. Daily noon–11pm. Moderate.

Meskerem 2434 18th St NW ☏202/462-4100; **Dupont Circle or Woodley Park-Zoo Metro.** One of the District's favorite Ethiopian hangouts, with funky decor and cheery staff. Eat with your hands, scooping food up with the sourdough *injera* bread. There are lots of vegetarian and seafood choices, and the *messob* platter gives you a taste of everything. Daily noon–midnight. Moderate.

Meze 2437 18th St NW ☏202/797-0017; **Dupont Circle or Woodley Park-Zoo Metro.** A wide array of delicious Turkish meze (the Middle East's answer to tapas), both hot and cold, is served in a fashionable restaurant-lounge setting. Kebabs, grape leaves, and apricot chicken are among the highlights. Mon–Thurs 5.30pm–2am, Fri 5.30pm–3am, Sat 11.30am–3am, Sun 11.30am–2am. Inexpensive (meze) to moderate (meals).

Mixtec 1792 Columbia Rd NW ☏202/332-1011; **Woodley Park-Zoo Metro.** Drab setting, but great-tasting, low-priced Mexican food like tacos and tortillas, plus roasted chicken and mussels steamed with chilis. You're unlikely to linger, but it's still worth a visit. Near the heart of Adams-Morgan. Sun–Thurs 10am–10pm, Fri & Sat 10am–11pm. Inexpensive.

Pasta Mia 1790 Columbia Rd NW ☏202/328-9114; **Woodley Park-Zoo Metro.** Expect long lines at this no-frills, family-run pasteria – it piles on the noodles and sauces at

13

EATING | Neighborhoods

Late-night eats

At the following eateries you'll be able to order a meal after midnight on at least one night of the week (usually Fri and/or Sat).

Afterwords Café (24hr Sat & Sun), Dupont Circle, p.271

Alberto's Pizza, Dupont Circle, p.271

America, Union Station, p.269

Art Gallery Bar & Grille, Foggy Bottom, p.273

Au Pied de Cochon (24hr), Georgetown, p.274

Ben's Chili Bowl, Shaw, p.279

Bistro du Coin, Dupont Circle, p.271

Bistro Français, Georgetown, p.274

Bukom Café, Adams-Morgan, p.266

Café Citron, Dupont Circle, p.272

Café la Ruche, Georgetown, p.275

Café Luna, Dupont Circle, p.272

Clyde's, Georgetown, p.275

Coppi's, Shaw, p.279

The Diner (24hr), Adams-Morgan, p.266

Fasika's, Adams-Morgan, p.266

Fish Market, Alexandria, p.268

Harambe Café, Adams-Morgan, p.266

Harry's, Old Downtown, p.278

J. Paul's, Georgetown, p.275

Jaleo, Old Downtown, p.278

Las Tapas, Alexandria, p.268

Martin's Tavern, Georgetown, p.275

Meze, Adams-Morgan, p.267

Mr Henry's, Capitol Hill, p.270

Old Ebbitt Grill, Old Downtown, p.278

Old Glory, Georgetown, p.275

Paolo's, Georgetown, p.275

Pizza Mart, Adams-Morgan, p.266

Sign of the Whale, New Downtown, p.277

Stoney's, New Downtown, p.277

U-topia, Shaw, p.279

prices so low it's worth the wait. Mon–Sat 6.30–10pm. Inexpensive.

Perry's 1811 Columbia Rd NW ☏202/234-6218; Woodley Park-Zoo Metro. Happening, in-crowd restaurant serving sushi and Asian-influenced American entrees like curried mussels and grilled salmon. Rooftop tables are always at a premium, and the drag queen brunch (Sun 11am–3pm) is a blast. Sun–Thurs 5.30–10.30pm, Fri & Sat 5.30–11.30pm; bar stays open 1hr later. Moderate.

Alexandria, VA

Cafés, snacks, and light meals

Ecco Café 220 N Lee St ☏703/684-0321; King Street Metro. Fine gourmet pizza and pasta joint with a neighborhood feel, featuring solid lunch specials, homemade noodles, decent steak and seafood, and a jazz brunch on Sunday. Mon–Thurs 11am–11pm, Fri & Sat 11am–midnight, Sun noon–10pm.

Five Guys 107 N Fayette St ☏703/549-7991; King Street Metro. This Old Town greasy spoon cooks its juicy hamburgers to order, piles on the fixings, and tucks 'em in a heavenly bun. The result? The best burger in the entire region, hands down. And don't forget the fries – the fresh, hand-cut, boardwalk-style chips boast their own loyal following. One of eight local branches. Daily 11am–10pm.

La Piazza 535 E Braddock Rd ☏703/519-7711; Braddock Road Metro. Straightforward Italian fare, and a good choice if a hoagie's what you crave, here made with generous portions of meat and cheese and just enough pepper, spice, and sauces to do the trick. Mon–Sat 11.30am–3pm & 5–10pm.

Restaurants

Blue Point Grill 600 Franklin St ☏703/739-0404; King Street Metro. Extremely fresh and delicious seafood earns this Old Town jewel its reputation as one of Alexandria's best restaurants. In warmer weather pass up sitting in the elegant dining room for a spot on the veranda. Daily 11am–3pm & 5.30–10pm. Expensive.

Cajun Bangkok 907 King St ☏703/836-0038; King Street Metro. The incendiary blend of Thai and Cajun fare served here goes straight for the jugular with items like a tasty Thai jerk chicken. While Thai dishes

dominate the appetizers (try the full-flavor Crying Tiger – grilled steak with a spicy sauce), Cajun dishes with Asian accents, like the zesty Cajun Bangkok Gumbo, make up the bulk of the entrees. Mon–Thurs 11.30am–10pm, Fri 11.30am–11pm, Sat 5–11pm, Sun 5–10pm. Moderate.

Fish Market 105 King St ☏703/836-5676; King Street Metro. Brick-walled restaurant with terrace a block from the water, serving oysters and chowder at the bar and fried-fish platters, pastas, and fish entrees, not to mention a mean spicy shrimp meal. Mon–Thurs 11am–midnight, Fri & Sat 11am–2am. Moderate.

Hard Times Café 1404 King St ☏703/837-0050; King Street Metro. Four styles of fiery chili; good wings, rings, and fries; tub-thumping country music; and savory microbrews – add up to one of Alexandria's better Tex-Mex/American restaurants. One of many in a local chain. Mon–Thurs 11am–10pm, Fri & Sat 11am–11pm, Sun noon–10pm. Inexpensive.

Las Tapas 710 King St ☏703/836-4000; King Street Metro. Best of the local tapas bars, with a wide selection of authentic small plates, plus rich paella, glass after glass of tasty sangria, and regular (free) flamenco sessions. Sun–Wed 11.30am–10pm, Thurs 11.30am–11pm, Fri & Sat 11.30am–1am. Moderate.

South Austin Grill 801 King St ☏703/684-8969; King Street Metro. Quality Tex-Mex fare packs lively crowds into this Old Town institution. The Cadillac-sized fajitas, stacked nachos, taste-bud-tingling salsas, and zesty margaritas make the long waits worthwhile. Sun & Mon 11.30am–10pm, Tues–Thurs 11.30am–11pm, Fri & Sat 11.30am–midnight. Moderate.

Southside 815 815 S Washington St ☏703/836-6222; King Street Metro. Deep-fried Southern cooking just the way you like it, heavy with good old-fashioned favorites like biscuits with ham gravy, thick and buttery cornbread, BBQ shrimp, crab fritters, and straight-up crawdads and catfish. Sun–Thurs 11.30am–10.30pm, Fri & Sat 11.30am–11pm. Moderate.

Arlington and Northern Virginia

Restaurants

Bombay Bistro 3570 Chain Bridge Rd, Fairfax, VA ☏703/359-5810; Vienna Metro. Though you'll have to truck way out to the suburbs west of Arlington, this Indian favorite is worth it for its delicious tandoori and vindaloo, plus more inventive entrees with lamb curry, mussels, and scallops. Mon–Fri 11.30am–2.30pm, Sat & Sun noon–3pm, Sun–Thurs 5–10pm, Fri & Sat 5–10.30pm. Inexpensive.

Café Dalat 3143 Wilson Blvd, Arlington ☎703/276-0935; Clarendon Metro. Brisk, Formica-tabled Vietnamese joint with a popular lunch buffet and some tasty menu specials like grilled lemon chicken and five-spice pork. Most dishes come with noodles and greens, making for pretty cheap eats. There's also a good selection of vegetarian dishes. Sun–Thurs 11am–9.30pm, Fri & Sat 11am–10.30pm. Inexpensive.

Carlyle Grand Café 4000 S 28th St, Arlington ☎703/931-0777. Steak and seafood with a nouveau twist, mixing in other, more exotic flavors to end up with tasty lobster potstickers, jambalaya, and crab fritters. Mon–Thurs 11.30am–11pm, Fri & Sat 11.30am–midnight, Sun 10.30am–11pm. Moderate.

Four Sisters 6769 Wilson Blvd, Falls Church, VA ☎703/538-6717; East Falls Church Metro. It's worth venturing out to this spot for delicious spicy squid, crispy shrimp, lemongrass beef, and other Vietnamese favorites. Sun–Thurs 10.30am–10pm, Fri & Sat 10.30am–11pm. Inexpensive.

Il Radicchio 1801 Clarendon Blvd, Arlington ☎703/276-2627; Court House Metro. Part of a chain that offers cheap wood-fired pizzas and spaghetti-and-sauce combos; three other citywide branches. Mon–Sat 11am–10pm. Inexpensive.

Mark's Duck House 6184 Arlington Blvd, Falls Church, VA ☎703/532-2125; East Falls Church Metro. More top-notch Asian fare in the 'burbs – this one offers primo Chinese food, such as Peking duck, salty shrimp, and lunchtime dim sum. Not to be missed if you're in the area. Sun–Thurs 10am–10pm, Fri & Sat 10am–11pm. Moderate.

Morton's of Chicago 1631 Crystal Square Ave, Arlington ☎703/418-1444; Crystal City Metro. Local branch of the chic steakhouse chain, with the standard array of delicious cuts of beef, veal, and lobster, plus a clubby atmosphere good for smoking and boozing. Mon–Sat 5–11pm, Sun 5–10pm. Expensive.

Queen Bee 3181 Wilson Blvd, Arlington ☎703/527-3444; Clarendon Metro. No question – the best Vietnamese food in town, with renowned crunchy spring rolls, seafood over crispy noodles, grilled pork, huge bowls of noodle soup, Saigon pancakes, and grilled shrimp. Expect to wait in line. Daily 11am–10pm. Inexpensive.

Red Hot & Blue 1600 Wilson Blvd, Arlington ☎703/276-7427; Court House Metro. Also 3014 Wilson Blvd, at Highland ☎703/243-1510; Clarendon Metro. Memphis barbecue joint that spawned a chain, serving the best ribs in the area. A rack, with coleslaw and beans, costs just ten bucks. Many other suburban branches. Sun–Thurs 11am–10pm, Fri & Sat 11am–11pm. Inexpensive.

Capitol Hill

Cafés, snacks, and light meals

Bread and Chocolate 666 Pennsylvania Ave SE ☎202/547-2875; Eastern Market Metro. Popular bakery and coffeehouse with solid sandwiches and street-view seating, located in this strip's main people-watching zone. Mon–Sat 7am–7pm, Sun 8am–6pm.

Le Bon Café 210 2nd St SE ☎202/547-7200; Capitol South Metro. Good for a wholesome lunch of soup, salad, or sandwich, and close to the Library of Congress. Mon–Fri 7.30am–4pm, Sat & Sun 8.30am–3.30pm.

Market Lunch Eastern Market, 7th Ave SE ☎202/547-8444; Eastern Market Metro. Excellent spot for munch-and-go, market hall-counter meals – sandwiches and fries, salads, crab cakes, and assorted fish platters – served to a loyal band of shoppers and suit-and-tie staffers. Tues–Sat 7.30am–3pm, Sun 11am–3.30pm.

Murky Coffee 660 Pennsylvania Ave SE ☎202/546-5228; Eastern Market Metro. Inspired by authentic Italian brewmaking, espresso drinks here pack an authentic punch, and are straight-up black – not murky. Also sells pastries and coffee by the pound. Mon–Sat 7am–9pm, Sun 8am–7pm.

Restaurants

America Union Station, 50 Massachusetts Ave NE ☎202/682-9555; Union Station Metro. Bustling restaurant-bar with a huge menu of regional staples from all corners of the US, but the people-watching is better than the

13

EATING | Neighborhoods

food – mostly regional staples and nothing too adventurous. Double-decker restaurant inside, concourse or gallery seating outside. Mon–Thurs & Sun 11.30am–11.30pm, Fri & Sat 11.30am–1am. Moderate.

B. Smith's Union Station, 50 Massachusetts Ave NE ☏202/289-6188; Union Station Metro. Southern cooking brings in folks hankering after fried-green tomatoes, Cajun paella, catfish, and red beans 'n' rice, though just as many come because of the glorious restaurant space (this was once the station's presidential waiting room). Mon–Thurs 11.30am–4pm & 5–11pm, Fri & Sat 11.30am–4pm & 5pm–midnight, Sun 11.30am–4pm & 5–9pm. Expensive.

Bistro Bis 15 E St NW ☏202/661-2700; Union Station Metro. One of the District's tastiest French restaurants connected to a chic boutique hotel (the *George*; see "Accommodation" chapter), with the requisite upmarket continental fare – traditional soups, seafood, and grilled meats – featuring the occasional twist. Mon–Sat 7–10am, Sun 7.30–10am, daily 11.30am–2.30pm & 5.30–10pm. Expensive.

Café Berlin 322 Massachusetts Ave NE ☏202/543-7656; Union Station Metro. The perfect spot to fill up on your favorite gut-busting German food, with all the savory, Old-World favorites from pork Jaegerschnitzel to potato pancakes to spiced herring with onions and apples. Mon–Thurs 11.30am–10pm, Fri & Sat 11.30am–11pm, Sun 4–10pm. Moderate.

Las Placitas 517 8th St SE ☏202/543-3700; Eastern Market Metro. Great-value Mexican standards and Salvadoran specials pack the tables nightly at this no-nonsense eatery. Another Capitol Hill branch at 723 8th St SE ☏202/546-9340. Mon–Thurs 11.30am–3pm & 5–10.30pm, Fri 11.30am–3pm & 5–11pm, Sat & Sun 4–11pm. Moderate.

The Monocle 107 D St NE ☏202/546-4488; Union Station Metro. Although some criticize this elegant saloon-bar-restaurant as stuffy, that's likely what draws the congressional patrons, who duck in for delicious crab cakes, steaks, and the like in between votes. Mon–Fri 11.30am–midnight. Expensive.

Mr Henry's 601 Pennsylvania Ave SE ☏202/546-8412; Eastern Market Metro. Saloon and restaurant with outside patio, charcoal grill, and loyal mixed gay and

straight crowd. Even the most expensive choices – the steak and shrimp plates – are typically below $10; burgers are half-price on Mon, and jazz trios play weekly. Sun–Thurs 11am–midnight, Fri & Sat 11am–1am. Inexpensive.

Taverna The Greek Islands 305 Pennsylvania Ave SE ☏202/547-8360; Capitol South Metro. Order something from the all-meat grill at this rustic, friendly Greek joint and you won't need appetizers, or choose from the pricier fish specialties; wine is by the carafe. A carryout section is in the basement. Mon–Sat 11am–11.30pm. Moderate.

Two Quail 320 Massachusetts Ave NE ☏202/543-8030; Union Station Metro. Romantic little bistro (spread over a trio of townhouses) serving changing menus of California Cuisine-styled food, including dinner entrees such as Cornish game hen with chipotle sauce. Lunches are a deal at $10–15. Reservations recommended. Mon–Fri 11.30am–2.30pm & 5.30–10.30pm, Sat & Sun 5.30–11.30pm. Expensive.

Chinatown

Restaurants

Burma 740 6th St NW ☏202/638-1280; Gallery Place-Chinatown Metro. Plain second-floor dining room with Burmese art, approachable staff, and very filling food. The noodle dishes are great (try the pork in black bean sauce), as is the Thai and Chinese beer; a handful of veggie meals are also on offer. Daily 6–10pm, also Mon–Fri 11am–3pm. Inexpensive.

Eat First 609 H St NW ☏202/289-1703; Gallery Place-Chinatown Metro. You should scour the menu first at this wide-ranging Cantonese diner, which has an array of Asian selections such as shrimp dumplings, roast duck, squid, pan-fried noodles, and on and on. Daily 10.30am–11pm. Moderate.

Hunan Chinatown 624 H St NW ☏202/783-5858; Gallery Place-Chinatown Metro. Sleekly furnished, Western-friendly restaurant (you'll have to ask for chopsticks) where spiciness replaces taste on occasion – though the tea-smoked duck is a definite standout. You probably won't need appetizers, but the wontons in chili sauce are tasty. Sun–Thurs 11am–10pm, Fri & Sat 11am–11pm. Moderate.

Lei Garden 629 H St NW ☏202/216-9696; Gallery Place-Chinatown Metro. Dumplings, dim sum, stir-fry, Peking duck, and even casseroles and barbecued meats fit the bill at this local favorite, which also features a great $12 buffet. Mon–Thurs 11.30am–11pm, Fri & Sat 11.30am–midnight, Sun noon–10.30pm. Moderate.

Matchbox 713 H St NW ☏202/289-4441; **Gallery Place-Chinatown Metro.** A good spot if, for some reason, you find yourself in Chinatown without a hankering for Chinese food. The gourmet pizzas are the undeniable high point, but the seafood and smallish hamburgers are savory as well. Mon–Thurs 11.30am–10pm, Fri & Sat 11.30am–11pm. Moderate.

Tony Cheng's 619 H St NW ☏202/842-8669 (Mongolian), ☏202/371-8669 (seafood); **Gallery Place-Chinatown Metro.** Downstairs is a fun, do-it-yourself, all-you-can-eat Mongolian barbecue, while upstairs is a Cantonese seafood restaurant with daily dim sum (11am–3pm) that's been visited by sundry sporting stars and every president since Carter. Mon–Thurs & Sun 11am–11.30pm, Fri & Sat 11am–midnight. Inexpensive (barbecue/dim sum); moderate (meals).

Dupont Circle

Cafés, snacks, and light meals

Afterwords Café 1517 Connecticut Ave NW ☏202/387-1462; **Dupont Circle Metro.** This spot in the back of Kramerbooks serves breakfast and brunch, great cappuccino, and full meals – salad, pastas, grills, and sandwiches, with plenty of vegetarian choices. Live blues and jazz Wednesday through Saturday. Sun–Thurs 7.30am–1am, Fri & Sat 24hr.

Alberto's Pizza 2010 P St NW ☏202/986-2121; **Dupont Circle Metro.** Little more than a basement-level take-out stand, *Alberto's* nevertheless draws major lines on weekend nights for its excellent deals on thin-crust pizza: a "slice" is one-quarter of an entire pie, and starts at just $3. Daily 11.30am–3pm, Sun–Thurs 4.30–10pm, Fri & Sat 4.30pm–4am.

Cyberstop Café 1513 17th St NW ☏202/234-2470; **Dupont Circle Metro.** One of DC's few cybercafés, this laid-back neighborhood coffee shop serves good java, cakes, and bagels, with seating inside the arty townhouse or out front on the sidewalk patio. Mon–Fri 7am–midnight, Sat & Sun 8am–midnight.

Firehook Bakery & Coffeehouse 1909 Q St NW ☏202/588-9296; **Dupont Circle Metro.** Renowned bakery-café serving up daily sandwich specials and a huge range of breads (also pies, desserts, and cookies), plus good coffee at reasonable prices. There's not much in the way of comfortable seating at this location, but there are plenty of other branches citywide if you'd prefer to pull up a chair. Mon–Fri 7am–9pm, Sat & Sun 8am–9pm.

Java House 1645 Q St NW ☏202/387-6622; **Dupont Circle Metro.** A local, gay-friendly favorite arguably serving the neighborhood's best coffee – grab a cup to go or scramble for a sunny seat on the packed patio, a good spot to read a book or have an afternoon chat. Muesli, bagels, and sandwiches are on offer throughout the day. Daily 7am–midnight.

Marvelous Market 1511 Connecticut Ave NW ☏202/332-3690; **Dupont Circle Metro.** Superb carryout deli with ready-made sandwiches, cheeses and olives, fresh produce, and very good brownies and bread. Mon–Sat 8am–9pm, Sun 8am–8pm.

Newsroom 1803 Connecticut Ave NW ☏202/332-1489; **Dupont Circle Metro.** Coffee, snacks, and pastries are served at this newsstand, which carries one of DC's best selections of hipster magazines, British and French imports, and hard-to-find newspapers. There's Internet access upstairs. Daily 7am–9pm.

Teaism 2009 R St NW ☏202/667-3827; **Dupont Circle Metro.** Serene Dupont Circle teahouse serving Japanese bentos, Thai curries, ginger scones, and, of course, lots of good tea. If you're looking to stock up on tea leaves, you'll find three dozen types on offer, as well as teapots and mugs. Also at 800 Connecticut Ave NW, New Downtown ☏202/835-2233, and 400 8th St NW, Old Downtown ☏202/638-6010. Mon–Thurs 8am–10pm, Fri 8am–11pm, Sat 9am–11pm, Sun 9am–10pm.

Restaurants

Bistro du Coin 1738 Connecticut Ave NW ☏202/234-6969; **Dupont Circle Metro.** Classic bistro with a superb bar, boisterous atmosphere, and genuine French food that actually tastes like continental cuisine. All at prices that won't cost you your Armani shirt. Mon–Wed 11.30am–11pm, Thurs–Sat 11.30am–1am, Sun 11am–11pm. Moderate–Expensive.

Café Citron 1343 Connecticut Ave NW
☎202/530-8844; Dupont Circle Metro. Hip
Dupont South restaurant serving tasty
Caribbean-influenced Latin food; try the
ceviche or fill up on one of the popular
fajitas. By ten, the dining crowd makes way
for smartly dressed partyers here to groove
to tunes provided by DJs or live Brazilian
or salsa/merengue bands – and to fuel up
on some of the best *mojitos* in town. Mon–
Thurs 11.30am–2am, Fri 11.30am–3am,
Sat 4pm–3am. Moderate.

Café Luna 1633 P St NW ☎202/387-4005;
Dupont Circle Metro. One of Dupont's best
spots. Soups, salads, sandwiches, pasta,
pizza, and Italian coffee are served in this
laid-back hangout with a handful of sunny
sidewalk tables. Caters especially to the
vegetarian crowd. Also breakfast and weekend brunches. Mon–Thurs 8am–11pm,
Fri 8am–1.30am, Sat 10am–1.30am, Sun
10am–11pm. Inexpensive.

**City Lights of China 1731 Connecticut Ave
NW** ☎202/265-6688; Dupont Circle Metro.
Well-regarded Chinese restaurant, with
spicy Szechuan and Hunan specialties
and a strong emphasis on seafood (try
the Hunan shrimp). It's also one of the few
Chinese spots that does vegetarian food
right – standouts include the steamed
dumplings and garlic eggplant. Mon–Fri
11.30am–11pm, Sat noon–11pm, Sun
noon–10.30pm. Moderate.

Gabriel 2121 P St NW ☎202/956-6690;
Dupont Circle Metro. New-wave Spanish
restaurant at the *Radisson Barceló* hotel
(see "Accommodation" chapter) that has
garnered plaudits for its inventive tapas
– like duck *taquitos* – and sherry list, great

Sunday brunch, and a full range of delicately flavored, lightly spiced grilled and
seared meat and fish entrees. Reservations recommended. Daily 7–10am, Sun
11am–3pm, Tues–Thurs 5.30–10pm, Fri &
Sat 5.30–10.30pm. Expensive.

Johnny's Half Shell 2002 P St NW ☎202/296-
2021; Dupont Circle Metro. Retro 1920s
decor and a swank marble bar make for an
agreeable atmosphere, in which you can
sample local specialties like crab cakes,
fried oysters, and seafood stew – go for the
gumbo or, in summer, the soft-shell crabs.
Mon–Thurs 11.30am–10.30pm, Fri & Sat
11.30am–11pm, Sun 5–10pm. Moderate–Expensive.

Luna Grill & Diner 1301 Connecticut Ave NW
☎202/835-2280; Dupont Circle Metro. Atypical
diner with bright decor, planetary murals
and mosaics, and wholesome blue-plate
specials, "green plate" (vegetarian) dishes,
and organic coffees and teas. Also makes
for an excellent weekend brunch spot; try
the "Eggs Neptune" – eggs Benedict with a
Maryland twist, crab cakes. Outdoor patio
adds to the allure. Mon–Thurs 8am–11pm,
Fri & Sat 8am–1am, Sun 8am–10pm. Inexpensive.

Nora's 2132 Florida Ave NW ☎202/462-5143;
Dupont Circle Metro. One of DC's best
eateries (with prices to match), set in a
converted store with folk-art quilts
decorating the walls. The all-organic fare
includes oddball Items like veal-and-
cashew curry and Amish duck confit.
Book ahead. Mon–Thurs 5.30–10pm. Fri
& Sat 5.30–10.30pm. Very expensive.

Pizzeria Paradiso 2029 P St NW ☎202/223-
1245; Dupont Circle Metro. Arguably DC's

Ten great places for brunch

Weekend brunch – mostly Sunday, but some Saturdays, too – is a Washington institution. The city's most prestigious hotels offer the best spreads and provide visitors
and locals with a relatively inexpensive way to experience their dining rooms. But
many non-hotel restaurants also pride themselves on their brunches. The places
listed below may not all offer the swanky surroundings and free champagne refills
of the hotels, but are still, in their own way, excellent.

best pizzeria, with lines forming nightly on the steps outside for a short list of familiar Italian staples. If you've simply got to have a slice but can't bear the wait and the crowd, cross the street to *Alberto's* (see p.271) for quick relief. Mon–Thurs 11.30am–11pm, Fri & Sat 11am–midnight, Sun noon–10pm. Inexpensive.

Sala Thai 2016 P St NW ☎202/234-5698; **Dupont Circle Metro.** Prominent Thai restaurant with stylish decor and a range of staples – the usual soups and pad thai – as well as surprises like soft-shell crab. Mon–Thurs 11.30am–10.30pm, Fri & Sat noon–11pm, Sun noon–10.30pm. Inexpensive.

Skewers 1633 P St NW ☎202/387-7400; **Dupont Circle Metro.** It has Dupont Circle's funkiest interior, but the food doesn't take a backseat to the decor. The restaurant (above *Café Luna*) is tops for kebabs, eggplant, seafood, and delicately flavored rice, but you can also put together a meal of Middle Eastern appetizers. Mon–Thurs 11.30am– 10.30pm, Fri 11.30am–midnight, Sat noon–midnight, Sun 11am–10pm. Moderate.

Sushi Taro 1507 17th St NW ☎202/462-8999; **Dupont Circle Metro.** One of DC's best Japanese restaurants; if raw fish isn't your thing, choose from the selection of tasty curries and noodles. When the cherry blossoms start to bloom, keep an eye out for the annual all-you-can-eat sushi-fest. Mon–Fri 11.30am–2pm & 5.30–10pm, Sat & Sun 5.30–10pm. Moderate–Expensive.

Zorba's Café 1612 20th St NW ☎202/387-8555; **Dupont Circle Metro.** Filling Greek combo platters, kebabs, pizzas, and pita-bread sandwiches, as well as daily specials and traditional dishes like bean casserole and spinach pie. Wash down one of the very good gyro sandwiches with pitchers of draft beer. Everything comes on plastic plates at this self-service spot. Hard-to-get sidewalk seating in summer. Mon–Sat 11am–11.30pm, Sun 11.30am–10.30pm. Inexpensive.

Foggy Bottom

Cafés, snacks, and light meals

The Breadline 1751 Pennsylvania Ave NW ☎202/822-8900; **Farragut West Metro.** DC's best sandwiches made with DC's best bread. This superb open bakery (with seats inside and out) also offers pizza, empana-

das, flatbreads, salads, smoothies, coffee, and tea, using (pricey) organic ingredients if possible. Mon–Fri 7am–3.30pm.

Café des Artistes 500 17th St NW ☎202/639-1700; **Farragut West or Farragut North Metro.** Corcoran Gallery café serving agreeable lunches. Go for the shrimp salad on a croissant or the grilled chicken Caesar salad. The highlight is its signature Gospel Brunch ($24), a famed Sunday morning event where you eat to the sound of musical evangelizing (10.30am–2pm). Mon, Wed & Fri–Sun 11am–2pm, Thurs 11am–3pm & 4–8pm.

Capitol Grounds 2100 Pennsylvania Ave NW ☎202/293-2057; **Foggy Bottom-GWU Metro.** A lively spot near George Washington University known for gourmet sandwiches and breakfast staples, plus good coffee and a convivial atmosphere. Also at 1455 Pennsylvania Ave NW (☎202/637-9618). Mon–Fri 7am–6pm, Sat 8.30am–4pm, Sun 9am–3pm.

Cosi 1700 Pennsylvania Ave NW ☎202/638-6366; **Farragut West Metro.** Just a short hop from both the White House and Corcoran, this chain lunch spot is good for a quick bite while on the tour circuit – though the other branches can be hit-or-miss. An assortment of tasty, if pricey, sandwiches on freshly baked flatbread. Mon–Fri 7am–6pm, Sat & Sun 9am–5pm.

Restaurants

Aquarelle 2650 Virginia Ave NW ☎202/965-2300; **Foggy Bottom-GWU Metro.** Now that George Dubya's favorite, *Jeffrey's*, has been driven away, this old standard is back in its original location in the *Watergate* hotel. A good thing, too, as it's an excellent choice for high-end Mediterranean cuisine in an upscale setting, with a complex blend of rice, pasta, and seafood dishes. Some good grilled offerings as well. Daily 7am–10.30am, 11am–2pm, 5–10pm. Very expensive.

Art Gallery Bar & Grille 1712 I St NW ☎202/298-6658; **Farragut West Metro.** Play the Wurlitzer jukebox and soak up the Art Deco ambience or sit on the outdoor patio as you tuck into breakfast, salads, burgers, sandwiches, omelets, pizza, and grills. Mon–Fri 6.30am–1am. Moderate.

Dish *River Inn* 924 25th St NW, ☎202/337-7600; **Foggy Bottom-GWU Metro.** Tasty newfangled versions of classic American fare, from fruit cobbler and fried chicken to steaks and pot roast, with a heftier price tag than you'll find in any diner. Given the posh atmosphere popular with the chattering classes, the restaurant name is as much a verb as a noun. Daily 11.30am–2.30pm & 5–11pm. Expensive.

Kinkead's 2000 Pennsylvania Ave NW ☎202/296-7700; **Foggy Bottom-GWU Metro.** One of DC's favorite, and priciest, restaurants, with a contemporary menu specializing in fish and seafood, from salmon stew to monkfish medallions. Since it's plenty popular, you'll need to book ahead. Daily 11.30am–2.30pm & 5.30–10pm. Very expensive.

Melrose 1201 24th St NW ☎202/955-3899; **Foggy Bottom-GWU Metro.** New-styled American-fusion food – Thai calamari, spicy duck confit, etc – at this ultra-chic hotel restaurant that draws crowds of foodies and diners in-the-know. Daily 7am–2.30pm, 5.30–10.30pm. Very expensive.

Nectar *GW University Inn,* **824 New Hampshire Ave NW** ☎202/337-6620; **Foggy Bottom-GWU Metro.** Quality hotel restaurant serving up delicious seafood and new American fare – from sushi and soft-shell crab to foie gras – though a bit on the pricey side at $25 per entree. Mon–Fri 11.30am–2.30pm, Sun–Thurs 5–10pm, Fri & Sat 5–11pm. Expensive.

Primi Piatti 2013 I St NW ☎202/223-3600; **Farragut West or Foggy Bottom-GWU Metro.** Major-league Italian restaurant with a knack for creating savory gourmet pizzas – with ingredients such as goat cheese and prosciutto – that are cheaper than the meat-and-pasta dishes. Daily 11.30am –2.30pm, 5.30–10.30pm. Moderate.

Georgetown

Cafés, snacks, and light meals

Booeymonger 3265 Prospect St NW ☎202/333-4810. Crowded deli-coffee shop at the corner of Prospect and Potomac streets. Excellent for its signature sandwiches like the Gatsby Arrow (roast beef and Brie) and the Patty Hearst (turkey and bacon with Russian dressing). Daily 8am–midnight.

Ching Ching Cha 1063 Wisconsin Ave NW ☎202/333-8288. Bright and pleasant tearoom transports teetotalers to Old Asia with black teas and herbal infusions, a menu of savory items like bentos and dumplings, and an

array of snazzy collectibles for sale. Tues–Sat 11.30am–9pm, Sun 11.30am–7pm.

Dean & Deluca 3276 M St NW ☎202/342-2500. Superior self-service café (and fantastic attached deli-market with sushi stand) in one of M Street's most handsome and historic red-brick buildings. Croissants and cappuccino, designer salads, pasta, and sandwiches. Café Mon–Thurs & Sun 8am–8pm, Fri & Sat 8am–9pm; market Mon–Thurs & Sun 10am–8pm, Fri & Sat 10am–9pm.

Furin's 2805 M St NW ☎202/965-1000. Georgetown's best bet for a home-cooked eggs-and-fries breakfast, blue-plate deli sandwiches, potato or chicken salads, and tasty desserts and pastries. Mon–Fri 7.30am–7pm, Sat 8am–5pm.

Restaurants

Amma Vegetarian Kitchen 3291 M St NW ☎202/625-6625. A safe haven for vegetarians and vegans, this South Indian joint specializes in *dosa* (lentil and rice-flour wraps) but also has very good curries and breads, along with veggie meatballs. Mon–Fri 11.30am–2.30pm & 5.30–10pm, Sat 11.30am–3.30pm & 5.30–10.30pm, Sun noon–3.30pm & 5.30–10pm. Inexpensive.

Au Pied de Cochon 1335 Wisconsin Ave NW ☎202/337-6400. Cheap French bistro-bar serving breakfast (until noon), $10 early-bird dinners (3–8pm), and à la carte eggs, fish, coq au vin, steaks, and the like. An old, weathered, Georgetown favorite. Daily 24hr. Inexpensive–Moderate.

Bangkok Bistro 3251 Prospect St NW ☎202/337-2424. In a stylish, often crowded, dining room, old favorites (tom yum, pad thai, shrimp cakes, and satay) are offered alongside spicy beef curries and chili prawns. Mon–Thurs noon–11pm, Fri & Sat noon–midnight, Sun noon–10.30pm. Moderate.

Bistro Français 3128 M St NW ☎202/338-3830. Renowned for its French cooking, from simple steak frites and rotisserie chicken to roast pigeon and lamb sausage. Early-bird (5–7pm) and late-night (10.30pm–1am) set dinners for around $20. Sun–Thurs 11am–3am, Fri & Sat 11am–4am. Moderate.

Busara 2340 Wisconsin Ave NW ☎202/337-2340. Designer Thai eatery with super-sleek decor and yuppie clientele. The food is a mix of authentic and inventive, including items like the Shrimp Bikini (deep-fried prawns in a spring roll) and flounder in chili sauce. Mon–Fri 11.30am–3pm, Sun–Thurs 5–11pm, Fri & Sat 5pm–midnight. Moderate.

Café la Ruche 1039 31st St NW ☎202/965-2684. Relaxing bistro with patio seating ideal for dining alone or in twos in warmer weather. Sample the onion soup, quiches, and croque monsieur, or drop by for pastries and espresso. Mon–Thurs 11.30am–11.30pm, Fri 11.30am–1am, Sat 10am–1am, Sun 10am–10.30pm. Inexpensive.

Citronelle in the Latham Hotel, 3000 M St ☎202/625-2150. Huge player on the DC dining scene, serving up French-inspired cuisine with a California flair, and set-price dinners starting at $125. Reserve in advance, dress chic, and bring plenty of attitude. Daily 7am–10.30am, Mon–Fri noon–2pm, Sun–Thurs 6.30–10pm, Fri & Sat 6.30–10.30pm. Very expensive.

Clyde's 3236 M St NW ☎202/333-9180. Classic New York-style saloon-restaurant featuring the obligatory checked tablecloths, Art Deco lampshades, and burnished wood interior. It's a Georgetown institution, which makes weekend dinner reservations essential. Book ahead for the great Sunday brunch too. Mon–Thurs 11.30am–midnight, Fri 11.30am–1am, Sat 10am–1am, Sun 9am–10.30pm. Moderate.

J. Paul's 3218 M St NW ☎202/333-3450. A "dining saloon" that offers the standard, but good, grill/barbecue menu, with some famous crab cakes and a great raw bar, plus its own-brewed Amber Ale. Last orders for food are taken around midnight. Mon–Thurs 11.30am–11.30pm, Fri & Sat 11.30am–midnight, Sun 10.30am–11.30pm. Moderate.

Martin's Tavern 1264 Wisconsin Ave NW ☎202/333-7370. Four generations have run this place and counted politicos from JFK to Nixon among their regulars. The old-fashioned, clubby saloon serves up steaks and chops, great burgers, linguine with clam sauce, and oyster platters. It's also known for its popular brunch (Sun 10am–3pm). Mon–Thurs 10am–1am, Fri 10am–1am, Sat 8am–1am, Sun 8am–11pm. Moderate–Expensive.

Morton's of Chicago 3251 Prospect St NW ☎202/342-6258. The premium steak-house

chain's Georgetown branch serves a fabulous porterhouse. Pick your cut – and make sure you've come with a huge appetite – or go for entrees ($25 and up) that range from chicken to swordfish. One of several local branches, including one in Arlington (see p.269). Mon–Sat 5.30–11pm, Sun 5–10pm. Very expensive.

Old Glory 3139 M St NW ☎202/337-3406. Rollicking barbecue restaurant with hickory smoke rising from the kitchen. Accompany your huge portions of ribs and chicken with one of the half-dozen sauces on every table and a shot of great bourbon. Sun–Thurs 11.30am–11pm, Fri & Sat 11.30am–midnight. Moderate.

Paolo's 1303 Wisconsin Ave NW ☎202/333-7353. Designer Italian dining with a few hotly contested tables open to the sidewalk. Gourmet pizzas (with toppings like feta cheese, goat cheese, salmon, spinach, and sun-dried tomato) and even better pastas are specialties. Sun–Thurs 11.30am–2am, Fri & Sat 11.30am–3am. Moderate.

Red Ginger 1564 Wisconsin Ave NW ☎202/965-7009. Crab cakes, seafood quesadillas, and oxtail stew are just some of the dishes at this hybrid Caribbean-African restaurant, with numerous "small plates" (à la tapas) at affordable prices. Tues–Fri 4–11pm, Sat 11.30am–11.30pm, Sun 11.30am–10pm. Moderate.

Saigon Inn 2928 M St NW ☎202/337-5588. The food served in this Vietnamese restaurant includes delicious crepes, noodles, and rolls. The lunch special (four dishes for $5, Mon–Fri 11am–3pm) is a real steal. Mon–Thurs 11am–10pm, Fri & Sat 11am–11pm, Sun noon–10pm. Inexpensive.

Vietnam Georgetown 2934 M St NW ☎202/337-4536. Tourist-friendly Vietnamese restaurant with decent food and solid specials that include grilled lemon chicken, stuffed crepes, and shrimp curry. Mon–Thurs 11am–11pm, Fri & Sat 11am–11.30pm, Sun noon–11pm. Moderate.

Zed's 1201 28 St NW ☎202/333-4710. The spot for Ethiopian food in Georgetown, and an intimate one at that. The set lunch is cheap but so are the dinner entrees. The *doro wot* (chicken stew in a red pepper sauce) is a good, spicy choice, as are the tenderloin beef cubes. Sun–Thurs 11am–10pm, Fri & Sat 11am–11pm. Inexpensive.

Cafés, snacks, and light meals

Julia's Empanadas 1221 Connecticut Ave NW
T 202/861-8828; Dupont Circle Metro. Savory
Mexican turnovers stuffed with the likes of
curry and spicy sausage, and so cheap
you'll barely notice the money leaving your
wallet. Mon–Fri 10.30am–6.30pm.

Loeb's Deli 832 15th St NW T 202/371-1150;
McPherson Square Metro. Classic New York-
style delicatessen, operating locally since
1959 and at this site since 1979. One of
the better places in the District to get a
decent pastrami or corned-beef sandwich,
plus all the usual bagel-and-lox staples.
Mon–Fri 6am–4pm.

Naan and Beyond 1710 L St NW T 202/466-
6404; Farragut North Metro. Mildly spiced but
flavorful Indian dishes, wrapped in freshly
baked naan, are tasty alternatives to traditional sandwiches for the Farragut lunch
crowd and Friday night clubgoers. Vegan
options available. Mon–Thurs 11am–9pm,
Fri 11am–4am.

Nooshi 1120 19th St NW T 202/293-3138;
Farragut North Metro. Lovers of "noodles
and sushi" looking for a cheap and hearty
meal should sample the full-flavor offerings
at this lunch favorite, with tamarind shrimp
and curry stir-fries among the highlights.
Mon–Thurs 11.30am–3pm & 5–10pm, Fri &
Sat 11.30am–3pm & 5–10.30pm.

Teaism 800 Connecticut Ave NW T 202/835-
2233; Farragut West or Farragut North Metro.
Pleasant spot for a pick-me-up chai or a
dose of Pan-Asian cuisine after a White
House tour. The light fare includes salads,
sandwiches, and bento boxes; afternoon
tea service is $15. Mon–Fri 7.30am
–5.30pm.

Restaurants

Bombay Club 815 Connecticut Ave NW
T 202/659-3727; Farragut North or Farragut West
Metro. Sleek Indian restaurant a block from
the White House (and a favorite of former
president Clinton), with Raj-style surroundings, piano accompaniment, and dishes that
are a little out of the ordinary, like tandoori
salmon. Sun–Fri 11.30am–2.30pm, Mon–Sat
6.30–10.30pm. Moderate.

Café Asia 1720 I St NW T 202/659-2696;
Farragut West Metro. Breezy Pan-Asian
restaurant that's an excellent choice for
budget sushi and sashimi, or try the big
plates of lemongrass-grilled chicken, seafood *bakar* (in banana leaf with spicy prawn
sauce), satay, or Thai noodles. Altogether,
something of a grab bag, though worth
a try. Mon–Thurs 11.30am–11pm, Fri
11.30am–midnight, Sat noon–midnight,
Sun noon–11pm. Inexpensive–Moderate.

Café Promenade *Mayflower* hotel, 1127 Connecticut Ave NW T 202/347-2233; Farragut
North Metro. A serenading harpist and pricey
but scrumptious Mediterranean menu set
the tone in this elegant hotel restaurant,
where you can expect to see all types of
political heavyweights at nearby tables;
the Friday night buffet ($39) – where you
can sup on anything from crab cakes to
oysters and steak salad – also draws an
eager crowd of hungry gourmands. Daily
6.30am–11pm. Expensive – Very expensive

Fran O'Brien's *Capital Hilton*, 1001 16th St NW
T 202/783-2599; McPherson Square Metro.
Former Redskins player's steak house-
saloon in the *Hilton* basement. Check out
the Hall of Fame, munch on a bountiful
steak or pasta, and watch the game on TV.
Mon–Fri 11.30am–3pm, daily 5–10.30pm.
Expensive.

Galileo 1110 21st St NW T 202/293-7191;
Foggy Bottom-GWU or Farragut West Metro.
Superb Northern Italian cuisine has made
this spot into a favorite for discerning foodies. Risotto makes a regular appearance
on the ever-changing menu. Service is
snappy, and the wine list impressive. Book
well in advance. Mon–Fri 11.30am–2pm &
5.30–10pm, Sat & Sun 5.30–10.30pm. Very
expensive.

Gerard's Place 915 15th St NW T 202/737-
4445; McPherson Square Metro. Accomplished French cuisine with a mix of classical and modern stylings. The fixed-price
dinners are predictably pricey (and delicious), so your best bet may be to indulge
in the $30 lunch. Mon–Fri 11.30am–2.30pm
& 5.30–10pm (Fri until 10.30pm), Sat
5.30–10.30pm. Very expensive.

Grillfish 1200 New Hampshire Ave NW
T 202/331-7310; Dupont Circle or Foggy
Bottom-GWU Metro. Industrial-chic eatery
offering casual dining and primo seafood,
with an attractive happy hour for cheap
eats (Mon–Fri 5.30–7pm). The daily catch
options might include sea bass, tuna, snap-
per, trout, mahi-mahi, shark, or calamari
– grilled, over pasta, or served in a sauté
pan. Mon–Fri noon–2.30pm, Sun–Thurs

Most of Washington's major sight-seeing attractions have their own cafés and fast-food restaurants, and often they're the only local option for lunch, especially on and around the Mall. Those listed below are particularly good.

Corcoran Gallery of Art (*Café des Artistes*) p.141, 273

Library of Congress p.112

National Gallery of Art p.79

National Museum of American History p.61

National Museum of Women in the Arts p.178

5.30–10pm, Fri & Sat 5.30pm–midnight. Moderate.

House of Kabob 1829 M St NW ☎202/293-5588; **Farragut North Metro.** Delicious and cheap Middle Eastern fare prepared according to Islamic rules. The meat and veggie kabobs are the main draw, and the goat curry is an adventure worth sampling, though the cramped setting offers zero atmosphere. Daily 11am–10pm. Inexpensive.

Malaysia Kopitiam 1827 M St NW ☎202/833-6232; **Dupont Circle or Farragut North Metro.** Despite the no-frills decor, this eatery's extensive selection of Indian, Malay, and Chinese fare is first class. Tuck into a bowl of noodles or, for heartier fare, try the spicy beef rendang, chili shrimp, or black pepper lamb. Mon–Thurs 11.30am–10pm, Fri & Sat 11.30am–11pm, Sun noon–10pm. Inexpensive.

McCormick & Schmick's 1652 K St NW ☎202/861-2233; **McPherson Square Metro.** Hugely popular seafood grill and raw bar, complete with Victorian stained glass and lamps and a buzzing bar. Best food deals are weekends from 10.30pm until closing, when two drinks get you access to the delicious bargain menu of clams, chowders, and fajitas, among other rotating snacks. Mon–Thurs 11am–11pm, Fri 11am–midnight, Sat 5–11pm, Sun 5–10pm. Expensive.

The Palm 1225 19th St NW ☎202/293-9091; **Dupont Circle or Farragut North Metro.** This "power meatery" is renowned for its New York strip and lobster – and for the power players and celebrities who wine and dine here. Reservations required for this DC branch of a New York institution. Mon–Fri 11.45am–10.30pm, Sat 6–10.30pm, Sun 5.30–9.30pm. Very expensive.

Sign of the Whale 1825 M St NW ☎202/785-1110; **Dupont Circle or Farragut North Metro.** Downtown saloon best known for its

supreme burgers grilled to perfection and dozens of beers on tap, though there's also famous jerk chicken, pasta, fish, and crab cakes, most around $10. A good spot to hear DJs spinning an eclectic batch of diner-friendly tunes. Mon–Thurs 11.30am–1.30am, Fri & Sat 11.30am–2.30am. Inexpensive.

Stoney's 1307 L St NW ☎202/347-9163; **McPherson Square Metro.** Down-to-earth saloon and bar that's more than three decades old. Revel in its big servings of burgers, fries, chili, and country fare, and be ready to wait cheek-to-jowl for a spot with the other hungry (and thirsty) patrons. Daily 11am–1am. Inexpensive.

Tabard Inn 1739 N St NW ☎202/785-1277; **Dupont Circle Metro.** Mellow Victorian inn's restaurant that rotates its creative New American fare – you might find anything from pan-seared salmon to ostrich to spicy shrimp – in dining rooms rich with Old World ambience. Its very pleasant garden is the perfect spot for brunch when the weather's right. Mon–Fri 7–10am, 11.30am–2.30pm & 6–10.30pm, Sat & Sun 11am–2pm & 6–9.30pm. Expensive.

Vidalia 1990 M St NW ☎202/659-1990; **Dupont Circle or Farragut North Metro.** The New American cuisine dished up with a decidedly Southern twang has garnered this eatery a reputation as one of the District's best. Be on the lookout for unique takes on barbecued pork, fried chicken, and the shrimp-and-grits combo. Mon–Fri 11.30am–2.30pm, Mon–Thurs 5.30–10pm, Fri & Sat 5.30pm–10.30pm, Sun 5.30–9.30pm. Expensive.

Old Downtown

Cafés, snacks, and light meals

Café Mozart 1331 H St NW ☎202/347-5732; **Metro Center Metro.** Worth seeking out if you have a taste for German food. A combination eatery and deli with the requisite schnitzels, bratwursts, roasted meats, and other favorites, plus sweets, cakes, and desserts. Mon–Fri 7.30am–10pm, Sat 9am–10pm, Sun 11am–10pm.

Corner Bakery The Shops at National Place, 529 14th St NW ☎202/662-7400; **Metro Center Metro.** Self-serve bakery-café close to the White House and with a full range of ciabatta sandwiches, cookies, salads, and pizza slices. Mon–Fri 7am–7pm, Sat & Sun 9am–5pm.

Dean & Deluca 1299 Pennsylvania Ave NW, in the Warner Theatre complex ☎202/628-8155; **Metro Center Metro.** Gourmet sandwiches, great homemade soups, hot dishes, and an appetizing salad bar in a boiler room turned café-carryout. Try to avoid the lunchtime crush. Mon–Fri 7am–4.30pm.

Ebbitt Express 675 15th St NW ☎202/347-8881; **Metro Center Metro.** Carryout eatery adjunct to the much pricier *Old Ebbitt Grill*. Excellent pastas, salads (Caesar and other faves), grilled and cold sandwiches, and snacks to go. Mon–Thurs 7.30am–8pm, Fri 7.30am–6pm.

Harry's *Hotel Harrington*, 436 11th St NW ☎202/624-0053; **Metro Center Metro.** Tasty, old-fashioned comfort food (meat loaf, spaghetti and meatballs), with even cheaper prices at the adjacent self-service *Harrington Café*. Sun–Thurs 11am–1am, Fri & Sat 11am–2am.

Reeve's Restaurant and Bakery 1306 G St NW ☎202/628-6350; **Metro Center Metro.** Classic diner, in business since 1886, with an all-you-can-eat breakfast and fruit bar, crisp-coated chicken at lunchtime, and famous pies. Mon–Sat 7am–6pm.

Restaurants

Andale 401 7th St NW ☎202/783-3133; **Archives-Navy Memorial Metro.** A Federal Triangle eatery with fine, fairly authentic Mexican cuisine, including the likes of pepper-roasted seafood and spicy chicken, plus some good mole sauces. Mon–Sat 11.30am–3pm, Mon–Thurs 5–10pm, Fri & Sat 5–11pm. Moderate.

Capitol City Brewing Company 1100 New York Ave NW, entrance at 11th and H ☎202/628-2222; **Metro Center Metro.** Best known as a brew-pub, though the kitchen serves up good burgers, sausages, pasta, salads, and other standards. Reserve on weekends. Sun–Thurs 11am–11pm, Fri & Sat 11am–midnight. Inexpensive.

District Chophouse & Brewery 509 7th St NW ☎202/347-3434; **Gallery Place-Chinatown Metro.** Classy Swing-era joint with great music and a grill-house menu. A bit on the pricey side for this kind of fare, but portions are huge, and you can order a burger (with a house salad) and soak up the atmosphere for less than twelve bucks. Reservations advised. Mon 11am–10pm, Tues–Thurs 11am–11pm, Fri 11am–midnight, Sat 10.30am–midnight. Expensive.

Haad Thai 1100 New York Ave NW, entrance on 11th St ☎202/682-1111; **Metro Center Metro.** Opposite the Convention Center, this classy, business-oriented Thai restaurant features coconut-milk curries, tasty steamed fish and shrimp, and spicy soups – all good staples, well made, and not too pricey. Mon–Fri 11.30am–2.30pm & 5–10.30pm, Sat noon–10.30pm, Sun 5–10.30pm. Moderate.

Jaleo 480 7th St NW ☎202/628-7949; **Gallery Place-Chinatown Metro.** Renowned upscale tapas bar-restaurant with flamenco dancing, seafood, and plentiful sangria. Limited reservation policy makes for long waits during peak hours. Mon & Sun 11.30am–10pm, Tues–Thurs 11.30am–11.30pm, Fri & Sat 11.30am–midnight. Moderate (tapas); expensive (restaurant).

Old Ebbitt Grill 675 15th St NW ☎202/347-4801; **Metro Center Metro.** In business in various locations since 1856, this plush re-creation of a nineteenth-century tavern features a mahogany bar (serving microbrews), gas chandeliers, leather booths, and gilt mirrors. Politico clientele indulges in everything from burgers to oysters, breakfasts to late dinners. Kitchen Mon–Fri 7.30am–1am, Sat 8.30am–1am, Sun 9.30am–1am, bar open until 2–3am. Expensive.

Red Sage 605 14th St NW ☎202/638-4444; **Metro Center Metro.** Landmark Southwestern restaurant, dripping with Santa Fe chic and featuring rotisserie-grilled meat, fish, and vegetarian specials. The funky café-bar is less exclusive, and the menu is more mainstream. Reservations essential for the restaurant. Restaurant daily 5.30–10pm & Mon–Fri 11.30am–2pm; café Mon–Sat 11.30am–11.30pm, Sun 5.30–10pm. Moderate (café); very expensive (restaurant).

Sky Terrace *Hotel Washington*, 515 15th St NW ☎202/638-5900; **Metro Center Metro.** A romantic spot to enjoy a sweeping view of the city, along with a simple sandwich.

Though the food is nothing special, it's a bargain considering the outdoor perch above the White House. Daily 11.30am–1am (May–Oct only). Moderate.

Ten Penh 1001 Pennsylvania Ave NW ☎202/393-4500; Federal Triangle Metro. Slick, high-profile Asian-fusion restaurant in the Federal Triangle, serving up pricey meals like roasted duck and pork wonton ravioli. Many dishes are worth the cost, but head north to Chinatown for more authentic entrees at less expensive prices. Daily 5.30–10.30pm, Mon–Fri 11.30am–2.30pm. Expensive.

Tosca 1112 F St NW ☎202/367-1990; Metro Center Metro. Upscale Northern Italian eatery with well-prepared meat and pasta staples from the Old Country, along with tasty desserts and flavorful juice drinks. Daily 5.30–10.30pm, Mon–Fri 11.30am–2.30pm. Moderate.

Shaw

Cafés, snacks, and light meals

Ben's Chili Bowl 1213 U St NW ☎202/667-0909; U Street-Cardozo Metro. Venerable U Street hangout across from the Metro, serving renowned chilidogs, burgers, milk shakes, and cheese fries at booths and counter stools. A number of Hollywood movies have been shot here, as photos on the wall attest. Mon–Thurs 6am–2am, Fri 6am–4am, Sat 7am–4am, Sun noon–8pm.

Cakelove 1506 U St NW ☎202/588-7100; U Street-Cardozo Metro. Popular, inventive bakery that makes some of the District's most appealing cakes, as well as a range of tasty cupcakes, pastries, and the like. U Street is well worth a visit for this place alone. Mon–Fri 8am–8pm, Sat 10am–6pm, Sun 11am–5pm.

Restaurants

Coppi's 1414 U St NW ☎202/319-7773; U Street-Cardozo Metro. Very chic and trendy little pizza palace with a brick oven, doling out organic pies with a range of fancy ingredients – goat cheese, pancetta, etc – along with spicy calzones. All this is more expensive than you might expect, though. Sun–Thurs 5–11pm, Fri & Sat 5pm–midnight. Moderate.

Florida Avenue Grill 1100 Florida Ave NW ☎202/265-1586; U Street-Cardozo Metro. Southern-style diner serving cheap and hearty meals for almost half a century to locals and stray celebs. Especially known for its eggs, ham, and grits. Tues–Sat 6am–9pm. Inexpensive.

U-topia 1418 U St NW ☎202/483-7669; U Street-Cardozo Metro. Arty, romantic bar-restaurant with regular live blues and jazz, art exhibits, good veggie dishes, and a popular weekend brunch. Eclectic entrees range from pasta and gumbo to steak and sausage. Sun–Thurs 11am–2am, Fri 11am–3am, Sat 5pm–3am. Inexpensive–Moderate.

Upper Northwest

Cafés, snacks, and light meals

Firehook Bakery & Coffeehouse 3411 Connecticut Ave NW ☎202/362-2253; Cleveland Park Metro. Breads, cakes, cookies, and very good coffee are all on offer at this DC institution's Upper Northwest outpost; seating in the wonderful garden completes the experience. Mon–Fri 7am–9pm, Sat & Sun 8am–9pm.

Krupin's 4620 Wisconsin Ave NW ☎202/686-1989; Tenleytown Metro. Jewish deli-diner that's a long way from anywhere, but devotees consider the trek worth it for the true tastes of hot corned-beef, lox and bagel platters, stuffed cabbage, pastrami, and the rest. Daily 8am–10pm.

Vace 3315 Connecticut Ave NW ☎202/363-1999; Cleveland Park Metro. Grab a slice of the excellent pizza or tasty sub sandwiches, or pack a picnic from the selection of sausages, tortellini salad, and olives, then head to the zoo. Mon–Fri 9am–9pm, Sat 9am–8pm, Sun 10am–5pm.

Restaurants

Ardeo 3311 Connecticut Ave NW ☎202/244-6750; Cleveland Park Metro. Ultra-trendy spot with "Modern American" cuisine – meaning lots of oddball hybrids like duck-confit cannelloni and pork loin with chickpeas – though the pricey experiments work most of the time; makes a good lobster sandwich too. Mon–Thurs 5.30–10.30pm, Fri & Sat 5.30–11.30pm, Sun 11am–10.30pm. Expensive.

Cactus Cantina 3300 Wisconsin Ave NW ☎202/686-7222; no nearby Metro stop. A festive Tex-Mex treat for Cathedral-goers, with a great veranda and fine eats like crab enchiladas, spicy chips and salsa, and other staples, and new twists on old favorites. Mon–Thurs 11.30am–11pm, Fri & Sat 11.30am–midnight, Sun 11am–11pm. Moderate.

Lebanese Taverna 2641 Connecticut Ave NW ☎202/265-8681; **Woodley Park-Zoo Metro.** Delicious Middle Eastern joint with soothingly dark, authentic decor inside. Sample something from the assortment of kebobs and grilled-meat platters, or go straight for the leg of lamb. Mon–Fri 11.30am–2.30pm & 5.30–10.30pm, Sat 11.30am–3pm & 5.30–11pm, Sun 5–10pm. Moderate.

Nam Viet 3419 Connecticut Ave NW ☎202/237-1015; **Cleveland Park Metro.** No-frills Vietnamese eatery in the heart of the Cleveland Park dining scene. The soups are good, as are the grilled chicken and fish, the caramel pork, the Vietnamese steak – really, you can't go wrong. Mon–Thurs 11am–3pm & 5–10pm, Fri & Sat 11am–11pm, Sun 11am–10pm. Moderate.

New Heights 2317 Calvert St NW ☎202/234-4110; **Woodley Park-Zoo Metro.** Fashionable, new-wave American restaurant serving an inventive, seasonal menu that is likely to include anything from buffalo to rockfish. Book ahead in summer to sit outside, especially for Sunday brunch (11am–2.30pm). Sun–Thurs 5.30–10pm, Fri & Sat 5.30–11pm. Expensive.

Sala Thai 3507 Connecticut Ave NW ☎202/237-2777; **Cleveland Park Metro.** Upper Northwest branch of a fine Southeast Asian eatery, with good, fairly traditional Thai noodle dishes and soups – though some are jazzed up with unexpected, trendy items like seared salmon and eggplant. Mon–Thurs 11.30am–10.30pm, Fri 11.30am–11pm, Sat noon–11pm, Sun noon–10.30pm. Inexpensive.

Spices 3333 Connecticut Ave NW ☎202/686-3833; **Cleveland Park Metro.** Stylish Pan-Asian place serving spicy bowls of *laksa*, stir-fried basil chicken, and sushi in a spacious, high-ceilinged dining room, complete with sushi bar. Mon–Fri 11.30am–3pm & 5–11pm, Sat noon–11pm, Sun 5–10.30pm. Moderate.

Woodley Café 2619 Connecticut Ave NW ☎202/332-5773; **Woodley Park-Zoo Metro.** Roomy neighborhood café-bar attracting a laid-back crowd, serving up the likes of pizza, burgers, calzones, and pasta. Breakfast

staples and Sunday brunch are also available. Daily 9am–10pm. Inexpensive.

Yanni's Greek Taverna 3500 Connecticut Ave NW ☎202/362-8871; **Cleveland Park Metro.** Popular pit stop before hitting the Cleveland Park bars. Offers bargain grilled-meat platters, a tasty tzatsiki, and pricier house specials like squid and octopus, plus the usual Greek favorites like souvlaki and baklava. Daily 11.30am–11pm. Inexpensive.

Yanyu 3433 Connecticut Ave NW ☎202/686-6968; **Cleveland Park Metro.** Celebrated for its inventive cuisine – rich with items like sea bass, shiitake mushrooms, and crab – and elegant decor, this spot ranks high among DC's upscale Asian restaurants. A meal here can get pricey fast. Sun–Thurs 5.30–10.30pm, Fri & Sat 5.30–11pm. Expensive.

Waterfront

Cafés, snacks, and light meals

Custis & Brown 12th St and Maine Ave SW ☎202/484-0168; **L'Enfant Plaza Metro.** Seafood stand serving sizable fried-fish sandwiches, steamed spiced shrimp, crab and lobster, clam chowder, and oyster platters to go – all at giveaway prices. Great for a lunch or sundowner picnic overlooking the Washington Channel. Located at the Fish Wharf, along with other fine eateries. Daily 8am–8pm.

Restaurants

H20 800 Water St SW ☎202/484-6300; **L'Enfant Plaza Metro.** One of the few decent choices in an area not known for its eateries. This marina restaurant has a swanky, newly remodeled interior and an attached lounge and stylish club. The appealing river view is the main attraction, along with tasteful entrees of crab cakes, steak, and pasta. The Captain's Platter features a welter of seafood faves for $33. Mon–Fri 11am–3pm & 5–10pm, Sat 3–10pm, Sun 11am–3pm. Expensive.

Phillips 900 Water St SW ☎202/488-8515; **L'Enfant Plaza Metro.** Another popular seafood spot on the tour-bus circuit, mainly worthwhile for those looking to pack away giant helpings of fish and crab from the lunch, dinner, and weekend brunch buffets. Good location not far from the Fish Wharf. Daily 11am–11pm. Moderate.

14

Bars and clubs

Nightlife in the District is not always the staid affair you might imagine – crowds of dark-suited lawyers and lobbyists swilling martinis as they circulate for the nightly networking session. Although some of this does occur, typically in the dreary hotel bars and corporate-dominated watering holes around New Downtown, in other areas you're likely to find a much livelier scene, attracting all types of revelers from beer-guzzling coeds and funky hipsters to graying hippies and sprightly clubkids. The mix depends largely on the neighborhood. Some of the most notable places to drop in for a drink or a dance include Capitol Hill, near Union Station and along Pennsylvania Avenue SE; Old Downtown, around the Penn Quarter; Georgetown, at M Street and Wisconsin Avenue; Dupont Circle, along 17th Street and Connecticut Avenue; Shaw, along U Street near the Metro; and Adams-Morgan, at 18th Street and Columbia Road. In northern Virginia, you can find good hangouts in Arlington, along Wilson and Clarendon boulevards, and in Alexandria, around Old Town. There's also a thriving – if relatively small – gay scene, with most of the action in Dupont Circle, especially on P Street (between 21st and 22nd) and 17th Street (between P and R); for more on these spots, turn to Chapter 16.

Note that while there's plenty of crossover between bars, lounges, clubs, and live-music venues – a well-soaked watering hole may have DJs on some nights, rock bands the next – we've categorized the following selections according to the main strength of each. If you're mostly interested in drinking and need little more than background music (live or canned) for your imbibing, look under "**Bars**"; if DJs and a frenetic social scene are the draw, try "**Clubs**"; and if you really want to groove on live jazz, rock, or anything else and don't care much about what cocktails or DJs are on tap, try "**Live music**." If you have multiple nightlife interests, we've also noted those spots that specialize in a range of after-dark entertainment.

Bars

As in other American cities, you'll increasingly find bars that have smoke-free policies, or at least segregate the puffers outside or in specially ventilated rooms. Obviously, true dive bars and grim, end-of-the-line holes may allow all sorts of indulgences to go with their rock-bottom prices for mainline brews, but offer no atmosphere that's worth seeking out – unless all you plan to do is get hammered and pass out. Thus, the selections below offer a spectrum of watering

Don't want to settle for just another Bud? **Microbrews** are big business these days, and you'll be able to get a decent selection of beers in many bars. For the best choice, hit one of the city's brew-pubs – *Capitol City Brewing Company* (see p.283), *District Chophouse & Brewery* (p.278), *John Harvard's* (p.286), *Founder's Brewing* (p.282), or the beer specialists *Brickskeller* (p.284) and *D.A.'s RFD Washington* (p.286). Elsewhere, keep an eye out for the following local brews: Foggy Bottom Ale (from DC), Virginia's Rock Creek, Potomac River, or Dominion; and from Maryland, Blue Ridge, Clipper City, and Wild Goose.

holes aimed at several different types of drinkers, from the chic yuppie palaces, offering brushed steel and glass surfaces and $10 cocktails, to the lower-end hangouts for casual revelry, where well drinks go for as little as $2 and the atmosphere is convivial, if not particularly inspired.

Most bars are open daily until 2am, often later on the weekends. Virtually all have **happy hours** during which drinks are two-for-one or at least heavily discounted; the optimum time for these is weekdays between 4pm and 7pm. Some bars also offer free snacks (and a few gourmet treats as well) to happy-hour drinkers.

Adams-Morgan

Bedrock Billiards 1841 Columbia Rd NW ☎202/667-7665; Dupont Circle or Woodley Park-Zoo Metro. A lively, if low-key, subterranean setting, quality bartenders, and quirky art set this funky pool hall apart from Adams-Morgan's more frenzied club scene. Mon–Thurs 4pm–1.30am, Fri & Sat 1pm–2.30am, Sun 1pm–1.30am.

Blue Room 2321 18th St NW ☎202/332-0800; Dupont Circle or Woodley Park-Zoo Metro. Classier than the typical Adams-Morgan fare, but far posier, too. This chi-chi bar and lounge enforces a dress code and offers nightly DJ selections from techno and house to acid jazz; Wednesdays brings out amateur turntablists for a spin at the decks. Wed, Thurs & Sun 7pm–2am, Fri & Sat 7pm–3am.

The Common Share 2003 18th St NW ☎202/588-7180; Dupont Circle Metro. Dedicated to cheap beers (starting at $3) drawn from mainline brews and microbrews, plus pricier cocktails. This boisterous (if a bit grimy) dive attracts what is perhaps the neighborhood's most diverse crowd. Mon–Thurs 6pm–2am, Fri 5.30pm–3am, Sat 7am–3am.

Millie and Al's 2440 18th St NW ☎202/387-8131; Woodley Park-Zoo Metro. The prototypical neighborhood tavern that locals dig and visitors avoid – plenty of cheap beer, not

much in the way of attitude, and folksy, old-fashioned decor. Mon–Thurs 5.30pm–2am, Fri & Sat 4pm–3am.

Toledo Lounge 2435 18th St NW ☎202/986-5416; Woodley Park-Zoo Metro. Cramped and barebones café-bar with attitude, featuring windows looking out on the local streetlife. The patio seats (best spot for hanging out) are like gold dust in summer. Mon–Thurs 6pm–2am, Fri & Sat 6pm–3am.

Alexandria, VA

Bayou Room 219 King St ☎703/549-1141; King Street Metro. Stone-walled dungeon making for a low-key local pub, with cheap, simple, and tasty Cajun eats, TVs tuned to sports, and classic rock blaring over the sound system. Above, in *Two Nineteen*, there's a jazz lounge that serves Creole food in a more stylish setting. Mon–Thurs 11.30am–1.30am, Fri & Sat 11.30am–2am.

Founder's Restaurant and Brewing 607 King St ☎703/684-5397; King Street Metro. Recent brew-pub arrival serving up a mix of American pale ales and stouts, along –with German-style Kolsch and altbier. Mon–Thurs 11am–midnight, Fri & Sat 11am–1am, Sun 10am–8pm.

Murphy's Grand Irish Pub 713 King St ☎703/548-1717; King Street Metro. Old Town's nightlife revolves around this boisterous pub, pouring the city's best pint of

Guinness. Local solo acts perform upstairs, while a central fireplace and chow like Irish stew add much Emerald-Isle atmosphere. Mon–Thurs 11am–12.30am, Fri & Sat 11am–1.30am.

Shenandoah Brewing Co. 652 S Pickett St ☎703/823-9508; **King Street Metro.** Fine combo pub and brewing academy, where you can learn how to make your own beer as well as munch on spicy chili and sample brews like Whitewater Wheat, Stony Man Stout, and Old Rag Mountain Ale. Thurs & Fri 4–11pm, Sat 10am–11pm.

Union Street Public House 121 S Union St ☎703/548-1785; **King Street Metro.** It's hard to miss this red-brick building with gas lamps. Good steak-and-seafood joint that's just as nice for drinking as eating, with its own handcrafted and hearty microbrews. Very popular on weekends. Daily 11.30am–1am.

Arlington and Northern Virginia

Clarendon Grill 1101 N Highland St ☎703/524-7455; **Clarendon Metro.** Solid old favorite for boozing, and something of a pickup joint. Music selections (Tues–Sat) include earnest acoustic strummers, alternative rockers, and occasional DJs – but the real focus is convivial drinking. Daily 11am–2am.

Dr Dremo's Taphouse 2001 Clarendon Blvd ☎703/528-4660; **Court House Metro.** This converted car showroom, right at the Metro station, is good for a tasty microbrew and a game of pool. The bar's the most fun on Tuesday nights, when the beer is just $1 a glass and "psychotronic" film showings offer nerve-jangling D-grade horror and kitsch classics. Tues, Wed & Sun 5pm–midnight, Thurs–Sat 5pm–2am.

Ireland's Four Courts 2051 Wilson Blvd, at N Courthouse Rd ☎703/525-3600; **Court House Metro.** One of the nicest of the area's Irish bars, drawing a cheery Arlington crowd for the live music (Tues–Sat), dozen beers on tap, decent whiskey selection, and filling food. Mon–Sat 11am–2am, Sun 10am–2am.

Mackey's Public House 23rd St and Crystal Drive ☎703/412-1113; **Crystal City Metro.** A relaxed bar in a prime shopping strip, with hefty Irish food like lamb stew and shepherd's pie, and good old Emerald Isle beers such as Guinness and Harp. Mon–Sat 11am–2am, Sun 11am–1am.

Old Dominion Brewing 44633 Guilford Drive, Ashburn, VA ☎703/724-9100. Mainly worth a

stop if you've got time to kill around Dulles Airport, though excellent for its twenty microbrewed lagers, ales, and stouts (it's the oldest such brewery in the state). Brewery tours available, too (Sat 2pm & 4pm, Sun 2pm). Mon–Thurs 11.30am–9pm, Fri 11.30am–10pm, Sat 11am–10pm, Sun noon–7pm.

Whitlow's on Wilson 2854 Wilson Blvd ☎703/276-9693; **Clarendon Metro.** Neighborhood retro lounge with good happy-hour drinks and food, plus pool and wraparound bar. Also good for its nightly selections of live rock, jazz, acoustic, blues, and reggae. Mon–Fri 11.30am–2am, Sat & Sun 9am–2am.

Capitol Hill

Bullfeathers 410 First St SE ☎202/543-5005; **Capitol South Metro.** Pol watchers just may catch a sighting at this old-time Hill favorite, a dark and clubby spot with affordable beer, and named for Teddy Roosevelt's favorite euphemism for bullshit during his White House days. Mon–Fri 11.15am–midnight, Sun 11.30am–9pm.

Capitol City Brewing Company 2 Massachusetts Ave NF ☎202/842-2337; **Union Station Metro.** Prime microbrewing turf offering average pub food but solid handcrafted beer, highlighted by the Amber Waves Ale, a rich and succulent beverage, and German-styled Capitol Kolsch and Prohibition Porter. Another branch in Old Downtown, 1100 New York Ave NW (see p.286). Sun–Thurs 11am–1am, Fri & Sat 11am–2am.

Capitol Lounge 229 Pennsylvania Ave SE ☎202/547-2098; **Capitol South Metro.** More sophisticated than most spots on the Hill – with cigars and martinis in the downstairs bar – but there's still plenty of life up in the brick-walled saloon thanks to happy hours and colorful campaign memorabilia, plus DJs who whip up the weekend action. Mon–Thurs 3pm–2am, Fri 11am–3am, Sat 9am–3am.

The Dubliner *Phoenix Park Hotel*, 520 N Capitol St NW ☎202/737-3773; **Union Station Metro.** A wooden-vaulted, good-time Irish bar, with draft Guinness, boisterous conversation, and live Irish music catering to the more refined Hill set. The patio is a nice summer hangout. Sun–Thurs 7am–2am, Fri & Sat 7am–3am.

Hawk 'n' Dove 329 Pennsylvania Ave SE ☎202/543-3300; Capitol South Metro. Iconic DC pub, a bit tatty at the edges now, hung with football pennants, bottles, and bric-a-brac. The young, loud crowd comes (depending on the night) for the cheap beer, half-price food, or football on TV. Sun–Thurs 10am–2am, Fri & Sat 10am–3am.

Kelly's Irish Times 14 F St NW ☎202/543-5433; Union Station Metro. Colorful folk music sets the stage (Wed–Sun nights) at this boisterous pub, which also features weekend club music on the downstairs dance floor and imperial pints of Guinness. Sun–Thurs 11am–2am, Fri & Sat 11am–3am.

Politiki and the Penn Ave Pourhouse 319 Pennsylvania Ave SE ☎202/546-1001; Capitol South Metro. Hill staffers and interns pour into this three-bars-in-one Hill hangout for the daily food and drink specials. There's a kitschy tiki bar with pool tables downstairs, plus an unexpected ode to the glories of Pittsburgh on the first floor, complete with Penn State pennants, sausage sandwiches, and Iron City beer on tap. Mon–Fri 4pm–1.30am, Sat & Sun 10am–2.30am.

Tune Inn 331 Pennsylvania Ave SE ☎202/543-2725; Capitol South Metro. Old-line neighborhood dive bar that's been around forever (or at least seventy years) and has a mix of grizzled regulars and wide-eyed newbies.

Restaurant bars

Some of DC's restaurants have very funky bars in their own right – you'll be welcome to stay for just a drink in any of the following.

America, Union Station, p.269

B. Smith's, Union Station, p.270

Bukom Café, Adams-Morgan, p.266

Café Citron, New Downtown, p.272

Cashion's Eat Place, Adams-Morgan, p.266

Gabriel, Dupont Circle, p.272

Grillfish, New Downtown, p.276

Jaleo, Old Downtown, p.278

Johnny's Half Shell, Dupont Circle p.272

Old Ebbitt Grill, Old Downtown, p.278

Perry's, Adams-Morgan, p.268

Red Sage, Old Downtown, p.278

Settle down in a booth, munch on the burgers, and feed the jukebox. Sun–Thurs 8am–2am, Fri & Sat 8am–3am.

Dupont Circle

Big Hunt 1345 Connecticut Ave NW ☎202/785-2333; Dupont Circle Metro. As well known for its eccentric decor, which includes a tarantula candelabra, as for its beer. More than 25 brews are on tap, and it has a good jukebox and a groovy crowd. Always busy during happy hour. Mon–Thurs 4pm–2am, Fri 4pm–3am, Sat 5pm–3am, Sun 5pm–2am.

Brickskeller 1523 22nd St NW ☎202/293-1885; Dupont Circle Metro. Renowned brick-lined basement saloon serving "the world's largest selection of beer" – up to 850 types, including dozens from US microbreweries. Knowledgeable bar staff can advise, or you can try your luck with the colossal menu. Also features its own inexpensive inn upstairs (see p.254). Mon–Thurs 11.30am–2am, Fri 11.30am–3am, Sat 6pm–3am, Sun 6pm–2am.

Buffalo Billiards 1330 19th St NW ☎202/331-7665; Dupont Circle Metro. Classy basement hangout with a seemingly endless sea of pool tables, plus darts, a good selection of tap beers, and tasty pub grub. There's even a lone snooker table. Mon–Thurs 4pm–2am, Fri 4pm–3am, Sat 1pm–3am, Sun 4pm–1am.

Childe Harold 1610 20th St NW ☎202/483-6700; Dupont Circle Metro. Friendly old red-brick pub with an outdoor patio; it draws a mixed crowd that comes to chew the fat and watch TV sports. There's a good restaurant, too. Sun–Thurs 11.30am–2am, Fri & Sat 11.30am–3am.

Fox and Hounds 1537 17th St NW ☎202/232-6307; Dupont Circle Metro. Smack in the middle of the 17th Street action, friends of this easygoing bar mostly kick back and enjoy the very stiff (and very cheap) rail drinks. Mon–Thurs 11.30am–2am, Fri 11.30am–3am, Sat 10.30am–3am, Sun 10.30am–2am.

Gazuza 1629 Connecticut Ave NW ☎202/667-5500; Dupont Circle Metro. See and be seen at this chic, attitude-driven lounge, whose perch above Connecticut Avenue attracts an eclectic mix for cocktails, electronica, and house. Sun–Thurs 5pm–2am, Fri & Sat 5pm–3am.

Foggy Bottom

Froggy Bottom Pub 2142 Pennsylvania Ave NW ⓣ 202/338-3000; **Foggy Bottom-GWU Metro.** Colorful, three-level bar catering to students at nearby GWU. Worth a visit if you're interested in shooting pool, munching on cheap pub grub, and knocking back a good brew or two (or more). Mon–Sat 11.30am–2am.

Lindy's Red Lion 2040 I St NW ⓣ 202/285-2766; **Foggy Bottom-GWU or Farragut West Metro.** No gimmicks, few frills – just a GWU student hangout doing a roaring trade in cheap food and drinks. Sun–Thurs 11am–2am, Fri & Sat 11am–3am.

Marshall's 2524 L St NW ⓣ 202/333-1155; **Foggy Bottom-GWU Metro.** Solid microbrews like Red Hook and beer faves like Guinness, plus a decent menu of steak, pasta, and seafood, make this upscale bar-and-grill a good spot for hanging out. The kitchen serves 'til midnight. Sun–Thurs 11.30am–2am, Fri & Sat 11.30am–3am.

Georgetown

Garrett's 3003 M St NW ⓣ 202/333-1033. Amid its brick-and-wood interior, *Garrett's* features a giant rhino head by the door, a pumping jukebox that keeps the young crowd in a party mood, and nightly drink specials, along with a few microbrews.

Saloons

DC has a wealth of traditional saloon-restaurants, bristling with checked tablecloths, paneled wood, good-value food, and crack waiters. The list below picks out those where the bar action is pretty good as well.

Clyde's, Georgetown, p.275

Fran O'Brien's, New Downtown, p.276

J. Paul's, Georgetown, p.275

McCormick & Schmick's, New Downtown, p.277

The Monocle, Capitol Hill, p.270

Mr Henry's, Capitol Hill, p.270

Old Glory, Georgetown, p.275

Sign of the Whale, New Downtown, p.277

Stoney's, New Downtown, p.277

Mon–Thurs 11.30am–2am, Fri 11.30am–3am, Sat noon–3am, Sun noon–2am.

Modern 3287 M St NW ⓣ 202/338-7027. Upscale lounge and club boasting a stylish bar and fittingly mod decor – all shiny metallic surfaces and posh designs – as well as a mix of hip-hop, house, and other beats. Tues–Thurs 8.30pm–2am, Fri & Sat 8.30pm–3am.

Mr Smith's 3104 M St NW ⓣ 202/333-3104. Most welcoming of Georgetown's saloons, with a splendid garden drinking-and-eating area, cheap beer-and-burger nights, live bands on weekends, and $1.50 rail drinks during weekday happy hour. Sun–Thurs 11.30am–2am, Fri & Sat 11.30am–3am.

Nathan's 3150 M Street NW ⓣ 202/338-2000. Longstanding Georgetown tradition for its sizable bar with plenty of potent choices, and steak-and-potatoes fare in its back dining room. Upstairs club has its own DJs and a festive atmosphere. Sun–Thurs 3pm–2am, Fri & Sat 3pm–3am.

Sequoia 3000 K St NW ⓣ 202/944-4200. Popular restaurant-bar with one of the best locations in the area – at the eastern end of Washington Harbor. Outdoor terrace seating overlooks the river. Arrive early on weekends. Daily 11.30am–12.30am.

The Tombs 1226 36th St NW, at Prospect ⓣ 202/337-6668. Busy student haunt adorned with rowing blades. Good for catching college football on Saturday afternoons in fall or just soaking up the Georgetown vibe. Occasional live bands and club nights. Mon–Thurs 11.30am–2am, Fri & Sat 11.30am–3am, Sun 9.30am–2am.

New Downtown

Dragonfly 1215 Connecticut Ave NW ⓣ 202/331-1775; **Dupont Circle Metro.** Sushi-and-cocktail lounge with ultra-swank decor and a crowd of beautiful young things on the make. Feels more like a transitional spot for Dupont scenesters, pausing for a drink and a smoke before serious club-hopping, than a destination in its own right. Mon–Thurs 5pm–1am, Fri 5.30pm–1.30am, Sat 6pm–1.30am, Sun 6pm–1am.

Lucky Bar 1221 Connecticut Ave NW ⓣ 202/331-3733; **Farragut North or Dupont Circle Metro.** Relaxed and earthy for this posey strip, with plenty of room and booths at the back to hang out and shoot pool. Dance nights, cheap drinks, and soccer on TV.

Mon–Thurs 3pm–2am, Fri 3pm–3am, Sat noon–3am, Sun 9pm–2am.

Madhatter 1831 M St NW ℡202/833-1495; **Farragut North or West Metro.** Homey saloon where an after-work crowd that comes for happy hour (4pm to 8pm) later gives way to a free-and-easy student set. Pop-oriented DJ tunes Tuesday through Friday from 9pm. Sun–Thurs 11am–2am, Fri & Sat 11am–3am.

Ozio 1813 M St NW ℡202/822-6000; **Farragut North or Dupont Circle Metro.** Ritzy cigar bar, lounge, and club popular with the District's well-polished and -varnished scenesters. A major player on the nightlife scene, and more fun if you love to pose. Mon–Thurs 5pm–2am, Fri 5pm–3am, Sat 6pm–3am.

Sign of the Whale 1825 M St NW ℡202/785-1110; **Dupont Circle or Farragut North Metro.** Downtown saloon with good food (see p.277) and dozens of beers on tap. Also a good spot to hear DJs spinning retro-pop anthems and corny Eighties knee-slappers. Mon–Thurs 11.30am–1.30am, Fri & Sat 11.30am–2.30am.

Tequila Grill 1990 K St NW ℡202/833-3640; **Farragut West Metro.** No one really comes to eat the Tex-Mex food; instead a young, after-work mob packs in for the very good happy-hour specials. Mon–Thurs 11am–1am, Fri & Sat 11am–3am.

Old Downtown

Capitol City Brewing Company 1100 New York Ave NW, entrance at 11th and H ℡202/628-2222; **Metro Center Metro.** Copper vats, pipes, and gantries adorn this microbrewery, serving a changing menu of home-brewed beers to an excitable bunch of drinkers. In September, the Mid-Atlantic Beer and Food Festival kicks off here. Also a branch at Union Station (see p.283). Sun–Thurs 11am–1am, Fri & Sat 11am–2am.

D.A.'s RFD Washington 810 7th St NW ℡202/289-2030; **Gallery Place-Chinatown Metro.** The leading edge in DC microbreweries, with three hundred bottled beers and forty locally crafted and international brews on tap – though the food tends to be mediocre. Centrally located near the MCI Center, so watch for heavy post-game crowds. Mon–Thurs 11am–2am, Fri 11am–3am, Sat noon–3am, Sun noon–2am.

District Chophouse & Brewery 509 7th St NW ℡202/347-3434; **Gallery Place-Chinatown Metro.** This stunningly converted old down-

town bank lends Swing-era style to the Penn Quarter. The busy bar serves five or six of its own brews. Also offers adequate food (see p.278). Mon–Thurs & Sun 11am–12.30am, Fri & Sat 11am–1.30am.

ESPN Zone 555 12th St NW ℡202/783-3776; **Metro Center Metro.** For some drinkers, the one unmissable chain sports bar, conspicuous in the Penn Quarter. For others, the purest sort of frat-boy torture. Sun–Thurs 11.30am–11pm, Fri & Sat 11.30am–midnight.

Fadó 808 7th St NW ℡202/789-0066; **Gallery Place-Chinatown Metro.** DC outpost of a national Irish-pub chain – with Victorian and Celtic decor – that's a good spot for a Guinness and a bite to eat, though more authentic Emerald Isle-themed haunts can be found on Capitol Hill near Union Station. Sun–Thurs 11am–2am, Fri & Sat 11am–3am.

Gordon Biersch Brewery 900 F St NW ℡202/783-5454; **Gallery Place-Chinatown Metro.** Yet another chain bar in the Penn Quarter. But its extravagant setting, in a restored 1891 Romanesque Revival bank that's a historic landmark, allows it to steal the show. Sun–Thurs 11.30am– midnight, Fri & Sat 11.30am–2am.

John Harvard's Warner Building, 1299 Pennsylvania Ave NW ℡202/783-2739; **Metro Center Metro.** Upscale basement brewhouse and restaurant, with half a dozen solid beers on tap; also a good place to power down home-styled food favorites like chicken pot pie and meatloaf. Mon–Thurs 11am–11pm, Fri 11am–midnight, Sat noon–midnight, Sun noon–10pm.

Sky Terrace *Washington Hotel*, 515 15th St NW ℡202/638-5900; **Metro Center Metro.** Superb rooftop views from the hotel's ninth-floor bar terrace. It's usually very busy – go early or late or expect to wait. Daily 11am–1am (May–Oct only).

Shaw

Exercise caution at night around all the places listed below. You can get to many of them in the evening by way of the U Street-Cardozo Metro, which operates on weekends until 3am, or by cab.

Polly's Café 1342 U St NW ℡202/265-8385; **U Street-Cardozo Metro.** Neat little brick-and-board café-bar with a few outdoor tables, good food, tap beers, and bottled micro-brews. Live music on Sundays. Mon–Thurs 6pm–2am, Fri 6pm–3am, Sat 10am–3am, Sun 10am–1am.

Red Room Bar *Black Cat*, **1811 14th St NW** ☎202/667-7960; **U Street-Cardozo Metro.** Independent, no-cover bar attached to the *Black Cat* music club with eponymous decor, plus pool, pinball, draft beers, and amiable, punky clientele. Sun–Thurs 8pm–2am, Fri & Sat 7pm–3am.

Velvet Lounge 915 U St NW ☎202/462-3213; **U Street-Cardozo Metro.** Schmooze-and-booze in this relaxed spot, with nightly live music upstairs (small cover) and an open-mike session every Tuesday. Sun–Thurs 8am–2am, Fri & Sat 8am–3am.

Upper Northwest

Aroma 3417 Connecticut Ave NW ☎202/244-7995; **Cleveland Park Metro.** For all its swell atmosphere, Cleveland Park's stylish cigar-and-martini bar still manages to feel like a neighborhood watering hole. Order a drink and take in the regular exhibits by local artists. Mon–Thurs 6pm–2am, Fri & Sat 6pm–3am.

Ireland's Four Provinces 3412 Connecticut Ave NW ☎202/244-0860; **Cleveland Park Metro.** Rollicking Irish music five nights a week brings in a college crowd. There's a good atmosphere, outdoor seats in the summer, thirteen beers on tap, and 20oz imperial pints of Guinness. Sun–Thurs 5pm–2am, Fri & Sat 4pm–3am.

Nanny O'Brien's 3319 Connecticut Ave NW ☎202/686-9189; **Cleveland Park Metro.** The other Irish tavern in Cleveland Park, this is a smaller, more personable joint, but with the same successful mix of heavy drinking and live music (usually no cover). Monday's jam night is good fun. Sun–Thurs 4pm–2am, Fri 4pm–3am, Sat noon–3am.

Zoo Bar (Oxford Tavern) 3000 Connecticut Ave NW ☎202/232-4225; **Woodley Park-Zoo Metro.** Timeless suburban saloon across from the zoo, with Guinness and microbrews and weekend performances by blues, jazz, and rock acts; open-mike night on Thursdays. Sun–Thurs 10am–2am, Fri & Sat 10am–3am.

Clubs

DC's **club** scene moves at a frenetic pace, and you can check out *City Paper*, the *Washington Post*'s "Weekend" section, and the gay-oriented *Metro Weekly* and *Washington Blade* for calendars, reviews, and ads. Although clubs come and go in all neighborhoods, DC's trendiest area is in New Downtown, near the intersection of Connecticut Avenue and 18th Street (just north of M St), in a part known as "Dupont South" due to its proximity to the Circle. The places listed below are some of the city's better-established venues; you're sure to find others that are new, or some that have changed hands and style. At many places the music and clientele can change radically on different nights, so you might want to call to confirm the lineup first.

Plenty of spots have low, and even no, **cover charges**, generally between $5 and $20 (highest on weekends). Upscale lounges and clubs are most likely to charge a steeper cover, and more often than not they have vague and at times completely arbitrary dress codes; if you avoid athletic gear, sneakers, sandals, and baseball caps, you'll greatly enhance your standing with the guardians of the velvet ropes – though at some places, merely being male may be enough to keep you out on evenings when the club decides to enforce a female-leaning 2-to-1 ratio.

There's not much point in listing **opening hours**; these vary wildly from night to night, and can change randomly from month to month. Generally, though, most places don't get going until well after 11pm and stay open until at least 3am, with some continuing (especially on weekends) until 5am. If you're going to be out this late, have a taxi number with you, since some clubs are in dubious parts of town where walking around in the wee hours invites trouble. Also remember to take photo ID or your passport with you; you won't get into many places without one. Lastly, you must be at least 21 to drink alcohol in DC.

Adams-Morgan and Shaw

2:K:9 2009 8th St NW ☎202/667-7750; U Street-Cardozo Metro. A flashy, multilevel nightclub close to Howard University that draws a diverse crowd of twentysomethings with its hip hop and house, velvet ropes, and dancers in cages.

Heaven & Hell 2327 18th St NW ☎202/667-4355; Woodley Park-Zoo or Dupont Circle Metro. While Hell (downstairs) would have trouble making Dante's hit list, Heaven features techno, dance, and live indie, reaching its cheesy best on Thursdays' Eighties night. Occasional cover.

Republic Gardens 1355 U St NW ☎202/323-2730; U Street-Cardozo Metro. Longstanding clubbers' favorite that recently reopened after being closed for two years, with DJs spinning hip hop, soul, and dance tunes in a stylishly converted townhouse. Live music some nights; the cover charge can zoom up to $20, so have a fat wallet in tow.

Spy Lounge 2408 18th St NW ☎202/483-3549; Woodley Park-Zoo Metro. The type of high-profile juggernaut dance club on the leading edge of Adams-Morgan gentrification – high-tech mod style, spy-themed decor, house and retro beats, and plenty of attitude. Connected to *Felix*, a snooty supper club.

Dupont Circle

Chaos 1603 17th St NW ☎202/232-4141; Dupont Circle Metro. Fun club at the heart of the Dupont scene, with cheap drinks and a well-stocked bar. Well-known events like drag bingo (Tues 9pm) and the Funky Divas cabaret show (Sat 10pm) serve to make this gay club increasingly straight.

MCCXXIII 1223 Connecticut Ave ☎202/822-1800; Dupont Circle Metro. The pinnacle of posing in DC, complete with strict velvet-rope and dress-code policies, throngs of youthful yuppie revelers, swank decor, a melange of music from hip hop to house, and attitude so thick you can cut it with a knife.

Red 1802 Jefferson Place NW ☎202/466-3475; Dupont Circle Metro. A diverse crowd shows up well past midnight at this hip underground hideout to get down to deep-house beats often until dawn. With sparse seating and a tiny bar, there's little space for anything but dancing.

Foggy Bottom and Georgetown

Lulu's Club Mardi Gras 1217 22nd St NW ☎202/861-5858; Foggy Bottom-GWU Metro. There's DJ rock and pop and a wild party scene every night at this amiable club, spread across three frenetic floors. Small cover on the weekend, when lines form early.

Third Edition 1218 Wisconsin Ave NW, near M St ☎202/333-3700. Gung-ho college scene with second-floor dance club featuring DJs and periodic live music. It's a cattle market on weekends, when you'll probably have to wait in line and pay a cover.

New Downtown

Andalu 1214 18th St NW ☎202/785-2922; Farragut North Metro. Stylish, dress-code-oriented place with a mix of moody deep-house and garage dance beats, and the occasional live musicians dabbling in jazz and electronica. Booze is on the expensive side.

Eighteenth Street Lounge 1212 18th St NW ☎202/466-3922; Dupont Circle Metro. Ultra-cool spot housed in Teddy Roosevelt's former mansion. While the attitude can be a bit thick at times, the music – mostly acid jazz, dub, and trip-hop, often served up by touring superstar DJs – is a big draw. Dress smart and look for the unmarked door next to the mattress shop. Come early (before 10pm) to avoid the cover and line.

Five 1214-B 18th St NW ☎202/331-7123; Farragut North Metro. Another staple on the New Downtown club scene, with several levels of party people dancing to the usual 4/4 beats – disco, house, pop, trance, and so on. Non-weekend nights sometimes feature jazz, reggae, and other styles.

Old Downtown

Diva 1350 I St NW ☎202/289-7300; McPherson Square Metro. What passes for an international club scene in DC, with a mix of Latin American and house sounds, plus a crowd of yuppies, foreign visitors, and leather-pant-wearing Eurotrash. Closes early (11pm), so more of a drop-in spot than a destination per se.

Platinum 915 F St NW ☎202/393-3555; Gallery Place-Chinatown Metro. Set in a converted bank, this stylish, multilevel dance club has a broad array of fans and sees its share of high rollers. Three DJs spin house and techno, and there's a VIP room for the self-appointed elite.

Dream 1350 Okie St NE T202/347-5255; no adjacent Metro station. A huge, four-level lounge-and-club scene with hip-hop and Latin music, and all the usual attitude. Take a cab to and from, as it's in one of DC's dicier areas, a fair distance from major sights. **Nation 1015 Half St SE** T202/554-1500; Waterfront or Navy Yard Metro. This hot,

two-floored club draws revelers to a dodgy part of town. During the week you're apt to hear a broad selection of bands and artists, while the weekend brings dance nights like Saturday's "Velvet Nation," highlighted by big-name DJs.
Zanzibar on the Waterfront 700 Water St SW T202/554-9100; L'Enfant Plaza Metro. African-American-oriented club that also draws an international crowd with live bands and DJs who kick out salsa, R&B, reggae, and jazz. Being on the water, it's a good spot to watch a sunset.

Live music

As with bars, the **live music** scene in Washington may surprise outsiders who come expecting a lackluster selection of retro-Vegas crooners and piano-bar hacks. Traditionally, such entertainment is found mainly in tourist zones, or anywhere visitors desire an "authentic" DC experience of patriotic anthems sung by frumpy matrons in old-fashioned concert halls. If you want to see the "official" side of culture in the District, there are plenty of opportunities at spots like the Kennedy Center and Constitution Hall (see the "Performing arts and film" chapter), but if you're really interested in head-banging, slam-dancing, or otherwise shaking your ass with abandon, the city has plenty of good choices. It isn't New York or LA, it's true, but DC is cool enough to have venues run by grunge superstars (like Dave Grohl of the Foo Fighters) and a number of classic joints that have left a historic mark on rock, jazz, and even punk history. Check local listings for opening times, cover charges, and ticket prices per show, which can vary widely depending on the night and the act.

Blues, folk, and country

Birchmere 3701 Mount Vernon Ave, Alexandria, VA T703/549-7500; no nearby Metro station. Excellent, longstanding club with an A-list of current and retro acoustic performers, as well as some up-and-comers.

Cowboy Café 2421 Columbia Pike, Arlington, VA T703/486-3467. All-American restaurant that's also a regional favorite for country & western music, rockabilly, and cowboy blues. Another Arlington branch at 4792 Lee Hwy (T703/243-8010).

Irish music

There are regular Irish (acoustic and folk) sessions in the following bars and clubs:
The Dubliner, Capitol Hill, p.283
IOTA, Arlington, p.291
Ireland's Four Courts, Arlington, p.283
Ireland's Four Provinces, Cleveland Park, p.287
Irish Times, Capitol Hill, p.287
Murphy's Grand Irish Pub, Alexandria, p.282–283
Nanny O'Brien's, Cleveland Park, p.287

J.V. Restaurant 6666 Arlington Blvd, Falls Church, VA ☎703/241-9504. Favorite honky-tonk joint that's a local haunt for its mix of live folk, country, blues, and rock - though located a ways out from DC.

New Vegas Lounge 1415 P St NW, Logan Circle ☎202/483-3971; Dupont Circle Metro. Neighborhood favorite that offers raunchy Chicago R & B in a decidedly funky setting. Cover can be steep – up to $15 for some acts.

Ragtime 1345 N Courthouse Rd, Arlington, VA ☎703/243-4003; Court House Metro. Relaxed bar-and-grill offering live music several nights a week, often in the blues, soul, and jazz vein.

State Theatre 220 N Washington St, Falls Church, VA ☎703/237-0300. Suburban venue in a stylish former moviehouse that rewards a drive out if you like country, folk, or blues music. Sometimes mixes things up with retread rockers and novelty acts as well.

Tiffany Tavern 1116 King St, Alexandria, VA ☎703/836-8844; King Street Metro. This Old Town haunt hosts open-mike nights during the week, but, on the weekends, it's all about bluegrass and its folk-flavored local and regional performers.

Jazz

Blues Alley 1073 Rear Wisconsin Ave NW, Georgetown ☎202/337-4141. This small, celebrated Georgetown jazz bar has been in business for over thirty years and attracts top names. Shows usually at 8pm and 10pm, plus midnight some weekends; cover can run to $40. Book in advance.

Bohemian Caverns 2003 11th St NW, Shaw ☎202/299-0800. U Street-Cardozo Metro. Legendary DC jazz supper club, reopened after three decades. The jazz happens in a basement grotto, below the stylish ground-level restaurant. Cover runs to $15 or more, with a limited number of reserved tickets for bigger acts.

Columbia Station 2325 18th St NW, Adams-Morgan ☎202/462-6040; Woodley Park-Zoo or Dupont Circle Metro. One of the better places in the area to listen to live jazz, along with blues, presented nightly in a sophisticated supper-club setting.

HR 57 1610 14th St NW, Logan Circle ☎202/667-3700; Dupont Circle Metro. Small but authentic club where jazz in many of its manifestations – classic, hard bop, free,

and cool – is performed on Wed, Fri, and Sun nights, often by newcomers on their way up. One of the essential cultural spots in this gentrifying neighborhood.

Laporta's 1600 Duke St, Alexandria, VA ☎703/683-6313; King Street Metro. Upscale seafood restaurant with a good range of jazz acts performing nightly.

The Saloun 3239 M St NW, Georgetown ☎202/965-4900. Cozy bar with 75 bottled beers and nightly jazz trios or bands, plus occasional R&B and soul acts. Free admission before 8pm, otherwise small cover charge.

Takoma Station Tavern 6914 4th St NW, Takoma Park, MD ☎202/829-1999; Takoma Metro. Laid-back club with live jazz several nights a week, showcasing mostly local acts. On some evenings reggae acts, comedians, or poetry slams take the spotlight.

Twins Jazz 1344 U St NW, Shaw ☎202/234-0072; U Steet-Cardozo Metro. Celebrated neighborhood jazz haunt drawing talented musicians Tues–Sun. Also serves decent Ethiopian, American, and Caribbean food. Associated with the equally appealing *Twins Lounge*, 5516 Colorado Ave NW (☎202/882-2523), though this is in a dicey area of north DC, so take a cab or drive there.

Rock and pop

9:30 Club 815 V St NW, Shaw ☎202/393-0930; U St–Cardozo Metro. Famous venue for indie rock and pop bands; book in advance for big names. Also has a separate no-cover bar. Not in a great part of town, but two blocks from the U Street-Cardozo Metro; take the Vermont Avenue exit.

Black Cat 1811 14th St NW, Shaw ☎202/667-7960; U St-Cardozo Metro. Part-owned by Foo Fighter Dave Grohl, this indie institution provides a showcase for veteran alternative acts and up-and-coming rock, punk, and garage bands alike, plus a sprinkling of world beat and retro-pop performers.

Chief Ike's Mambo Room 1725 Columbia Rd NW, Adams-Morgan ☎202/332-2211; Woodley Park-Zoo or Dupont Circle Metro. Ramshackle mural-clad bar with live bands playing rock, reggae, and R&B, or DJs hosting theme nights. Makes for an unpretentious, fun spot to dance. The upstairs bar has live indie music and a pool table.

Live music in restaurants and bars

The following restaurants and bars all feature regular live performances, from jazz to R&B to rock; there's usually no charge other than the price of the meal or drink.

Afterwords Café (jazz/blues), Dupont Circle, p.271

Bukom Café (African), Adams-Morgan, p.266

Café des Artistes (gospel), Foggy Bottom, p.273

Chi-Cha Lounge (Latin), Shaw, p.291

Columbia Station (jazz), Adams-Morgan, p.290

Kinkead's (jazz), Foggy Bottom, p.274

Mr Henry's (jazz), Capitol Hill, p.270

Mr Smith's (rock/piano bar), Georgetown, p.285

Polly's Café (eclectic), Shaw, p.286

Rumba Cafe (Latin), Adams-Morgan, p.291

U-topia (jazz/blues/Brazilian), Shaw, p.279

Whitlow's on Wilson (rock/jazz), Arlington, p.283

Zanzibar on the Waterfront (jazz/reggae), p.289

Clarendon Grill 1101 N Highland St, Arlington, VA ☎703/524-7455; Clarendon Metro. Old favorite for boozing, and something of a pickup joint. Musical offerings (Wed–Sat) include earnest acoustic strummers, alternative rockers, and occasional DJs.

Galaxy Hut 2711 Wilson Blvd, Arlington, VA ☎703/525-8646; Clarendon Metro. Regular lineup of local indie talent takes the stage at this tiny neighborhood hangout, with a bevy of beers on tap.

IOTA 2832 Wilson Blvd, Arlington, VA ☎703/522-8340; Clarendon Metro. One of the area's better choices for clubbing, this warehouse-style music joint has nightly performances by local and national indie, folk, and blues bands. A great bar and attached restaurant, too.

Madame's Organ 2461 18th St NW, Adams-Morgan ☎202/667-5370; Woodley Park-Zoo Metro. Straightforward hangout featuring live blues, raw R&B, and bluegrass, plus a small cover. Upstairs, there's a pool table and a rooftop bar.

Nation 1015 Half St SE, Waterfront ☎202/554-1500; Water Front or Navy Yard Metro. Mid-sized warehouse concert venue with a state-of-the-art sound system. It doubles as a popular dance club boasting an assortment of star guest DJs from around the globe. The neighborhood's a bit dicey, so take a cab home.

Zig's Bar & Grill 4531 Duke St, Alexandria, VA ☎703/823-2777. Though located in a cultural no-man's-land between Old Town and the freeway, this is a prime venue for regional bands of all stripes – with good mainstream and indie rock and some jazz acts, plus biweekly Sunday-night "jazz pootry" events.

Salsa and Latin American

Chi-Cha Lounge 1624 U St NW, Shaw ☎202/234-8400; U Street-Cardozo Metro. Swank candlelit lounge oozing atmosphere, with live Latin music and regulars toking on fruit-cured tobacco from Middle Eastern-style hookahs. Sink into a sofa and sample the excellent Andean tapas.

Habana Village 1834 Columbia Rd NW, Adams-Morgan ☎202/462-6310; Woodley Park-Zoo or Dupont Circle Metro. Intoxicating Latin-dance joint infused with the eclectic spirit of the Adams-Morgan of old. Tango and salsa lessons are available, and a good downstairs lounge/bar serves a fine *mojito*.

Rumba Cafe 2443 18th St NW, Adams-Morgan ☎202/588-5501, Woodley Park-Zoo Metro. A Latin oasis, this sliver of a café-bar, its walls rich with paintings and photographs, is a good bet for a night of sipping *caipirinhas* and grooving to live Brazilian bossa nova and Afro-Cuban rhythms.

Performing arts
and film

Washington **high culture** is inevitably associated with an institutional regime second only to New York in government funding,
prestige, and media exposure. Indeed, the city's cultural beacons
– from its concert halls to its award ceremonies – regularly make
appearances on public television and radio, giving the impression that after
a performer "makes it" in DC, he or she is artistically cast in stone, a living
legend on the road to national canonization. This, of course, is all properly
uplifting and enriching, but also has the effect of making the city's cultural
scene seem staid, a place where artists long past their prime go to receive medals and ribbons from the president and other important public figures.

That said, the livelier elements of high culture in DC do exist, but do take
some effort to find beyond all the grand institutional showpieces. The prime
mover in such matters is, naturally, the **John F. Kennedy Center for the
Performing Arts** – popularly known as the Kennedy Center – encom-
passing a concert hall, opera house, three theaters, and a film center. Home
to the National Symphony Orchestra, it stages seasonal productions by the
city's top opera and ballet companies, and also has a full program of visiting
national and international artists, companies, and ensembles. The other main
artistic promoter in town is the **Washington Performing Arts Society**
(WPAS), which sponsors music, ballet, and dance productions across the
city.

When Washington tries to free itself from institutional ossification, it scores
with its host of **smaller theaters** and **performance spaces** dedicated to contemporary, experimental, ethnic, or left-field productions, where tickets tend to
be cheaper (and more available) and the productions often more spontaneous
and compelling. Well away from the world of officially approved culture and
corporate largesse, **comedy clubs** have made slow headway in the District in
recent years, while the city's unique **moviehouses** present a range of interesting fare – foreign to indie to avant-garde – that you might not find in the
blander suburban multiplexes.

To find out **what's going on** in any of these categories, consult the Friday edition of the *Washington Post*, the monthly *Washingtonian*, or the free
weekly *City Paper*. Other sources include flyers and posters in bookstores
and cafés.

Tickets

Prices vary considerably according to the event or production. You can expect to shell out a lot for the high-profile events at the Kennedy Center, National Theatre, Arena Stage, and the like, and tickets at any price for major opera and ballet productions will be hard to come by unless you book well in advance. But many places offer half- or cut-price tickets on the day if there's space. In all instances it's worth a call to the box office: students (with ID), senior citizens, military personnel, and people with disabilities qualify for discounts in most theaters and concert halls. You can also buy tickets over the phone from various **ticket agencies**, which sell advance-reserved, full-price tickets (plus surcharge). Usually no changes or refunds are allowed.

Ticket agencies

Tickets.com ☎703/218-6500 or 1-800/955-5566, ⓦwww.tickets.com. Full-price tickets for performing arts, music, and sports events, by phone or online.
Ticketmaster ☎202/432-7328 or 1-800/551-7328, ⓦwww.ticket master.com. Full-price tickets for performing arts, music, and sports events, by phone or online, with a service charge.

TicketPlace, Old Post Office Pavilion, 1100 Pennsylvania Ave NW, Old Downtown ☎202/842-5387, ⓦwww .ticketplace.org. On-the-day (Sun and Mon tickets sold on Sat), **half-price** (plus ten percent surcharge) cash-only tickets for theater and music performances; credit-card bookings for full-price advance tickets. Tues–Sat 11am–6pm.

Box office numbers

Arena Stage ☎202/488-3300
DAR Constitution Hall ☎202/628-4780
Kennedy Center ☎202/467-4600
Lisner Auditorium ☎202/994-1500
National Theatre ☎202/628-6161
Shakespeare Theatre ☎202/547-1122
Smithsonian Institution ☎202/357-2700

Warner Theatre ☎202/628-1818
Washington Ballet ☎202/362-3606
Washington Opera ☎202/295-2420 or 1-800/876-7372
Washington Performing Arts Society ☎202/785-9727
Wolf Trap Farm ☎703/255-1860 (Filene Center), 703/938-2404 (Barns) 703/218-6500 (tickets)

Classical music, opera, and dance

The major trio of **classical music, opera**, and **dance** are predictably well represented in the nation's capital, where a less-than-respectable showing would be embarrassing to a city with such worldly cultural pretensions. Classical music is performed at the Kennedy Center and a half-dozen other concert halls, while concerts by popular performers and all-star ensembles take place in a variety of major venues (see box overleaf) in and outside the city.

Tickets for these big-name concerts tend to be pricey ($20–100) and need to be booked in advance, either direct from the venues or from one of the major ticket agencies (see "Tickets" box above). Because costs tend to be all over the map – from just a few bucks for no-name up-and-comers to $80 or more for international heavyweights – you're encouraged to visit each site's or company's website to check ticket prices for each event. As a rule, any performances at

The big-name concert venues in DC and beyond are scattered all over the place, thwarting your desire, if you have one, to see multiple shows or performances within a limited time frame. Indeed, you might find yourself driving back and forth from Virginia to Maryland to attend performances, or devoting significant lead time to secure tickets. Whatever the case, prices vary broadly according to the site, the section of the venue where you plan to sit, the nature of the program, and of course the performance itself. For more details, call the box office numbers listed below, or Ticketmaster, Tickets.com or Ticket Place (see p.293).

In the District

Carter Barron Amphitheater 4850 Colorado Ave NW, Upper Northwest ☎202/426-0486, ⓦwww.nps.gov/rocr /cbarron. Popular summer amphi-theater in Rock Creek Park that offers a mix of free and paid events, including Shakespeare plays, rock, pop, and blues concerts, dance, and classical-music performances, and much more.

DAR Constitution Hall 1776 D St NW, Foggy Bottom ☎202/628-4780, ⓦwww.dar.org/conthall; Farragut West Metro. Widely known as one of the best concert halls in the city, only usurped in the 1960s by the Kennedy Center. Now, with its 4000 seats, hosts uneventful mainstream concerts of pop, country, and jazz acts.

Kennedy Center 2700 F St NW, Foggy Bottom ☎202/467-4600, ⓦwww.kennedy-center.org; Foggy Bottom-GWU Metro. The National Symphony Orchestra performs in the 2800-seat Concert Hall (Sept–June); there are less expensive chamber recitals in the Terrace Theater, and

free concerts in the Grand Foyer. See also p.149–152.

Lincoln Theatre 1215 U St NW, Shaw ☎202/328-6000, ⓦwww .thelincolntheatre.org; U Street-Cardozo Metro. Renovated movie/ vaudeville house featuring touring stage shows; pop, jazz, soul, and gospel concerts; and dance, with a focus on multicultural productions.

Lisner Auditorium George Washing-ton University, 730 21st St NW, Foggy Bottom ☎202/994-1500; Foggy Bot-tom-GWU Metro. A 1500-seat audit-orium with regular classical and cho-ral concerts on campus; often quite good, sometimes free. Rock, pop, and indie acts also take the stage.

MCI Center 601 F St NW, Old Down-town ☎202/628-3200, ⓦwww .mcicenter.com; Gallery Place-Chinatown Metro. Downtown 20,000-seater hosts big-name rock, pop, and country gigs. For more, see p.172.

National Theatre 1321 Pennsylvania Ave NW, Old Downtown ☎202/628-6161, ⓦwww.nationaltheatre.org

the major venues will cost $30 or more for anything resembling a decent seat. However, free shows at other DC concert halls – just like exhibitions at DC museums – often tend to be free, and where this is true we've noted it below.

Classical music

The Concert Hall of the Kennedy Center (see pp.149–152) is the most prestigious in town for **classical music** – it's also the home of the National Symphony Orchestra – and DAR Constitution Hall is another longstanding favorite. Other com-panies and venues, large to small,

are noted below for their respective programs and characteristics.

Major companies

Aside from those **major companies** listed below, there are any number of small- and mid-sized entities perform-ing classical music in DC, from virtu-osi-in-training on college campuses, to church members singing in their own

Metro Centre Metro. One of the country's oldest theaters, it's been on this site (if not in this building) since 1835. Today, it features flashy new premieres, pre- and post-Broadway productions, and musicals.

RFK Stadium 2400 E Capitol St SE (east of Capitol Hill) ☎202/547-9077; Stadium-Armory Metro. A 55,000-seater stadium and temporary home of DC's new baseball team, RFK is

Outside the District

FedEx Field 1600 FedEx Way, Landover, MD ☎301/276-6050. Redskins football stadium hosts occasional summer pop and rock concerts.

Merriweather Post Pavilion 10475 Little Patuxent Parkway, Columbia, MD ☎202/397-SEAT, ⑩www .merriweathermusic.com. Mid-league and major pop, jazz, country, and middle-of-the-road acts perform in spring and summer only. There's pavilion and open-air seating.

Nissan Pavilion at Stone Ridge 7800 Cellar Door Drive, Bristow, VA ☎1-800/455-8999 or 703/754-6400, ⑩www.nissanpavilion.com. Outdoor summer stadium (25,000 seats) plays host to many of the major summer tours, though a bit removed from DC out near Manassas, VA.

Patriot Center George Mason University, Fairfax, VA ☎703/993-3000, ⑩www.patriotcenter.com. A 10,000

the occasional site of concerts by big-name pop stars and mainstream rock acts.

Warner Theatre 1299 Pennsylvania Ave NW, Old Downtown ☎202/783-4000, ⑩www.warnertheatre.com; Metro Center Metro. Glorious 1920s movie palace that's been remodeled and is now staging post-Broadway productions, musicals, and major concerts.

-seat venue for big concerts and family entertainment.

Strathmore Music Center 10701 Rockville Pike, North Bethesda, MD ☎301/530-0540 or 581-5100, ⑩www .strathmore.org; Grosvenor-Strathmore Metro. The latest big-league concert center to open (in Feb 2005), **Strathmore** plans an ambitious set of performances from regional groups, notably the Baltimore Symphony Orchestra and National Philharmonic. Beyond this, genres range broadly from musicals and show tunes to pop, folk, jazz, and world-beat.

Wolf Trap Farm Park Filene Center and The Barns, 1624 Trap Rd, Vienna, VA ☎703/255-1860 (Filene Center), ☎703/938-2404 (Barns), ☎703/218-6500 (tickets), ⑩www .wolftrap.org. US Park Service gem plays host to a variety of jazz, country, folk, zydeco, and pop acts. See p.246 for details.

public choirs, to handfuls of chamber musicians giving concerts in museums, cathedrals, mansions, and embassies. Check local listings for more details.

Note also that the **armed forces** have their own performing ensembles, which tend to be quite accomplished and more varied in their repertoire than you might expect. All groups play weekly during the summer in front of the US Capitol; the big names (Navy and Marine bands) are listed below, but the Army (☎703/696-3399, ⑩www.army.mil

/armyband) has a solid reputation, too, and performs throughout the region, and the Air Force (☎202/767-5658, ⑩www.usafband.com) has its own group of fans, and can often be seen at the National Air and Space Museum on the Mall (see pp.83–87).

Choral Arts Society of Washington ☎202/244-3669, ⑩www.choralarts.org. The District's major choir, performing at the Kennedy Center, Wolf Trap, and other region-wide locations. Usually offers traditional pieces (classical to current), and seasonal favorites, especially at Christmas (Handel's *Messiah*, and so on).

Friday Morning Music Club 2233 Wisconsin Ave NW, Suite 326 ☎202/333-2075, ⓦwww.fmmc.org. Longstanding cultural group (est. 1886) that gives performances of classical, romantic, and (traditional) contemporary pieces by major composers. Performs at the Charles Sumner School (see p.184) as its primary venue, along with area churches and Dumbarton Oaks.

National Symphony Orchestra 2700 F St NW ☎1-800/444-1324, ⓦwww.kennedy-center .org/nso; Foggy Bottom-GWU Metro. Performs in the Kennedy Center, serving up the big names in classical music under the baton of conductor Leonard Slatkin, who's best known for championing American composers. Tickets to performances run from $25 to $60, though the orchestra also performs free outside the Capitol on the West Terrace on Memorial Day, July 4, and Labor Day.

US Marine Band 8th and I St SE, Marine Barracks ☎202/433-4011, ⓦwww.marineband.usmc.mil; Navy Yard Metro. The oldest professional music organization in the country (dating from 1798) and an accomplished champion of all kinds of classical music – John Philip Sousa was a legendary director. Smaller ensembles perform folk and jazz, and there are also fall and winter chamber recitals – all concerts are free and take place at either the US Capitol or Marine Corps War Memorial (see p.232).

US Navy Band 617 Warrington Ave, Navy Yard SE ☎202/433-2525, ⓦwww.navyband.navy.mil. Offers free weekly summer concerts at the US Capitol and Navy Memorial (see p.158), with eight different performing groups and seven chamber ensembles. Genres range widely, from sea chanties and drum-corps pieces to jazz, big-band, country, and bluegrass – even rock and R&B. The classical-oriented Concert Band has been going strong for 70 years and regularly receives the big notices.

Washington Performing Arts Society 2000 L St NW, Suite 510 ☎202/833-9800, tickets ☎202/785-9727, ⓦwww.wpas.org. Not a performing group per se, but a co-ordinator of high-cultural events that puts together shows at twelve prominent venues and offers ticket packages based on the interest of each audience member. Categories (and prices) range widely from jazz to world-beat, but usually involve at least two to five classical shows per month.

Washington Symphony Orchestra 1225 I St NW, Suite 110 ☎202/546-9787, ⓦwww .washingtonsymphony.org. Started in the 1930s, an agreeable group presenting four concerts per year, usually in the traditional vein – waltzes, Bach, Mozart, etc – and occasional free outdoor concerts at Dupont Circle and other District locations.

Smaller venues

There's much worth seeking out at the many **smaller venues** for the performing arts in DC. Events take place at university halls (like Lisner Auditorium), as well as museums (the Corcoran Gallery of Art, p.140), historic houses (Dumbarton House, p.226), churches (Washington National Cathedral, p.209) and embassies (see "Embassy events," p.21). For details about Smithsonian Institution concerts, call ☎202/357-2700, or check ⓦwww.si.edu.

Arts Club of Washington 2017 I St NW, Foggy Bottom ☎202/331-7282, ⓦwww.artsclubofwash-ington.org; Foggy Bottom-GWU Metro. Based in a historic Federal house where President James Monroe lived briefly in 1817, the club presents free Friday concerts at noon during selected months (often June–July & Oct–Nov), tending toward chamber music, sonatas, and small ensembles.

Coolidge Auditorium Jefferson Building, Library of Congress, 1st St and Independence Ave SE, Capitol Hill ☎202/707-5502, ⓦwww.loc.gov; Capitol South Metro. Free chamber music concerts in a historic venue (see p.112). Sept–May.

Folger Shakespeare Library 201 E Capitol St SE, Capitol Hill ☎202/544-7077, ⓦwww .folger.edu; Capitol South Metro. Medieval and Renaissance music from the Folger Consort ensemble. Oct–May.

National Academy of Sciences 2101 Constitution Ave NW, Foggy Bottom ☎202/334-2436, ⓦwww.nationalacademies.org/arts; Foggy Bottom-GWU Metro. Pleasing 700-seat auditorium with free chamber recitals, often monthly from Oct–April.

National Gallery of Art West Building, West Garden Court, Constitution Ave NW at 7th St ☎202/842-6941, ⓦwww.nga.gov; Archives-Navy Memorial Metro. Free concerts every Sunday at 7pm (Oct–June) in the lovely

West Garden Court. First-come-first-served basis; doors open at 6pm. Also jazz performances in July & Aug.
Phillips Collection 1600 21st St NW; Dupont Circle ☎202/387-2151, ⓦwww .phillipscollection.org; Dupont Circle Metro. Classical music concerts in the museum's Music Room (Sept–May Sun 5pm); free with museum admission (see p.190). Arrive early.
Society of the Cincinnati at Anderson House 2118 Massachusetts Ave NW, Dupont Circle ☎202/785-2040; Dupont Circle Metro. Free chamber recitals once or twice a week in fine mansion surroundings (see p.189), performed by the accomplished Air Force Chamber Players (Oct–May, Sun or Wed 1.30pm).

Opera

The District's version of **opera** is similar to that of other major American cities – one institutional heavyweight supported by a few small companies and entities. Unlike a lot of other performing arts in DC, opera is not one that can be put on casually at a museum, historic mansion, or institution. It requires significant investment and a sizable facility – for that reason, the options here are much fewer than they are for classical music in general. The listings below offer a representative selection of the limited operatic possibilities.
Opera Camerata 1819 Shepherd St NW, Suite 100 ☎202/722-5335, ⓦwww.operacamerata .org. Small institution that offers periodic (once or twice yearly) productions of German operetta and historically minor or forgotten works. Rotating venues, but often held at the Austrian Embassy at 3524 International Court NW (ⓦwww.austria.org).
Summer Opera Theater Company Hartke Theater, Catholic University, Michigan Ave and 4th St NE ☎202/526-1669, ⓦwww.summeropera .org; Brookland Metro. Independent company staging two operas each summer (usually June, July and/or Aug), mostly familiar staples from the nineteenth-century canon; located near the National Shrine of the Immaculate Conception (see p.204).
Washington Opera ☎202/295-2400 or 1-800/876-7372, ⓦwww.dc-opera.org. Tickets for one of the country's finest resident opera companies (artistic director: Placido Domingo) sell out well in advance, though you may get standing-room tickets at the box office. Performances are mainly

Free open-air concerts

Summer is a good time to catch a free **open-air concert** in Washington, though certain locations host events all year round. Check the following places and see DC's festival calendar (pp 307–310) for more information.

C&O Canal, Georgetown. Varied Sunday afternoon summer concerts take place between 30th and Thomas Jefferson St.
Freedom Plaza, Pennsylvania Ave NW. Year-round venue for folk events and music festivals.
National Zoological Park, Connecticut Ave NW. "Sunset serenades" in summer, featuring a variety of musical performances.
Netherlands Carillon, Marine Corps (Iwo Jima) War Memorial, Arlington, VA. Carillon concerts every Saturday and on national holidays May through September; regular summer concerts at War Memorial by US Marine Band.
Sylvan Theatre, Washington Monu-

ment grounds. Army, Air Force, Navy, and Marine Corps bands perform four nights a week June through August (including annual *1812 Overture* performance in Aug). Other musical events throughout the year, too.
US Capitol. Armed forces bands perform four nights a week (June–Aug) on the East Terrace. National Symphony Orchestra concerts on the West Terrace on Memorial Day, July 4, and Labor Day.
US Navy Memorial, 701 Pennsylvania Ave NW. Spring and summer concert series featuring Navy, Marine Corps, Coast Guard, and high-school bands. Regular performances Tues 8pm June–Aug.

Romantic European warhorses, with an occasional exception or two, and given in the Opera House and the other Kennedy Center theaters. Sept–June season.

Dance

You can find **dance** from ballet to hip hop in any number of good Washington venues, from international stylings at the various Smithsonian institutions to avant-garde pieces put on by modern galleries and museums. These are generally noted throughout the text and this chapter; the companies below are stricter in their focus on dance, and make it a central concern.

Dance Institute of Washington 128 M St NW #300 ☎ 202/371-9656, ⓦ www.danceinstitute. org. Presents five to ten performances per year at major venues in DC, Maryland, and Virginia, and offers a range of dance classes.

The Dance Place 3225 8th St NE, Brookland ☎ 202/269-1600, ⓦ www.danceplace.org; Brookland Metro. Contemporary and modern dance productions, mainstream and experimental, with a bent toward African- and African-American-themed shows. Also hosts the Dance Africa festival every June.

Momentum Dance Theatre 651 E St NE, Capitol Hill East ☎ 202/543-0945, ⓦ www.momentumdancetheatre.com. Small troupe presenting inventive spins on the classics (such as a jazz hip hop *Nutcracker*) and jazz- and modern-oriented productions, often with a satiric twist. Irregular shows take place throughout the year at regional venues.

Washington Ballet 3515 Wisconsin Ave NW ☎ 202/362-3606 or 467-4600, ⓦ www .washingtonballet.org. Classical and contemporary ballet performed in rep by the city's major ballet company at the Kennedy Center. Every December *The Nutcracker* is performed at the Warner Theatre.

Theater

As with other performing arts, **theater** in the District is alive and well, and has proven to be a revitalizing force for many formerly down-at-the-heel neighborhoods, with areas from Adams–Morgan to Logan Circle to the Penn Quarter to Arlington, VA, experiencing cultural renaissances that at least partially owe to the presence of independent theaters and troupes. For major-league shows, most Broadway productions either preview or tour in Washington, typically in grand concert halls or renovated moviehouses. Quite simply, you're never at a loss to see drama in DC, and there's often something engaging playing on any given night, and usually at a Metro-accessible location. As with other arts, tickets vary depending on the event and location; call for details.

Adams-Morgan and Shaw

DC Arts Center 2438 18th St NW, Adams -Morgan ☎ 202/462-7833, ⓦ www.dcartscenter .org; Woodley Park-Zoo Metro. Performance art, drama, poetry, dance, and a whole range of multicultural activities are held in this small northern Adams-Morgan space.

Lincoln Theatre 1215 U St NW, Shaw ☎ 202/328-6000, ⓦ www.thelincolntheatre.org; U Street-Cardozo Metro. Renovated movie/vaudeville house features touring stage shows, concerts, and dance, with a focus on multicultural productions.

Arlington, VA

Gunston Arts Center 2700 S Lang St ☎ 703/228-1850. Featuring two theaters – a proscenium stage and smaller "black box" – this facility hosts a range of drama, novelties, and cultural events from local and regional troupes.

Rosslyn Spectrum 1611 N Kent St ☎ 703/525-7550, ⓦ www.arlingtonarts.org; Rosslyn Metro. Near the last Arlington Metro stop before DC, a good venue for theater, concerts, and cultural events. With classics, multimedia experiments, and off-kilter new plays, you're likely to see almost anything here.

Signature Theatre 3806 S Four Mile Run
☎703/218-6500, ⓦwww.signature-theatre
.org. Award-winning theatrical group
putting on premieres of new works, as
well as straightforward revivals of classics
and musicals, and irreverent adaptations
of them.

Logan Circle

Source Theatre 1835 14th St NW ☎202/462-
1073, ⓦ www.sourcetheatre.com; U-Street-
Cardozo Metro. New and contemporary
works and classic reinterpretations. Promotes the Washington Theater Festival, a
showcase for new works, every summer.
Take a taxi here at night.
Studio Theatre 1333 P St NW ☎202/332-3300,
ⓦwww.studiotheatre.org; Dupont Circle Metro.
Independent theater with two stages presenting classic and contemporary drama as
well as comedy.

Old Downtown

Ford's Theatre 511 10th St NW ☎202/426-
6924, ⓦwww.fordstheatre.org; Metro Center
Metro. The site of Lincoln's assassination
(see p.175), this restored nineteenth-
century theater stages mainstream musicals
and dramas; rehearsals or matinees usually
Thurs, Sat & Sun.
Gala Hispanic Theatre Warehouse Theatre,
1021 7th St NW ☎202/234-7174, ⓦwww
.galatheatre.org; Mount Vernon Square-UDC
Metro. Specializes in works by Spanish/
Latin American playwrights, performed in
Spanish or English, as well as performance art and poetry. Note that in 2005 the
theater plans to open a facility at the classic Tivoli Theatre in Columbia Heights; see
website for details.
National Theatre 1321 Pennsylvania Ave NW
☎202/628-6161, ⓦ www.nationaltheatre.org;
Metro Center Metro. One of the country's
oldest theaters, it's been on this site (if not
in this building) since 1835. Premieres,
pre- and post-Broadway productions, and
musicals.
Shakespeare Theatre in the Lansburgh, 450 7th
St NW ☎202/547-1122, ⓦwww
.shakespearedc.org; Gallery Place-Chinatown
Metro. Four annual plays by Shakespeare
and his contemporaries. Each June the
company stages free, outdoor performances at the Carter Barron Amphitheater in
Rock Creek Park (see p.294).

Warner Theatre 1299 Pennsylvania Ave NW
☎ 202/628-1818, ⓦ www.warnertheatre.com;
Metro Center Metro. Glorious 1920s movie
palace that's been remodeled and is now
staging post-Broadway productions, musicals, and major concerts.
Woolly Mammoth Theatre 7th and D sts
☎202/289-2443, ⓦwww.woollymammoth.
net; Archives-Navy Memorial. Metro. Increasingly popular theater troupe that's recently
moved to splashy new downtown digs.
Stages budget- and mid-priced shows of
contemporary and experimental plays.

Other locations

African Continuum Theater Company 3523
12th St NE, Outer Northeast ☎202/529-5763,
ⓦwww.africancontinuumtheatre.com. Specializes in productions reflecting the African-
American experience. Call for schedules
and venues; usually four to five shows per
year.
Arena Stage 1101 6th St SW, Waterfront
SW ☎202/554-9066, ⓦwww.arenastage.org;
Waterfront Metro. One of the most popular,
and well-respected, of DC's major theatrical
institutions and a centerpiece of waterfront
redevelopment. Presents an eclectic selection of modern, classical, musical, and
avant-garde works on its three stages (Arena
Stage, Kreeger Theater and Old Vat Room).
Discovery Theater Arts and Industries Building, 900 Jefferson Drive SW, National Mall
☎ 202/357-1500, ⓦ www.discoverytheater
.si.edu; Smithsonian Metro. Year-round daytime children's theater, offering musicals
and puppet shows at budget prices.
Folger Shakespeare Library 201 E Capitol St SE,
Capitol Hill ☎ 202/544-7077, ⓦwww
.folger.edu; Capitol South Metro. A full program
is presented at the Elizabethan library-
theater (Sept–June), not solely Shakespeare,
but often including his contemporaries and
more modern playwrights as well.
Kennedy Center 2700 F St NW, at Virginia and
New Hampshire Ave, Foggy Bottom ☎202/467-
4600, ⓦwww.kennedy-center.org; Foggy
Bottom–GWU Metro. Site of three theaters:
the Eisenhower (drama and Broadway
productions), the Terrace (experimental/
contemporary works) and the Theater Lab
(almost permanently home to the long-run-
ning *Shear Madness*, a comedy-whodunit;
plus children's shows and cabaret). The
Opera House also hosts musicals.

Comedy

When it comes to comedy, several clubs offer the usual mix of big-name stand-up acts, improv, local or regional circuit appearances and open-mike nights. These apart, there are occasional stand-up nights at spots as diverse as Adams-Morgan bars like *Madame's Organ* (see p.291) and *Chief Ike's Mambo Room* (see p.290) or the Arena Stage, Studio Theatre, and the Kennedy Center; local listings papers have all the latest details.

Keep an eye out, too, for comedy troupes that appear in cabaret or improv shows at various venues around town, including major hotels like the *Four Seasons*, the *Mayflower*, and the *Washington Hilton*. Capitol Steps is the best-known (and most unavoidable) of these troupes, but there are also regular shows by ensembles like ComedySportz and Gross National Product.

Cabaret performances can be expensive, since there's often a drinks-and-food minimum charge on top of the ticket price. A big weekend show can cost as much as $40–50, though tickets for basic stand-up and improv nights are more like $15. Reservations are essential.

Capitol Steps Ronald Reagan Building and International Trade Center, 1300 Pennsylvania Ave NW, Old Downtown ☏202/408-8736, ⓦwww.capsteps.com; Metro Center Metro. Well-established political satire by a group of Capitol Hill staffers on Friday and Saturday nights at 7.30pm.

Improv 1140 Connecticut Ave NW ☏202/296-7008, ⓦwww.dcimprov.com; Farragut North Metro. DC's main comedy stage, part of a chain of eight such venues nationwide. Draws both up-and-coming performers and the occasional veteran from the TV humor circuit.

Film

As with most American cities, the great majority of **moviehouses** in Washington are owned by a handful of major corporations (in this case operators such as AMC and Loews Cineplex Odeon), and program the same tired Hollywood action schlock and teen sex comedies you can see anywhere. Multiplexes are growing in number and size throughout the DC region, and usually feature raked seating, $8–10 tickets, and the same bland neon-and-pastel designs. What follows below, by contrast, are those unique theaters that, either by their historic pedigree or inventive programming, offer a good reason to venture beyond the big-box mainstream cinemas.

Although nighttime tickets are increasingly pricey, afternoon matinees come in at a few dollars cheaper – while cheapest of all are the free films showing at museums and galleries; indeed, these programs are often among the best in DC, focusing on a single director, genre, style, movement, or national cinema, with a range of films showing over several days or weeks. Also don't forget the IMAX screens at the National Air and Space Museum (see p.83) and the National Museum of Natural History (see p.68), especially if you've got kids to entertain. If you happen to be here in April, be on the lookout for screenings tied to DC's annual Filmfest (ⓦ www.filmfestdc.org), which premieres national and international movies in theaters across town.

American Film Institute Kennedy Center, 2700 F St NW, Foggy Bottom ☏202/785-4600, ⓦwww.afi.com; Foggy Bottom-GWU Metro. Institutional film heavyweight with regular programs of art, foreign, and classic films, usually built around certain directors, countries, and themes, often with associated lectures and seminars. A second branch in Silver Spring, MD (two blocks from the eponymous Metro stop) shows similar programs, and makes for a nice evening jaunt.

Arlington Cinema 'n' Drafthouse 2903 Columbia Pike ☎703/486-2345. Grab a brew or munch on food while you watch a second-run movie at this combination pub-theater, with one screen showing three or four movies during the week. You'll need transportation, though – it's a quarter-mile east of Glebe Road.

Avalon Theatre 5612 Connecticut Ave NW, Upper Northwest ☎202/966-6000, ⓦwww .theavalon.org; Friendship Heights Metro. Near the Maryland border (a 10–15min walk from the Metro), a marvelously refurbished 1930s movie palace with handsomely redecorated lobby, lovely ceiling mural, and old-fashioned charm, now showing independent films and Hollywood classics.

Dr. Dremo's Taphouse 2001 Clarendon Blvd ☎703/528-4660, ⓦwww.drdremo.com; Court House Metro. Tasty microbrews and pool in a converted car showroom, where weekly cult film showings (Tues 8pm; $2) offer nerve-jangling D-grade horror and kitsch classics

– brought to you by the Washington Psychotronic Film Society (ⓦwww.wpfs.org).

Mary Pickford Theater Madison Building, Library of Congress, 1st St and Independence Ave SE, Capitol Hill ☎202/707-5677, ⓦwww .loc.gov; Capitol South Metro. Free classic and foreign historic movies from the library's voluminous archives.

Uptown Theater 3426 Connecticut Ave NW, Upper Northwest ☎202/966-5400; Cleveland Park Metro. Along with the Avalon, this is the District's other extant 1930s moviehouse, with one marvelously large screen, plenty of balcony seating, and slate of contemporary Hollywood movies.

Visions Cincma Bistro Lounge 1927 Florida Ave NW ☎202/667-0090, ⓦwww.visionsdc .com; Dupont Circle Metro. Excellent spot that's one of the few places in DC showing independent and foreign films; the attached bistro serves good food and potent drinks, which can be taken into the theater. Also features Bar Noir with dance DJs, and Midnight Movies on weekends.

16

Gay DC

For a smallish East Coast city better known for its policy prattle than its Pride parades, Washington DC's **gay and lesbian scene** is surprisingly vibrant – though you'll find it a bit more buttoned-down than the ones in New York, LA, or San Francisco. But times have certainly changed in the nation's capital since 1975, when gay federal employees risked being fired from their government jobs for engaging in "immoral conduct." Within the past decade, the first openly gay city official has been elected, the alternative weekly *Washington Blade* has grown to more than one hundred pages, and, in April 2000, hundreds of thousands descended upon DC to attend the Millennium March on Washington for Equality.

The heart of DC's gay community is **Dupont Circle**, where the greatest concentration of shops, bars, and restaurants catering to a gay clientele can be found. Most of the action takes place along P Street, just west of the Circle between 21st and 22nd streets, and on 17th Street, where gay and gay-friendly establishments form a lively strip between P and R streets. It's here that stilettoed sprinters in drag line up each October for the High-Heel Race (see p.304), a vivacious sporting event/street carnival. Across town in **Capitol Hill**, a handful of gay-friendly spots are clustered in the vicinity of the Eastern Market Metro station, near the intersection of Pennsylvania Avenue and 8th Street, while in the somewhat dodgy **Southeast** quadrant you'll find a few noteworthy dance clubs (just take care to come and go by cab when partying in this part of town).

To get a reading on the local pulse, grab a copy of the *Washington Blade* (⊛www.washblade.com) for news, listings, and classified ads. For an insider's guide to the nightlife, turn to the *Metro Weekly* for up-to-date listings of dining and partying hot spots – including information on special events, DJs, and happy hours – accompanied by a map. Both publications are free and can be picked up at Lambda Rising, 1625 Connecticut Ave (☎202/462-6969, ⊛www .lambdarising.com), or at various restaurants and clubs in Dupont Circle and Capitol Hill. A list of other gay resources and organizations in DC appears on p.305.

Accommodation

While only a handful of places in DC bill themselves exclusively as gay **hotels** or B&Bs, gay-friendly accommodation is scattered throughout the city. You can count on feeling welcome at most of the hotels in the Dupont Circle area listed in Chapter 12, plus a few recommended spots are listed below, with page references to their fuller descriptions.

Bull Moose B&B 101 Fifth St NE, Capitol Hill ☎202/547-1050 or 1-800/261-2768, ⓦwww .bullmoose-b-and-b.com; see p.253.
Carlyle Suites 1731 New Hampshire Ave NW, Dupont Circle ☎202/234-3200 or 1-866/468-3532, ⓦwww.carlylesuites.com; see p.254.
Dupont at the Circle 1604 19th St NW, Dupont Circle ☎202/332-5251 or 1-888/412-0100, ⓦwww.dupontatthecircle.com; see p.254.
Embassy Inn 1627 16th St NW, Dupont Circle ☎202/234-7800 or 1-800/423-9111; see p.254.
Kalorama Guest House at Woodley Park 2700 Cathedral Ave NW, Upper Northwest ☎202/328-0860; see p.260.
Tabard Inn 1739 N St NW, New Downtown ☎202/785-1277, ⓦwww.tabardinn.com; see p.258.
William Lewis House 1309 R St NW, Logan Circle ☎202/462-7574 or 1-800/465-7574, ⓦwww.wlewishous.com; see p.258.

Restaurants and cafés

While more than a few places reviewed in the main "Eating" chapter (see p.262) have won loyal gay followings – including *Pizzeria Paradiso* and *Afterwords Café* in Dupont Circle, *Two Quail* in Capitol Hill, and *The Diner* and *Perry's* in Adams–Morgan – the handful of spots listed below have become fixtures on the capital's gay and lesbian scene.

Annie's Paramount Steakhouse 1609 17th St NW, Dupont Circle ☎202/232-0395; Dupont Circle Metro. A local institution, in business since the 1940s, serving inexpensive steaks, good burgers, and brunch – including a midnight brunch on weekends. Sun–Thurs 11am–11pm, Fri & Sat 24hr. Moderate.

Banana Café & Piano Bar 500 8th St SE, Capitol Hill ☎202/543-5906; Eastern Market Metro. A tropical spot serving uneventful Tex-Mex staples alongside some fine Caribbean and Cuban standouts, such as *ropa vieja* (a hearty shredded-beef delight), cod-fish fritters, and plantain soup, the house specialty. Stop by the upstairs *Piano Bar* on weekdays for happy hour, when the celebrated margaritas go for $2 and a piano man is in the house. Mon–Thurs 11.30am–2.30pm & 5–10.30pm, Fri 11.30am–2.30pm & 5–11pm, Sat 5–11pm, Sun 11am–3pm & 5–10.30pm. Moderate.

Hamburger Mary's 1337 14th St NW, Logan Circle ☎202/232-7010; Dupont Circle Metro. East Coast branch of a West Coast chain, serving juicy burgers along with very good spicy fries in a converted garage decked out with kitschy memorabilia and a very long bar. Daytime draws a mixed crowd; after dark it gets very cruisey. Upstairs, in the *Titan* bar, DJs spin tunes from 5pm to 2am daily. Mon–Thurs 11am–midnight, Fri & Sat 11am–2am, Sun 10am–midnight. Inexpensive.

Jolt 'N Bolt 1918 18th St NW, Adams-Morgan ☎202/232-0077; Dupont Circle Metro. Townhouse tea- and coffeehouse with side-alley patio tucked away up 18th Street. Wraps and sandwiches, pastries, and fresh juices are served. Sun–Thurs 6.30am–12.30am, Fri & Sat 6.30am –1.30am. Inexpensive.

L'Enfant 2000 18th St NW, Adams-Morgan ☎202/319-1800; Dupont Circle Metro. A bagel-and-crepe spot that's better for hanging out (sipping coffee perhaps) than for having an overpriced meal. On "Wine-and-Wig Wednesdays" (Sept–May), there's half-priced vino and plenty of fake hair on show. Mon–Thurs 7.30am–11pm, Fri–Sun 10am–midnight. Moderate.

Mr Henry's 601 Pennsylvania Ave SE, Capitol Hill ☎202/546-8412; Eastern Market Metro. Saloon and restaurant with outside patio, charcoal grill, and loyal gay crowd. Even the most expensive choices – the steak and shrimp plates – are typically below $10. Sun–Thurs 11am–midnight, Fri & Sat 11am–1am. Inexpensive.

SoHo Tea & Coffee 2150 P St NW, Dupont Circle ☎202/463-7646; Dupont Circle Metro. Trendy, late-night hangout for P Street clubbers refueling on coffee, cakes, and sandwiches. Occasional drag and open-mike nights, plus a computer terminal with Internet access. Tues & Thurs–Sat 7.30am–4am; Sun, Mon & Wed 7.30am–2am. Inexpensive.

The District's gay community hosts any number of freewheeling **parties** and **festivals** (as well as more sober-minded fundraisers) throughout the year, usually packed with throngs of locals, and sometimes with the odd closeted politico dropping in for a peek.

Cherry (April): Weekend dance party with top DJs, benefiting various gay and AIDS organizations. ⓦwww.cherryfund.com.

Capital Pride (early June): Weeklong festival still going strong after thirty years that features cultural, political, and community events, including films, pageants, a parade, and a street festival along Pennsylvania Avenue NW. ⓦwww.capitalpride.org.

Atlantic Stampede (September): The East Coast's largest gay rodeo, sponsored by the Atlantic States Gay Rodeo Association. The weekend-long affair comprises two days of rodeo, plus evening dinner-and-dance

events. Shuttles available from Shady Grove Metro out to rodeo grounds at Gaithersburg, MD. ⓦwww.asgra.org.

Reel Affirmations (October): One of the nation's largest gay and lesbian film festivals, held at various venues. Inquire also about monthly "RAXtra" gay-film screenings and Pride Festival cinema events. ⓦwww.reelaffirmations.org.

High-Heel Race (Tues before Halloween): Colorful street festival featuring a carnival-like atmosphere, drag queens in all manner of mind-blowing outfits, and a mad dash down 17th Street in three- to six-inch heels.

Bars and clubs

The focus of gay **bars and clubs** in DC is unquestionably Dupont Circle, though Capitol Hill SE and the Southeast quadrant (in general) have scattered points of interest, too. With the latter area, though, try to take a cab around at night, as some of the back streets can get rather dodgy.

Unless otherwise indicated, there's no cover charge at the places listed below.

Capitol Hill

Phase One 525 8th St SE ☎202/544-6831; Eastern Market Metro. Longstanding neighborhood lesbian bar with relaxed and convivial atmosphere, DJs, dancing, and pool table. Sun–Thurs 7pm–2am, Fri & Sat 7pm–3am.

Remington's 639 Pennsylvania Ave SE ☎202/543-3113; Eastern Market Metro. Signature gay country & western club with four bars and two dance floors; events include cornpone singing competitions, spirited hoe-downs, and "cowgirl"-themed drag pageants. Sun–Mon & Wed–Thurs 4pm–2am, Fri 4pm–3am, Sat 8pm–3am.

Dupont Circle

Apex 1415 22nd St NW ☎202/296-0505; Dupont Circle Metro. Well-located dance club

with DJs spinning pop, house, tribal, and garage for a party crowd; at its best on Friday and Saturday nights. Get here early on weekends to beat the $8 cover charge. Mostly men. Thurs 9pm–2am, Fri & Sat 9pm–3am.

Chaos 1603 17th St NW ☎202/232-4141; Dupont Circle Metro. Free-spirited club at the heart of the 17th Street scene, where inexpensive drinks are poured from a finely stocked bar. There are drag-king and -queen shows, a cabaret, and drag bingo – the latter popular with the straight crowd, too. Tues–Thurs 5pm–2am, Fri & Sat 5pm–3am, Sun 11am–3pm & 8pm–1am.

Cobalt 1639 R St NW ☎202/462-6569; Dupont Circle Metro. Another fixture on the local scene. The first floor has a bar called "Thirty Degrees," and upstairs there's a more frenetic and engaging club with theme nights and all kinds of yuppie types gyrating to house and trance tunes. Sun–Thurs 5pm–2am, Fri & Sat 5pm–3am.

Fireplace 2161 P St NW ☎202/293-1293; Dupont Circle Metro. Good-time corner bar with a vibrant crowd, and atypical staging ground for the cruisey P Street scene. Mostly men. Sun–Thurs 1pm–2am, Fri & Sat 1pm–3am.

JR's 1519 17th St NW ☎202/328-0090; Dupont Circle Metro. A young, mostly male, professional crowd packs into this narrow saloon-bar, which boasts a great location along the 17th Street cruise strip. Very much the place to be seen for cocktails. Mon–Thurs 11.30am–2am, Fri & Sat 11.30am–3am, Sun noon–2am.

Lizard Lounge 1223 Connecticut Ave NW ☎202/331-4422; Dupont Circle Metro. Very popular Sunday evening dance and cruise scene at the *MCCXXIII* club, which caters to a mixed crowd and is one of DC's top spots for house and techno grooves. Sun 8pm–2am.

Mr P's 2147 P St NW ☎202/293-1064; Dupont Circle Metro. Longest-serving gay bar in the neighborhood, though some say it's seen better days. Mirrored walls and dance tunes downstairs, hustling naked go-go dancers upstairs, Saturday- and Sunday night drag shows (11pm), plus an outdoor patio decorated with kitsch like pink flamingos. Mostly men. Mon–Thurs 3pm–2am, Fri & Sat 3pm–3am.

Omega 2122 P St NW, in the rear alley ☎202/223-4917; Dupont Circle Metro. Gay-oriented, techno-swanky spot with four bars, pool tables, and a dark video room upstairs. Stop in for happy hour or for a kickoff drink on the weekends. Mon–Thurs 4pm–2am, Fri 4pm–3am, Sat 8pm–3am, Sun 7pm–2am.

Southeast

The Edge & Wet 56 L St SE ☎202/488-1200; Navy Yard Metro. Frenetic club with multiple bars and special dance nights – the Edge is home to African-American-oriented gay club nights, while Wet has foam parties, nude dancing, and other colorful activities. Cover. Mostly men. Mon–Thurs 8pm–2am, Fri & Sat 8pm–3am.

Nation 1015 Half St SE, near K St and S Capitol St ☎202/554-1500; Navy Yard Metro. Star DJs churn out deep-house grooves for Saturday-night dance parties called "Velvet Nation". $12 cover. Mostly men. Sat 10pm–4am.

Ziegfields/Secrets 1345 Half St SE ☎202/554-5141; Navy Yard Metro. Techno and house DJs provide the soundtrack, but the focus here is definitely on the twice-nightly weekend drag shows, which make up in energy what they lack in polish. Thurs & Sun 9pm–2am, Fri & Sat 9pm–3am.

Gay organizations and resources

Gay and Lesbian Hotline ☎202/833-3234. Information, advice, and peer counseling service provided by volunteers under the aegis of the Whitman-Walker Clinic (see below). Anonymity of both caller and operator is respected so that both may speak freely on any topic; no subject is off-limits. Daily 7am–11pm.

Human Rights Campaign Store and Action Center 1640 Rhode Island Ave NW, New Downtown ☎202/628-4160, ⓦwww.hrc.org; Farragut North Metro. HRC is a national organization that educates people on political issues affecting gay, lesbian, bisexual, and transgender people; its store sells Equality Wear merchandise to raise funds for its programs.

Lambda Rising 1625 Connecticut Ave NW, Dupont Circle ☎202/462-6969, ⓦwww

.lambdarising.com; **Dupont Circle Metro.** The city's best-known gay and lesbian bookstore, which acts as a clearinghouse for information and events.

Metro Weekly ⓦwww.metroweekly.com. Free magazine that makes an excellent guide to DC's gay nightlife scene, stuffed with ads and listings about the latest spots and specials. Available at Lambda Rising (above) and various Dupont and Capitol Hill venues.

Rainbow History Project ☎202/907-9007, ⓦwww.rainbowhistory.org. Preserves and promotes community history through exhibits, talks, and archives, and publishes Web-based DC timeline and database of gay and lesbian "places and spaces" from the 1920s to the present. Also offers downloadable walking-tour brochures of neighborhoods such as Capitol Hill and Dupont Circle.

Washington Blade ⊛ www.washblade.com. News, listings, and classified ads are featured in this free weekly paper, available at bookstores, restaurants, and cafés around town.

Whitman-Walker Clinic 1407 S St NW, Shaw ℡ 202/797-3500, ⊛ www.wwc.org; **U Street-Cardozo Metro.** Nonprofit community health organization for the gay and lesbian community, providing accessible health care and services, including 24hr AIDS information line (℡ 202/332-2437 or 1-877/939-2437). Check website for information on four other regional facilities.

Women's Monthly ⊛ www.womo.com. Independent magazine by and about women that focuses on lesbian issues, with literary works, feature articles, and event listings. Available at Lambda Rising and select cafés and bars.

17

Festivals and parades

Washington has a huge variety of annual **festivals and parades**, many of them national in scope: America's Christmas Tree is lit each December on the Ellipse in front of the White House; the grandest Fourth of July Parade in the country takes place along and around the Mall; and every four years in January the newly inaugurated president takes part in a triumphal parade up Pennsylvania Avenue, from the US Capitol to the White House. Many of the national holidays are celebrated with special events and festivities in the city – for a comprehensive list contact the Washington DC Convention and Visitors Association (see p.21) or seek out the events calendar at ⓦwww.washington.org.

Open days at museums, galleries and attractions are covered in the relevant parts of the guide; for a list of **national public holidays**, see Basics, p.36. For a list of gay-oriented festivals, see "Gay DC," p.304.

January

Dr Martin Luther King Jr's Birthday 15th
☎202/619-7222 Wreath-laying at the Lincoln Memorial, a reading of the "I have a dream" speech, concerts, and speeches.
Robert E. Lee's Birthday 18th ☎703/548-1789 Music, food, and exhibits at Arlington House in Arlington Cemetery; special events in Old Town Alexandria, VA, including guided tour of Lee-Fendall House (see p.239).

February

African-American History Month Special events, exhibits, and cultural programs. Information from Martin Luther King Memorial Library (☎202/727-1186) or the Smithsonian or National Park Service (see box opposite).
Chinese New Year varies ☎202/638-1041 Dragon dancers, parades, and fireworks light up H Street NW in Chinatown.
Abraham Lincoln's Birthday 12th ☎202/619-7222 Wreath-laying and reading of the Gettysburg Address at the Lincoln Memorial.
Frederick Douglass's Birthday 14th ☎202/426-

5961 Wreath-laying, history exhibits, and music at Cedar Hill, Anacostia.
George Washington's Birthday Parade 22nd
☎703/838-9350 Spectacular parade and events in Old Town Alexandria, VA. Also, concerts and wreath-laying at Mount Vernon (☎703/780-2000).

March

St Patrick's Day 17th Big parade down Constitution Avenue NW on the Sunday before

Information lines

National Park Service ☎202/619-7222
Post-Haste (*Washington Post*) ☎202/334-9000
Smithsonian ☎202/357-2700
Washington DC Convention and Visitors Association ☎202/789-7000
Washington DC Events Office ☎202/619-7222
For more details on these organizations, see p.20.

the 17th (call ☎202/637-2474 for grand-stand seats) and another through Old Town Alexandria on the first Saturday of the month (☎703/237-2199). There's also a celebration on the 17th at Arlington House, Arlington National Cemetery, VA (☎703/557-0614).
Smithsonian Kite Festival late March/early April ☎202/357-2700, ⊛www.kitefestival.org Kite-flying competitions at the Washington Monument, with games and prizes.

April

Blessing of the Fleet early ☎202/737-2300 Nautical celebrations and services at US Navy Memorial, including sailors serving navy bean soup. Boat-related displays and races at Southwest Waterfront marina.
National Cherry Blossom Festival early ⊛www.nationalcherryblossomfestival.org The famous trees around the Tidal Basin (see p.54) bloom in late March/early April; celebrated by a massive parade down Constitution Avenue NW, the crowning of a festival queen, free concerts, lantern-lighting, dances, and races. Parade ticket information ☎202/728-1137; other events ☎202/547-1500.
Thomas Jefferson's Birthday 13th ☎202/619-7222 Wreath-laying and military ceremonies at the Jefferson Memorial.
Easter Sunrise Service Easter Sun ☎703/695-3250 or 202/685-2851 Sunrise memorial service at Arlington National Cemetery.
White House Easter Egg Roll Easter Mon ☎202/456-2200, ⊛www.whitehouse.gov Entertainment and egg rolling (eggs provided) on the White House South Lawn. Special garden tours one weekend after Easter; call well in advance.
Filmfest DC late ☎202/724-5613, ⊛www.filmfestdc.org Two-week festival premiering national and international movies in theaters and museums across the city.
Smithsonian Craft Show late ☎202/357-2700 for information, ☎1-888/832-9554 for tickets, ⊛www.smithsoniancraftshow.org Fascinating craft exhibitions by regional artisans in the National Building Museum, 401 F St NW, Old Downtown.
William Shakespeare's Birthday 25th ☎202/544-7077 The Bard is praised in song, word, and food at the Folger Shakespeare Library (see p.111).
Duke Ellington's Birthday 29th ☎202/331-9404, ⊛www.smithsonianjazz.org Music and events at Freedom Plaza, Pennsylvania

Avenue NW. Music and lectures are given at some Smithsonian museums.

May

Flower Mart first weekend ☎202/537-6200 Flowers, booths, children's entertainment, and displays at Washington National Cathedral.
Garden Day early ☎202/333-4953, ⊛www.georgetowngardentour.com Self-guided tours to see private patches of lush greenery at Georgetown's houses and mansions. Tickets go for $25 (or $30 in May).
Malcolm X Day mid ☎202/396-1021 Commemorative concerts, films, and speeches in honor of the Sixties black revolutionary leader in Anacostia Park.
Mount Vernon Wine Festival/Sunset Tour mid ☎703/780-2000, ⊛www.mountvernon.org George Washington's estate hosts this celebration of early America's homegrown wine-making, featuring music, food, and a trip to the first president's own cellar vaults.
Memorial Day last Mon Wreath-layings, services, and speeches at Arlington Cemetery (☎202/685-2851), Vietnam Veterans Memorial (☎202/619-7222), and US Navy Memorial (☎202/737-2300). The National Symphony Orchestra performs on the Capitol's West Lawn on the Sunday before, and there's a jazz festival in Old Town Alexandria (☎703/883-4686).

June

Dupont Kalorama Museum Walk early ☎202/387-4062 ext 12, ⊛www.dkmuseums.com/walk Colorful music, food, and historic displays provide the backdrop to tours of area museums and private homes and estates, around the Dupont Circle-Embassy Row-Kalorama neighborhoods.
Dance Africa mid ☎202/269-1600, ⊛www.danceplace.org Festival of African dance, open-air market, and concerts at Dance Place, 3225 8th St NE.
Marvin Gaye Jr Appreciation Day mid ☎202/789-7000 Street events and music on Pennsylvania Avenue NW between 13th and 14th streets, honoring the R&B great born in the District in 1939.
DC Caribbean Carnival mid-to-late ☎202/829-1477, ⊛www.dccaribbeancarnival.com Caribbean-style parade spread over consecutive weekends, with masqueraders and live

music, from Georgia and Missouri avenues to Banneker Park near Howard University.
Red Cross Waterfront Festival mid ☏703/549-8300, ⓦwww.waterfrontfestival.org Major Alexandria, VA, event with music, food, and kids' events, plus visits from tall ships along the Potomac River.
Smithsonian Festival of American Folklife late June/early July ☏202/357-2700, ⓦwww.folklife.si.edu One of the country's biggest festivals, loaded with American music, crafts, food, and folk heritage events on the Mall.

July

National Independence Day Celebration 4th ☏202/619-7222 Reading of the Declaration of Independence at National Archives, parade along Constitution Avenue NW, free concerts at the Sylvan Theatre near the Washington Monument, National Symphony Orchestra performance on west steps of the Capitol, finishing with a superb fireworks display. Get there as early as possible for all events.
Mary McLeod Bethune Celebration varies ☏202/673-2402, ⓦwww.nps.gov/mamc/Bethune Wreath-laying, gospel choir, and speakers at Bethune statue, Lincoln Park; ongoing exhibits at Bethune Council House.
Virginia Scottish Festival late ☏703/912-1943, ⓦwww.vascottishgames.org Alexandria and Arlington, VA, are the spots for the wearing of kilts, playing of bagpipes, and eating of haggis. Also features dancing competitions and a British car show.

August

Arlington County Fair mid ☏703/920-4556, ⓦwww.arlingtoncountyfair.org Traditional fair with rides, crafts, entertainment, food stalls, and concerts at Thomas Jefferson Community Center, 3501 2nd St, Arlington, VA.
Georgia Avenue Day end ☏202/723-5166 Parade along Georgia Avenue (at Eastern Ave NW), plus carnival rides, music, and food stalls.
DC Blues Festival late Aug or early Sept ☏202/828-3028, ⓦwww.dcblues.org Free music at Rock Creek Park's Carter Barron Amphitheater, the spectrum from folky acoustic to Chicago electric.

September

Labor Day Weekend Concert Sun before Labor Day ☏202/619-7222 The National

Symphony Orchestra plays on west lawn of the Capitol to mark the end of the summer season.
National Frisbee Championships around Labor Day ☏301/645-5043 Frisbee-related activities – including amazing disc-catching pooches – on the Mall near the Air and Space Museum.
Adams-Morgan Day first Sun after Labor Day ☏202/328-9451, ⓦwww.adamsmorganday.org One of the best of the neighborhood festivals, with live music, crafts, and cuisine along 18th Street NW – always packed and great fun.
Black Family Reunion second weekend ☏202/737-0120, ⓦwww.ncnw.org Weekend festival on the Mall featuring food, dance performances, and music.
Constitution Day Commemoration 17th ☏202/501-5215, ⓦwww.archives.org The US Constitution is displayed at the National Archives to celebrate the anniversary of its signing; naturalization ceremonies, parade and concerts.
Oktoberfest late Sept/early Oct ☏202/310-4691, ⓦwww.geocities.com/saengerbund Plenty of high-spirited beer drinking, song, and dance at area locations, including Arlington, VA, and several DC restaurants and microbreweries.

October

Taste of DC varies ☏202/789-2002, ⓦwww.tasteofdc.org Restaurant festival mixing tastings – from haute cuisine to fast food – with arts and crafts displays, children's shows, and entertainment on Pennsylvania Avenue NW.
Columbus Day second Mon ☏202/371-9441, ⓦwww.unionstationdc.com Wreath-laying, speeches and music at the Columbus Memorial in front of Union Station.
White House Fall Garden Tours mid ☏202/456-2200, ⓦwww.whitehouse.gov Free garden tours and military band concerts. Call well in advance for reservations.
Halloween 31st ☏703/549-2997 or 838-4242 Unofficial block parties, costumed antics, and fright-nights in Georgetown, Dupont Circle, and other neighborhoods. Historic "Alexandria Hauntings" give you the lowdown on the spook scene in that city, with tours of appropriately eerie or chilling places.

November

Annual Seafaring Celebration varies ☎ 202/433-4882 The Navy Museum hosts a family-oriented event with maritime activities, food, arts, and children's performances.

Veterans Day 11th Solemn memorial services and wreath-laying at 11am at Arlington Cemetery (usually with the president in attendance), Vietnam Veterans Memorial, and US Navy Memorial.

December

Candlelight Tours varies Call well in advance for reservations at these extremely popular evening events, which take place at the White House (Dec 26–28; free; ☎202/456-2200 or 619-7222, ⓦwww.whitehouse .gov), Mount Vernon (early-to-mid ☎703/780-2000), Old Town Alexandria (mid ☎703/838-4242), and Gunston Hall (mid ☎703/550-9220).

Christmas Tree Lightings beginning ☎202/619-7222 Separate ceremonies for the lighting of the Capitol (west side) and National (Ellipse) Christmas trees – the latter lit by the president. The entire month on the Ellipse sees Nativity scenes, choral groups, and other seasonal displays.

Pearl Harbor Day 7th ☎202/737-2300 Wreath-laying ceremony at the US Navy Memorial to commemorate the attack on Pearl Harbor.

Christmas Services all month ☎202/537-6247, ⓦwww.cathedral.org/cathedral Carols, pageants, choral performances, and bell-ringing at Washington National Cathedral. There is also much ceremony and ritual at the National Shrine of the Immaculate Conception (☎202/526-8300, ⓦwww .nationalshrine.com).

18

Sports and outdoor activities

V isitors to Washington may be surprised to find that the nation's capital is one of its greenest cities, with easy access to a multitude of woodsy trails and a major waterway, the Potomac River. Thanks to these natural attributes, DC is a great place for people who like to cycle, sail, hike, paddle, skate, run, or just stroll in the great **outdoors** – all a welcome relief from pounding the pavement between monuments and museums.

The capital also has a lot to offer those who prefer to enjoy their **sports** from the sidelines – or from in front of the TV set in a sports bar. Unfortunately, the two regional teams that have had any kind of success in recent years, football's Washington Redskins and college basketball's Maryland Terrapins, have waiting lists for tickets that are several years long. The situation isn't remedied by the area's other teams, who are often not just mediocre – as with baseball's Baltimore Orioles – but sometimes downright awful (basketball's Wizards and hockey's Capitals come to mind). Thus, the more you take spectator sports as casual entertainment instead of a feverish pursuit, the less frustrated you'll be as a fan.

As of 2004, the former Montreal Expos are scheduled to become DC's new baseball team, but a permanent stadium site, owner, and financing plan have yet to be settled – so check the papers for details on getting tickets for future games.

Outdoor activities

Those looking to stretch their legs after a day on a Tourmobile will find plenty to keep them busy. The green expanse of **Rock Creek Park** – which stretches from the city's northern edge to the Potomac River (see p.213) – and the network of trails heading out from the capital to Virginia and Maryland together offer miles of routes for biking, walking, and inline skating. Downtown, the **Mall** and the **Ellipse** provide the city with a central playground, particularly in summer when softball season swings into gear, and are good spots to go for a run.

Forming DC's southern boundary, the Potomac offers everything from heady Class VI rapids to guided tours for novice paddlers to sunset sails, making it easy to take in spectacular views of DC from the water.

Bicycling

For a pleasant outdoor excursion, the best option might be to rent a bike for short rides along the **Potomac River** or the **C&O Canal towpath**, something you can do at Big Wheel Bikes' Georgetown branch; Thompson Boat Center, near the Watergate Complex; and Fletcher's Boat House, two miles farther up the towpath (see details, p.223). Bicycle rentals run anywhere from $4/hour for a cruiser to $50/day for a flashy mountain bike.

Among DC's long-distance cycle paths are one in Rock Creek Park, the 18.5-mile **Mount Vernon Trail** (see p.234), and the entire 184-mile length of the C&O towpath (see p.223). The Washington & Old Dominion Trail (ⓦwww.nvrpa.org/wod) starts a bit further out in Vienna, VA, but offers 45 miles of pavement following the route of an old-time railway, heading westward into northern Virginia.

The eleven-mile **Capital Crescent Trail**, starting at Thompson Boat Center, branches off the C&O towpath after three miles and follows the course of an old railway line up into Bethesda and on to Silver Spring, both in Maryland. Once in Bethesda, cyclists can turn this trip into a 21-mile loop by returning via Rock Creek Park – follow the signs to the unpaved Georgetown Branch Trail, which cuts across Connecticut Avenue, to find the park. On the southern end, the trail links up with the Mount Vernon Trail (via the Key Bridge) and the Rock Creek Trail (via K St). Be warned that this trail is extremely popular on weekends; for more information, call ⓉT202/234-4874 or check out ⓦwww.cctrail.org.

Many trails and bicycle paths criss-cross the Metrorail system, giving you the option of cutting short a trip or avoiding backtracking. Keep in mind that while bikes are permitted on the Metro at any time during the weekend, they are prohibited during weekday rush hours (7–10am & 4–7pm) and on major holidays.

Rentals

Better Bikes ⓉT202/293-2080, ⓦwww.betterbikesinc.com. Delivers anywhere in DC.
Big Wheel Bikes 1034 33rd St NW, Georgetown ⓉT202/337-0254; 2 Prince St, Alexandria, VA ⓉT703/739-2300; 3119 Lee Hwy, Arlington, VA ⓉT703/522-1110; 6917 Arlington Rd, Bethesda, MD ⓉT301/652-0192; ⓦwww.bigwheelbikes.com.
Blazing Saddles 445 11th St NW, Old Downtown ⓉT202/544-0055.
Fletcher's Boat House 4940 Canal Rd NW, Georgetown ⓉT202/244-0461, ⓦwww.fletchersboathouse.com.
Thompson Boat Center 2900 Virginia Ave NW, Georgetown ⓉT202/333-4861, ⓦwww.thompsonboatcenter.com.
Washington Sailing Marina 1 Marina Drive, George Washington Memorial Parkway, Alexandria, VA ⓉT703/548-9027, ⓦwww.washingtonsailingmarina.com. Located along the Mount Vernon Trail (see also below, p.234).

Tours and resources

Bike the Sites ⓉT202/842-BIKE, ⓦwww.bikethesites.com. Two- to six-hour guided bike tours of the city's major sights ($40 and up, including bike and helmet), plus tours of Mount Vernon and customized tours of the District. No fixed schedule; also rents bikes for $25–60 per hour. Tour reservations required.
Bike Washington ⓦwww.bikewashington.org. Online recreational bicycling guide loaded with tips on local routes and trails.
Washington Area Bicyclist Association ⓉT202/628-2500, ⓦwww.waba.org. Advocacy group whose website offers info on trails, gear, and local events.

Rollerblading

The Capital Crescent and Mount Vernon trails are both traveled by **rollerbladers** as well as cyclists, but one of the best spots for inline skaters on the weekends is forested **Beach Drive** in Rock Creek Park, which is closed to vehicular traffic on weekends from 7am Saturday to 7pm Sunday. Near Parking Lot 6, just north of the intersection of Beach and Military roads and near the Public Golf

If you'd prefer to sweat it out indoors, Olympus, Gold's Gym, and Bally's are but a few of the big-name **health clubs** that have made their mark on DC. Several other spots open their doors to nonmembers, although it will cost you from $25 per visit.

Results the Gym 1612 U St NW, Shaw ☎202/518-0001, ⊛www .resultsthegym.com; U Street-Cardozo Metro; also at 315 G St SE, Capitol Hill ☎202/234-5678. Mon–Fri 5am–11pm, Sat & Sun 8am–9pm.

Washington Sports Club 1211 Connecticut Ave NW, New Downtown ☎202/296-7733. Mon–Fri 6am–10pm, Sat & Sun 8.30am–8.30pm. Also at 214 D St SE, Capitol Hill ☎202/547-2255. Mon–Thurs 6am–11pm, Fri 6am–10pm, Sat & Sun 8.30am–8.30pm.

Course, a gently hilly six-mile stretch is a popular training and cruising ground for local bladers. Skilled skaters shouldn't have too much trouble getting there from the Van Ness-UDC Metro station, though it's probably easier to drive or catch a cab.

Those accustomed to slicing through urban traffic will find the roads and sidewalks in the vicinity of downtown hit-or-miss in terms of pavement quality, though you will feel a bit safer than you would, say, blading down Fifth Avenue in New York. Good areas include the Tidal Basin and National Mall, and selected parts of the Waterfront, East and West Potomac parks, and the riverside sections of Georgetown and Alexandria, VA. The **Washington Area Roadskaters** (☎202/466-5005, ⊛www.skatedc.org) are a local club that organizes frequent group-skates of varying lengths, as well as free weekly inline skate clinics (April–Oct) in Rock Creek Park.

Jogging and walking

Of course you can walk or jog on any of the trails described under "Bicycling" or "Rollerblading," and many choose to simply put on their running shoes and hit the Mall, where the imperial buildings and monuments provide an inspiring backdrop for a daily workout. The gravel path circumscribing the mammoth front lawn of the city center provides a surface easier on the knees than your typical city pavement.

Those looking for a quieter place for a constitutional should head to **Theodore Roosevelt Island** (see p.234), a nature park with 2.5 miles of trails that meander through marsh, swamp, and forest. Access to the island, which lies at the start of the Mount Vernon Trail, is via a footbridge on the Arlington side of the Potomac. Other relaxing spots include **Great Falls Park** (see p.223), the **National Arboretum** (see p.205), and **Rock Creek Park**. Of course, merely wandering around DC itself from neighborhood to neighborhood provides its own sort of workout, and a combination of foot and Metrorail travel can take you to most places worth visiting in the District.

Water activities

The **Potomac River** provides plenty of chances to get out on the water. North of the city, twenty minutes beyond the Beltway, lies **Seneca Creek State Park** (⊛www .dnr.state.md.us/publiclands), where a flat expanse of river is ideal for canoeing. The current picks up and the crowds emerge a bit farther downstream as the Potomac races through **Great Falls**, where Class VI rapids provide ample challenges for whitewater **kayakers** – though make sure you have plenty of experience, as a 2004 fatality proved the dangers of the swift current.

Near Georgetown, several boat-rental shops offer the means to explore the calmer waters on either side of the Key Bridge and around Roosevelt Island, a stretch of the river that provides a worthy afternoon retreat. From here, it's easy enough to paddle your way into the **Tidal Basin**, an outing especially pretty in spring, when the cherry blossoms are in bloom. Landlubbers keen on staying closer to shore can head to the Tidal Basin Boat House near the Jefferson Memorial and rent a **paddleboat** (☏202/484-0206; March–Sept Mon–Fri 10am–6pm, Sat & Sun 10am–7pm; 2-seaters $8/hr, 4-seaters $16/hr).

Going south, the river widens as it flows past Alexandria toward the Wilson Bridge, an area popular with sailors, windsurfers and sea-kayakers. South of the bridge on the Virginia side, you can glide into **Dyke Marsh Wildlife Preserve** (ⓦwww.nps.gov /gwmp/dyke-marsh.htm), a freshwater wetland home to osprey, great blue heron, and many other birds.

Rentals, as you'd expect, vary in price with the size and type of boat, with discounted rates offered for booking an entire day. Kayaks, canoes, and rowboats go for anywhere from $10 per hour to $40 per day. **Sailboats** range from $10 to $20 per hour (though you may find that there's a two-hour minimum rental) to $140 per day. As rental service tends to be seasonal (March–Nov), you'd do well to call in advance in early spring or late fall before heading to the waterfront.

Boat rentals

Fletcher's Boat House 4940 Canal Rd NW, Georgetown ☏202/244-0461, ⓦwww .fletchersboathouse.com. Rents rowboats, canoes, and bikes and sells bait and tackle to the fishing crowd.
Jack's Boats 3500 K St NW, Georgetown ☏202/337-9642, ⓦwww.jacksboats.com. Located under the Key Bridge. Rents canoes, kayaks, and rowboats April–Oct.
Thompson Boat Center 2900 Virginia Ave NW, Georgetown ☏202/333-9543, ⓦwww .thompsonboatcenter.com. Single and double

kayaks, canoes, and recreational and racing rowing shells, plus bikes.

Canoeing and kayaking tours and instruction

Atlantic Kayak Company 1201 N Royal St, Alexandria, VA ☏703/838-9072 or 1-800/297-0066, ⓦwww.atlantickayak.com. Kayak tours along the Potomac, including 2.5-hour sunset tours exploring the monuments and bridges of Georgetown or the Dyke Marsh Wildlife Preserve ($44–54 each). Also moonlight tours, full-day trips, and overnight excursions to wildlife areas. April–Oct.
Outdoor Excursions Boonsboro, MD ☏1-800/775-2925, ⓦwww.outdoorexcursions .com. Located below Great Falls, with rafting ($30–47) and tubing ($26) trips, plus white-water kayaking and sea-kayaking instruction (each $90 per day) – the latter on the Chesapeake Bay, near Annapolis.

Sailing and windsurfing

Alexandria Seaport Foundation Zero Thompson Alley, between Queen and Cameron at waterfront, Alexandria, VA ☏703/549-7078, ⓦwww .alexandriaseaport.org. Sunset sails twice a week aboard a Potomac River dory, a work boat common on the river a century ago. The wooden vessel, a replica launched in 1995 by the foundation, is one of two of this class currently afloat. Reservations required; donations requested.
Belle Haven Marina at Belle Haven Park off George Washington Parkway, Alexandria, VA ☏703/768-0018, ⓦwww.saildc.com. Rentals (8.30am–sunset) include canoes, kayaks, and rowboats, plus sailboats – Flying Scots, Hobie Cats, and Sunfish – and windsurfers. A 34-foot sloop is available for charter ($90/hour including captain). Also offers sailing instruction.
Washington Sailing Marina 1 Marina Drive, George Washington Memorial Parkway, Alexandria, VA ☏703/548-9027, ⓦwww.washingtonsailing marina.com. Seasonal sailboat rentals (11am–4pm, by reservation only) include Islands, Flying Scot, and Sunfish. Also rents bikes. Located along the Mount Vernon Trail.

Spectator sports

Although they're not as rabid as the most red-blooded fanatics in New York or Philadelphia, DC's own sports-crazed fans still make a good show – the

Redskins have sold out their games for years to come and Washingtonians pine for the days when baseball season meant something more than Hill staffers swatting at softballs on the Mall. Encouragingly, as of press time the former Montreal Expos are officially on their way to town, plus recent years have brought other new franchises as well: soccer's DC United and basketball's Mystics have given the capital something new to cheer – or boo, this being the East Coast.

An outing to a sporting event can be expensive, however, once the cost of tickets, snacks, and beer are tallied. Seats for Caps and Wizards games can run as high as $100, though admission to soccer matches and WNBA games tends to be much cheaper. Buy your tickets through Ticketmaster (☎202/432-SEAT, ⓦwww.ticketmaster.com) or directly through the team's or stadium's box office. If going to the game in person isn't your thing, you can always head to a downtown sports bar and catch your team on television – or in the case of *ESPN Zone* (see p.286), some two hundred of them.

Baseball

The capital was without a **baseball** team after the Washington Senators packed their bags for Texas in 1971. However, local politicians and business leaders clamored for a team for several years, and Washington's most recent attempts to secure a squad have resulted in the landing of the Montreal Expos. This process, however, was not always a smooth one – involving political wrangling over funding, regional squabbles with Virginia towns and counties (Arlington dropped out of the running, but neighboring Loudon County and downstate Norfolk both

made bids), and an open threat from Baltimore Orioles' owner Peter Angelos to sue if baseball located a franchise so close to his own turf. Ultimately, DC got what it wanted, though as of press time no permanent stadium site has been selected, nor an owner picked out (Major League Baseball owns the Expos and can sell it to whomever it desires). When and if baseball is played in the District in 2005, it will take place (temporarily) at RFK Stadium; see box for details.

Alternately, you can head up the road to cheer for the **Baltimore Orioles** (☎410/685-9800, ⓦwww .theorioles.com; April–Oct season; tickets $8–50), whose downtown Camden Yards offers a chance to catch a game in a prime setting – although the team's recent struggles may make for a less than riveting outing. Built in 1992, the park is a stylish throwback to the classic baseball stadiums of old and proved so popular that it sparked a nationwide push to relocate local clubs in old-fashioned fields.

Basketball

Now that basketball legend Michael Jordan's days of playing with, and partly owning, the terminally dismal **Washington Wizards** (☎202/661-5050, ⓦwww.nba.com/wizards; Nov–April season) are over, the capital is left with just another mediocre sports squad. Simply put, the best reason to

Where the pros play

Camden Yards 333 W Camden St, Baltimore, MD ☎ 410/685-9800, ⓦ www.theorioles.com. Baltimore Orioles baseball.
FedEx Field 1600 Raljon Rd, Landover, MD ☎301/276-6050, ⓦwww .fedex.com/us/sports/fedexfield. Redskins football.
MCI Center 601 F St NW, Old Downtown ☎202/628-3200, ⓦwww .mcicenter.com; Gallery Place-Chinatown Metro; see p.172. Wizards and Mystics basketball, Capitals hockey.
RFK Stadium 2400 E Capitol St SE, Southeast ☎202/547-9077, ⓦwww .rfkstadium.com; Stadium-Armory Metro. DC United soccer, temporary baseball site.

△ Kayaking on the Potomac River

show up is to catch one of the NBA's powerhouses rolling into the MCI Center to push the team around. For this you can expect to pay extra; tickets average $10–105, but you can expect a higher charge to watch an actual good team on the hardwood.

In summer, the focus swings to the **Washington Mystics** (☎202/661-5050, ⊛www.wnba.com/mystics; June–Aug season; tickets $10–50), DC's pro women's team, led by all-star Chamique Holdsclaw. Despite struggling since the inception of the WNBA in 1997, the Mystics draw one of the largest crowds in the league to the MCI Center.

If you're really interested in seeing a solid b-ball squad take to the floor, you'll have to look beyond the pro ranks. Up the road in College Park, Maryland, just beyond the DC border, the excellent **Maryland Terrapins** (☎301/314-7070, ⊛www.umterps .com; tickets $5–30) put on a fine show for their young student fans and alumni at the **Comcast Center**. They won their ACC Conference in 2004 and an NCAA title just two years before – making a ticket for them about as hard to come by as one for football's Redskins. By contrast, the dominant team from the mid-1980s, the **Georgetown Hoyas** (☎202/628-3200, ⊛www.guhoyas.com; tickets $5–25), has had a more difficult recent history, and pines for the glory days when Patrick Ewing brought Washington a championship of its own.

Football

The **Washington Redskins** (☎301/276-6050, ⊛www.redskins .com; Sept–Dec season; tickets $45 –100-plus) are the dominant obsession of the capital's sports fans. One of American football's oldest franchises, the team has also been one of the most successful since arriving in DC in 1937, with a total of five championships under its belt – the most recent in 1992. Its fortunes have dimmed of late, however, hampered by poor play,

salary mismanagement, and a meddling owner. Despite all its woes, though, Redskins games, played at 80,000-seat FedEx Field (see p.315) in Landover, MD, remain among DC's hardest tickets to snag – indeed, tickets are sold by the season only and the waiting list is years long. So, unless you're prepared to pay ridiculous prices to scalpers, or know someone in DC with an extra ticket, chances are slim that you'll see the 'Skins in action.

Hockey

The MCI Center's other main tenant, hockey's **Washington Capitals** (☎202/266-2277, ⊛www.wash ingtoncapitals.com; Oct–April season; tickets $10–99), has been even more disappointing than basketball's Wizards, finishing the 2003–04 season tied for the fewest wins of any Eastern Conference team. The Caps have yet to win the coveted Stanley Cup since they joined the league in the 1970s (though they did reach the championship round in 1998), and it looks as if they'll be among the league's cellar-dwellers for many more years to come.

Soccer

The city's only major-league soccer team, **DC United** (☎703/478-6600; ⊛www.dcunited.com; March–Nov season; $18–40), was once among the most successful in the United States. Since the inaugural MLS season in 1996, the team has won the title three times (last in 1999) and was also the first American club to win the CON-CACAF Champions Cup (1998), the major competition for clubs from North and Central America and the Caribbean. The team has fallen off in recent years, though average home attendance is still around 25,000. If you want to go and cheer teenage phenomenon Freddie Adu and the rest of the Black-and-Red, the noisiest fans – the self-styled Screaming Eagles – usually occupy sections 133 and 134 at RFK Stadium.

Kids' DC

t's possible that there may be no friendlier and accommodating major city in the nation, perhaps the world, than Washington DC. Unlike some cities, such as Las Vegas, which have tried (and failed) to reinvent themselves for the family tourist trade, such traffic is intrinsic to DC, and there are practically no significant areas where **children** are off-limits. Indeed, you can bring a tot to practically any museum, historic mansion, art exhibit, memorial, monument, or institution without the staff batting an eyelash. In fact, the District is ruled by children to such a degree that you might find some of its major sights – especially the National Mall – unbearable because of it. Certain neighborhoods, such as Adams–Morgan, Shaw, and Dupont Circle, are notable for their relative lack of rugrats pounding the pavement - "relative lack" because there's no place where tourists and their kids are entirely absent.

Instead of dividing Washington into adult- and kid-oriented zones, it's more useful to consider the breakdown between places catering to mature, thought-

Practicalities

Given the broad scope of children's activities in the nation's capital, it's not too surprising that kids are accommodated in various ways when it comes to actually staying in and visiting the city. As for **hotels**, you may find that younger children (12 and under) are sometimes allowed to stay in their parents' room for free or a reduced rate; these and other facilities may even offer special games, entertainment, or diversions aimed at their apple-cheeked guests. The only way to know for sure is by calling or checking websites for each hotel; policies may change depending on the corporate owner.

Kids are generally accepted in most Washington **restaurants**, though such tolerance may be contingent on their maturity level and the hour of night – immature imps will be accorded little slack at an upscale restaurant or lounge at 10pm. In many cases, though, eateries may offer reduced-rate meals to children, or even a separate menu filled with all kinds of kid-friendly favorites like peanut-butter-and-jelly sandwiches and macaroni-and-cheese – though not exactly the healthiest sorts of meals.

One of the reasons DC is so popular with families and others with kids in tow is because so many sites and attractions are free. The Smithsonian is noted for charging no admission at its facilities, as are places like the US Capitol, government parks, the White House, National Gallery of Art, and countless other museums, galleries, and parks. Where admission is charged, it's usually under $10 (except for the International Spy Museum) and children may even be given a break here, too, with reduced- or half-price rates. The same is true when it comes to **transportation** in and around the District, with many operators charging lower rates for kids; to cite but one example, the Metro allows two very young kids (age 4 and under) to ride free with their parents without paying a fare; see ⓦ www.wmata.com for details.

ful young visitors and those throwing open their gates to all manner of scream-ing youth. Even childless adult couples will find no difficulty in frequenting sights attended by the former, while the latter are apt to drive even parents with bountiful families to hopeless distraction. What follows, then, is a short overview of the best and most appropriate places to bring kids in DC, keeping in mind the above considerations, as well as the fact that children are welcomed almost everywhere in town – outside of bars and clubs, of course.

Museums

Ground zero for kids in DC is undoubtedly the **National Mall**, and in some stretches school groups, Bible-study troupes, huge families, and ran-dom flocks of urchins are so thick on the ground you can barely wade through them – especially during the high season. That said, there's a definite delineation between Mall museums aimed at inquisitive young learners and those designed more as giant playpens. In the former category, institutions like the **National Gallery of Art** (p.71), **Hirshhorn Museum** (p.87), and the **national museums of Asian and African art** (p.92 and p.91) are excellent spots to educate the mind and get a sense of American and inter-national art and culture; some even provide pamphlets or guides aimed at young patrons. By contrast, the national museums of **Natural Histo-ry** (p.68), **American History** (p.60), and **Air and Space** (p.83) are cha-otic environments where ill-behaved hellions often run amok with interac-tive exhibits and hands-on displays; it's not always so frenetic, of course, but with few museum staff members or adult chaperones around to stop them, the brats often hold sway.

Away from the Mall, the other major site that attracts all kinds of young enthusiasts – both well- and ill-mannered – is the **International Spy Museum** (p.173), which entic-es visitors with its displays of Cold War gizmos and exotic weaponry; unlike the Mall museums, though, this one isn't free, and is among the priciest in town. Also around the Penn Quarter, the new **Koshland Science Museum** (p.166) is much more valuable for young learn-ers, presenting scientific concepts and controversies in a way that is refreshingly straightforward and not dumbed-down. Likewise, the **National Postal Museum** (p.116), near Union Station, is engaging and educational without being mindless.

At other scattered locations around DC, the museums are aimed at more mature children, or at least those with an appreciation or sense of history and art. The harrowing **US National Holocaust Museum** (see p.121) is not really aimed at young children, though it does have sections directed toward younger visitors, while the **Renwick** (p.138), **Corcoran** (p.140), and **National Portrait** (p.167) galleries will be enjoyed most by kids whose parents or guardians take an active role in guiding them through the displays. Finally, the **National Geographic Society's Explorers' Hall** (p.183) is off the beaten path a bit from the major attractions (though not from the major hotels), and offers intelligent, kid-friendly exhibits focus-ing on the environment, medicine, science, and world cultures.

Historic sites

Most **historic sites** – be they famous mansions, monuments, or memori-als – can be appreciated by a young audience, and as with the museums, many of these big names are located on the Mall. Typically, the **presiden-tial memorials** (Jefferson, Lincoln, and FDR) are fairly wide-open, so children's behavior can be less inhib-ited than it would be inside. However, the war memorials demand a cer-tain sort of quietude and reverence

– which can be in irritatingly short supply around some high-traffic sites like the **Vietnam Veterans Memorial** (p.59), where chatty schoolkids are routinely told to hush by adults mourning family members commemorated on the wall. The same is true to an even greater degree at **Arlington National Cemetery** (p.228), where the solemn tone is occasionally broken by unsupervised children yelling or running around the grounds. Although this behavior is stopped by rangers when spotted, it's definitely something concerned parents should beware of when bringing underage visitors to such a sombre location.

There are countless other historic sites in the city where well-behaved kids, with a knack for learning, can find interest and edification – these include **Dumbarton Oaks** (p.226), **Tudor Place** (p.225), and the **C&O Canal** (p.222) in Georgetown; the **Woodrow Wilson** (p.192) and **Heurich** (p.188) houses, around Dupont Circle; the **US Supreme Court** (p.108), **Folger Shakespeare Library** (p.111), and **Library of Congress** (p.112) on Capitol Hill; **Ford's Theatre** (p.175) and **Old Post Office Pavilion** (p.157) in Old Downtown; **The Octagon** (p.147) in Foggy Bottom; the **Charles Sumner School** (p.184) and **Bethune Council House** (p.186) in New Downtown; and the various classic historic and architectural sights in the region, from **Gunston Hall** (p.245), **Mount Vernon** (p.241), and Old Town Alexandria in Virginia, to **Takoma Park** in Maryland (p.204). However, almost all children and their parents will want to attempt to visit the **US Capitol** (p.99) and the **White House** (p.130) – though with security at a premium these days, you're well advised to have a backup plan (preferably including some of the above sights) in case your plans are thwarted.

Parks and gardens

Aside from the National Mall itself – a wondrous spot for strolling and relaxing amid monuments and museums – the District's assorted **parks and gardens** afford a welcome respite from overdosing on history, art, and culture. Here, beleaguered parents can let their unruly spawn run wild amid forested surroundings, or spread out on flowing lawns and hillsides once they've spent their energy. The city's urban park squares near the White House – such as Lafayette and Franklin – are not the best places for this sort of activity, so you'll have to venture further out. Good choices for nature-based activity – which may involve bicycling, hiking, water activities, or even Frisbee-playing, depending on the site – include **West and East Potomac parks** (p.58 and p.125), the **Ellipse** (p.136), **Theodore Roosevelt Island** (p.234), the **Mount Vernon Trail** (p.234), **Georgetown waterfront** (p.224), and especially **Rock Creek Park** (p.213) – perhaps the best place to do everything under the sun. Other nature-oriented locations are more contemplative in character, less for burning off energy than taking in the natural splendor; these include the **National Arboretum** (p.205), which has the added historical attraction of the Capitol Columns; **Kenilworth Aquatic Gardens** (p.206); the **US Botanic Garden** (p.106), and **Green Springs Gardens Park** (p.244).

Another spot children will inevitably want to see in the outdoors is the **National Zoological Park** (p.211), which despite some recent troubles continues to be a major draw for kids and adults – with the added benefit of free admission, as with all Smithsonian facilities. However, one spot vaguely involving nature, the National Aquarium (p.159), is worth avoiding, no matter how enthusiastic the kids are about undersea life – the cramped fish tanks and bureaucratic hallways of the Commerce Building are hardly the best places to show off nature in all its glory.

Shops and galleries

t's pretty obvious that no one comes to DC to shop, and for the most part shopping here is associated with museum stores, government trinkets, and T-shirts, plus a handful of big-box malls on the border with Maryland, in **Friendship Heights**. Beyond this, the best areas for browsing are Adams-Morgan, Dupont Circle, Georgetown, and around **Eastern Market**, where arts-and-crafts shops coexist with specialty book and music stores and student-oriented clothes-and-accessories hangouts. **Adams–Morgan** has a strong ethnic flair, and some good shops to match, while in **Shaw and Logan Circle** a number of hipster boutiques have begun to crop up amid the funky bars, nightclubs, and fringe theaters. Farther out, in the small liberal enclave of **Takoma Park**, there's a range of funky clothing stores along Carroll Avenue. Across the river, you'll find a fair share of retailers in **Alexandria**, with many specializing in antiques and arts and crafts.

The shopping heart has been ripped out of Old Downtown, however, as all the major department stores have given up the ghost – with the honorable exception of Hecht's, which nonetheless relocated to a new high-rise near the Treasury Building. This situation may improve over the next few years (development plans for the Penn Quarter around the MCI Center include new retail units), but for the foreseeable future you're best off at one of the mega-malls on the outskirts of the city for clothing and most other day-to-day items: what shopping complexes DC does have are fairly depressing, the half-vacant precinct of **The Shops at National Place** being the most conspicuous example.

Usual store hours are Monday through Saturday 10am to 7pm; some have extended Thursday night hours. In Georgetown, Adams-Morgan, and Dupont Circle many stores open on Sunday, too (usually noon–5pm).

Arts, crafts, and antiques

The only indigenous local craft is politics, but specialist **arts-and-crafts** stores in DC let you take home a piece of historic memorabilia or American Victoriana, if you wish. Richest pickings are in Dupont Circle, Georgetown (which also has a run of antiques shops), and Old Town Alexandria, loaded with antiques/bric-a-brac places aimed at the weekend-visitor market. Another great spot to poke around for arts, crafts, and other funky finds is the weekend flea market held at Eastern Market (see p.114). For works of art, visit the **galleries** of Dupont Circle and those downtown on 7th Street – see p.329.

Affrica 2010 R St NW, Georgetown ☎202/745-7272. Traditional and stylish African apparel, totems, pottery, fabrics, and masks, with information provided about the origin of, and tribal craftworkers responsible for, each item.
Appalachian Spring 1415 Wisconsin Ave NW, Georgetown ☎202/337-5780; Union Station, 50 Massachusetts Ave NE ☎202/682-0505. A colorful array of handmade ceramics, jewelry, rugs, glassware, kitchenware, quilts, toys, and other eclectic examples of American craftwork.
Art & Soul 225 Pennsylvania Ave SE, Capitol Hill ☎202/548-0105. Handmade clothes and contemporary ceramics, toys, and crafts by more than two hundred regional artists.
Artcraft Collection 132 King St, Alexandria, VA ☎703/299-6616. A strange and impressive collection of handcrafted artifacts, like furniture painted in unique colors, exquisitely detailed atomizers, oddball sculptures, anthropomorphic teapots, and high-heeled doorstops.
Beadazzled 1507 Connecticut Ave NW, Dupont Circle ☎202/265-2323. New and antique beads from all over the world, plus ethnic jewelry, folk art, and related books.
Indian Craft Shop Department of the Interior, Room 1023, 1849 C St NW, Foggy Bottom ☎202/208-4056. One of the city's best gift boutiques in a rather bleak stretch for shopping, selling rugs, crafts, beadwork, jewelry, and pottery by artisans from native tribes in the US. The shop is inside the Department.
Old Print Gallery 1220 31st NW, Georgetown ☎202/965-1818. A favorite local seller of historic landscapes, antique maps, old charts and prints, plus political cartoons, DC scenes, and early American artisan work.
Wake Up Little Susie 3409 Connecticut Ave, Upper Northwest ☎202/244-0700. Trinket emporium with a broad range of interesting items, including homemade jewelry and ceramics, arty novelty items, curious puppets, and more.

Beauty supplies and services

Blue Mercury 3059 M St NW, Georgetown ☎202/965-1300. If you find yourself desperate for fancy face creams, hair products, scents, and salves, this is your shop. There's an attached spa for on-the-spot pampering.
Celadon 1180 F St NW, Old Downtown ☎202/347-3333. Swanky downtown salon good for getting your hair cut, styled, or dyed, your brows plucked, or your entire look made over.
Norbert Hair Designers 1050 Connecticut Ave NW, New Downtown ☎202/466-2111. Along with hair styling, this upscale salon offers a laundry list of services – from acid peels and body bronzing to lip, bikini, and back waxing, to French manicures and pedicures. Just have a full wallet at the ready.
Sephora 3065 M St NW, Georgetown ☎202/338-5644. French makeup boutique offering fragrances, well-being products, and brand-name cosmetics.

Books

Washington's array of **bookstores** is one of the high points of its shopping scene: you'll find a place to suit you whether you're looking for discounted new novels or political science tomes, flagship superstores with coffee bars or cozy secondhand shops. The weekly *City Paper* and Friday's *Washington Post* list bookstore lectures, concerts, readings, and events.

General

Barnes & Noble 3040 M St NW, Georgetown ☎202/965-9880; 555 12th St NW, Old Downtown ☎202/347-0176. Familiar chain-store heavyweight with three floors, offering sizable discounts, one of the better crime/mystery sections in the city, and, fittingly, Starbucks coffee.
Borders 1800 L St NW, New Downtown ☎202/466-4999. Huge bookstore with voluminous selection of magazines, news-

papers, and discount books, a full CD and tape selection, plus readings, events, and an espresso bar.

Chapters Literary Bookstore 455 11th St NW, Old Downtown ☎202/737-5553. Downtown spot with a high-quality selection of poetry and fiction titles and a supporting program of readings and events.

Kramerbooks 1517 Connecticut Ave NW, Dupont Circle ☎202/387-1400. City institution with a good general selection, a great café-restaurant called *Afterwords Café* (see p.271), and long hours (24hr on weekends).

Olsson's Books and Records 1307 19th St NW, Dupont Circle ☎202/785-1133; **2211 Wilson Blvd, Arlington, VA** ☎703/525-4227. High-speed Internet access ($6/hr) at **418 7th St NW, Old Downtown** ☎202/638-7610; and **1735 N Lynn St, Arlington, VA** ☎703/812-2103. Massive range in one of Washington's oldest independent bookstore chains; it's a great spot to browse. Other pluses include tapes and CDs, regular book signings, and a café in the 7th Street branch.

Politics & Prose 5015 Connecticut Ave NW, Tenleytown ☎202/364-1919. Located in the northern reaches of Upper Northwest, a good independent bookstore/coffee shop with one of the best programs of author appearances and readings in the city.

Vertigo Books 7346 Baltimore Ave, College Park, MD ☎301/779-9300. Covers everything from local to world politics, social and cultural studies, and modern literature. Regular signings and readings, too.

Secondhand

Bryn Mawr Lantern Bookshop 3241 P St NW, Georgetown ☎202/333-3222. Although its stock is all donated, this rare and vintage dealer has a great general selection of secondhand books – though it's only open four or five hours a day.

Idle Time Books 2467 18th St NW, Adams-Morgan ☎202/232-4774. Local favorite for used and vintage titles, with a bent toward fiction, left-leaning politics, science, and the off-beat. Late hours, often until 10pm or beyond.

Second Story Books 2000 P St NW, Dupont Circle ☎202/659-8884. Large range of used books, antiques, and records; also a good spot to find out what's going on in the city, with events listings, bulletin boards, etc.

Specialty

ADC Map & Travel Center 1636 I St NW, New Downtown ☎202/628-2608. Wide selection of maps, atlases, and travel guides.

AIA Bookstore 1735 New York Ave NW, Foggy Bottom ☎202/626-7475. Operated by the American Institute of Architects, this is a good spot to visit if you're interested in local or national architecture, and if you want to learn the difference between Federal, Georgian, and Colonial Revival building styles for your walks throughout DC.

Big Planet Comics 3145 Dumbarton Ave NW, Georgetown ☎202/342-1961. An extensive comic-book store specializing in alternative comics, manga, and graphic novels.

Bridge Street Books 2814 Pennsylvania Ave NW, Georgetown ☎202/965-5200. Volumes on politics, literature, history, philosophy, and film, with author readings of fiction and poetry.

Brookings Institution Bookstore 1775 Massachusetts Ave NW, Dupont Circle ☎202/797-6258. Political science and policy studies from the prestigious think tank.

Card and Comic Collectorama 2008 Mount Vernon Ave, Alexandria, VA ☎703/548-3466. Worth a trip for its stock of ancient Disney memorabilia, long-forgotten trading cards and rare comics, and all manner of other curious castoffs.

Franz Bader 1911 I St NW, Foggy Bottom ☎202/337-5440. Visually evocative books – many large-format – focusing on photography, fine arts, architecture, prints, and the history of art movements and concepts.

InfoShop in the World Bank, 1818 H St NW, Foggy Bottom ☎202/458-5454. An excellent bookstore for serious readers and viewers, with a compendious selection of volumes on finance, education, international relations, the Third World, and environment, with many educational videos, too.

International Language Centre 1803 Connecticut Ave NW, Dupont Circle ☎202/332-2894. Specializing in foreign-language books and self-instruction cassettes, and offering a generous helping of foreign-language magazines.

Lambda Rising 1625 Connecticut Ave NW, Dupont Circle ☎202/462-6969. Extensively stocked gay and lesbian bookstore; see also p.305.

Reiter's 2021 K St NW, New Downtown ☎202/223-3327. Books on business,

Although there are some uninspiring **malls** around downtown DC, you'll have to head for the suburbs for the best ones (and lower local sales taxes); there's direct Metro access to the stores at Friendship Heights, Crystal City, and Pentagon City that are listed below. Opening hours are usually Monday through Saturday from 10am to 8pm, Sunday from noon to 6pm.

Downtown

Old Post Office Pavilion, 1100 Pennsylvania Ave NW ☎202/289-4224; Federal Triangle Metro; see also p.157.

The Shops at National Place, 1331 Pennsylvania Ave NW ☎202/662-1250; Metro Center Metro.

Union Station Mall, 50 Massachusetts Ave NE ☎202/371-9441; Union Station Metro; see also p.115.

Georgetown

Georgetown Park, 3222 M St NW ☎202/298-5577; Foggy Bottom-GWU Metro or Georgetown Shuttle (see p.219).

Out of town

Chevy Chase Pavilion, 5345 Wisconsin Ave NW ☎202/686-5335; Friendship Heights Metro.

Crystal City Shops, Crystal Drive at Jefferson Davis Hwy, Arlington, VA ☎703/922-4636; Crystal City Metro.

Fashion Center at Pentagon City, 1100 S Hayes St, Arlington, VA ☎703/415-2400; Pentagon City Metro.

Mazza Gallerie, 5300 Wisconsin Ave NW ☎202/966-6114; Friendship Heights Metro.

Potomac Mills Outlet Mall, 2700 Potomac Mills Circle, Prince William, VA ☎1-800/826-4557; Wed–Sun shuttle from Metro Center, Rosslyn and Pentagon City Metro stations.

Tysons Corner Center, 1961 Chain Bridge Rd, McLean, VA ☎703/893-9400; Capital Beltway (Hwy 495) exit 47B.

Tysons Galleria, 2001 International Drive, McLean, VA ☎703/827-7700; Capital Beltway (Hwy 495) exit 46A.

White Flint Mall, 11301 Rockville Pike, Bethesda, MD ☎301/468-5777; shuttle from White Flint Metro.

computing, finance, engineering, and other professional and scientific topics.

Sisterspace 1515 U St NW, Shaw ☎202/332-3433. Books by African-American women; locally and nationally known authors frequently drop by to promote their work.

US Government Bookstore 710 N Capitol St NW, Old Downtown ☎202/512-0132. All the official facts and figures you could ever want, and, as of 2004, the only government printing-office bookstore still operating in the nation. Open Mon–Fri only 8am–4pm.

Yawa 2206 18th St NW, Adams-Morgan ☎202/483-6805. African and African-American books, magazines, crafts, and cards.

Clothing

The best areas for browsing for **clothing** are in New Downtown, along Connecticut Avenue; Dupont Circle, also along Connecticut; and Georgetown, along M Street and Wisconsin Avenue. Tucked among the ubiquitous Gaps and Banana Republics, you'll find a handful of unique boutiques worth a look. Even gentrifying Adams-Morgan has begun to get in on the act, with a growing number of ultra-hip clothing shops appearing along 18th Street, amid the trendy bars and restaurants.

But nearly every serious shopper winds up heading to **Georgetown**, the District's retail epicenter. Here you'll find the greatest concentration of the national retail chains, as well as local boutiques and more exclusive shops. There are a few deals to be had here, though, with vendors setting up shop along the sidewalks to sell knock–off designer handbags and the like.

For still more places to enhance your wardrobe, also see "Malls," p.324, and "Department stores," p.326.

Women's boutiques

All About Jane 2438 18th St NW, Adams-Morgan ☎703/797-8719. With contemporary clothes ranging from sophisticated to sexy, Jane spares women-on-the-go the trip to New York. Good for big-name designers as well as stylish T-shirts and handbags. Closed Tues.

American in Paris 1225 King St, Alexandria, VA ☎703/519-8234. As the name suggests, this is one of the top spots in town to get your fix of fashionable European wear, as well as unique clothes from local designers.

Betsey Johnson 1319 Wisconsin Ave, Georgetown ☎202/338-4090. The upscale but whimsical creations of this well-known, rather manic designer of women's fashions call out from behind a colorful facade.

Betsy Fischer 1224 Connecticut Ave, New Downtown ☎202/785-1975. Sophisticated women's attire, from conservative to hip, comes with sage advice from the owner herself. Popular with urban professionals on the prowl for chic designer names.

Daisy 1814 Adams Mill Rd NW, Adams-Morgan ☎202/797-1777. Stylish women's shop in a trendy zone that features hot items from the latest designers and an ass-kicking selection of grrrl shoes. Closed Tues.

Donna Lewis 309 Cameron St, Alexandria, VA ☎703/548-2452. Hip yet classy women's clothes, and a handful of Italian bags and shoes.

Kaur Three 2102 18th St NW, Adams-Morgan ☎202/299-0404. Trendy, sophisticated women's boutique featuring designer samples and a back lounge stocked with vintage accessories. Closed Mon.

Nuevo Mundo 313 Cameron St, Alexandria, VA ☎703/549-0040. Globetrotting mother-daughter team offers jewelry, unique "wearable art" from around the world, and easy-care travel clothing for men and women.

Pua Naturally 444 7th St NW, Old Downtown ☎202/347-4543. Upmarket boutique brings a splash of ethnic flair to downtown DC, with fine hand-woven skirts, jackets, and scarves, most of which hail from South Asia.

Saks Jandel Watergate complex, 2522 Virginia Ave NW ☎202/337-4200. Women's formal wear and cocktail dresses from noted designer collections.

Funky clothing

Backstage 545 8th St SE, Capitol Hill ☎202/544-5744. Whether you're at a loss on Halloween or looking for an elaborate disguise, this costume shop – teeming with wigs, boas, and cat suits – may be able to help. Also sells makeup, masks, dance shoes, and books on the theater.

Dream Dresser 1042 Wisconsin Ave NW, Georgetown ☎202/625-0373. One of the racier operations along this commercial stretch; an eye-popping emporium for all kinds of naughty lingerie, corsets, and fetish-wear.

Imagine Artwear 1124 King St, Alexandria, VA ☎703/548-1461. Colorful array of fashions bridging the gap between the aesthetic and the functional – brightly colored and detailed garments that could pass for tapestries, unique handcrafted jewelry and accessories, and more.

Leather Rack 1723 Connecticut Ave NW, Dupont Circle ☎202/797-7401. Chaps, vests, boots, and more (about as many ways to skin a cow as you can imagine), plus fetish items and sexual accessories too bizarre to describe.

Red River Western Wear 641 Pennsylvania Ave SE, Capitol Hill ☎202/546-5566. One of DC's few Western-wear stores carries everything from boots and Stetsons to Native American jewelry and Southwestern clothing – and not just for cowpoke congressmen on parade.

Smash! 3285 1/2 M St NW, Georgetown ☎202/337-6274. Punks gasping for air amid Georgetown's well-scrubbed shops can take refuge in the racks of leather pants, zebra-stripe Creepers, and studded belts, or select a vinyl classic from the tidy selection of punk records.

Men's clothing

Beau Monde 1814 K St NW, New Downtown
☏202/466-7070. The place on K Street to
help you look like you belong here, amid
the high-powered lawyers and lobbyists.
European suits and ties and a stylish range
of upscale accessories give you a flush and
fearsome appearance.
**Everett Hall 1230 Connecticut Ave NW, Dupont
Circle** ☏202/467-0003. Big-name designer
for men's Italian suits and contemporary
sportswear, outfitting countless high rollers,
celebrities, and athletes – and you, too, if
you have the money.
Universal Gear 1601 17th St NW, Dupont Circle
☏202/319-0136. Gay men's pit stop for current fashion along the 17th Street strip, with
T-shirts, swimwear, casual duds, and a full
line of skivvies.

Secondhand and vintage

Meeps Fashionette 1520 U St NW, Shaw
☏202/265-6546. This renovated classic
building houses a neighborhood favorite
that offers a cool and groovy selection of
men's and women's vintage attire, some of
which dates as far back as the 1940s.
**Rage Clothing 1069 Wisconsin Ave NW, George-
town** ☏202/333-1069. Vintage clothing shop
with jeans galore, plus T-shirts, shorts, and
so on – some of it a fashion bargain.

**Secondi 1702 Connecticut Ave NW, Dupont
Circle** ☏202/667-1122. Agreeable selection
of high-flying designer names, marked
down to a more affordable level.

Shoes and accessories

**Commander Salamander 1420 Wisconsin Ave
NW, Georgetown** ☏202/337-2265. Funky
T-shirts, sneakers, sportswear, wigs,
gimcrack jewelry, and various eclectic and
oddball accessories. Open late.
Fleet Feet 1841 Columbia Rd NW, Adams-Morgan
☏202/387-3888. Fleet's friendly, experienced
staff first outfits you in the proper shoes for
running, walking, playing soccer, or doing
aerobics, then lets you test-drive the pair
outside. An assortment of sports clothes and
accessories are also on hand.
**Kenneth Cole 1259 Wisconsin Ave NW, George-
town** ☏202/298-0007. Big name for men's
and women's shoes, belts, and jackets.
**Proper Topper 1350 Connecticut Ave NW, New
Downtown** ☏202/842-3055. A sleek spot with
a hip and stylish assortment of purses, bags,
makeup, hats, watches, knickknacks, and
accessories. A second location in Georgetown at 3213 P St NW ☏202/333-6200.
**Shake Your Booty 2439 18th St NW, Adams-
Morgan** ☏202/518-8205; **3225 M St NW,
Georgetown** ☏202/333-6524. Hip shoes and
one-of-a-kind accessories add a kick to the
District's limp shoe scene.

Department stores

The glory days of Washington DC's **department stores** are long gone, and
you'll have to travel to out-of-town malls (see p.324) if you're looking for
flagship stores like Neiman Marcus, Nordstrom, Saks Fifth Avenue, Lord &
Taylor, Bloomingdale's, and Macy's. Only Hecht's and Filene's Basement have
maintained their downtown outposts.

**Filene's Basement 1133 Connecticut Ave NW,
New Downtown** ☏202/872-8430; **The Shops at
National Place, 529 14th St NW, Old Downtown**
☏202/638-4110. Famed Boston-based
bargain fashion retailer with good deals on
men's and women's clothing, shoes and
accessories; also at Mazza Gallerie (p.324).

Hecht's 1201 G St NW, Old Downtown
☏202/628-6661, **and several suburban locations.** Classic downtown department store
with a full range of clothing and home furnishings. The store is a century old, though
this more modern building was put up in
1985.

Museum and gallery stores

Virtually all of DC's museums – in particular the Smithsonians – have well-
stocked **gift shops**. The list below picks out some of the best; see the relevant

pages for transport and museum details. (Smithsonian stores can also be found at National Airport.) Note that every other major attraction – from the US Capitol to the White House – also has its own gift shop, selling enough name-emblazoned souvenirs to satisfy even the most avid collectors.

Arthur M. Sackler Gallery 1050 Independence Ave SW, National Mall ☎202/357-4880. Jewelry, prints, fabrics, Asian art, ceramics, rugs, beads ,and calligraphy.

B'nai B'rith Klutznick National Jewish Museum 2020 K St NW, New Downtown ☎202/857-6583. Jewelry, goblets, ceramics, T-shirts, arts and crafts, linen and embroidered goods, all with Jewish motifs.

Bureau of Engraving and Printing 14th and C sts SW, south of the Mall ☎1-800/456-3408. Just the place for that presidential engraving, those prints of Washington DC, copies of famous texts, and even bags of shredded cash.

National Air and Space Museum Independence Ave and 6th SW, National Mall ☎202/357-1387. Fantastic array of air- and space-related goodies, from science-fiction books to ray-guns and spaceman "ice cream."

National Gallery of Art Constitution Ave, between 3rd and 7th St NW, National Mall ☎202/842-6002 or 1-800/697-9350. Perhaps DC's best art shop, with thousands of books, prints,

slides, posters, and postcards featuring famous artists and movements.

National Museum of African Art 950 Independence Ave SW, National Mall ☎202/986-2147. Rich and splendid displays of African arts and crafts, including great fabrics and jewelry.

National Museum of American History 14th St and Constitution Ave NW, National Mall ☎202/357-2700. The Smithsonian's biggest store is great for souvenirs. Offers music, books, T-shirts, kitchenware, ceramics, posters, toys, crafts, jewelry, and reproductions from the museum.

National Museum of Natural History 10th St NW and Constitution Ave, National Mall ☎202/357-2700. Though crawling with kids, worth a visit for its huge selection of tomes relating to science, geology, biology, paleontology, and other related fields.

Textile Museum 2320 S St NW, Kalorama ☎202/667-0441. Unique T-shirts, ethnic fabrics, textile books, silks, cushion covers, ties, kimonos, and jewelry.

Music

CD Warehouse 3001 M St NW, Georgetown ☎202/625-7101. Good across-the-board selection of used CDs.

DC CD 2423 18th St NW, Adams-Morgan ☎202/588-1810. One of the better bets for new and used vinyl and CDs – from the mainstream to the utterly obscure – with late hours and a knowledgeable staff, especially about the local music scene.

DJ Hut 2010 P St NW, Dupont Circle ☎202/659-2010. Caters to turntablists, with a focus on unique or hard-to-find vinyl and a bent toward funk, hip hop, breakbeat, jungle, and so on.

Kemp Mill Music 1113 F St NW, Old Downtown ☎202/638-7077; 1028 19th St NW, New Down-

town ☎202/223-5310; and 1619 Connecticut Ave NW, Dupont Circle ☎202/986-0300. Local chain for mainstream and chart releases, often with good discounts. Also three nearby outlets in Maryland.

Smash! 3285 1/2 M St NW, Georgetown ☎202/337-6274. Punk, hardcore, new wave, and indie music, along with T-shirts, boots, and clothes (see p.325).

Tower Records 2000 Pennsylvania Ave NW, Foggy Bottom ☎202/331-2400. Like it or not, the biggest music store in DC, with regular in-store appearances by mid-level musicians. Open daily until midnight. Another nearby branch at 20F 6200 Little River Turnpike in Alexandria, VA ☎703/256-2500 (call for directions).

Specialty shops

Discovery Channel Store 50 Massachusetts Ave NE, Union Station ☎202/842-3700; 1100 S

Hayes St, Arlington, VA ☎703/413-3425; 118 King St, Alexandria, VA ☎703/549-1352.

Washington isn't exactly known for its delis, though a few good places do stand out. Good **coffee**, at least, isn't hard to find – many of the coffee bars listed in Chapter 13 can sell you the beans. For quality **tea**, try one of *Teaism*'s branches (p.271 and p.276) or *Ching Ching Cha* (p.274) in Georgetown.

Old-style **markets** are thin on the ground: Eastern Market (p.114) is your best bet, while the Fish Wharf (p.125) has a great selection of Chesapeake Bay seafood. There are weekend farmers' markets in Adams-Morgan, Alexandria, Dupont Circle, Takoma Park, and Arlington.

For bread, you can't beat the *Breadline* (p.273) or *Firehook Bakery & Coffeehouse* (p.279). The best general deli is the splendid *Dean & Deluca* (p.274) in Georgetown, although Dupont Circle's homespun *Marvelous Market* (p.271) is a great local find; other solid delis are *Loeb's* (p.276) and *Krupin's* (p.279). Southwest fanciers should visit the *Red Sage* restaurant's shop (p.278).

Curious items you never knew you wanted, from African art and flight jackets to space-ship models, teapots, games, jewelry, and books.

Ginza 1721 Connecticut Ave NW, Dupont Circle ☎202/331-7991. Longstanding neighborhood favorite for all things Japanese, including chopsticks, art screens, woodblock prints, kimonos, and sandals.

Go Mama Go! 1809 14th St NW, Shaw ☎202/299-0850. Funky home-furnishings store featuring cool and upscale Asian-styled art, wall hangings, and dinnerware, some of it designed by the store's owner.

Movie Madness 1083 Thomas Jefferson St NW, Georgetown ☎202/337-7064. Thousands of movie posters, old and new, plus vintage advertising, celebrity pics, political bric-a-brac, and other visual oddments.

Orioles Baseball Store 1666 K St NW, New Downtown ☎202/296-2473. Stock up on jerseys honoring the legendary Cal Ripken Jr and other O's paraphernalia, or buy tickets to see the team up the highway in Camden Yards.

Political Americana 50 Massachusetts Ave NE, Union Station ☎202/547-1685. A good spot to pick up everything from historic and topical buttons and bumper stickers to gifts, books, and videos from every side of the political scene.

Pulp 1803 14th St NW, Shaw ☎202/462-7857. Eye-popping, purple-fronted shop thick with trinkets and souvenirs, but best for its wide selection of greeting cards – from the mundane to the freakish – which it allows you to make, too, if you have the zeal for it.

Galleries

DC has a massive range of commercial art **galleries** that often host (usually free) rotating exhibitions of paintings, prints, sculpture, photography, applied art, and folk art. The galleries listed below are some of the more notable; call for details of current shows or check *City Paper* or the *Washington Post*'s "Weekend" section. There's also a monthly guide available in bookstores with comprehensive listings of DC's art galleries called, appropriately enough, *Galleries* (❂www.artlineplus.com/gallerymagazine).

The venues themselves are grouped in distinct city areas. Downtown, those along 7th Street NW specialize in the works of contemporary regional artists, though the major concentration of galleries is in Dupont Circle, where more than thirty are clustered in a defined **Gallery District** (mainly R Street between 21st and 22nd). Georgetown has a number of art galleries as well. Most are closed on Monday and many are also closed on Tuesday.

Downtown and Foggy Bottom

406 7th Street NW Archives-Navy Memorial or Gallery Place-Chinatown Metro. A grouping of galleries featuring the works of fine DC-area artists – paintings, sculpture, photograhs, mixed-media pieces. Galleries include Apex ☎202/638-7001, Marnin Art ☎202/347-3327, and Touchstone ☎202/347-2787.

Arts Club of Washington 2017 I St NW ☎202/331-7282; **Foggy Bottom–GWU or Farragut West Metro.** Eclectic exhibits of works by local artists; see also "Performing arts and film" chapter, p.296, for its occasional classical-music concerts.

George Washington University Brady Gallery, 805 21st St NW, 2nd Floor ☎202/994-1525; **and Dimock Gallery, Lower Lisner Auditorium, 730 21st St NW** ☎202/994-1525; **Foggy Bottom-GWU Metro.** Regular rotating shows by local, student, national, and international artists.

Signal 66 926 N St NW ☎202/842-3436; **Mount Vernon Square-UDC Metro.** Alternative space run by local artists where a wide range of multimedia events are held, including irreverent gallery shows, mainstream and avant-garde musical shows, video presentations, and more; see Ⓦwww.signal66.com for the lowdown.

Zenith Gallery 413 7th St NW ☎202/783-2963; **Archives-Navy Memorial or Gallery Place-Chinatown Metro.** Prints, paintings, and sculpture (both traditional and more off-beat), a good portion of which is by city-based artists.

Dupont Circle

Fondo del Sol Visual Arts Center 2112 R St NW ☎202/483-2777; **Dupont Circle Metro.** Nonprofit museum featuring Latino-Caribbean art; also hosts lectures, poetry, and performance art, and sponsors the DC Caribbean Festival (see p.308).

Irvine Contemporary Art 1710 Connecticut Ave NW, Dupont Circle Metro ☎202/332-8767. Broad, often interesting selection of modern or contemporary paintings, prints, and other visual art.

Kathleen Ewing Gallery 1609 Connecticut Ave NW ☎202/328-0955; **Dupont Circle Metro.** Highly regarded gallery featuring nineteenth- and twentieth-century photography, plus some mixed works.

Marsha Mateyka Gallery 2012 R St NW ☎202/328-0088; **Dupont Circle Metro.** Contemporary painting and sculpture by American and European artists.

Tartt Gallery 2023 Q St NW ☎202/332-5652; **Dupont Circle Metro.** Nineteenth- and early twentieth-century photography, plus American folk art. By appointment.

Washington Printmakers' Gallery 1732 Connecticut Ave NW ☎202/332-7757; **Dupont Circle Metro.** Original prints by contemporary artists, plus monotypes, relief works, and other inventive uses of the print medium.

Georgetown

Addison/Ripley Gallery 1670 Wisconsin Ave NW ☎202/333-5180. Contemporary fine art – oil paintings, photography, sculpture, and prints.

Atlantic Gallery The Foundry Building, 1055 Thomas Jefferson St NW ☎202/337-2299. Traditional fine art, featuring landscapes, hunting scenes, and seascapes.

Fine Art & Artists 2920 M St NW ☎202/965-0780. Pop and Abstract Expressionist art, with a bent toward big international names from the 1960s and more contemporary minimalists, metal sculptors, and neo-abstract painters.

Spectrum Gallery 1132 29th St NW ☎202/333-0954. Local artists' co-op with regular exhibitions of prints, photos, sculpture, and mixed media.

Other locations

Arts Afire 102 N Fayette St, Alexandria, VA ☎703/838-9785. Major dealer in art glass, with a full complement of work from regional and national designers on display; includes everything from jewelry and home decor to kaleidoscopes, vases, and trinkets.

Fusebox 1412 14th St NW, Logan Circle ☎202/299-9220. A chic and popular spot to sample the latest in avant-garde artwork in a variety of media, with a strong emphasis on the abstract, irreverent, and inexplicable.

Village on Capitol Hill 705 N Carolina Ave SE ☎202/546-3040; **Eastern Market Metro.** Oddball set of art-related items, from abstract paintings to quirky sculptures made by international artisans to colorful hats and jewelry. A good example of an Eastern Market gallery straddling the thin line between high art and cheesy kitsch.

Directory

Addresses The US Capitol – which itself doesn't have an address – is the center of the District's street-numbering system, and the four quadrants of the city (NW, SW, SE, NE) relate to their position respective to the building. North and South Capitol streets divide the city by east and west, and the National Mall and East Capitol Street divide it by north and south.

Airlines Air Canada, US and Canada ☎1-888/247-2262, Ⓦwww.aircanada.ca; Air France, UK ☎0845/359 1000, Ireland ☎01/605 0383, Ⓦwww.airfrance.com; Air New Zealand, Australia ☎13 24 76, Ⓦwww.airnz.com.au, New Zealand ☎0800/737 000, Ⓦwww.airnz.co.nz; Air Tran ☎1-800/247-8726, Ⓦwww.airtran.com; Alaska ☎1-800/252-7522, Ⓦwww.alaskaair.com; America West ☎1-800/235-9292, Ⓦwww.americawest.com; American ☎1-800/433-7300, Ⓦwww.aa.com; American Trans Air (ATA) ☎1-800/435-9282, Ⓦwww.ata.com; British Airways, UK ☎0870/850 9850, Ireland ☎1800/626 747, Ⓦwww.britishairways.com; British Midland (BMI), UK ☎0870/607 0555, Ireland ☎01/407 3036, Ⓦwww.flybmi.com; Cathay Pacific, Australia ☎13 17 47, New Zealand ☎0508/800 454 or 09/379 0861, Ⓦwww.cathaypacific.com; Continental ☎1-800/523-3273, Ⓦwww.continental.com; Delta ☎1-800/221-1212, Ⓦwww.delta.com; Frontier ☎1-800/432-1359, Ⓦwww.flyfrontier.com; JetBlue ☎1-800/JET-BLUE, Ⓦwww.jetblue.com; Lufthansa, UK ☎0845/773 7747, Ireland ☎01/844 5544, Ⓦwww.lufthansa.com; Midwest ☎1-800/452-2022, Ⓦwww.midwestairlines.com; Northwest/KLM ☎1-800/225-2525, Ⓦwww.nwa.com; Qantas, Australia ☎13 13 13, New Zealand ☎0800/808 767 or 09/357 8900, Ⓦwww.qantas.com; Southwest ☎1-800/435-9792, Ⓦwww.southwest.com; United ☎1-800/241-6522, Ⓦwww.united.com; US Airways, US and Canada ☎1-800/428-4322, Ⓦwww.usairways.com.

American Express ☎1-800/528-4800, Ⓦwww.americanexpress.com; offices at 1150 Connecticut Ave NW, New Downtown ☎202/457-1300; Pentagon City Mall, Arlington, VA ☎703/415-5400.

Area code Phone numbers in Washington DC are prefixed by the area code ☎202, while those in Arlington and Alexandria use ☎703. Numbers over the Maryland border require a ☎301 area code.

Banks Citibank ☎1-800/926-1067, Ⓦwww.citibank.com. Main service center at 435 11th St NW, Old Downtown; other branches at 600 Pennsylvania Ave SE, Capitol Hill; 1400 G St NW, Old Downtown; 1000 Connecticut Ave NW, New Downtown; and 1901 Wisconsin Ave NW, Georgetown. Riggs ☎301/887-6000 or 1-800/368-5800, Ⓦwww.riggsbank.com; branches at 650 Pennsylvania Ave SE, Capitol Hill; 800 17th St NW, Foggy Bottom; 1913 Massachusetts Ave NW, Dupont Circle; 301 (and 833) 7th St NW, Old Downtown; 1503 Pennsylvania Ave NW, Old Downtown; 1101 15th St NW, New Downtown. SunTrust ☎1-888/786-8787 or 1-800/SUNTRUST, Ⓦwww.suntrust.com; branches at 300 Pennsylvania Ave SE and 2 Massachusetts Ave NW, both in Capitol Hill; 1275 K St NW, New Downtown; 1250 U St NW, Shaw. Wachovia ☎1-800/922-4684, Ⓦwww.wachovia.com. 801 (and 1301) Pennsylvania Ave NW, Federal Triangle; 1310 G St NW, Old Downtown; 215 Pennsylvania Ave SE, Capitol Hill; 1700 Pennsylvania Ave NW, Foggy Bottom; 1800 K St NW, New Downtown.

Bus info Call Greyhound (☎1-800/231-2222, in DC ☎202/289-5154) or Peter Pan Trailways (☎1-800/343-9999). Departures to Baltimore, Philadelphia, New York, Boston, and beyond are from the terminal at 1005 1st St NE.

Cell phones In 2004 Washington became one of the few US cities to ban cell-phone use while driving; early enforcement of the law may bring warnings, but by 2005 stiffer fines may result.

Doctors and dentists Lists of doctors can be found in the *Yellow Pages* under "Clinics" or "Physicians and Surgeons." For a doctor referral service call Washington Hospital Center (☎202/877-3627) or George Washington University Hospital (☎1-888/449-3627), or contact your embassy (see below). Contact the DC Dental Society (Mon–Fri 8am–4pm; ☎202/547-7615) for dentist referral.

Electricity 110 volts AC. Plugs are standard two-pins – foreign visitors will need an adaptor and voltage converter for their own appliances.

Embassies Australia: 1601 Massachusetts Ave NW, 20036 ☎202/797-3000, ⓦwww .austemb.org; Canada: 501 Pennsylvania Ave NW, 20001 ☎202/682-1740, ⓦwww .canadianembassy.org; Ireland: 2234 Massachusetts Ave NW, 20008 ☎202/462-3939, ⓦwww.irelandemb.org; New Zealand: 37 Observatory Circle NW, 20008 ☎202/328-4800, ⓦwww.nzembassy.com; United Kingdom: 3100 Massachusetts Ave NW, 20008 ☎202/588-6500, ⓦwww .britainusa.com.

Floor terminology The first floor in the US is what would be the ground floor in Britain; the second floor would be the first floor and so on. However, the design of certain DC buildings and institutions (including various Mall museums and galleries) incorporates underground and mezzanine levels, so some buildings do have a "ground floor" on the level at which you enter.

Hospital George Washington University Hospital, 901 23rd St NW (☎202/715-4000, general patient information), has a 24hr emergency department (☎202/715-4911).

Internet access Available at the Martin Luther King Memorial Library, 901 G St NW, Old Downtown (Mon–Thurs 9.30am–9pm, Fri & Sat 9.30am–5.30pm, Sun 1–5pm; ☎202/727-1186, ⓦwww.dclibrary.org), or at one of the following outlets:

Cyberlaptops.com, 1636 R St NW, Dupont Circle (☎202/462-7195, ⓦwww .cyberlaptops.com); Cyberstop Café, 1513 17th St NW, Dupont Circle (closes midnight; ☎202/234-2470, ⓦwww .cyberstopcafe.com); FedEx Kinko's, 325 7th St, Old Downtown (24hr; ☎202/544-4796, ⓦwww.kinkos.com), 715 D St SE, Capitol Hill (24hr; ☎202/547-0421), 1612 K St NW, New Downtown (☎202/466-3777), 3329 M St NW, Georgetown (☎202/965-1415); and The Newsroom, 1803 Connecticut Ave NW, Dupont Circle (☎202/332-1489).

Libraries The general public can register with ID and use the Library of Congress (see p.112), while the main city library is the Martin Luther King Memorial Library, 901 G St NW, Old Downtown (see above).

Pharmacies CVS has many different locations throughout DC (information at ⓦwww .cvs.com), with convenient downtown and Georgetown sites and 24hr stores at 1199 Vermont Ave NW, New Downtown (☎202/737-3962); 7 Dupont Circle (☎202/833-5704); and 4555 Wisconsin Ave, Upper Northwest (☎202/537-1459).

Police In an emergency call ☎911. For non-emergency help, information, and the location of police stations call ☎202/727-1010. The Metro Transit Police can be contacted at ☎202/962-2121.

Post offices and mail services DC's main downtown post office is across from Union Station at 2 Massachusetts Ave NE, 20002 (Mon–Fri 7am–midnight, Sat & Sun 7am –8pm; ☎202/523-2368). There are also convenient branches at 1800 M St NW, New Downtown, 20036 (Mon–Fri 9am–5pm; ☎202/523-2506), and 1200 Pennsylvania Ave NW, 20004 (Mon–Fri 7.30am–5.30pm, Sat 8am–12.30pm; ☎202/842-1444). Service counters offering stamps are in the Old Post Office building (see p.157), the National Museum of American History (p.60), and the US Capitol (p.99). For other locations and more information, visit ⓦwww.usps.com.

Tax DC sales tax is 5.75 percent; restaurant tax, 10 percent; hotel tax, 14.5 percent.

Taxis Capitol Cab ☎202/546-2400, Diamond Cab ☎202/387-6200, Yellow Cab ☎202/544-1212. Information at ⓦwww.dctaxi.dc.gov.

Time Washington DC is on Eastern Standard Time, five hours behind Greenwich

DIRECTORY

Mean Time (-5 GMT). Daylight saving time, when clocks are turned back an hour, operates between April and October (check newspapers for specific dates).

Train departures Amtrak (☎1-800/872-7245 ⓦwww.amtrak.com) operates out of Union Station, offering service along the Northeast Corridor and beyond. For more detailed information on this and regional railways, see "City transportation," p.29.

Travelers Aid Society Useful help, emergency, and information desks run by a voluntary, nonprofit agency (ⓦwww.travelersaid.org). Main office is at Union Station (Mon–Sat 9.30am–5.30pm, Sun 12.30–5.30pm; ☎202/371-1937); other offices at National Airport (Mon–Fri 9am–9pm, Sat & Sun 9am–6pm; ☎703/417-3972) and Dulles Airport (Mon–Fri 8am–9pm, Sat & Sun 8am–7pm; ☎703/572-8296).

Travelex and Thomas Cook ☎1-800/287-7362, ⓦwww.travelex.com; branches at 1800 K St NW (Mon–Fri 9am–6pm, ☎202/872-1428); Union Station, Massachusetts Ave NE (Mon–Sat 9am–5pm, Sun noon–6pm; ☎202/371-9220); and at National Airport (daily 7am–9pm; ☎703/417-3200) and Dulles Airports (daily 7am–9pm; ☎703/572-2946).

Weather For five-day city weather forecasts check the *Washington Post's* Post-Haste information line at ☎202/334-9000.

Western Union ☎1-800/325-6000, ⓦwww .westernunion.com; offices at 1405 G St NW, Old Downtown (☎202/783-7878); 3821 Mount Vernon Ave, Alexandria, VA (☎703/683-0396); and 2425 N Harrison St, Arlington, VA (☎703/237-0331). Also inquire about local stores that offer Western Union services.

Contexts

Contexts

A history of Washington DC

I n the two centuries since Washington DC was founded, it has been at the heart of American government, a showcase city embodying the ideals and aspirations of the United States. Among the mighty monuments and memorials, however, it's often easy to forget it's also a city where people live and work. The **history** below provides a brief exposition of the main themes in the city's development. For more detail on specific matters – from biographies of famous people to histories of buildings – follow the pointers at the end of each section.

Native peoples

The area that is now the nation's capital was, for most of its history of human habitation, populated by native peoples like the **Piscataway** tribe, who spoke an Algonquin dialect and lived on both banks of the Chesapeake Bay. They were content to live a fairly peaceful existence in teepees, hunting and fishing for game, and their dugout canoes and handwoven baskets are evidence of their longstanding culture in the region. They did, however, have their enemies – the belligerent **Susquehannocks** were perhaps the most fearsome fellow tribe, scheming and attacking their settlements such as Nacotchtant, around present-day Anacostia. The war-mongering of the Susquehannocks, however, could not alone drive the tribe from the region; predictably, it took the presence of **European settlers** to do that. Although Spanish explorer Pedro Menendez cruised around the southern Chesapeake inlets in the sixteenth century, English colonists were to have more interest in the land, and prove to be a more formidable foe for the Piscataway than any other they'd encountered.

European settlement

Sponsored by King James I, **English settlers** under Captain John Smith of the Virginia Company in 1608 established the first successful English colony in America at **Jamestown** on the coast to the south. What is now DC was mostly overlooked – though Smith did explore the Potomac River as far as Great Falls, and perhaps beyond. It wasn't until the 1630s that European settlement in the Chesapeake really took off, with the granting to Lord Baltimore of a royal charter establishing a Catholic colony in the region, **Maryland**, that would welcome members of that persecuted denomination from other parts of the British Empire. This grant was timely, since just eight years later, Parliament under Puritan domination would prove openly hostile to any even remotely Catholic enterprises.

Despite early setbacks, the colonists flourished on the back of a thriving **tobacco trade**. In the later seventeenth century both Virginia and Maryland expanded as English, Irish, and Scottish settlers poured into the region, displacing the indigenous population of Piscataways. Although Baltimore and other Catholics attempted at first to convert the tribe to Christianity, much like Protestant colonizers they soon drove them further into the wilderness, where they became prey for larger, more dominant tribes. The Europeans also introduced **slaves** from West Africa to work the plantations. Among these slave-holding planters was one Captain John Washington, George's great-grandfather, who in 1656 arrived from Essex in England and immediately set about establishing a plantation on the river. The Potomac remained an important commercial thoroughfare, and vibrant new towns sprang up alongside it: notably **Alexandria** in Virginia (1749) and **Georgetown** in Maryland (1751).

War and aftermath

Increasing hostilities with England throughout the 1770s led to the colonies – now calling themselves states – drafting the Declaration of Independence in 1776. The **American Revolutionary War** (1775–83), however, had already begun, and Virginia's George Washington was leading troops of volunteer militia, which later formed into something resembling a continental army. The battle that basically guaranteed American independence – Yorktown, in 1781 – was fought just to the south in Virginia, within 25 miles of the founding colonial site of Jamestown.

After the war some revolutionary leaders proposed the establishment of a permanent capital city, but there was no obvious site: the exigencies of war and conflicting political interests in the new republic meant that early meetings of Congress had gathered in several different cities. The 1787 **Constitutional Convention** in Philadelphia devised a permanent system of government for the nation and drafted a permanent Constitution, which replaced the dysfunctional Articles of Confederation, something of a wartime leftover that lacked an executive branch of government. After **George Washington** was inaugurated as the first president of the United States in New York City in 1789, extended political wrangling between the increasingly mercantile North and agrarian South, both of which wanted the capital, ended in compromise when a general site on the Potomac was chosen (near Washington's beloved estate at Mount Vernon), with land to be donated by Virginia and Maryland. Washington himself picked the exact site and hired surveyors **Andrew Ellicot** and **Benjamin Banneker**, an African American, to conduct the preliminary survey.

Building and re-building

In 1791, French engineer **Pierre Charles L'Enfant** began work on a grand master plan for the new city, and though he was fired the following year, his blueprint was largely followed by his successors. The first stone of the Executive Mansion (later known as the **White House**) was laid in 1792, construction of the **US Capitol** followed in 1793, and in 1800 **Congress** and second president John Adams – just months before he left office – moved from Philadelphia to the nascent city. The following year, **Thomas Jefferson** became the first president to be inaugurated in Washington DC.

The population of 3500 was then little more than that of a village, based largely around Capitol Hill and the Executive Mansion, overseen by a mayor and council. Its numbers were boosted by more than three thousand slaves who labored on the new buildings, wharves, and streets and lived in the swamp-ridden reaches near the river. Progress was interrupted by the **War of 1812** with England. Although the war was largely fought in far-flung places like Quebec and upstate New York, the British did score a propaganda coup when

L'Enfant's city plan	pp.48–49	The Octagon and the War of 1812	pp.147–148
White House, history	p.131	Presidential inaugurations	p.154
US Capitol, history	p.101		

in 1814 they sailed up the Potomac to burn the White House, the Capitol, and other public buildings to the ground – though they were stopped before they could do the same to Baltimore. President James Madison was forced to relocate to a private DC house, known as the Octagon, where the peace treaty ending the war was signed in 1814. Congress met in a hastily assembled Brick Capitol until the original was fully restored in 1819.

The Antebellum Era

Between the War of 1812 and the Civil War, the new capital struggled to make its mark; it was designed to be America's commercial and industrial showpiece, but was consistently overshadowed by Philadelphia and New York, and scarcely had enough residents to make it much of anything except a paper tiger of bureaucracy. **The Mall** – L'Enfant's central thoroughfare – remained a muddy swamp, and construction was slow and piecemeal. Foreign ambassadors collected hardship pay while stationed in this marshy outpost, and criticism was heaped upon the place; early snide detractors included such notable visitors as Charles Dickens (in the 1840s) and Anthony Trollope (1860s).

Despite its critics, however, the capital city was slowly beginning to look the part. **Pennsylvania Avenue** was spruced up as a grand link between the White House and Capitol, monumental buildings like the US Treasury and Patent Office (both by Robert Mills) were added in the 1830s and 1840s, and work started on the **Washington Monument** in 1848. British gentleman scientist and philanthropist James Smithson made a huge bequest in 1829, which led to the founding of the Smithsonian Institution; its first home, the **Smithsonian Institution Building** (or the "Castle"), was completed on the Mall in 1855.

Despite these advancements, Virginia demanded its share of the capital back in 1846, and the District of Columbia lost two of its major components – Arlington and Alexandria. Only Georgetown remained as an independent city in the District outside of Washington.

Though DC's population increased slowly, throughout the first half of the century it never breached 60,000. The balance of the steadily rising black population shifted, however, as the number of runaway slaves and free blacks (migrants from Southern plantations) jumped dramatically. Separate black schools and churches were established as debate intensified between abolitionists and pro-slavery adherents – the so-called **Snow Riots** (1835) saw intimidation and destruction by white mobs intent on maintaining slavery in the capital. Indeed, as it grew, Washington became a microcosm of the divisions searing the country at large – ideologically polarized residents, each eyeing the other with suspicion; political combat so fractious as to make dialogue nearly impossible; and the increasing threat of secession in the air. When the domination of the pro-slavery **Democratic Party** – which had ruled the country for all but eight years since 1800 – came to an end in 1860, so too did the bonds of the nation.

The Civil War

Following the Confederate attack on Fort Sumter in South Carolina, which finally propelled the country into civil war, **Abraham Lincoln**'s call to defend the Union in 1861 brought thousands of volunteer soldiers to Washington, virtually doubling the city's population. Others left to join the Confederate cause, among them **Robert E. Lee**, who abandoned his estate at Arlington and his Union Army post to take command of the Virginia military. Washington DC became the epicenter of the Union effort and the North's main supply depot, surrounded by defensive forts (now known as the Fort Circle Parks), its grand Neoclassical buildings turned over to massive makeshift hospitals. Lincoln determined to continue construction in the capital (symbolically, the **Capitol dome** was added in 1863), despite fear of imminent attack by Southern forces – the city was never overrun, though several of the bloodiest battles (including Bull Run/Manassas, Antietam, and Gettysburg) were fought within ninety miles of it. Because of these factors, an atmosphere of paranoia developed in the capital, as reports of spies, saboteurs, and assassins became legion, which led Lincoln to take such drastic measures as suspending certain civil liberties (such as habeas corpus) for residents of nearby Maryland – thought to be a hotbed of rebel intrigue.

As it dragged on, the Civil War became as much a war about slavery as about preserving the Union (Lincoln's initial war goal). Slavery was outlawed in DC in 1862, and in 1863 the **Emancipation Proclamation** freed all slaves in rebel states – though not those of pro-Union slave states like Maryland and Kentucky. Eventually the South was defeated by the North's superior strength and economic muscle, not to mention the striking, yet bloody, strategy of attrition by Union commander **Ulysses S. Grant**, who realized pure, unending carnage – and not elegant battlefield victories of the kind won by Lee – was the way to bring the South to its knees. The war ended in April 1865 with Lee's surrender to Grant at Appomattox Court House in Virginia, not far from the initial battle of the war. Five days later, **Lincoln was assassinated** in Washington while attending a play at Ford's Theatre.

Reconstruction and expansion

The period after the Civil War was an era of tremendous growth in DC, as ex-slaves from the South and returned soldiers settled here; within thirty years, the population stood at 300,000, and distinct neighborhoods began to emerge. Black residents now constituted forty percent of the population and enjoyed unprecedented rights and privileges in the aftermath of emancipation. **Suffrage** was extended to all adult men for local DC elections (1866), black public schools were established, the all-black **Howard University** was founded (1867), segregation was prohibited (1870), and ex-slave, orator, and abolitionist **Frederick Douglass** was appointed marshal (and, later, recorder of deeds) of DC (1877). In 1867, after Congress granted the District of Columbia **territorial status**, for the first time the city embarked on a coherent public works program under Alexander "Boss" Shepherd – a short-lived exercise in local democracy that ended in 1874, when control of the debt-ridden city passed back to Congress. Although residents had been able to elect their own officials since 1802, Congress now reserved this right for itself, and denizens were politically disenfranchised for another century.

Washington's cultural profile, however, went from strength to strength, boosted after the 1876 Philadelphia Centennial Exhibition when the Smithsonian Institution built America's first **National Museum** (now the Arts and Industries Building) on the Mall to provide a permanent home for the exhibition's artifacts. The **Renwick** and **Corcoran** galleries – two of the earliest public art museums in the country – both opened during this period. The Washington Monument, first of the city's grand presidential memorials, was finally completed in 1884, as DC began to reshape itself as a national showpiece. As its stock rose, place-seekers and lobbyists (a term first coined during Grant's presidency) flooded into the city, seeking attachment to the administration of the day. One such aspirant, Charles Guiteau was so incensed at being denied a civil-service post that he assassinated **President James Garfield** in 1881, just four months after his inauguration.

The turn of the century

By the turn of the nineteenth century, Washington had established itself as a thriving, modern capital with civic and federal buildings to match: in a flurry of construction from the 1870s to the 1890s, fine premises for the **Old Post Office**, **Pension Building**, and **Library of Congress** were erected, while Theodore Roosevelt carried out the first full-scale expansion and renovation of the White House (1901). Meanwhile, LeDroit Park, Adams-Morgan, and Cleveland Park became fashionable suburbs, Georgetown was formally merged with DC, and the Smithsonian branched out again with the establishment of the **National Zoo**.

In 1901, a committee under Senator James McMillan proposed the development and extension of the city's park system. Later, the National Commission of Fine Arts was established to co-ordinate public improvements and new building design: the country's largest train station, **Union Station**, was completed in the prevailing monumental Beaux Arts style in 1908, and in 1910, height restrictions were imposed on downtown buildings to preserve the cityscape – ensuring that the Capitol remained the tallest and most prominent government edifice. However, after the high hopes of the Reconstruction years, the city's black population suffered from increasing segregation and loss of civil rights. Housing in black neighborhoods like Foggy Bottom and Georgetown was in poor shape, federal jobs became harder to come by, and the black population actually decreased.

World War I and the Depression

The US entered World War I in 1917, despite President **Woodrow Wilson**'s avowed efforts to remain neutral; after the war, Washington's population increased again as soldiers returned home. The post-war years were as troubled for DC as they were for the rest of the US. Under Wilson, **Prohibition** was imposed in a futile attempt to improve the morality of the nation, and a number of strikes were violently broken. **Racial tension** increased in this uneasy climate, which saw segregation become entrenched, the Ku Klux Klan parading at the Washington Monument, and race riots, fanned by demobilized white soldiers, breaking out in the city in 1919. Ironically, segregation also worked to boost the fortunes of DC's black neighborhoods: prevented from socializing elsewhere, blacks made Shaw's U Street famous as the "Black Broadway," nurturing stars like Duke Ellington. The **Phillips Collection**, America's first modern art museum, opened in 1921, while the building of the **Lincoln Memorial** (1922) and the **Freer Gallery** (1923) represented the last cultural gasps of the McMillan Commission – though the Mall itself soon turned into a giant parking lot to serve an increasing amount of automotive commuters.

Washington, with its government agencies and large federal payroll, was not as hard hit as rural or industrial areas by the **Great Depression**; unemployed marchers from the rest of the country descended on the Capitol to register their distress in 1931 and 1932 (the latter march being dispersed by the army). President Franklin Roosevelt's **New Deal**, and, specifically, the **Works Progress Administration** (WPA), put thousands of jobless men to work – in DC, building the Federal Triangle and Supreme Court (1935), among other projects. Despite this kind of progressive economic uplift, racial injustice proved a thornier issue. As but one example, in 1939 the **Daughters of the American Revolution** (DAR) infamously banned black contralto Marian Anderson from singing in their Constitution Hall; Anderson subsequently appeared in front of a huge, desegregated crowd at the Lincoln Memorial, in an early hint of the civil-rights battles to come.

Woodrow Wilson	p.192	Federal Triangle, construction	p.159
U Street, history	p.201	Supreme Court, history	p.108
Lincoln Memorial, history	p.56	Marian Anderson and the DAR	p.143

World War II to the 1968 riots

In 1941, the US entered World War II and a third great wartime influx boosted the population of Washington DC. Guards were posted at the White House and Capitol, air defenses installed in case of Axis attack, and the **Pentagon** built in 1943 to accommodate the expanding War Department. The war years also saw the opening of the **National Gallery of Art** (1941), one of the nation's finest museums, and the completion of the **Jefferson Memorial** (1943). Following the war, Washington grew as the federal government expanded under presidents Truman and Eisenhower, growing as a result of both the maintenance of New Deal-era programs and fresh military and economic funds to fight the **Cold War**. By 1960, the city's population reached 800,000, the White House was completely overhauled, neighboring Foggy Bottom became the seat of various departments and international organizations, and new housing proliferated in suburban Maryland and Virginia.

The war had gone some way to changing racial perceptions in America, as black soldiers had again enlisted in droves to fight for freedom, and in the post-war years the **civil rights movement** began to gain strength. Segregation of public facilities was finally declared illegal by the Supreme Court ruling on **Brown v. Board of Education**, and schools in DC were desegregated in 1954. In the South, however, the ruling was obeyed in name only, leading to an increasingly politicized, nationwide stream of demonstrations, boycotts, sit-ins, and marches in the 1950s and early 1960s. A feeling of progressive hope culminated in the close 1960 election victory of **John F. Kennedy** – the youngest president ever elected, and the only Catholic – and was epitomized by **Dr Martin Luther King Jr**'s famous "I have a dream" speech during the **March on Washington for Jobs and Freedom** at the Lincoln Memorial in August 1963. Just three months later, however, JFK was assassinated in Dallas and buried in Arlington Cemetery. In 1964, DC citizens voted in a presidential election for the first time, following the 23rd Amendment of 1961, which gave them new electoral rights. The contest was won in a landslide by Lyndon Johnson, who, as vice president, had become president after Kennedy's death.

By the late 1960s, despite the partial enactment of Johnson's **Great Society**, including new civil-rights and Medicare legislation, the growing **Vietnam War** was taking a huge toll on the president's popularity and national cohesion. Demonstrations in Washington were called against poverty (notably the **Poor People's March**, in 1968) and the war itself, and the assassination of Dr Martin Luther King Jr in Memphis in 1968 led to nationwide **race riots**, including the worst in DC's history: parts of Shaw, Logan Circle, and Old Downtown were devastated. The white flight to the suburbs began in earnest, and DC became a predominantly black city.

Growth and malaise

The 1970s were a time of momentous political upheaval in Washington DC. In 1970, DC got its first nonvoting delegate to the House of Representatives; three years later, the Home Rule Act paved the way for the city's first elected mayor – **Walter Washington** – in more than a century; and the **Watergate scandal** of 1974 led to the resignation of President Richard Nixon – still the only such occurrence in US history.

Meanwhile, divisions within the city became increasingly stark. Downtown continued to reshape itself – the **Kennedy Center** opened in 1971, the **Hirshhorn Museum** (1974) and East Wing of the **National Gallery of Art** (1979) were added to the Mall, the K Street business and lobbyist district in New Downtown thrived, and artsy **Dupont Circle** became one of the city's trendiest neighborhoods – while Shaw and areas of southeast and northeast Washington slipped further into degradation, with a drug and crime problem that earned DC the enduring tag of "**Murder Capital of America**." Such contradictions were largely ignored, however, and in 1976, Bicentennial year, the city celebrated by opening its **Metrorail** system and the **National Air and Space Museum** – still the top museum attraction in America. Jimmy Carter was sworn in as president in 1977 and, after his inauguration, famously walked the distance from the Capitol to the White House, though his tenure was eventually marked by what he called a "malaise," signified by high gas prices, inflation, and unemployment, plus the taking of American hostages in Iran in 1979 – an act which Carter was helpless to stop. In November 1980 he lost his job to ex-California governor and *Bedtime for Bonzo* co-star Ronald Reagan.

The Reagan era

Under **Ronald Reagan**, the nation's economy boomed and busted as taxes (and welfare and entitlement programs) were slashed and the federal budget deficit soared. In DC, the souped-up economy paved the way for drastic downtown urban-renewal projects: the building of the **Convention Center** (1980) signaled the revitalization of Old Downtown; Pennsylvania Avenue and its buildings – eyesores for three decades – were restored; and yuppies began moving into Adams-Morgan. Reagan survived an assassination attempt at the *Washington Hilton* in 1981, but his reputation (and that of his successor, George Bush) was put in question by later Iran-Contra proceedings, whose revelations (involving the funneling of illegal arms sales to the official "enemy" of Iran to finance right-wing Nicaraguan guerrillas) were carried live on TV from hearings in the city. At the same time, as American military spending increased dramatically, major new **memorials** were built to the Vietnam veterans (1982) and US Navy (1987).

Culturally, the city went from strength to strength. The Smithsonian expanded its collections on the Mall with the addition of the **Sackler Gallery** and **African Art Museum** (both in 1987), the **National Postal Museum** opened (1986), and Union Station was restored (1988). City politics took a colorful turn with the successive mayoral terms of Marion Barry (first elected in 1978), whose initial success in attracting investment soon gave way to conflict with Congress, which was to become the hallmark of the following decade. The city began its slide into insolvency just as Bill Clinton was elected president in 1992 on promises to turn the economy around and restructure welfare.

The Clinton years

To the casual eye, it was business as usual in the 1990s in DC – now one of the most touristed cities in America, with almost 20 million visitors a year – as new attractions continued to open: the **National Law Enforcement Officers Memorial** in 1991, the **US Holocaust Memorial Museum** in 1993, the **Korean War Veterans Memorial** and the **White House Visitor Center** in 1995, and the **FDR Memorial** and **MCI Center** in 1997. Behind the scenes, though, Washington lurched into crisis in the first half of the 1990s, as the federal budget deficit spiraled. Amazingly, Marion Barry returned from a drug-related prison sentence to be re-elected as mayor in 1994 – only for a new ultra-right-wing Republican Congress (under Newt Gingrich) to revoke Washington's home rule charter a year later and place a congressionally appointed financial control board in charge of the city's affairs.

The city did, however, rebound under the control board, which by virtue of its success put itself out of a job in 2001, restoring power to the city council and the mayor. During this period, as the city was grappling with its financial woes, the public exposure of President Clinton's affair with intern **Monica**

Lewinsky put DC in the national spotlight in a way not seen since the Watergate hearings of the 1970s. As always, the cover-up seemed worse than the crime, but Clinton, who had scored a political victory in the congressional elections of 1998, survived later impeachment hearings. The situation was different, though, in 2000, when the Supreme Court for the first time decided a presidential election. The Court, in a still-controversial 5-4 decision, awarded the White House to conservative Texas Governor George W. Bush, whose public fight was successfully shepherded by family crony (and former Secretary of State) James Baker, while his opponent, Vice President Al Gore, was content to appear before cameras nonchalantly playing touch football with his family.

Contemporary DC

The events and aftermath of 9/11 are well known: **on September 11, 2001**, terrorists hijacked a United Airlines jet and crashed it into the Pentagon, killing nearly 200 people, including those on the plane. A second aircraft, probably headed for the US Capitol, crashed in a Pennsylvania field before reaching its target, while two other hijacked planes destroyed New York City's World Trade Center, killing nearly 3000. Soon after, **anthrax** spores were found in a letter mailed to Senate leader Tom Daschle, heightening tensions in an already shaken DC. The House suspended its session for a week and several federal buildings were closed pending investigation and fumigation. In the aftermath, security was tightened throughout the capital and tourism slowed to a trickle.

Paradoxically, even while the city was on lockdown its economic fortunes – beyond tourism – continued to revive. **Anthony Williams**, a former chief financial officer of the council board, had won election as mayor in 1998 and proceeded to get credit for lower crime rates, newly paved roads, and a revitalized downtown where restaurants and sports and cultural events began to attract visitors to places once overrun by crime. Areas such as Adams-Morgan, Dupont Circle, and especially the Penn Quarter attracted new investment and saw their stately, once-decaying old buildings re-emerge as modern showpieces. Perhaps most tellingly, DC's population stabilized at just above half a million after decades of decline, and the city's property values began to soar in places. Still, many parts of the city remained poverty-stricken, and areas of northeast DC – well away from the capital investment zones – sunk even further into economic blight.

In 2004 Washington is very much a city in transition: even as construction barricades go up throughout downtown, heralding the renovation of classic structures into modern offices and hotels, security barricades have followed them, and in some spots the capital resembles an armed camp surrounded by chain-link fences and concrete planters. Amid all this construction, the visitors have returned in droves, and flock to popular areas like the Mall and Capitol Hill even as they stay in stylish hotels in the Penn Quarter and New Downtown. Washington's **growth and economic renaissance** are even having an effect on the suburbs, where residents priced out of living in the city itself jostle for decent houses near the Metrorail, the thought of doing battle with car commuters on the gridlocked Beltway just too onerous to imagine. The opening of new memorials and museums has also improved the city's optimistic, if fearful, sense of itself. The Memorial Day unveiling of the **National World War II Memorial** drew thousands of veterans, diplomats, and politicians from around the world who came to hear America's leader praise the warriors of the past for their fearless defense of democracy, and warn the current generation of the endless terrorist threats of its future.

In November 2004, owing largely to his own canny political skills and the absence of a follow-up terrorist strike after 9/11, George W. Bush was **re-elected** to the presidency and his Republican party expanded its grip on Congress. Whether this victory will translate into long-term conservative dominance, however, depends for the most part on whether the president is able to keep the upper hand on global terrorism and, especially, find a way to extricate the US from its increasingly bloody entanglement in **Iraq**, invaded by Bush in spring 2003.

The American system of government

The **American system of government** derives squarely from the Constitution of the United States, sorted out by the original thirteen states at the Constitutional Convention in Philadelphia and signed on September 17, 1787. Deriving its authority from the essential force of popular sovereignty – "We the People" – the Constitution gave a federal administration certain designated powers so that it could both resist attack from abroad and prevent the fragmentation of the nascent nation. Two centuries and 27 amendments later, its provision of "checks and balances" on the exercise of power still provides the basis for the fundamental stability of a country that has often looked less than united.

The idea was simple enough. The earlier **Articles of Confederation** (adopted during the Revolution) had joined a loose grouping of independent states together in Congress under a weak central legislature with no executive branch, but by the late 1780s it was clear that the system lacked efficiency and coherence. With no separation of powers, Congress had to request permission from the states every step of the way; each state retained the right to refuse consent (whether for money, soldiers, or permission for new laws) and exercised the power in its own interest. What was needed, according to arch-Federalists like Alexander Hamilton, was a strong central government buttressed by a supreme **Constitution**. The anti-Federalists who opposed them (such as fiery orator Patrick Henry, rabble-rouser Sam Adams, and the crafter of Virginia's bill of rights, George Mason) feared encroachment upon the sovereignty of the states and citizens' liberties, but many were appeased by the promise of the ratification of various amendments (adopted in 1791 in the ten-point **Bill of Rights**) that would encompass many of their demands. What was produced at the Constitutional Convention was nothing less than a triumph: eighty percent of the original text of the Constitution remains unchanged today; only seventeen more amendments have been added in the two centuries following the Bill of Rights; and the United States remains one of the world's most enduring democracies – technically since 1789, but in practice since 1865.

As a **federal republic**, the country splits its powers between the government and the fifty individual states, basically protecting the states from unnecessary intrusions from an overbearing central government while allowing federal decisions to be made to benefit (or protect) the whole country, and to manage interstate commerce. Thus the states can police themselves, make local laws and raise taxes, but they can't issue currency, conclude foreign treaties, maintain armed forces, or levy taxes against other states. On the other hand, the Constitution pledges that the federal government shall protect each of the states against invasion or "domestic violence." Moreover, those who framed the Constitution took great pains to emphasize that individual states should retain all powers not specifically "enumerated" by the Constitution; reinforced by the 10th Amendment, this notion remains a fundamental tenet of American democracy, in which local and national powers are stringently defined within the framework of a federal, and not centralized, republic. Thus each state has a significant amount of autonomy, while the states' political structures duplicate the federal system, with their own legislative chambers, state courts and constitutions.

The branches of federal government

The **federal government** itself comprises three distinct branches: the **legislative**, **executive**, and **judiciary**. Each operates as a check and balance on the other, and each directly affects individual liberties and not just those of the states.

Article 1 of the Constitution vests all **legislative** powers in a bicameral **Congress** made up of a House of Representatives and a Senate, both of which meet in the US Capitol. When established in the eighteenth century, the House of Representatives was conceived as the body whose directly elected members would represent the people and all their presumably angry, fickle tendencies – essentially the democratic part of the equation. The Senate, or upper house, however, would not only be a check on the House's power, but also a way of balancing the interests of the smaller states against the larger, since each state in the Senate has an equal vote; it was also designed as an elite protector of republican liberty by being a means of controlling the "hot tempers" blowing through the House. Not surprisingly, early senators were sent to Congress by state legislatures – not by direct vote of the people – and were white, property-owning men, largely by design. The separation of roles between House and Senate was institutionalized from the start: representatives and senators are elected at different times, from differently sized constituencies for different terms of office.

The **House of Representatives** (or simply the "House") has 435 members (this size was fixed in 1929), with states allocated a number of representatives based on their population (which is reassessed, or "reapportioned," every ten years; each state is entitled to at least one representative). Members are elected from defined congressional districts (each containing, at present, about 650,000 people, except for the smallest states), serve for two years and receive $154,700 per annum, rising about three percent annually. The House is still the more representative of the two chambers: more frequent elections mean a closer convergence with the general public's mood, while the House always has a significantly higher percentage of women and ethnic minorities than the Senate (though neither remotely reflects the demographic make-up of the modern US). Apart from the fifty states thus represented, there are also nonvoting delegates in the House, representing the territories of Samoa, Guam and the Virgin Islands, and, since 1973, Washington DC itself (see p.164 for more on Washington's peculiar status within the Union). The chief officer of the House is the Speaker – chosen from the ranks of the majority party and paid about $200,000 a year. Each party also elects a leader in the House, known accordingly as the House Majority or House Minority leader, and a House Whip (whose job is to ensure that party members vote the right way).

The **Senate** comprises two senators from each state. In 1913, the 17th Amendment allowed for the direct election of senators by state voters, though the job remains essentially an aristocratic one – this legislative branch is often, and accurately, described as a "millionaire's club." Senators are elected for six years, with one third being elected every two years; like members of the House, they get paid $154,700 a year, with three-percent annual raises. The presiding officer in the Senate is the US vice president, but he doesn't have a vote unless it's to break a tie. However, the President Pro

Tempore – traditionally the oldest member of the Senate majority party – is by law only two steps below the VP in order of succession to the presidency, with the House Speaker between them.

In Congress, the House and the Senate share certain **responsibilities**, like assessing and collecting taxes, borrowing money, overseeing commerce, minting currency, maintaining the armed forces, declaring war and, crucially, making "all Laws which shall be necessary and proper for carrying into Execution" of these matters. But each separate chamber also has its own responsibilities: all revenue-raising (ie tax) bills originate in the House of Representatives, though the Senate can propose changes to such bills; only the Senate can "advise and consent" to the president's foreign treaties, nominations or appointments. While the House has the sole power of impeachment of the president or other federal officer, the Senate is the body that acts as jury in a political trial, deciding whether or not to remove the office-holder.

The House and Senate have separate chambers in the US Capitol, in which their official debates take place. In practice, however, the **bills** that Congress debates as a prelude to making laws are generally put together and taken apart ("marked up," in the jargon) by more than 250 smaller standing **committees** and **subcommittees** (not to mention ad hoc committees and joint committees) that meet in rooms in the Capitol or in the various relevant House or Senate office buildings. The committees are made up of members from both parties, in rough accordance with their overall strength, and are usually chaired by senior members of the controlling party.

If a bill survives this process (and many don't), it is "reported" to the full House for consideration; at that point **amendments** may be added before the particular bill is voted upon. If it passes it's sent to the Senate, which can also make amendments before returning it to the House. Any differences are resolved by wrangles in a joint House–Senate **conference committee**, which produces a final bill, acceptable to a majority in Congress. In addition to the standing committees of Congress, on occasion **select committees** are established to deliberate on special congressional investigations or matters of national importance – most famously, perhaps, the unraveling of the Watergate affair.

Voting in Congress doesn't always divide up according to party as it usually does in parliamentary democracies. The Speaker and the Rules Committee (which arranges the work of the House) can ensure that the majority party influences the make-up of various committees, the order of debates and the nature of proposed amendments. In the House, members often vote along state or regional lines on particular issues, while specific matters are increasingly agreed and voted upon by members grouped into caucuses, which can cut across party loyalties.

Once a bill passes Congress it goes to the **executive** branch of government – whose head is the president, or chief executive – for approval. The **president** can either sign the bill, at which point it becomes law, or veto it, in which case the bill goes back to the chamber where it originated. With two-thirds majority votes in both houses, Congress can override the president to make the bill law. The powers of the president (whose annual salary is $400,000, plus $50,000 in expenses; the vice president gets $200,000) are defined in Article 2 of the Constitution. As well as being chief executive, the president is also **commander-in-chief** of the armed forces; he can make treaties with foreign powers – provided two-thirds of the Senate agrees – and can appoint ambassadors, Supreme Court justices and other federal officers – with a majority of the Senate approving. Lest the chief executive get too bold, though, the

Constitution provides **parameters** for presidential power: under the terms of the 22nd Amendment, ratified in 1951, the president (and the vice president) is elected to office for four years and may only serve two terms. The amendment was a direct result of the presidency of Franklin Delano Roosevelt, who, determined to preserve his New Deal programs and wary of impending war, was elected for an unprecedented four terms, and served twelve years until his death. Moreover, the president is not above the law and can be removed from office by Congress "on impeachment for, and conviction of, treason, bribery, or other high crimes and misdemeanors."

This, however, is rarely attempted. The **impeachment** of President Clinton in 1999 was only the second such attempt in the country's history (the first was against Andrew Johnson, Lincoln's ill-fated successor; Nixon resigned before he could be impeached), and its failure was due in part to the nebulous nature of the defined standards of impeachment as laid down by the Constitution. "High crimes and misdemeanors" can essentially mean anything the House wants it to – in the eighteenth century, it probably referred to offenses against the state, but thanks to the Clinton impeachment, it now apparently means lying about adulterous affairs with interns as well.

This entire system is underpinned by the third arm of government, the **judiciary**, whose highest form is manifested in the **Supreme Court**, established by Article 3 of the Constitution. From the outset, the Court was designed as the final protector of the Constitution; its task is to uphold its articles and the laws made under it – in effect, to maintain what the Constitution calls "the supreme law of the land." All members of Congress, and all executive and federal officers, are bound by oath to support and uphold the Constitution since they derive their powers from it. Ultimately, although the Court did not initially have the power to strike down Congressional legislation, it gave itself this "judicial review" in the famous case of Marbury v. Madison in 1803. Since then, this notion of judicial supremacy has boiled down to the Constitution being what the Supreme Court says it is: the country has an "inferior" federal court system, in which legal decisions are made, and states are empowered to pass their own laws, but the appointed justices of the Supreme Court have the absolute right to throw out any legislation or legal argument that, in their opinion alone, violates the Constitution (or for that matter conflicts with the letter of an act passed by Congress). Naturally, for this reason, the executive branch in the shape of each president is keen to appoint sympathetic justices to the Supreme Court bench. This, fortunately for the system, is not as easy or as predictable as it might appear. For more on the make-up of the Supreme Court itself, see p.108.

Over the years, constitutional developments have also taken place outside the Constitution as **informal changes** have been introduced to the system of government through custom or historical event. The Constitution makes no mention of political parties, primary elections or congressional committees, for example, though all are now firmly entrenched in the system.

Real-world politics

That's the theory of American government. In practice, depending on whom you listen to, the entire structure is in a state somewhere between bare working order and terminal decline, with some even claiming that the framers of the Constitution designed gridlock to be built into the system, so as to slow down the pace of coercive legislation. Political historian David McKay puts his finger on the nub when he says that the "federal system, with its myriad governments and what amounts to fifty-one distinct constitutional structures, is the very essence of fragmentation." The most obvious drawback of the system of "**checks and balances**" is that it can work both for and against political progress. The Constitution forces the president to work with Congress on policy, and some of the wilder presidential excesses are certainly curtailed by congressional deliberations. But in an entrenched **two-party system** such as exists today, much depends on the prevailing political climate in either House or Senate: stalemate or compromise tend to be the natural outcomes of the checks-and-balances system.

Real-world congressional politics, as opposed to the theoretical marvel of American democracy, can be an unedifying spectacle, involving the often squalid trading of political favors, known as "**logrolling**." Moreover, the people are increasingly isolated from their elected representatives by the simple fact that candidates now need to be very rich to stand in the first place. Partly in response to the Watergate revelations, the 1974 Federal Election Campaign Act limited party and corporate contributions to a candidate's campaign, though failed to place a limit on the candidate's own contributions (with a subsequent Supreme Court decision upholding unlimited self-financing) – a campaign for a prospective House seat can now cost $250,000, up to ten times that for a Senate seat, and in 2004, a quarter-billion for the presidency. Hardly surprisingly, becoming a member of Congress is now seen as a career move: having invested the time and money, incumbent members are less likely to stand down whatever their personal or political failings and, statistically, much more likely to be re-elected than a challenger (who doesn't have the same access to the media and to the reflected political glories of Congress colleagues). At the presidential level, institutional ossification has meant that races for the nation's highest office end up being contests between incumbents of one kind or another – in the last 76 years only one election (1952) has paired two presidential candidates who didn't happen to include one sitting president or vice president.

Though Democrats and Republicans are increasingly polarized in liberal and conservative camps, third-party candidates have failed to make any enduring impact. A reasonably high (though ultimately futile) protest vote went to Ross Perot in 1992 and again in 1996 (though in 2004, Ralph Nader got less than one percent of the vote). Moreover, the voters are becoming less willing to give a president an overwhelming mandate. Since Richard Nixon's landslide in 1972, the presidential victor's share of the popular vote has bobbed under and around fifty percent – the only one to buck the trend was Ronald Reagan, who, in 1984, gained almost 59 percent of the vote. In the end, though, the general indifference felt for what happens on Capitol Hill is perhaps best indicated by the fact that the turnout for presidential and House elections ranges from only 30 to 55 percent – one of the lowest in any democracy in the world.

Presidents of the USA

Name	Party	Date	State of birth	Notable facts
George Washington	–	1789–97	Virginia	Only president unaffiliated by party
John Adams	Federalist	1797–1801	Massachusetts	First to occupy White House; died on July 4
Thomas Jefferson	Democratic-Republican	1801–09	Virginia	Wrote Declaration of Independence; died on July 4
James Madison	Democratic-Republican	1809–17	Virginia	Co-wrote US Constitution; started War of 1812
James Monroe	Democratic-Republican	1817–25	Virginia	Presided over "Era of Good Feelings"; died on July 4
John Quincy Adams	Democratic-Republican	1825–29	Massachusetts	Elected by Congress, not popular majority
Andrew Jackson	Democrat	1829–37	South Carolina	"Old Hickory"; last to have fought in Revolutionary War
Martin Van Buren	Democrat	1837–41	New York	Nickname "Old Kinderhook" may have led to word "OK"
William H. Harrison	Whig	1841	Virginia	"Old Tippecanoe"; died a month after inauguration
John Tyler	Whig	1841–45	Virginia	First unelected president; first to face impeachment attempt
James Polk	Democrat	1845–49	North Carolina	Started Mexican–American War; died 3 months after leaving office
Zachary Taylor	Whig	1849–50	Virginia	"Old Rough and Ready"; died after two years in office
Millard Fillmore	Whig	1850–53	New York	"His Accidency"; not nominated for re-election
Franklin Pierce	Democrat	1853–57	New Hampshire	Friends with Nathaniel Hawthorne; not nominated for re-election
James Buchanan	Democrat	1857–61	Pennsylvania	Only bachelor president; not nominated for re-election
Abraham Lincoln	Republican	1861–65	Kentucky	Preserved Union during the Civil War; first president killed in office
Andrew Johnson	Union	1865–69	North Carolina	Military governor of Tennessee; first president to be impeached
Ulysses S. Grant	Republican	1869–77	Ohio	"Galena Tanner"; Civil War commander of Union forces
Rutherford B. Hayes	Republican	1877–81	Ohio	Elected by Congress, not popular majority
James A. Garfield	Republican	1881	Ohio	Last president born in a log cabin; second killed in office
Chester A. Arthur	Republican	1881–85	Vermont	Diagnosed with fatal kidney disease; not nominated for re-election
Grover Cleveland	Democrat	1885–89	New Jersey	"Uncle Jumbo"; only president married in White House
Benjamin Harrison	Republican	1889–93	Ohio	Elected by Congress, not popular majority
Grover Cleveland	Democrat	1893–97	New Jersey	Only president to serve two non-consecutive terms

William McKinley	Republican	1897–1901	Ohio	First to campaign from front porch; third killed in office
Theodore Roosevelt	Republican	1901–09	New York	Fought at San Juan Hill; Teddy Bear named for him
William H. Taft	Republican	1909–13	Ohio	Got stuck in a White House bathtub; became Chief Justice of Supreme Court
Woodrow Wilson	Democrat	1913–21	Virginia	First directly re-elected Democrat in 84 years; retired and died in DC
Warren G. Harding	Republican	1921–23	Ohio	Widely considered worst US president; died in office
Calvin Coolidge	Republican	1923–29	Vermont	"Silent Cal"; last Republican not to seek re-election
Herbert Hoover	Republican	1929–33	Iowa	First president born west of Mississippi; second longest-lived
Franklin D. Roosevelt	Democrat	1933–45	New York	Only president to serve more than two terms; died in office
Harry S. Truman	Democrat	1945–53	Missouri	"Give 'em hell Harry"; dropped atomic bomb, fought Cold War
Dwight D. Eisenhower	Republican	1953–61	Texas	Supreme Allied Commander in WWII; last general to be elected
John F. Kennedy	Democrat	1961–63	Massachusetts	Youngest elected president; fourth killed in office
Lyndon B. Johnson	Democrat	1963–69	Texas	"Landslide Lyndon"; last Democrat not to seek re-election
Richard M. Nixon	Republican	1969–74	California	Re-elected with 49 states in 1972; resigned two years later
Gerald Ford	Republican	1974–77	Nebraska	Served as vice president and president; not elected to either position
James (Jimmy) Carter	Democrat	1977–81	Georgia	First Democrat defeated for re-election since Cleveland
Ronald Reagan	Republican	1981–89	Illinois	"The Gipper"; longest-lived former president (93)
George Bush	Republican	1989–93	Massachusetts	First sitting VP to be elected president since Van Buren
William (Bill) Clinton	Democrat	1993–2001	Arkansas	First Democrat to serve two full terms since FDR; first impeached since Andrew Johnson
George W. Bush	Republican	2001–	Connecticut	Chosen by US Supreme Court in 2000; (re-)elected in 2004

Books

here are plenty of **books** that touch upon the history, politics, and personalities of Washington DC; the problem is in getting an over-all picture of the city. There's no one single, straightforward, and up-to-date history of the District, and visitors through the ages have tended only to include their observations of the capital as part of wider works about America. However, every book on American history contains at least a few pages about the founding of DC; Civil War treatises highlight the city as Lincoln's headquarters (and place of assassination); and presidential autobiographies and biographies, from those of George Washington onwards, necessarily recount the daily experience of political and social life in the District.

Although assembling any selection of books on the US capital can be akin to taking a chip off the tip of an iceberg, what follows are some of the better volumes about Washington DC, including novels set in the city. Many are available in good bookstores everywhere, and most in stores in DC itself (see p.322 for a list). Every major museum, gallery, and attraction here sells related books, too, and these are a good first stop if you're looking for something arcane or specific. The selection in the National Museum of American History is perhaps the finest, while the Smithsonian Institution publishes a wide range of titles on a variety of city-related topics. Finally, the White House Historical Association (740 Jackson Place, DC 20503 ☎202/737-8292, ⊛www.whitehousehistory .org) publishes a series of informative accounts of the White House, its archi-tecture and contents, and historical occupants.

Note that titles marked "o/p" are not currently in print, though with suf-ficient effort on the Web (on sites such as Abebooks.com or Bookfinder.com) you may be able to locate them.

Guidebooks

★ **Thomas J. Carrier** *Washington DC: Historic Walking Tour* (US, Arcadia). Photographic record of the development of DC, incorporat-ing informed walking tours around downtown areas. Carrier's *Historic Georgetown* is another excellent book in this fine Arcadia series on DC history.

Alzina Stone Dale *Mystery Reader's Walking Guide: DC* (US, Backinprint .com). Eight guided walks around the city in the company of the words of mystery writers, taken from some 200 volumes; one of several city-mystery volumes by this author.

Federal Writers Project *WPA Guide to Washington DC* (o/p, Pan-theon). Classic volume detailing a history and survey of then-contem-porary DC, from the view of the

1930s New Deal. Interesting obser-vations penned when many of the Neoclassical structures (such as the Supreme Court and Lincoln Memo-rial) were relatively new.

Kathryn Allamong Jacob *Testament to Union* (US, Johns Hopkins Univer-sity Press). Exhaustive record of the District's Civil War monuments and memorials, with over 90 photographs by Edwin Harlan Remsberg and accompanying historical text.

John J. Protopappas and Alvin R. McNeal *Washington on Foot* (US, Smithsonian). The latest edition of a regularly updated volume provid-ing historic treks around DC, with good maps and diagrams; includes coverage of lesser-known spots like LeDroit Park, Meridian Hill, and Takoma Park.

Travel accounts

Christopher Buckley *Washington Schlepped Here* (US, Crown). Republican's lighthearted view of the capital in a slim volume focusing mainly on the Mall and Capitol Hill. Somewhat amusing short account – the stylings of a poor man's P.J. O'Rourke.

David Cutler *Literary Washington* (US, Madison). The words and wisdom of celebrated writers, past and present, who have visited, worked in, and lived in DC.

★ **Charles Dickens** *American Notes* (US & UK, Penguin). One of the most quoted of all DC visitors, Dickens came here in the early 1840s, when it was still, famously, a "City of Magnificent Intentions." Amusing satirical commentary about the US that's lighter in tone than the author's later, more scabrous *Martin Chuzzlewit*.

Jan Morris *Destinations* (US & UK, OUP). Typically dry observations of Washington high- and low-life; one of a series of pieces (about international cities) first written in the early 1980s for *Rolling Stone* magazine.

Anthony Trollope *North America* (US, Penguin/UK, Granville). Two-volume account of Trollope's visit to the US in the early 1860s. Picking up where his pioneering mother, Fanny, had left off in her contentious *Domestic Manners of the Americans* (1832; Da Capo/Alan Sutton), Trollope offers much carping and moaning about irredeemably vulgar Yanks.

Art and architecture

Marjorie Hunt *The Stone Carvers: Master Craftsmen of Washington National Cathedral* (US, Smithsonian). Eye-opening volume about two Italian-American artisans who transformed the look of Washington and other cities with their fluid, detailed stonework. Features many fine photos of their work at the Cathedral.

George Kousoulas *Washington: Portrait of a City* (US, Norfleet). Elegant black-and-white pictures of some of the most classic and stylish buildings in the District; includes an introduction by late New York senator Patrick Moynihan.

David Ovason *The Secret Architecture of Our Nation's Capital: The Masons and the Building of Washington, DC* (US, Perennial). Better researched than it sounds, but still controversial in its thesis that Masons like Washington and Jefferson designed the capital according to the blueprint of Freemasonry – a wild theory some might say, though there's lots of evidence for it.

★ **Pamela Scott and Antoinette J. Lee** *Buildings of the District of Columbia* (US & UK, OUP). Though now a decade old, still the best and most comprehensive guide to the structures in the city, with countless stories and facts behind each, and a narrative explaining the development of the capital.

Christopher Weeks *AIA Guide to the Architecture of Washington DC* (US, Johns Hopkins University Press). Useful illustrated guide to the architecture of the city, covering buildings from every period since its founding, though less comprehensive for outlying areas.

District history

Catherine Allgor *Parlor Politics* (US, University Press of Virginia). As nineteenth-century DC developed from backwater to capital, the arrival of high society in the shape of the First Ladies and their social circles began to have a growing influence on politics – a thesis encapsulated in the book's subtitle: "In which the ladies of Washington build a city and government."

Mark Anderson and Mark Jenkins *Dance of Days: Two Decades of Punk in the Nation's Capital* (US, Soft Skull). Long-overdue story of DC's impact on subversive culture – in this case, the various forms of punk, as practiced by seminal acts like Bad Brains, Minor Effect, Henry Rollins, and, in more current times, Fugazi.

★ **David Brinkley** *Washington Goes to War* (US, Ballantine/UK, Deutsch). Acclaimed account of the capital during World War II under FDR, charting its emergence onto the international stage with countless anecdotes and stories of life in the era.

Francine Curro Cary *Urban Odyssey: A Multicultural History of Washington DC* (US, Smithsonian). A compelling historical account of settlement in the city by all manner of peoples from around the world, as well as of the capital's deeply set racial discrimination.

Alistair Cooke *Alistair Cooke's America* (US, Carroll & Graf; UK, Weidenfeld & Nicolson). The author's overview of American life and customs occasionally touches on DC, as well as US politics. The latest (2002) updated edition of a long-

standing classic. Also worth a look are any of Cooke's other volumes on the American experience.

★ **Harry S. Jaffe and Tom Sherwood** *Dream City: Race, Power, and the Decline of Washington DC* (o/p, Simon & Schuster). Still the best volume devoted to contemporary politics in DC, though now a decade old. Focuses on the way the riots of 1968, combined with oppressive social conditions, gave rise to demagogues such as Marion Barry and all his attendant antics.

David L. Lewis *District of Columbia: A Bicentennial History* (o/p, Norton). Useful – if now rather dated (1976) – history of the District providing a snapshot of the slowly rejuvenating city at the time.

Jeffrey Meyer *Myths in Stone: Religious Dimensions of Washington DC* (US, University of California). Examines the lesser-known spiritual side of the capital, evident in its rituals, culture, and architecture, and places the city in a global religious context.

Anthony S. Pitch *The Burning of Washington: The British Invasion of 1814* (US, Naval Institute Press). Recounting of the dramatic events of the summer of 1814 as the British set fire to the young capital and Francis Scott Key was inspired to write the "Star-Spangled Banner."

Paul K. Williams *Greater U Street* (US, Arcadia). Another in an excellent series on DC neighborhoods, this one focusing on the history and culture of Shaw in the days of "Black Broadway," the Lincoln Theatre, Duke Ellington, and so on.

Presidents

See also the *American Presidents* series (Times Books; Arthur Schlesinger, ed.), which cover a number of overlooked presidents, from John Quincy Adams to James Polk to Grover

Cleveland, in slim volumes written by noted writers and historians.

Jonathan Aitken *Nixon: A Life* (US, Regnery). Not quite the Tricky

Dick-bashing book that some may prefer (for such choices, see box, p.358), but a good, well-rounded view of one of the nation's most controversial, and paranoid, chief executives.

★ **Robert Caro** *The Years of Lyndon Johnson* (US, Vintage). Essential (and ongoing) history of the champion of the Great Society and purveyor of the Vietnam War. So far the three volumes only cover LBJ from childhood to election as vice president, but these are still compelling, and revealing, volumes about the developing character of this larger-than-life figure.

David Herbert Donald *Lincoln* (US, Touchstone). Hands-down the definitive volume covering the life and legend of the Railsplitter, who guided the Union through its most traumatic period, the Civil War. Lincoln's biography is also covered by authors ranging in the hundreds.

Joseph Ellis *American Sphinx: The Character of Thomas Jefferson* (US, Vintage). Recent, thoughtful volume describing the contradictory aspects of the third president, as a proponent of states' rights who expanded the federal government, and as a champion of liberty who owned slaves. Also outstanding is the author's latest, *His Excellency: George Washington* (US, Knopf), providing additional insight on a familiar American icon.

Frank Friedel *Franklin D. Roosevelt: Rendezvous with Destiny* (US, Back Bay). One of the few decent one-volume histories of the twentieth century's greatest president; the author's own set of four FDR volumes is now out of print.

★ **Ulysses S. Grant** *Personal Memoirs* (US, Modern Library). Indispensable classic written (with the aid of Mark Twain) while the ex-president was dying, covering his life from childhood to the end of the Civil War. A highly readable and illuminating view of war and

sacrifice – by far the best book written by, and one of the best written about, any president.

Lloyd Lewis *The Assassination of Lincoln: History and Myth* (US, University of Nebraska). Lyrical, minute-by-minute account of the city's most notorious assassination and the conspiracy's aftermath, first published in 1929 as *Myths After Lincoln*.

David Maraniss *First in His Class: A Biography of Bill Clinton* (US, Simon & Schuster). Fine, balanced look at the strengths and weaknesses of the 42nd president, prescient in some ways in foreseeing his successes and pitfalls. Winner of the Pulitzer Prize.

David McCullough *John Adams* and *Truman* (both US & UK, Simon & Schuster). Folksy historian and public-TV personality who's made a career out of resurrecting the reputations of underestimated presidents from the past. The Truman claim to presidential greatness is an easier one to swallow than that of Adams.

Edmund Morris *The Rise of Theodore Roosevelt* and *Theodore Rex* (both US, Random House/UK, Harper-Collins). Still the essential accounts of the rise of the New York governor, Spanish-American war hero, corporate trust-buster, and "accidental" two-term US president.

Robert V. Remini *Andrew Jackson* (US, Johns Hopkins University). Three thick volumes on the life and times of the seventh president, from his dark side supporting slavers and Indian removal, to his paradoxical role as a fervent democratizer who threw a chaotic inauguration party for the public, which nearly ruined the White House.

Henry Wiencek *An Imperfect God: George Washington, His Slaves, and the Creation of America* (US, Farrar Straus and Giroux). Of the hundreds of volumes dealing with the first president, this is the first to focus, quite incisively, on his actions regarding slavery and thoughts on emancipation. A compelling recent work.

Bob Woodward and Carl Bernstein *All the President's Men* (US & UK, Touchstone); *The Final Days* (US & UK, Touchstone).

America's most famous journalistic sleuths tell the gripping story of the unraveling of the Nixon presidency. Although both men have written investigative books since, none has matched these early classics.

DC people and politics

Paul F. Boller *Presidential Anecdotes; Presidential Campaigns; Presidential Wives; Congressional Anecdotes* (all US & UK, OUP); *Presidential Inaugurations* (US, Harcourt Brace). Amusing, inconsequential political factoids – who did what, where, and when, and with whom. Good for a round of trivia while you're waiting in line at the Mall.

Ben Bradlee *A Good Life* (US & UK, Touchstone). Autobiography of the executive editor of the *Washington Post*, covering the years between 1968 and 1991, during which Watergate and its fallout made the author America's most famous editor.

Ron Chernow *Alexander Hamilton* (US, Penguin). Standout work that looks at the colorful life, controversial politics, and far-sighted economic policies of America's first Treasury Secretary – better known as that wig-wearing fellow on the $10 bill.

George Crile *Charlie Wilson's War* (US, Atlantic Monthly Press). Good and instructive primer on Washington politics, in which the dogged efforts of a sex-scandalized congressman and a shadowy CIA agent help secretly funnel millions of dollars to Afghanistan's Communist-fighting mujahedin – who later became the Taliban and aided America's current crop of enemies.

★ **Frederick Douglass** *The Life and Times of Frederick Douglass* (US & UK, various). The third volume (1881) of statesman, orator, and ex-slave Frederick Douglass's autobiography sees him living in DC as US marshal and recorder of deeds. But the first volume, *Narrative of the Life of Frederick Douglass: An*

American Slave (1845), which covers part of the author's early life, is actually more gripping.

Katherine Graham *Personal History* (US, Vintage/UK, Phoenix). Pulitzer Prize-winning autobiography of the *Washington Post* owner and Georgetown society hostess lifts the lid on DC's social and political niceties.

Meg Greenfield *Washington* (US, Public Affairs). Posthumously published memoir by long-time columnist, editorial writer, and, eventually, editor of the *Washington Post*. Greenfield writes perceptively about the cocoon-like qualities of DC life and the range of its beguiling personalities.

David Halberstam *The Best and the Brightest* (US, Ballantine). Unforgettable portrait of the proud, swaggering brain trust of secretaries and advisers to JFK and LBJ, who, despite their brilliance and advanced college degrees, led the nation into a disastrous war in Vietnam. A chilling tale with many modern implications.

★ **Richard Hofstadter** *The American Political Tradition* (US, Vintage). One of the twentieth century's finest and most insightful volumes on American presidents and politicians and the economic forces behind them. Also essential is the author's *Paranoid Style in American Politics* (US, University of Chicago), now more relevant than ever.

David McKay *American Politics and Society* (UK, Blackwell). Best introduction to who does what, why, and when in the United States government, with diversions into American beliefs and values, and coverage of social, economic, and foreign policy.

Norman Mailer *The Armies of the Night* (US, Plume). Despite the author's now-caricatured bluster, his 1967 Pulitzer Prize-winning description of the March on the Pentagon, protesting the Vietnam War, is still essential reading, full of drama and color – as well as plenty of surly antics by Mailer himself.

P.J. O'Rourke *Parliament of Whores* (US, Vintage/UK, Picador). Demented political insights and raving right-wing prejudices, brought together in a scabrous, amusing critique of the American political system as practiced in Washington DC.

Hunter S. Thompson *Fear and Loathing on the Campaign Trail '72* (US, Warner Books). More than three decades after its release, still a dark and hilarious look at how campaigns are waged in the media age, with evil, glowering Nixon administering an electoral whipping to George McGovern – with whom the normally cynical Thompson had tragically placed his hopes.

Theodore H. White *The Making of the President 1960* (US, Buccaneer). Still one of the quintessential books for understanding American politics, using the Kennedy–Nixon race as a synonym for the manufactured stagecraft and imagery of contemporary elections. Subsequent, less groundbreaking but still diverting, volumes cover the next three campaigns through 1972.

Fiction and poetry

★ **Henry Adams** *Democracy* (US & UK, Meridian). A story of electioneering and intrigue set in 1870s Gilded Age-era DC, written (anonymously) by the historian grandson of John Quincy Adams.

Anonymous *Primary Colors* (US, Warner/UK, Vintage). Highly readable, barely disguised account of a presidential primary campaign by young, charismatic, calculating, philandering, Southern governor Jack Stanton. Published amid great controversy in 1996, its author was eventually unmasked as Washington insider Joe Klein. *The Running Mate* (US, Delta/UK, Vintage) was his follow-up satire, a presidential-campaign

---

Watergate

If Washington has one domestic scandal that still towers above all others, it's **Watergate** (see p.150), whose various aspects have been exhaustively covered since Woodward and Bernstein first set the ball rolling with *All the President's Men*. For the full story, you could consult Fred Emery's *Watergate: The Corruption of American Politics and the Fall of Richard Nixon* (US, Touchstone) or a host of other eyewitness accounts, including Nixon's own *Memoirs* (US, Simon & Schuster); Robert Haldeman's *Haldeman Diaries: Inside the Nixon White House* (US, Berkley); John Dean's *Blind Ambition* (US, Simon & Schuster) and *Lost Honor* (US, Stratford Press); John Erlichman's *Witness to Power* (US, Simon & Schuster); and G. Gordon Liddy's *Will: The Autobiography of G. Gordon Liddy* (US & UK, St Martin's Press) – all first-hand (if not completely reliable) testimony from those who were there at the time. Virtually everyone else involved has written about the affair at some point or other, too, from Watergate burglar James McCord to Judge John Sirica, while *Nixon: An Oliver Stone Film* (US, Hyperion) presents the original screenplay of said movie alongside transcripts of taped Watergate conversations, previously classified memos, and essays by key protagonists. More of the secret tapes recorded by Nixon, betraying his deep prejudices, turn up in Stanley Kutler's *Abuse of Power: The New Nixon Tapes* (US & UK, Touchstone).

novel with even more backstabbing and scandal on every page.

John Barth *The Tidewater Tales* (US, Johns Hopkins University Press). A couple goes sailing in the waters of Chesapeake Bay, only to become immersed in picaresque stories of local history and lore, Eastern legends, and the CIA. Worthwhile for anyone with a taste for postmodern fiction – playing narrative games and turning words and meanings inside out.

William Peter Blatty *The Exorcist* (US, HarperCollins/UK, Corgi). Seminal horror story about the possession of a teenage girl, written in 1971, set around Georgetown University and made into one of the scariest films ever produced.

Allen Drury *Advise and Consent* (US, Avon). Blackmail and slippery politics in Washington's upper echelons in the late 1950s; the novel – a great read once you adapt to the measured pace – was turned into a fine film by Otto Preminger starring Henry Fonda.

James Ellroy *American Tabloid* (US, Vintage). Epic scandal–mongering conspiracy tale of biblical proportions, tying the Mafia, JFK, renegade Cubans, and rogue FBI and CIA officers into an infernal web of lies and deception, with all manner of Washington wickedness at the epicenter.

Sebastian Faulks *On Green Dolphin Street* (US, Random House/ UK, Vintage). A British diplomat's wife embarks on an affair with an American reporter during the 1960 presidential election. The Cold War politics of the period act as a chilly backdrop to this taut tale of love and deception.

Edward P. Jones *Lost in the City* (US, Amistad Press). Fourteen moving short stories about residents trying to get by in the depressed under- and working-class world of DC in the 1960s and 1970s, well away from the showpiece tourist zones and halls of political power.

Ward Just *Echo House* (US, Mariner Books). Elegiac, epic novel of a DC political dynasty, with much to say about the nature of power in the city.

Sinclair Lewis *It Can't Happen Here* (o/p, Signet). Disturbing, oddly humorous tale of the coming of fascism to the US, brought by a goofy yet conniving politician with a folksy, homespun style – perhaps hitting a little too close to home these days.

Gore Vidal *Burr*; *Lincoln*; *1876*; *Empire*; *Hollywood*; *Washington DC*; *The Golden Age* (all US, Vintage/ UK, Abacus). DC's – and America's – most potent and cynical chronicler sustains a terrific burst of form in seven hugely enjoyable novels tracing the history of the US from the Revolution to modern times and relying heavily on Washington set-piece scenes. The moving epic *Lincoln* is the real tour de force. Vidal's other DC-related books include *Palimpsest* (US, Penguin/UK, Abacus), a terrific memoir chronicling his life and loves, and his novel, *The Smithsonian Institution* (US, Harvest/UK, Abacus).

★ **Walt Whitman** *Leaves of Grass* (US & UK, various). The first edition of this poetic juggernaut appeared in 1855, and Whitman added sections to it for the rest of his life. His war poems, *Drum-Taps* (1865), were directly influenced by his work in DC's Civil War hospitals. *Memories of President Lincoln* were added after the assassination – including the famous and affecting *O Captain! My Captain!*

Crime and thrillers

Jeffrey Archer *Shall We Tell the President?* (US & UK, HarperCollins); *The Eleventh Commandment* (US & UK,

HarperCollins). Serves up the usual offerings – risible characterization, feeble plot development, and leaden prose wrapped around tales of assassination plots and Cold War shenanigans set in the capital.

Tom Clancy Blockbuster thriller writer who weaves DC scenes (or at least the White House, Capitol building, FBI, and CIA headquarters at Langley, VA) into nearly every tale of spook and terrorist intrigue. *Debt of Honor* (US, Berkeley/UK, HarperCollins), in which the president, his Cabinet, and most of Congress perish in a terrorist attack on the US Capitol, now seems eerily prophetic; *Executive Orders* (US, Berkeley/UK, HarperCollins) sees Jack Ryan take over as president of a shattered US.

Richard Timothy Conroy *The India Exhibition*; *Mr Smithson's Bones*; *Old Ways in the New World* (all US, St Martin's Press). Murder, mystery, and labyrinthine goings-on in a series of engaging thrillers set in the Smithsonian Institution.

John Grisham DC pops up in most of Grisham's work, notably in *The Pelican Brief* (US, Dell/UK, Arrow), a renowned legal whodunit starting with the assassination of two Supreme Court judges and delving into dodgy politics and murky land deals, and in *The Street Lawyer* (US, Dell/UK, Arrow), a rather good exposé of city homelessness and poverty.

David Ignatius *A Firing Offense* (US, Ivy Books). Former *Washington Post* journalist puts his newspaper experience to good use in an intelligent espionage thriller that jumps from DC locations to France and China.

Charles McCarry *Shelley's Heart* (US, Ivy Books). Page-turning thriller detailing stolen elections, secret societies, and other political shenanigans. His *Lucky Bastard* (US, Random House) details the rise of a (rather familiar) charismatic, liberal, womanizing, presidential hopeful.

James Patterson *Along Came A Spider*; *Kiss the Girls*; *Cat and Mouse*; *Pop Goes the Weasel*; *Jack and Jill*; *Roses Are Red*; *Violets Are Blue* (all US, Warner/UK, HarperCollins). High-profile thriller writer whose dreadful prose style and crude characterization do nothing to blunt his success. These seven books all feature black DC homicide detective Alex Cross.

William D. Pease *Playing the Dozens*; *The Monkey's First*; *The Rage of Innocence* (all US, Signet). A former Assistant US Attorney in DC, Pease writes legal/police thrillers that range across all the usual city locations and power sites.

★ **George P. Pelecanos** Hip raconteur Pelecanos writes pointedly and beautifully about the city in a series of great thrillers, spanning the years and ethnic divide. *A Firing Offense* (his first), *Nick's Trip*, and *Down By the River Where the Dead Men Go* (all US & UK, Serpent's Tail) introduce feisty private eye Nick Stefanos; *King Suckerman* (US, Bantam/UK, Serpent's Tail) is a tour de force of Seventies drugs and racial tension; while *The Sweet Forever* (US, Dell/UK, Serpent's Tail) updates Suckerman's characters to coke-riddled 1980s DC. Later novels include the vivid *Hard Revolution* (US, Little, Brown/UK, Orion).

Phyllis Richman *The Butter Did It* (US & UK, HarperCollins). The *Washington Post's* longtime restaurant critic turns her hand to mystery, introducing Chas Wheatley, the "*Washington Examiner*" restaurant reviewer-turned-detective.

Elliott Roosevelt *Murder in the . . .* (US & UK, St Martin's Press & Avon). White House murder tales (with the dark deed committed in the *Blue Room*, *West Wing*, etc) by FDR's son, with the highly improbable First Lady-turned-sleuth Eleanor riding to the rescue every time.

Margaret Truman *Murder . . .* (US & UK, Fawcett). Harry's daughter churns out wooden murder-mystery stories set in various neighborhoods and buildings of DC, from Georgetown to the National Cathedral.

Film

I t's quite possible that more **films** have been set in the District of Columbia than any American city outside of LA or New York. However, despite this celluloid familiarity, few movies have ever really examined life in DC, gotten to the core of its politics, or looked beyond Capitol Hill, the White House, and, occasionally, the National Mall. Indeed, aside from a few showpieces, very little of the District itself has actually attracted the interest of filmmakers. Therefore, the list of relevant DC films is much shorter than one might expect, and basically revolves around the decisions, personalities, and antics of fictional presidents; the untrustworthy plotting of politicians on the Hill and generals at the Pentagon; and the lovely historic backdrop of Georgetown. Except for a few penetrating documentaries, that's basically all there is to Washington's on-screen life, so for insight into the city, you're better off reading a book. What's listed below, though, are the various worthwhile tales that leave an impression of DC, and don't just show chase scenes with the Washington Monument in the background. Following the film title are its year of release and director's name – though not all films can be said to have a definite "auteur" style.

Comedies and musicals

1776 (Peter H. Hunt, 1972). Amazingly, this musical view of the American Revolution is one of the very few memorable films on the subject – but if you don't enjoy history set to tub-thumping show tunes, you're out of luck.

Americathon (Neal Israel, 1979). Memorably bad "comedy" (with music) in which a down-on-his-luck presidential sap must rescue the floundering US by holding an oddball telethon; features a cast that somehow includes John Ritter, Meat Loaf, Harvey Korman, Elvis Costello, and Jay Leno.

⭐ **Being There** (Hal Ashby, 1979). Unforgettable comedy about a simple-minded gardener (Peter Sellers) who leaves the Washington estate of his deceased employer and unwittingly becomes a political pawn and, possibly, presidential candidate.

Dr. Strangelove (Stanley Kubrick, 1964). For many film-goers, this is the archetypical satire of the Cold War Pentagon gone berserk, in which a power-mad general brings the world to the brink of annihilation, fearing a Communist takeover of his "precious bodily fluids."

The President's Analyst (Theodore Flicker, 1967). Political cult film in which James Coburn plays the title character, who gets into all sorts of trouble when various spies and thugs want to find out what he knows. A classic conspiracy-theory satire.

State of the Union (Frank Capra, 1948). Republican bigwig Spencer Tracy asks his estranged wife to return to him to aid his election, putting on a public show for the media and causing all manner of hijinks.

Documentaries

Fahrenheit 9/11 (Michael Moore, 2004). The ultimate liberal attack on the controversial policies of George W. Bush, which won the top prize at Cannes and became the most successful documentary in history.

⊡ ★ **The Fog of War** (Errol Morris, 2003). A film that deservedly won the Oscar for Best Documentary, giving a look at the now-aged former Defense Secretary Robert McNamara, who plunged the US deeper into the Vietnam War despite his own misgivings. Told in the Secretary's own paradoxical, ambivalent words.

Milhouse – A White Comedy (Emile de Antonio, 1971). Dark documentary satire about the foibles and trickery of Richard Nixon, whose own words and deeds are used to indict him. Made three years before his resignation and long before Watergate was a household word.

A Perfect Candidate (David Van Taylor, 1996). Stark and chilling examination of the 1994 Virginia senatorial campaign of Oliver North, accused Iran-Contra conspirator and champion of the far-right. Uses telling details and behind-the-scenes access to craft an indelible portrait of a campaign that relied on fear and scare tactics, and almost triumphed.

Point of Order (Emile de Antonio, 1964). Stark black-and-white documentary with images taken from the McCarthy hearings of the 1950s, in which the Wisconsin senator's own ranting paranoia and deceptions are made clear before the cameras.

The Trials of Henry Kissinger (Eugene Jarecki, 2003). Angry polemic about the former Secretary of State's alleged misdeeds in toppling the government of Chile, illegally bombing Cambodia, and countless other acts of official wickedness. Based on the book and magazine articles by arch-contrarian Christopher Hitchens.

Fantasy and sci-fi

⊡ ★ **The Day the Earth Stood Still** (Robert Wise, 1951). Classic sci-fi in which an alien makes the mistake of landing his spaceship in Washington DC, demanding earthlings give up their warlike ways or else. He is, of course, killed, which sends his trusty robot companion Gort out for vengeance against the town that wronged him. More somber and compelling than it sounds.

Independence Day (Roland Emmerich, 1996). Wildly successful, though crude and ham-fisted, action flick about aliens who greet earth with a barrage of destruction, including blowing up the White House in one of the more famous images of 1990s Hollywood overkill.

Werewolf of Washington (Milton Ginseberg, 1973). Semi-cult film about a White House Press Secretary who goes lupine and bites the prez and other victims. More interesting as a period piece than compelling cinema.

Partisan politics

⊡ ★ **Advise and Consent** (Otto Preminger, 1962). Lengthy, close-in view of the tortuous process that Secretary-of-State-nominee Henry Fonda must undergo when subjected to the machinations of Congress – vividly personified in the figure of a drawling Southern pol played with aplomb by Charles Laughton.

Bob Roberts (Tim Robbins, 1992). Dark satire about a right-wing senatorial candidate who uses charm and folksiness to reach the Capitol. Prescient and still amusing, if a bit ponderous in spots.

Citizen Cohn (Frank Pierson, 1992). Incisive look at arch-McCarthyite Red-hunter and right-wing operative Roy Cohn (James Woods), who, despite his public persona, was a closeted gay, Jewish man – who reviews his life while dying of AIDS.

Mr. Smith Goes to Washington (Frank Capra, 1939). An exercise in earnest, apple-cheeked faith in the body politic, made before World War II. Still loved for its image of populist hero Jimmy Stewart fighting wags and charlatans on Capitol Hill and triumphing with his honesty and courage.

Wag the Dog (Barry Levinson, 1997). Political satire that sounds better than it plays – a president desperate to recover from a sex scandal reacts by declaring war and seeing his popularity jump. All well and good, until the movie limps along to the end.

Presidents

★ **All the President's Men** (Alan J. Pakula, 1976). Appearing just a few years after the Watergate scandal, one of the few Hollywood films with a premise drawn from real-life politics (crusading journalists exposing a baleful president) that actually made money; shot at many sites across the city.

American President (Rob Reiner, 1995). Dewy-eyed portrait of the life and loves of vaguely Clintonesque president Michael Douglas, who wines and dines tough-gal lobbyist Annette Bening, drawing cheers and tears in equal measure.

Dave (Ivan Reitman, 1993). Another strangely affectionate 1990s portrait of a fictional president, this one being Kevin Kline. An earnest Everyman who's also a lookalike for the president subs after the Chief Exec has a stroke.

Gabriel Over the White House (Gregory La Cava, 1933). Eerie period piece about a corrupt president who sees the eponymous angel and gets inspired to clean up his act, reform the nation, imprison - and execute – his enemies, and force peace upon other countries at the barrel of a gun.

The Man (Joseph Sargent, 1972). James Earl Jones stars as the president pro tempore of the Senate who, after a national tragedy, suddenly becomes US president and has to battle racists and thick-headed politicians determined to dethrone him.

Nixon (Oliver Stone, 1995). Unlike the director's *JFK*, this presidential flick is set mainly in DC, offering a dark look into the brooding mind of the only US president to resign. Anthony Hopkins plays Tricky Dick, doing a gallant job of stifling his British accent and looking appropriately sweaty and paranoid.

Primary Colors (Mike Nichols, 1998). John Travolta plays Jack Stanton, a Southern governor seeking the White House with dangerous libidinal tendencies. Mildly amusing and strongly familiar.

The Tall Target (Anthony Mann, 1951). Excellent, nearly forgotten film about an early murder plot against Abraham Lincoln, scheduled to take place on a train headed to his Washington inauguration. Dick Powell plays the hero – oddly enough, named John Kennedy – who must thwart the assassination.

★ **Thirteen Days** (Roger Donaldson, 2001). Riveting insider story – supposedly based on newly released documents – detailing how the brothers Kennedy and their crony (Kevin Costner) outflanked the Russians in the potentially world-ending nuclear duel of 1962's Cuban Missile Crisis.

Thrillers and horror

Arlington Road (Mark Pellington, 1999). Washington terrorism expert Jeff Bridges sees danger in his well-scrubbed neighbor, Tim Robbins, and thinks he may have stumbled onto an authentic homegrown killer. Complications ensue in this riveting, somewhat uneven thriller.

★ **The Exorcist** (William Friedkin, 1973). The lodestar of religious-horror movies, filmed along 36th Street in Georgetown, giving us unforgettable scenes of evil-possessed Linda Blair speaking and retching with satanic intensity, as well as a famously "head-turning" moment.

Fail Safe (Sidney Lumet, 1964). President Henry Fonda plays a slow, excruciating game of nuclear chicken with the Russians as a US bomber crew is sent on a fatal, erroneous errand to destroy cities in the USSR.

In the Line of Fire (Wolfgang Petersen, 1993). Top-notch action-thriller with Service Service agent Clint Eastwood racing around to protect an undeserving president from the homemade bullets of psycho assassin John Malkovich; filmed around Dupont Circle and Capitol Hill.

No Way Out (Roger Donaldson, 1987). A Pentagon-oriented thriller in which Kevin Costner must investigate a crime whose trail leads squarely back to himself, featuring scenes set in Georgetown and a memorable twist ending. Remake of film-noir classic *The Big Clock*.

★ **Seven Days in May** (John Frankenheimer, 1964). Striking conspiracy thriller about thuggish general Burt Lancaster plotting a coup to achieve nefarious right-wing ends; Kirk Douglas fights to stop his evil deeds.

Rough
Guides
advertiser

small print and Index

A Rough Guide to Rough Guides

In the summer of 1981, Mark Ellingham, a recent graduate from Bristol University, was traveling round Greece and couldn't find a guidebook that really met his needs. On the one hand there were the student guides, insistent on saving every last cent, and on the other the heavyweight cultural tomes whose authors seemed to have spent more time in a research library than lounging away the afternoon at a taverna or on the beach.

In a bid to avoid getting a job, Mark and a small group of writers set about creating their own guidebook. It was a guide to Greece that aimed to combine a journalistic approach to description with a thoroughly practical approach to travelers' needs —a guide that would incorporate culture, history and contemporary insights with a critical edge, together with up-to-date, value-for-money listings. Back in London, Mark and the team finished their Rough Guide, as they called it, and talked Routledge into publishing the book.

That first *Rough Guide to Greece*, published in 1982, was a student scheme that became a publishing phenomenon. The immediate success of the book – with numerous reprints and a Thomas Cook prize shortlisting – spawned a series that rapidly covered dozens of destinations. Rough Guides had a ready market among low-budget backpackers, but soon also acquired a much broader and older readership that relished Rough Guides' wit and inquisitiveness as much as their enthusiastic, critical approach. Everyone wants value for money, but not at any price.

Rough Guides soon began supplementing the "rougher" information about hostels and low-budget listings with the kind of detail on restaurants and quality hotels that independent-minded visitors on any budget might expect, whether on business in New York or trekking in Thailand.

These days the guides – distributed worldwide by the Penguin group – offer recommendations from shoestring to luxury and cover more than 200 destinations around the globe, including almost every country in the Americas and Europe, more than half of Africa and most of Asia and Australasia. Our ever-growing team of authors and photographers is spread all over the world, particularly in Europe, the USA and Australia.

In 1994, we published the *Rough Guide to World Music* and *Rough Guide to Classical Music*; and a year later the *Rough Guide to the Internet*. All three books have become benchmark titles in their fields – which encouraged us to expand into other areas of publishing, mainly around popular culture. Rough Guides now publish:

- Travel guides to more than 200 worldwide destinations
- Dictionary phrasebooks to 22 major languages
- History guides ranging from Ireland to Islam
- Maps printed on rip-proof and waterproof Polyart™ paper
- Music guides running the gamut from Opera to Elvis
- Restaurant guides to London, New York and San Francisco
- Reference books on topics as diverse as the Weather and Shakespeare
- Sports guides from Formula 1 to Man Utd
- Pop culture books from *Lord of the Rings* to Cult TV
- World Music CDs in association with World Music Network

Visit **www.roughguides.com** to see our latest publications.

Rough Guide credits

Text editor: Amy Hegarty
Layout: Umesh Aggarwal
Cartography: Katie Lloyd-Jones, Miles Irving
Picture research: Jj Luck
Proofreader: Derek Wilde
Editorial: **London** Martin Dunford, Kate
Berens, Helena Smith, Claire Saunders,
Geoff Howard, Ruth Blackmore, Gavin
Thomas, Polly Thomas, Richard Lim, Clifton
Wilkinson, Alison Murchie, Fran Sandham,
Sally Schafer, Karoline Densley, Andy Turner,
Ella O'Donnell, Keith Drew, Edward Aves,
Andrew Lockett, Joe Staines, Duncan Clark,
Peter Buckley, Matthew Milton, Daniel Crewe;
New York Andrew Rosenberg, Richard Koss,
Chris Barsanti, Steven Horak, AnneLise
Sorensen, Amy Hegarty
Design & Pictures: London Simon Bracken,
Dan May, Diana Jarvis, Mark Thomas,
Jj Luck, Harriet Mills, Chloë Roberts;
Delhi Madhulita Mohapatra, Umesh
Aggarwal, Ajay Verma, Jessica Subramanian,
Amit Verma

Production: Julia Bovis, Sophie Hewat,
Katherine Owers
Cartography: London Maxine Repath,
Ed Wright, Katie Lloyd-Jones, Miles Irving;
Delhi Manish Chandra, Rajesh Chhibber,
Jai Prakash Mishra, Ashutosh Bharti,
Rajesh Mishra, Animesh Pathak, Jasbir
Sandhu, Karobi Gogoi
Online: New York Jennifer Gold, Suzanne
Welles, Benjamin Ross; **Delhi** Manik Chauhan,
Narender Kumar, Shekhar Jha, Rakesh Kumar,
Lalit K. Sharma
Marketing & Publicity: London Richard Trillo,
Niki Hanmer, David Wearn, Chloë Roberts,
Demelza Dallow, Kristina Pentland; **New York**
Geoff Colquitt, Megan Kennedy, Milena Perez
Custom publishing and foreign rights:
Philippa Hopkins
Finance: Gary Singh
Manager India: Punita Singh
Series editor: Mark Ellingham
PA to Managing Director: Julie Sanderson
Managing Director: Kevin Fitzgerald

Publishing information

This fourth edition published May 2005 by
Rough Guides Ltd,
80 Strand, London WC2R 0RL.
345 Hudson St, 4th Floor,
New York, NY 10014, USA.
Distributed by the Penguin Group
Penguin Books Ltd,
80 Strand, London WC2R 0RL
Penguin Putnam, Inc.
375 Hudson Street, NY 10014, USA
Penguin Group (Australia)
250 Camberwell Road, Camberwell
Victoria 3124, Australia
Penguin Books Canada Ltd,
10 Alcorn Avenue, Toronto, Ontario,
Canada M4V 1E4
Penguin Group (New Zealand)
Cnr Rosedale and Airborne Roads
Albany, Auckland, New Zealand
Typeset in Bembo and Helvetica to an original
design by Henry Iles.

Printed in China

384pp includes index
A catalogue record for this book is available from
the British Library

ISBN 1-84353-401-0

The publishers and authors have done their best
to ensure the accuracy and currency of all the
information in **The Rough Guide to Washington
DC**, however, they can accept no responsibility
for any loss, injury, or inconvenience sustained
by any traveller as a result of information or
advice contained in the guide.

1   3   5   7   9   8   6   4   2

Help us update

We've gone to a lot of effort to ensure that
the seventh edition of **The Rough Guide
to Washington DC** is accurate and up-to-
date. However, things change – places get
"discovered", opening hours are notoriously
fickle, restaurants and rooms raise prices or
lower standards. If you feel we've got it wrong
or left something out, we'd like to know, and if
you can remember the address, the price, the
time, the phone number, so much the better.

   We'll credit all contributions, and send a
copy of the next edition (or any other Rough

Guide if you prefer) for the best letters.
Everyone who writes to us and isn't already a
subscriber will receive a copy of our full-color
thrice-yearly newsletter. Please mark letters:
"Rough Guide Washington DC Update" and
send to: Rough Guides, 80 Strand, London
WC2R 0RL, or Rough Guides, 4th Floor, 345
Hudson St, New York, NY 10014. Or send an
email to **mail@roughguides.com**.

   Have your questions answered and tell
others about your trip at
www.roughguides.atinfopop.com.

Acknowledgments

The editor would like to thank JD Dickey for his excellent work on this book, and for being so dedicated and reliable throughout; Derek Wilde for superb proofreading; Umesh Aggarwal for typesetting; Katie Lloyd-Jones, Miles Irving, and Maxine Repath for cartography; Jj Luck for photo research; Karoline Densley and Mark Rogers for support; Richard Koss for much-appreciated help and humor; and Andrew Rosenberg for valued guidance, feedback, and encouragement throughout.

Readers' letters

Thanks to all the readers who have taken the time to write in with comments and suggestions (and apologies if we've inadvertently omitted or misspelt anyone's name):

Michelle Cooper, Adam Teller, Will Roney

SMALL PRINT

Photo credits

Cover credits

Main picture Franklin Delano Roosevelt Memorial © Corbis

Small front top East Building, National Gallery of Art © Corbis

Small front lower US Capitol © Pictures Colour Library

Back top Washington Monument © Corbis

Back lower Reading Room, Library of Congress © Corbis

Color introduction

Cherry blossoms and Washington Monument © Corbis

Vendor selling patriotic neckties © Michael Macor/San Francisco Chronicle/Corbis

Fountain, National Gallery Sculpture Garden © Reuters/Corbis

Korean War Veterans Memorial, Advancing Soldiers © J. Isachsen/Trip

Vietnamese spring rolls © Trevor Wood/ Robert Harding Picture Library

Rally on Capitol Hill © Todd A. Gipstein/ Corbis

Georgetown © Adam Woolfitt/Robert Harding Picture Library

Scottish Rite House of the Temple © Joseph Sohm; ChromoSohm Inc/Corbis

Things not to miss

1. Ford's Theatre © Rough Guides
2. Interior of the Old Supreme Court Chamber in the US Capitol © Bettmann/ Corbis
3. Mount Vernon © Rough Guides
4. Supreme Court © Paul Quayle/Axiom
5. Fourth of July fireworks over the Jefferson Memorial © Robert Harding Picture Library
6. Thomas Jefferson Building, Library of Congress © E.Young/Trip
7. Blue crabs, Fish Wharf © J. Isachsen/Trip
8. Arlington National Cemetery © Rough Guides
9. Cyclists along the Chesapeake and Ohio (C&O) Canal © J. Isachsen/Trip
10. National World War II Memorial at night © Molly Riley/Corbis

11. US Botanic Garden © Rough Guides
12. Vietnam Veterans Memorial © Alison Wright/Robert Harding Picture Library
13. The White House © Neil Setchfield
14. National Air and Space Museum © Richard T. Nowitz/Corbis
15. Rock Creek Park © Rough Guides
16. Koto players at the Cherry Blossom Festival © Catherine Karnow/Corbis
17. Home of Frederick Douglass © Adam Woolfitt/Robert Harding
18. *Fasika's*, Adams-Morgan © J.Isachsen/ Trip
19. Light through stained glass window, Washington National Catheral © J.Isachsen/Trip
20. National Symphony Orchestra © Chuck Pefley/Alamy
21. *Eleazer Tyng* by John Singleton Copley © Burstein Collections/Corbis
22. National Museum of American History © Rough Guides
23. *Ben's Chili Bowl*, U Street © J. Isachsen/ Trip
24. Lincoln Memorial © J. Isachsen/Trip
25. Giant panda, National Zoological Park © J. Isachsen/Trip
26. Peacock Room, Freer Gallery of Art © Rough Guldes
27. Flower stall, Eastern Market © J. Isachsen/Trip

Black and white photos

Washington DC at twilight © Charles O'Rear/ Corbis, p.69

National Postal Museum © Lee Snider/Photo Images/Corbis, p.107

Fish Market © Rough Guides, p.124

Renwick Gallery © Rough Guides, p.142

National Building Museum © Rough Guides, p.171

Canal boat on the C&O Canal © Rough Guides, p.220

Lobby of Willard InterContinental Hotel © Kelly-Mooney Photography/Corbis, p.257

Kayaking on the Potomac River © Rough Guides, p.316

Index

Map entries are in color.

D

E

F

Map symbols

maps are listed in the full index using colored text

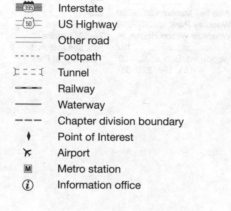

Interstate	Post office
US Highway	Gardens
Other road	Memorial
Footpath	Statue
Tunnel	Hospital
Railway	Restroom
Waterway	Grave
Chapter division boundary	Building
Point of Interest	Church
Airport	Cemetery
Metro station	Park
Information office	

THE METRORAIL SYSTEM

Shady Grove
Rockville
Twinbrook
White Flint
Grosvenor
Medical Center
Bethesda
Friendship Heights
Tenleytown-AU
Van Ness-UDC
Cleveland Park
Woodley Park-Zoo
Dupont Circle
Farragut North
Foggy Bottom -GWU

Glenmont
Wheaton
Forest Glen
Silver Spring
Takoma

Greenbelt
College Park-U of Md
Prince George's Plaza
West Hyattsville

Georgia Ave-Petworth
Columbia Heights
U Street-Cardozo
Shaw-Howard Univ

Fort Totten
Brookland-CUA
Rhode Island Ave
New York Ave

New Carrollton
Landover
Cheverly

McPherson Square
Mt Vernon Square
Union Station
Gallery Pl-Chinatown
Judiciary Square

Deanwood
Minnesota Ave
Largo Town Center

Potomac River

Rosslyn
Ballston   Clarendon
Virginia Sq -GMU
Court House
East Falls Church
West Falls Church AIRORT TRANSFER
Dunn Loring
Vienna

Farragut West
Metro Center
Federal Triangle
Smithsonian
L'Enfant Plaza

Archives-Navy Meml

Stadium Armory
Potomac Ave
Federal Center SW
Capitol South
Eastern Market

Morgan Blvd
Addison Rd
Capitol Heights
Benning Road

Arlington Cemetery
Pentagon
Pentagon City
Crystal City

Waterfront

Navy Yard
Anacostia
Congress Heights

National Airport
Braddock Road
Van Dorn Street
King Street
Eisenhower Ave
Huntington

Southern Ave
Naylor Road
Suitland
Branch Ave

Franconia-Springfield

Potomac River

N

Red Line
Glenmont / Shady Grove
Orange Line
New Carrollton / Vienna
Blue Line
Addison Road / Van Dorn Street
Yellow Line
Mt Vernon Sq-UDC / Huntington
Green Line
U Street-Cardozo / Anacostia
Greenbelt / Fort Totten
Interchange transfer station

For Metro information
call ☎ 202/637-7000

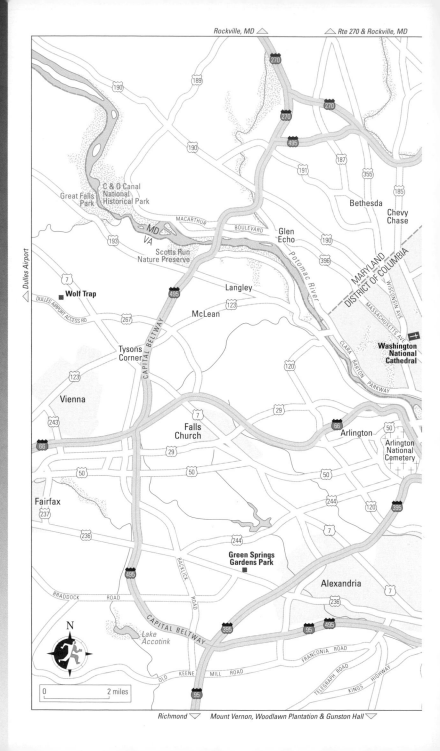

△ Dulles Airport

270

189

190

270

270

495

190

191

187

355

185

C & O Canal
National
Historical Park

Great Falls
Park

MD
VA

MACARTHUR

BOULEVARD

Bethesda

Chevy
Chase

193

Scotts Run
Nature Preserve

Glen
Echo

190

396

Potomac River

MARYLAND
DISTRICT OF COLUMBIA

WISCONSIN AVE

7

Wolf Trap

DULLES AIRPORT ACCESS RD

267

495

Langley

123

McLean

MASSACHUSETTS AVE

Washington
National
Cathedral

CLARA BARTON PARKWAY

Tysons
Corner

CAPITAL BELTWAY

123

120

Vienna

243

66

Falls
Church

7

29

66

Arlington

50

Arlington
National
Cemetery

50

29

50

50

50

Fairfax

237

244

120

395

236

7

236

244

Green Springs
Gardens Park

BACKLICK ROAD

Alexandria

236

7

495

BRADDOCK   ROAD

CAPITAL BELTWAY

Lake
Accotink

395

95

495

N

FRANCONIA ROAD

TELEGRAPH ROAD

OLD   KEENE   MILL   ROAD

KINGS   HIGHWAY

0   2 miles

95

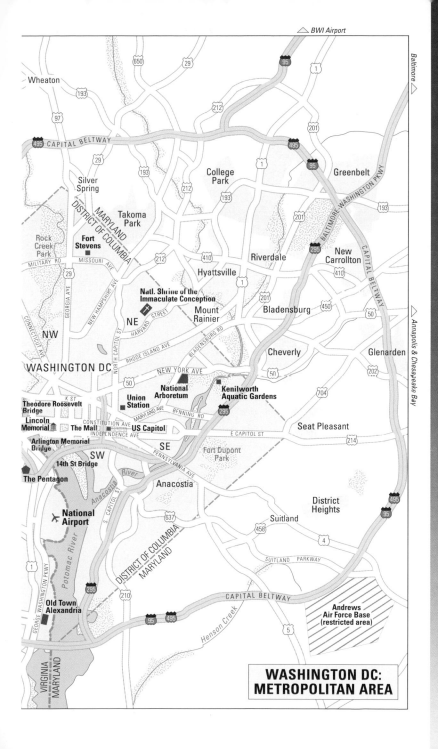

WASHINGTON DC: METROPOLITAN AREA

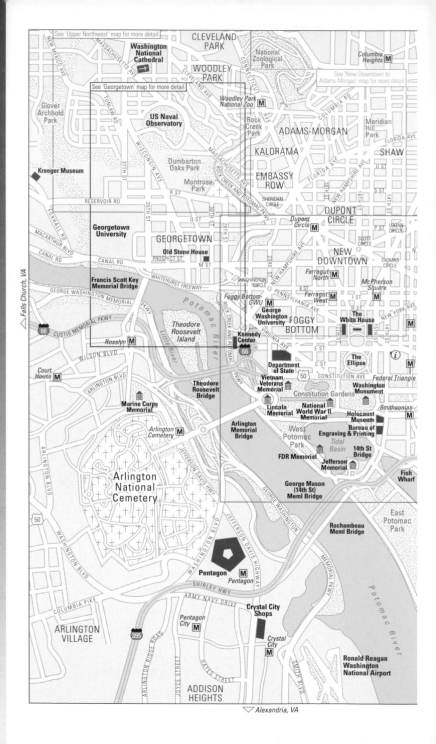

◁ Falls Church, VA

CLEVELAND PARK

Washington National Cathedral

National Zoological Park

Columbia Heights Ⓜ

See 'Upper Northwest' map for more detail

WOODLEY PARK

See 'New Downtown to Adams-Morgan' map for more detail

See 'Georgetown' map for more detail

Woodley Park National Zoo Ⓜ

Glover Archbold Park

US Naval Observatory

Rock Creek Park

ADAMS-MORGAN

Meridian Hill Park

FLORIDA AVE

KALORAMA

SHAW

Kreeger Museum

Dumbarton Oaks Park

EMBASSY ROW

U ST

Montrose Park

RESERVOIR RD

R ST

SHERIDAN CIRCLE

S ST

DUPONT CIRCLE

Georgetown University

Q ST

Dupont Circle Ⓜ

P ST

LOGAN CIRCLE

SCOTT CIRCLE

GEORGETOWN

Old Stone House

PROSPECT ST

M ST

NEW DOWNTOWN

THOMAS CIRCLE

Francis Scott Key Memorial Bridge

WHITEHURST FREEWAY

WASHINGTON CIRCLE

Farragut North Ⓜ

McPherson Square

CANAL RD

Potomac River

Foggy Bottom-GWU Ⓜ

Farragut West Ⓜ

GEORGE WASHINGTON MEMORIAL PKWY

Theodore Roosevelt Island

George Washington University

The White House

FOGGY BOTTOM

Rosslyn Ⓜ

Kennedy Center

Court House Ⓜ

WILSON BLVD

ARLINGTON BLVD

The Ellipse

Ⓜ

ⓘ

Theodore Roosevelt Bridge

Department of State

CONSTITUTION AVE

Federal Triangle

Vietnam Veterans Memorial

Washington Monument

Marine Corps Memorial

Lincoln Memorial

National World War II Memorial

Holocaust Museum

Smithsonian Ⓜ

Arlington Memorial Bridge

West Potomac Park

Bureau of Engraving & Printing

Constitution Gardens

14th St Bridge

Arlington National Cemetery

Tidal Basin

FDR Memorial

Jefferson Memorial

Fish Wharf

George Mason (14th St) Meml Bridge

East Potomac Park

Rochambeau Meml Bridge

Potomac River

Pentagon

Pentagon Ⓜ

SHIRLEY HWY

ARMY NAVY DRIVE

Crystal City Shops

COLUMBIA PIKE

ARLINGTON VILLAGE

395

Pentagon City Ⓜ

Crystal City Ⓜ

Ronald Reagan Washington National Airport

ADDISON HEIGHTS

▽ Alexandria, VA

Silver Spring, MD & Takoma Park

29

National Shrine of the
Immaculate Conception
Brookland CUA

0   500 yds

N

MICHIGAN AVE
FRANKLIN ST
McMillan
Reservoir

GEORGIA AVE
NORTH CAPITOL ST
13TH ST
8TH ST

Howard
University

RHODE ISLAND AVE
W ST

Rhode Island
Avenue

U Street
Cardozo

VERMONT AVE

LEDROIT PARK

Shaw-
Howard
University

RHODE ISLAND AVE

NEW YORK AVE
Brentwood
Park

WEST VIRGINIA AVE
BLADENSBURG RD

US National
Arboretum

Gallaudet
University

See 'Central Washington DC' map for more detail

New
Convention
Center

ST
M ST

New York
Ave

50

FLORIDA AVE

M ST

Mt Vernon
Sq-UDC

NEW JERSEY AVE
NORTH CAPITOL ST

MARTLAND AVE
BENNING RD

MT VERNON
SQUARE

Convention
Center
Gallery
Place

Metro
Center

Judiciary
Square

MASSACHUSETTS AVE

Greyhound
Bus Terminal

K ST

See 'Capitol Hill and Waterfront' map for more detail

H ST

Union
Station

Union
Station

4TH ST

F ST

395

OLD
DOWNTOWN

PENNSYLVANIA AVE

AVE

Archives-Navy Meml

Senate
Offices

STANTON
SQUARE

CONSTITUTION AVE

CAPITOL
HILL

C ST

MADISON DR

JEFFERSON DR

The Mall

US Capitol

US Capitol

US Supreme Court

EAST CAPITOL ST

EAST CAPITOL ST

LINCOLN
PARK

MASSACHUSETTS AVE

RFK
Stadium

Library of
Congress

MARYLAND AVE

E ST

Federal
Center SW

INDEPENDENCE AVE

House Offices

NEW JERSEY AVE

Eastern
Market

N CAROLINA AVE
11TH ST

CENTURY RD

Stadium
Armory

L'Enfant
Plaza

395

SEWARD
SQUARE

Capitol
South

Eastern
Market

SOUTH CAROLINA AVE

PENNSYLVANIA AVE

Potomac
Ave

SOUTHWEST/
WATERFRONT

SOUTH CAPITOL ST

VIRGINIA AVE

Thomas
Law House

Waterfront

M ST

Navy Yard

John Phillip
Sousa Bridge

295

Wheat Row

Washington
Navy Yard

Navy
Museum

ANACOSTIA DRIVE

ANACOSTIA FREEWAY

MINNESOTA AVE

11th St
Bridge

Anacostia River

Fort
McNair

Washington Channel

Frederick
Douglass
Meml Bridge

ROBBINS ROAD

Anacostia

ANACOSTIA

NAYLOR RD

GOOD HOPE RD

Frederick Douglass
National Historic Site

Naval District
Washington
Anacostia

295

MARTIN LUTHER KING JR AVE

MORRIS ROAD

Fort Stanton
Park

Anacostia
Museum

ALABAMA AVE

GARFIELD
HEIGHTS

SUITLAND PARKWAY

△ Adams-Morgan

R ST

Phillips Collection

CORCORAN ST

Q ST

MASSACHUSETTS AVE

CONNECTICUT AVE

Dupont Circle
M

DUPONT CIRCLE

Anderson House

Patterson House

P ST

16TH ST

14TH ST

△ Georgetown

28TH ST

ROCK CREEK & POTOMAC PARKWAY

21ST ST

N ST

Heurich Mansion

NEW DOWNTOWN

SCOTT CIRCLE

18TH ST

CONNECTICUT AVE

NEW HAMPSHIRE AVE

St. Matthew's Cathedral

NGS Explorers Hall

Bethune Council House

THOMAS CIRCLE

M ST

25TH ST

24TH ST

23RD ST

Mayflower Hotel

Farragut North
M

Washington Post

VERMONT AVE

L ST

National Jewish Museum

16TH ST

15TH ST

WASHINGTON CIRCLE

K ST

PENNSYLVANIA AVE

Foggy Bottom-GWU
M

I ST

Farragut West
M

I ST

M McPherson Square

H ST

H ST

Watergate Complex

VIRGINIA AVE

George Washington University

FOGGY BOTTOM

IMF

World Bank

Renwick Gallery

Old Executive Office

Treasury

NEW YORK

ROCK CREEK AND POTOMAC

H ST

G ST

F ST

22ND ST

21ST ST

20TH ST

19TH ST

18TH ST

17TH ST

Octagon

Corcoran Gallery of Art

The White House

14TH ST

National Place

Kennedy Center

66

23RD ST

Dept of State

Dept of the Interior

E ST

D ST

DAR Museum

C ST

Boy Scout Memorial

The Ellipse

Original Patentees Monument

National Aquarium

District Building
i

22ND ST

National Academy of Sciences

Federal Reserve

50

CONSTITUTION AVE

Dept of Commerce

Vietnam Veterans Memorial

National Museum of American History

Constitution Gardens

Reflecting Pool

Washington Monument

Lincoln Memorial

Korean War Veterans Memorial

DC War Memorial

National World War II Memorial

US Holocaust Memorial Museum

Arlington Memorial Bridge

INDEPENDENCE AVE

West Potomac Park

Bureau of Engraving & Printing

Dept of

△ Arlington, VA

Potomac River

WEST BASIN DR

OHIO DRIVE

Tidal Basin

14th St Bridge

FDR Memorial

Jefferson Memorial

1

MEMORIAL PARKWAY

BOUNDARY CHANNEL ROAD

George Mason (14th St) Meml Bridge

East Potomac Park

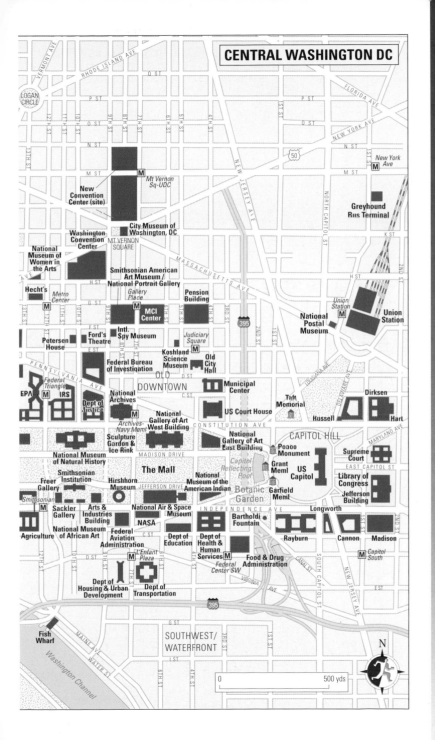

CENTRAL WASHINGTON DC

LOGAN CIRCLE

New Convention Center (site)

Washington Convention Center

National Museum of Women in the Arts

Hecht's
Metro Center

Petersen House

Ford's Theatre

Intl. Spy Museum

Federal Bureau of Investigation

Federal Triangle

EPA   IRS

Dept of Justice

Mt Vernon Sq-UDC

City Museum of Washington, DC

MT VERNON SQUARE

Smithsonian American Art Museum / National Portrait Gallery

Gallery Place

MCI Center

Pension Building

Judiciary Square

Koshland Science Museum

Old City Hall

DOWNTOWN

National Archives

Archives-Navy Meml

National Gallery of Art West Building

Municipal Center

National Gallery of Art East Building

Peace Monument

Taft Memorial

US Court House

Greyhound Bus Terminal

New York Ave

National Postal Museum

Union Station

Dirksen

Russell   Hart

CAPITOL HILL

Supreme Court

EAST CAPITOL ST

Library of Congress

Jefferson Building

Sculpture Garden & Ice Rink

MADISON DRIVE

National Museum of Natural History

Smithsonian Institution

Freer Gallery

Hirshhorn Museum

The Mall

JEFFERSON DRIVE

National Museum of the American Indian

Botanic Garden

Washington Monument

US Capitol

Grant Meml

Capitol Reflecting Pool

Garfield Meml

Longworth

Sackler Gallery

Arts & Industries Building

National Museum of African Art

National Air & Space Museum

NASA

Federal Aviation Administration

L'Enfant Plaza

Dept of Education

INDEPENDENCE AVE

Bartholdi Fountain

Dept of Health & Human Services

Federal Center SW

Food & Drug Administration

Rayburn

Cannon   Madison

Capitol South

Agriculture

Dept of Housing & Urban Development

Dept of Transportation

Fish Wharf

Washington Channel

SOUTHWEST/ WATERFRONT

0   500 yds

N

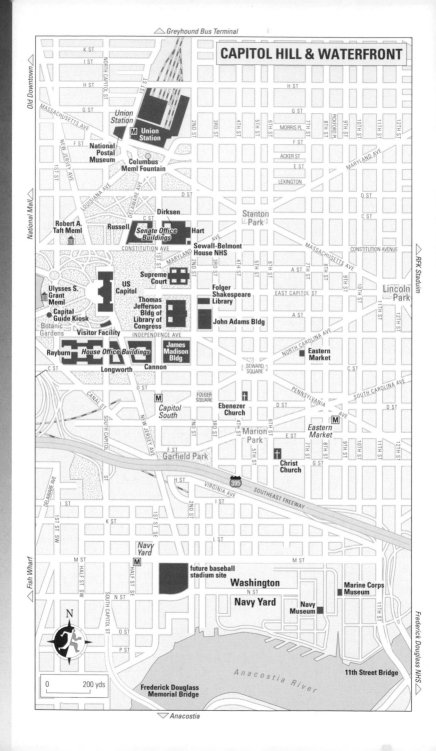

△ Greyhound Bus Terminal

CAPITOL HILL & WATERFRONT

◁ Old Downtown

△ National Mall

▷ RFK Stadium

K ST
I ST
H ST
G ST
H ST
G ST

NORTH CAPITOL ST
1ST ST
2ND ST
3RD ST
4TH ST
5TH ST
6TH ST
7TH ST
8TH ST
9TH ST
10TH ST
11TH ST
12TH ST

MASSACHUSETTS AVE

Union Station
Ⓜ Union Station

MORRIS PL
PICKFORD P

F ST
ACKER ST

National Postal Museum
Columbus Meml Fountain

E ST
LEXINGTON

NEW JERSEY AVE
1ST ST
LOUISIANA AVE
DELAWARE AVE

D ST

D ST

MARYLAND AVE

Dirksen

Stanton Park

C ST

C ST

Robert A. Taft Meml
Russell
Senate Office Buildings
Hart

Sewall-Belmont House NHS

CONSTITUTION AVE

1ST ST
MARYLAND AVE
2ND ST
3RD ST
4TH ST
5TH ST
6TH ST
7TH ST
8TH ST
9TH ST

MASSACHUSETTS AVE

CONSTITUTION AVENUE

Lincoln Park

Ulysses S. Grant Meml
Capital Guide Kiosk
US Capitol
Supreme Court

Thomas Jefferson Bldg of Library of Congress

Folger Shakespeare Library

EAST CAPITOL ST

A ST

10TH ST
11TH ST
12TH ST

Botanic Gardens
Visitor Facility

INDEPENDENCE AVE

John Adams Bldg

A ST

Rayburn
House Office Buildings
James Madison Bldg

NORTH CAROLINA AVE

Eastern Market

Longworth
Cannon

SEWARD SQUARE

C ST

C ST

D ST

CANAL ST
SOUTH CAPITOL ST
NEW JERSEY AVE
2ND ST
3RD ST

FOLGER SQUARE

PENNSYLVANIA AVE

SOUTH CAROLINA AVE

D ST

Ⓜ Capitol South

Ebenezer Church

D ST

Ⓜ Eastern Market

4TH ST
5TH ST
1ST ST SE
2ND ST

Marion Park

E ST

7TH ST
8TH ST
9TH ST
10TH ST
11TH ST
12TH ST

F ST
Garfield Park

Christ Church

G ST

H ST

VIRGINIA AVE

SOUTHEAST FREEWAY

395

I ST

DELAWARE AVE
1ST ST
1ST ST SE
2ND ST

K ST

L ST

Navy Yard

M ST

M ST

◁ Fish Wharf

M ST
HALF ST SW
HALF ST SE
SOUTH CAPITOL ST

Ⓜ

future baseball stadium site

Washington

N ST

Marine Corps Museum

N

Navy Yard

Navy Museum

O ST

P ST

Anacostia River

11th Street Bridge

Frederick Douglass NHS ▷

0   200 yds

Frederick Douglass Memorial Bridge

▽ Anacostia

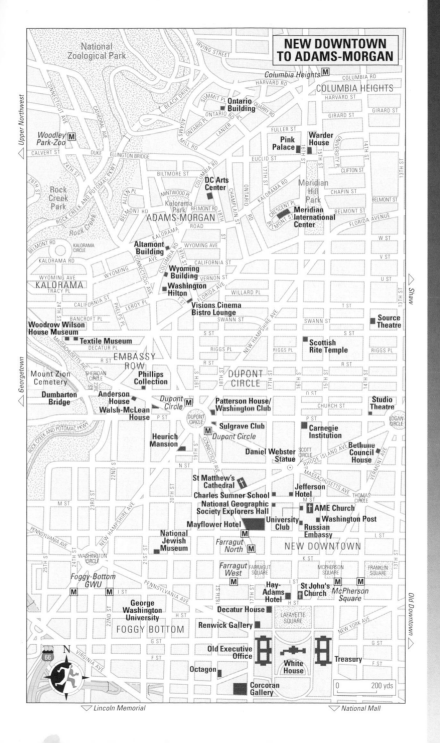

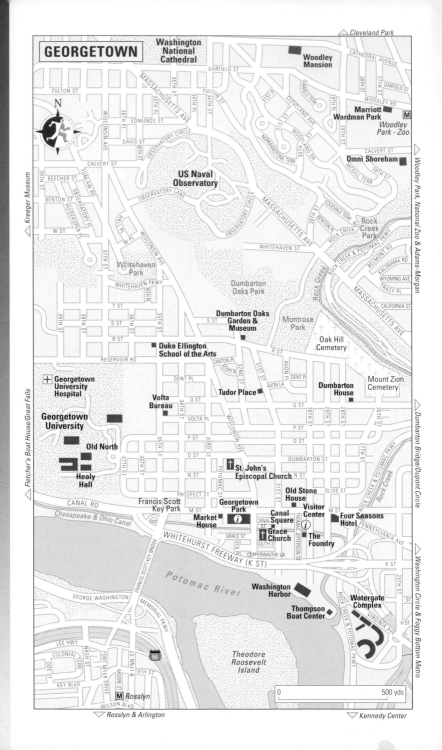

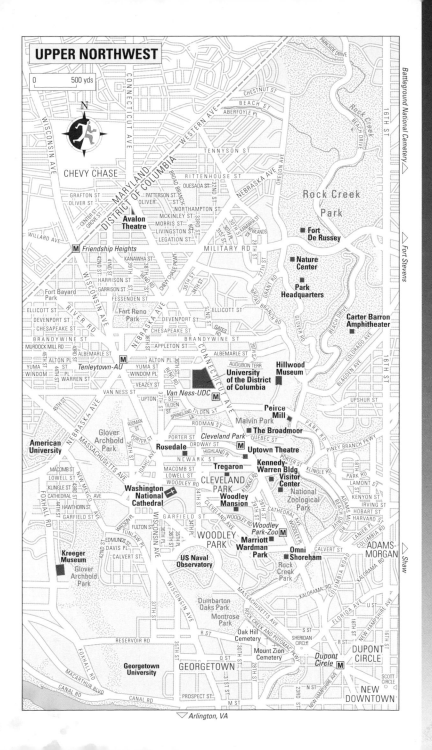

UPPER NORTHWEST

0   500 yds

N

CHEVY CHASE

Battleground National Cemetery ▽

Fort Stevens ▽

Shaw ▽

PARKSIDE DRIVE

CHESTNUT ST

BEACH ST

ABERFOYLE PL

CONNECTICUT AVE

WESTERN AVE

TENNYSON ST

RITTENHOUSE ST

OUESADA ST

BROAD BRANCH RD

32ND ST

NEBRASKA AVE

OREGON AVE

Rock Creek Park

NORTHAMPTON ST

McKINLEY ST

MORRIS ST

LIVINGSTON ST

LEGATION ST

GRAFTON ST

OLIVER ST

PATTERSON ST

OLIVER ST

CENTER ST

DRIVE

MARYLAND

DISTRICT OF COLUMBIA

Avalon Theatre

ROWLANDS

31ST ST

33RD ST

30TH ST

28TH ST

27TH ST

MILITARY RD

■ **Fort De Russey**

WILLARD AVE

M *Friendship Heights*

WISCONSIN AVE

42ND ST

41ST ST

39TH ST

KANAWHA ST

HARRISON ST

GARRISON ST

FESSENDEN ST

CHEVY CHASE PKWY

38TH ST

34TH ST

KANAWHA ST

■ **Nature Center**

GRANT RD

BROAD BRANCH RD

GLOVER RD

■ **Park Headquarters**

Fort Bayard Park

RIVER RD

RENO RD

Fort Reno Park

ELLICOTT ST

DEVENPORT ST

CHESAPEAKE ST

BRANDYWINE ST

MURDOCK MILL RD

45TH ST

43RD ST

ALTON PL

YUMA ST

WINDOM

4TH ST

NEBRASKA AVE

ELLICOTT ST

32ND ST

DEVENPORT ST

CHESAPEAKE ST

APPLETON ST

ALBEMARLE ST

GATES RD

BRANDYWINE ST

36TH ST

34TH ST

REED ST

ALTON PL

YUMA ST

WINDOM PL

VEAZEY ST

M Tenleytown-AU

39TH ST

Carter Barron Amphitheater ■

COLORADO AVE

16TH ST

BLAGDEN AVE

UPSHUR ST

AUDUBON TERR

University of the District of Columbia

Hillwood Museum ■

VAN NESS ST

UPTON ST

Van Ness-UDC M

37TH ST

38TH ST

SPRINGLAND LA

TILDEN ST

CONNECTICUT AVE

29TH ST

PARK RD

Peirce Mill ■

Malvin Park

RODMAN ST

Glover Archbold Park

PORTER ST

Cleveland Park

PORTER ST

ORDWAY ST

■ **The Broadmoor**

QUEBEC ST

PINEY BRANCH PKWY

18TH ST

American University

NEBRASKA AVE

MASSACHUSETTS AVE

39TH ST

Rosedale ■

NEWARK ST

HIGHLAND PL

M *Cleveland Park*

Uptown Theatre ■

KLINGLE RD

PARK RD

LAMONT ST

KENYON ST

MACOMB ST

LOWELL ST

KLINGLE ST

42ND ST

NEW MEXICO AVE

43RD ST

CATHEDRAL AVE

HAWTHORN ST

MACOMB ST

LOWELL ST

WOODLEY ST

Tregaron ■

CLEVELAND AVE

Kennedy-Warren Bldg ■

Visitor Center ■

National Zoological Park

KLINGLE RD

IRVING ST

HOBART ST

HARVARD ST

LANIER PL

ADAMS-MORGAN

GARFIELD ST

FULTON ST

TUNLAW RD

EDMUNDS ST

DAVIS PL

CALVERT ST

Washington National Cathedral ✚

Woodley Mansion

36TH ST

35TH ST

34TH ST

CLEVELAND AVE

28TH ST

WOODLEY RD

CLEVELAND PARK

WOODLEY RD

Woodley Park-Zoo M

CATHEDRAL AVE

24TH ST

WOODLEY PARK

Marriott Wardman Park ■

Omni Shoreham ■

CALVERT ST

KALORAMA RD

CALVERT ST

COLUMBIA ROAD

BELMONT RD

Kreeger Museum ■

Glover Archbold Park

WISCONSIN AVE

37TH ST

US Naval Observatory

Rock Creek Park

MASSACHUSETTS AVE

KALORAMA RD

FLORIDA AVE

19TH ST

18TH ST

NEW HAMPSHIRE AVE

RESERVOIR RD

FOXHALL RD

Dumbarton Oaks Park

Montrose Park

35TH ST

ROCK CREEK AND POTOMAC PKWY

Oak Hill Cemetery

S ST

SHERIDAN CIRCLE

R ST

DUPONT CIRCLE

Georgetown University

GEORGETOWN

Mount Zion Cemetery

Q ST

31ST ST

30TH ST

28TH ST

S ST

23RD ST

NEW HAMPSHIRE AVE

Dupont Circle M

SCOTT CIRCLE

MACARTHUR BLVD

CANAL RD

CANAL RD

PROSPECT ST

M ST

N ST

NEW DOWNTOWN

▽ Arlington, VA

Wolf Trap National Park

VIRGINIA METRO REGION

Dulles Int'l Airport

Central Washington, DC

29

7 FALLS CHURCH

ARLINGTON
Arlington National Cemetery
Crystal City M

66

29

50

50

120

7 244

National Airport
M
Reagan National Airport

395

Baileys Crossroads

236 Annandale

244

Green Springs Gardens Park

7 ALEXANDRIA

Braddock Road
M

Washington Masonic Memorial
King Street M
Old Town Alexandria

236

495

BACKLICK ROAD

395

Van Dorn St M

Eisenhower Ave
M

95 495

ROAD

M
Huntington

FRANCONIA

Springfield

Franconia Springfield M

Franconia

KINGSTOWNE BLVD

Rose Hill

TELEGRAPH ROAD

1 Grovetown

VIRGINIA
MARYLAND

FAIRFAX COUNTY PARKWAY

Huntley Meadows Park

Hybla Valley

Mount Vernon Trail

Newington

95

Woodlawn Plantation/ Pope Leighey House

235

Pohick

Lorton

1

Fort Belvoir (US Army restricted area)

235

Mount Vernon Grist Mill

Mount Vernon

Piscataway National Park

242

Gunston Cove

VA MD

Potomac River

277

N

Gunston Hall

Mason Neck State Park

0   2 miles

Fairfax, Vienna, VA

Manassas, VA

Fredericksburg, VA